Henn on Copyright Law

A Practitioner's Guide

Henn on Copyright Law
A Practitioner's Guide

Third Edition

Harry G. Henn

Date of Publication: May 1991

G1-1016
Practising Law Institute

"This publication is designed to provide accurate and authoritative information in regard to the subject matter covered. It is sold with the understanding that the publisher is not engaged in rendering legal, accounting or other professional service. If legal advice or other expert assistance is required, the services of a competent professional person should be sought."

—from Declaration of Principles jointly adopted by Committee of American Bar Association and Committee of Publishers and Associations.

Library of Congress Catalog Card Number: 91-061040

ISBN: 0-87224-020-7

About the Author

Harry G. Henn is the Edward Cornell Professor of Law Emeritus at Cornell University, where he taught copyright, trademark, and patent law, as well as corporation law from 1953 to 1985. His annual copyright seminar guest lecturers included leaders of the Copyright Bar.

He has been an active practitioner and consultant in connection with copyright matters. Besides serving on the UNESCO Panel on International Copyright (concerned with the Universal Copyright Convention) and Panel of Consultants to the Librarian of Congress on General Revision of the Copyright Law, Professor Henn was the author of one of the pilot Copyright Law Revision studies in 1955.

A charter trustee of The Copyright Society of the U.S.A., Professor Henn was President of the Society for two terms, and is now a life trustee. In 1986, he received the Society's annual award. He also served on several copyright committees of the Association of the Bar of the City of New York and American Bar Association, as chairman of the ABA's Copyright Subsection, and as a member of Association Littéraire et Artistique Internationale and Internationale Gesellschaft für Urheberrect EV.

Professor Henn was the eighth Brace Lecturer in 1978 ("Cassandra Considers Copyright," 25 Bull. Copyright Soc'y 453 (1978)).

Professor Henn received a Bachelor of Arts, summa cum

laude, with Honors in Political Science degree, from New York University, and a Bachelor of Laws, with Distinction, degree from Cornell, where he was Editor-in-Chief of the *Cornell Law Quarterly*. For his doctorate of juridical science from New York University, his copyright thesis was under the graduate committee chairmanship of the late Professor Walter J. Derenberg.

Table of Chapters

Table of Contents

Chapter 26—"Statutory" Secondary Transmission by Satellite Carriers for Private Home Viewing License

Table of Appendixes

Preface

Henn on Copyright Law: A Practitioner's Guide (initially entitled *Copyright Primer*) was the successor to the 1965 revised edition of *Copyrights* by Barbara A. Ringer, then Assistant Register of Copyrights for Examining, and Paul Gitlin, an active copyright and tax practitioner.

A completely new presentation was required by the fundamental changes effected by the 1976 Act, effective January 1, 1978, principally drafted by Ms. Ringer, then the Register of Copyrights. Developments after the *Primer's* publication in 1979 justified a second edition in 1988 reflecting changes in the law and its interpretation.

The second edition added chapters on the anomalous "copyright" protection for semiconductor soft chips and on satellite cable programming, both legislated in 1984. Neither legislation is part of the Copyright Law, although the former is administered by the Copyright Office.

The Berne Convention Implementation Act of 1988, effective March 1, 1989, made some fundamental changes, most applicable to all works and one limited to "Berne Convention works" whose "country of origin" is *not* the United States (i.e., registration as prerequisite for infringement actions). These changes, summarized in our 1989 Supplement on the Berne Act, were not retroactive.

Thus, the copyright status of a work may depend on when it was created or first published, and its compliance with the then existing laws, especially formalities like copyright notice.

This third edition integrates the Berne Act changes into the text, and discusses the Satellite Home Viewer Act of 1988 and other developments, through January 1, 1991.

The 1965 exegesis of the twenty-three-page 1909 Act required 187 pages. The 1988 second edition attempted to explain the sixty-two-page 1976 Act and its amendments in some 350 pages [exclusive of appendixes], divided into thirty-three chapters. This third edition comprises 436 pages in thirty-four chapters. A new chapter on protection of American works in foreign countries has been added. The chapter on the National Commission on New Technological Uses of Copyrighted Works (CONTU) has been eliminated, and references to it have been included where appropriate.

A seasoned statute does not require appendices of secondary materials commenting—not always disinterestedly—on new legislation. Hence, appendices have been reduced substantially from the second edition. Up-to-date versions may be found in the latest 17 U.S.C.A. cumulative pocket supplement, CCH COPYRIGHT L. REP., and elsewhere, especially from the Copyright Office, without charge. The table of contents of the current Copyright Office "Information Kit" appears in appendix F *infra*.

Beginning with the first edition in 1979, the description of the copyright statute has closely adhered to the statutory language, any accompanying congressional discussion, and Copyright Office explanatory material. This still seems desirable. Rather than indicate every borrowed phrase by quotation marks, only the more important words and phrases usually are so set off. Sources, however, are attributed.

Well-financed lobbying has added many "refinements" to the statute. As a result, this third edition must deal with an inflated statute and a judicial gloss of uneven quality.

Many segments of copyright-related industries and institutions have their own sets of "guidelines," often self-serving and drafted by "consultants." No attempt has been made here to collect, collate, and evaluate those.

This one-volume text attempts to explain one of the most sophisticated aspects of property law and freedom of expression at various levels. The text is a restatement, with the footnotes buttressing the text. Anticipated copyright problems may be resolved easily; *ex post facto* resolutions may be costly and ineffective.

Any review of the copyright decisions of the past decade must raise the question whether the United States Court of Appeals for the Ninth Circuit is replacing the Second Circuit as the premier copyright court. But no judge with the copyright insights—no matter how imperfect—of a Learned Hand has yet to emerge.

A new edition always presents problems to its author, as to coverage and methods of presentation. Computer litigation pervades our "copyright" system. This third edition, like its predecessors, reflects the copyright law interface with patent law and other legal and equitable principles, under rather perfunctory "copyright law" computer provisions. Quaere, as to "writings of authors" versus "discoveries of inventors"; "aesthetic" versus "utilitarian" distinctions; "expression" versus "ideas"; "originality" versus "nonobvious" "novelty"; means of securing and maintaining protection; duration of protection; tests of infringement; available remedies; judicial attitudes.

The problem is complicated by the historical "turf" fact that the Copyright Office is part of the Library of Congress (legislative branch) and the Patent and Trademark Office is part of the Department of Commerce (executive branch).

Both the 1976 Act and 1909 Act, as amended, appear in 17 U.S.C.A. (West 1977 & Supps.) The former is cited as "17 U.S.C.A. § ______"; the 1909 Act as "1909 Act § ______."

The Berne Convention Implementation Act, effective March 1, 1989 (also *not* retroactive), is cited as "Berne Act § ______".

Recent years have witnessed the premature losses of many long-time friends and stalwarts of the Copyright Bar, especially Professors Walter J. Derenberg, Alan Latman, and Melville Nimmer, not to mention many other mentors, who were specialists, subspecialists, or subsubspecialists in copyright law. In the 1940s there were few "copyright lawyers."

Responsible for the first edition was Selma Arnold of the Practising Law Institute. She joined the author in envisaging a new, one-volume text based on the comprehensive revision of the copyright statute in 1976, effective January 1, 1978. The older texts seemed wedded to the pre-1978 law or at least earlier outlines and terminology, and even concepts. Encouraging this third, and the second, edition were William C. Cubberley, ably supported by Henry W. Enberg, of PLI.

For their contributions to the initial treatment of scope of protection and copyright ownership, acknowledgment is due Stephen C. Clancy, Albert J. Givray, and Steven W. Korn, all of the Cornell Law School Class of 1978. Credit for research assistance is also due Bruce M. Kennedy, D. Alan Diefenbach and the Cornell Law Library staff, and N. Jeffrey Klauder, Jr., also of the Class of 1978, and George M. Dentes, of the Class of 1979.

The guidance afforded by Peter D. Rosenberg, the users and reviewers of earlier editions, and by incisive questioning and discourse with my Cornell Law School students, are gratefully acknowledged. Appreciation is also due my Congressman, Peter H. Goss, for facilitating the receipt of publicly available information from the Copyright Office.

And, as usual, gratitude is expressed to my former secretaries, Mary D. Mignano, Judith B. Oltz, and my present secretary, Virginia R. Fredrickson, and also to Nancy L. Sparrow.

Harry G. Henn

Naples, Florida
January 1, 1991

1. Introduction

1.1 Copyrights Distinguished from Patents and Trademarks

Copyrights and patents, in return for their promotion of the progress of the arts and sciences, provide incentives for limited times to authors and inventors. Trademarks prevent confusion of the public and protect the goodwill of their owners. All three serve public and private interests, requiring delicate legislative, judicial, and administrative compromises between the needs of the public and the property rights of the owners.[1]

The three, with related or neighboring concepts, are sometimes called "intellectual property" or "industrial property." Some purists would argue that copyrights are intellectual property, and that trademarks and patents are industrial property. All three have antitrust implications.

1. Most members of Congress know little about copyright. *See Litman, Copyright, Compromise, and Legislative History,* 72 CORNELL L. REV. 857, 860, 862 (1987). For many years, the copyright "guru" has been Representative Robert W. Kastenmeier of Wisconsin. However, in 1990, he was defeated for a seventeenth term. For twenty-one years, he was the dominant chairman of the House subcommittee on copyrights, trademarks, and patents. On copyright matters, the Senate usually deferred to the House. Substantial PAC funds have been established by major copyright interests. Most federal judges have had little copyright background.

1.1[1] Copyrights

Copyright protects the "writings" of "authors" against unauthorized copying. It protects "expression" as distinguished from "ideas," even of identical works as long as they are "original," meaning independently conceived and not copied. Even "expression" is not protected when an idea can be expressed in only a limited number of ways; otherwise the idea itself would be preempted.

The "works of authorship" include literary, musical, and dramatic works; pantomimes and choreographic works; pictorial, graphic, and sculptural works; motion pictures and other audiovisual works; and sound recordings.[2]

Copyright begins when a work is "created," in the sense of being "fixed" in a "copy" or "phonorecord" for the first time. Protection starts with creation and for most works is for the life of the author plus fifty years.

The copyright law is found in title 17 of the United States Code (Copyrights). Copyright administration is in the Copyright Office directed by the Register of Copyrights, whose principal functions are to accept deposits of copies, register copyright claims, and record documents relating to copyright. The Copyright Office is part of the Library of Congress in the legislative branch of the federal government.

The Copyright Royalty Tribunal, also part of the Library of Congress, administers or is otherwise involved with the compulsory and "statutory" licenses under the Copyright Law.

1.1[2] Patents

A patent protects the "discoveries" of "inventors" against unauthorized making, using, or selling the invention in the United States. A patent is more of a monopoly than a copy-

2. And, arguably, "mask works." *See* chapter 32 *infra.*

right since the first inventor of the invention prevails over any subsequent "inventor" even though the latter independently conceived and reduced to practice the "invention." Thus, a patentee with an improvement patent may not practice the improvement without a license from the holder of the basic patent.

There are three kinds of patents:

1. Utility patents
2. Plant patents
3. Design patents (which may overlap with copyright)

The invention must be useful, new, and non-obvious, compared to the prior art. Novelty and non-obviousness of an invention require much more than the "originality" for a work of authorship.

Patent protection begins when the patent is issued. While the application is pending ("patent pending"), there is no protection. The duration of protection, except for design patents, which have a fourteen-year period, is seventeen years (up to five-year extension for certain "products" subject to regulatory review) with no renewal.

The Patent Act of 1952, as amended, is found in title 35 of the United States Code (Patents). Patent matters are administered by the Patent and Trademark Office (whose functions involve examination rather than mere registration), which is in the Department of Commerce, part of the executive branch. The Office is headed by the Commissioner of Patents and Trademarks.

1.1[3] Trademarks

A trademark or other mark is a trade symbol adopted and used (first use in a trademark or service mark sense or bona fide intent to use being critical) by a person to identify that person's goods or services and to distinguish them from the goods or services of others. While "intent to use" may be the basis for an application "bona fide use" "in the ordinary course of trade" is prequisite to registration. Protection is against probability of confusion, protecting the first trader's goodwill and the public against deception. A mark may include words or designs or a combination thereof, or sounds.

There are four kinds of marks:

1. Trademarks, used in connection with goods;
2. Service marks, used in connection with services;
3. Certification marks, used to certify characteristics of goods or services; and
4. Collective marks, used to indicate membership in a group.

Unlike copyrights and patents, which are federally preempted, trademarks and other marks are subject to state law and also to federal law when interstate or foreign commerce is involved.

Rights in a mark are acquired by adoption and use in commerce, and implemented by federal and possibly state registrations. Federal registration (on "Principal Register" for stronger marks or "Supplemental Register" for weaker marks) is for ten years, renewable for additional ten-year periods as long as the mark continues to be used.

The Federal Trademark Act of 1946 (called the "Lanham Act"), as amended, enacted under the power of Congress to regulate interstate and foreign commerce and not the copyright-patent power, is found in title 15 of the United States Code (Commerce and Trade), sections 1051 *et seq.* Federal trademark matters are administered by the Patent and Trademark Office (of the Department of Commerce), which combines registration and examination procedures. Even absent federal registration, there may be federal protection against false designation of origin,[3] and state protection against "dilution" without state registration.[4]

1.2 Constitutional Copyright Aspects

The constitutional basis for federal copyright and patent legislation is the power of Congress:[5]

> To promote the Progress of Science and useful Arts, by securing for limited Times to Authors and Inventors the exclusive Right to their respective Writings and Discoveries.

1.2[1] "To Promote the Progress of Science and Useful Arts"

Copyright is only a means to promote the public interest—the "Progress of Science and useful Arts"—which is paramount.[6] This raises doubts as to the constitutionality

---

3. 15 U.S.C.A. § 1125(a).
4. *E.g.*, N.Y. GEN. BUS. LAW §§ 360 *et seq.* (McKinney)
5. U.S. CONST. art. I, § 8, cl.8. The Constitution does not use the term "copyright" or "patent." The 1976 Act Transitional and Supplementary Provisions sec. 115 provides that if any provision of title 17, United States Code, as amended by the 1976 Act, is declared unconstitutional, the remainder of the title is not affected. For background, see Fenning, *The Origin of the Patent and Copyright Clauses of the Constitution*, 17 GEO. L.J. 109 (1929); Crawford, *Pre-Constitutional Copyright Statutes*, 23 BULL. COPR. SOC'Y 11 (1975). *See also* B. KAPLAN, AN UNHURRIED VIEW OF COPYRIGHT (1967).
6. L. EVANS, COPYRIGHT AND THE PUBLIC INTEREST (1949); Phillips, *The Berne Convention and the Public Interest*, 11 COLUM.-V.L.A. J.L. & ARTS 165 (1986); Richards, *Value of the Copyright Clause in Construction of Copyright Law*, 2 HASTINGS CONST. L.Q. 221 (1975). Despite the constitutional phrase "useful arts," utility has never been a requirement for copyright protection. Bleistein v. Donaldson Lithographing Co., 188 U.S. 239, 249 (1903) (circus poster) ("A picture is none the less a subject of copyright that it is used for an advertisement."). Justice Douglas has questioned whether the "novelty" requirement for

of any legislation that revives copyright in a work in the public domain,[7] extends copyright in works in which copy-

---

patents should apply to copyrights, since both derive from the same constitutional clause. Lee v. Runge, 404 U.S. 887 (1971) (Douglas, J., dissenting from denial of certiorari). Like design patents, copyrights protect aesthetic as distinguished from "utilitarian" aspects, the subject of utility patents. Trademark protection does not extend to "functional" aspects. Some commentators have suggested that "Science" in the Constitution refers to the "Writings" of "Authors" and "useful Arts" to the "Discoveries" of "Inventors." Both would seem "to promote the Progress" of both the sciences and the arts, which together comprise knowledge. Quaere, as to the copyrightability of odors (odor microencapsulation) and of sequencing of nucleotides in molecules of genetically engineered micro-organisms.

7. At least nine Congressional private acts have revived copyrights in works of John Rowlett (3), Levi H. Corson, Thomas H. Summer, Ms. Henry R. Schoolcraft, Mrs. William L. Herndon, William Tod Helmuth, Judson Jones (between 1828 and 1898) and Mary Baker Eddy (in 1971). *See, e.g.;* Priv. L. No. 92-60, 92d Cong., 1st Sess. (Dec. 15, 1971) (*Science and Health with Key to the Scriptures* by Mary Baker Eddy); *see also* chapter 2, note 7 *infra*. *See generally* M. NIMMER, NIMMER ON FREEDOM OF SPEECH (1983); Nimmer, *Does Copyright Abridge the First Amendment Guarantees of Free Speech and Press?* 17 U.C.L.A. L. REV. 1180, 1194-96 (1970); *cf.* Goldstein, *Copyright and the First Amendment*, 70 COLUM. L. REV. 983, 1007-08 (1970). *See* Wang, *The First Amendment Exception to Copyright: A Proposed Test*, 1977 WIS. L. REV. 1158. Arguably, the limitation of copyright protection to "expression" and the "fair use" exception may be construed as avoiding any first amendment-copyright conflict. *But see* Jartech, Inc. v. Clancy, 666 F.2d 403 (9th Cir.), *cert. denied*, 459 U.S. 826 (1982); Mitchell Bros. Film Group v. Cinema Adult Theatre, 604 F.2d 852 (5th Cir. 1979) (obscenity no defense because of varying community standards and need for national copyright uniformity), *cert. denied*, 445 U.S. 917 (1980); Comment, *Problems in Giving Obscenity Copyright Protection: Did* Jartech *and* Mitchell Brothers *Go Too Far?* 36 VAND. L. REV. 403 (1983). *Cf.* Belcher v. Tarbox, 486 F.2d 1087 (9th Cir. 1973)(2-1) (copyright protection for false and fraudulent material not precluded by "clean hands" doctrine). *See* Patterson, *Free Speech, Copyright, and Fair Use*, 40 VAND. L. REV. 1 (1987). The Visual Artists Rights Act of 1990 expressly requires compliance with the First Amendment!

right is already subsisting,[8] or, as once thought, affords copyright protection to an obscene work.[9]

1.2[2] "Writings" of "Authors"

The term "Writings" connotes at least some fixation in a tangible medium of expression capable of perception directly or with the aid of a device,[10] and that expression, as distinguished from ideas, is copyrightable. Implicit in the word "Authors"[11] is the requirement that the expression be that of the author and be not copied.

1.2[3] "Exclusive Right"

Copyright is a "bundle of rights," most of them exclusive, but subject to a growing number of compulsory and "statutory" licenses. The constitutional phrase "the exclusive Right" raises some doubt as to the constitutionality of statutory compulsory licenses. The 1909 Act compulsory license

---

8. *See* note 7 *supra*. For ten extensions since 1962 and actuarily increased duration, see chapter 16, note 13 *infra*.

9. 1 M. NIMMER, COPYRIGHT §§ 1.03[B], 2.17 (1978). Obscenity was a defense under common-law copyright. Note, 46 FORDHAM L. REV. 1037 (1978).

10. 17 U.S.C.A. § 102; Derenberg, *et al.*, *The Meaning of "Writings" in the Copyright Clause of the Constitution* (1956), *reprinted in* 1 STUDIES ON COPYRIGHT—ARTHUR FISHER MEMORIAL EDITION 43 (1963); Note, *Study of the Term "Writings" in the Copyright Clause of the Constitution*, 31 N.Y.U. L. REV. 1263 (1956).

11. The law, in its elimination of masculine and feminine, excepting in the definition of "work made for hire" in § 101 and in the added § 119 (c)(3)(D)(ii), where "his or her" is redundant, does not mention the neuter case. Quaere, whether a corporation can be an author. Presumably, it can. *See* chapter 6, note 5 *infra*. The 1976 Act eliminated gender as a tribute to Barbara Ringer, its principal drafter. Gender was reintroduced by the copyright riders to the Judicial Improvements Act of 1990 ("his or her" or "his" alone).

provision for recording musical works was effective only after the right was exercised by, or with the authority of, the copyright owner, meaning that the right was exclusive until then. There are newer provisions encouraging negotiation of licenses.[12] Quaere, as to the constitutionality of compulsory or "statutory" licenses.[13]

1.2[4] "For Limited Times"

Perpetual statutory copyright would clearly contravene the Constitution. The "limited Times" for copyrights under the 1976 Act has been the life of the author plus fifty years, with several variations, compared to a twenty-eight-year original term and possible renewal for another twenty-eight years under the 1909 Act, compared to a single seventeen-year term for most patents.

---

12. 17 U.S.C.A. §§ 116 A, 119.

13. *See* Cassler, *Copyright Compulsory Licenses—Are They Coming or Going?* 37 J. COPYRIGHT SOC'Y 231 (1990). Goldstein, *Preempted State Doctrines, Involuntary Transfers and Compulsory Licenses: Testing the Limits of Copyright,* 24 U.C.L.A. L. REV. 1107 (1977). Compulsory licenses have been introduced when certain new rights were recognized or previously recognized rights were broadened: (1) recording rights for music, (2) elimination of juke-box exemption, (3) elimination of "for profit" limitation on public performance rights for music and nondramatic literary works, and (4) broadening of definition of performance to include cable television secondary transmissions. Proposed amendments often would involve new types of compulsory licenses. Diamond, *The Compulsory Licenses and the Copyright Royalty Tribunal,* 6 A.P.L.A. Q.J. 46 (1978). A fifth complusory license, called "statutory license," was added by the Satellite Home Viewer Act of 1988. Denial of preliminary injunctions has been deemed equivalent to compulsory licenses. Note, 10 COLUM.–V.L.A. J.L. & ARTS 277 (1986).

1.3 Background of 1976 Revision (Effective January 1, 1978)

The Copyright Law of 1976, signed by President Ford on October 19, 1976,[14] became effective for most purposes on January 1, 1978.[15] It replaced the Act of March 4, 1909,[16] although many of the sections of the 1909 Act, not to mention common-law copyright principles, will be relevant for decades to come.[17]

The new legislation was the culmination of more than twenty years of revision effort, involving thirty-five scholarly monographs on major copyright problems,[18] twelve years of congressional consideration, tremendous lobbying,

---

14. Pub. L. No. 94-553, 94th Cong., 90 Stat. 2541 (Oct. 19, 1976), reprinted, as amended, in appendix A *infra*. The new law is found in title 17 of the United States Code (U.S.C.) and in title 17 of the United States Code Annotated (West 1977 & Supp.) (U.S.C.A.). The "Transitional and Supplementary Provisions," although part of the 1976 Act, are not included as such in title 17. For highlights of the 1976 Act, *see* former Copyright Office Circular R99.
15. 17 U.S.C.A. § 102. Effective upon enactment were § 118 (use of certain works in connection with noncommercial broadcasting), § 304(b) (extension to seventy-five-year term of copyrights in their renewal between December 31, 1976 and December 31, 1977), and chapter 8 (Copyright Royalty Tribunal). Absent was any provision for giving a notice of termination prior to January 1, 1978. *See* chapter 16, note 15 *infra*. *See* Beckett, *The Copyright Act of 1976: When Is It Effective?* 24 BULL. COPYRIGHT SOC'Y 391 (1977).
16. Rev. Stat. ch. 320, 35 Stat. 1075 (1909), reprinted as appendix in 17 U.S.C.A. Appropriate references to the 1909 Act are included herein.
17. *See* chapter 2 *infra*.
18. The copyright law revision studies and reports are cited herein when appropriate. They are listed in appendix G of the second edition of this *Guide*. They are reprinted, with some additional materials, in STUDIES ON COPYRIGHT—ARTHUR FISHER MEMORIAL EDITION (2 vols.) (1963) (in-depth exegesis of pre-1978 law).

substantial drafting and redrafting,[19] and lengthy congressional subcommittee hearings and reports.[20] Earlier versions had been passed by the House in 1967[21] and by the Senate in 1974.[22] It was essentially the House substitute bill[23] (amending the Senate bill) that emerged from conference[24] and became the new law.

The 1976 Act was the fourth major[25] copyright law revision since the first federal copyright statute was enacted by the first Congress in 1790.[26] Other revisions occurred at approximately forty-year intervals in 1831,[27] 1870,[28] and 1909.[29] The 1909 statute, drafted in flexible language, re-

---

19. For list of copyright law revision bills, *see* appendix H of the second edition of this *Guide*.
20. For list of copyright law revision hearings, *see* appendix H of the second edition of this *Guide*. For selective excerpts from congressional committee reports, including guidelines, *see* appendix I of the second edition of this *Guide*.
21. H.R. 2512, 90th Cong., 1st Sess. (April 11, 1967). The copyright riders on architectural works, computer software rental, and moral rights, tacked on to the Judicial Improvements Act, enacted December 1, 1990, used "his or her" in several provisions and even a "his" alone.
22. S. 22, 94th Cong., 2d Sess. (Feb. 19, 1976); S. 1361, 93d Cong., 2d Sess. (Sept. 9, 1974); S. REP. No. 94–473, 94th Cong., 1st Sess. (Nov. 20, 1975) (hereinafter cited as 1975 Senate Report).
23. H.R. REP. No. 94–1476, 94th Cong., 2d Sess. (Sept. 3, 1976) (hereinafter cited as 1976 House Report).
24. H.R. REP. No. 94–1733, 94th Cong., 2d Sess. (Sept. 29, 1976) (hereinafter cited as Conference Report).
25. The 1909 Act was amended in 1912, 1913, 1914, 1919, 1926, 1928, 1938, 1939, 1940, 1941, 1947, 1948, 1949, 1952, 1954, 1957, 1962, 1965, 1970, 1971, 1972, and 1974. *See* Goldman, *The History of U.S.A. Copyright Law Revision 1901 to 1954* (1955), *reprinted in* 2 STUDIES ON COPYRIGHT—ARTHUR FISHER MEMORIAL EDITION 1101 (1963).
26. Act of May 31, 1790, 1 Stat. 124–26 (1790).
27. Act of Feb. 3, 1831, 4 Stat. 436–39 (1831).
28. Act of July 8, 1870, 16 Stat. 212–17 (1870).
29. Act of March 4, 1909, 35 Stat. 1075–88 (1909).

mained in effect longer than any of its predecessors, during a period of unprecedented technological advances.[30]

1.4 Overview of 1976 Act, as Amended

The 1976 Act comprises sixty-two pages in the Statutes at Large compared with twenty-three pages for the 1909 Act.

The twenty-year copyright revision program has a voluminous "legislative history."[31] Reliance on the "legislative his-

---

30. *See* 1976 House Report 47:

> Motion pictures and sound recordings had just made their appearance in 1909, and radio and television were still in the early stages of their development. During the past half century a wide range of new techniques for capturing and communicating printed matter, visual images, and recorded sounds have come into use, and the increasing use of information storage and retrieval devices, communications satellites, and laser technology promises even greater changes in the near future. The technical advances have generated new industries and new methods for the reproduction and dissemination of copyrighted works, and the business relations between authors and users have evolved new patterns.

Even before its effective date, however, the 1976 Act was out of date in terms of existing and developing technologies. *See* Henn, *Cassandra Considers Copyright,* 25 BULL. COPYRIGHT SOC'Y 453 (1978).

31. A. LATMAN & J. LIGHTSTONE, THE KAMINSTEIN LEGISLATIVE HISTORY PROJECT: A COMPENDIUM AND ANALYTICAL INDEX OF MATERIALS LEADING TO THE COPYRIGHT ACT OF 1976 xxxi–xliii (1981). The Kaminstein Project (6 vols.) indexes more than 160 items of legislative history, much of which is collected on 143 microfiche cards in G. GROSSMAN, OMNIBUS COPYRIGHT REVISION (1976). *See* Litman, *Copyright, Compromise, and Legislative History,* 72 CORNELL L. REV. 857 (1987). Goldstein, *Outline of the Legislative History of Copyright Law Revision from 1955 to 1976,* 6 A.P.L.A. Q.J. 74 (1978); Lehman, *Legislative Background,* 25 BULL. COPYRIGHT SOC'Y 192 (1978); Marke, *United States Copyright Revision and Its Legislative History,* 70 LAW LIB. J. 121 (1977); Brennan, *Legislative History and Chapter 1 of S.22,* 22 N.Y.L. SCH. L. REV. 193 (1977).

tory," especially when based on a report of a subcommittee of a committee of one branch of Congress, could be misplaced. The reports contain some internal inconsistencies[32] and misstatements of prior law.[33] The language in the reports occasionally does not keep abreast of congressional changes in the language of the bills.[34] On the other hand, language sometimes is changed in the reports when the legislative language has not been changed.[35] The reports also include self-serving declarations of various lobbying groups and "guidelines"; to some extent they are a law unto themselves.[36]

---

32. *E.g.*, variations between the 1975 Senate Report and the 1976 House Report interpreting fair use (§ 107) and library and archives provisions (§ 108), detailed in Copyright Office Circular R21 (Reproduction of Copyrighted Works by Educators and Librarians). *See also* 1976 House Report 122, 124 (presumptions as to rights transferred); *id.* at 147 (stating that omission of copyright notice "whether intentional or unintentional" does not invalidate the copyright if either of two conditions is met).
33. *E.g.*, 1976 House Report 122 (basic presumption that, unless there has been express transfer of more, owner of collective work acquires only privilege to use in that particular collective work, etc., is "fully consistent with present law and practice"). *See id.* at 144 (name of "copyright owner" in copyright notice, when name of "owner of copyright" is required).
34. *E.g.*, *id.* at 132 (discussion of nonpreemption of "misappropriation"; reference to "misappropriation" deleted by conference committee without clarifying explanation in Conference Report).
35. *E.g.*, *compare* 1976 House Report 77 ("daily newscasts of the national television networks, which report the major events of the day," excluding documentaries, magazine-format and other public affairs programs "dealing with subjects of general interest to the viewing public"), *with* Conference Report 73 ("local, regional, or network newscasts, interviews concerning current news events, and on-the-spot coverage of news events").
36. *E.g.*, 1976 House Report 65–74 (fair use), 86–87 (Twentieth Century Music Corp. v. Aiken, 422 U.S. 151 [1975]; Buck v. Jewell-LaSalle Realty Co., 283 U.S. 191 [1931]), 159–60 (vicarious liability for infringing performances). *See* Litman, *supra* note 31; Katz, *The General Revision of the Copyright Law—From Bare Bones to Corpulence—A Partial Overview*, 4 PEPPERDINE L. REV. 213 (1917); Katz, *The 1976*

1.5 Summary of Berne Convention Implementation Act of 1988 (Effective March 1, 1989)

The Berne Convention Implementation Act of 1988 (Berne Act[37]) was enacted to enable the United States to adhere to the Berne Convention of 1886, as revised (Berne Convention[38]).

The Berne Act became effective on March 1, 1989, "the date on which the Berne Convention (as defined in section 101 of title 17, United States Code)[39] entered "into force

---

Copyright Revision Act and Authors' Rights: A Negative Overview, 4 PEPPERDINE L. REV. 171 (1977). Views have been expressed that copyright legislation is crafted by lobbyists for major copyright interests and rubber-stamped by Congress. The political clout and contributions of such interests await analysis. Some have contended that the congressional subcommittee reports, mostly drafted by others and not always accurate as to the pre-existing law and reflective or revisions in the wording of the statute as eventually enacted, are more important than the statute itself. *Cf.* A & M Records, Inc. v. A.L.W. Ltd. 855 F.2d 368 (7th Cir. 1988) (congressional lobbying not conspiracy in restraint of trade).

37. Berne Convention Implementation Act of 1988, Pub. L. No. 100-568. 102 Stat. 2853 (1988) (effective March 1, 1989) (hereinafter referred to as Berne Act).

38. Each adhering nation applies to so-called Berne Convention works its domestic law, which must meet minimal Berne Convention requirements. Hence, the need for the United States to enact implementing legislation to minimize formalities and amplify rights.

    A Berne Convention work is defined at length in the Berne Act, which expands the classes of published works eligible for protection. 17 U.S.C.A. § 104 (Supp.) Unpublished works regardless of "country of origin" enjoy protection. For published works, nationality of the author and nationality of the work are recognized. Nationality of the work depends on first or "simultaneous" "publications" in a Berne Convention nation. *See* chapter 6, *infra*.

    For protection of American works in foreign countries, *see* chapter 34 *infra*.

39. "The Convention for the Protection of Literary and Artistic Works, signed at Berne, Switzerland, on September 8, 1886, and all acts, protocols, and revisions thereto," of which the Paris revision of 1971, as amended in 1979, is the latest version.

with respect to the United States."[40] The Convention, by its terms, entered into force with respect to any country outside the Union three months after the date on which the Director General has notified the deposit of its instrument of accession."[41] Until the effective date of March 1, 1989, United States law was not affected.

The Berne Act states that the Convention is not self-executing in the United States,[42] that the obligations of the United States under the Convention "may be performed only pursuant to appropriate domestic law,"[43] that the domestic law as amended by the Berne Act satisfies the "obligations of the United States" in adhering to the Convention, and that "no further rights or interests shall be recognized or created for that purpose."[44]

The Convention provisions are not to be given effect under title 17, as amended by the Berne Act, "and any other relevant provisions of Federal or State law, including the common law,"[45] and are not enforceable in any act brought pursuant to the provisions of the Convention "itself."[46]

Title 17 of the United States Code, as amended by the Berne Act (17 U.S.C.), does not provide "copyright protection for any work that is in the public domain in the United States."[47] Causes of action arising under 17 U.S.C. before March 1, 1989, are governed by 17 U.S.C. "as in effect when the cause of action arose."[48]

Since the Berne Convention has no direct application to copyright law in the United States, this summary of the

40. Berne Act § 13(a).
41. Berne Convention art. 29(2)(a) (footnotes omitted).
42. Berne Act § 2(1).
43. Berne Act § 2(2).
44. Berne Act § 2(3).
45. Berne Act § 3(a)(1).
46. Berne Act § 3(a)(2).
47. Berne Act § 12.
48. Berne Act § 13(b).

Berne Act focuses on its provisions as they affect the copyright statute as amended prior to the Berne Act. The Berne Act has no retroactive effect; therefore, the requirements of the law as it existed prior to March 1, 1989, will continue to apply to preexisting issues.

The text of the Berne Convention For the Protection of Literacy and Artistic Works, as revised at Paris, France, July 24, 1971, since it is not self-executing, is not appended. Its text may be found in *Corporation Law Reports* (CCH) ¶ 11.402 and other sources (e.g., WIPO).

The Berne Act purports to qualify the United States for Berne Convention protection.[49] The Convention states two essential conditions for adherence thereto:

1. That Berne Union authors enjoy, for works protectible under the Convention, in Union countries "other than the country of origin," the rights which their respective laws grant to their nationals (reciprocal national treatment), as well as the rights "specially granted" by the Convention;[50]
2. That the enjoyment and exercise of such rights "shall not be subject to any formality."[51]

The Berne Act, although entitled "Implementation," may not adequately recognize every right "specially granted" by the Convention (e.g., noneconomic, or moral, rights). Also, the Berne Act eliminates or relaxes formalities beyond Convention requirements (e.g., for works whose "country of origin" is the United States) and includes some other provisions (e.g., negotiated licenses for public performances by means of coin-operated phonorecord players, doubling statutory damages).

49. Berne Act § 2(1).
50. Berne Convention art. 5(1).
51. Berne Convention art. 5(2).

On December 1, 1990, Congress passed the Judicial Improvements Act, Pub. L. No. 101-650, with copyright riders prohibiting the unauthorized commerical rental of computer software, protecting constructed architectural works, and specifying moral rights for visual artists. The Computer Software Rental Amendments Act, the Architectural Works Copyright Protection Act, and the Visual Artists Rights Act have differing effective dates and periods of duration.

1.6 Comparative View of Copyright, Trademark, and Patent Laws

COMPARATIVE VIEW OF COPYRIGHT, TRADEMARK, AND PATENT LAWS

Excluded from Analysis: Hybrid Protection of Semiconductor Chip Products.

	COPYRIGHTS	TRADEMARKS (See S. KANE, TRADEMARK LAW: A PRACTITIONER'S GUIDE (1987) (Supp)	PATENTS (See R. HILDRETH, PATENT LAW: A PRACTITIONER'S GUIDE (1988) (Supp.); P. ROSENBERG, PATENT LAW FUNDAMENTALS (rev. 2d ed. 1991) (3 vols.)
1. Federal Constitutional Basis	U.S. Const. art. I, § 8, cl. 8: Congress shall have power "To promote the Progress of Science and the useful Arts by securing for limited Times to authors . . . the exclusive Right to their respective Writings . . ."	U.S. Const. art. I, § 8, cl. 3: Congress shall have power to regulate commerce with foreign nations and among the several states and with the Indian tribes.	U.S. Const. art. I, § 8, cl. 8: Congress shall have power "To promote the Progress of Science and the useful Arts by securing for limited Times to . . . Inventors the exclusive Right to their respective . . . Discoveries."

continued

COMPARATIVE VIEW OF COPYRIGHT, TRADEMARK, AND PATENT LAWS
Excluded from Analysis: Hybrid Protection of Semiconductor Chip Products. (*Continued*)

	COPYRIGHTS	TRADEMARKS	PATENTS
2. Statutory Provisions			
(a) Federal	17 U.S.C. §§ 101 *et seq.* (1976 Act, effective Jan. 1, 1978, as amended, including Berne Convention Implantation Act of 1988 [Berne Act], effective Mar. 1, 1989). (Pre-1978 statute was 17 U.S.C. §§ 1 *et seq.* (1909 Act, as amended).	15 U.S.C. §§ 1051 *et seq.*; Trademark Act of 1946 (Lanham Act), somewhat amended by Trademark Revision Act of 1988 (effective Nov. 16, 1989, with focus on registration procedure); false designation of origin or false statements about competitor's goods actionable under § 43(a) without registration; no antidilution provision or consumer standing to sue under § 43(a).	35 U.S.C. §§ 1 *et seq.*
(b) State	Some state statutes, e.g., distinction between ownership of copyright and ownership of material object, moral rights, *droit de suite.*	State trademark statutes (some with antidilution provisions not necessarily dependent on state registration).	No state patent statutes

3. Common-Law Principles	Subsisting state common-law copyrights became federal statutory copyrights on Jan. 1, 1978; absent "fixation," common-law rights exist.	State common-law rights provide basis for federal registration with its substantive and procedural rights.	State trade secret protection; state contractual protection for confidential information and reasonable covenants not to compete (unless in restraint of trade).
4. Degree of Federal Preemption	17 U.S.C. § 301; *See* Goldstein v. California, 412 U.S. 546 (1973); *cf.* International News Serv. v. Associated Press, 248 U.S. 215 (1918).	Federal statutes limited to commerce that Congress lawfully may regulate; intrastate commerce subject to state law, absent conflict with paramount federal law; registration on federal principal register precludes innocent adoption of common-law rights anywhere in the United States. *See* Trade-Mark Cases, 100 U.S. 82 (1879).	*See* Sears, Roebuck & Co. v. Stiffel Co., 376 U.S. 225 (1964); Compco Corp. v. Day-Brite Lighting, Inc., 376 U.S. 234 (1964); Kewanee Oil Co. v. Bicron Corp., 416 U.S. 470 (1974); Aronson v. Quick Point Pencil Co., 446 U.S. 257 (1979); Bonito Boats, Inc. v. Thunder Craft Boats, 109 S. Ct. 971 (1989).
5. Subject Matter	U.S. Const.: "Writings" of "Authors"; Statute: Original works of authorship fixed in any tangible medium of expression (§ 102); *cf.* Semiconductor Chips Protection Act of 1984.	Trademarks, service marks, certification marks, collective marks (§ 45); *cf.* trade names and commercial names under §§ 43(a), 44.	U.S. Const.: "Discoveries" of "Inventors"; Statute: invention, discovery; new and useful process, machine, manufacture, composition of matter, or improvement thereof; new,

continued

COMPARATIVE VIEW OF COPYRIGHT, TRADEMARK, AND PATENT LAWS

Excluded from Analysis: Hybrid Protection of Semiconductor Chip Products. (*Continued*)

	COPYRIGHTS	TRADEMARKS	PATENTS
			original and ornamental design for articles of manufacture; asexually reproduced distinct and new variety of plant. *Cf.* Plant Variety Protection Act of 1970, administered by Department of Agriculture.
6. Eligibility	Unpublished works without regard to nationality or domicile of author; published works eligible under 17 U.S.C. § 104, to which Berne Act added "Berne Convention works."	Natural or juristic person, American or foreign national of country of origin extending reciprocal rights to American nationals.	"Whoever invents or discovers . . ." [*cf.* claim for foreign priority].
7. Protectible Elements	"Expression" versus "ideas"; not ideas, procedures, processes, systems, methods of operation, concepts, principles, discoveries, facts, news, material in the	Distinctive, not descriptive or generic, to identify (certify or indicate membership) (see §§ 2, 23, 45); nonfunctional; abandoned mark may be adopted and used by	New and useful; nonobvious; not anticipated by prior art (can be dominant patent or narrower improvement patent).

	public domain; not intrinsic utilitarian functions; not "work of the United States Government."	another who can acquire rights therein.	
8. Ownership	Author (employer in case of "work made for hire") (also coauthors of "joint work").	First user in area (*see* § 22: constructive notice of registrant's claim of ownership thereof by registration on principal register; retroactivity to date of filing of intent-to-use application—with exceptions—upon acceptance of statement of use).	Inventor (possibility of co-inventors); employer of person hired to invent; application must be by inventor although application or the resulting patent can be assigned.
9. Acquisition of Protection	"Creation" ("fixed") by or under authority of author in copy or phonorecord for first time (§§ 302, 101).	Adoption and use in area or bona fide intent to use; additional protection by federal registration, especially on principal register. *Cf.* state trademark statutes.	Issue of patent (pending application affords no protection) (§ 154).
10. Formalities			
(a) Effective Jan. 1, 1978	None for unpublished works (registration prerequisite to infringement	None for common-law rights (possibly "Trademark" or "TM"); if	Notice: "Patent" or "Pat." together with number of patent (§ 287) ("Patent

continued

COMPARATIVE VIEW OF COPYRIGHT, TRADEMARK, AND PATENT LAWS

Excluded from Analysis: Hybrid Protection of Semiconductor Chip Products. (*Continued*)

	COPYRIGHTS	TRADEMARKS	PATENTS
	action, and statutory damages and attorney's fees); for published works, copyright notice ("©" or "℗"; year of publication; name of owner of copyright), deposit of copies, registration of claim (prerequisite to infringement action and possibly statutory damages and attorney's fees); renewal for copyrights in their first term on Jan. 1, 1978; recordation of transfer prerequisite to pre-Mar. 1, 1989 infringement action by transfers.	federally registered, "®" or "Reg. U.S. Pat. & Tm. Off." notice (§ 29); if state registered, possibly "Registered Trademark"; filing and processing of application for registration, subject to interference and opposition; cancellation after registration, subject to degree of incontestability.	pending" lawful if true, but without legal effect); filing and prosecution of application, subject to Patent and Trademark Office responses and interferences.
(b) Effective Mar. 1, 1989	Copyright notice for works published after effective date of Berne Act not mandatory, but permissive;		

	notice given evidentiary effect; registration not prerequisite for infringement action for Berne Convention works whose country of origin is not United States. Recordation of transfer requirement eliminated for all works.		
11. Administration	United States Copyright Office (part of Library of Congress, i.e., legislative branch); headed by Register of Copyrights; administrative action relatively prompt.	United States Patent and Trademark Office (part of Department of Commerce, i.e., executive branch); headed by Commissioner of Patents and Trademarks; *cf* state trademark statutes, e.g., N.Y. GEN. BUS. LAW §§ 360 *et seq.* (secretary of state); more than one-year average federal administrative delay.	United States Patent and Trademark Office (part of Department of Commerce, e.g., executive branch), headed by Commissioner of Patents and Trademarks; more than two-year average administrative delay.
12. Fees	$20 for registration of copyright claim; for other fees, see § 708 (e.g., $12 for renewal).	(As effective Aug. 26, 1986): e.g., application per class: $200, renewal per class: $300	(As effective Nov. 5, 1990):* e.g., for utility patent Basic filing fee: $630 Issue fee: $1,050

continued

COMPARATIVE VIEW OF COPYRIGHT, TRADEMARK, AND PATENT LAWS

Excluded from Analysis: Hybrid Protection of Semiconductor Chip Products. (*Continued*)

	COPYRIGHTS	TRADEMARKS	PATENTS
			Maintenance fee: $830, $1,670, $2,500 For design patent Basic filing fee: $250 Issue fee: $370 For plant patent Basic filing fee: $420 Issue fee: $520 *Fees for "small entity" usually are 50 percent of above fees.
13. Commencement of Protection	"Creation" ("fixation").	First use or bona fide intent to use; additional procedural and substantive rights on registration.	Issue of patent.
14. Duration	Post-Jan. 1, 1978, works: life of author plus fifty years (with refinements); pre-Jan. 1, 1978, works (neither published nor copyrighted before then): life plus fifty years, but at least until 2002/2027; works	So long as used and not abandoned; federal registration for ten years, renewable for additional ten-year periods (within six months before expiration), as long as still in use (§ 9) timely verified statement of	Seventeen years for utility patent (§ 154 (extendable for up to five years if regulatory delay for certain pharmaceutical and similar patents)); fourteen years for design patents (§§ 154, 161); seventeen years for

	in first term on Jan. 1, 1978: twenty-eight years unless renewed (as extended); renewal for forty-seven years—seventy-five-year total—renewable during last year; all copyright terms run to end of calendar year; works in renewal term on Jan. 1, 1978: seventy-five years from date of original copyright secured.	use required to support intent-to-use application.	plant patents (§ 173) [no renewals of patents]
15. Premature Loss of Protection	Omission before effective date of Berne Act (Mar. 1, 1989) of copyright notice unless excused or rectified under statute; termination by author, surviving spouse, children, grandchildren (§§ 203, 304(c)); failure to renew (§ 304). Omission of copyright notice from copies or phonorecords after effective date of Berne Act (Mar. 1, 1989) no longer results in	Discontinuance of use (abandonment); mark's becoming generic (§ 45); protection under registration lost on lapse of registration (e.g., failure to file affidavit of continued use in sixth year or to renew; cancellation; 1989 redefinition of "use in commerce").	Dedication (e.g., failure to apply within one year of commercial use—"statutory bar"); abandonment; disclaimer; fraud on Patent and Trademark Office; abandonment of application also is possible.

continued

COMPARATIVE VIEW OF COPYRIGHT, TRADEMARK, AND PATENT LAWS
Excluded from Analysis: Hybrid Protection of Semiconductor Chip Products. (*Continued*)

	COPYRIGHTS	TRADEMARKS	PATENTS
	possible loss of protection. Fraud on Copyright Office.		
16. Transfers of Rights			
(a) Assignments	*Cf.* "Transfer of copyright ownership" ("signed writing")—*See* §§ 201-204; for recordation, see § 205; transfer of copyright versus material object (§ 202); Recordation-of-transfer requirements as condition precedent to infringement action eliminated for all works after effective date of Berne Act (Mar. 1, 1989).	*See* § 10 (assignable by writing with goodwill of business or part thereof); recordation within three months for protection against subsequent purchaser without notice.	*See* § 261 (assignable by instrument in writing); recordation within three months for protection against subsequent purchaser or mortgagee).
(b) Licenses	Exclusive—*see* §§ 201-204 (signed writing required); nonexclusive. For recordation, *see* § 205.	*See* provisions on "related companies"—§§ 5, 45.	Transfers of exclusive or nonexclusive rights less than assignment; employer's nonexclusive, royalty-free "shop rights."

17. Exclusive Rights	*See* § 106 ("to do and to authorize" reproduction, preparation of derivative works—*cf.* §§ 103, 101), public distribution, public performance, public display; access and copying essential; independent creation not infringement and protectible.	To prevent use of mark, etc., likely to cause confusion or to cause mistake or to deceive (§ 32). *See* § 43(a) (unfair competition regardless of registration); "antidilution" protection under some state trademark statutes regardless of registration.	*See* § 154 (right to exclude others from making, using, or selling invention throughout United States); for plant patents, right to exclude others from asexually reproducing plant or selling or using plant so reproduced (§ 163); copying not required; independent creation no defense.
(a) "Fair Use," etc.	*See* § 107.	Collateral, nondenominative, nonmark use (e.g., comparative advertising; reference to ingredients).	Exception for "experimental use."
(b) Other Limitations or Exemptions	*See* §§ 108–119; antitrust limitations.	Antitrust limitations.	Antitrust limitations.
(c) Contributory	No statutory basis; *but cf.* Sony Corp. of Am. v. Universal City Studios, Inc., 104 S. Ct. 774 (1984) (patent law analogy); actively aiding and abetting direct infringement).	*Cf.* § 32(b); actively aiding and abetting direct infringement.	*See* § 271(c) (knowingly selling nonstaple item especially adapted for use in patented combination or for practicing patented process—not by selling unpatented parts for use in repairing patented goods).

continued

COMPARATIVE VIEW OF COPYRIGHT, TRADEMARK, AND PATENT LAWS
Excluded from Analysis: Hybrid Protection of Semiconductor Chip Products. (*Continued*)

	COPYRIGHTS	TRADEMARKS	PATENTS
18. Compulsory Licenses	§ 111 (cable television secondary transmission license); § 115 (musical recording license); § 116 (coin-operated phonorecord players license) (suspended); § 118 (noncommercial broadcasting license); [others being proposed]; [role of Copyright Office and Copyright Royalty Tribunal]. Some cases award damages but deny injunction, in effect, a compulsory license.	No statutory basis; *cf.* abortive attempts by FTC; some cases award damages, but deny injunction, in effect, a compulsory license.	No patent statutory basis; *cf.* judicial imposition in antitrust cases; there are some specific references in other statutes that permit compulsory licenses; some cases award damages, but deny injunction, in effect, a compulsory license.
19. "Statutory" Licenses	§ 116A (negotiated licenses for public performances by means of coin-operated phonorecord players). § 119 (negotiated licenses for secondary transmissions by satellite carriers for		

	private home viewing license; voluntary negotiation; compulsory arbitration, subject to Copyright Royalty Tribunal review).		
20. Infringement			
(a) Direct	Violation of any of exclusive rights under §§ 106–118 (§ 501); impliedly within United States	Use of mark, etc., likely to cause confusion or mistake or to deceive (probability, not actuality or possibility, of confusion); impliedly within United States	Making, using, or selling invention "within United States" during term of patent (§ 271(a)).
(b) Inducing	No statutory basis; *cf.* "to authorize" in § 106 and cases	No statutory basis.	Actively inducing infringement (§ 271(b)).
21. Suits for Infringement			
(a) Federal Courts	Exclusively in federal courts (registration prerequisite), except for Berne Convention works whose country of origin is not United States) (*cf.* contract claims, etc.)	Concurrently in state and federal courts; federal court jurisdiction dependent upon federal registration, diversity of citizenship with increased jurisdictional amount ($50,000); or pendent/ancillary	Exclusively in federal courts; *cf.* contract claims, etc.

continued

COMPARATIVE VIEW OF COPYRIGHT, TRADEMARK, AND PATENT LAWS
Excluded from Analysis: Hybrid Protection of Semiconductor Chip Products. *(Continued)*

	COPYRIGHTS	TRADEMARKS	PATENTS
		jurisdiction; federal registration not required for alleged violation of § 43(a) or § 44.	
(b) State Courts	Federal court jurisdiction exclusive for infringement; state law contract and other claims.	Concurrent with federal courts for infringement; other rights within state court jurisdiction.	Federal court jurisdiction exclusive for infringement; state law contract and other claims.
(c) Standing to Sue	Legal or beneficial owner of any exclusive right infringed (notice to Copyright Office and possible other claimants).	Registrant for infringement of registered mark; protection under § 43(a) by any person or under § 44 by persons eligible thereunder; common-law protection by owner of common-law rights infringed.	Patentee; exclusive licensee of rights infringed; patentee as indispensible party.
(d) Pendent Claims	"[O]riginal jurisdiction of any civil action asserting a claim of unfair competition	[same]	[same]

when joined with a substantial and related claim under the copyright, patent, plant variety protection or trade-mark laws." (28 U.S.C. § 1338); federal court, as incident to disposition of matter properly before it, has "ancillary" or "pendent" jurisdiction to decide other matters raised by case, so long as there is "common nucleus of operative fact."

1.7 Problems of New Technologies

To claim copyright protection for newly developed technologies, their "authors," whoever they might be, would be seeking protection for all or some aspects of whatever "writings" they have produced, under a legal system devised to protect printed matter, expanded to "writings," against "copying."

Distortion of the copyright system already is evident.[52] Protectionists prefer the ease and longer duration of copyrights over patents. The Copyright Office, with its traditional copyright functions greatly reduced, has not been reluctant to serve a Procrustean function, at least as a temporary expedient. New technologies require a more sophisticated balance between public and competing private interests.

As a result, the copyright system is being overwhelmed. Required is a modern system designed to meet unique unprecedented needs consistent with the public interest. Those concerned should resolve their problems and propose reasonable compromises for Congress to enact within its powers.[53] Required is competent administration subject to knowledgeable judicial review.[54]

---

52. *See* chapter 32 *infra.*
53. *See* chapter 32, notes 2 and 3, *infra.* Quaere, as to constitutional basis.
54. The Copyright Office, now a vestige of the British Stationers Company of 1710, can be abolished. Its functions of serving as an intermediary for free Library of Congress deposits and keeping of records, with the personnel involved, could be absorbed by the Library of Congress itself. Its intermediate functions for the Copyright Royalty Tribunal, also, would seem expendable. The current Register of Copyright, with a Library of Congress background, would seem qualified to direct such absorption.

2. Relevance of Prior Laws

For most purposes, there have been three somewhat-overlapping copyright systems in the United States since 1909. Prior to January 1, 1978 (when the 1976 Act became effective), there was a federal-state dual system: exclusively federal for "published" works and state common law for "unpublished" works; since exclusively federal for "fixed" works:

1. 1909 Act, effective July 1, 1909, with its amendments—expressly preserving the rights of authors and proprietors of unpublished works;
2. 1976 Act, effective January 1, 1978, subject to "Transitional and Supplementary Provisions," with its amendments—expressly preempting copyright for all fixed works whenever created and whether published or unpublished; and
3. Berne Convention Implementation Act of 1988, effective March 1, 1989—expressly stating that certain rights (moral rights), "whether Federal, State, or the common law," are not affected by United States adherence to the Berne Convention.

As a general rule, all such legislation was prospective only and did not apply retroactively to revive works in the public domain or to cure past noncompliance with then applicable copyright requirements.

For many decades, the pre-January 1, 1978, and pre-March 1, 1989, laws will continue to be relevant. Continuing copyright law amendments are enacted with differing effective dates and durations of protection. Sometimes copyright bills are passed by Congress as riders to major bills of nongermane subject matter, *e.g.*, the copyright riders to the Judicial Improvements Act of 1990, Pub. L. 101-650 (Dec. 1, 1990), which had varying effective dates for prohibiting the unauthorized commerical rental of computer software, protecting constructed architectural works, and specifying moral rights for visual artists ("attribution and integrity" rights).

2.1 Federal Preemption

The law provides for federal preemption of rights that are equivalent to any of the exclusive rights within the general scope of copyright in works of authorship that are fixed in a "tangible medium of expression" and come within the subject matter of copyright,[1] and abolishes state common-law copyrights in the preempted areas, transforming subsisting state common-law copyrights into federal statutory copyrights. "Fixation" has replaced "publication" as the general dividing line between federal and state law; absent fixation, there is no federal preemption.

2.2 Viability of Common-Law Copyright

Works under common-law copyright when the 1976 Act became effective on January 1, 1978, are protected as statutory copyrights for the life of the author and fifty years after

1. 17 U.S.C.A. § 301; Abrams, *The Historic Foundation of American Copyright Law: Exploding the Myth of Common Law Copyright*, 29 *Wayne L. Rev. 1119 (1983). See* chapter 4 *infra.*

the author's death (or alternative statutory durations), but at least until December 31, 2002, and, if published on or before then, until December 31, 2027.[2] Also, common-law copyright infringement causes of action arising from undertakings commenced before January 1, 1978, are not affected.[3] These works should be registered, because registrations may be prerequisite to an infringement suit and no award of statutory damages or attorney's fees would be available for infringement of copyright in an unpublished work commenced before the effective date of registration.[4] Thus, whether or not common-law copyright was subsisting on January 1, 1978, can be relevant until 2027 or even thereafter.

2.3 Viability of 1909 Act

2.3[1] Transitional and Supplementary Provisions

The 1976 Act stated that it amended the 1909 Act "in its entirety."[5] Fourteen more qualifying sections ("secs." as distinguished from "§§"), however, were contained in the Transitional and Supplementary Provisions.[6]

2.3[1][a] Nonrevival of Copyright

For works in the public domain before January 1, 1978, no protection was provided by the 1976 Act.[7] In short, there was no revival of copyright protection. Whether or not a

2. 17 U.S.C.A. § 303.
3. 17 U.S.C.A. § 301(b)(2) (subject to applicable state statute of limitations—usually ranging from one to six years—for bringing action, and until final disposition).
4. 17 U.S.C.A. §§ 411, 412(1). *See* chapter 12 *infra*.
5. Pub. L. No. 94-553, sec. 101 (1976).
6. *See* annotations to relevant sections in 17 U.S.C.A. *See also* chapter 3, note 2, *infra*.
7. Pub. L. No. 94-553, sec. 101 (1976). *Compare* Priv. L. No. 92-60 (1971)

work was in the public domain before January 1, 1978, must be determined under the 1909 Act.[8]

2.3[1][b] Reciprocity with Foreign Nations

Presidential proclamations confirming the existence of reciprocal copyright conditions with foreign nations under the 1909 Act and previous copyright statutes[9] "continue in force until terminated, suspended, or revised by the President."[10]

(reviving and extending copyrights in *Science and Health with Key to the Scriptures* by Mary Baker Eddy). Quaere, as to its constitutionality because not promotive of the progress of science and useful arts, violative of freedom of speech and press, and violative of the principle of separation of church and state. Priv. L. No. 92-60 was held unconstitutional in United Christian Scientists v. Christian Science Bd. of Directors, 616 F. Supp. 476 (D.D.C. 1985), *aff'd*, 829 F.2d 1152 (D.C. Cir. 1987) (impermissible aid to religion). Religious scriptures and other works are entitled to the same copyright protections as other works. Religious Technology Center v. Scott, 66. F. Supp. 515 (S.D. Cal. 1987). Of course, there may be problems of authorship, duration, etc. *See* chapter 1, note 7 *supra*.

8. *E.g.*, publication without proper copyright notice; failure to register and deposit on demand; noncompliance with manufacturing clause; failure to renew. *See* Copyright Office Circular R22 (How to Investigate the Copyright Status of a Work). Copyrights in their renewal terms on or after September 19, 1962, meaning works that were copyrighted on or after September 19, 1906, and renewed, did not expire until December 31, 1982. For the 1962-1976 extensions, *see* chapter 16, note 13, *infra*. *See* Nimmer, *The Old Copyright Act as a Part of the New Act*, 22 N.Y.L. SCH. L. REV. 471 (1977).

9. The list of Presidential proclamations, and whether they include mechanical reproduction rights for music, is set out following 17 U.S.C.A. § 109 (Supp.). *See* Copyright Office Circulars R38a, (International Copyright Relations of the United States) and R38c (International Copyright Conventions).

   American statutory copyright protection was not afforded to foreign authors prior to July 1, 1891. Act of March 3, 1891, § 13, 26 Stat. 1106 (March 3, 1891) (Chace Act). *See* chapter 6 *infra*.

10. Pub. L. No. 94-553, sec. 104 (1976).

2.3[1][c] Sound Recordings Under Compulsory License

Persons who have lawfully made sound recordings under the compulsory license provision of the 1909 Act[11] may continue to make and distribute them without the need for any new compulsory license.[12] However, sound recordings made on or after January 1, 1978, constitute phonorecords and are otherwise subject to section 115.[13]

2.3[1][d] Extension of Ad Interim Copyright

Ad interim copyright, whether subsisting or capable of being secured on December 31, 1977, was extended for the term or terms provided by section 304.[14]

2.3[1][e] Copyright Notice

In the case of a work published before January 1, 1978, compliance with the copyright notice provisions of either the 1909 Act or the 1976 Act "is adequate with respect to copies publicly distributed after December 31, 1977."[15]

2.3[1][f] Registration

The registration of claims to copyright for which the required deposit, application, and fee were received in the Copyright Office before January 1, 1978, were to "be made in accordance" with the 1909 Act.[16]

---

11. 1909 Act § 1(e).
12. Pub. L. No. 94-553, sec. 106 (1976).
13. *Id. See* chapter 22 *infra.*
14. *Id.* sec. 107. *See* text accompanying chapter 14, notes 10–15, *infra.*
15. *Id.* sec. 108.
16. *Id.* sec. 109.

2.3[1][g] Recordation

The recordation of assignments of copyright or other instruments received in the Copyright Office before January 1, 1978, were to "be made in accordance" with the 1909 Act.[17]

2.3[1][h] Demand and Penalty for Failure to Deposit

The demand and penalty provisions of the 1909 Act applied "to any work in which copyright has been secured by publication with notice of copyright" on or before December 31, 1977.[18]

2.3[1][i] Pre-1978 Federal Statutory Causes of Action

All "causes of action" that arose under the 1909 Act before January 1, 1978, are to be governed by the 1909 Act.[19] Both the 1976 Act and the 1909 Act provided for three-year statutes of limitations for a criminal "cause of action"[20] and for a civil "claim."[21] Thus, as to preexisting criminal "causes of action," the 1909 Act may continue in full force until December 31, 1980, for bringing the action and thereafter until final disposition. Presumably, the same would be true of civil "claims."

2.3[2] Freezing and Codification of Pre-1978 Law

The 1976 Act expressly froze the law as of December 31, 1977, concerning:

---

17. *Id.*
18. *Id.* sec. 110 (but any deposit and registration made after December 31, 1977 in response to demand under 1909 Act must "be made in accordance" with 1976 Act).
19. *Id.* sec. 112. Pre-1978 common-law copyright infringement causes of action are governed by state common law prior to its preemption. *See* note 3 *supra.*
20. 17 U.S.C.A. § 507(a); 1909 Act § 115(a).
21. 17 U.S.C.A. § 507(b); 1909 Act § 115(b).

1. Rights to make, distribute, or display a useful article portrayed in a copyrighted work;[22]
2. Rights to use a copyrighted work in conjunction with computers and similar information services;[23] and
3. Rights with respect to specified activities by a public broadcasting entity with respect to published nondramatic musical works and published pictorial, graphic, and sculptural works.[24]

In various other areas, the 1976 Act, according to frequent statements in the congressional reports,[25] was intended to codify preexisting law.

2.4 Viability of Pre-Berne Act Laws

2.4[1] Nonretroactivity of Berne Act

The Berne Act, effective March 1, 1989, eliminated many formalities retained by the 1976 Act, but was not retroactive.

Works in the public domain on March 1, 1989, were not revived,[26] and causes of action for copyright infringement accrued prior to such date were not affected by the Berne Act.[27]

---

22. 17 U.S.C.A. § 113(b).
23. 17 U.S.C.A. § 117.
24. 17 U.S.C.A. §§ 118(b)(4), 118(d).
25. E.g., 1976 House Report: § 102(a) (standard of originality) (at 51), § 102(b) (dichotomy between expression and idea) (at 57), § 107 (fair use) (at 66), § 109(a) (disposition of lawfully acquired noninfringing copies and phonorecords) (at 79), § 113(a) (copyright in pictorial, graphic, or sculptural work not affected if work is employed as design of useful article) (at 105), § 201(a) (author as source of copyright ownership) (at 120), § 201(a) (coauthors as coowners of copyright) (at 120), and § 406(b) (effect of antedated copyright notice) (at 149).
26. Berne Conventions § 12.
27. Berne Conventions § 13(b).

2.4[2] Applicability of Older Laws

Thus, copyright status and remedies under older laws may continue to be relevant.

In short, various works may be subject to laws prior to January 1, 1978, from January 1, 1978, to March 1, 1989, and after March 1, 1989. Statutory changes, now at an annual rate, generally are prospective in application.

2.5 Due Process Limitations

The foregoing discussion reflects less than all of the continuing applicability of the 1909 Act with its seventy-year judicial gloss[28] and other pre-Berne Act Laws.

For example, the "work made for hire" concepts may have been changed.[29] Arguably, where a work was made by an employee or on commission prior to 1978, the 1909 Act concepts should control on due process grounds.

Also the "presumption" of rights acquired in a contribution to a collective work by the owner of the collective work[30] conceivably may have been changed, in which case pre-1978 transfers should also be governed by the pre-1978 law on due process grounds.

The 1976 Act recognized due process considerations by its verbatim retention of the 1909 Act renewal provisions for copyrights in their first term on January 1, 1978.[31]

The Berne Act confirmed "moral rights" recognized under federal and state laws.[32]

---

28. *See Decisions of the United States Courts Involving Copyright, 1909–____,* COPYRIGHT OFF. BULL. NOS. 17____ *(1928–____).*
29. 17 U.S.C.A. Act §§ 101, 201(b). *See* text accompanying chapter 7, notes 15–41, *infra.*
30. 17 U.S.C.A. § 201(c). *See* text accompanying chapter 7, notes 38–41, *infra.*
31. 17 U.S.C.A. § 304(a) (with renewal term extended from twenty-eight to forty-seven years, subject to possible termination during last nineteen years). *See* text accompanying chapter 15, notes 30, 31, *infra.*
32. *See* chapter 17, notes 57–60, *infra.*

3. Outline of Copyright Statute

Public Law No. 94-553, 90 Statutes at Large 2541-602 (1976 law), enacted October 19, 1976, is entitled "An Act for the general revision of the Copyright Law, title 17, of the United States Code, and for other purposes."

The 1976 law contained only one title: "Title I—General Revision of Copyright Law."[1]

1. Earlier drafts of the legislation contained two other titles: (1) for the establishment of the National Commission on New Technological Uses of Copyrighted Works (CONTU), and (2) for the protection of ornamental designs of useful articles. The former was enacted in 1974, Pub. L. No. 93-573, 93d Cong., 2d Sess. (Dec. 31, 1974), and CONTU began in July 1975. The ornamental design protection title passed the Senate, as separate legislation in 1962, 1963, and 1966, and as part of the general copyright revision bill in 1974 and 1976, but was deleted by the House. *See* 1976 House Report 50. *See* Copyright Office Circulars R1 (Copyright Basics), former R99 (Highlights of the Current Copyright Law); Henn, *Cassandra Considers Copyright*, 25 BULL. COPYRIGHT SOC'Y 453 (1978); Gorman, *An Overview of the Copyright Act of 1976*, 126 U. PA. L. REV. 856 (1978); Moore, *The Most Significant Changes Effected by Copyright Law Revision*, 6 A.P.L.A. Q.J. 10 (1978); Latman, *A Glimpse at the New Copyright Act*, 24 BULL. COPYRIGHT SOC'Y 77 (1976); Brennan, *An Overview of Copyright and the Copyright Bill*, 17 IDEA 5 (Fall 1975); Henn, *Copyright Law Revision: Paragon or Paradox?* 44 N.Y.U. L. REV. 477 (1969).

3.1 "Sec." and"§"

Title I, which amended title 17 in its entirety, was divided into two sets of provisions:

1. Sec. 101 and fourteen other provisions, each designated by the abbreviation "Sec.," known as the "Transitional and Supplementary Provisions"; and
2. New title 17, with each section designated by a section symbol, "§."

3.2 Secs. 101–115

Sec. 101 amended title 17 of the United States Code in its entirety, followed by the seventy-three sections of a new title 17. These seventy-three sections were each designated by a section symbol, "§." Title 17 was amended in 1977, 1980, 1982, 1984, 1988, 1989, and 1990. The 1984 amendment added a new chapter 9 for the protection of semiconductor chip products (Pub. L. No. 98-620, 98 Stat. 334-756, effective Nov. 8, 1984), which is not part of the copyright statute.

After § 810, the last section of title 17 as enacted in 1976, appear secs. 102–115, known as the "Transitional and Supplementary Provisions." These provisions do not appear in title 17 U.S.C.A. as such. Instead, they appear as scattered notes to particular sections.[2]

---

2. Secs. 102 and 103 appear in a note preceding § 101; sec. 104 in a note following § 104; sec. 106 in a note following § 115; sec. 107 in a note following § 304; sec. 108 in a note following § 401; sec. 109 in a note following § 410; sec. 110 in a note following § 407; sec. 112 in a note following § 501; secs. 114 and 115 in notes preceding § 101. Secs. 105 and 111 amend other titles of the United States Code. Sec. 113 provides for the American Television and Radio Archives. The Transitional and Supplementary Provisions are reprinted in appendix *B infra*.

3.3 §§ 101–914 (Present Title 17 U.S.C.)

3.3[1] Outline of Present Title 17 U.S.C.

Present title 17 has nine chapters divided into ninety-one sections, captioned as follows:

Chapter	*Caption*	§§
1	Subject Matter and Scope of Copyright	101–120
2	Copyright Ownership and Transfer	201–205
3	Duration of Copyright	301–305
4	Copyright Notice, Deposit, and Registration	401–412
5	Copyright Infringement and Remedies	501–511
6	Manufacturing Requirements and Importation	601–603
7	Copyright Office	701–710
8	Copyright Royalty Tribunal	801–810
9	Protection of Semiconductor Chip Products	901–914

The Berne Act, besides adding §116A, changed the headings and text of some sections. The Satellite Home Viewer Act of 1988 added § 119; the 1990 legislation added §§ 511, 106A, and 120. In 1986, § 601 lapsed.

3.3[2] Definitions

Forty-five definitions for "terms and their variant forms" are found in § 101:[3]

3. 17 U.S.C.A. § 101, compared to two definitions in the original 1909 Act. 1909 Act § 26 ("author" in the case of a work made for hire; "date of publication"). Five definitions were added to the 1909 Act in 1971 in connection with the limited protection for sound recordings. The current definitions will be treated in the discussion of the sections where the defined terms are used.

"Anonymous work"
"Architectural works" (added in 1990)
"Audiovisual works"
"Berne Convention" (added by Berne Act);
"Berne Convention work" (added by Berne Act);
"Best edition"
"Children"
"Collective work"
"Compilation"
"Computer program" (added in 1980 out of alphabetical order)
"Copies"
"Copyright owner"[4]
"Country of origin" (added by Berne Act for purposes of § 411)
"Created"
"Derivative work"
"Device"
"Display"
"Fixed"
"Including"
"Instructional text" (in definition of "work made for hire")
"Joint work"
"Literary works"
"Machine" (in definition of "device")
"Motion pictures"
"Perform"
"Phonorecords"
"Pictorial, graphic, and sculptural works" (amended by Berne Act)

---

4. Undefined is the term "owner of copyright," used in 17 U.S.C.A. §§ 106, 113(b), 114(a), 114(b), 115(a)(1), 117, 118(b), 118(c), 201(c), 205(d), 401(b)(3), 402(b)(3), 404(a), 404(b), 406(a), 407(a), 408(a), 408(c)(2)(A), 602(a). *See* chapter 7, note 5, *infra*.

"Process" (in definition of "device")
"Pseudonymous work"
"Publication"
"Publicly"
"Sound recordings"
"State"
"Such as" (in definition of "including")
"Supplementary work" (in definition of "work made for hire")
"Transfer of copyright ownership"
"Transmission program"
"Transmit"
"United States"
"Useful article"
"Widow"
"Widower" (in definition of "widow")
"Work of visual art" (added in 1990)
"Work of the United States Government"
"Work made for hire"

In addition, there are nine definitions in § 111,[5] three in § 116,[6] one in § 118,[7] ten in § 119,[8] one in § 501(a) ("anyone"), nine in § 901, and one in § 910 ("any person").[9]

---

5. 17 U.S.C.A. § 111(e)(4) ("videotape"); *id.* § 111(f) ("cable system"; "distant signal equivalent"; "independent station"; "local service area of a primary transmitter"; "network station"; "noncommercial educational station", "primary transmission"; "secondary transmission"). *See* chapter 25 *infra*.
6. 17 U.S.C.A. § 116(e) ("coin-operated phonorecord player"; "operator"; "performing rights society"). *See* chapter 23 *infra*.
7. 17 U.S.C.A. § 118(g) ("public broadcasting entity"). *See* chapter 24 *infra*.
8. Satellite Home Viewer Act of 1988, 17 U.S.C.A. § 119(d) ("distributor"; "network station"; "primary network station"; "primary transmission"–per §111[f]; "private home viewing"; "satellite carrier"; "secondary transmissions"–per § 111[f]; "subscriber"; "superstation"; "unserved household").
9. 17 U.S.C.A. § 901(a) ("semiconductor chip product"; "mask work";

The definitions provide some basic distinctions:

1. "Works" of "authorship" are distinguished from the "material objects" in which the works are "fixed."
2. The "material objects" are either visually perceptible "copies" or aurally perceptible "phonorecords," with fixed sounds accompanying "motion pictures" or other "audiovisual works" being treated as "copies."
3. Copyright subsists from "creation," in the sense of "fixation" in a "copy" or "phonorecord."
4. "Fixation" "in a tangible medium of expression" is embodiment in a "copy" or "phonorecord" "by or under the authority of the author" for "more than transitory duration," but "fixation" simultaneously with "transmission" is sufficient.
5. The portion of the work fixed at any particular time constitutes the work "as of that time," and "each version constitutes a separate work."
6. Federal "preemption" is of the "exclusive rights" in "works" of "authorship" "fixed" in a "tangible medium of expression."
7. "Sound recordings" are distinguished from sounds accompanying "motion pictures or other audiovisual works."
8. "Compilations," including "collective works" (e.g., "periodical issue"), are distinguished from "derivative works."
9. "Collective works" are assembled collections of a number of "contributions" constituting "separate and independent works in themselves."

"fixed"; "distribute"; "commercially exploit"; "owner"; "innocent purchaser"; "notice of protection"; "infringing semiconductor chip product"). *See* chapter 32 *infra*. The terms "anyone" (as used in § 501) and "any person" (as used in § 910) expressly were defined in the Copyright Remedy Clarification Act of 1990.

10. Features of "pictorial, graphic, and sculptural works" incorporated in "useful articles" are "pictorial, graphic, and sculptural works" if identifiable "separately from," and "capable of existing independently of," the "utilitarian aspects of the article."
11. "Work of the United States Government" is a work "prepared" by a government employee "as part of that person's official duties."
12. "Work made for hire" is a work "prepared by an employee within the scope of his or her employment," and enumerated "specially ordered or commissioned" works "if the parties expressly agree in a written instrument signed by them that the work shall be considered a work made for hire."
13. "Copyright owner" is defined, "with respect to any one of the exclusive rights," as the "owner of that particular right," but the term "owner of copyright" is not defined.
14. "Transfer of copyright ownership" is defined as any grant other than a nonexclusive license, but the term "transfer of copyright" is not defined.
15. "Publication" is the "public" "distribution" of "copies" or "phonorecords"; "public performance or display" does not "of itself" constitute "publication."
16. "Performance" is reciting, rendering, playing, dancing, or acting a work, either directly or by means of any "device" or "process," including showing of the images of a "motion picture" or other "audiovisual work" "in any sequence" or making "the sounds accompanying it audible," and may be or not be "publicly."
17. "Display" is the showing of a copy, either directly or by means of any "device" or "process," including the nonsequential showing of individual images of a "motion picture" or other "audiovisual work," and may be or not be "publicly."

18. "Performance" or "display" may be face-to-face or by "transmission."
19. "Transmission" of a "performance" or "display" is the communication of it by any "device" or "process" whereby images or sounds are "received beyond the place from which they are sent."
20. "Publicly" means *at* a "place open to the public" or "any place where a substantial number of persons outside of a normal circle of a family and its social acquaintances is gathered," or by "transmission" or other communication *to* such a place or "the public, by means of any device or process, whether the members of the public capable of receiving the performance or display receive it in the same place or in separate places and at the same time or at different times."
21. The concept of "commercially exploit" as applied to a mask work" is defined.
22. The concept of "owner" of a "mask work" as a person with "all the rights" or as employer to whom all rights are transferred is defined.

4. Federal Preemption

The pre-1978 dual copyright system, with its dichotomy between state common-law protection for unpublished works and federal statutory protection for published works,[1] has been changed to a national copyright system with federal statutory protection for both unpublished and published works, automatically subsisting from creation, meaning "fixation" in a "copy" or "phonorecord" for the first time. The consequence is federal preemption for fixed works of authorship.

4.1 Preemption of Common-Law Copyright

4.1[1] Common-Law Copyright

At common law, protection accrued automatically upon the creation of the work, vested in the author regardless of the author's nationality or the place of creation of the work,

1. The 1909 Act permitted copyright for certain classes of works of which copies were not reproduced for sale by registration and deposit. 1909 Act § 12. Upon such event, the common-law copyright ended. *See generally* Wheaton v. Peters, 33 U.S. (8 Peters) 591 (1834). Questions of preemption, copyright subject matter, scope of exclusive rights, and infringement are correlative dimensions of the basic problem of promoting the public interest by recognizing the rights of authors in their writing by balancing freedom of expression with property interests.

and included full control over all uses of the work perpetually, prior to publication.[2]

"Publication"[3] was the dividing line, divestitive of common-law protection and investitive of statutory copyright. Under

---

2. Strauss, *Protection of Unpublished Works* (1957), *reprinted in* 1 STUDIES ON COPYRIGHT—ARTHUR FISHER MEMORIAL EDITION 189 (1963). Judicial opinions, legislative reports, law review articles, and treatises tend to refer cavalierly to "common-law copyright," despite some paucity of precedent, especially in the forum jurisdiction, e.g., England or a particular state. In many common-law jurisdictions, there are few precedents. Oddly, Louisiana, a civil-law jurisdiction, may have the most reported decisions. Certainly, the British House of Lords and United States Supreme Court opinions in landmark cases reflected great uncertainty. *See* Donaldson v. Becket, 4 Burr. 2408, 98 Eng. Rep. 257 (H.L. 1774) (12–11, 10–1, 7–4, 6–5, 7–4, 6–5) (Mansfield, L.J. recusing on two vital 6–5 issues), *overruling* Millar v. Taylor, 4 Burr, 2303, 98 Eng. Rep. 201 (K.B. 1769) (3–1) (Mansfield, L.J., dissenting—only dissent of Mansfield period) (English common law); Wheaton v. Peters, 33 U.S. (Peters) 591 (1834) (5–2) (Pennsylvania common law during waning Marshall Court); Abrams, *The Historic Foundation of American Copyright Law: Exploding the Myth of Common Law Copyright*, 29 WAYNE L. REV. 1119 (1983); Whicher, *The Ghost of Donaldson v. Becket*, 9 BULL. COPYRIGHT SOC'Y 102 (1961).
3. "Publication" is defined in 17 U.S.C.A. § 101 as "the distribution of copies or phonorecords of a work to the public by sale or other transfer of ownership, or by rental, lease, or lending," including the "offering to distribute copies or phonorecords to a group of persons for purposes of further distribution, public performance, or public display." However, a "public performance or display of a work does not of itself constitute publication." The 1909 Act defined only "the date of publication" as "the earliest date when copies of the first authorized edition were placed on sale, sold, or publicly distributed by the proprietor of the copyright or under his authority." 1909 Act § 26. The emphasis was on "copies" and whether the "publication" was "general" or "limited," "limited publication" being a contradiction in terms. Two cases involving the greatest distributors of copies with findings of nonpublication were King v. Mister Maestro, Inc., 224 F. Supp. 101 (S.D.N.Y. 1963) (distribution of press kit of ''advance copies" of "I Had a Dream" speech without then mandatory copyright notice held nonpublication) and Jackson v. MPI Home Video, 694 F. Supp. 483 (W.D. Ill. 1988) (omission of notice from several hundred copies of speech at National Democratic Convention cured by efforts to add notice to copies distributed after omission of notice discov-

the 1909 Act, publication with correct copyright notice secured statutory copyright, while publication without such notice placed the work irretrievably in the public domain.

"Publication" has been replaced by "fixation" as the dividing line between federal copyright and nonpreempted state statutory and decisional law.

---

ered). *Cf.* Public Affairs Assocs. v. Rickover, 284 F.2d. 262, 271 (D.C. Cir. 1960) (performance, distribution to press, copies sent on recipient's request, and batches of fifty copies sent to sponsors held publication), *judgment vacated*, 369 U.S. 111 (1962), *on remand*, 268 F. Supp. 444 (D.D.C. 1967). "Publication" ended common-law copyright, and publication with the required copyright notice was the usual means of securing statutory copyright under the 1909 Act. "Divestitive" publications, which ended common-law copyright, was defined differently from "investitive publication" to secure statutory copyright. However, statutory copyright could be secured under the 1909 Act for limited classes of works e.g., lecture or similar production; dramatic, musical, or dramatic-musical composition; motion-picture photoplay; motion picture other than a photoplay; work of art or plastic work or drawing; not reproduced for sale by registration and deposit, terminating common-law copyright. If the work were later published, a second registration and deposit were required. 1909 Act § 12.

The concept of "publication" has had a more limited function since 1978. *Quaere*, whether "publication" should be defined by federal or state laws for events prior to 1978. Published works are protected only if of eligible national origin. Publication on or before December 31, 2002, of works under common-law copyright on December 31, 1977, extends protection to December 31, 2027. The copyright notice had to be on published works, prior to March 1, 1989, and an element of the statutory copyright notice is the year of first publication. Deposit of copies is required within three months after publication. Failure to register within three months after publication may result in no award of statutory damages or attorney's fees. *See* Academy of Motion Picture Arts and Sciences v. Creative House Promotions, Inc., 728 F. Supp. 1442 (C.D. Cal. 1989) (Oscar award statuette in public domain because of general publication prior to 1978); Moore v. Columbia Pictures Indus., Copyright L. Rep. (CCH) ¶ 26,586 (D. Minn. 1990) (submission to record company of demo tape and lyric sheets not publication; attorneys' fees denied for lack of registration before infringement); Cary, *The Troublesome Concept of Publication: A Look at Some of the Forgotten Provisions of the Copyright Revision Bill*, 17 IDEA 69 (Fall 1975).

Common-law copyright, expressly preserved by the 1909 Act,[4] has been preempted for "fixed" works by the 1976 Act.[5]

4.1[2] Continuing Relevance

Since works that were under common-law copyright on January 1, 1978, are statutorily protected for the life, and fifty years after the death, of the author or alternative statutory provisions and at least until December 31, 2002, and, if published on or before then, until December 31, 2027,[6] whether or not common-law copyright was subsisting on January 1, 1978, can be relevant until 2002, 2027, or even thereafter. Also, state-law causes of action arising before January 1, 1978, are preserved.[7]

4.2 Federal Preemption

The 1976 Act provides for federal preemption of rights equivalent to copyright, combining a subject matter test with an equivalent rights test.

---

4. 1909 Act § 2. Common-law copyright was not preempted, at least for unpublished works ("at common-law or in equity") by earlier federal copyright statutes. Wheaton v. Peters, note 1 *supra*.
5. 17 U.S.C.A. § 301. The scope of federal preemption under section 301 is not affected by the adherence of the United States to the Berne Convention or the satisfaction of obligation of the United States thereunder. Berne Act §§ 6, 13. Such satisfaction remains questionable. Brown, *Unification: A Cheerful Requiem for Common Law Copyright*, 24 U.C.L.A. L. REV. 1070 (1977); Mentlik, *Federal Preemption in the Field of Intellectual Creations—An End to the Common Law Copyright*, 23 ASCAP COPYRIGHT L. SYMP. 115 (1977).
6. 17 U.S.C.A. § 303.
7. 17 U.S.C.A. § 301(b)(2). The state statutes of limitations range from one to six years, permitting the commencement of suits until December 31, 1978 to December 31, 1983, with the litigation continuing until final disposition.

4.2[1] Positive Statement in Section 301(a)

Expressly preempted on and after January 1, 1978, are "all legal or equitable rights":[8]

1. "Equivalent to any of the exclusive rights within the general scope of copyright";[9]
2. In "works of authorship. . . fixed in a tangible medium of expression. . . within the subject matter of copyright";[10]

---

8. 17 U.S.C.A. § 301(a) (mirror image of § 301[b]). The exclusive rights in architectural works under new § 120 have been preemptive since December 1, 1990; the rights of "attribution and integrity" in works of visual art under new § 301(f) have been preemptive since May 1, 1991. § 301(f)(1). To avoid preemption claims, one must allege rights qualitatively different from reproduction, performance, distribution, or display. Brignoli v. Balch Hardy & Scheinman, Inc., 645 F. Supp. 1201 (S.D.N.Y. 1986); James v. Delilak Films, Inc., 544 N.Y.S. 2d 447 (Sup. Ct. 1989). *See* note 31 *infra*. Diamond, *Preemption of State Law,* 25 BULL. COPYRIGHT SOC'Y 204 (1978). For copyright infringement actions the federal courts have exclusive jurisdiction. 28 U.S.C.A. § 1338. State trade secret laws, laws of contracts, and protection for ideas arguably are not preempted. 17 U.S.C.A. § 102(b); M. Bryce & Assocs. v. Gladstone, 107 Wis. 2d 241, 319 N.W.2d 907, *cert. denied,* 459 U.S. 944 (1982)(state trade secret law not preempted by federal copyright law); *but see* Foresight Resources Corp. v. Pfurtmuller, 719 F. Supp. 1006 (D. Kan. 1989) (injunction under state trade secret law preempted by copyright law on adaptation of computer program). Baltimore Orioles v. Major League Players Ass'n, 805 F.2d 663 (7th Cir. 1986); (rights of publicity in televised performances held preempted), *cert. denied,* 107 S. Ct. 1593 (1987); Brown, *Copyright and Its Upstart Cousins: Privacy, Publicity, Unfair Competition,* 33 J. COPYRIGHT SOC'Y 301 (1986).
9. *17 U.S.C.A. ("as specified by section 106"). See* chapter 17 *infra*. The phrase "equivalent to" is not defined.
10. 17 U.S.C.A. ("as specified by sections 102 and 103"). The phrase "that are fixed in a tangible medium of expression" appears redundant. *See* 17 U.S.C.A. § 102(a) defining subject matter of copyright. *See* chapter 5 *infra*. *See* note 15 *infra*. If the work is fixed and within the subject matter of copyright, state law protection is preempted even if the work lacks sufficient originality or is in the public domain. 1976 House Report 131.

3. Whether created before or after January 1, 1978;[11] and
4. Whether published or unpublished.[12]

Thereafter, no person is entitled to any such right or equivalent right in any such work under the common law or statutes of any state.[13]

4.2[2] Negative Statement in Section 301(b)

Expressly not preempted are "any rights or remedies" under the common law or statutes of any state with respect to:[14]

1. Subject matter "not. . . within the subject matter of copyright. . . including works of authorship not fixed in any tangible medium of expression;[15]
2. Any cause of action arising from undertakings commenced before January 1, 1978;[16]
3. Activities violating legal or equitable rights "not equivalent to any of the exclusive rights within the general scope of copyright";[17]

---

11. 17 U.S.C.A. *But see* text accompanying note 6 *supra*.
12. 17 U.S.C.A. *See* note 3 *supra*. An unfixed work of authorship, such as an improvisation or an unrecorded choreographic work, performance, or broadcast, continues to be subject to protection under state common law or statute. 1976 House Report 52.
13. 17 U.S.C.A. "State" is defined as including the District of Columbia, the Commonwealth of Puerto Rico, and any territories to which the 1976 Act is made applicable by an act of Congress. 17 U.S.C.A. § 101.
14. 17 U.S.C.A. § 301(b) (mirror image of § 301[a]).
15. 17 U.S.C.A. § 301(b)(1) (obverse of preempted "works of authorship . . . within the subject matter of copyright"), note 10 *supra*.
16. 17 U.S.C.A. § 301(b)(2). *See* note 7 *supra*. For nonpreemption of pre-1978 common-law causes of action, *see* note 7 *supra*.
17. 17 U.S.C.A. § 301(b)(3) (obverse of preempted rights "equivalent to any of the exclusive rights within the general scope of copyright," note 9 *supra*). Many state law doctrines developed from common-law

4. "State and local landmarks, historic preservation, zoning, or building codes" relating to "architectural works."[18]

4.2[3] Sound Recordings Fixed Before February 15, 1972

State law rights and remedies in sound recordings fixed before February 15, 1972,[19] are not annulled or limited until February 15, 2047, but are preempted thereafter.[20]

4.2[4] Other Federal Statutes

Expressly preserved are any rights or remedies under any other federal statute.[21]

---

copyright, notable examples being right of privacy and right of publicity.

18. 17 U.S.C.A. § 301(b)(4) (Architectural Works Copyright Protection Act of 1990).

19. Until February 15, 1972, sound recordings were not protected under the 1909 Act, although there was state-law protection against unauthorized duplication. *See* Goldstein v. California, 412 U.S. 546 (1973)(upholding California antipiracy statute for sound recording fixed before February 15, 1972). In 1971, federal statutory provision for protection against unauthorized duplication for sound recordings fixed on or after February 15, 1972, and before January 1, 1975, was enacted. In 1974, the before-1975 limitation was eliminated. *See* text accompanying chapter 5, notes 26–28, *infra*.

20. Preempted thereafter are any such rights or remedies pertaining to any cause of action arising from undertakings commenced on and after February 15, 2047. Sound recordings fixed before February 15, 1972, are not subject to copyright. 17 U.S.C.A. § 301(c); 1976 House Report 133. Forty-eight states (Iowa and Vermont being the exceptions) and the District of Columbia have record-piracy statutes, applicable to original recordings properly fixed prior to February 15, 1972. Copyright L. Rep. (CCH) ¶¶ 10,901 *et seq.*

21. 17 U.S.C.A. § 301(d). *E.g.*, Federal Patent Law, Federal Trademark Law, Federal Communications Act (quaere, as to FCC regulations and deregulation), proposed federal unfair competition law, state unfair competition or unfair trade practices statutes, some of which prescribe some activities resembling copyright concepts. *See* Pacific & S. Co. v. Satellite Broadcast Networks, Inc. 594 F. Supp. 1565 (N.D.Ga. 1988) (federal trademark law–Lanham Act–not preempted). *Cf.* state trademark statutes.

4.2[5] Legislative History

The last Senate[22] and House[23] bills prior to conference contained express examples of nonequivalent rights:

1. Rights against misappropriation "not equivalent to any of such exclusive rights";[24]
2. Breaches of contract;
3. Breaches of trust;
4. Trespass;
5. Conversion;
6. Invasion of privacy;
7. Defamation;
8. Deceptive trade practices, such as passing off and false representation.

These examples were deleted in the substitute bill passed by the House and the Conference Report adopted the House

22. S. 22, 94th Cong., 1st Sess. (passed Feb. 19, 1976); 1975 Senate Report 133.
23. Substitute for S. 22, 94th Cong., 1st Sess. (1976); 1976 House Report 132.
24. Nonequivalency was mentioned twice: "activities violating legal or equitable rights that are not equivalent to any of the exclusive rights within the general scope of copyright . . . including rights against misappropriation not equivalent to any of such exclusive rights." The cases are legion in both federal and state courts.

Misappropriation, by doing something akin to the exclusive rights of copyright, without more, is preempted. Unfair competition, absent passing off is preempted. Walher v. Time Life Films, Inc. 784 F.2d 44 (2d Cir. 1985), *cert. denied*, 476 U.S. 1159 (1986). "Passing off" ("Palming off") is *not* preempted. Raffoler, Ltd. v. Peabody & Wright, Ltd., 671 F. Supp. 947 (E.D.N.Y. 1987); Ippolito v. Ono-Lennon, 139 Misc. 2d 230, 526 N.Y.S. 2d 877 (Sup. Ct. 1988) Quaere, whether "reverse passing off" is preempted. *See* note 26 *infra*. Association of Am. Medical Colleges v. Carey, 728 F. Supp. 873 (N.D.N.Y. 1990) (New York "Truth-in-Testing" Act requiring disclosure of test questions, answers, etc. held preempted). State community property laws applicable to ownership of works authored by spouse are not preempted. Worth v. Worth, 195 Cal. App. 3d 768 (1987).

version without clarifying explanation.[25] The congressional discussion is no more helpful.[26]

---

25. Conference Report 78–79.

26. 122 CONG. REC. H-10910 (daily ed. Sept. 22, 1976) (colloquy among Congressmen Seiberling, Railsback, and Kastenmeier):

Mr. SEIBERLING. Mr. Chairman, I offer an amendment.

The Clerk read as follows:

Amendment offered by Mr. SEIBERLING: Page 127, line 16, strike "including" and all that follows down through line 20, and insert in lieu thereof a period.

Mr. SEIBERLING. Mr. Chairman, my amendment is intended to save the "Federal preemption" of State law section, which is section 301 of the bill, from being inadvertently nullified because of the inclusion of certain examples in the exemptions from preemption.

This amendment would simply strike the examples listed in section 301(b)(3).

The amendment is strongly supported by the Justice Department, which believes that it would be a serious mistake to cite as an exemption from preemption the doctrine of "misappropriation." The doctrine was created by the Supreme Court in 1922, and it has generally been ignored by the Supreme Court itself and by the lower courts ever since.

Inclusion of a reference to the misappropriation doctrine in this bill, however, could easily be construed by the courts as authorizing the States to pass misappropriation laws. We should not approve such enabling legislation, because a misappropriation law could be so broad as to render the preemption section meaningless.

* * *

Mr. RAILSBACK. Mr. Chairman, may I ask the gentleman from Ohio, for the purpose of clarifying the amendment that by striking the word "misappropriation," the gentleman in no way is attempting to change the existing state of the law, that is as it may exist in certain States that have recognized the right of recovery relating to "misappropriation"; is that correct?

Mr. SEIBERLING. That is correct. All I am trying to do is prevent the citing of them as examples in a statute. We are, in effect, adopting a rather amorphous body of State law and codifying it, in effect. Rather I am trying to have this bill leave the State law alone and make it clear we are merely dealing with copyright laws, laws applicable to copyrights.

Mr. RAILSBACK. Mr. Chairman, I personally have no objection to

Judicial construction will be required to define the bounds of preemption, especially in the areas of misappropriation[27] and state law rights relating to the ownership of

---

the gentleman's amendment in view of that clarification and I know of no objections from this side.

* * *

Mr. KASTENMEIER. Mr. Chairman, I too have examined the gentleman's amendment and was familiar with the position of the Department of Justice. Unfortunately, the Justice Department did not make its position known to the committee until the last day of markup.

* * *

I think that the amendment the gentleman is offering is consistent with the position of the Justice Department and accept it on this side as well.

* * *

The amendment was agreed to.

27. Confusion from mere act of copying without "palming off" has been held preempted. Patsy, Aiken Designs, Inc. v. Baby Toys, Inc., 701 F. Supp. 108 (E.D.N.C. 1988); Abrams, *Copyright, Misappropriation, and Preemption: Constitutional and Statutory Limitations of State Law Protection*, 1983 SUP. CT. REV. 509; Fetter, *Copyright Revision and the Preemption of State "Misappropriation" Law*, 27 COPYRIGHT L. SYMP. (ASCAP) 1 (1982); Mitchell, *Misappropriation and the New Copyright Act: An Overview*, 10 GOLDEN ST. U.L. REV. 587 (1980); Comment, *Misappropriation Doctrine After the Copyright Revision Act of 1976*, 81 DICK. L. REV. 469 (1977). State courts, as well as federal courts, are faced with issues of what state laws are preempted.

California, Maine, Massachusetts, Navada, New Hampshire, New Jersey, New York, Oregon, and Rhode Island have statutory provisions on subject matter and rights not preempted. *E.g.*, CAL. CIV. CODE §§ 980–983; N.Y. ARTS & CULT. AFF. LAW art. 11. Copyright L. Rep. (CCH) ¶¶ 10,861 *et seq.*

Compare Bonito Boats, Inc. v. Thundercraft Boats, Inc., 109 S. Ct. 971 (1989), Kewanee Oil Co. v. Bicron Corp., 416 U.S. 470 (1974); Goldstein v. California, 412 U.S. 546 (1973); Sears, Roebuck & Co. v. Stiffel Co., 376 U.S. 225 (1964); Compco Corp. v. Day-Brite Lighting, Inc., 376 U.S. 234 (1964); *and* their progeny. Quaere, as to viability of International News Serv. v. Associated Press, 248 U.S. 215 (1918)(protection of news against misappropriation; reaping where one has not sown; passing off in reverse—by defendant of plaintiff's goods as those of defendant). *Compare* Tracy v. Skate Key, Inc., 697 F. Supp.

748 (S.D.N.Y. 1988) (reverse "passing-off" like passing-off, involves element of misrepresentation, and therefore not preempted) *with* Ortho-Vision v. H.B.O. 474 F. Supp. 672, 682 n.12 (S.D.N.Y. 1979) (reverse "passing off" claims preempted). Bavid, *Common Law Intellectual Property and the Legacy of* International News Service v. Associated Press, 50 U. CHI. L. REV. 429 (1983). "Misappropriation" traditionally has been part of state laws of unfair competition. To state a truism, equivalent misappropriation has been preempted, but nonequivalent misappropriation has not been preempted. 1976 House Report 131–32.

See H.R. REP. NO. 98-781, 98th Cong., 2d Sess. 28–29 (1984) (reference to nonpreempted state law, including breaches of contract, breaches of trust, trade secrets, trespass, conversion, and such deceptive trade practices as passing off and false misappropriation).

A state-law claim, to be not preempted, must involve extra elements in addition to copyrightable subject matter (*see* chapter 5 *infra*) and rights equivalent to the exclusive rights of copyright (*see* chapter 17 *infra*). Valente-Kritzer Video v. Pinckney, 881 F.2d 772 (9th Cir. 1989), *cert. denied,* 110 S. Ct. 879 (1990) (state-law fraud claim for breach of oral promise to transfer copyright ownership held not preempted because of element of misrepresentation); Del Madera Properties v. Rhodes & Gardner, Inc., 820 F.2d 973 (9th Cir. 1987). *See* Acorn Structures, Inc. v. Sevantz, 846 F.2d 923 (4th Cir. 1988) (breach of agreement to purchase plans or materials held not preempted); Vault Corp. v. Quaid Software, Ltd., 847 F.2d 255 (5th Cir. 1988) (provisions in Louisiana Software License Enforcement Act in conflict with Copyright Act preempted); Buchwald v. Paramount Pictures Corp., 13 U.S.P.Q. (BNA) 2d 1497 (Cal. Super. Ct. 1990) (defendants' film held based upon plaintiffs' strong treatment and breach of express contract; no issue of access; less similarity required for breach of contract than for copyright infringement); Gemcraft Homes, Inc. v. Sumurdy, 633 F. Supp. 289 (E.D. Tex. 1988) (conversion claims for copying architectural plans and using plans to build homes held preempted). There were states laws on moral rights which were held preempted, at least in reproduction rights aspects. Tracy v. Skate Key, Inc., 697 F. Supp. 748 (S.D.N.Y. 1988) (N.Y. Arts & Cultural Affairs Law art. 14); Ronald Litoff, Ltd. v. American Express Co., 621 F. Supp. 981 (S.D.N.Y. 1985). Quaere, whether California Art Preservation Act and New York Artists Authorship Rights Act, prohibiting physical mutilation, preempted because of equivalence to adaptation rights. *But see* Berne Act § 3(b), discussed in text accompanying chapter 17, notes 60, 81–83, *infra*. *See* Francione, The California, Art Preservation Act and Federal Preemption by the 1976 Copyright Act—Equivalence and Actual Conflict, 31 COPYRIGHT L. SYMP. (ASAP) 105 (1984).

any material object in which a copyrighted work is embodied.[28]

"Fixation"[29] replaces "publication" as the dividing line between common-law and statutory protection. An unfixed work of authorship, such as an extemporaneous expression

---

Presumably, state laws relating to the *droit de suite* are not preempted, since they deal with tangible rather than intangible property, but then so do public distribution rights. *See* text accompanying chapter 17, notes 18–23, 81, *infra*. State community property laws have been held not preempted, although the copyright laws deal with "authors" and ownership. *See* chapter 7 *infra*. Worth v. Worth, 24 Cal. Rptr. 135 (Ct. App. 1987). Not preempted are state right-of-privacy and right-of-publicity laws. Midler v. Ford Motor Co., 849 F.2d 460 (9th Cir. 1988). Nor federal or state trademark laws. Tracy v. Skate Key, Inc., 697 F. Supp. 748 (S.D.N.Y. 1988) (including state "antidilution" provisions). *See also* Ehat v. Tanner, 780 F.2d 876 (10th Cir. 1985), *cert. denied*, 479 U.S. 820 (1986); Crow v. Wainwright, 720 F. 2d. 1224 (11th Cir. 1983); Towle Mfg. Co. v. Godinger Silver Art Co., 612 F. Supp. 986 (S.D.N.Y. 1985); McGhan v. Ebersol, 608 F. Supp. 277 (S.D.N.Y 1985); Mayer v. Josiah Wedgwood & Sons, 601 F. Supp. 1523 (S.D.N.Y 1985); Videotronics, Inc. v. Bend Elecs., 564 F. Supp. 1471 (D. Nev. 1983) Meyers v. Waverly Fabrics, 65 N.Y.2d 75, 479 N.E.2d 236, 489 N.Y.S.2d 891 (1985); Editorial Photocolor Archives, Inc. v. Granger Collection, 61 N.Y.2d 517, 463 N.E.2d 365, 474 N.Y.S.2d 964 (1984). Consistent with preemption are the provisions that jurisdiction over actions under the copyright and patent laws is exclusively in the federal courts as compared to concurrent jurisdiction over trademark cases, even when there is federal court jurisdiction.

28. 17 U.S.C.A. expressly distinguishes between "ownership of a copyright" and "ownership of any material object in which the work is embodied." Several states have statutes applicable to the ownership of the material object, but sometimes also applicable to ownership of the exclusive rights of copyright. Comment, *The* Droit de Suite *Has Arrived: Can It Thrive in California as It Has in Calais?* 11 CREIGHTON L. REV. 529 (1977). Quaere, as to state moral rights legislation.

29. "Fixed" when embodied in a "copy" or "phonorecord" "by or under the authority of the author," 17 U.S.C.A. § 101 ("more than transitory duration"). *See* Brown, *Publication and Preemption in Copyright Law: Elegiac Reflections on* Goldstein v. California, 22 U.C.L.A. L. REV. 1022 (1975).

or improvisation, or an unrecorded choreographic work, performance, or broadcast continues to be subject to protection under state statute[30] or state common law (quaere, whether this should be called "common-law copyright").

Only when there is the requisite "fixation,"[31] may there be preemption, and then only if there is the requisite "equivalence"[32] to the "subject matter of copyright"[33] and "exclusive rights."[34]

When Congress amended § 117 in 1980, there was an express intention of no preemption of state law protection of computer software, especially unfair competition and trade secrets laws.[35]

The Berne Covention Implementation Act expressly stated that it did not affect the scope of federal preemption.[36]

---

30. 1976 House Report 52–53. *Cf.* Zacchini v. Scripps-Howard Broadcasting Co., 433 U.S. 562 (1977)(state law right of publicity for "human cannon ball" upheld). *See* note 6 *supra.*
31. Thrice-mentioned is "fixed in a tangible medium of expression." 17 U.S.C.A. §§ 101 (definition of "fixed"), 301(a), 301(b)(1) ("any").
32. "Equivalent to" is not defined.
33. *See* chapter 5 *infra.*
34. *See* chapter 17 *infra.*
35. *See* text accompanying chapter 17, note 53, *infra.*
36. Berne Act § 6.

5. Subject Matter of Copyright

The subject matter of copyright is first treated "in general."[1]

5.1 In General

Copyright subsists in:

1. "Original works of authorship";[2]

---

1. 17 U.S.C.A. § 102(a) (followed by three sections on compilations and derivative works, national origin, and United States government works). The two essential elements—"original work" and "tangible object"—must merge through "fixation" to produce copyrightable subject matter. 1976 House Report 53. Only copyrightable elements of such subject matter are protected against infringement. Questions of subject matter, scope of exclusive rights, and infringement, like preemption, are correlative to each other. *See* Levine, *Subject Matter of Copyright*, 25 BULL. COPYRIGHT SOC'Y 201 (1978); Nimmer, *The Subject Matter of Copyright Under the Act of 1976*, 24 U.C.L.A. L. REV. 978 (1977). As Holmes, J., wrote in Bleistein v. Donaldson Lithographing Co., 188 U.S. 329 (1903):

   > . . . some new collocation of visible or audible points,—of lines, colors, sounds, or words. The restraint is directed against reproducing this collocation, although but for the . . . statute any one would be free to combine the contents of the dictionary, the elements of the spectrum, or the notes of the gamut in any way that he had the wit to devise. The restriction is confined to the specific form, to the collocation devised. . . .

2. 17 U.S.C.A. § 102(a). The phrase "original works of authorship" was

2. "Fixed in any tangible medium of expression, now known or later developed, from which they can be perceived, reproduced, or otherwise communicated, either directly or with the aid of a machine or device."[3]

5.1[1] "Original Works of Authorship"

The term "original works of authorship" was purposely left undefined. Decisional law indicates that authorship has two essential components:

1. Expenditure of a modicum of intellectual effort
2. Originality

Ingenuity, uniqueness, and esthetic merits are not required.[4] Nor are the patent law requirements of utility, novelty, and nonobviousness. Authorship involves expression, as distinguished from the ideas expressed.[5]

---

used in place of the 1909 Act phrase "all the writings of an author" [1909 Act § 4] to avoid exhausting the constitutional copyright power with respect to the "writings" of "authors." Legislatively, copyrightable subject has been expanded over the years: books, maps, and charts (1790); prints (1802); musical compositions (1831); dramatic compositions (1856); photographs (1865); paintings, drawings, sculptures, models, and designs for the fine arts (1870); photoplays and motion pictures other than photoplays (1912); sound recordings (1972); pantomimes, choreographic works, and audiovisual works (1978); computer programs (1980); semiconductor chip products (1984).

3. 17 U.S.C.A. § 102(a). "Machine" and "device" are defined as those "now known or later developed." *Id.* § 101.
4. Bleistein v. Donaldson Lithographing Co., 188 U.S. 239 (1903) (circus poster). The Court, per Holmes, J., discussing the constitutional phrase "useful Arts," stated, "The Constitution does not limit the useful to that which satisfies immediate bodily needs." *Id.* at 249. *See* chapter 1, note 6 *supra*.
5. *See* 17 U.S.C.A. § 102(b); E. Misham & Son v. Marycana, Inc., 622 F. Supp. 1339 (S.D.N.Y. 1987) (independent assemblage held copyrightable despite lack of novelty). *See* text accompanying note 38 *infra*;

Hoehling v. Universal City Studios, Inc., 618 F.2d 972 (2d Cir.) ("*scénes á faire*, that is, 'incidents, characters or settings which are as a practical matter indispensable, or at least standard, in the treatment of a given topic' " are not copyrightable as a matter of law), *cert. denied*, 449 U.S. 841 (1980). *See* Gentien v. John Muller & Co., 712 F. Supp. 740 (W.D.Mo. 1989) (copyrightable elements of photograph include selection of background, lighting, shading, positioning, timing—expression, not idea, of poses); Chuck Blore & Dan Richman, Inc. v. 20/20 Advertising Inc., 674 F. Supp. 671 (D. Minn. 1987) (artistic choices in television commercials of montage style, camera angle, framing, hairstyle, jewelry, decor, makeup, and background held aspects of expression); Kisch v. Ammirati & Puris, Inc., 657 F. Supp. 380 (S.D.N.Y. 1987) (photograph's copyright protects selection of lighting, shading, positioning, timing, angles, pose, background, camera, film, lens setting; second photograph duplicating first photograph with live subject held to state claim); Kurtz, *Copyright: The Scénes á Faire Doctrine*, 41 FLA. L. REV. 79 (1989). The idea-expression dichotomy offers an acceptable balance between copyright and free speech. Fisher v. Dee, 794 F.2d 431 (9th Cir. 1986). A bolstering factor is the doctrine of fair use. *See* chapter 18 *infra*.

Protection of characters often involves questions of sufficient authorship: the less developed the characters, the less their copyrightability. Pictorial characters are more readily protected than literary characters, although both must be delineated in a sufficiently distinctive manner. Anderson v. Stallone, Copyright L. Rep. ¶ 26, 427 (CCH) (C.D. Cal. 1989) (Rocky, Adrian, Apollo, Creed, Clubber Lang, Paulie "highly delineated group of characters"). Walt Disney Prods. v. Air Pirates, 581 F.2d 751 (9th Cir. 1978), *cert. denied*, 439 U.S. 1133 (1979). Exclusive rights to a work do not necessarily include such rights in the characters that are the vehicles of the story. Warner Bros. Pictures v. Columbia Broadcasting Sys., 216 F.2d 945 (9th Cir. 1954) (*The Maltese Falcon*). Kurtz, *The Independent Legal Lives of Fictional Characters*, 1986 WIS. L. REV. 429; Clark, *Of Mice and Men, and Superman: The Copyrightability of Graphic and Literary Characters*, 28 ST. LOUIS U.L.J. 959 (1983); Zissu, *Whither Character Rights: Some Observations*, 29 J. COPYRIGHT SOC'Y 121 (1981); Marks, *The Legal Rights of Fictional Characters*, 25 COPYRIGHT L. SYMP. (ASCAP) 35 (1980); Note, 68 HARV. L. REV. 349 (1954). Names of characters may be protected on trademark or unfair competition principles; portrayals of actual persons may be protected under the "right of publicity." Parody of characters may or may not constitute fair use. *See* chapter 18, note 16 *infra*.

If the idea may be expressed in limited ways, the expression may not be protected lest the idea itself be protected ("merger doctrine"). Ring v. Estee Lauder, Inc., 874 F.2d 109 (2d Cir. 1989); Whelan Assocs.

Originality means that the work owes its creation to the author, which in turn means that the work is not slavishly or mechanically copied from others.[6]

These concepts have not been changed.[7]

5.1[2] Fixation

A work is defined as "fixed" in a tangible medium of expression when its embodiment in a copy or phonorecord, by or under the authority of the author, is sufficiently permanent or stable to permit it to be perceived, reproduced, or otherwise communicated for a period of more than transitory duration."[8] If it consists of sounds, images, or both

---

v. Jaslow Dental Laboratory, Inc., 797 F.2d 1222 (3d Cir. 1986), *cert. denied*, 107 S. Ct. 877 (1987); Toro Co. v. R & R Prods. Co., 787 F.2d 1208 (8th Cir. 1986); M. Kramer Mfg. Co. v. Andrews, 783 F.2d 421 (4th Cir. 1986); Cooling Sys. & Flexibles, Inc. v. Stuart Radiator, Inc., 777 F.2d 485 (9th Cir. 1985); Herbert Rosenthal Jewelry Corp. v. Kalpakian, 446 F.2d 738 (9th Cir. 1971); Morrissey v. Procter & Gamble Co., 370 F.2d 675 (1st Cir. 1967). Similar issues arise in determining whether copyrighted subject matter has been infringed. *See* chapter 27 *infra*.

6. *Compare* Original Appalachian Artworks, Inc. v. Toy Loft, Inc., 684 F.2d 821 (11th Cir. 1982)(soft sculpture dolls marketed as "The Little People" held to exhibit requisite degree of originality) *with* L. Batlin & Son v. Snyder, 536 F.2d 486 (2d Cir.)(en banc)(6-3)(requiring substantial, not merely trivial, originality for plastic "Uncle Sam" bank copied from antique cast iron bank in public domain), *cert. denied*, 429 U.S. 857 (1976). The term "author" in the Constitution had previously been defined as one "to whom anything owes its origin." Burrow-Giles Lithographic Co. v. Sarony, 111 U.S. 53, 58 (1884)(photograph of Oscar Wilde in "aesthete" clothing before ornate studio background). Later cases have protected photographs without much inquiry into the photographer's original authorship. *E.g.*, Pagano v. Chas. Beseler Co., 234 F. 963 (2d Cir. 1916).
7. 1976 House Report 51.
8. 17 U.S.C.A. § 101 (overruling White-Smith Publishing Co. v. Apollo Co., 209 U.S. 1 [1908]); Production Contractors, Inc. v. WGN Continental Broadcasting Co., 622 F. Supp. 1500 (N.D. Ill. 1985)(parade held not work of authorship). Fixation is probably required by the term "writings" in the Constitution. *See* chapter 1, note 10 *supra*. The

sounds and images that are being transmitted, the work is "fixed" if "a fixation of the work is being made simultaneously with the transmission."[9]

5.2 "Works of Authorship"

"Works of authorship" "include" (defined as "illustrative" and "not limitative")[10] the following eight categories:[11]

1. Literary works
2. Musical works, including any accompanying words
3. Dramatic works, including any accompanying music
4. Pantomimes and choreographic works

---

original work of authorship (e.g., literary work or musical composition) should be distinguished from the material objects—"copy" or "phonorecord"—in which it may be embodied (e.g., book, periodical, microfilm, computer punch card). Preparation of materials in the process of production may amount to both fixations and infringement. Walt Disney Prods. v. Filmation Assoc., 628 F. Supp. 871 (C.D. Cal. 1986).

9. 17 U.S.C.A. § 101. Absent fixation, a work of authorship is not protected under the statute and state-law protection is not preempted. *See* chapter 4, note 10 *supra*. The definition of "fixation" would exclude evanescent or transient reproductions such as those projected briefly on a screen, shown electronically on television or other cathode ray tubes, or captured momentarily in the "memory" of a computer. 1976 House Report 53. *See* Baltimore Orioles, Inc. v. Major League Baseball Players Ass'n, 805 F.2d 663 (7th Cir. 1986) (live performance of professional baseball players held not to create right for players independent of copyright in videotaped telecast of game), *cert. denied*, 107 S. Ct. 1593 (1987).

10. 17 U.S.C.A. § 101.

11. 17 U.S.C.A. § 102(a) (divided into four classes for administrative registration purposes and a fifth class for renewal). *See* text accompanying chapter 12, notes 8–10, *infra*. Compare fourteen categories and classes under 1909 Act: former classes A, B, and C, now class TX (textual); former classes D, E, L, and M, now class PA (performing arts); former classes F, G, H, I, J, and K, now class VA (visual arts); and former class N, now class SR (sound recordings). The four classes are somewhat overlapping.

5. Pictorial, graphic, and sculptural works
6. Motion pictures and other audiovisual works
7. Sound recordings
8. Architectural works

5.2[1] Literary Works

The first category of protectible works of authorship[12] comprises literary works.

"Literary works" are defined as "works, other than audiovisual works, expressed in words, numbers, or other verbal or numerical symbols or indicia, regardless of the nature of the material objects, such as books, periodicals, manuscripts, phonorecords, film, tapes, disks, or cards, in which they are embodied."[13]

---

12. 17 U.S.C.A. § 102(a)(1). This category (now class TX) under the 1909 Act encompassed books, including composite and cyclopedic works, directories, gazetteers, and other compilations (class A); periodicals, including newspapers (class B); and lectures, sermons, and addresses (prepared for oral delivery) (class C).
13. 17 U.S.C. § 101. Computer bases and programs that satisfy other requirements are copyrightable. 1976 House Report 54; R. SALTMAN, COPYRIGHT IN COMPUTER-READABLE WORKS: POLICY IMPACTS OF TECHNOLOGICAL CHANGE (National Bureau of Standards Special Publication 500-17) (1978). Keplinger, *Computer Intellectual Property Claims: Computer Software and Data Base Protection,* 1977 WASH. U.L.Q. 461; Squires, *Copyright and Compilations in the Computer Era: Old Wine in New Bottles,* 24 BULL. COPYRIGHT SOC'Y 18 (1976); Note, *Protection of Computer Software—A Hard Problem,* 26 DRAKE L. REV. 180 (1977); Copyright Office Circular R61 (Copyright Registration for Computer Programs). Test questions and their answers may be copyrighted. Educational Testing Serv. v. Katzman, 793 F.2d 533 (3d Cir. 1986) (individual questions covered); National Conference of Bar Examiners v. Multistate Legal Studies, Inc., 692 F.2d 478 (7th Cir. 1982)(multistate bar examination held copyrightable; § 102(a) not all-inclusive), *cert. denied,* 464 U.S. 814 (1983); Association of Am. Medical Colleges v. Mikaelian, 571 F. Supp. 144 (E.D. Pa. 1983)(medical college admission test questions based on scientific facts held copyrightable); Harcourt, Brace, World, Inc. v. Graphic Controls Corp., 329 F. Supp. 517 (S.D.N.Y. 1971)(printed test answer sheets for optical scanning). Tests may be subject to the secure test deposit provisions. *See* chapter 11, note 9 *infra.*

5.2[2] Musical Works, Including Any Accompanying Words

The second category is designated "musical works, including any accompanying words."[14] Nondramatic musical works should be distinguished from dramatic musical works,[15] the former being in this second category, while the latter are in the third category of "dramatic works, including any accompanying music."

5.2[3] Dramatic Works, Including Any Accompanying Music

Comprising the third category are "dramatic works, including any accompanying music."[16] Operas, operettas, musical comedies, and other dramatic musical compositions are in this third category.[17]

5.2[4] Pantomimes and Choreographic Works

"Pantomimes and choreographic works" constitute the fourth category.[18] The previously mentioned statutory re-

---

14. 17 U.S.C.A. § 102(a)(2). This category (now part of class PA) under the 1909 Act comprised musical compositions (class E).
15. Known as "dramatico-musical compositions" under the 1909 Act, not subject to the compulsory mechanical license for musical compositions. 1909 Act § 1(e).
16. 17 U.S.C.A. § 102(a)(3). This category (now part of class PA) under the 1909 Act included dramatico-musical compositions as well as dramatic compositions (class D). *See* note 15 *supra*. Dramatic musical works no longer are subject to compulsory musical recording licenses and compulsory coin-operated phonorecord players licenses (latter now suspended).
17. *See* note 16 *supra*.
18. 17 U.S.C.A. § 102(a)(4). The 1909 Act did not refer to choreographic works, which administratively were accepted for registration beginning in 1959 (class D, usually). Included were ballets or similar theatrical works of a dramatic nature. Not included were social dance steps or simple routines. Fixation in some legible written form was required. Varmer, *Copyright in Choreographic Works* (1959), *reprinted in* 1 STUDIES ON COPYRIGHT—ARTHUR FISHER MEMORIAL EDITION 103 (1963);

quirement that the work be "fixed"[19] is especially troublesome for this category.[20]

5.2[5] Pictorial, Graphic, and Sculptural Works

"Pictorial, graphic, and sculptural works" are the fifth category.[21]

Singer, *In Search of Adequate Protection for Choreographic Works: Legislative and Judicial Alternatives vs. the Custom of the Dance Community*, 38 U. MIAMI L. REV. 287 (1984); Fisher, *The Copyright in Choreographic Works: A Technical Analysis of the Copyright Act of 1976*, 31 COPYRIGHT L. SYMP. (ASCAP) 145 (1984); Traylor, *Choreography, Pantomime and the Copyright Revision Act of 1976*, 16 NEW ENG. L. REV. 227 (1980–81); Note, 33 U.C.L.A. L. REV. 1442 (1986). Comment, *Moving to a New Beat: Copyright Protection for Choreographic Works*, 24 U.C.L.A. L. REV. 128 (1977). They are part of class PA. In 1990, Gerald Alpino resigned as director of the Joffrey Ballet and purported to withdraw the ballets he and the late Robert Joffrey choreographed over five years. Joffrey died in 1988, willing his rights to Alpino. Some of the ballets were commissioned by outside parties. Whether or not a specific ballet is a "work made for hire" with the hirer being considered the author and, absent an express written agreement to the contrary, the owner of all the rights of copyright, would present factual and legal questions. *See* text accompanying chapter 7, notes 15–41, *infra*. The Joffrey Ballet controversy was amicably resolved. Choreography involves long intensive perfecting of a ballet in the studio.

19. *See* text accompanying note 8 *supra*. *See also* Horgan v. Macmillan, Inc., 789 F.2d 157 (2d Cir. 1986) (choreography copyright upheld on basis of still photographs in book on Balanchine's "Nutcracker").
20. Fixation could be by detailed verbal description, dance notation (Laban system, known as "Labanotation, devised in 1928), motion picture, pictorial, or graphic diagrams. Absent fixation, 17 U.S.C.A. does not apply and state-law protection is not preempted. 1976 House Report 131.
21. 17 U.S.C.A. § 102(a)(5); 37 C.F.R. § 202.10. This category (now class VA) under the 1909 Act included maps (class F), works of art and models or designs for works of art (class H), reproductions of a work of art (class I), photographs (class J), and prints and pictorial illustrations (class K). *See* Copyright Office Circular R44 (Cartoons and Comic Strips); *see also* Mazer v. Stein, 347 U.S. 201 (1954)(upholding copyrightability of work of art incorporated into useful article: meet-

"Pictorial, graphic, and sculptural works" were defined in the 1976 Act as including "two-dimensional and three-dimensional works of fine, graphic, and applied art, photographs, prints and art reproductions, maps, globes, charts, technical drawings, diagrams, and models . . . insofar as their form but not their mechanical or utilitarian aspects are concerned." The Berne Act struck out in the first sentence "technical drawings, diagrams, and models" and inserted in lieu thereof "diagrams, models, and technical drawings, including architectural plans,"[22] a change which did not make architectural plans any more copyrightable, and did not address their exclusive rights.

---

ing ground of copyrights and design patents); Masquerade Novelty, Inc. v. Unique Indus., Copyright L. Rep. (CCH) ¶ 26,624 (3d Cir. 1990) (nose masks whose only utilitarian function was humorous portrayal of animal noses held not useful articles); Reader's Digest Ass'n v. Conservative Digest, Inc., 821 F.2d 800 (D.C. Cir. 1987) (distinctive arrangement and layout of magazine cover held protectible as graphic work). *See* R. LERNER & J. BRESLER, ART LAW: THE GUIDE FOR COLLECTORS, INVESTORS, DEALERS, AND ARTISTS (1989).

22. 17 U.S.C.A. § 101. A design of a "useful article" is considered a pictorial, graphic, or sculptural work "only if, and only to the extent that," the design incorporates pictorial, graphic, or sculptural features that can be "identified separately from," and are "capable of existing independently of, the utilitarian aspects" of the article. *Id.* Artistic or aesthetic features thus may be relevant concerning useful articles. *See* Brandir Int'l, Inc. v. Cascade Pac. Lumber Co., 834 F.2d 1142 (2d Cir. 1987) (2–1) (aesthetic elements not conceptually separable where original design modified to serve functional purpose); Carol Barnhart Inc. v. Economy Cover Corp., 773 F.2d 411 (2d Cir. 1985)(2–1)(clothing mannequins held not copyrightable); Poe v. Missing Persons, 745 F.2d 1238 (9th Cir. 1984)(whether work of art or clothing left to trier of fact); Gay Toys, Inc. v. Buddy L Corp., 703 F.2d 970 (6th Cir. 1983)(toys held not useful articles); Fabrica Inc. v. El Dorado Corp., 697 F.2d 890 (9th Cir. 1983)(carpet display books not copyrightable); Morris Indus., Inc. v. International Tel. & Tel. Corp., 696 F.2d 918 (8th Cir. 1983) (wire-spoked automobile wheel cover held not copyrightable because useful article with no physically or conceptually separable work of art); Kieselstein-Cord v. Accessories by Pearl, Inc., 632 F.2d 989 (2d Cir. 1980)(2-1)(ornamental aspects of belt buckles analogized

5.2[6] Motion Pictures and Other Audiovisual Works

"Motion pictures and other audiovisual works" make up the sixth category.[23]

---

to jewelry and held copyrightable; dissent found functional and useful article); Beverly Hills Design Studio (NY) Inc. v. Morris, 126 F.R.D. 33 (S.D.N.Y. 1989) (clothing pattern held useful article); Animal Fair, Inc. v. AMFESCO Indus., Inc., 620 F. Supp. 175 (D. Minn. 1985) (design features need not be physically, but may be conceptually, separable from useful article). *Compare* Kieselstein-Cord v. Accessories by Pearl, Inc., *supra* ("conceptual separability" sufficient) *with* Esquire, Inc. v. Ringer, 591 F.2d 796 (D.C. Cir. 1978), *cert. denied*, 440 U.S. 908 (1979). Useful article is defined as an article having "an intrinsic utilitarian function that is not merely to portray the appearance of the article or to convey information." 17 U.S.C.A. § 101. This is to distinguish works of applied arts from industrial designs. Architectural plans are copyrightable as "graphic works" to the extent that they combine original elements of authorship. But only such elements are protected. Utilitarian or functional aspects—concepts of patent law—are not copyrightable, e.g., concepts of living, family, dining, or bedrooms, bathrooms, kitchens, dens, rumpus rooms, walk-through closets, or windows-within-windows, as such. The copyrightable elements are protected against substantial copying, shown by direct evidence or indirect evidence of copying and substantial similarity. Plans, except for some aberrant decisions, were not protected prior to 1990 against a building or structure based on the plans. Also, until 1990, a structure, unless itself a work of art, is not protected. Demetriades v. Kaufmann, 680 F. Supp. 658 (S.D.N.Y. 1988) (absent design protection not protectible in useful article depicted by plans). Perlmutter, *Conceptual Separability and Copyright in the Designs of Useful Articles*, 8 CARDOZO ARTS & ENT. L.J. 683 (1990). *Copyright Protection for Architecture and the Berne Convention*, 65 N.Y.U. L. REV. 403 (1990). Strauss, *Copyright in Architectural Works* (1959), *reprinted in* 1 STUDIES ON COPYRIGHT—ARTHUR FISHER MEMORIAL EDITION 87 (1963); Brenner, *Two-Phase Approach to Copyrighting the Fine Arts*, 24 BULL. COPYRIGHT SOC'Y 85 (1976). *But see* Intown Enters. v. Barnes, 721 F. Supp. 1263 (N.D. Ga. 1989); Aitken, Hazen, Hoffman, Miller, P.C. v. Empire Constr. Co., 542 F. Supp. 252 (D. Neb. 1982)(copying architectural plans and using them in construction of building held infringement). The Architectural Works Copyright Protection Act of 1990 provided protection for architectural plans against unauthorized construction. *See* notes 29, 30 *infra*.

23. 17 U.S.C.A. § 102(a)(6). New class part of class PA. The 1909 Act (by 1912 amendment) distinction between motion picture photoplays

"Motion pictures" are defined as "audiovisual works consisting of a series of related images that, when shown in succession, impart an impression of motion, together with accompanying sounds, if any."[24]

"Audiovisual works" are defined as "works that consist of a series of related images which are intrinsically intended to be shown by the use of machines or devices such as projectors, viewers, or electronic equipment, together with accompanying sounds, if any, regardless of the nature of the material objects, such as films or tapes, in which the works are embodied."[25]

5.2[7] Sound Recordings

"Sound recordings" are the seventh category.[26]

They are defined as "works that result from the fixation of a series of musical, spoken, or other sounds, but not

---

(class L) and motion pictures other than photoplays (class M), has been abolished, and, with it, the differing exclusive rights afforded to the two classes by assimilating the former to "dramatic works" and the latter to nondramatic works. *See* Nolan, *A Brighter Day for the Magic Lantern: Thoughts on the Impact of the New Copyright Act on Motion Pictures,* 11 LOY. L.A.L. REV. 1 (1977); Holland, *Audiovisual Package: Handle with Care,* 22 BULL. COPYRIGHT SOC'Y 104 (1974).

24. 17 U.S.C.A. § 101.
25. *Id.* M. Kramer Mfg. Co. v. Andrews, 783 F.2d 421 (4th Cir. 1986) (audiovisual copyright may protect computer program implementing audiovisuals).
26. 17 U.S.C.A. § 102(a)(7); Diamond, *Sound Recordings and Phonorecords: History and Current Law,* 1979 U. ILL. L. REV. 337; Goldberg, *Sound Recordings,* 25 BULL. COPYRIGHT SOC'Y 227 (1978); Meyers, *Sound Recordings and the New Copyright Act,* 22 N.Y.L. SCH. L. REV. 573 (1977). Sound recordings were not protected under the 1909 Act until February 15, 1972, and then only if they were fixed between that date and January 1, 1975. Pub. L. No. 92–139, 85 Stat. 391 (Oct. 15, 1971)(effective Feb. 15, 1972); Shaab v. Kleindienst, 345 F. Supp. 589 (D.D.C. 1972)(upholding constitutionality of 1971 legislation). *See* Copyright Office Circular 56a (Copyright for Sound Recordings). In 1974, the January 1, 1975, limitation was deleted. Pub. L. No. 93–573, 88 Stat. 1873 (Dec. 31, 1974). The 1971 legislation introduced the

including the sounds accompanying a motion picture or other audiovisual work, regardless of the nature of the material objects, such as disks, tapes, or other phonorecords, in which they are embodied."[27]

Thus, the statute distinguishes between:

1. Sounds accompanying motion pictures (e.g., sound tracks or other audiovisual works), which are assimilated to motion pictures and other audiovisual works; and
2. Sound recordings, which are treated differently under the statute.[28]

---

concept of the "℗" copyright notice to be affixed to "reproductions" of sound recordings. The defined term "phonorecords" is used for the material objects in which "sound recordings" are fixed. 17 U.S.C.A. § 101. Federal preemption of protection of sound recordings fixed before February 15, 1972, is deferred until February 15, 2047. 17 U.S.C.A. § 301(c). Authorship of sound recordings often is shared by the performer and the record producer. Sound recordings, covered by neither the Universal Copyright Convention nor the Berne Convention, are the subject of the UNESCO Geneva Convention of 1971, which was ratified by the United States in 1974.

27. 17 U.S.C.A. § 101. A sound recording is a "derivative work" distinguishable from the underlying work performed in the recording.

28. Motion pictures and other audiovisual works, together with any accompanying sounds (class PA), unlike sound recordings (class SR), are protectible against unauthorized public performance. 17 U.S.C.A. §§ 106(4), 114. *See* chapter 17, notes 23–29, *infra*. Sound recordings are protected only against unauthorized reproduction, adaptation, and distribution. Although the 1909 Act did not protect sound recordings in any way, some protection against unauthorized duplication was provided under common-law principles, often implemented by state statutes. *See* Ringer, *The Unauthorized Duplication of Sound Recordings* (1957), *reprinted in* 1 Studies on Copyright—Arthur Fisher Memorial Edition 117 (1963). The Register of Copyrights has recommended recognition of performance rights in sound recordings, and legislation to that effect has been introduced in several sessions of Congress. *See* chapter 17, notes 30–31, *infra*.

5.2[8] Architectural Works

"Architectural works" comprise the eighth category.[29]

"Architectural works" are defined as the "design of a building" as "embodied" in any tangible medium of expression, including a "building, architectural plans, or drawings." Included is the "overall form as well as the arrangement and composition of spaces and elements in the design." Excluded are "individual standard features."[30]

5.3 "Compilations" and "Derivative Works"

"Compilations" and "derivative works" are included within the subject matter of copyright.[31]

A "compilation" is defined as a "work formed by the collection and assembling of preexisting materials or of data that are selected, coordinated, or arranged in such a way that the resulting work as a whole constitutes an original work of authorship," including "collective works."[32]

---

29. 17 U.S.C.A. § 102(.8), as amended by the Architectural Works Copyright Protection Act of 1990 (eff. Dec. 1, 1990).
30. 17 U.S.C.A. § 101, as amended in 1990.
31. 17 U.S.C.A. § 103. To be copyrightable, a compilation or derivative work must represent an original work of authorship. A compilation results from selecting, bringing together, organizing and arranging existing materials of any kind, whether individually copyrighted or not. A compilation of copyrightable works is called a collective work. A derivative work, on the other hand, recasts, transforms, or adapts one or more existing copyrightable work: for example, a telephone directory might be a compilation; an anthology, a collective work; a motion picture, a derivative work based on an underlying work. The existing materials selected, arranged, and organized in a compilation, like the materials recast, transformed, or adapted in a derivative work, might or might not be copyrighted.
32. 17 U.S.C.A. The 1909 Act referred to "compilations" and "other versions." 1909 Act § 7. *See* Original Appalachian Artworks, Inc. v. Toy Loft, Inc., 684 F.2d 821 (8th Cir. 1982)(derivative work written after

1977 held governed by 1976 Act even though underlying work published without notice required by Act); Ehat v. Tanner, 780 F.2d 876 (10th Cir. 1985)(compilations of uncopyrightable material held copyrightable), *cert. denied*, 479 U.S. 820 (1986); Illinois Bell Tel. Co. v. Haines & Co., 905 F.2d 1081 (7th Cir. 1990); Konor Enters., Inc. v. Eagle Publications, Inc., 878 F.2d 138 (4th Cir. 1989) (telephone directory protected as unique compilation); United Tel. Co. v. Johnson Publishing Co., 855 F.2d 604 (8th Cir. 1988) (white pages held copyrightable "compilation"). Southern Bell Tel. & Tel. Co. v. Associated Tel. Directory Publishers, 756 F.2d 801 (11th Cir. 1985)(compilation of facts held copyrightable because of sufficient originality in selection, arrangement, or both selection and arrangement); Signo Trading Int'l v. Gordon, 535 F. Supp. 362 (N.D. Cal. 1981)(list of words translated from English into Arabic and then from Arabic into Roman letters held not copyrightable where translation of word list was fairly mechanical process requiring little if any originality, as did choice of words and phonetic spelling).

Compilations of factual information are protectible if they exhibit sufficient subjective "selection, organization, and arrangement" or "industrious collection." Compare the "selection, creativity, judgment, and arrangement" test (originality) in Rockford Map Publishers, Inc. v. Directory Serv. Co., 768 F.2d 145 (7th Cir. 1985), *cert. denied*, 106 S. Ct. 806 (1986), with the "industrious collection" test ("sweat of brow") in Schroeder v. William Morrow & Co., 566 F.2d 198 (7th Cir. 1977). *See also* Nash v. CBS, 899 F.2d 1537 (7th Cir. 1990) (research and hard work not protectible expression); Worth v. Selchow & Richter Co., 827 F.2d 569 (9th Cir. 1987) (rejecting "sweat of brow" test); Financial Information, Inc. v. Moody's Investors Serv., Inc., 808 F.2d 204 (2d Cir. 1986)(copyrightability of compilation of facts—daily bond cards with some five items of information each—dependent not upon author's efforts ("industrious collection," ["sweat of researcher's brow"] but rather upon nature of final result ["independent creation"]), *cert. denied*, 484 U.S. 820 (1987); Eckes v. Card Price Update, 736 F.2d 859 (2d Cir. 1984); *Compare* Miller v. Universal City Studios, 650 F.2d 1365 (5th Cir. 1981)(copyright in directory rests on originality of selection and arrangement of factual information rather than on industriousness of efforts to develop information) *with* Stanford Univ. v. Associated Business Consultants, Inc., Copyright L. Rep. (CCH) ¶ 26,243 (D. Kan. 1988) (vocational inventory test and scoring held protectible expression). *See* Note, 62 NOTRE DAME L. REV. 763 (1987). Copyright in a compilation does not protect the individual facts, only their selection, arrangement, and expression. *See* Denicola, *Copyright in Collections of Facts: A Theory for the Protection of Nonfiction Literary Works*, 8 COLUM. L. REV. 516 (1981). Gorman, *Copyright Protection for the Collection and Representation of Facts*, 76 HARV. L. REV. 1569 (1963).

A three-dimensional work derived from a two-dimensional work, and vice versa, assuming originality, may be copyrightable. W. Goebel Porzellanfabrik v. Action Indus., Inc., 589 F. Supp. 763 (S.D.N.Y. 1984)(converting two-dimensional drawings into three-dimensional Hummel figures held to involve sufficient creative effort to justify copyright in derivative works).

Color reproductions of black-and-white works are more likely to be protected than black-and-white reproductions of color work. Alfred Bell & Co. v. Catalda Fine Arts, Inc., 74 F. Supp. 973 (S.D.N.Y. 1940)(mezzotints of old masters), *aff'd*, 191 F.2d 99 (2d Cir. 1951); Storm v. Kennington, Ltd., 223 U.S.P.Q. (BNA) 790 (N.D. Cal. 1984)(black-and-white copies of unprotected color plates held not entitled to copyright protection). Quaere, as to "colorization."

Maps traditionally have been held to a higher standard of original authorship. *See* former Copyright Office Circular R40f (appreciable amount of cartographic surveying and field work or computations resulting therefrom). *But see* United States v. Hamilton, 583 F.2d 448 (9th Cir. 1978)(holding that "elements of compilation which amount to more than a trivial selection, may, either alone or when taken into consideration with direct observations" support copyrightability of map, declining to follow "direct observation rule"; same standard for maps as for other works). *See also* Kern River Gas Transmission Co. v. Coastal Corp. 899 F.2d 1458 (5th Cir. 1990) (idea and expression in maps showing location of proposed pipelines merged); Amsterdam v. Triangle Publications, 93 F. Supp. 79 (E.D. Pa. 1950), *aff'd on opinion below*, 189 F.2d 104 (3d Cir. 1951); Rand McNally & Co. v. Fleet Management Sys., Inc., 634 F. Supp. 604 (N.D. Ill. 1986)(on remand) (compilation copyrightable on basis of contribution, not industriousness).

Randomly selected numbering systems are not protectible. Toro Co. v. R & R Prods. Co., 787 F.2d 1208 (8th Cir. 1986)(manufacturer's parts). *Compare* Clark Equip. Co. v. Lift Parts Mfg. Co., Copyright L. Rep. (CCH) ¶ 25,989 (N.D. Ill. 1986)(replacement parts; "industrious collection" doctrine applied); West Publishing Co. v. Mead Data Central, Inc., 799 F.2d 1219 (8th Cir. 1986)(2–1) (starred page numbering in National Reporter System, being key to self-index by which West's arrangements are accessed, is within meaning of phrase "taken as a whole" within definition of "compilation"; arrangement of cases involves considerable planning, labor, talent, and judgment; self-indexing nature of editorial work based on volume number, series designation, and page number court-approved confidential settlement and case law license agreement, July 31, 1988; antitrust *et al.* actions similarly settled), *cert. denied*, 479 U.S. 1069 (1987); Locke, *A Critical Analysis of* West Publishing Co. v. Mead Data Central, Inc., 36 J. COPYRIGHT SOC'Y 182 (1989); Patterson & Joyce, *Monopolizing the Law: The Scope of Copyright Protection for Law Reports and Statutory Compilations*, 36 U.C.L.A. L. REV. 719 (1989) (control of key to access

"Collective work" is defined as a "work, such as a periodical issue, anthology, or encyclopedia, in which a number of contributions, constituting separate and independent works in themselves, are assembled into a collective whole."[33]

"Derivative work" is defined as a "work based upon one or more preexisting works, such as a translation, musical arrangement, dramatization, fictionalization, motion picture version, sound recording, art reproduction, abridgment, condensation, or any other form in which a work may be recast, transformed, or adapted," including a "work consisting of editorial revisions, annotations, elaborations, or other modifications which, as a whole, represent an original work of authorship."[34]

---

to law through numbering of internal pages in National Reporter Series by asterisks); Comments, 64 CHI.-KENT L. REV. 37 (1988); 71 MINN. L. REV. 991 (1987).

Labels, stickers, slogans, and jingles may be protected if there is sufficient authorship, in which case there may be questions of infringement. Higgins v. Keuffel, 140 U.S. 428 (1891)(label not copyrightable; possibility of trademark protection); Goodson-Todman Enters. v. Kellogg Co., 513 F.2d 913 (9th Cir. 1975)("Will the real . . . please stand up?"); Alberto-Culver Co. v. Andrea Dumon, Inc., 466 F.2d 705 (7th Cir. 1972)("most personal part of deodorant"); Original Appalachian Artworks, Inc. v. Topps Chewing Gum, Inc., 642 F. Supp. 1031 (N.D. Ga. 1986)("Cabbage Patch Dolls" versus "Garbage Pail Kids" stickers); Dr. Pepper Co. v. Sambo Restaurants, Inc. 517 F. Supp. 1202 (N.D. Tex. 1981)("Wouldn't you like to be a Pepper, too?" commercial tagline).

33. 17 U.S.C.A. § 101. Typically, collective works incorporate two different sorts of materials: (1) the collective work as a whole (including any material not written independently, but prepared by employees and the elements of compilation, revision, editing, arrangement, and similar authorship that went into putting the work into final form); and (2) individual, self-contained contributions written independently by nonemployees. These contributions are considered to be separately copyrightable works, different from the collective work in which they appear. The 1909 Act used the term "composite work." 1909 Act § 3.

34. 17 U.S.C.A. § 101; Oppenheimer, *Originality in Art Reproductions: "Variations" in Search of a Theme*, 26 BULL. COPYRIGHT SOC'Y 1 (1978);

Protection for a work employing preexisting material in which copyright subsists does not extend to "any part" of the work in which such material has been used unlawfully.[35]

The copyright in a compilation or derivative work extends only to the material contributed by the author of the work ("incremental additions of originality"), as distinguished from the preexisting material employed in the work, and does not imply any exclusive right in the preexisting material. The copyright in such a work is independent of, and does not affect or enlarge the scope, duration,

---

Hearn v. Meyer, 664 F. Supp. 832 (S.D.N.Y. 1987) (reproductions of illustrations in public domain held not original and therefore not copyrightable, even if reproduction involved difficult, time-consuming artistic effort to recreate precise colors). *But see* note 32 *supra*. International Film Exch., Ltd. v. Corinth Films, Inc., 621 F. Supp. 631 (S.D.N.Y. 1985)(dubbed or subtitled versions of foreign-language film in public domain held to create derivative work translation). Presumably, an adaptation, even under the first sentence of the definition of "derivative work," must "represent an original work of authorship." Sufficient originality to qualify as a copyrightable derivative work must be more than trivial; the standard for infringement is substantial similarity of protectible elements. Mirage Editions, Inc. v. Albuquerque A.R.T. Co., 856 F.2d 1341 (9th Cir. 1988), *cert. denied*, 109 S.Ct. 1135 (1989) (mounting art reproduction on ceramic tile held infringement of exclusive right to make derivative work; quaere, whether mounting represented original work of authorship); Eden Toys, Inc. v. Florelee Undergarment Co., 697 F.2d 27 (2d Cir. 1982).

35. 17 U.S.C.A. § 103(a). The 1909 Act protected new versions containing copyrighted matter "when produced with the consent of the proprietor of the copyright" in the preexisting matter. 1909 Act § 7. JBJ Fabrics, Inc. v. Brylane, Inc., 714 F. Supp. 107 (S.D.N.Y. 1989) (derivative work copyrightable despite unauthorized use of preexisting work). Not protectible as derivative works are transmission programs embodied in a copy or phonorecord made under 17 U.S.C.A. § 112 (except with express consent of "owners of copyright" in preexisting works employed in programs) (§ 112(e)) and arrangements made under compulsory musical recording license (except with express consent of "copyright owner") (§ 115(a)(2)).

ownership, or subsistence of any copyright protection in the preexisting material.[36]

The status of a derivative work after the termination of the license to produce it or after renewal when the license did not apply to any renewal term or when the licensee is not the owner of the renewal copyright has posed some challenging questions.[37]

---

36. 17 U.S.C.A. § 103(b). Copyright in a new version covers only material added by the later author, and has no effect one way or the other on the copyright or public domain status of the preexisting material. 1976 House Report 57. "Others are free to copy the original. They are not free to copy the copy." Bleistein v. Donaldson Lithographing Co., 188 U.S. 239, 249 (1903)(Holmes, J.). The copyright notice is not required to distinguish new from preexisting matter, except where the new work consists "preponderantly" of "works of the United States Government." 17 U.S.C.A. § 403. However, the application for copyright registration is required to include an identification of any preexisting work or works that it is based on or incorporates, and a brief, general statement of the additional material covered by the copyright claim being registered. 17 U.S.C.A. § 409(9). *See* Weissmann v. Freeman, 868 F.2d 1313 (2d Cir. 1989) (unauthorized use by one co-author of joint work of derivative work prepared by other co-author held infringement of new protectible elements in derivative work).
37. Stewart v. Abend, 110 S. Ct. 1750 (1990) (6–3) (public performance of motion picture unauthorized by owner of renewal copyright in underlying work held infringement of renewal copyright; author of underlying work had included renewal rights in motion picture grant, but that expectancy did not survive author's death before renewal period; applying conventional approach that copyrights in derivative works are subservient to copyrights in underlying works; dissenters [110 S. Ct. at 1769] emphasized that 1909 Act section 7 ["versions"] provided that new versions "shall be regarded as new works subject to copyright under the provisions of this title" and contended that the renewal provisions were affected by the 1976 Act termination provisions despite the fact that the pre-1978 renewal language was retained for pre-1978 copyrights to preserve existing rights), *aff'g* Abend v. MCA, 863 F.2d 1465 (9th Cir. 1988) (2–1). The dissent appears to beg the question, and, in the process, ignores possible deprivation of renewal copyright property retroactively without due process of law. The fact that the renewal copyright owner had purchased renewal expectancies for $650 plus a percentage of proceeds from uses like rereleases of films in a variety of media, including videocassettes and cable TV,

5.4 Nonprotectible Matter

Excluded from copyright protection for an original work of authorship is "any idea, procedure, process, system, method of operation, concept, principle, or discovery," regardless of the form in which it is described, explained, illustrated, or embodied in the work.[38]

---

was emphasized by the dissent. But the 1976 Act nineteen-year exception for termination during the extended renewal term (from twenty-eight to forty-seven years) was persuasive. By analogy to patent law, an improvement patent is always subservient to the dominant original patent.

Unauthorized use of a derivative work in the public domain may infringe any subsisting copyright in the underlying work to the extent of the inclusion of protected material from the underlying work. Filmvideo Releasing Corp. v. Hastings, 668 F.2d 91 (2d Cir. 1981), Russell v. Price, 612 F.2d 1123 (9th Cir. 1979) (Pygmalion). Mills Music, Inc. v. Snyder, 469 U.S. 105 (1985)(5–4)("derivative work exception" held to protect music publisher's contractual right to share in recording royalties despite termination of authors' grant to publisher; dissent construed exception to apply to users of derivative works and not intermediaries). *See* chapter 16, note 34 *infra*. *See also* Colby, *Rohauer Revisited: "Rear Windows," Copyright Reversions, Renewals, Terminations, Derivative Works and Fair Use*, 13 PEPPERDINE L. REV. 569 (1986); Goldstein, *Derivative Rights and Derivative Works in Copyright*, 30 J. COPYRIGHT SOC'Y 209 (1982); Fabe, *Fine Artist's Right to the Reproductions of His Original Work*, 9 J. BEVERLY HILLS B.A. 59 (1975), *reprinted in* 23 COPYRIGHT L. SYMP. (ASCAP) 81 (1977).

38. 17 U.S.C.A. § 102(b); 37 C.F.R. § 202.1. Copyright protects the expression of the author and not the ideas expressed. Thus the expression adopted by the computer programmer is the copyrightable element in the program, and the processes and methods embodied in the program are not within the scope of copyright law. 1976 House Report 57. Computer software may be protected by patent law, copyright law, and other legal principles. The application of traditional copyright principles would not result in the protection of ideas, procedures, processes, systems, methods of operations, concepts, principles, discoveries, or useful articles so far as their mechanical or utilitarian aspects are concerned. Copyright includes specified exclusive rights for works of authorship, as distinguished from their material embodiment.

In 1988, the Copyright Office decided to accept a single registration for computer programs with screen displays as one work, although separate registrations are still permissible. Copyright Notice of Policy Decision, 53 FED. REG. 21,817–20 (1988). *See* Manufacturers Technologies, Inc. v. Cams, Inc., 706 F. Supp. 894 (D. Conn. 1989) (single copyright registration as compilation for computer covered both program as such and screen displays or user interface of program to extent of creative authorship; screen displays generated by program constituted expression beyond functional considerations); Broderbund Software, Inc. v. Unison World, Inc., 648 F. Supp. 1127 (N.D. Cal. 1986). *See* chapter 32 *infra* (Semiconductor Chip Products). Noncopyrightable are trademarks, ideas, plans, methods, systems, inventions, computing and measuring devices, names, titles, other short phrases or expressions, general ideas or outlines for radio and television programs. Distinctive computer 1-2-3 spread sheet programs have been held protectible. Lotus Dev. Corp. v. Paperback Software, Copyright L. Rep. (CCH) ¶ 26,595 (D. Mass. 1990). *See generally* Goldberg & Burleigh, *Computer Programs: The Patent/Copyright Interface*, 17 A.I.P.L.A. Q.J. 173 (1989); Menell, *Analysis of the Scope of Copyright Protection for Application Programs*, 41 STAN. L. REV. 1045 (1989); Einhorn, *The Scope of Computer Software Copyrights*, 35 COPYRIGHT L. SYMP. (ASCAP) 13 (1989); Halvey, *A Rose by Any Other Name: Computer Programs and the Idea–Expression Distinction*, 35 COPYRIGHT L. SYMP. (ASCAP) 1 (1989); Perelman, *Proving Copyright Infringement of Computer Software: An Analytical Framework*, 34 COPYRIGHT L. SYMP. (ASCAP) 99 (1987), Clapes, Lynch & Steinberg, *Silicon Epics and Binary Bards: Determining the Proper Scope of Protection for Computer Programs*, 34 U.C.L.A. L. REV. 1495 (1987); Rashind, *The Uncertain Case for Special Legislation Protecting Computer Software*, 47 U. PITT. L. REV. 1131 (1986). Various legal principles from other than copyright law have been involved. *See* Maher, *The Shrink-Wrap License: Old Problems in a New Wrapper*, 34 J. COPYRIGHT L. SOC'Y 292 (1987). Quaere, as to preemption. *See* chapter 4 *supra*.

Ideas may be protected under principles of express, implied-in-fact or implied-in-law contract (quasi contract) or confidential relationship. Hopkins, *Ideas. Their Time Has Come: An Agreement and a Proposal for Copyrighting Ideas*, 46 ALBANY L. REV. 443 (1982). *But see* McCulloch v. Albert E. Price, Inc., 823 F.2d 316 (9th Cir. 1987) (protecting red plate and "You Are Special Today" around rim); Nash v. CBS, Inc., 899 F.2d 1537 (7th Cir. 1990) (plaintiff's "interpretative historical theory" that gangster John Dillinger was not shot and was alive held unprotectible facts and ideas); Silverman v. C.B.S., Inc., 870 F.2d 40 (2d Cir. 1989) ("Amos 'n Andy" trademark abandoned for nonuse for one year with no intent to resume in reasonably foreseeable future; scripts containing names and characters no longer under copyright); Murray v. NBC, Inc., 844 F.2d 988 (2d Cir. 1988) (2–1) (NBC employee's idea for Cosby show not sufficiently novel for protectible interest); Burcourt, *No Titles to Titles: An Analysis of the Lack of Copyright Protection for Literary Titles*, 32 COPYRIGHT L. SYMP. (ASCAP) (1986). *See* Copyright Office Circulars R13 (Trademarks), 31 (Ideas, Methods or Systems), 32 (Blank Forms and Other Works Not Protected by Copyright), 33 (Computing and Measuring Devices), R34 (Copyright Protection Not Available for Names, Titles, or Short Phrases). Trademarks, service marks, certification marks, collective marks, brand names, trade names, slogans, and phrases may be protected under state unfair competition law, and may be registrable under federal or state trademark statutes. *See* 15 U.S.C.A. §§ 1051 *et seq.* Inventions may be patentable under the patent statute. *See* 35 U.S.C. §§ 1 *et seq.* The issue of patents for inventions and registration of trademarks and other marks are within the jurisdiction of the Patent and Trademark Office of the Department of Commerce and not of the Copyright Office. *See* chapter 1 *supra.* For noncopyrightability of works of the United States government, see text accompanying chapter 6, notes 18–23, *infra.*

The leading case is Baker v. Selden, 101 U.S. 99 (1879). *See* Bibbero Sys., Inc. v. Colwell Sys., Inc., 893 F.2d 1104 (9th Cir. 1990) (forms for applications for medical insurance benefits held not copyrightable under blank-forms rule); Kregos v. Associated Press, 731 F. Supp. 113 (S.D.N.Y. 1990). John H. Harland Co. v. Clarke Checks, Inc., 711 F.2d 966 (11th Cir. 1983)(check manufacturer's "Memory Stub" blank form designed for recording information held lacking in original pictorial expression); Kregos v. Associated Press, 731 F. Supp. 113 (S.D.N.Y. 1990) (baseball pitching form); Safeguard Business Sys., Inc. v. Reynolds & Reynolds Co., Copyright L. Rep. (CCH) ¶ 26,576 (E.D. Pa. 1990) (health care day sheets); Januz Mktg. Communications, Inc. v. Doubleday & Co., 569 F. Supp. 76 (S.D.N.Y. 1982). *Compare* Merritt Forbes & Co. v. Newman Inv. Sec., Inc., 604 F. Supp. 943 (S.D.N.Y. 1985)(bond underwriting documents held copyrightable against contentions of use of boilerplate, information required by disclosure laws, and precedents).

Games, being basically ideas, are not copyrightable, but some of their elements may be, e.g., rules (literary works), playing boards (pictorial works), sounds (audiovisual works). Anti-Monopoly, Inc. v. General Mills Fun Group, 611 F.2d 296 (9th Cir. 1979) (game concept not copyrightable), *on remand*, 515 F. Supp. 448 (N.D. Cal. 1981). For discussion of protection of computerized audiovisual game, *see* chapter 17, note 53 *infra.* Game names may be protected under trademark and other laws. For books of game strategy, *see* Landsberg v. Scrabble Crossword Game Players, Inc., 736 F.2d 485 (9th Cir.), *cert. denied*, 469 U.S. 1037 (1984).

5.5 Deferred Matter

Deferred for future Congresses has been protection for typeface designs,[39] National Technical Information Service (NTIS) publications,[40] and ornamental designs.[41]

---

39. 1976 House Report 54; Eltra Corp. v. Ringer, 579 F.2d 294 (4th Cir. 1978)(affirming nonregistrability of typeface designs). Photocopying of composed type may constitute unfair competition. Computer programs to control digitigation process may be registrable even though the resulting typefonts are not protectible.
40. 1976 House Report 59–60.
41. Conference Report 82. Lehrer, *The Design of Design Law Today,* 37 COPYRIGHT L. SYMP. (ASCAP) 145 (1989); Brown, *Design Protection—An Overview,* 34 UCLA L. REV. 1341 (1987); Reichman, *Design Protection After the Copyright Act of 1976: A Comparative View of the Emerging Interim Models,* 31 J. COPYRIGHT SOC'Y 267 (1984); Denicolar, *Applied Art and Industrial Design: A Suggested Approach to Copyright in Useful Articles,* 67 MINN. L. REV. 707 (1983); Levine & Meyer, *Unfinished Business—Copyright Issues Unresolved by the Act of 1976,* 6 A.I.P.L.A. Q.J. 61, 68 (1978). *See* S.791 and H.R.1179, 100th Cong., 1st Sess. (1987).

6. Eligible Works

This chapter deals with protection of works *in the United States* of American, foreign, or mixed origin. Copyright status depends on the statutory provisions applicable at the time:

1. Under the 1909 Act, as amended in 1955 when the United States adherered to the Universal Copyright Convention;
2. Under the 1976, effective January 1, 1978; and
3. Under the 1976 Act, as amended by the Berne Convention Implementations Act of 1988, effective March 1, 1989.[1] The revisions and amendments were not retroactive. Protection is based on the applicable statutory provision, since the Convention provisions were not self-executing and the implementing legis-

1. The converse—protection of American works in foreign countries—is discussed in chapter 34 *infra*. Prior to 1891, foreign works were not protected in the United States. *See* chapter 2, note 9, *supra*. Over the years, reciprocal copyright relations based on national treatment were established with foreign countries, first by bipartite arrangements (see note 17 *infra*), and then by Pan-American conventions (see text accompanying chapter 34, notes 30–40 *infra*), the Universal Copyright Convention in 1955 (see text accompanying chapter 34, notes 16–29, *infra*), and the Berne Convention (see text accompanying chapter 34, notes 4–15, *infra*).

lation controls. Protection of American works in other countries is discussed in chapter 34.

Eligibility for protection in the United States varies, depending upon whether the work is:

1. Unpublished
2. Published

"Publication" is defined as:[2]

> the distribution of copies or phonorecords of a work to the public by sale or other transfer of ownership, or by rental, lease, or lending. . . . A public performance or display of a work does not of itself constitute publication.

6.1 Unpublished Works

Unpublished works are entitled to protection "without regard to the nationality or domicile of the author,"[3] and without regard to place of publication.[4]

6.2 Published Works

Eligibility for protection of published works depends on "national origin," meaning:

1. Eligibility of the author
2. Eligibility of the work

---

2. 17 U.S.C.A. § 101. The offering to distribute copies or phonorecords to a group of persons for purposes of further distribution, public performance, or public display constitutes publication.
3. 17 U.S.C.A. § 104(a).
4. Presumably, this is so, although § 104(a) does not contain the phrase, "without regard to the nationality of the work." Prior to January 1, 1978, common-law protection extended to the writings of all authors, with no national limitations.

Published works are entitled to protection if they are eligible under any of the following provisions:

6.2[1] Eligibility of One or More Authors[5]

The work is entitled to protection if on the date of first publication, one or more of the authors is a national or domiciliary of the United States, or is a national, domiciliary, or sovereign authority of a foreign nation that is a party to a copyright treaty to which the United States is also a party,[6] or is a stateless person, wherever that person may be domiciled.[7]

---

5. The phrase "one or more of the authors" qualifies "joint works" by two or more co-authors so long as one of the authors is eligible. In the case of a "work made for hire," the employer or other person for whom the work was prepared is considered the author. 17 U.S.C.A. § 201(b). An express agreement in a written instrument signed by the parties that the employee or person preparing the work owns all of the rights does not affect the authorship status. Neither does an assignment. Protection for an assignee depends upon the eligibility of the author. The 1909 Act referred to "author or proprietor." 1909 Act § 9. Presumably, a corporation may still be an author in the case of a "work made for hire," despite the current statute's addition of feminine but not neuter references. *Cf.* 1 U.S.C. § 1A (unless context indicates otherwise, words importing masculine gender include feminine as well).
6. The current copyright relations between the United States and a foreign country are charted in the latest Cummulative Annual Pocket Part to 17 U.S.C.A. *See also* Copyright Office Circular R–38a. The World Intellectual Property Organization (WIPO) provides information on adherents to the Berne Convention, revisions, and other arrangements sponsored by it or its predecessors, and tests of the more relevant agreements in various languages. Concerning the Universal Copyright Convention and other arrangements sponsored by UNESCO, the latter offers information on signatory countries and copies of conventions. Where international copyright relations are "unclear," the Copyright Office will not apply its "rule of doubt" in favor of the claimant. *See also* Bogsch, *Protection of Works of Foreign Origin* (1959), *reprinted in* 1 STUDIES ON COPYRIGHT—ARTHUR FISHER MEMORIAL EDITION 737 (1963).
7. 17 U.S.C.A. § 104(b)(1). *See* Houghton Mifflin Co. v. Stackpole Sons, 104 F.2d 306 (2d Cir.), *cert. denied*, 308 U.S. 597 (1939) (protecting Hitler's *Mein Kampf*).

6.2[2] Eligibility Dependent on Place of First Publication

The work is entitled to protection if it is first published in the United States[8] or in a foreign nation that, on the date of first publication, is a party to the Universal Copyright Convention.[9]

6.2[3] Eligibility of Works First Published by United Nations or Organization of American States

The work is entitled to protection if it is first published by the United Nations or any of its specialized agencies, or by the Organization of American States.[10]

6.2[4] Eligibility of Berne Convention Works

The work is entitled to protection if it is a "Berne Convention work."[11]

"Berne Convention work"[12] includes an "unpublished work" if "one or more of the authors" is a national of a nation adhering to the Berne Convention,[13] and a "published work" if "one or more of the authors" is such a

---

8. First publication in the United States provided no basis for protection under the 1909 Act except for alien authors or proprietors domiciled in the United States. *See* 1909 Act § 9.

9. 17 U.S.C.A. § 104(b)(2). For reference to list of countries adhering to the Universal Copyright Convention, *see* note 6 *supra*.

10. 17 U.S.C.A. § 104(b)(3). Required by the Second Protocol of the Universal Copyright Convention to which the United States has adhered.

11. 17 U.S.C.A. § 104(b)(4), effective March 1, 1989.

12. Defined in 17 U.S.C.A. § 101 (added by Berne Act § 4(a)(1)(B). "Country of origin" is defined for purposes of Berne Act § 411. *Id.*

13. "Berne Convention" is defined as the "Convention for the Protection of Literary and Artistic Works, signed at Berne, Switzerland, on September 9, 1886, and all acts, protocols, and revisions thereto." 17 U.S.C.A. § 101. The Convention is not self-executing. Reliance upon, or United States adherence to, the Convention has no effect upon any rights or interests in a work under federal or state statutes or the common law. 17 U.S.C.A. § 104(c); Berne Act § 4(a)(3).

national "on the date of first publication," or the work was "first published" in a Berne Convention nation or was "simultaneously first published" in a Berne Convention nation and a nonadhering foreign nation.[14]

An author domiciled in or having "habitual residence" in a nation adhering to the Berne Convention is "considered" to be a national thereof. A work is "considered" to have been "simultaneously published" in two or more nations if "its dates of publication are within thirty days of one another."[15]

Also included as a "Berne Convention work" is an "audiovisual work" if "one or more of the authors is a legal entity" with its headquarters" in a nation adhering to the Berne Convention, or if "one or more of the authors is an individual" whose domicile or "habitual residence" is in such a nation; in the case of a "pictorial, graphic, or sculptural work" "incorporated in a building or other structure" "located" in such a nation; and in the case of an "architectural work" "embodied in a building" such building is "erected" in a "country" adhering to the Berne Convention.[16]

6.2[5] Eligibility Dependent upon Presidential Proclamation

The work is entitled to protection if it comes within the scope of a Presidential proclamation. Whenever the President finds that a particular foreign nation extends, to works by authors who are nationals or domiciliaries of the United States or to works that are first published in the United States, copyright protection "on substantially the same basis as that on which the foreign nation extends protection to

14. 17 U.S.C.A. § 101.
15. *Id.*
16. *Id.*

works of its own nationals and domiciliaries and works first published in that nation," the President may by proclamation extend protection to works of which one or more of the authors is, on the date of first publication, a national, domiciliary, or sovereign authority of that nation, or that was first published in that nation. The President may revise, suspend, or revoke any such proclamation or impose any conditions or limitations on protection under a proclamation.[17]

6.3 Ineligibility of Works of United States Government

"Works of the United States Government," whether unpublished or published, are precluded from copyright protection,[18] as compared with the 1909 Act prohibition against

---

17. 17 U.S.C.A. § 104(b)(4). Protection under this provision is based on nationality of the author or nationality of the work. A single proclamation now covers all rights. Under the 1909 Act a general proclamation would not cover mechanical (recording) rights. Specific declaration of mechanical rights reciprocity was required. For reference to list of proclamations, and whether they included mechanical reproduction rights for music, *see* note 6 *supra*. All pre-1978 proclamations continue in force until terminated, suspended, or revised by the President. 17 U.S.C.A. § 104. The existence of the proclamation is controlling. New York Chinese TV Programs, Inc. v. U.E. Enters, Inc. Copyright L. Rep. (CCH) ¶ 26,398 (S.D.N.Y. 1989) (Taiwanese films held protected under Taiwan Relations Act).
18. 17 U.S.C.A. § 105. Legislation to provide limited copyright protection for publications of the Department of Commerce National Technical Information Service (NTIS) was deferred. Conference Report 69–70; Ringer, *The Unfinished Business of Copyright Revision,* 24 U.C.L.A. L. REV. 951, 956-60 (1977). The section does not affect protection abroad of United States government works. Apart from statutes, federal, state, and local governmental enactments consistently have been held not copyrightable, as have judicial opinions. Callaghan v. Myers, 128 U.S. 617 (1888)(judicial opinions and other materials prepared by court); Georgia v. Harrison Co, 548 F. Supp. 110 (N.D. Ga. 1982)(state statutes not copyrightable); *cf.* DEL. GEN. CORP. LAW § 397 (penalty for unauthorized publications of law). Quaere, as to the

copyright in "any publication of the United States Government."[19] "Work of the United States Government" is defined as a work prepared by a United States government officer or employee "as part of that person's official duties."[20] Neither the government nor the officer or employee enjoys

---

effect of a private law publisher's arrangement of state laws on a state's interest in returning its statutory law to the public domain. Texas v. West Publishing Co., 882 F.2d 171 (5th Cir. 1989) (lack of controversy) *cert. denied*, 110 S. Ct. 869 (1990); West Publishing Co. v. Aaron/Smith Assocs., Copyright L. Rep. (CCH) ¶ 26,554 (N.D. Ga. 1990) (consent decree permanently enjoining retrieval of infringing materials in publisher's copyrighted case reporters). The selection, editing, arrangement, synopses, headnotes, additional citations, and even pagination may be protected. West Publishing Co. v. Mead Data Cent. Inc., 799 F.2d 1219 (8th Cir. 1986) (2–1), *cert. denied*, 479 U.S. 1069 (1987); N.Y. JUD. LAW § 438; *cf.* Lipman v. Massachusetts, 475 F.2d 565 (1st Cir. 1973)(verbatim transcription by freelance reporter of Kennedy Chappaquiddick incident held not copyrightable, but protected on contract principles against sale by state court clerk). *See also* Building Officials & Code Adm'rs v. Code Technology, Inc., 628 F.2d 730 (1st Cir. 1980)(legislatively enacted model building code, at least to extent of inclusion in state regulations, held not copyrightable). Telephone directories (white pages and, a fortiori, Yellow Pages, possibly subject to rights of listees in their ads) are copyrightable, even when publication of information in white pages is required by state. Hutchinson Tel. Co. v. Frontier Directory Co., 770 F.2d 128 (8th Cir. 1985). *See* Illinois Bell Tel. Co. v. Haines & Co., 905 F.2d 1081 (7th Cir. 1990); Rocky Mountain Motor Tariff Bureau, Inc. v. G.R. Leonard & Co., 652 F. Supp. 1473 (D. Colo. 1987). Patterson & Joyce, *Monopolizing the Law: The Scope of Copyright Protection for Law Reports and Statutory Compilations*, 36 U.C.L.A L. REV. 719 (1989); Nodiff, *Copyrightability of Works of the Federal and State Governments Under the 1976 Act*, 32 COPYRIGHT L. SYMP. (ASCAP) 43 (1986).

19. 1909 Act § 8; Berger, *Copyright in Government Publications* (1959), *reprinted in* 1 STUDIES ON COPYRIGHT—ARTHUR FISHER MEMORIAL EDITION 169 (1963); Smith, *Government Documents: Their Copyright and Ownership*, 22 ASCAP COPYRIGHT L. SYMP. 147 (1977); Price, *Copyright in Government Publications: Historical Background, Judicial Interpretation, and Legislative Clarification*, 74 MIL. L. REV. 19 (1976).
20. 17 U.S.C.A. § 101. Compare definition of "work made for hire." Despite some difference in language in definitions of "work of the United States Government" and "work made for hire," the concepts

copyright protection, and anyone, including the officer, employee, or public, is free to use the work.

Government-funded works are not within the statutory ban, but are subject, of course, to administrative regulations of the funding government agency or contractual restrictions.[21] The 1976 Act expressly provides that the government is not precluded from receiving and holding copyrights transferred to it by assignment, bequest, or otherwise.[22]

Any published work consisting "preponderantly of one or more works of the United States Government" must include in its notice of copyright "a statement identifying either affirmatively or negatively, those portions" embodying any protected work.[23]

---

are intended to be construed in the same way. 1976 House Report 58. Relevant are the concepts of an employer-employee as distinguished from an independent-contractor relationship. *See* RESTATEMENT (SECOND) OF AGENCY §§ 2, 220 (1958). *See* text accompanying chapter 7, note 21, *infra*. Publications of the United States Postal Service, including postage stamps, under the terms of the Postal Reorganization Act, of 1970, are not "works of the United States Government." 1976 House Report 60. Sheets of United States postal stamps bear copyright notices. Special legislative exemptions are provided congressional parliamentarians. *See also* 15 U.S.C.A. § 290(e) (Standard Data Reference Act exception).

21. 1976 House Report 59; Schnapper v. Foley, 667 F.2d 102 (D.C. Cir. 1981), *cert. denied*, 455 U.S. 948 (1982)(federally commissioned work held not United States Government work). *See* University of Minn. v. Applied Innovations, Inc., 876 F.2d 626 (8th Cir. 1989) (test statements involving sufficient authorship copyrightable despite United States government funding; state affiliation irrelevant; WPA regulations never published in *Federal Register*); Simon, *A Constitutional Analysis of Copyrighting Government-Commissioned Work*, 34 COPYRIGHT L. SYMP. (ASCAP) 39 (1987). Copyright and exclusive licensing of government software, with sharing of royalties with federal researchers, has been suggested as stimulating transfer and use of software and facilitating public access, thus improving world market competitiveness.
22. 17 U.S.C.A. § 105 (somewhat redundant if the work were not prepared by an employee within the employee's official duties).
23. 17 U.S.C.A. § 403.

7. Copyright Ownership

7.1 Copyright Distinct from Copies and Phonorecords

Two types of property rights must be distinguished:

1. Ownership of copyright;[1] and

---

1. Including any of the exclusive rights under a copyright, 17 U.S.C.A. § 202. Weisbond, *Highlights of Ownership and Transfer Provisions of the New Copyright Law,* 25 BULL. COPYRIGHT SOC'Y 221 (1978). A non-exclusive license does not involve a property right, but is a covenant or promise by the licensor not to sue the licensee. A copyright is intangible and incorporeal, without physical existence. A "sole and exclusive license" is a contract by the licensor not to exercise personally or authorize others to exercise the licensed rights; an "exclusive license" literally means not to grant similar licenses to others; a nonexclusive license constitutes authorization, in effect a covenant not to sue. Licenses do not amount to copyright ownership or, under the 1909 Act, proprietorship. Licensing agreements, like other contracts, are subject to an implied covenant of good faith and fair dealing. Original Appalachian Artworks, Inc. v. S. Diamond Assocs., 911 F.2d 1548 (11th Cir. 1990) (exclusive licensee under license barring licensee from suing infringer without licensor's written consent, held entitled to share in settlement proceeds paid to licensor by infringer; copyright licensor under fiduciary obligation [implied covenant of good faith and fair dealing] to licensee); SAS Inst., Inc. v. S & H Computer Sys., Inc., 606 F. Supp. 816 (M.D. Tenn. 1985). The extent of permissible editing or other changes depends on the scope of the license. S.O.S., Inc. v. Payday, Inc., 886 F.2d 1081 (9th Cir. 1981); Silliam v. ABC, 538 F.2d 14 (2d Cir. 1976) (contractual provisions requiring consultation and limiting editing). Quaere, as to the

2. Ownership of the material object in which the copyrighted work is embodied.[2]

---

duties of a book publisher in licensing "subsidiary rights" (use in other media): the publisher acts not only pro se, but as agent (fiduciary) for the author. *See also* Cohen v. Paramount Pictures Corp., 845 F.2d 851 (9th Cir. 1988) (pre-VCR-era license to use in film and exhibit film in theatres and on TV held not to authorize taping and use in videocassettes). United States v. King Features Entertainment, Inc., 843 F.2d 394 (9th Cir. 1988) (license to sell films for use on military bases in United States and territories "free of charge and not on television or cable" held not to cover noncommercial closed circuit military television use); Major League Baseball Promotion Corp. v. Colour-Tex, Inc., 629 F. Supp. 1035 (D.N.J. 1990).

2. 17 U.S.C.A. § 202. The material object—"copy" or "phonorecord"—is tangible and corporeal and has physical existence. Protection for the material objects is not preempted. *See* chapter 4, note 15 *supra*. Absent "fixation," there is no preemption. *See* chapter 4, note 5 *supra*. The terms "copy" and "phonorecord" are mutually exclusive. Control over the transfer of a particular copy after the initial transfer of the copy's ownership is limited by the "first sale doctrine." 17 U.S.C.A. § 109; Bobbs-Merrill Co. v. Strauss, 210 U.S. 339 (1908)(after first sale no breach of contract actionable as copyright infringement). The first-sale doctrine limits the copyright owner's control of transfer of a particular copy after the initial transfer of the copy's ownership. There are limitations on the "first sale doctrine," e.g., rental of phonograph records (17 U.S.C.A. § 109[b], and 1980 amendment of § 117 (computer programs); rental of computer software (17 U.S.C.A. § 109(b)(1)(a) [eff. Dec. 1, 1990]). Large-scale commercial resale of used copies of books, especially textbooks, is a common practice. *See* Sebastian Int'l, Inc. v. Consumer Contacts (Pty.) Ltd., 847 F.2d 1093 (3d Cir. 1988) (manufacturer selling its goods with copyrighted labels to foreign distributors barred under "first-sale doctrine" from recovery for unauthorized importation, regardless of place of manufacture and sale); once a lawfully made copy is sold, the exclusive right to "vend" or "distribute," the "first-sale doctrine," applies. This is consistent with the basic distinction between the usual rights in *tangible* personal property—the physical fixation of the expression of the author. Under copyright law, copies and phonorecords are tangible. In contrast, copyright is *intangible* personal property. In a sense, all rights (like duties and privileges) are intangible, but what the rights apply to may be tangible (real property or chattels) or intangible (besides copyrights, patents, choses in action, shares of stock as distinguished from the certificates representing them, etc.). United States v. Wise, 550 F.2d 1180 (9th Cir.), *cert. denied*, 434 U.S. 929

Transfer of ownership of the material object does not of itself convey any rights in the copyrighted work embodied in the object.[3] Conversely, transfer of copyright, absent agreement,[4] does not convey property rights in the material object.[5]

(1977). *See* United States v. Minor, 756 F.2d 731 (9th Cir. 1985); Columbia Pictures Indus. Inc. v. Redd Horne, Inc., 568 F. Supp. 494 (W.D. Pa. 1983), *aff'd*, 749 F.2d 154 (3d Cir. 1984). *Compare* Fawcett Publications, Inc. v. Elliot Publishing Co., 46 F. Supp. 717 (S.D.N.Y. 1942) (binding two second-hand copies of comic magazines with defendant's cover entitled "Double Comics"—without removing plaintiff's copyright notice—held within "first-sale doctrine" and not unlawful adaptation) *with* National Geographic Soc'y v. Classified Geographic, Inc., 27 F. Supp. 655 (D. Mass. 1949) (classification and rebinding of plaintiff's magazine articles into defendant's book on various topics held infringement); Colby, *The First Sale Doctrine–the Defense that Never Was?* 32 J. COPYRIGHT SOC'Y 77 (1984). Copies, such as original paintings, musical manuscripts, and compositions of authors, can themselves be very valuable.

3. 17 U.S.C.A. § 202. Transfers of copyright ownership, other than by operation of law, to be "valid," must be by signed writings. 17 U.S.C.A. § 204(a). *See* chapter 8 *infra*. Overruled is the tenuous common-law presumption that transfer of some material objects absent specific reservation, transferred the common-law copyright, overruling Pushman v. New York Graphic Soc'y, 287 N.Y. 302, 39 N.E.2d 249 (1942). 17 U.S.C.A. §§ 202, 204(a), 301 (federal preemption); N.Y. Arts & Cultural Affairs Law §§ 14.01 *et seq.* (reproduction rights reserved by grantor on transfer of work of art). The transferee of a lawfully made copy or, until 1990, a copy of a computer software program or, until 1984, a phonorecord may dispose of it by sale, rental, or any other means, and display it under certain circumstances. 17 U.S.C.A. § 109(a). Breach of any contractual restrictions would be governed by contract, not copyright, law, and therefore actionable in state courts and in federal courts only when there is diversity of citizenship or pendent (ancillary) jurisdiction. 1976 House Report 79–81.
4. 17 U.S.C.A. § 202. Conveyances of rights in the material object are not subject to copyright law, but may be subject to state statutes of frauds (e.g., sale of personal property for $500 or more, or contract not to be performed within one year) and other state statutes.
5. 17 U.S.C.A. § 202. The 1909 Act had a similar provision. 1909 Act § 27. The provision assumably did not apply to works under common-law copyright. There were common-law cases raising presumptions

There is a third type of ownership of noneconomic rights (*droit moral*, "moral rights," "attribution and integrity" rights), which is distinct from ownership of any copy or of a copyright or any exclusive right thereunder.[6]

---

that transfers of material objects, depending on classes of works, did or did not, of themselves, transfer common-law copyrights. In the case of letters, the author was held to retain the copyright, with the recipient owning the tangible letter. *See* Salinger v. Random House, Inc., 811 F.2d 90 (2d Cir. 1987). For magazine articles, *see* Dam v. Kirke La Shelle Co., 175 F. 902 (2d Cir. 1910) (pre-1909 law) (acceptance by author of manuscript of sum "in full payment thereof" held to include all rights of copyright), *quoted in* Pushman case, *infra. But see* Best Medium Publishing Co. v. National Insider, Inc., 385 F.2d 384 (7th Cir. 1967) (absent restrictions, sale by author to magazine included all rights). For works of art, Pushman v. New York Graphic Soc'y, 287 N.Y. 302, 39 N.E.2d 249 (1942), arguably created the common-law presumption that an "unconditinal sale" of a painting transferred rights in the tangible painting and the reproduction rights, quoting the *Dam* case, *supra*, admittedly not in point. In *Pushman*, the policy of the selling agency was expressly to reserve reproduction rights except for sales to universities and others not in the reproduction business, such as the original purchaser of the painting involved in the case.

One can argue that letters may be personal, typescripts of literary works usually of little value, and original works of art often of present or future value. Quaere, as to application of state laws to right of first publication, "publication" until 1978 being the dividing line between federal and state protection. The 1909 Act (former 17 U.S.C.A. § 27) had a provision similar to present 17 U.S.C.A. § 202. However, the current law extends Federal preemption to unpublished works in contrast to the 1909 Act which expressly preserved common-law rights in unpublished works. *See* Tracy v. Skate Key, Inc., 697 F. Supp. 748 (S.D.N.Y. 1988) (preempting state statute on transfers).

6. 17 U.S.C.A. § 106A(e)(2) (effective June 1, 1991). Such rights may not be transferred but may be waived by the author only by a signed written instrument as specified in the statute. A waiver by one co-author is a waiver for all co-authors.

7.2 Authors

7.2[1] Initial Ownership

The "author or authors"[7] are the persons in whom copyright "vests initially."[8]

7.2[2] Joint Works

In the case of a "joint work,"[9] the authors are co-owners of copyright.[10] A "joint work" is defined as a work prepared by two or more authors "with the intention that their contributions be merged into inseparable or interdependent parts of a unitary whole."[11] The intention at the time of writing controls.[12] One or more of the authors of a joint work may work for hire.[13]

---

7. 17 U.S.C.A. § 201(a). The term "author" is not defined. For discussion of "original works of authorship," *see* text accompanying chapter 5, notes 4–7 *supra*.
8. 17 U.S.C.A. § 201(a). Normal editing should not affect authorship; quaere, as to ghostwriting.
9. 17 U.S.C.A. § 201(a). *See* note 11 *infra, cf.* "collective work," note 54 *infra*.
10. *Id.*
11. *Id.* § 101.
12. 1976 House Report 120. Cases under the 1909 Act had stressed "fusion of effort" rather than intent at the time of writing. *Compare* Shapiro Bernstein & Co. v. Jerry Vogel Music Co. ("Melancholy Baby"), 161 F.2d 406 (2d Cir. 1946)(contemporaneous mutual intention to write joint work) *with* Shapiro Bernstein & Co. v. Jerry Vogel Music Co. ("12th Street Rag"), 221 F.2d 569, *modified on rehearing*, 223 F.2d 252 (2d Cir. 1955). *See* Sinkler v. Goldsmith, 623 F. Supp. 727 (D. Ariz. 1985)(exchange of correspondence held not joint work); Kenbrooke Fabrics, Inc. v. Material Things, Copyright L. Rep. (CCH) ¶ 25,679 (S.D.N.Y. 1984)(no joint work found where second alleged co-author independently repeated first alleged co-author's designs). *See* Community for Creative Non-Violence v. Reid, *infra* note 21 (remanded on issue of intention).
13. *See* 17 U.S.C.A. § 302(b) (fixing duration for life and fifty years after last surviving author's death for post-1977 "joint work prepared by two or more authors who did not work for hire").

There is no elaboration of the respective rights of co-owners, and the subject is left to decisional law, presumably property law (at least tangible personal property law) dealing with co-ownership.[14]

---

14. 1976 House Report 121. Picture Music, Inc. v. Bourne, Inc., 314 F. Supp. 640, 645–47 (S.D.N.Y. 1970), *aff'd*, 457 F.2d 1213 (2d Cir.), *cert. denied*, 409 U.S. 997 (1972); Cary, *Joint Ownership of Copyright* (1958), *reprinted in* 1 STUDIES ON COPYRIGHT—ARTHUR FISHER MEMORIAL EDITION 689 (1963). Each co-owner is akin to a tenant in common. A co-author cannot be liable for copyright infringement to the other co-owner. Compensation from unilateral exploitation of the joint work by one of the co-owners without the permission of the other is held in constructive trust for the mutual benefit of all co-owners, and there is under a duty to account therefor. No right of survivorship has been suggested.

A co-owner of a joint work does not ipso facto become a co-owner of a derivated work based thereon written by author or co-owner. *See* Ashton-Tate Corp. v. Ross, Copyright L. Rep. (CCH) ¶ 26,640 (9th Cir. 1990); Weismann v. Freeman, 868 F.2d 1313 (2d Cir. 1989), *cert. denied*, 110 S. Ct. 219 (1989); Novak v. NBC, 724 F. Supp. 141 (S.D.N.Y. 1989) (copyright registered in name of one co-owner held in trust for other; both may sue for infringement); Werbungs & Commerz Union Austalt v. Le Shufy, 6 U.S.P.Q. 2d 1153 (S.D.N.Y. 1987) (license of one co-author of joint work held defense to infringement by other co-author); Weinstein v. University of Ill., 811 F.2d 1091 (7th Cir. 1987) (each co-owner of joint work may make derivative work and may publish either work); Weissman v. Freeman, 868 F.2d 1313 (2d Cir. 1989) (derivative work by one co-author of joint work not itself joint work, infringed by other co-author of joint work); Fantasy, Inc. v. Fogerty, 654 F. Supp. 1129 (N.D. Cal. 1987) (songwriter who sold exclusive rights for royalties capable of infringement of legal owner's copyright; beneficial owner with only economic interest not joint owner with right to use or license work). A beneficial owner may be liable for infringing the legal owner's rights. SBK Catalogue Partnership v. Orion Pictures Corp., 723 F. Supp. 1053 (D.N.J. 1989); For joint authorship of commissioned works, see Notes, 89 COLUM. L. REV. 867 (1989); 137 U. PA. L. REV. 1251 (1989) (computer software). The laws of many foreign countries require co-owners of joint works to join in any license.

7.2[3] Works Made for Hire

In the case of a "work made for hire,"[15] the employer or other person for whom the work was prepared is considered the author,[16] and, unless the parties have expressly agreed otherwise in a "written instrument signed by them,"[17] "owns all of the rights comprised in the copyright."[18] Such a written instrument does not affect the "work made for hire" status of the work,[19] but only the ownership of the rights.

A "work made for hire" is defined as:[20]

1. A work prepared by an employee within the scope of employment;
2. A work specially ordered or commissioned for a statutorily prescribed use, if the parties expressly agree in a "written instrument signed by them" that the work *shall* be considered a work made for hire.

7.2[3][a] Work Prepared by Employee Within Scope of Employment

Traditional concepts of employer-employee (or master-servant) law apply, the basic question being whether, using

---

15. Angel & Tannerbaum, *Works Made for Hire Under S.22*, 22 N.Y.L. SCH. L. REV. 209 (1977); Rudell, *Works for Hire Under New Copyright Law*, 177 N.Y.L.J., March 14, 1977, at 1, col. 1; Copyright Office Circular R9 (Works-Made-for-Hire Under the 1976 Copyright Act).
16. 17 U.S.C.A. § 201(b).
17. 17 U.S.C.A. § 201(b). Such written instrument must be contemporaneous with the preparation of the work. Otherwise, the parties retroactively could alter the status of the work in a manner not contemplated by the statute. *See* text accompanying notes 31–37 *infra*. Quaere, whether such written instrument is a "transfer of copyright ownership" within the recordation provisions. *See* chapter 9 *infra*.
18. 17 U.S.C.A. § 201(b).
19. *See* text accompanying notes 31–37 *infra*.
20. 17 U.S.C.A. § 101 (longest definition).

principles of the "general common law of agency," the work was prepared by an employee or independent contractor.[21] If the work was prepared by an employee within the scope of employment, it is a "work made for hire," and the parties

---

21. Community for Creative Non-Violence v. Reid, 109 S. Ct. 362 (1989) (rejecting right-to-control, exercise-of-control, and formal-salaried-employees tests; "conventional employment relationship" under "general [federal] common law of agency" essential to maintain dichotomy between employees and independent contractors in work made for hire provisions; Court characterized "work for hire doctrine" as carrying "profound significance for freelance creators—including artists, writers, photographers, designers, composers, and computer programmers—and for the publishing, advertising, music, and other industries which commission their works"; case remanded on issue of joint work). The Court suggested that the parties involved with specially ordered or commissioned works "at the outset" should "settle relevant contractual terms, such as the price for the work and the ownership of reproduction rights"—a more comprehensive term would be "ownership of copyright and all the rights thereunder." *See* Notes, 74 CORNELL L. REV. 559 (1989); 22 IND. L. REV. 619 (1989).

The pre-1978 cases had held that the test of "employer"/"employee" (like traditional "master"/"servant") was the right of "control," whether or not exercised.

Murray v. Gelderman, 566 F.2d 1307 (5th Cir. 1978); Epoch Producing Corp. v. Killiam Shows, Inc., 522 F.2d 737 (2d Cir. 1975), *cert. denied*, 424 U.S. 955 (1976); Picture Music, Inc. v. Bourne, 314 F. Supp. 640, 650–51 (S.D.N.Y. 1970), *aff'd*, 457 F.2d 1213 (2d Cir.), *cert. denied*, 409 U.S. 997 (1972); Scherr v. Universal Match Corp., 417 F.2d 497 (2d Cir. 1969), *cert. denied*, 397 U.S. 936 (1970).

Several factors are to be considered in determining whether one acting for another is a servant or independent contractor. *See* RESTATEMENT (SECOND) OF AGENCY §§ 2, 220, 228 ("scope of employment") (1958) (non-exhaustive list in section 220—no one factor being determinative: skill required; source of instrumentalities and tools; location of work; duration of relationship; right of hiring party to assign additional projects; extent of hired party's discretion over when and how long to work; method of payment; role in hiring and paying assistants; whether work is part of regular business of hiring party; whether hiring party is in business; provision of employee benefits; tax treatment of hired party). Quaere, as to relevance of withholding income, Social Security, and unemployment insurance taxes, providing employee retirement and health benefits, and workers' compensation coverage, typical indicia or effect of employer-employee

cannot alter that status by agreement, although, by a signed writing, they may agree that the employer will not own all or any of the rights.[22]

---

relationships. Early social legislation referred to "employees" and the issues were whether the workers were "servants" or "independent contractors" and subject to such legislation. Subjectability to such legislation has become part of the definition. The plaintiff in the *Reid* case *supra*, a nonprofit organization, did not comply with such legislation.

See note 40 *infra*. An employer is liable for an employee's copyright infringement, United States v. Shabazz, 724 F.2d 1536 (5th Cir. 1984), but usually not for an independent contractor's infringement.

For unauthorized public performance of music, judicial exceptions have been created, sometimes on a theory of contributing infringement. Mitch Leigh v. Sakkaris, 215 U.S.P.Q. (BNA) 113 (W.D. Cal. 1982) (lack of control by proprietor of establishment over independent contractors engaged to perform music held no defense).

As for "professorial" writings ("Publish or Perish!"), "work made for hire" status presents many problems, not only for pre-1989 works (see note 21 *supra*) but for pre-1978 works (see text), and what admissible evidence exists or proves convincing as to the rights of university or college "faculty" members of various standings—scholars; fellows; assistants; instructors; assistant, associate, or "full" professors, tenured or not; endowed professors; emeriti, or emeritae, professors; visiting faculty—is very complex. *See* Hays v. Sony Corp. of Am., 847 F.2d 412 (7th Cir. 1988); Weinstein v. University of Ill., 811 F.2d 1091 (7th Cir. 1987), Rome, *Scholarly Writings in the University Setting: Changes in the Works and on the Books*, 35 COPYRIGHT L. SYMP. (ASCAP) 41 (1989); Note, 39 SYRACUSE L. REV. 1351 (1988). University and college policies are being changed to enhance university rights in the marketing of computer and other uses of faculty writings—with some faculty resistance. Quaere, as to the effect of any change purporting to be retroactive.

Presidential memoirs have been held not written within the scope of official duties (and not a work of the United States government). Harper & Row, Publishers, Inc. v. Nation Enters., 471 U.S. 539 (1985). Recall that the first "fair use" case (see chapter 18 *infra*) involved some alleged authorship by George Washington.

22. 17 U.S.C.A. § 201(b). *Cf.* Baltimore Orioles, Inc. v. Major League Baseball Players Ass'n, 805 F.2d 663 (7th Cir. 1986) (baseball telecasts held "work for hire" owned by club owners; players' rights of publicity preempted by fixation of performance), *cert. denied*, 107 S. Ct. 1593 (1987).

7.2[3][b] Work Specially Ordered or Commissioned

Specially ordered or commissioned works by nonemployees are "works made for hire" only if:[23]

1. The works are in one of the nine categories listed below;
2. The parties expressly agree in a written instrument signed by them that the work "shall" be considered a "work made for hire."

Such a work must be specially ordered or commissioned for use as:[24]

1. A contribution to a "collective work";[25]
2. A part of a "motion picture" or other "audiovisual work";[26]
3. A translation;
4. A "supplementary work";[27]
5. A "compilation";[28]

---

23. 17 U.S.C.A. § 101. Under the provision, the maker would be an independent contractor rather than an employee. See note 21 *supra*.
24. 17 U.S.C.A. § 101. Among the many types of work not included are photographs, paintings, and sculptures.
25. "Collective work" is defined in 17 U.S.C.A. § 101. See text accompanying chapter 5, notes 31–33 *supra*.
26. "Motion pictures" and "audiovisual works" are defined in 17 U.S.C.A. § 101. See text accompanying chapter 5, notes 23–25, *supra*.
27. "Supplementary work" is defined in the definition of "work made for hire." 17 U.S.C.A. § 101 (work "prepared for publication" as "secondary adjunct" to work) by "another author" for "purpose" of introducing, concluding, illustrating, explaining, revising, commenting upon, or assisting in use of other work, such as forewords, afterwords, pictorial illustrations, maps, charts, tables, editorial notes, musical arrangements, answer material for tests, bibliographies, appendixes, and indexes).
28. "Compilation" is defined in 17 U.S.C.A. § 101. See text accompanying chapter 5, notes 31–33 *supra*.

6. An "instructional text";[29]
7. A test;
8. Answer material for a test; or
9. An atlas.

The signed written instrument, probably in advance, is required to make such an otherwise qualified specially ordered or commissioned work a "work made for hire."[30]

7.3 Status of "Works Made for Hire"

"Work made for hire" status arises when the work is "created,"[31] by being within the definition, and cannot be changed thereafter, even by a signed written instrument,

29. "Instructional text" is defined in the definition of "work made for hire." 17 U.S.C.A. § 101 ("literary, pictorial, or graphic work prepared for publication" and with "purpose" of use in "systematic instructional activities"). *See* chapter 20, note 23 *infra.*
30. Use of the word "shall" suggests that the instrument must be contemporaneous with the preparation of the work. Quaere, whether such a written instrument is a "transfer of copyright ownership" within the recordation provisions. *See* chapter 9 *infra.* Compare the function of the signed written instrument that can affect the ownership of rights in a "work made for hire." In Community for Creative Non-Violence v. Reid, 109 S. Ct. 362 (1989), the Court suggested that parties involved in "specially ordered or commissioned works" (quaere, as to the distinction between "specially ordered" and "commissioned" works) should "at the outset settle on relevant contractual terms," e.g., price, royalties, remainder, derivative works, ownership of copyright, and all the present or *future* rights therein. Thousands of works have been registered as "works made for hire" that were not such even under some cases prior to the *Reid* case, *supra.* Quaere, as to fraud on the Copyright Office by those registrations. Registrations after the *Reid* case obviously should comply with its holding. Quaere, as to correcting earlier registrations. *See* chapter 12, notes 8, 12, *infra. See* text accompanying notes 23–26 *supra.*
31. 17 U.S.C.A. §§ 201, 101 (definition of "created"). See chapter 14, note 17 *infra.*

which can only affect the ownership of rights.[32] Several statutory provisions treat "works made for hire" differently from other works:

1. Eligibility for copyright of a "work made for hire," when dependent upon the eligibility of the author, is based on the eligibility of the employer;[33]
2. Duration of a "work made for hire" is for seventy-five years from first publication or 100 years from creation, whichever expires first;[34]
3. "Works made for hire" are not subject to the termination provisions;[35]
4. If the renewal provisions apply, a "work made for hire" is renewable under the first provision by the "proprietor" rather than under the second proviso with its four priorities of renewal claimants;[36] and
5. A "work made for hire" was not exempted from the importation restrictions unless a substantial part of the work was prepared for a non-United States national or domiciliary.[37]
6. Any "work made for hire" is excluded from the definition of "work of visual art" added in 1990 when moral rights were defined in section 106A.

7.4 Relevance of Pre-1978 Law

The "work made for hire" concept has been changed definitionally by the 1976 Act.[38] For example, the 1909 Act

---

32. Comment of Harry Filler, Copyright Law Revision pt. 3, Discussions and Comments on the Preliminary Draft for Revised U.S. Copyright Law 362, 88th Cong., 2d Sess. 146 (1964).
33. 17 U.S.C.A. § 104. *See* chapter 6 *supra*.
34. 17 U.S.C.A. § 302(c). *See* chapter 14 *infra*.
35. 17 U.S.C.A. §§ 203, 304(c). *See* chapter 16 *infra*.
36. 17 U.S.C.A. § 304(a). *See* chapter 15 *infra*.
37. 17 U.S.C.A. § 601(b)(1). *See* chapter 29 *infra*.
38. 1976 House Report 121–23; Varmer, *Works Made for Hire and on Commission* (1958), *reprinted in* 1 STUDIES ON COPYRIGHT—ARTHUR FISHER MEMORIAL EDITION 717 (1963).

stated only that the word "author" will "include an employer in the case of works made for hire."[39] Decisional law developed to the effect that the employee and the commissioned independent contractor should be treated similarly, with the employer or other person for whom the work was prepared presumptively owning all of the rights. In either case, the presumption was rebuttable by even an oral agreement to the contrary.[40]

The statute allows for no change of "work made for hire" status if prepared in the course of employment, and permits an allocation of rights only by a signed written instrument. For commissioned works by nonemployees, the statute limits "work made for hire" status to nine narrow categories of works, and then only if there is a signed written instrument that the work "shall be considered" a "work made for hire."

As to pre-1978 works, the "work made for hire" concepts developed under the pre-1978 law, rather than those of the 1976 Act, should control, on due process grounds, to avoid adversely affecting the rights of the employer or other person for whom the work was prepared or successors in interest.[41]

---

39. 1909 Act § 26; Annot., A.L.R. Fed. 457 (1972) ("works for hire" under 1909 Act).

40. Real Estate Data, Inc. v. Sidwell Co., 907 F.2d 770 (7th Cir. 1990) (work for hire presumptions not rebutted); Brattleboro Publishing Co. v. Winmill Publishing Corp., 369 F.2d 565 (2d Cir. 1966); Picture Music, Inc. v. Bourne, 457 F.2d 1213 (2d Cir.), *cert. denied*, 409 U.S. 997 (1972); Dielman v. White, 102 F. 892 (C.C. Mass. 1900). See note 21 *supra*.

41. Real Estate Data, Inc. v. Sidwell Co., 809 F.2d 366 (7th Cir. 1987) (pre-1979 work governed by 1909 Act work-for-hire concept); Ruth v. Pritikin, 710 F.2d 934 (2d Cir.)(work-for-hire provision in 1976 Act applicable prospectively and not retroactively), *cert. denied*, 104 S. Ct. 394 (1983). The United States Supreme Court avoided this issue in Community for Creative Non-Violence v. Reid, *note 21 supra*, invoking for federal statutory interpretation "the general common law of agency" without considering any due process aspects. Federal "common law" was once decried as a "brooding omnipresence in the

7.5 Divisible Copyright Ownership

The 1909 Act was premised on the theory that copyright was indivisible in the sense that there was a single legal title held by the "proprietor."[42] The "proprietor" was the one who secured the copyright by publishing with the name of the "copyright proprietor" in the copyright notice, registered the copyright, and deposited the copies. The "proprietor" had standing to sue for infringement, and was an indispensable party to an infringement action. Critical under the indivisible copyright theory was the "assignment"-"license" distinction in determining whether the "copyright" had been transferred.

The 1976 Act rendered copyright divisible by defining "copyright owner," as referring, with respect to any one of the exclusive rights, to the owner of that particular right,[43] and giving such "copyright owner" standing to sue for infringement of that right.[44] Also, "transfer of copyright ownership" is defined as an assignment, exclusive

---

sky" (Holmes, J.). the term "employer" and "employee" were given expansive meanings in social legislation of the 1930s, but the copyright cases for the next generation, when there was not much emphasis on basic agency law, applied or misapplied the "control" test, and overgeneralized the *Restatement* "control of physical conduct" test. RESTATEMENT (SECOND) OF AGENCY § 2 (1958). *See* H. HENN, AGENCY, PARTNERSHIP AND OTHER UNINCORPORATED BUSINESS ENTERPRISES 296–324 (2d ed. 1985).

42. Kaminstein, *Divisibility of Copyright* (1957), *reprinted in* 1 STUDIES ON COPYRIGHT—ARTHUR FISHER MEMORIAL EDITION 623 (1963); Even an "indivisible" copyright was subject to legal ownership and to split legal-equitable ("beneficial") property interests. A legal owner may hold rights in trust for beneficial owners. Rights held in trust are dependent on prevailing fiduciary concepts. *See* Henn, *"Magazine Rights": A Division of Indivisible Copyright*, 40 CORNELL L.Q. 411 (1955).
43. 17 U.S.C.A. § 101; Mayer, *Transfer of Copyright Ownership to Periodicals*, 46 FORDHAM L. REV. 907 (1978); Note, *Copyright—The Doctrine of Indivisibility: The Final Chapter*, 7 MEM. ST. U.L. REV. 637 (1977).
44. 17 U.S.C.A. § 501(a). *See* chapter 27 *infra*.

license, and any other grant except a nonexclusive license.[45]

Vestiges of the indivisible copyright theory, whether intended or not,[46] remain in the statute. The owner of all of the exclusive rights is called the "owner of copyright,"[47] suggesting that a "copyright owner" possesses something less than all of the rights. The name in the copyright notice should be that of the "owner of copyright."[48] Deposit of copies is required by the "owner of copyright or of the exclusive right of publication."[49] Registration may be made by the "owner of copyright or of any exclusive right."[50] Elsewhere in the statute[51] and in the regulations,[52] these terms and their variants are used.

---

45. 17 U.S.C.A. § 101. Even an exclusive license for a particular geographical area for a particular period of time, such as the right of first publication in the remotest hamlet. 1976 House Report 123. *See* Dannay, *Annotated Case List: Book Publishing Contracts and Related Matters,* in PLI, LEGAL AND BUSINESS ASPECTS OF BOOK PUBLISHING 1986, at 11 (1986).
46. 1976 House Report 61 refers to the "copyright owner" in discussing the exclusive rights in copyrighted works. The section itself uses the term "owner of copyright." 17 U.S.C.A. § 106. The 1976 House Report, at 144, states that copyright notice must contain the name of the "copyright owner," although the statute prescribes the name of the "owner of copyright." 17 U.S.C.A. §§ 401(b)(3), 402(b)(3). *See* note 51 *infra.*
47. 17 U.S.C.A. § 106.
48. 17 U.S.C.A. §§ 401(b)(3), 402(b)(3).
49. 17 U.S.C.A. § 407(a).
50. 17 U.S.C.A. § 408(a).
51. The term "owner of copyright" occurs in 17 U.S.C.A. §§ 106, 113(b), 114(a), 114(b), 115(a)(1) (where "owner of copyright" and "copyright owner" are both used), 117, 118(b) (both terms), 118(e), 201(c), 205(d), 401(b)(3), 402(b)(3), 404(a), 404(b), 406(a), 407(a), 408(a), 408(c)(2)(A), 602(a). Other undefined phrases used are "owners" of "copyrighted materials," "copyright owners of copyrighted materials" (§ 114(d)), "owner of the rights conveyed" (§ 204(a)), "owner . . . of any exclusive right under a copyright" (§ 205(d)), "owner . . . of the exclusive right of publication" (§ 407(a)), "owner . . . of any exclusive right in the work" (§ 408(a)), "legal or beneficial owner of an exclusive right under a copyright" (§ 501(b)), owner of "such exclusive rights" (§ 601(d)), "copyright owner of record" (§ 704(e)).
52. *E.g.,* compare 17 U.S.C.A. § 118(b)(2) ("copyright owners") with its

7.6 Transfers of Copyright Ownership

7.6[1] Formalities

To be "valid," any transfer or grant, other than by operation of law, except a nonexclusive license, must be in writing and signed by the owner of the rights conveyed or that owner's duly authorized agent.[53] To be fully effective, any transfer of copyright ownership or other document pertaining to copyright should be recorded.[54]

7.6[2] Contributions to Collective Works

In the case of a contribution to a "collective work,"[55] absent an express transfer[56] of the copyright or of any rights under it, the owner of copyright in the collective work[57] is

---

supplementing regulations in 37 C.F.R. § 201.9(a) (title to section reads "copyright owners," but text reads "owners of copyright").

53. 17 U.S.C.A. § 204(a). *See* chapter 8 *infra*. Under the common law, specific reservation was required to preserve the author's copyright in some but not all classes of works. Any such presumption is overruled by the statute (now applicable to all unpublished works as well as published works; a written instrument is required for transfer of copyright). 1976 House Report 124. *Cf.* Best Medium Publishing Co. v. National Insider, Inc., 385 F.2d 384 (7th Cir. 1967)(when freelance author sells article to periodical, all rights are transferred unless other restrictions are indicated). *See* note 3 *supra*.
54. 17 U.S.C.A. § 205. *See* chapter 9 *infra*.
55. Defined in 17 U.S.C.A. § 101 as including periodical issues, anthologies, or encyclopedias, in which a number of contributions constituting separate and independent works in themselves, are assembled into a collective whole. Not included are compositions of words and music, works with front matter or illustrations, or three one-act plays. 1976 House Report 122. A species of "compilation," a "collective work," is distinguishable from other types of "compilation." 17 U.S.C.A. § 101. A "collective work" is also distinguishable from a "joint work," the former being unintegrated and disparate while the latter is a "unitary whole." 1976 House Report 122.
56. Subject to signed writing and recordation provisions. *See* note 53 *supra*.
57. Copyright in each separate contribution is distinct from copyright in the collective work as a whole. 17 U.S.C.A. § 201(c). The latter

"presumed"[58] to have acquired "only the privilege of reproducing and distributing the contribution as part of that particular collective work, any revision of that collective work, and any later collective work in the same series."[59]

7.7 Involuntary Transfers

When an "individual author's" "ownership of copyright," or of any of the exclusive rights under a copyright, has not previously been transferred voluntarily by that individual author, no action by any governmental body or other official or organization purporting to seize, expropriate, transfer, or exercise rights of ownership with respect to the copyright, or any of the exclusive rights under a copyright, shall be given effect.[60] This somewhat cryptic provision is to counteract seizure of American copyrights of foreign authors, especially dissidents, by foreign governments to suppress the works.

---

included elements of compilation, selection, arrangement, and editing, any contributions written for hire, and any other contributions in which ownership has been transferred in writing by the authors. 1976 House Report 122.

58. Quaere, as to rebuttability and the required evidence.

59. 1976 Act § 302(c); 1976 House Report 122–23. Mayer, *The Transfer of Copyright Ownership to Periodicals*, 46 FORDHAM L. REV. 907 (1978); Quinto v. Legal Times of Wash., Inc., 506 F. Supp. 554 (D.D.C. 1981). There is an advertisement exception. *See* Brattleboro Publishing Co. v. Winmill Publishing Corp., 369 F.2d 565 (2d Cir. 1966). For notice requirements, *see* chapter 10, note 37 *infra*.

60. 17 U.S.C.A. § 201(e); Goldstein, *Preempted State Doctrine, Involuntary Transfers and Compulsory Licenses: Testing the Limits of Copyright*, 24 U.C.L.A. L. REV. 1107, 1123-27 (1977). Not within the scope of the provision are such traditional legal actions as bankruptcy proceedings (involuntary as well as voluntary) and foreclosure of mortgages and pledges. 1976 House Report 124. Whether a transfer is voluntary or coerced by covert pressure may present a factual issue. *See* Intellectual Property Bankruptcy Protection Act of 1988 (licensee of "intellectual property" broadly defined, retains all rights despite bankruptcy of licensor and trustees determination to terminate), *overruling* Lubrizol Enters., Inc. v. Richmond Metal Finishers, 756 F.2d 1043 (4th Cir. 1985).

8. Execution of Transfers

8.1 Signed Writing Requirement

A "transfer of copyright ownership,"[1] other than by operation of law, is "not valid"[2] unless an "instrument of conveyance," or a "note or memorandum of the transfer," is "in

1. Defined as any grant except a nonexclusive license. *See* note 4 *infra.* For waiver by an author of exclusive rights of "attribution and integrity," a signed written instrument of specified content is required under the Visual Artists Rights Act of 1990.
2. 17 U.S.C.A. § 204(a); Dean v. Burrows, 732 F. Supp. 816 (E.D. Tenn. 1989) (endorsed check qualifies as transfer document). Transfers within the operation-of-law exception include those resulting from corporate mergers or dissolutions. Forry, Inc. v. Neundorfer, Inc., 837 F.2d 259 (6th Cir. 1988); Fantasy, Inc. v. Fogerty, 664 F. Supp. 1345 (N.D. Cal. 1987). *See also* Maxtone-Graham v. Burtchaell, 631 F. Supp. 1432 (S.D.N.Y.), *aff'd*, 803 F.2d 1253 (2d Cir. 1986) (quoted oral interviews held protectible by interviewing author despite lack of writing and recordation of transfers from interviewees who were promised anonymity), *cert. denied*, 481 U.S. 1059 (1987); Valente-Kritzer Video v. Pinckney, 881 F.2d 772 (9th Cir. 1989) (letter from author's attorney to producer's agent construed as less than transfer). The requirement goes to validity and is more than a statute of frauds. Valante-Kritzer Video v. Pinckney, 881 F.2d 772 (9th Cir. 1989). *Compare* Mellencamp v. Riva Music, Ltd. 698 F. Supp. 1154 (S.D.N.Y 1988) *with* Gushkin v. Guralnik, Copyright L. Rep. (CCH) ¶ 26,086 (S.D.N.Y. 1987) (state statute of frauds inapplicable to agreement to transfer copyright ownership). *But see* Rothenberg, *Oral Copyright Contracts and the Statute of Frauds,* 25 BULL. COPYRIGHT SOC'Y 159 (1977). Otherwise, little has

writing and signed by the owner of the rights conveyed or such owner's duly authorized agent."[3]

A "transfer of copyright ownership" is defined as an assignment, mortgage, exclusive license, or any other conveyance, alienation, or hypothecation of a copyright or of any of the exclusive rights comprised in a copyright, whether or not it is limited in time or place of effect, but not including a nonexclusive license.[4]

Thus, any transfer of rights under copyright, except a nonexclusive license, to be "valid" must be in a signed

---

been written on the new requirements of signed express grants and the implications of the new signed writing requirements and the recordation complications. Oral grants under common-law copyright were valid. Statutory copyright under the 1909 Act could be "assigned, granted, or mortgaged by an instrument in writing signed by the proprietor of the copyright or may be bequeathed by will." 1909 Act § 28. However, the requirement of a writing in order to validate a copyright assignment was subject to some qualifications. Callaghan v. Myers, 128 U.S. 617, 638 (1888); 2 M. & D. NIMMER, COPYRIGHT § 120.2. (An oral license, whether exclusive or nonexclusive, was valid). 3 M. & D. NIMMER, COPYRIGHTS § 10.03(B); Effects Assocs. v. Cohen, 908 F.2d 555 (9th Cir. 1990) (no writing required for implied nonexclusive license to use special effects footage); Harris v. Emus Records Corp., 734 F.2d 1329 (9th Cir. 1984) ("bare" copyright license, because nontransferable, held not to vest in trustee-in-bankruptcy). Under the Intellectual Property Bankruptcy Protection Act of 1988, section 365 of the Bankruptcy Act was amended to provide that a licensee of "intellectual property" retains all rights under the license agreement despite the licensors bankruptcy and the trustee's election to disaffirm).

3. 17 U.S.C.A. § 204(a). The authorization is not required to be in writing. The phrase is "such owner's duly authorized agent," not "such owner's agent thereunto duly authorized in writing." This may be inconsistent with a few common-law cases requiring some reservation, at least for some classes of work, to preserve the author's rights. 1976 House Report 124. Licenses and other contracts not to be performed within one year may be subject to state statutes of frauds.

4. 17 U.S.C.A. § 101; Library Publications, Inc. v. Medical Economics Co., 548 F. Supp. 1231 (E.D. Pa. 1982)(transfer of exclusive rights, no matter how narrow, must be in writing even for breach-of-contract action), *aff'd without opinion*, 714 F.2d 123 (3d Cir. 1983).

writing. The right of first publication in the smallest hamlet would be an exclusive license for that geographical area until exercised and, therefore, would have to be in writing. Even a nonexclusive license must be "evidenced by a written instrument signed by the owner of the rights licensed or such owner's duly authorized agent"[5] to be effective against a "transfer of copyright ownership."[6]

8.2 Effect of Acknowledgment

A certificate of acknowledgment is not required for the validity of a transfer. However, a certificate of acknowledgment is prima facie evidence of the execution of the transfer if:[7]

1. For transfers executed in the United States, the certificate is issued by a person authorized to administer oaths within the United States; or
2. For transfers executed in a foreign country, the certificate is issued by a diplomatic or consular officer of the United States, or by a person authorized to administer oaths whose authority to administer oaths is proved by a certificate of such an officer.

---

5. The authorization is not required to be in writing. *See* note 3 *supra*.
6. 17 U.S.C.A. § 205(f). *See* Dan Dee Imports, Inc. v. Well-Made Toy Mfg. Corp. 524 F. Supp. 615 (E.D.N.Y. 1981)(written evidence of transfer not prerequisite to issuance of copyright registration).
7. 17 U.S.C.A. § 204(b). Under the 1909 Act, acknowledgement was required for an assignment executed in a foreign country. 1909 Act § 29.

9. Recordation of Documents

Recordation of documents in the Copyright Office is to be distinguished from registration of copyright claims.[1]

Documents "pertaining to a copyright," if they meet certain conditions, "may" be recorded in the Copyright Office.[2]

1. *See* chapter 12 *infra*.
2. 17 U.S.C.A. § 205(a); 37 C.F.R. § 201.4 (excluding specified recordations). Since January 1, 1978, the recordation provisions have applied to unpublished works, whether registered or not. The recordation fees, including issuance of certificate of recordation, are $20 for a document covering no more than one title and $10 for each group of not more than ten additional titles. 17 U.S.C.A. § 708(a)(4). The effective date of recordation is when all the statutory requisites are received by the Copyright Office. Quaere, as to the retroactivity of the recordation provisions. *See* Pub. L. No. 94–553 (1976) sec. 109. Arguably, agreements as to the ownership of rights in works made for hire are subject to the recordation provisions. 17 U.S.C.A. § 201(b). Quaere, as to instruments agreeing that specially ordered or commissioned works be considered works made for hire. Also recordable are statements revealing the identity of an author of an anonymous or pseudonymous work under § 302(c) or relating to the death of an author under § 302(d). Notices of intention to make phonorecords are filed under § 115(b). Copyright Office Circulars R12 (Recordation of Transfers and Other Documents), R96 (Recordation of Transfers and Certain Other Documents); Patch Factory, Inc. v Broder, 586 F. Supp. 132 (N.D. Ga. 1984) (receipt by Copyright Office of transfer for recordation held not to constitute recordation). *See* chapter 30 *infra*. (Copyright Office). The Computer Software Rental Amendments Act of 1990 included an elaborate provision entitled "Recordation of Software."

Although recordation is permissive, prompt recordation is desirable, for several reasons:

1. To provide constructive notice of the facts stated in the recorded document;[3]
2. As a prerequisite to an infringement suit;[4]
3. To determine the priority between conflicting transfers;[5]
4. To determine the priority between a conflicting transfer of copyright ownership and a nonexclusive license;[6]
5. To preclude the defense of error in name in the copyright notice;[7]
6. To identify the "copyright owner" for service of notice of intention to obtain a compulsory musical recording license,[8] and for entitlement to receive royalties under such license.[9]

9.1 Constructive Notice

Constructive notice of the facts stated in the recorded document is given to all persons if:[10]

---

3. 17 U.S.C.A. § 205(c).
4. 17 U.S.C.A. § 205(d) (repealed Mar. 1, 1989).
5. 17 U.S.C.A. § 205(e).
6. 17 U.S.C.A. § 205(f).
7. 17 U.S.C.A. § 406(a)(2). *See* text accompanying ch. 10, notes 47–53, *infra*.
8. 17 U.S.C.A. § 115(b)(1). *See* text accompanying ch. 22, notes 11–15, *infra*.
9. 17 U.S.C.A. § 115(c). *See* text accompanying ch. 22, notes 22–31, *infra*.
10. 17 U.S.C.A. § 205(c). *See In re* Peregrine Entertainment, 16 U.S.P.Q. 2d (BNA) 1017 (S.D. Cal. 1990) (state Uniform Commercial Code filing provisions for perfecting security interest in copyright held preempted by copyright law requirement of Copyright Office recordation).

1. The recorded material specifically identifies the work so that, after indexing, the document would be revealed by a reasonable search under the title or registration number of the work; and
2. Registration has been made for the work.

9.2 No Longer Prerequisite to Infringement Suit

Recordation of instruments of transfer has not been prerequisite to an infringement suit by a transferee[11] since March 1, 1989.[12]

11. Former 17 U.S.C.A. § 205(d) was deleted by Berne Act § 5. Its requirements were easily circumvented, and the recorded information could be incomplete. Literally, only recordation of the immediate instrument of transfer was required, permitting missing recordations of links in a chain of transfers. Sevarouski Am. Ltd. v. Silver Deer Ltd., 537 F. Supp. 1201 (D.D.C. 1982) (only "instrument of transfer" under which party claims, not full claim of title, need be recorded); Eden Toys, Inc. v. Florelee Undergarment Co., 697 F.2d 27 (2d Cir. 1982) (written confirmation after suit commenced of oral exclusive license held sufficient); Kenbrooks Fabrics, Inc. v. Soho Fashions, Inc., 690 F. Supp. 298 (S.D.N.Y. 1988) (letter from transferee to Copyright Office recorded eight months after action held sufficient); Metafilm Assocs. v. MCS Inc. 586 F. Supp. 1346 (C.D. Cal. 1984) (filing of transfer after suit instituted held to relate back, curing initial failure); Northern Songs, Ltd. v. Distinguished Prod., Inc., 581 F. Supp. 638 (S.D.N.Y. 1984) (lack of recording no bar where alleged infringer had actual notice of transfer). Corporate mergers that involves transfers "by operation of law" need not be in writing (see 17 U.S.C.A. § 204[a]); nor recorded. Forry, Inc. v. Neudorfer, Inc., 837 F.2d 259 (6th Cir. 1988); Raffoler, Ltd. v. Peabody & Wright, Ltd., 671 F. Supp. 949 (E.D.N.Y. 1987). *See also* Maxtone-Graham v. Burtchaell, 631 F. Supp. 1432 (S.D.N.Y. 1986), aff'd, 803 F.2d 1253 (2d Cir. 1986) (recordation of transfers from oral interviewees promised anonymity held not required), *cert. denied*, 481 U.S. 1059 (1987); Dean v. Burrows, 732 F. Supp. 816 (E.D. Tenn. 1989) (endorsed check qualifies as transfer document).
12. Berne Act § 5 (deleting former 17 U.S.C.A. § 205[d] [for *all* works]).

9.3 Priority Between Conflicting Transfers

As between two conflicting "transfers,"[13] the one executed first prevails if it is recorded, in the manner required to give constructive notice,[14] within one month after its execution in the United States or within two months after its execution outside the United States, or at any time before recordation in the manner of the later transfer. Otherwise the later transfer prevails if recorded first in that manner, and if taken in good faith, for valuable consideration or on the basis of a binding promise to pay royalties, and without notice of the earlier transfer.[15]

In short, the first transfer to be recorded in the manner required to give constructive notice prevails, with the earlier transfer being allowed a one-month grace period if executed in the United States or a two-month grace period if executed outside the United States.[16]

---

13. Compare the term "transfers" in 17 U.S.C.A. § 205(e) and the use of the term "transfer of copyright ownership" in section 205(f). The latter is a term defined in section 101.
14. 17 U.S.C.A. § 205(c).
15. 17 U.S.C.A. § 205(e).
16. The 1909 Act referred only to an "assignment of copyright," not mentioning exclusive and nonexclusive licenses under statutory copyright and all grants under common-law copyright. *But see* Macloon v. Vitagraph, Inc., 30 F.2d 634 (2d Cir. 1929); Photo-Drama Motion Picture Co. v. Social Uplift Film Corp., 213 F.374 (S.D.N.Y. 1914), *aff'd*, 220 F.448 (2d Cir. 1915); Vidor v. Serlin, 7 N.Y.2d 502, 166 N.E.2d 680, 199 N.Y.S.2d 669 (1960). The 1909 Act also provided for grace periods of three and six calendar months. 1909 Act § 30; Latman, *The Recordation of Copyright Assignments and Licenses* (1958), reprinted in STUDIES ON COPYRIGHT—ARTHUR FISHER MEMORIAL EDITION 761 (1963). Failure to record was not available to an infringer in an action brought by an assignee and did not affect the rights as between the parties to the assignment. New Fiction Publishing Co. v. Star Co., 220 F. 994 (S.D.N.Y. 1915). *But see* Group Publishers, Inc. v. Winchell, 86 F. Supp. 573 (S.D.N.Y. 1949) (substitutions of assignee's name in copyright nature, without first recording license, held fatally defective).

9.4 Priority Between Conflicting Transfer of Ownership and Nonexclusive License

A nonexclusive license,[17] whether recorded or not, prevails over a conflicting "transfer of copyright ownership"[18] if the license:[19]

1. Is evidenced by a written instrument signed by the owner of the rights licensed or such owner's duly authorized agent;
2. Was taken either:
   a. Before execution of the transfer;
   b. In good faith before recordation of the transfer and without notice of it.

In summary, oral nonexclusive licensees have no defense against prior or subsequent transferees, at least when without notice thereof. If evidenced by a signed writing, the nonexclusive license prevails if taken:

1. Prior to the transfer;
2. In good faith before recordation of the transfer and without notice of the transfer.

9.5 Precluding Defense of Error in Name in Copyright Notice

When the person named in the prescribed copyright notice is not the "owner of copyright,"[20] a person who "inno-

---

17. A nonexclusive license is expressly excluded from the definition of "transfer of copyright ownership." 17 U.S.C.A. § 101. To be valid, a nonexclusive license need not be in writing and signed. 17 U.S.C.A. § 204(a). However, it should be for purposes of priority and proof. *See* note 19 *infra*.
18. *See* note 13 *supra*.
19. 17 U.S.C.A. § 205(f).
20. *Id. See* text accompanying chapter 10, notes 47–53, *supra*.

cently begins an undertaking" that infringes has a "complete defense" by proof of having been "misled" by the notice and having begun "the undertaking in good faith" under a "purported transfer or license" from the person named in the notice, unless "before the undertaking was begun" either the work had been registered in the name of the "owner of copyright" or a document executed by the person named in the notice and showing the "ownership of the copyright" had been recorded.[21]

9.6 Identification of "Copyright Owner" for Purposes of Compulsory Musical Recording License

The "notice of intention" to obtain a compulsory musical recording license[22] must be served on the "copyright owner," but if the "public records" of the Copyright Office do not "identify" the "copyright owner" and include an address at which notice can be served, it is sufficient to file the notice in the Copyright Office.[23]

To be entitled to receive royalties under the compulsory license, the "copyright owner" must be "identified" in the "public records" of the Copyright Office. Only for phonorecords "made and distributed after" being so identified is the owner entitled to royalties.[24]

---

21. 17 U.S.C.A. § 406(a)(2).
22. See chapter 22 *infra*.
23. 17 U.S.C.A. § 115(b)(1).
24. 17 U.S.C.A. § 115(c).

10. Copyright Notice

10.1 In General

10.1[1] As of March 1, 1989

The Berne Act[1] made notice permissive for copies and phonorecords publicly distributed by authority of the copyright owner after March 1, 1989. The change applies regardless of "country of origin".[2]

If a notice in specified form and position appears on the published copy or phonorecord to which a defendant in a copyright infringement suit had access, no weight may be

1. Berne Act § 7(a)(2), (b)(2) (by substituting "may" for "shall" in 17 U.S.C.A. §§ 401[a] ["visually perceptible copies"] and 402[a] ["phonorecords of sound recordings"]). The critical copyright notice question is the time of publication of the copies or phonorecords at issue, *not* the time of first publication of the work:
   - Before Jan. 1, 1978: 1909 Act notice requirements apply;
   - Jan. 1, 1978—Mar. 1, 1989: 1976 Act notice requirements apply, subject to transitional section 108 provision allowing 1909 Act provisions to apply with respect to work published before January 1, 1978; and
   - As of Mar. 1, 1989: Copyright notice permissive. Therefore, with respect to any work not in the public domain as of such time periods, the respective copyright notice provisions apply to copies or phonorecords publicly distributed in such time periods.
2. "Country of origin" is defined for purposes of Berne Act § 411. *See* chapter 6, note 13, *supra* and chapter 12, note 39, *infra*.

given to a defense based on innocent infringement in mitigation of actual or statutory damages.[3]

10.1[2] Before March 1, 1989

The 1976 Act,[4] while still requiring notice on copies published by authority of the "copyright owner," more significantly provided that omission or errors would no longer result in immediate forfeiture of the copyright, and could be cured by registration within five years. Innocent infringers misled by the omission or error would be shielded from liability. The 1909 Act rule was "no copyright notice, no copyright" (with some exceptions). Any user of a work without a copyright notice before March 1, 1989, will have to search the Copyright Office records to be sure that there has been no curative registration.

Copyright notice provisions refer to authorized, "publicly distributed":

---

3. Berne Act § 7(a)(4), (b)(4) ("Evidentiary weight of notice"); 17 U.S.C.A. §§ 401(d), 402(d). An exception refers to 17 U.S.C.A. § 504(c)(2).
4. 37 C.F.R. § 202.2; Goldstein, *Copyright Formalities: Notice, Deposit, and Registration*, 6 A.P.L.A. Q.J. 18 (1978); Hadl, *Notice, Deposit and Registration*, 25 BULL. COPYRIGHT SOC'Y 218 (1978); Levine & Squires, *Notice, Deposit and Registration; The Importance of Being Formal*, 24 U.C.L.A. L. REV. 1232, 1236 (1977); Gottlieb & Cooper, *Copyright Notice, Deposit and Registration under S.22*, 22 N.Y. L. SCH. L. REV. 255 (1976). *See also* Doyle, Cary, McCannon & Ringer, *Notice of Copyright* (1957), *reprinted in* 2 STUDIES ON COPYRIGHT—ARTHUR FISHER MEMORIAL EDITION 229 (1963); Blaisdell, *Commercial Use of the Copyright Notice* (1959), *reprinted in* 2 STUDIES ON COPYRIGHT—ARTHUR FISHER MEMORIAL EDITION 275 (1963); Rogers, *Use of the Copyright Notice by Libraries* (1959), *reprinted in* 1 STUDIES ON COPYRIGHT—ARTHUR FISHER MEMORIAL EDITION 307 (1963). For notice required on "mask works" [*M* or Ⓜ], *see* chapter 32 *infra*. Many "copyright notices" contain meaningless hyperbolic verbiage. *See* Fischer, *Reserving All Rights Beyond Copyright: Nonstatutory Restrictive Notices*, 34 J. COPYRIGHT SOC'Y 249 (1987).

1. Visually perceptible copies
2. Phonorecords of sound recordings

10.1[3] Visually Perceptible Copies

All "visually" perceptible copies[5] "publicly distributed"[6] anywhere[7] by "authority" of the "copyright owner"[8] prior to

---

5. "Copies" are defined as "material objects, other than phonorecords, in which a work is fixed" and from which it "can be perceived, reproduced, or otherwise communicated, either directly or with the aid of a machine or device." 17 U.S.C.A. § 101.
6. "Publicly distributed" is not defined. "Publication," however, is defined. *See* chapter 4, note 3 *supra*. No copyright notice is required in connection with the public display of copies by any means, including projectors, television, or cathode ray tubes connected with information storage and retrieval systems, or in connection with the public performance of works by means of copies or phonorecords, whether in the presence of an audience or through television, radio, computer transmission, or any other process. 1976 House Report 143.
7. The 1909 Act required copyright notice on each copy published or offered for sale *in the United States*, except in case of books seeking ad interim copyright. 1909 Act § 10. There were other exceptions under the 1909 Act, e.g.,
   1. Infringing copies;
   2. Copies from which licencee had improperly omitted notice;
   3. Copies from which notice had been omitted by accident or mistake;
   4. Copies republished abroad;
   5. Copies published by the United States government;
   6. Copies of works originating in a country adhering to the Pan American Copyright Convention of 1910.

   Hasbro Bradley, Inc. v. Sparkle Toys, Inc., 780 F.2d 189 (2d Cir. 1985) (extended discussion of impact of foreign omission on copyright claim by American assignee).
8. "Copyright owner" is defined, with respect to any one of the exclusive rights, as referring "to the owner of that particular right." 17 U.S.C.A. § 101. The authority to publish triggering the copyright notice requirement thus would seem to have to come from the owner of the exclusive right of publication being exercised, but the law does not so state.

March 1989, were required to bear the copyright notice prescribed for "copies."[9]

As of March 1, 1989, notice became permissive as to copies thereafter published.

10.1[3][a] Form of Notice

The form of notice on visually perceptible copies consists of three elements:[10]

1. "©," "Copyright," or "Copr."[11]
2. Year of first publication[12]

---

9. 17 U.S.C.A. § 401(a). The statutory language literally states that if there is an authorized publication, the notice must be placed on all "publicly distributed copies," the latter phrase not being qualified by the words "by authority of the copyright owner." The Transitional and Supplementary Provisions (sec. 108) provide that in the case of a work published before 1978, a notice complying with the provisions of either the 1976 Act or the 1909 Act "is adequate with respect to copies publicly distributed after December 31, 1977."

10. *Id.* § 401(b).

11. 17 U.S.C.A. § 401(b)(1) (no change). The letter "c" alone has been held insufficient. Holland Fabrics, Inc. v. Delta Fabrics, Inc., Copyright L. Rep. (CCH) ¶ 26,052 (S.D.N.Y. 1987). Quaere as to a "c" in parentheses, "(c)." *Compare* Forry, Inc. v. Neundorfer, Inc., 837 F.2d 259 (6th Cir. 1988) ("(c)" arguably sufficiently similar to "©") *with* Videotronics v. Bend Elecs., 586 F. Supp. 478 (D. Nev. 1984) (upholding C in hexagon; questioning C in parenthesis for incomplete enclosure). "©" should be used for Universal Copyright Convention purposes. "All Rights Reserved" might be added to avoid any possible problem under the Buenos Aires Convention requirement that the work contain a statement reserving the property right.

12. 17 U.S.C.A. § 401(b)(2). In the case of compilations or derivative works incorporating previously published material, the year date of first publication of the compilation or derivative work is sufficient. 1976 House Report 144. However, the copyright registration application must identify any pre-existing works and briefly state the additional material. 17 U.S.C.A. § 409(9). The year date may be omitted where a pictorial, graphic, or sculptural work, with accompanying text matter, if any, is reproduced in or on greeting cards, post cards, stationery, jewelry, dolls, toys, or any useful articles. *Id.* § 401(b)(2).

3. Name of "owner of copyright" in the work[13]

10.1[3][b] Position of Notice

Affixation of the copyright notice should be "in such manner and location as to give reasonable notice of the claim of copyright."[14]

The year date was required by the 1909 Act only for printed literary, musical, or dramatic works. 1909 Act § 19. Even when the date was required, the year date of a new version, without earlier year dates of underlying works, was sufficient. Wrench v. Universal Pictures Co., 104 F. Supp. 374 (S.D.N.Y. 1952). For purposes of the Universal Copyright Convention, the year date should be included on all works, and should be the year of "publication" as defined in the Convention. Under the 1976 Act, as under the 1909 Act, the original year date is adequate in the case of renewed copyrights, but the better practice is to include both dates.

13. 17 U.S.C.A. § 401(b)(3) ("or an abbreviation by which the name can be recognized, or a generally known alternative designation of the owner"). The 1909 Act permitted some alternative designations for limited classes of works. 1909 Act § 19; Pudder v. Buonamici Statuary, Inc., 450 F.2d 401 (2d Cir. 1971) ("ARP and nondecipherable markings purporting to be name of owner held inadequate notice under 1909 Act even though defendant knew identity of 'ARP' ") "Owners of copyright," unlike "copyright owner," is not defined. *See* chapter 3 note 4; chapter 7, notes 46, 51, *supra*. The 1909 Act required the "name of the copyright proprietor" Quaere, as to the use under current law of the name of any assignee or owner of renewal copyright. Arguably, one would then be the "owner of copyright."

14. 17 U.S.C.A. § 401(c). The Register of Copyrights is required to prescribe by regulation, "as examples," specific methods of affixation and positions on various types of works. *Id;* former Copyright Office Circular R96 (Method of Affixation and Positions of the Copyright on Various Types of Works). The 1909 Act was very specific as to place of application of the notice on certain classes of works. 1909 Act § 20. Gardenia Flowers, Inc. v. Joseph Markovits, Inc., 280 F. Supp. 776 (S.D.N.Y. 1968)(notice on removable paper tags slipped into stems of plastic flower in corsage held not to meet affixation requirement of 1909 Act); United Merchants & Mfrs., Inc. v. Sarno Co., 157 U.S.P.Q. (BNA) 331 (S.D.N.Y. 1967)(upholding notice on selvage of fabric absent showing of alternative location). The Universal Copyright Convention has the same language as the 1976 Act, suggesting that Copyright Office practices in accepting deposits and registrations of

10.1[4] Phonorecords of Sound Recordings

All phonorecords[15] of sound recordings[16] "publicly distributed"[17] anywhere[18] by "authority" of the "copyright owner",[19] prior to March 1, 1989, were required to bear the copyright notice prescribed for "phonorecords."[20]

10.1[4][a] Form of Notice

The form of copyright notice on phonorecords consists of three elements:[21]

---

works under the Convention should help construe the 1976 Act provision. Universal Copyright Convention art. III(1). *See* 37 C.F.R. § 201.20. *See also* Koontz v. Jaffarian, 787 F.2d 906 (4th Cir. 1986)(copyright notice on manual sold with computer software held to cover latter under "unit publication doctrine"); Videotronics, Inc. v. Bend Elecs., 586 F. Supp. 478 (D. Nev. 1984)(random display notice flashed on videogame's display scene held inadequate); Midway Mfg. Co. v. Dirkschneider, 543 F. Supp. 466 (D. Neb. 1981) (copyright notice on coin-operated electronic video games sufficient despite omission from games' printed circuit boards); Central Tel. Co. v. Johnson Publishing Co., 526 F. Supp. 838 (D. Colo. 1981)(notice on spine of cover and inside front cover of telephone directory held sufficient).

15. "Phonorecords" are defined as the "material objects in which sounds, other than those accompanying a motion picture or other audiovisual work, are fixed." 17 U.S.C.A. § 101. *See* chapter 5, note 26 *supra*.
16. "Sound recordings" are defined as "works that result from the fixation of a series of musical, spoken, or other sounds, but not including the sounds accompanying a motion picture or other audiovisual work." 17 U.S.C.A. § 101. *See* chapter 5, note 28 *supra*.
17. *See* note 6 *supra*. Public distribution of phonorecords constitutes publication of the phonorecord. The pre-1978 rationale was that the public sale of a phonorecord was not publication of a *copy* and, therefore, not divestive of common-law copyright in the recorded material.
18. *See* note 7 *supra*.
19. *See* note 8 *supra*.
20. 17 U.S.C.A. § 402(a). Since "phonorecords" are not "copies," there is no need to place the copyright notice prescribed for "copies" on "phonorecords" to protect the literary or musical works embodied in the "phonorecords." 1976 House Report 145.
21. 17 U.S.C.A. § 402(b).

1. "℗";[22]
2. Year of first publication;[23]
3. Name of "owner of copyright" in the sound recording.[24]

10.1[4][b] Position of Notice

The notice should be placed on the surface, label, or container of the phonorecord "in such manner and location as to give reasonable notice of the claim of copyright."[25]

10.2 Publications Incorporating United States Government Works

10.2[1] As of March 1, 1989

The Berne Act[26] deleted the former section 403 and substituted language that the "Evidentiary Weight of Notice" provisions[27] should not apply to works consisting "predominantly" of one or more "works of the United States Government"[28] unless the copyright notice on the copies or phonorecords to which a defendant in a copyright infringe-

---

22. 17 U.S.C.A. § 402(b)(1). The "℗" symbol has been adopted as the international symbol for the protection of sound recordings by the "Phonograms Convention" (Convention for the Protection of Producers of Phonograms Against Unauthorized Duplication of Their Phonograms, done at Geneva October 29, 1971), to which the United States is a party. 1976 House Report 145. *See* Innovative Concepts in Entertainment, Inc. v. Entertainment Enters., Ltd., 576 F. Supp. 457 (E.D.N.Y. 1983) (omission of "℗" symbol not fatal).
23. 17 U.S.C.A. § 402(b)(2).
24. 17 U.S.C.A. § 402(b)(3) ("or an abbreviation by which the name can be recognized, or a generally known alternative designation of the owner; if the producer of the sound recording is named on the phonorecord labels or containers, and if no other name appears in conjunction with the notice, the producer's name shall be considered a part of the notice").
25. 17 U.S.C.A. § 402(c).
26. Berne Act § 7(c).
27. *See* note 3 *supra*.
28. *See* text accompanying chapter 6, notes 18–23, *supra*.

ment suit had access includes "a statement identifying, either affirmatively or negatively," the copyrighted portions.[29]

10.2[2] Before March 1, 1989

The deleted provision stated the copyright notice on such works "shall" include such an identifying statement.

10.3 Copyright Notice on Contributions to Collective Works

A "separate contribution" to a "collective work"[30] may "bear its own notice of copyright."[31] However, a "single notice applicable to the collective work as a whole" is "sufficient"[32] with "respect to the separate contributions it contains,"[33] "regardless of the ownership of copyright in the contributions and whether or not they have been previously published."[34]

---

29. 17 U.S.C.A. § 403.
30. "Collective work" is defined as a work "such as a periodical issue, anthology, or encyclopedia, in which a number of contributions, constituting separate and independent works in themselves, are assembled into a collective whole." 17 U.S.C.A. § 101.
31. 17 U.S.C.A. § 404(a) (no change).
32. "Sufficient to invoke" the "Evidentiary Weight of Notice" provisions (see note 3 *supra*). Berne Act § 7(d); 17 U.S.C.A. § 404(a).
33. 17 U.S.C.A. § 404(a). ("not including advertisements inserted on behalf of persons other than the owner of copyright in the collective work"); Donald Frederick Evans & Assocs. v. Continental Homes, Inc., 785 F.2d 897 (11th Cir. 1986)(advertisement exception to collective copyright provision not applicable on facts); Canfeld v. Ponchatoula Times, 759 F.2d 493 (5th Cir. 1985)(advertisement in newspaper not protectible under masthead notice); Brattleboro Publishing Co. v. Wimmill Publishing Corp., 369 F.2d 685 (2d Cir. 1966); Triangle Publications, Inc. v. Knight-Ridder Newspapers, Inc., 626 F.2d 1171 (5th Cir. 1980)(covers of publications included in copyright); Frederick Warne & Co. v. Book Sales, Inc., 481 F. Supp. 1191 (S.D.N.Y. 1979).
34. 17 U.S.C.A. § 404(a) (no change, except where owner of collective work had no authority, express or implied, to secure copyright in

But, with respect to copies or phonorecords publicly distributed before March 1, 1989,[35] where the person named in a "single notice applicable to a collective work as a whole" is not the "owner of copyright"[36] in a "separate contribution" that does not bear its own notice, the case is governed by the error-in-name provisions.[37]

10.4 Inadequate Notice

Inadequate notice under the 1976 Act, since January 1, 1978, in contrast to the 1909 Act,[38] did not invalidate the copyright.[39]

10.4[1] Omission of Notice

10.4[1][a] Effect of Omission on Copyright on Certain Copies and Phonorecords

Even before March 1, 1989,[40] omission did not invalidate the copyright if:

---

contribution). Goodis v. United Artists Television, Inc., 425 F.2d 397 (2d Cir. 1970) (general copyright notice in periodical in name of publisher held to secure copyright in licensed contribution).

35. Berne Act § 7(d); 17 U.S.C.A. § 404(b).
36. 17 U.S.C.A. § 404(b). *See* notes 13, 34 *supra*.
37. 17 U.S.C.A. § 404(b). *See* note 36 *supra*. *Compare* 1909 Act §§ 3, 20. *See* Quinto v. Legal Times of Washington, Inc., 506 F. Supp. 554 (D.D.C. 1981)(contribution to periodical held protected by periodical's blanket notice; periodical publisher presumed, absent express transfer, owner of rights to use in collective work; no good faith reliance on false name in notice).
38. See Doyle, Cary, McCannon & Ringer, *Notice of Copyright* (1959), *reprinted in* 1 STUDIES ON COPYRIGHT—ARTHUR FISHER MEMORIAL EDITION 229 (1963); Hasbro Bradley, Inc. v. Sparkle Toys, Inc., 780 F.2d 189 (2d Cir. 1985) (2–1)(omission of notice, even if deliberate, curable under section 405[a][2]).
39. 17 U.S.C.A. §§ 405(a), 406(a).
40. Berne Act § 7(e); 17 U.S.C.A. § 405.

1. Omission was "from no more than a relatively small number" of publicly distributed copies or phonorecords.[41]
2. The work was registered "before" or "within five years" after the publication without notice, and a "reasonable effort" was made to add notice after the omission has been "discovered."[42]

---

41. 17 U.S.C.A. § 405(a)(1). Lifshitz v. Walter Drake & Sons, 806 F.2d 1426 (9th Cir. 1986) (discussion of provisions of section 405[a]). The 1976 Act substituted "relatively small number" for "a particular copy or copies" in the 1909 Act. 1909 Act § 21. Presumably "relative small number" may refer to percentages as well as numbers. *See* Sunset Lamp Corp. v. Alsy Corp., 698 F. Supp. 1146 (S.D.N.Y. 1988) (omission of notice on between 3 and 10 percent of lamps held to invalidate copyright). Efforts to add notice to copies no longer in possession, although relevant on question of reasonableness, is not required. Forry Inc. v. Neundorfer, Inc., 837 F.2d 259 (6th Cir. 1988); M. Krayer Mfg. Co. v. Andrews, *supra*; the House Report refers to omission, "whether intentional or unintentional." 1976 House Report 147. M. Kramer Mfg. Co. v. Andrews, 783 F.2d 421 (4th Cir. 1986) (innocent infringer must be misled by omission of notice); Shapiro & Son Bedspread Corp. v. Royal Mills Assocs., 764 F.2d 69 (2d Cir. 1985) (action to cure defective notice on goods in hands of retailer not unreasonable effort where all in inventory had been corrected); Original Appalachian Artworks, Inc. v. Toy Loft, Inc., 684 F.2d 821 (8th Cir. 1982) (upholding copyright notice on detachable name tags where only one percent lacked sewn-in copyright notices; "relatively few" exceptions); Rachel v. Banana Republic, Inc., 228 U.S.P.Q. (BNA) 416 (N.D Cal 1985)(omission on sixty copies, or 39 percent sold, not excused under § 405(a)(1); insufficient efforts made under § 405(a)(2)); Jackson v. MPI Home Video, 694 F. Supp. 483 (N.D. Ill. 1988) (omission of notice from several hundred copies of speech at National Democratic Convention cured by efforts to add notice to copies distributed after omission of notice discovered).
42. 17 U.S.C.A. §405(a)(2) (no similar provision in 1909 Act). The "reasonable effort" need extend only to copies or phonorecords "distrib-

3. The omission was in violation of an "express" written "condition" of the "authorization" of the "copyright owner."[43]

10.4[1][b] Effect of Omission on Innocent Infringers

Innocent infringers relying on the omission of notice on distributions before March 1, 1989,[44] incurs no liability for "actual or statutory damages" for any infringing acts committed before receiving "actual notice" of timely registration, by proof of having been misled by the omission. The court may allow or disallow recovery of any profits, may enjoin the continuation of the infringement, or may require the payment of a reasonable license fee as a condition for permitting continuation.[45]

---

uted to the public in the United States." 17 U.S.C.A. § 405(a)(2); Werlin v. Reader's Digest Ass'n, 528 F. Supp. 451, 461 (S.D.N.Y. 1981) (upholding redemptive registration to cure lack of copyright notice). *Compare* Hasbro Bradley, Inc. v. Sparkle Toys Inc., 780 F.2d 189 (2d Cir. 1985).

43. 17 U.S.C.A. § 405(a)(3) (no express provision in 1909 Act, but probably no change, except for requirement of express writing, on theory that noncompliance with condition of license resulted in publication's constituting infringement and not being by authority of the copyright proprietor); Fantastic Fakes, Inc. v. Pickwick Int'l, Inc., 661 F.2d 479 (5th Cir. 1981)(licensee's negligent designation of self as copyright owner in notice held not to destroy copyright or constitute infringement).

44. Berne Act § 7(e), 17 U.S.C.A. § 405(b).

45. 17 U.S.C.A. § 405(b).

10.4[1][c] Removal of Notice

Copyright protection is not affected by the removal of the notice without the authorization of the "copyright owner."[46]

10.4[2] Error in Name on Certain Copies and Phonorecords

Even before March 1, 1989,[47] in case of an error in name,[48] an innocent infringer had "a complete defense" by proof of having been "misled" by the notice and having begun the undertaking in good faith under a purported transfer or license from the person named in the notice unless, before the "undertaking was begun":[49]

1. Registration had been made in the name of the "owner of copyright."[50]
2. A document executed by the person named in the notice and showing the "ownership of the copyright"[51] had been recorded.[52]

For all receipts from transfers or licenses purportedly made by the person named in the notice, the recipient was liable to account to the "copyright owner."[53]

---

46. 17 U.S.C.A. § 405(c) (no express provision in 1909 Act, but probably no change, since notice was on when work was publicly distributed). The removal or alteration "with fraudulent intent" of any copyright notice appearing on a copy of a copyrighted work is subject to a fine of up to $2,500. 17 U.S.C.A. § 506(d).
47. Berne Act § 7(f),(g); 17 U.S.C.A. § 406(a).
48. 17 U.S.C.A. § 406(a) (no similar provision in 1909 Act).
49. 17 U.S.C.A. § 406(a).
50. 17 U.S.C.A. § 406(a)(1) (no similar provision in 1909 Act). *See* chapter 12, note 5 *infra*.
51. The terms "ownership of the copyright" and "copyright ownership" are used but not defined. *See* note 13 *supra*.
52. 17 U.S.C.A. § 406(a)(2).
53. 17 U.S.C.A. § 406(a) (no express provision in 1909 Act, but probably no change). *See* note 8 *supra*.

10.4[3] Error in Date

The effect of an error in the year date in the notice depends upon whether the notice is antedated or postdated.

10.4[3][a] Antedated Notice

When the year date in the notice in distributions before March 1, 1989,[54] was *earlier* than the year of first publication, any duration period computed from the year of first publication was to be "computed from the year in the notice."[55]

10.4[3][b] Postdated Notice

When the year date in the notice was "more than one year later than the year of first publication," the work was "considered to have been published without any notice."[56]

10.4[4] Omission of Name or Date

For distributions before March 1, 1989,[57] when there was no name or date "that could reasonably be considered a part of the notice," the work was "considered to have been published without any notice."[58]

---

54. Berne Act § 7(f); 17 U.S.C.A. § 406(b).
55. 17 U.S.C.A. § 406(b) (no express provision in 1909 Act, but probably no change).
56. 17 U.S.C.A. § 406(b) (no express provision, but probably no change). Decisional law and the Copyright Office regulations under the 1909 Act tolerated postdating by not more than one year. White Metal Castings Corp. v. Cornell L & L Metal Corp., 353 F. Supp. 1170 (E.D.N.Y. 1972); Davis v. E. I. duPont de Nemours & Co., 240 F. Supp. 612 (S.D.N.Y. 1965); former 37 C.F.R. § 202.2(b)(6).
57. Berne Act § 8(f)(3); 17 U.S.C.A. § 406(c).
58. 17 U.S.C.A. § 406(c), and governed by § 405 as in effect on Feb. 28, 1989. *See* text accompanying notes 39–45 *supra*.

10.5 Fraudulent Copyright Notice

Any person who, "with fraudulent intent":[59]

1. Places on any article a copyright notice or "words of the same purport" that such person "knows to be false"
2. "Publicly distributes or imports for public distribution" any article bearing such notice or words that such person "knows to be false"

is subject to a fine of up to $2,500.

---

59. 17 U.S.C.A. § 506(c). *See* Berger, *False Use of the Copyright Notice* (1959), *reprinted in* 1 STUDIES ON COPYRIGHT—ARTHUR FISHER MEMORIAL EDITION 307 (1963); Donald Frederick Evans & Assocs. v. Continental Homes Inc., 785 F.2d 897 (11th Cir. 1986)(no private right of action for fraudulent copyright notice). For comparable provisions, see 1909 Act §§ 105, 106.

11. Deposit of Copies and Phonorecords

The deposit requirements, separate but related to registration, while mandatory, are not conditions of copyright protection.[1]

Deposit of copies or phonorecords in the Copyright Office for the use or disposition of the Library of Congress is required:[2]

---

1. 17 U.S.C.A. § 407(a); 37 C.F.R. § 202.19; Copyright Offce Circular R7d (Mandatory Deposit of Copies or Phonorecords for the Library of Congress); Hadl, *Notice, Deposit and Registration*, 25 BULL. COPYRIGHT SOC'Y 218, 219 (1978); Levine & Squires, *Notice, Deposit and Registration: The Importance of Being Formal*, 24 U.C.L.A. L. REV. 1232, 1255 (1977); Gottlieb & Cooper, *Copyright Notice, Deposit and Registration under S.22*, 22 N.Y.L. SCH. L. REV. 255, 264 (1976); Dunne, *Deposit of Copyrighted Works* (1960), *reprinted in* 1 STUDIES ON COPYRIGHT—ARTHUR FISHER MEMORIAL EDITION 409 (1963). The exemption from mandatory deposit for works published solely in machine-readable form was revoked as of October 16, 1989, to improve the Library of Congress's services. Only IBM and Macintosh formats are now acceptable as "best editions." *See* note 7 *infra*. The Computer Software Rental Amendments Act of 1990 provided for optional deposit of two complete copies of "public domain computer software" for the benefit of the Library's Machine-Readable Collections Reading Room.
2. 17 U.S.C.A. § 407. The nexus between free copies for the Library of Congress and copyright has been almost eliminated. Quaere, as to how free copies can be required apart from the federal copyright power. *See* Ladd v. Law & Technology Press, 762 F.2d 809 (9th Cir.

1. Apart from registration of the copyright claim
2. As part of registration

However, deposit to satisfy the deposit requirements ("deposit for the Library of Congress") may also satisfy the deposit provisions of the registration section ("deposit for copyright registration") if the deposited copies or phonorecords are accompanied by the prescribed application (or written request that they be held in connection with an application), fee, and additional identifying material.[3]

1985), (deposit requirement held not to violate first or fifth amendments), *cert. denied,* 475 U.S. 1045 (1986).

3. 17 U.S.C.A. § 408(b); 37 C.F.R. §§ 202.19(f), 202.20(e). If copies or phonorecords are received without an application or written request: (1) they will not be held to await connection with the application; (2) they will be used to satisfy the mandatory deposit requirements; and (3) the deposit of additional copies or phonorecords will be necessary if an application for copyright registration is received at a later time. To be effective, the "written request" must be clear and must appear in a letter or similar document accompanying the deposit. A request or instructions appearing on the packaging, wrapping, or container for the deposit is insufficient. Copies or phonorecords sent in reply to correspondence concerning a pending application should be accompanied by either a covering letter referring to the pending case by number and date or a copy of the copyright Office letter. Former Copyright Office Circular R7a. The free mailing privilege under the 1909 Act was abolished by the 1976 Act. However, books mailed to the Copyright Office by publishers and distributors can be mailed at the fourth-class library rate. For mailing at the fourth-class library rate, the package must bear the statement "LIBRARY RATE," placed conspicuously on the address side. For any accompanying copyright registration application, postage should include the extra first-class rate and there should be an endorsement reading "FIRST CLASS MAIL ENCLOSED" on the package below the postage and above the address. Copyright Office Circular R30.

11.1 Deposit Requirements

Deposit is required by the "owner of copyright or of the exclusive right of publication"[4] in a work "published in the United States"[5] within three months after the date of such publication.[6]

Required to be deposited are:

1. Two complete copies of the "best edition";[7]
2. If the work is a sound recording, two complete phonorecords of the "best edition," together with any "printed or other visually perceptible material" published with such phonorecords.[8]

---

4. Neither "owner of copyright" nor "owner . . . of the exclusive right of publication" is defined. *See* chapter 7, note 51 *supra*. Compare the terminology of the registration section: "the owner of copyright or of any exclusive right in the work." 17 U.S.C.A. § 408(a).
5. Until March 1, 1989, the requirement was limited to publication "with notice of copyright." Berne Act § 8; 17 U.S.C.A. § 407(a). "Country of origin" is irrelevant. Compare the copyright notice requirement whenever a work is published "in the United States or elsewhere." 17 U.S.C.A. §§ 401(a), 402(a).
6. 17 U.S.C.A. § 407(a). The provision does not state that the publication must be authorized. *Cf.* § 401(a).
7. *Id.* § 407(a)(1). "Best edition" is defined as "the edition, published in the United States, at any time before the date of deposit, that the Library of Congress determines to be most suitable for its purposes." 17 U.S.C.A. § 101; 37 C.F.R. § 202.19(b); Copyright Office Circular R7b ("Best Edition" of Published Copyrighted Works for the Collections of the Library of Congress).
8. 17 U.S.C.A. § 407(a)(2) (entire "package," including sleeve, album, and any accompanying leaflets or booklets, not just "phonorecord"); Davies, *Compulsory Deposit of Sound Recordings*, 10 COPYRIGHT BULL. (No. 3) 29 (1976). Upon request and payment of the $4 fee, a receipt for the deposit will be issued. 17 U.S.C.A. §§ 407(b), 708(a)(3).

Limited exemptions from the deposit requirements may be provided by regulation.[9]

11.2 Penalties for Failure to Deposit

Written demand for the required deposit may be made "at any time after publication" by the Register of Copyrights "on any of the persons obligated to make the deposit."[10]

If deposit is not made within three months after receipt of the demand, the "person or persons on whom the demand was made" are liable:[11]

1. For a fine of not more than $250 for each work;[12]
2. To pay to the Library of Congress the total retail price of the copies or phonorecords demanded, or, if no price has been fixed, the reasonable cost to the Library of acquiring them;[13]

---

9. 17 U.S.C.A. § 407(c); 37 C.F.R. §§ 202.19(c), 202.19(d), 202.21.

For "secure test" regulation for trade secrets in computer programs and tests, *see* 37 C.F.R. § 202.20(c)(2)(vi); Copyright Office Circular R64 (Copyright Registration for Secure Tests); National Conference of Bar Examiners v. Multistate Legal Studies, Inc., 692 F.2d 478 (7th Cir. 1982)(upholding "secure test" copyright regulation permitting return of deposit after examination except sufficient portions for archival record), *cert. denied sub nom.* Multistate Legal Studies, Inc. v. Ladd, 464 U.S. 814 (1983); Association of Am. Medical Colleges v. Carey, 482 F. Supp. 1358 (N.D.N.Y. 1980)(disclosure under state "truth in testing" law enjoined because of copyright in Medical College Admissions Test); Stern Elecs., Inc. v. Kaufman, 669 F.2d 852 (2d Cir. 1982)(deposit of video tapes of "attract" and "play" modes of electronic video game without computer program held sufficient); Atari, Inc. v. Amusement World, Inc., 547 F. Supp. 222 (D. Md. 1981).

10. 17 U.S.C.A. § 407(d). *See* note 4 *supra*.

11. 17 U.S.C.A. §407(d). Failure to deposit after demand under the 1909 Act made the copyright void. 1909 Act § 14. *See* Transitional and Supplementary Provisions, sec. 110.

12. 17 U.S.C.A. § 407(d)(1).

13. 17 U.S.C.A. § 407(d)(2) ("into a specially designated fund").

3. To pay a $2,500 fine in addition for willful or repeated failures or refusal to comply with such demand.[14]

11.3 Acquisition of Unpublished Transmission Programs

"Transmission programs"[15] "fixed"[16] and "transmitted"[17] to the public in the United States, but not published, may be acquired, through deposit or otherwise, for the collections of the Library of Congress.[18]

14. 17 U.S.C.A. § 407(d)(3).
15. For definition of "transmission program," *see* 17 U.S.C.A. § 101.
16. For definition of "fixed," *see* 17 U.S.C.A. § 101.
17. For definition of "transmit," *see* 17 U.S.C.A. § 101.
18. 17 U.S.C.A. § 407(e); 37 C.F.R. § 202.22. These acquisition provisions are not conditions of copyright protection. 17 U.S.C.A. § 407(a). *See* 17 U.S.C.A. § 408(b) (satisfaction of deposit provisions of registration section). 1976 House Report 152.

12. Registration of Copyright Claims

Registration is not a condition of copyright protection.[1] Although registration is called "permissive,"[2] failure to register can adversely affect the remedies for infringement and have other negative effects.[3] Registration may be obtained at

1. 17 U.S.C.A. § 408(a); 37 C.F.R. § 202.3. Omission of copyright notice, if required, may be cured by registration within five years after publication. 17 U.S.C.A. § 405(a)(2). Hence, the Copyright Office registration records should be checked before using a work without a copyright notice. Hadl, *Notice, Deposit and Registration*, 25 BULL. COPYRIGHT SOC'Y 218, 220 (1978); Levine & Squires, *Notice, Deposit and Registration: The Importance of Being Formal*, 24 U.C.L.A. L. REV. 1232, 1260 (1977); Gottlieb & Cooper, *Copyright Notice, Deposit and Registration Under S. 22*, 22 N.Y.L. SCH. L. REV. 255, 265 (1976). Under the 1909 Act, registration and deposit constituted a single procedure, which was the means of securing statutory copyright in limited classes of works not reproduced for sale and of making enforceable copyrights secured by publication with copyright notice. 1909 Act §§ 11–14. Although the 1909 Act specified "promptly" after publication, compliance at any time before suit or renewal, absent unrequited demand for deposit by the Register of Copyrights, was sufficient. Washingtonian Publishing Co. v. Pearson, 306 U.S. 30 (1939); Kaplan, *The Registration of Copyright* (1958), *reprinted in* 1 STUDIES ON COPYRIGHT—ARTHUR FISHER MEMORIAL EDITION 325 (1958).
2. 17 U.S.C.A. Act § 408(a).
3. *See* text accompanying notes 32–46 *infra*.

any time during the subsistence of copyright in any published or unpublished work.[4]

The "owner of copyright or of any exclusive right in the work"[5] may obtain registration by delivering to the Copyright Office:[6]

1. The application for copyright registration;
2. The $20 fee for registration and issuance of a certificate of registration;[7]
3. The required deposit copies or phonorecords.

---

4. 17 U.S.C.A. § 408(a); 37 C.F.R. § 202.20; Hagendorf v. Brown, 699 F.2d 478 (9th Cir. 1983).
5. 17 U.S.C.A. § 408(a). Neither "owner of copyright" nor "owner . . . of any exclusive right" is defined. *See* chapter 7, note 51 *supra*. Compare the terminology of the deposit section: "the owner of copyright or of the exclusive right of publication in a work." § 407(a). The Copyright Office permits submission of an application for registration "by any author or other copyright claimant . . ., or the owner of any exclusive right. . ., or the duly authorized agent of any such author, other claimant, or owner." 37 C.F.R. § 202.3(c); Sinkler v. Goldsmith, 623 F. Supp. 727 (D. Ariz. 1985) (mental competence of registrant irrelevant). *See* note 45 *infra*. Error in name in the copyright notice can be corrected by registration "in the name of the owner of copyright." 17 U.S.C.A. § 406(a)(1).
6. 17 U.S.C.A. § 408(a), (b). Application (or written request that they be held in connection with an application), fee, and deposit copies or phonorecords should accompany each other. *See* chapter 11, note 3, *supra*. No longer practical is the 1909 Act practice of shipping deposit copies and application forms from different places. Registration of claims for which the required deposit, application, and fee were received in the Copyright Office before January 1, 1978, were to be made "in accordance with" the 1909 Act. Transitional and Supplementary Provisions sec. 109. After January 1, 1991 (fee having been doubled as of Jan. 1, 1991), copyright registration dates could be established by paying the old $10 fee if the additional $10 had been received "promptly after notification of the short fee."
7. 17 U.S.C.A. § 708(a)(1). Remittance in the form of a check, money order, or bank draft should be payable to the "Register of Copyrights." The fee for foreign works is no longer waived by sending one additional copy and a catalog card. Foreign remittances should be payable

12.1 Application

Application for copyright registration must be made on a form prescribed by the Register of Copyrights.[8] There are

---

immediately in United States dollars. Registrations are cancelled if the checks for them are uncollectable. Deposit accounts for at least twelve transactions per year and with minimum $250 deposits are possible. Depletion of the deposit account can delay the effective date of registration. Copyright Office Circular R5 (including form to open account).

8. 17 U.S.C.A. § 409. The forms are required by statute to include at least ten items of information bearing upon the preparation and identifcation of the work and the existence, ownership, and duration of the copyright. *Id.* Among the required information are the names, addresses, nationalities or domiciles of the authors, and the dates of any of their deaths; if the work was made for hire, a statement to such effect; if the claimant is not the author, how ownership was obtained; the present and any previous or alternative titles of the work; the year when creation was completed; the date and nation of first publication; in the case of a compilation or derivative work, identification of any preexisting works and a "brief, general statement" of the additional material; and "any other information" required by the Register of Copyrights. An application for a periodical issue on form SE, short form SE must name the "author." It may name the author of the collective work as a whole (possibly with the names of the authors of independently written contributions so long as the copyright claimant for the issue as a whole has acquired ownership of all rights belonging to each of the authors listed). In the case of collective works, the Copyright Office does not require that all authors and contributions covered by the copyright claim be identifed on the application. For any listing of individual authors, separate lines should be used for each author.

When the owner of copyright in a periodical issue as a whole has not obtained ownership of all rights initially belonging to the author of a particular contribution, it is not the "claimant" of copyright in that contribution. In order to make registration for the contribution in such a case, it is necessary to submit a separate application (Form TX). The "claimant" identified in that application should be the author of the contribution, or a person or organization that has obtained ownership of all of the rights in the contribution that the author originally owned. Former Copyright Office Circular R60a. Either the citizenship or domicile of the author should be given. For business enterprises organized under American laws, "U.S.A." is sufficient. The

five "administrative classes" for purposes of registration, including renewal,[9] with a different application form for each:[10]

1. Class TX—Nondramatic literary works [textual] (formerly classes A, B, and C);
2. Class PA—Works of the performing arts (formerly classes D, E, L, and M);
3. Class VA—Works of the visual arts (formerly classes F, G, H, I, J, and K);

---

new format of application forms no longer requires completion by the applicant of two parts, with the second part, after Copyright Office processing, being issued as the certificate of registration. Instead, a photocopy of the application is issued as the certificate of registration. Since January 1, 1978, the new forms have been required. They, with Copyright Office circulars, are obtainable free of charge by writing to the Information and Publications Section, Copyright Office, Library of Congress, Washington, D.C. 20559. False representation "knowingly made" of a material fact in the application for copyright registration is subject to a fine of up to $2,500. 17 U.S.C.A. § 506(e) Urantia Found. v. Burton, 210 U.S.P.Q. (BNA) 217 (W.D. Mich. 1980) (misstatement of authorship in registration certificate, unless fraudulent, held not to invalidate copyright).

9. 37 C.F.R. § 202.3; Copyright Office Circulars R1e, R45, R50, R55, R56, R61, R62, R65. The administrative classification has no significance with respect to the subject matter of copyright or the exclusive rights. 17 U.S.C.A. § 408(c). Under the 1909 Act there were fifteen specified classes, including renewal, stated not to limit the phrase "all the writings of an author" in § 4 or to invalidate or impair copyright protection. 1909 Act § 5. The courts gave little effect to such qualifying language. Renewal was not enumerated in the 1909 Act classification.

10. Forms TX, PA, VA, SR, and RE. In addition to the five basic application forms, there are other forms for use in special cases: form CA (for supplementary registration to correct or amplify information given in the copyright record of an earlier registration), form GR/CP (for group registration for contributions to periodicals), form SE or short form SE (for registration of each individual issue of a serial), and form JB (for recordation of coin-operated phonorecord players). The Copyright Office maintains a twenty-four-hour telephone hotline for accepting requests for copyright forms: (202)287–9100.

4. Class SR—Sound recordings (formerly class N); and
5. Class RE—Renewal registration.

12.1[1] Class TX—Nondramatic Literary Works

Except for dramatic works and certain kinds of audiovisual works, Class TX includes all types of published and unpublished works written in words (or other verbal or numerical symbols). A few of the many examples of "nondramatic literary works" include: fiction, nonfiction, poetry, periodicals, textbooks, reference works, directories, catalogs, advertising copy, and compilations of information.

12.1[2] Class PA—Works of Performing Arts

Class PA includes published and unpublished works prepared for the purpose of being "performed" directly before an audience or indirectly "by means of any device or process." Examples of works of the performing arts are: musical works, including any accompanying words; dramatic works, including any accompanying music; pantomimes and choreographic works; and motion pictures and other audiovisual works.

12.1[3] Class VA—Works of Visual Arts

Class VA consists of published and unpublished "pictorial, graphic, or sculptural works," including two-dimensional and three-dimensional works of fine, graphic, and applied art, photographs, prints and art reproductions, maps, globes, charts, technical drawings, diagrams, and models. Within this class are pictorial or graphic labels and advertisements, as well as "works of artistic craftsmanship." The "design of a useful article" may be registrable in Class VA, but "only if, and only to the extent that, such design incorporates pictorial, graphic, or sculptural features that can be identified separately from, and are capable of existing independently of, the utilitarian aspects of the article."

12.1[4] Class SR—Sound Recordings

Class SR is appropriate for registration for both published and unpublished works in two situations:

1. Where the copyright claim is limited to the sound recording itself;
2. Where the same copyright claimant is seeking to register not only the sound recording but also the musical, dramatic, or literary work embodied in the sound recording.

With one exception, "sound recordings" are works that result from the fixation of a series of musical, spoken, or other sounds. The exception is for the audio portions of audiovisual works, such as a motion picture soundtrack or an audio cassette accompanying a filmstrip. These are considered an integral part of the audiovisual work as a whole and are registrable in Class PA. Sound recordings fixed before February 15, 1972, are not eligible for registration, but may be protected by state law.

12.1[5] Class RE—Renewal Registration

Class RE covers renewal registration for copyrights that were already in their first term on January 1, 1978 (i.e., renewals for works originally copyrighted between January 1, 1950, and December 31, 1977). Class RE is appropriate for all renewal registrations, regardless of the class in which the original registration was made.

12.1[6] Most Appropriate Class

If a work contains copyrightable material falling into two or more classes, registration should be in the class most appropriate for the work as a whole. Any predominating material should determine the class for registration. However, registration should be in Class SR whenever the same copyright claimant is seeking to register both a sound recording and also the musical, dramatic, or literary work embodied in the sound recording.

The proper class for a work published as a contribution to a collective work or other compilation depends on the nature of the contribution, and not of the collective work or other compilation in which it appears.

12.1[7] Registration Numbering System

Beginning January 1, 1978, the Copyright Office started a new numbering system for all registrations:

1. Classes TX, PA, VA, and SR are given registration numbers in separate series, preceded by the double letters identifying the class. Unpublished works are identified by adding a small "u" after the double letters.
2. Class RE constitutes a separate numbering series, without indication of whether the work being renewed is published.

12.2 Deposit

Required to be deposited are:

1. For an unpublished work, one complete copy or phonorecord;[11]
2. For a published work, two complete copies or phonorecords of the "best edition";[12]

---

11. 17 U.S.C.A. § 408(b)(1).
12. 17 U.S.C.A. § 408(b)(2). *But see* chapter 11, note 7 *supra,* for the definition of "best edition."

3. For a work first published outside the United States, one complete copy or phonorecord "as so published";[13]
4. For a contribution to a "collective work,"[14] one complete copy or phonorecord of the "best edition of the collective work."[15]

These deposit provisions may be satisfied by copies or phonorecords deposited for the Library of Congress under the deposit requirements, if accompanied by the prescribed application, fee, and additional identifying material.[16]

The nature of the copies or phonorecords to be deposited in the various classes may be specified by regulation, which may require or permit, for particular classes, the deposit of identifying material instead of copies or phonorecords, the deposit of only one copy or phonorecord when two would normally be required, or a single registration for a group of related works.[17]

---

13. 17 U.S.C.A. § 408(b)(3).
14. *See* chapter 11, note 7 *supra*.
15. 17 U.S.C.A. § 408(b)(4).
16. 17 U.S.C.A. § 408(b); 37 C.F.R. § 202.21. Acquisitions under § 407(e) may also satisfy the deposit provisions of the registration section.
17. 17 U.S.C.A. § 408(c)(1); 37 C.F.R. § 202.20(c)(2). Such optional deposits might include the deposit of phonorecords for musical compositions, print-outs of computer programs, or one volume of an encyclopedia for purposes of registration of a single contribution, and single registrations for the various editions or issues of a daily newspaper, a work published in serial installments, a group of related jewelry designs, a group of photographs by one photographer, a series of related greeting cards, or a group of poems by a single author. 1976 House Report 153-54; Copyright Office Circular 40a (Deposit Requirements for Registration of Claims to Copyright in Visual Arts Material).

12.3 Group Registration

A single "adjunct" registration is specifically permitted for a group of works by "the same individual author,"[18] all "first published as contributions to periodicals, including newspapers, within a 12-month period," on the basis of a single application, fee, and deposit, under three specified conditions:[19]

1. Each of the works as first published bore a separate copyright notice with the same name or designation of the "owner of copyright."[20]
2. The deposit consists of one copy of the "entire issue," or "entire section" of a newspaper, in which each contribution was published.[21]
3. The application identifies each work separately, "including the periodical containing it and its date of first publication."[22]

If the copyright is infringed before registration not made within three months after first publication of the work, however, award of statutory damages and attorney's fees is precluded.[23]

12.4 Supplementary Registration

Supplementary registration may correct an error or amplify the information in a copyright registration. Once a

---

18. 17 U.S.C.A. § 408(c)(2); 37 C.F.R. § 202.3(a)(5); Form GR/CP. Excluded are "employers for hire." *See* Copyright Office Circular R15.
19. 17 U.S.C.A. § 408(c)(2). Two forms must be submitted: (1) form GR/CP and (2) the basic application on form TX, form PA, or form VA, as the case may be. The publications need not occur within the same calendar year.
20. 17 U.S.C.A. § 408(c)(2)(A).
21. 17 U.S.C.A. § 408(c)(2)(B).
22. 17 U.S.C.A. § 408(c)(2)(C).
23. 17 U.S.C.A. § 412(2).

basic registration has been made for a work, "any author or other copyright claimant, or any owner of an exclusive right in the work," may "correct" or "amplify" the basic registration by filing an application for supplementary registration that "clearly identif[ies] the registration to be corrected or amplified." The information contained in a supplementary registration augments but does not supersede that contained in the earlier registration. The basic registration will not be expunged or cancelled; rather, the two registrations, each with its own registration number, will both stand in the Copyright Office, calling to the public's attention possible errors or omissions in the basic registration, and placing the correct facts or additional information on official record.[24]

---

24. 17 U.S.C.A. 408(d); 37 C.F.R. § 201.5; Copyright Office Circular R8. Supplementary registration may also be made by the duly authorized agent of any such author, other claimant, or owner. 37 C.F.R. § 201.5(b)(1). A "correction" is appropriate if information in a basic registration was incorrect at the time that basic registration was made, e.g., where the basic registration identifed someone incorrectly as an author of the work, or the work was registered as published when publication has not actually taken place. Copyright Office Circular R8. A correction is inappropriate if the error is "one that the Copyright Office itself should have recognized." 37 C.F.R. § 201.5(b)(2)(i). Where it is discovered that the record of basic registration contains such a recognizable error, the Office itself will take "appropriate measures" to rectify its error. 37 C.F.R. § 201.5(a)(2). "Amplifications" fall into three general categories: (1) additional information that could have been given, but was omitted at the time of basic registration (e.g., a co-author was omitted); (2) changes in facts that have occurred since the basic registration (e.g., change of title); and (3) explanations clarifying information given in the basic registration (e.g., statement of changes or additions in the version being registered was not sufficiently explicit). Copyright Office Circular R8; 37 C.F.R. § 201.5(b)(ii). The fee is $20, 17 U.S.C.A. § 708(a)(1). The correct application form is form CA. Theoretically any completed registration, even a completed renewal registration, can be the subject of a supplementary registration, but supplementary registration is *not appropriate:* (1) where changes have been made in statements on copies or phonorecords, or in the work itself; (2) as a substitute for renewal registration; and (3) as a substitute for recording a transfer or

12.5 Double Registration

Registration for the first published edition of a work previously registered in unpublished form may be made even though the work as published is substantially the same as the unpublished version.[25]

12.6 Certificate of Registration

The certificate of registration is issued after examination and determination that the material deposited constitutes copyrightable subject matter and that the "other legal and formal requirements" of the law have been met.[26] The certificate contains the information given in the application, together with the number and "effective date" of the registration.[27]

If registration is refused, the applicant will be notified in writing of the reasons for that refusal.[28]

---

other document pertaining to copyright ownership. Copyright Office Circular R8; 37 C.F.R. § 201.5(b)(2)(iii). If the person on whose behalf the application for supplementary registration is submitted is the same as the person identified as copyright owner in the basic registration, the Copyright Office will place a note referring to the supplementary registration in its records of the basic registration. Copyright Office Circular R8. *See also* 37 C.F.R. § 201.5(d).

25. 17 U.S.C.A. § 408(e). Such double registration is permissible. It was required by the 1909 Act.
26. 17 U.S.C.A. § 410(a). *See* Berger, *Authority of the Register of Copyrights to Reject Applications for Registration* (1959), *reprinted in* 1 STUDIES ON COPYRIGHT—ARTHUR FISHER MEMORIAL EDITION 393 (1963); Schneider, *Authority of the Register of Copyright to Deny Registration of a Claim to Copyright on the Ground of Obscenity,* 51 CHI.[-]KENT L. REV. 691 (1975); Reed, *The Role of the Register of Copyrights in the Registration Process: A Critical Appraisal of Certain Exclusionary Regulations,* 18 COPYRIGHT L. SYMP. (ASCAP) 1 (1970).
27. 17 U.S.C.A. § 410(d). *See* note 6 *supra.*
28. 17 U.S.C.A. § 410(b). The applicant should exhaust the administrative remedies by requesting re-examination before commencing a

The evidentiary weight to be accorded the certificate of registration in any judicial proceeding depends upon when registration was made:[29]

1. If made before or within five years after publication, the certificate constitutes "prima facie evidence" of "the validity of the copyright" and of the facts stated in the certificate.[30]
2. If made after five years after first publication, the evidentiary weight to be accorded the certificate shall be within the discretion of the court.

---

mandamus proceeding, but the applicant may sue an infringer by having delivered to the Copyright Office the required deposit, application, and fee. For discussion as to whether the increased executive and regulatory powers of the Register of Copyrights are violative of the principle of separation of powers, *see* Brylawski, *The Copyright Office: A Constitutional Confrontation,* 44 GEO. WASH. L. REV. 1 (1975). *But see* Eltra Corp. v. Ringer, 579 F.2d 294 (4th Cir. 1978). *See also* Atari Games Corp. v. Oman, 888 F.2d 878 (D.C. Cir. 1989) ("abuse of discretion" standard applicable to review of Copyright Office refusal to register video game).

29. 17 U.S.C.A. § 410(c). Prima facie effect of registration may be neutralized by any supplemental registration.

30. The 1909 Act made the certificate "prima facie evidence of the facts stated therein." 1909 Act § 209. Some courts, however, treated the certificate as evidence of the validity of the copyright. Under current law, timely registration generally constitutes prima facie evidence of originality, authorship, and compliance with statutory formalities. Gaste v. Kaiserman, 863 F.2d 1061 (2d Cir. 1988) (presumption of validity of copyright, including initial publication with notice); Business Trends Analysists, Inc. v. Freedonia Group, Inc. 700 F. Supp. 1213 (S.D.N.Y. 1988) (presumption of originality). Supplemental registrations may neutralize prima facie effect. For burdens of proof and going forward with the evidence, see text accompanying chapter 27, note 28, *infra*. *See* Cooling Sys. & Flexibles, Inc. v. Stuart Radiator, Inc., 777 F.2d 485 (9th Cir. 1985) (registration of derivative work held not to create presumption of validity of copyright in underlying work).

12.7 Effect of Failure to Register

Although registration is "not a condition of copyright protection,"[31] prompt registration is encouraged by various provisions in the law:

1. If the registration was made before or within five years after publication without any required copyright notice, it can prevent invalidation of the copyright ("curative registration").[32]
2. If the registration was made "in the name of the owner of copyright"[33] before an innocent infringer starts an undertaking in reliance on a transfer or license from the person named in the copyright notice when that person is not the "owner of copyright," the infringer may not defend because of the error in name.[34]
3. If the registration was made before or within five years after first publication, the certificate of registration is "prima facie evidence" of "the validity of the copyright" and of the facts stated therein.[35]
4. If the registration was made before commencement of infringement of copyright in an unpublished work, statutory damages and attorney's fees may be awarded.[36]
5. If the registration was made within three months after the first publication of the work, statutory damages and attorney's fees may be awarded for any

31. 17 U.S.C.A. § 408(a).
32. 17 U.S.C.A. § 405(a)(2) (curative provision). *See* note 1 *supra*, and chapter 10, note 42 *supra*.
33. 17 U.S.C.A. § 406(a)(1). *See* note 5 *supra*.
34. 17 U.S.C.A. *See* text accompanying chapter 10, notes 48–53, *supra*.
35. 17 U.S.C.A. § 410(c). *See* text accompanying notes 26–36 *supra*.
36. 17 U.S.C.A. § 412(1). *See* chapter 28, note 20, *infra*.

infringement of copyright commenced after first publication and before registration.[37]

6. If the registration was made, constructive notice may be given documents recorded in the Copyright Office.[38]

Registration, whether the work is published or unpublished, is prerequisite to an infringement suit,[39] with three exceptions:

1. For "Berne Convention works" "whose country of origin" is *not* the United States;[40]

---

37. 17 U.S.C.A. § 412(2). *See* chapter 28, note 21 *infra*. Quaere, as to retroactive effect and whether a registration under the 1909 Act would satisfy the section. *See* 1975 Senate Report 160-61; Tanmock v. Review Trading Corp., 231 U.S.P.Q. (BNA) 798 (D.N.J. 1986) (infringement "commenced" before registration; no damages or attorney's fees).
38. 17 U.S.C.A. § 205(c)(2).
39. 17 U.S.C.A. § 411(a). The registration, as under 1909 Act, may be made after the infringement.
40. Berne Act § 9(b), 17 U.S.C.A. § 411. For purposes of § 411 (making registration prerequisite to infringement actions except for "Berne Convention works" whose "country of origin" is not the United States), "country of origin" is the United States if a "published work" is "first published" in the United States; "simultaneously" in the United States and in another nation or nations with the same of longer term of protection; "simultaneously" in the United States and a "foreign nation" that does not adhere to the Berne Convention; or in a "foreign nation" that does not adhere to the Berne Convention and "all" of the authors of the work are "nationals, domiciliaries, or habitual residents" of, or in the case of an "audiovisual work," "legal entities with headquarters" in the United States. "Country of origin" is the United States of an "unpublished work," if all of its authors are "nationals, domiciliaries, or habitual residents" of the United States; or in the case of an "unpublished audiovisual work," "all the authors are legal entities with headquarters" in the United States; or in the case of a "pictorial, graphic, or sculptural work" if "incorporated in a building or structure" "located" in the United States. Otherwise, for section 411 purposes, the "country of origin" of any other "Berne Convention work" is not the United States. Berne Act § 4(a)(1)(C); 17 U.S.C.A. § 101.

2. When application, deposit, and fee were delivered to the Copyright Office in proper form and registration was refused;[41] or
3. For a work consisting of sounds, images, or both, the first fixation of which is made simultaneously with its transmission.[42]

Registration is also required for the filing of a renewal claim,[43] and may identify the "copyright owner" for service of notice of intention to obtain a compulsory musical recording license[44] and for entitlement to royalties thereunder.[45] Registration of an authorized edition manufactured in the United States or Canada before infringement was commenced may, in a civil action or criminal proceeding for

41. 17 U.S.C.A. § 411(a). A copy of the complaint must be served on the Register of Copyrights, who has the option to enter an appearance within sixty days to become a party with respect to the issue of registrability. The Register's failure to become a party does not deprive the court of jurisdiction to determine that issue. Overruled by the new law is Vacheron & Constantin-Le Coultre Watches, Inc. v. Benrus Watch Co., 260 F.2d 637 (2d Cir. 1958).
42. 17 U.S.C.A. § 411(b) (permitting institution of an infringement suit either before or after such fixation if the copyright owner: (1) serves the required notice upon the infringer; and (2) makes registration within three months after the first transmission). 37 C.F.R. § 201.22; NBC Subsidiary (KCNC-TV), Inc. v. Broadcast Servs, 717 F. Supp. 1449 (D. Colo. 1988) (section 411(b) inapplicable to pretaped material).
43. Simultaneous original and renewal registrations are possible if the required applications, copies, and fees are all received in the Copyright Office during the last calendar year of the original term. Copyright Office Circular R15.
44. 17 U.S.C.A. § 115(b)(1). If the "public records" of the Copyright Office do not "identify" the "copyright owner," and include an address at which notice can be served, the notice may be filled in the Copyright Office. Since registration should be in the name of the "owner of copyright or of any exclusive right," registration might not identify the "copyright owner" in the sense of the owner of the exclusive recording rights. *See* note 5 *supra*.
45. 17 U.S.C.A. § 115(c). The owner is entitled to royalties for phonorecords "made and distributed" after, but not before, being "identified."

infringement, preclude the "complete defense" possibility available under the manufacturing clause.[46]

12.8 Cancellation of Registrations

Registrations may be cancelled on specified grounds, under recent regulations.[47]

---

46. 17 U.S.C.A. § 601(d). As to the expiration of the manufacturing clause, *see* chapter 12 *infra*. Quaere, as to noncompliance prior to July 1, 1986.
47. 37 C.F.R. § 201.7 (cancellation of completed registrations); Lack of adequate disclosure to the Copyright Office in registration may invalidate or render unenforceable the copyright ("fraud on Copyright Office"). Whimsicality, Inc. v. Rubie's Costume Co., 891 F.2d 452 (2d Cir. 1989) (fanciful costumes registered as "soft sculpture" held useful articles; fraud on Copyright Office). Often claimants (applicants for registration) do not know all the facts and circumstances relevant to copyright status, e.g., publication (none, "limited," general), affixation of copyright notice when required, transfer or transfers of copyright ownership, work-made-for-hire status. *But see* Xerox Corp. v. Apple Computer, Inc., 734 F. Supp. 1542 (N.D. Cal. 1990) (suit for declaratory judgment to cancel competitor's registrations and other relief—fear of suit by potential licensees no actual controversary; courts without power to order cancellation); Kiddie Rides, U.S.A., Inc. v. Curran, 231 U.S.P.Q. (BNA) 210 (D.D.C. 1986) (Copyright Office cancellation of registration before examination of all deposits held not justified); Knickerbocker Toy Co. v. Westerbrook Corp., 554 F. Supp. 1309 (D.N.H. 1982) (alleged fraudulent conduct before Copyright Office precluding copyright). *Compare* Wondura Prods., Inc. v. Dart Indus., Inc., 215 U.S.P.Q. (BNA) 94 (N.D. Miss. 1981) *with* Vogue Ring Creations, Inc. v. Harman, 410 F. Supp. (D.R.I. 1976) (fraudulently procured copyright as defense).

13. Manufacturing Requirements (Lapsed July 1, 1986)

The manufacturing requirements of the 1976 Act, considerably more limited than those of the 1909 Act,[1] after an extension, expired by their own terms on July 1, 1986.[2]

1. 1909 Act § 16. The "manufacturing clause" was introduced in 1891 when American statutory copyright was made available to foreign authors. McCannon *et al.*, *The Manufacturing Clause of the U.S. Copyright Law* (1963), *reprinted in* 2 STUDIES ON COPYRIGHT—ARTHUR FISHER MEMORIAL EDITION 1123 (1963); Herman, *The Manufacturing Clause: A History and Critique of a Sophism in the Copyright Act,* 17 IDEA 5 (Summer 1975); Tucker, *The Validity of the Manufacturing Clause of the United States Copyright Code as Challenged by Trade Partners and Copyright Owners,* 3 VAND. J. TRANSNAT'L L. 577 (1985).
2. 17 U.S.C.A. § 601(a), as amended by Pub. L. No. 97–215, 96 Stat. 178 (July 13, 1982); A review by the Register of Copyrights of the impact of the elimination of the manufacturing clause was made by July 1, 1981. Letter from Senators McClellan and Scott, 122 CONG. REC. S17,225-53 (daily ed. Sept. 30, 1976). In 1982, the manufacturing requirement was extended from July 1, 1982, to July 1, 1986. *See* Authors League of Am., Inc. v. Oman, 790 F.2d 220 (2d Cir. 1986) (upholding constitutionality of manufacturing clause). A panel of the General Agreement on Tariffs and Trade (GATT) had concluded that the clause violated GATT rules. Quaere, as the effect of noncompliance with the manufacturing clause prior to July 1, 1986.

13.1 Works Subject to Manufacturing Requirements Prior to July 1, 1986

Manufacture in the "United States"[3] or Canada[4] was required of copies imported into or publicly distributed in the United States of a copyrighted work "consisting preponderantly of nondramatic literary material"[5] in the English language.[6]

There was exemption from the manufacturing requirements:[7]

1. When the author of "any substantial part of such material" was a non-United States national or domiciliary,[8] except a "work made for hire"[9] unless "a substantial part" of the work was prepared for a non-United States national or domiciliary;[10]
2. When an import statement[11] issued by the Copyright Office was presented to the United States Customs

---

3. For definition of "United States," *see* 17 U.S.C.A. § 101.
4. The 1909 Act did not equate manufacture in Canada with manufacture in the United States. The change was in contemplation of the Florence Agreement and removal of high Canadian tariffs and other restraints on United States printed matter. Conference Report 80–81.
5. 17 U.S.C.A. § 601(a); 1976 House Report 164–69; Stonehill Communications, Inc. v. Martuge, 512 F. Supp. 349 (S.D.N.Y. 1981).
6. 17 U.S.C.A. § 601(a).
7. 17 U.S.C.A. § 601(b) (not amended).
8. 17 U.S.C.A. § 601(b)(1) (not amended) ("on the date when importation is sought or public distribution in the United States is made"). Also exempted *were* United States nationals domiciled outside the United States for a continuous period of at least one year preceding that date. *Id.*
9. *See* text accompanying chapter 7, notes 15–41, *supra.*
10. 17 U.S.C.A. § 601(b)(1) (not amended). A "work made for hire" for a "domestic corporation or enterprise" was not exempted. *Id. See* Cooling Sys. & Flexibles, Inc. v. Stuart Radiator, Inc., 777 F.2d 848 (9th Cir. 1986).
11. 17 U.S.C.A. § 601(b)(1). *See* former Copyright Office Form IS ($3 fee; *id.* § 708(a)(7)).

Service, allowing entry of a total of no more than 2,000 copies of any one such work;[12]

3. When importation was sought under the authority or for the use, other than in schools, of the government of the United States or of any "State"[13] or political subdivision of a state;[14]
4. When importation, for use and not for sale, was sought by:[15]
   - Any person with respect to no more than one copy of any work at any one time;
   - Any person arriving from outside the "United States," with respect to copies forming part of that person's personal baggage;
   - An organization operated for scholarly, educational, or religious purposes and not for private gain, with respect to copies intended to form a part of its library;
5. When the copies were reproduced in raised characters for the use of the blind;[16]
6. When, in addition to copies imported under clauses (3) and (4), no more than 2,000 copies of any one such work, which had not been manufactured in the United States or Canada, were publicly distributed in the United States;[17]
7. When, on the date that importation was sought or public distribution in the United States was made:[18]

---

12. 17 U.S.C.A. § 601(b)(2) (not amended). The import statement was issued upon request to the "copyright owner" or to a person designated by such owner at the time of registration or at any time thereafter.
13. For definition of "State," *see* 17 U.S.C.A. § 101.
14. 17 U.S.C.A. § 601(b)(3) (not amended).
15. 17 U.S.C.A. § 601(b)(4) (not amended).
16. 17 U.S.C.A. § 601(b)(5) (not amended).
17. 17 U.S.C.A. § 601(b)(6) (not amended).
18. 17 U.S.C.A. § 601(b)(7) (not amended).

- The author "of any substantial part of such material" was "an individual" and received compensation for the transfer or license of the right to distribute the work in the United States;
- The first publication of the work had previously taken place outside the United States under a transfer or license granted by that author to a transferee or licensee who was not a national or domiciliary of the United States or a domestic corporation or enterprise;
- There had been no publication of an authorized edition of the work of which the copies were manufactured in the United States;
- The copies were reproduced under a transfer or license granted by that author or by the transferee or licensee of the right of first publication, and the transferee or the licensee of the right of reproduction was not a national or domiciliary of the United States or a domestic corporation or enterprise.

13.2 Satisfaction of Manufacturing Requirements

The requirement that copies be manufactured in the United States or Canada was satisfied if:[19]

1. For copies printed directly from set type or from plates made from such type, the type was set and the plates made in the United States or Canada.
2. For copies printed from plates made by a lithographic or photoengraving process as a final or intermediate step preceding the printing, the plates were made in the United States or Canada.

19. 17 U.S.C.A. § 601(b)(8) (not amended).

3. The printing or other final process of producing multiple copies and any binding were performed in the United States or Canada.

Compliance with the manufacturing requirements did not have to be supported by an affidavit as part of the application for registration.[20] The application had to include the names of the persons or organizations who performed the required processes and the places where those processes were performed.[21] Similar information had to be set forth in the complaint in any action for infringement of the exclusive rights to reproduce and distribute copies of a work required to be manufactured in the United States or Canada.[22]

13.3 Effect of Noncompliance with Manufacturing Requirements

Copyright protection was not invalidated by the importation or public distribution of copies in violation of the manufacturing requirements.[23]

In any civil action or criminal proceeding for infringement of the exclusive rights to reproduce and distribute copies of the work, however, the infringer had a complete defense with respect to all of the nondramatic literary material comprised in the work and any other parts of the work in which the exclusive rights to reproduce and distribute copies were owned by the same person who owned the

20. 1909 Act § 17.
21. 17 U.S.C.A. § 409(10) (not amended).
22. 17 U.S.C.A. § 601(e) (not amended).
23. 17 U.S.C.A. § 601(d) (not amended). Quaere, as to the validity of copyrights in works manufactured in violation of the manufacturing clause under the 1909 Act. Cases were lacking because, absent registration, no infringement action could be brought.

exclusive rights in the nondramatic literary material, if the infringer proved that:[24]

1. Copies had been imported into or publicly distributed in the United States in violation of the manufacturing requirements by or with the authority of the "owner of such exclusive rights."
2. The infringing copies had been manufactured in satisfaction of the manufacturing requirements.
3. The infringement had been commenced before the effective date of registration for an authorized edition of the work, the copies of which had been manufactured in satisfaction of the manufacturing requirements.

Copies manufactured in violation of the manufacturing requirements were subject to the importation restrictions.[25]

---

24. 17 U.S.C.A. § 601(d) (not amended). The 1909 Act sections 22 and 23 provided for five-year "ad interim" protection. *See* 1976 Act. sec. 109.
25. *See* chapter 29 *infra*.

14. Duration

The duration of copyright under the 1976 Act varies, depending upon whether the work was:[1]

1. Created but not published or copyrighted before January 1, 1978;[2]

---

1. Copyright Office Circulars R15a (Duration of Copyright), R15t (Extension of Copyright Terms); Levine, *Preemption and Duration*, in PLI, PRACTICING UNDER THE COPYRIGHT LAW OF 1976, at 47 (1978); Goldberg, *Preemption and Duration Under the New Copyright Law, Public Law 94-553*, in 1 PLI, CURRENT DEVELOPMENTS IN COPYRIGHT LAW 1977, at 209, 287 (1977); Bricker, *Duration of Copyright*, 25 BULL. COPYRIGHT SOC'Y 213 (1978); Cohen, *Duration*, 24 U.C.L.A. L. REV. 1180 (1977); Jackson, *Duration of Copyright under S.22*, 22 N.Y.L. SCH. L. REV. 241 (1977); Under the 1909 Act, copyright endured for 28 years, and, if renewed, for an additional twenty-eight-year renewal term, subject to the 1962 and subsequent extensions. *See* note 13 *infra*. Works in which statutory copyright was secured before 1949 and for which no renewal registration was made are in the public domain. The numerous extensions did not extend first terms. Guinan, *Duration of Copyright* (1957), *reprinted in* 1 STUDIES ON COPYRIGHT—ARTHUR FISHER MEMORIAL EDITION 473 (1963). The 1790 Act provided for a fourteen-year term with a fourteen-year renewal by the author, if living. From 1834 to 1909, the first term was twenty-eight years, subject to a fourteen-year renewal by the author, if living, or by any surviving spouse, child, or children. Life expectancies were much shorter in those days.
2. 17 U.S.C.A. § 303 (works under common-law copyright as of January 1, 1978).

2. Under subsisting first term copyright on January 1, 1978;[3]
3. Under subsisting renewal copyright on January 1, 1978;[4]
4. Created on or after January 1, 1978.[5]

All "terms of copyright" run to the end of the calendar year in which they would otherwise expire.[6]

14.1 Works Created but Not Published or Copyrighted Before January 1, 1978

These works were under common-law copyright as of January 1, 1978, when common-law copyright was preempted.[7] Their perpetual protection prior to publication has been limited to protection for the life of the author plus fifty years or variously seventy-five or 100 years for "anonymous works," "pseudonymous works," and "works made for

---

3. 17 U.S.C.A. § 304(a).
4. 17 U.S.C.A. § 304(b) (including works for which renewal registration was made between December 31, 1976 and December 31, 1977). Section 304(b) took effect on October 19, 1976. Transitional and Supplementary Provisions sec. 102. Copyrights in their renewal terms on September 19, 1962, were extended by ten extensions. *See* note 13 *infra*.
5. 17 U.S.C.A. §§ 101, 302 (works "fixed in a copy or phonorecord for the first time" on or after January 1, 1978).
6. 17 U.S.C.A. § 305 ("terms of copyright provided by sections 302 through 304"). The periods provided in § 304(c) with respect to termination of grants are not affected by § 305. Copyright now "subsists" from "creation" *(id.* § 302(a)), compared to the 1909 Act under which copyright was "secured" by publication with copyright notice or, for limited classes of works, by registration and deposit. The Visual Artists Rights Act of 1990 provides for duration for the life of the author for "attribution and integrity" rights (life of last surviving author for joint works); terms run to end of calendar year in which they would otherwise expire. 17 U.S.C.A. § 106A(d).
7. 17 U.S.C.A. § 301. (at least where there was no fixation).

hire,"[8] but at least for another twenty-five years until December 31, 2002, and, if published on or before then, for another twenty-five years until December 31, 2027.[9]

14.2 Works Under Subsisting First-Term Copyright on January 1, 1978

Works under a subsisting first-term copyright on January 1, 1978, have a twenty-eight-year first term, and are subject to renewal under provisions that are identical to the renewal provisions of the 1909 Act.[10] Absent renewal during the twenty-eighth calendar year, the work falls irretrievably into the public domain at the end of the first term. The renewal term was extended by the 1976 Act from twenty-eight to forty-seven years, or a potential total of seventy-five years,[11] subject to possible termination of transfers and licenses covering the extended renewal term.[12]

14.3 Works Under Subsisting Renewal Copyright on January 1, 1978

Works under a subsisting renewal copyright on January 1, 1978, defined as those in which renewal copyright was subsisting at any time between December 31, 1976 and December 31, 1977,[13] or for which renewal registration was made

---

8. 17 U.S.C.A. §§ 303, 302 (or, in the case of "anonymous works," "pseudonymous works," or "works made for hire," seventy-five years from year of first publication or 100 years from year of creation, whichever expires first). *See* note 25 *infra.*
9. 17 U.S.C.A. § 303. For discussion of due process considerations, *see* 1976 House Report 139.
10. 17 U.S.C.A. § 304(a) *See* chapter 15 *infra.*
11. 17 U.S.C.A.
12. 17 U.S.C.A. § 304(c). *See* chapter 16 *infra.*
13. 17 U.S.C.A. § 304(b).

Beginning September 19, 1962, copyrights in their renewal terms as

in that period, have a renewal term automatically extended to forty-seven years or a total of seventy-five years from the date copyright was originally secured,[14] subject to possible termination of transfers and licenses covering the extended renewal term.[15]

14.4 Works Created on or After January 1, 1978

Works created on or after January 1, 1978, have a duration, except for "works made for hire," "anonymous works," and "pseudonymous works," from creation[16] "for a term

---

of the following dates received ten extensions:

	Subsisting as of	*Extended to*	*Law*
1.	September 19, 1962	December 31, 1965	Public Law 87-668
2.	August 28, 1965	December 31, 1967	Public Law 89-142
3.	November 16, 1967	December 31, 1968	Public Law 90-141
4.	July 23, 1968	December 31, 1969	Public Law 90-416
5.	December 16, 1969	December 31, 1970	Public Law 91-147
6.	December 17, 1970	December 31, 1971	Public Law 91-555
7.	November 24, 1971	December 31, 1972	Public Law 92-170
8.	October 25, 1972	December 31, 1974	Public Law 92-566
9.	December 31, 1974	December 31, 1976	Public Law 93-573
10.	December 31, 1976 December 31, 1977 (or for which renewal registration was made during such period)	75 years from date copyright was originally secured	Public Law 94-553 § 304(b) (effective Oct. 19, 1976; sec. 102)

Under these extensions, copyright in any work copyrighted on or after September 19, 1906, and renewed would be subsisting on January 1, 1978. If copyrighted on September 19, 1906, the copyright would not have expired until December 31, 1981. *See* Copyright Office Circular R15t (Extension of Copyright Terms). In the nineteenth century, there were nine private-bill extensions, the last in 1888. *See* chapter 1, note 7, and chapter 2, note 7, *supra*. *See also* Southern Bell Tel. & Tel. Co. v. Associated Tel. Directory Publishers, 756 F.2d 801 (11th Cir. 1985).

14. 17 U.S.C.A. § 304(b).
15. 17 U.S.C.A. § 304(c). *See* chapter 16 *infra*.
16. 17 U.S.C.A. § 302.

consisting of the life of the author and fifty years after the author's death."[17] There is a single term with no renewal.

14.4[1] Joint Works

A "joint work prepared by two or more authors"[18] "who did not work for hire"[19] has a duration for a term "consist-

---

17. 17 U.S.C.A. § 302(a). The "life-plus-50 term" has been called the "most important legislative goal in copyright law revision" and the "foundation of the entire bill." 1976 House Report 133. The arguments for the change are listed at *id.* 134-35. An assortment of durations was added by copyright riders to the Judicial Improvements Act of 1990:
    - *Architectural work.* Protection under § 120 for "any architectural work created on or after" December 1, 1990, and unreconstructed but embodied in unpublished plans "terminates" on December 31, 2002, "unless the work is constructed by that date."
    - *Computer software.* Rental provisions effective December 1, 1990, do not affect rights to software acquired before December 1, 1990, and "terminate" on October 1, 1997, except for audiovisual games software (December 1, 1991, with October 1, 1995, termination).
    - *Work of visual art.* Rights of "attribution and integrity" for work created on or after June 1, 1991, life of the author; for work created before June 1, 1991, and the "title" of which, as of June 1, 1991, has not been transferred from the author, the same as for other "rights conferred by section 106."

    A work is "created" when it is fixed in a copy or phonorecord for the first time; where a work is prepared over a period of time, the portion of it that has been fixed at any particular time constitutes the work as of that time, and where the work has been prepared in different versions, each version constitutes a separate work, 17 U.S.C.A. § 101.
18. "Joint work" is defined as a work prepared by two or more authors with the "intention" that their "contributions be merged into inseparable or interdependent parts of a unitary whole." 17 U.S.C.A. § 101. *See* text accompanying chapter 7, notes 19–24, *supra*. Quaere, as to the status of a work coauthored by an employee and an individual author. *See* § 302(b).
19. 17 U.S.C.A. § 302(b).

ing of the life of the last surviving author and fifty years after such surviving author's death."[20]

14.4[2] Works Made for Hire, Anonymous Works, and Pseudonymous Works

"Works made for hire,"[21] "anonymous works,"[22] and "pseudonymous works"[23] have a duration of seventy-five years from the year of first publication, or 100 years from the year of creation,[24] whichever expires first.[25]

---

20. 17 U.S.C.A. (suggesting possible desirability of collaboration with younger coauthor).
21. 17 U.S.C.A. § 302(c). *See* text accompanying chapter 7, notes 14–20, *supra*. A "work made for hire" is defined at some length, and differently from the case law under the 1909 Act. *See* text accompanying chapter 7, notes 21, 38–41 *supra*.
22. 17 U.S.C.A. § 302(c). "Anonymous work" is defined as "a work on the copies or phonorecords of which no natural person is identified as author." *Id.* § 101. For changing status on special Copyright Office Registry, *see id.* §§ 302(c), 708(a)(6) (minimum $20 fee).
23. 17 U.S.C.A. § 302(c). "Pseudonymous work" is defined as "a work on the copies or phonorecords of which the author is identified under a fictitious name." *Id.* § 101. For changing status on special Copyright Office registry, *see id.* §§ 302(c), 708(a)(6) (minimum $20 fee).
24. 17 U.S.C.A. § 302(c). For definition of "created," *see* note 17 *supra*.
25. 17 U.S.C.A. § 302(c). If, before the end of that term, the identity of one or more of the authors of an anonymous or pseudonymous work is revealed in the records of a registration or supplementary registration made for that work, or in the records provided by § 302(c), the copyright in the work endures for the life-plus-fifty-year term based on the life of the author or authors whose identities have been revealed. Any person having an interest in the copyright in an anonymous or pseudonymous work may at any time record, in records to be maintained by the Copyright Office for that purpose, a statement identifying one or more authors of the work; the statement shall also identify the person filing it, the nature of that person's interest, the source of the information recorded, and the particular work affected, and shall comply in form and content with requirements that the Register of Copyrights shall prescribe by regulation. *See* 17 U.S.C.A. § 708(a)(6) (minimum $20 fee).

14.4[3] Obituary Records

Current records of information relating to the death of authors of copyrighted works are required to be maintained by the Copyright Office.[26]

14.4[4] Presumption as to Author's Death

After seventy-five years from the year of first publication, or 100 years from the year of its creation, whichever expires first, any person who obtains from the Copyright Office a certified report that the obituary records disclose nothing to indicate that the author is living, or died less than fifty years before, is entitled to the benefit of a presumption that the author has been dead for at least fifty years. Reliance in good faith upon this presumption shall be a complete defense to any infringement action.[27]

14.5 Constitutional Aspects of Extended Copyright

In the balancing of freedom of speech and press, on the one hand, and copyright, on the other, there is a constitutional question concerning extensions of copyright duration for works in which copyright is already subsisting.[28] Revival of copyright in a work in the public domain presents a greater problem.[29]

---

26. 17 U.S.C.A. § 302(d). Any person having an interest in a copyright may at any time record in the Copyright Office a statement of the date of death of the author of the copyrighted work, or a statement that the author is still living on a particular date. The statement shall identify the person filing it, the nature of that person's interest, and the source of the information recorded, and shall comply in form and content with requirements that the Register of Copyrights shall prescribe by regulation. *See* 17 U.S.C.A. § 708(a)(6) (minimum $20 fee).
27. 17 U.S.C.A. § 302(e).
28. *See* text accompanying chapter 1, note 8, *supra*.
29. *See* chapter 1, note 7, and chapter 2, note 7, *supra*.

15. Renewal

15.1 Renewal Concept

The renewal concept, dating back to the first federal copyright statute of 1790, for works created on or after January 1, 1978, has been abolished, replaced by the termination concept. For first-term copyrights subsisting on January 1, 1978, the renewal provisions of the 1909 Act, for due process reasons, have been retained, with the renewal term extended from twenty-eight to forty-seven years, or by nineteen years.[1] The 1909 Act language should be interpreted by the judicial decisions under the 1909 Act.[2]

Absent timely renewal,[3] copyrights in their first term on January 1, 1978 (*i.e.*, works originally copyrighted between January 1, 1950, and December 31, 1977), will expire twenty-eight years from the date copyright "was originally

1. 17 U.S.C.A. § 304(a); Copyright Office Circular R15. *See* 1976 House Report 139.
2. 1909 Act § 24; Ringer, *Renewal of Copyright* (1960), *reprinted in* 1 STUDIES ON COPYRIGHT—ARTHUR FISHER MEMORIAL EDITION 503 (1963); Bricker, *Renewal and Extension of Copyright,* 29 S. CAL. L. REV. 23 (1955); Note, *Renewal of Copyright,* 44 COLUM. L. REV. 712 (1944).
3. Renewal must be effected during the last calendar year of the original term. *See* note 25 *infra*. Under the 1909 Act, only about 15 percent of copyrighted works were renewed, but these comprised most of the more currently significant works. *See* 1976 House Report 136.

secured,"[4] except that all terms of copyright run to the end of the calendar year in which they would otherwise expire.[5]

Renewal is governed by two provisions:[6]

1. For a "work made for hire"[7] copyrighted by the employer or a composite or "posthumous work" originally copyrighted by the "proprietor";[8]
2. For any other work, "including a contribution by an

---

4. 17 U.S.C.A. § 304(a). A special transitional situation arose with respect to first-term copyrights that were originally secured in 1950, and that became eligible for renewal during the calendar year 1977. If renewal registration was made before January 1, 1978, the duration of the copyright was extended to the full period of seventy-five years without the need for further renewal. However, even if renewal registration had not been made before January 1, 1978, renewal for the second forty-seven-year term could have been made under the 1976 Act at any time between January 1, 1978 and December 31, 1978.
5. 17 U.S.C.A. § 305. The term "renewal period" refers to the period during which application by the appropriate claimant may be made (twenty-eight years from date copyright "was originally secured") under pre-1978 law; to end of calendar year in which copyright would otherwise expire since 1978. "Renewal rights" vest in the appropriate claimant "at the beginning of the renewal period, perfected by timely registration of the renewal application in the name of the appropriate claimant, who may hold some or all of the copyright ownership in trust for beneficial owners during the forty-seven-year "renewal term." Quaere, as to when a renewal expectancy vests: (1) at the commencement of the renewal *period*; (2) when the renewal application is timely filed and registered; or (3) at the commencement of the renewal *term*. See note 20 *infra*.
6. 17 U.S.C.A. § 304(a); Harris v. Coca-Cola Co., 73 F.2d 370 (5th Cir. 1934), cert. *denied*, 294 U.S. 709 (1935)(renewal copyright held not to include illustrations owned by others).
7. 17 U.S.C.A. § 304(a). For discussion of "work made for hire," *see* text accompanying chapter 7, notes 15–41, *supra*.
8. Also under the first proviso is "any work copyrighted by a corporate body (otherwise than as assignee or licensee of the individual author)." *See* Schmid Bros. v. W. Goebel Porzellanfabrik A.G., 589 F. Supp. 497 (E.D.N.Y. 1984)("corporate body" meaning; renewal registrant held renewal as trustee for next of kin).

individual author to a periodical or to a cyclopedic or other composite work."[9]

15.2 First Renewal Proviso

Works, the renewal of which is governed by the first proviso, are:

1. Any "posthumous work";[10]
2. Any periodical, cyclopedic, or other composite work upon which the copyright was originally secured by the "proprietor" thereof;[11]
3. Any work "copyrighted by a corporate body (otherwise than as assignee or licensee of the individual author)";[12]

---

9. Quaere, whether a contribution to a periodical, when the contribution was published not under its own separate copyright notice, but under the general notice of the periodical, is subject to renewal under the first or second proviso. *See* Brylawski, *Renewal of Copyright in a Magazine Contribution: A Belated View,* 42 GEO. WASH. L. REV. 737 (1974). The Copyright Office accepts separate renewal registration for a contribution to a periodical, whether the contribution was copyrighted separately or as part of the periodical issue. Except for group renewal, each contribution published in a separate issue requires a separate renewal registration. Copyright Office Circular R15.
10. The term "posthumous work" is not defined in the 1976 Act or 1909 Act. *See* Bartok v. Boosey & Hawkes, Inc., 523 F.2d 941 (2d Cir. 1975)(2-1)(construing "posthumous work" as one in which no assignment occurred during author's lifetime rather than one simply first published after author's death). This construction was confirmed in the 1976 House Report at 139. *See* Shapiro, Bernstein & Co. v. Bryan, 123 F.2d 697 (2d Cir. 1941)(definition of "posthumous work" and "composite work"; successor of proprietor in case of work made for hire held to have renewal rights).
11. Under the 1909 Act, copyright was secured in the name of the "copyright proprietor." 1909 Act § 19. *See* note 9 *supra* and note 15 *infra,* Cadence Indus. Corp. v. Ringer, 450 F. Supp. 59 (S.D.N.Y. 1978)(holding that renewal application could identify work as both a "periodical, cyclopedic or other composite work" and a "work made for hire").
12. The Copyright Office considers this type of claim appropriate in relatively few cases. Copyright Office Circular R15.

4. Any "work made for hire" copyrighted by the employer.[13]

Such renewal should be by the "proprietor of such copyright."[14] By assignment of copyright, renewal rights can be transferred.

15.3 Second Renewal Proviso

Works, the renewal of which is governed by the second proviso, are "any other copyrighted work, including a contribution by an individual author to a periodical or to a cyclopedic or other composite work."[15]

Such renewal should be by:

1. The author, if still living;

---

13. *See* text accompanying chapter 7, notes 15–41, *supra*.
14. 1976 Act § 304(a); Shapiro, Bernstein & Co. v. Bryan, 123 F.2d 697 (2d Cir. 1941)(meaning "proprietor" at time of renewal, not at time of original copyright). "Proprietor" refers to the 1909 Act nomenclature under the indivisible-copyright theory. *See* text accompanying chapter 7, notes 42–52 *supra*.
15. 17 U.S.C.A. § 304(a). Until 1940, the "including" phrase read: "including a contribution by an individual author to a periodical . . . when such contribution has been separately registered." *See* White-Smith Music Publishing Co. v. Goff, 187 F. 247 (1st Cir. 1911)(author and others named in second proviso, not proprietor, held to enjoy renewal expectancy). *See* notes 9, 11 *supra*. Quaere, as to vested rights, to the extent of any retroactive change in the law. For renewal of "joint works," *compare* Shapiro, Bernstein & Co. v. Jerry Vogel Music Co., 161 F.2d 406 (2d Cir. 1946) (renewable by either joint author or both), *cert. denied*, 331 U.S. 820 (1947) *with* Shapiro, Bernstein & Co. v. Jerry Vogel Music Co., 221 F.2d 569 (2d Cir. 1955)("intention test" for joint work) *and* Shapiro, Bernstein & Co. v. Jerry Vogel Music Co., 223 F.2d 252 (2d Cir. 1955)(composer and later lyricist held to enjoy joint rights in renewal, with each entitled to accounting from exploitation of renewal of joint work).

2. The author's surviving spouse or children,[16] if the author is dead;
3. The author's executor, absent surviving spouse or children;[17]

---

16. Under decisional law under the 1909 Act, surviving spouse and children constituted a single class, with each entitled to share in the renewal term (presumably as tenants in common), Bartok v. Boosey & Hawkes, Inc. 523 F.2d 941 (2d Cir. 1975); and the status of illegitimate children depended upon state domestic relations law. DeSylvia v. Ballentine, 351 U.S. 570 (1956); Saroyan v. William Saroyan Found., 675 F. Supp. 843 (S.D.N.Y. 1987) (fact that children were estranged from father-author immaterial), *aff'd*, 862 F.2d 304 (2d Cir. 1989); Hill & Range Songs, Inc. v. Fred Rose Music, Inc., 570 F.2d 554 (6th Cir. 1978)(widow's interest in renewal terms of husband's works held not assets of deceased husband but statutory rights created by copyright law); Jerry Vogel Music Co. v. Edward B. Marks Music Corp, 425 F.2d 834 (2d Cir. 1969) (illegitimate child denied inheritance rights; widow prevailed over child); Tobani v. Carl Fischer, Inc., 98 F.2d 57 (2d Cir.), *cert. denied*, 305 U.S. 650 (1938)(author's son who renewed held to hold renewal copyrights for benefit of all surviving children); Stone v. Williams, 873 F.2d 401 (2d Cir. 1989) (five-year delay by illegitimate daughter in seeking declaration of renewal rights in father's songs renewed by songwriter's widow and son held laches barring suit), *reh'g granted*, 891 F.2d 401 (2d Cir. 1989) (issue of illegitimate daughter's knowledge and prejudice to others), *vacated on rehearing*, Copyright L. Rep. (CCH) ¶ 26,516 (2d Cir. 1989) (delay induced by fraud), *motion to defer consideration of petition for cert. granted*, 110 S. Ct. 2558 (1990); Sweet Music, Inc. v. Melrose Music Corp., 189 F. Supp. 655 (S.D. Cal. 1960)(surviving co-author and widow of deceased co-author held to hold renewal copyright as tenants-in-common); Edward B. Marks Music Corp. v. Bost Music Publishing Co., 110 F. Supp. 913 (D.N.J. 1953)(widow who remarried held to retain status as widow of author-first husband); *In re* Williams, 156 U.S.P.Q. (BNA) 704 (Ala. Cir. Ct. 1968)(illegitimate child held entitled to inherit under Alabama law, but rights lost as result of adoption by third party; therefore, child not entitled to renewal rights). The statute defines "widow" and "widower" as the surviving spouse under the law of the author's domicile at the time of death, "whether or not the spouse has later remarried," and "children" as "immediate offspring, whether legitimate or not, and any children legally adopted." 17 U.S.C.A. § 101. Quaere, as to vested rights, to the extent of any retroactive change in the law.
17. The executor would take the renewal, subject to the terms of the will and otherwise according to the rules of intestacy, unbound by any

4. The author's next of kin, in the absence of a will.[18]

Such renewal expectancy is assignable[19] and effective if

---

agreement of the testator. Miller Music Corp. v. Charles N. Daniels, Inc., 362 U.S. 373 (1960) (5-4); Fox Film Corp. v. Knowles, 261 U.S. 326 (1923); Gibran v. Natural Comm. of Gibran, 225 F.2d 121 (2d Cir.) (legatee of author who died without widow or children held to take renewal copyright over next of kin where copyright renewed by administrator c.t.a.), *cert. denied,* 358 U.S. 828 (1958); Capano Music v. Myers Music, Inc., 605 F. Supp. 692 (S.D.N.Y. 1985)(renewal rights in next of kin rather than author's legatee widow when widow died before time of renewal).

18. Quaere, if there is a will that makes no provision by bequest or residuary clause and there is no executor, as to the role of an administrator c.t.a. Presumably the next of kin share according to the laws of intestate succession. Silverman v. Sunrise Pictures Corp., 273 F. 609 (2d Cir. 1921) (next of kin where executor discharged), *cert. denied,* 262 U.S. 758 (1922); Danks v. Gordon, 272 F. 821 (2d Cir. 1921)(administrator c.t.a. held to have no renewal rights where author left widow and children); Fitch v. Shubert, 20 F. Supp. 314 (S.D.N.Y. 1937) (next of kin held to hold renewal copyright free of author's grants of rights).

19. Fred Fisher Music Co. v. M. Witmark & Sons, 318 U.S. 643 (1943) (5-4). The renewal expectancy may be assigned, even though not expressly transferred, if the language of the assignment or the circumstances surrounding the transaction indicate an intention to assign such rights. Paige v. Banks, 80 U.S. 608 (1871) (under 1790 and 1831 Acts)(assignment of copyright "forever" held to include author's renewal expectancy); Followay Prods., Inc. v. Maurer, 603 F.2d 72 (9th Cir. 1979) (plaintiff found not to have carried burden of showing that it had protectable interest in renewal copyright allegedly infringed); Rohauer v. Friedman, 306 F.2d 933 (9th Cir. 1962)(evidence of intention to transfer renewal expectancy sufficient without express mention in assignment; right of employer to renew copyright in work made for hire does not depend upon employer-employee relationship at time of renewal); Rose v. Bourne, 279 F.2d 79 (2d Cir.) (assignment construed to combine renewal expectancy with implied power of attorney to file for renewal), *cert. denied,* 364 U.S. 880 (1960); Venus Music Corp. v. Mills Music, Inc., 261 F.2d 577 (2d Cir. 1958)(evidence of intention to transfer renewal expectancy held sufficient; express reference to renewal not required; recorded assignment of right to renew for nominal consideration where it was not paid held not entitled to prevail over earlier unrecorded assignment); Edward B. Marks Music Corp. v. Charles K. Harris Music Publishing Co., 255 F.2d 518 (2d Cir.) (renewal

the assignor is the proper renewal claimant at the time of renewal.[20]

15.4 Group Renewal

Single renewal registration may be made for a group of works by the "same individual author,"[21] "all first published as contributions to periodicals, including newspapers,"

---

expectancy held not included in general transfer of copyright without mention of renewal rights—or other evidence of their inclusion), *cert. denied*, 358 U.S. 831 (1958); Jerry Vogel Music Co. v. Forster Music Publisher, Inc., 147 F.2d 614 (2d Cir.)(defendant held not to have satisfied burden of showing co-ownership in copyright and renewal), *cert. denied*, 325 U.S. 880 (1945); Siegel v. National Periodical Publications, Inc., 364 F. Supp. 1032 (S.D.N.Y. 1973)(state court decision construing renewal rights under agreement held res judicata). Interpretation of contracts, including assignment of renewal expectancy, is within state court jurisdiction. Lewis Publishing Co. v. Shapiro, Bernstein & Co., 27 N.Y.2d 682, 262 N.E.2d 213, 314 N.Y.S.2d 5 (1970); April Prods., Inc. v. G. Schirmer, Inc., 308 N.Y. 366, 126 N.E.2d 283 (1955) (4-3) (assignment held not to include renewal expectancy); Annot., 2 A.L.R.3d 1403 (1965).

20. Miller Music Corp. v. Charles N. Daniels, Inc., 362 U.S. 373 (1960) (5-4) (ambiguous reference to "renewal period"); *compare* Marascalco v. Fantasy, Inc., 6 Copyright L. J. 46 (S.D. Cal. 1990) (author's renewal expectancy held not to vest until commencement of renewal term, i.e., end of calendar year in which original term would have otherwise expired) *with* Frederick Music Co. v. Sickler, 708 F. Supp. 587 (S.D.N.Y. 1989) (death before renewal term of author who renewed during renewal period held not to affect author's assignee's renewal interest; assignment to another by author's widow without effect). A licensee with "rights of renewal" may renew in the name of the author, but has no standing to renew in the licensee's own name. International Film Exch., Ltd. v. Corinth Films, Inc., 621 F. Supp. 631 (S.D.N.Y. 1985); Edward B. Marks Music Corp. v. Jerry Vogel Music Co., 140 F.2d 268 (2d Cir. 1944)(beneficial owners of renewal copyright held not indispensable parties in infringement action); Edward B. Marks Music Corp. v. Jerry Vogel Music Co., 140 F.2d 266 (2d Cir. 1944)(renewal by one co-owner held valid; applicant acting as constructive trustee for other co-author).

21. Not an employer for hire. Copyright Office Circular R15. *See* text accompanying chapter 7, notes 15–41, *supra*.

upon the filing of a single application[22] and fee,[23] under all of the following conditions:[24]

1. The renewal claimant or claimants and the basis of claim or claims are the same for each of the works.
2. The works were all copyrighted upon their first publication, either through separate copyright notice and registration or by virtue of a general copyright in the periodical issue as a whole.
3. The renewal application and fee are received not more than twenty-eight or less than twenty-seven years after December 31 of the calendar year in which all of the works were first published.
4. The renewal application identifies each work separately, including the periodical containing it and its date of first publication.

15.5 Application for Renewal

Application for renewal may be made during the last calendar year of the first term of copyright. If the renewal is not effective by December 31 of the twenty-eighth calendar year,[25] the work falls irretrievably into the public domain.

---

22. *See* Copyright Office Form RE.
23. 17 U.S.C.A. § 408(c)(3).
24. *Id.* All of the contributions must have been published during the same calendar year. Thus, if six contributions by the same author were published on April 1, 1970; July 1, 1970; November 1, 1970; February 1, 1971; July 1, 1971, and March 1, 1972, the three 1970 copyrights can be combined and renewed at any time during 1998, and the two 1971 copyrights can be renewed as a group during 1999, but the 1972 copyright must be renewed by itself, in 2000.
25. 37 C.F.R. § 202.17; Copyright Office Circular R15. The effective date is the day on which an acceptable application, deposit, and fee have all been received in the Copyright Office, which has no discretion to extend the renewal time limits. Under the 1909 Act, renewal was

The Copyright Office has prescribed the form for copyright renewal.[26] Registration of the copyright claim and deposit are prerequisite to renewal.[27] The fee for renewal, including certificate of renewal, is $12.[28]

15.6 Rights of Assignees and Licensees

Under the second renewal proviso, if an assignment does not cover the renewal term, or if the assignor does not survive, the assignee has no rights in the renewal copyright. Similarly, a licensee's rights might not exist under a re-

---

required during the twenty-eighth year after the securing of copyright. Quaere, as to the eligibility of a person, eligible during that year, but not during the one calendar year prior to the expiration of the original term of copyright. Renewal must be in name of an eligible person; a member of the class renews for the class as tenants-in-common. Quaere, as to renewal in trust or by agent. Dolch v. United Cal. Bank, 702 F.2d 178 (9th Cir. 1983)(federal courts without jurisdiction to decide whether assignment of renewal expectancy without consideration is valid, since interpretation of copyright law or federal policies not involved).

26. Copyright Office Form RE (in class RE regardless of class in which original registration was made). Redeposit is not required and copies of the work need not accompany the renewal application.

27. Copyright Office Circular R15. Quaere, as to the statutory basis for the registration and deposit requirement for renewal. Simultaneous original and renewal registrations are permissible. Under the 1909 Act registration was allowed as late as the last year of the first term. Shapiro, Bernstein & Co. v. Jerry Vogel Music Co., 161 F.2d 406 (2d Cir. 1946), *cert. denied,* 331 U.S. 820 (1947). Universal Copyright Convention works need not be registered before renewal; a proper showing of entitlement to renewal is sufficient.

28. 17 U.S.C.A. § 708(a)(2). Although each copyrighted work, other than for group renewal, requires separate application and fee, a single remittance for the total amount may accompany them all. The original copyright notice should continue to be used after renewal. More informative would be an *additional* reference to renewal, e.g.:

©Copyright 1961 John Doe.
©Copyright renewed 1989 Mary Doe.

newal copyright. The renewal claimant takes the renewal free and clear of all rights, interests, and licenses.[29]

15.7 Termination of Transfers and Licenses Covering Extended Renewal Term

Grants of transfers or licenses, whether exclusive or non-exclusive, of renewal copyrights or of any right thereunder,

29. Ringer, *Renewal of Copyright* (1960), *reprinted in* 1 STUDIES ON COPYRIGHT—ARTHUR FISHER MEMORIAL EDITION 503, 564–66 (1963). The disposal of copies during the renewal term by the assignee or licensee for the first term, and the use during the renewal term of new versions, created under an assignment or license limited to the first term present complications. *But see* Russell v. Price, 612 F.2d 1123 (9th Cir. 1978), *cert. denied sub nom.* Drebin v. Russell, 846 U.S. 952 (1980) (copyright of stage play "Pygmalion" held to preclude exhibition of derivative motion picture after copyright on latter was not renewed, since material from stage play in motion picture was not dedicated to public); *accord*, Filmvideo Releasing Corp. v. Hastings, 668 F.2d 91 (2d Cir. 1981)(Hopalong Cassidy books and films); Classic Film Museum, Inc. v. Warner Bros., 597 F.2d 13 (1st Cir. 1979)(duplication of motion picture on which statutory copyright had expired held not to infringe common-law copyright in underlying story (and screenplay), since common-law copyright not for limited time). The United States Supreme Court has held that the owners of a derivative motion picture had no rights to perform the motion picture publicly during the renewal term without authorization from the assignee of the testamentary trustee under the will of the deceased author of the underlying work. The author died without surviving spouse or children, and had assigned his renewal expectancy to the motion picture producers, but died one year before the time for renewal. Renewal was made by the executor under a will leaving the author's estate in trust for Columbia University. Abend, a literary agent, had acquired some 100 renewal copyrights in works made into films for modest sums and percentages of all proceeds from the exploitation of those works. Stewart v. Abend, 110 S. Ct. 1750 (1990), *aff'g* 863 F.2d 465 (9th Cir. 1988). Rejected was the Second Circuit's analogizing of the 1976 termination provisions to renewal. Rohauer v. Killiam Shows, Inc., 551 F.2d 484 (2d Cir.)(renewal copyright in underlying work where renewal expectancy assigned by author not infringed by performance of derivative work after au-

executed before January 1, 1978, by any renewal claimant under the second proviso of the renewal provision, otherwise than by will, may be terminated by those with termination interests.[30]

Such termination may be effected at any time during a period of five years beginning at the end of fifty-six years from the date copyright was "originally secured."[31]

---

thor's death and renewal by statutory successor), *cert. denied,* 431 U.S. 949 (1977). Renewal of copyright in a new version covers only the new matter. Elements of the original versions not under copyright remain in the public domain available to all. *See* Silverman v. CBS, Inc., 870 F.2d 40 (2d Cir. 1989).

30. 17 U.S.C.A. § 304(a). *See* chapter 16 *infra.*

31. 17 U.S.C.A. § 304(c)(3).

16. Termination

Termination, to protect authors against "unremunerative transfers,"[1] is a concept introduced by the 1976 Act, to replace the renewal concept for *future* copyrighted works created on or after January 1, 1978. The termination concept is not retroactive except with respect to certain pre-1978 grants covering renewal terms for their lengthened duration.

The renewal concept resulted in 85 percent of copyrighted works' going into the public domain after twenty-eight years for lack of renewal, and the potential renewal claimants included all persons from the author to the author's remotest next of kin. Under the termination concept, the author, or surviving spouse, and surviving children and surviving children of any deceased child, may reclaim future copyright ownership by terminating an affected transfer or license, whether exclusive or nonexclusive, of rights made by any of them. Termination is not automatic, but

1. 1976 House Report 124; Curtis, *Caveat Emptor in Copyright: A Practical Guide to the Termination-of-Transfers Provisions of the New Copyright Code*, 25 BULL. COPYRIGHT SOC'Y 19 (1977); Nimmer, *Termination of Transfers Under the Copyright Act of 1976*, 125 U. PA. L. REV. 947 (1977); Stein, *Termination of Transfers and Licenses under the New Copyright Act: Thorny Problems for the Copyright Bar*, 24 U.C.L.A. L. REV. 1141 (1977); Melniker & Melniker, *Termination of Transfers and Licenses Under the New Copyright Law*, 22 N.Y.L. SCH. L. REV. 589 (1977).

requires advance notice. Whether reclaimed or not, the copyright subsists for its full duration.

Transfers covering "works made for hire"[2] are not subject to termination.[3] Nor are transfers by will.[4]

16.1 Two Termination Provisions

There are two provisions for termination:

1. For transfers and licenses "by the author" "on or after January 1, 1978";[5]
2. For transfers and licenses covering extended renewal terms by any of the renewal claimants under the "second proviso" of the renewal provision[6] "before January 1, 1978."[7]

In either case, termination is not waivable in advance. Termination may be effected notwithstanding any agreement to the contrary, including an agreement to make a will or to make any future grant.[8] Agreements for earlier termination are effective.

---

2. One or more authors of a joint work may work for hire. *See* text accompanying chapter 7, notes 15–41, *supra*.
3. 17 U.S.C.A. §§ 203(a), 304(a).
4. *Id.*
5. 17 U.S.C.A. § 203.
6. *See* text accompanying chapter 15, notes 15–20, *supra*.
7. 17 U.S.C.A. § 304(c). Section 304(c) is a close, but not exact, counterpart of § 203. For summary of distinction between § 304(c) and § 203, *see* A. LATMAN, THE COPYRIGHT LAW: HOWELL'S COPYRIGHT LAW REVISED AND THE 1976 ACT 105 (5th ed. 1979).
8. 17 U.S.C.A. §§ 203(a)(5), 304(c)(5). In contrast, the renewal expectancy was and is conditionally assignable. *See* chapter 15, note 19, *supra*.

16.2 Transfers and Licenses "by the Author" "on or After January 1, 1978"

Subject to termination are exclusive and nonexclusive grants of transfers or licenses of copyright or of any right under a copyright *executed* "by the author" "on or after January 1, 1978."[9]

16.2[1] Persons Who May "Effect" Termination

Termination may be "effected" by the author who executed the grant or, if the author is dead, by the person or persons entitled to exercise a total of more than one-half of that author's "termination interest."[10]

The "termination interest" of a dead author is owned, and may be exercised, by the surviving spouse and children or grandchildren as follows:

1. By the author's surviving spouse alone if there are no surviving children or grandchildren;[11]
2. By the author's surviving children and the surviving

9. 17 U.S.C.A. § 203(a). *Cf.* oral nonexclusive license not "executed" by author.
10. 17 U.S.C.A. § 203(a)(1). In the case of a grant executed by one author, termination of the grant may be effected by the author or, if the author is dead, by the person or persons who own and are entitled to exercise a total of more than one-half of that author's termination interest. In the case of a grant executed by two or more authors of a joint work, termination of the grant may be effected by a majority of the authors who executed it; if any of such authors is dead, the termination interest of any such author may be exercised as a unit by the person or persons who own and are entitled to exercise a total of more than one-half of that author's interest. *Id.*
11. 17 U.S.C.A. § 203(a)(2)(A). For definitions of "widow," "widower," and "children," *see id.* § 101.

children of any dead child of the author, "on a per stirpes basis," if there is no surviving spouse;[12]

3. If there are a surviving spouse and surviving children or grandchildren, the author's "termination interest" is owned:
   - One-half by the surviving spouse;
   - One-half by the surviving children and surviving children of any dead child, "on a per stirpes basis."[13]

16.2[2] Time for Effecting Termination

Termination may be effected at any time during a period of five years beginning at the end of thirty-five years from the date of execution of the grant. If the grant covers the right of publication, the period begins at the end of thirty-five years from the date of publication under the grant or at the end of forty years from the date of execution of the grant, whichever term ends earlier.[14]

16.2[3] Required Notice of Termination

Termination is effected by serving an advance notice in writing, signed by the required number and proportion of

12. 17 U.S.C.A. § 203(a)(2)(B). The 1909 Act renewal provision used the vague phrase "widow, widower, or children" with no reference to "per stirpes" or "per capita." The language is varied in the current renewal provision. *See* chapter 15, note 16, *supra*.
13. 17 U.S.C.A. § 203(a)(2)(A), (B), (C). The share of the children of a dead child can be exercised only by the action of a majority of them. *Id.* § 203(a)(2)(C). To illustrate the per stirpes principle: assume that an author dies, leaving a widow, two children, and three children of a deceased child. The widow and two of the grandchildren would constitute more than one-half of the author's termination interest (one-half for the spouse plus one-sixth for a majority of the three grandchildren, since each of the two living children and the three grandchildren—children of the deceased child—have a one-sixth interest, that is, one-third of one-half).
14. 17 U.S.C.A. § 203(a)(3).

owners of termination interests, or by their duly authorized agents, upon the grantee or the grantee's "successor in title."[15]

The notice must state "the effective date of the termination," which must fall within the specified five-year period. The notice must be served not less than two or more than ten years before that date.[16] As a condition to its taking effect, a copy of the notice shall be recorded in the Copyright Office before the effective date of termination.[17]

16.2[4] Effect of Termination

Upon the "effective date of termination," all rights covered by the terminated grants "revert" to the author, authors, and other persons owning termination interests, "including those owners who did not join in signing the notice of termination," subject to the following limitations:[18]

1. A derivative work prepared under authority of the grant before its termination may continue to be uti-

15. 17 U.S.C.A. § 203(a)(4). The notice must comply in form, content, and manner of service with the requirements prescribed by the Register of Copyrights. *Id.* § 203(a)(4)(B). Quaere, whether a "successor in title" must have full title. Subject to termination immediately on January 1, 1978, were transfers and licenses covering renewal copyrights already extended by the several extensions. *See* chapter 15, note 14, *supra*. Without any basis in the Transitional and Supplementary Provisions for notices of termination prior to January 1, 1978, the Copyright Office has recorded them after October 13, 1977. *See* 37 C.F.R. § 201.10.
16. 17 U.S.C.A. §§ 203(a)(4)(A), 304(c)(4)(A); 37 C.F.R. § 201.10. Early notice may result in different vesting of the ownership of the reverted rights than later notice. *See* note 20 *infra*.
17. 17 U.S.C.A. §§ 203(a)(4)(A), 304(c)(4)(A). The recording fee has been $10, with an additional charge of fifty cents for each page over six and each title over one. 37 C.F.R. § 201.10(f)(ii)(2).
18. 17 U.S.C.A. § 203(b).

lized under the terms of the grant after its termination.[19]

2. The "future rights" that "will revert upon termination" become "vested" on the date the "notice of termination" has been "served," vesting "in the author, authors, and other persons" with termination interests according to their "proportionate shares."[20]
3. A further grant, or agreement to make a further grant, of any right covered by a terminated grant is valid only if it is signed by the "same number and proportion of the owners," in whom the right has "vested," as are required to terminate the grant.[21]
4. A further grant, or agreement to make a further grant, of any right covered by a terminated grant is "valid" only if it is made after the "effective date of the termination."[22]
5. Termination of a grant affects only those rights covered by the grants arising under the copyright statute, and in no way affects rights arising under any other federal, state, or foreign laws.[23]

---

19. 17 U.S.C.A. § 203(b)(1). This privilege does not extend to the preparation after the termination of other derivative works based upon the copyrighted work covered by the termination grant. *See* Abrams, *Who's Sorry Now? Termination Rights and the Derivative Rights Exception*, 62 U. DET. L. REV. 181 (1985).
20. 17 U.S.C.A. § 203(b)(2). Such vested reverted future rights, upon the death of their owners, pass to the owners' estates, the beneficiaries of which may differ from the statutory successors of the termination interests.
21. 17 U.S.C.A. § 203(b)(3). Such further grant or agreement is effective with respect to all of the persons in whom the right it covers has vested, including those who did not join in signing. If any person dies after rights under a terminated grant have vested in that person, that person's legal representatives, legatees, or heirs at law represent the person. *Id.*
22. 17 U.S.C.A. § 203(b)(4). One exception is provided. An agreement for such a further grant may be made between the persons provided by § 203(b)(3) and the original grantee or that grantee's successor in title after the notice of termination has been served.
23. 17 U.S.C.A. § 203(b)(5).

6. Unless and until termination is effected, the grant, if it does not provide otherwise, continues in effect for the term of copyright.[24]

16.3 Transfers and Licenses Covering Extended Renewal Terms by Any Renewal Claimants Under "Second Proviso" of Renewal Provision "Before January 1, 1978"

Subject to termination are exclusive and nonexclusive grants of transfers or licenses of renewal copyrights or any right thereunder, executed "before January 1, 1978," by any renewal claimant under the "second proviso" of the renewal provision.[25]

16.3[1] Persons Who May "Effect" Termination

Termination may be "effected" under the following conditions:[26]

1. For a grant executed by a person (or persons) other than the author, by the surviving person (or persons)

---

24. 17 U.S.C.A. § 203(b)(6).
25. 17 U.S.C.A. § 304(c). The renewal claimants under the second proviso are successively the author, the author's surviving spouse or children, the author's executor, and the author's next of kin. *See* text accompanying chapter 15, notes 15–20, *supra*. Pre-1978 transfers and licenses by renewal claimants under the first proviso are not subject to termination. *See* Freedman v. Select Information Sys., Inc., 221 U.S.P.Q. (BNA) 848 (N.D. Cal. 1983) (termination provisions held applicable only to executed and not nonexclusive oral licenses; under California law, oral contracts not to be performed within one year involved); Burroughs v. Metro-Goldwyn-Mayer, Inc., 683 F.2d 610 (2d Cir. 1982)(works not listed in termination notice not affected). Bourne Co. v. MPL Communications, Inc., 675 F. Supp. 859 (1987) (§ 304(a) section termination provision for nineteen-year extension applicable despite specific bequest of royalties), *modified*, 678 F. Supp. 70 (S.D.N.Y. 1988).
26. 17 U.S.C.A. § 304(c).

"who executed it";[27] for a grant executed by one or more of the authors of the work, "to the extent of a particular author's share in the ownership of the renewal copyright," by the author who executed it or, if such author is dead, by the person (or persons) who own and are entitled to exercise a total of more than one-half of that author's "termination interest."[28]

2. Where an author is dead, the author's "termination interest" is owned, and may be exercised, by the surviving spouse and children or grandchildren, in the same manner as for transfers and licenses by authors on or after January 1, 1978.[29]

16.3[2] Time for Effecting Termination

Termination may be "effected" at any time during a period of five years beginning at the end of fifty-six years from the date copyright was originally secured.[30]

---

27. 17 U.S.C.A. § 304(c)(1).
28. 17 U.S.C.A. § 304(c)(1). Since it is not clear how the shares of a class of renewal beneficiaries are to be divided under the 1909 Act (presumably as tenants in common), and greater difficulties would be presented if any attempt were made to apply the majority principle to further beneficiaries in cases where one or more of the renewal beneficiaries are dead, the majority principle is not applicable where the grant was executed by a person or persons other than the author. Termination can be effected only by the unanimous action of the survivors of those who executed it. 1976 House Report 141. Those who control a deceased joint author's termination interest may terminate without joining the other joint authors or their representatives, in the same manner as would be permitted if all of the joint authors had survived.
29. 17 U.S.C.A. § 304(c)(2). *See* note 11 *supra*.
30. 17 U.S.C.A. § 304(c)(3) (applicable to additional nineteen full years added to renewal term). These provisions, since they do not involve "terms of copyright," are not affected by § 305 (all "terms of copyright" to run to end of calendar year).

16.3[3] Required Notice of Termination

Termination is "effected" by serving an advance written notice upon the grantee or the grantee's "successor in title," signed:[31]

1. For a grant executed by a person (or persons) other than the author, by "all of those entitled to terminate the grant" or by their duly authorized agents;
2. For a grant executed by one or more of the authors, as to any one author's share, by that author or the author's duly authorized agent, or, if that author is dead, by the "required number and proportion of the owners" of the author's "termination interest," or by their duly authorized agents.

The requirements for the notice, time of service, vesting of rights, and recordation of the notice of termination are the same for terminating pre-1978 grants covering extended renewal terms[32] as for grants by authors on or after January 1, 1978.[33]

16.3[4] Effect of Termination

Upon the "effective date of termination":[34]

---

31. 17 U.S.C.A. § 304(c)(4). The notice shall be signed: (1) for a grant executed by persons other than the author, by all those entitled to terminate the grant, or by their duly authorized agents; or (2) for a grant executed by one or more of the authors, as to any one's share by that author or the author's duly authorized agent or, if that author is dead, by the required number and proportion of the owners of the author's termination interest, or by their duly authorized agents. *Id.* *See* Burroughs v. Metro-Goldwyn-Mayer, Inc., 683 F.2d 610 (2d Cir. 1982)(works not listed in termination agreement not affected).
32. 17 U.S.C.A. § 304(c)(4)(A), (B); 37 C.F.R. § 201(10).
33. *See* text accompanying notes 14–17 *supra*.
34. 17 U.S.C.A. § 304(c)(6).

1. For grants executed by a person (or persons) other than the author, all grants covered by the terminated grant "revert" to "all of those entitled to terminate the grant."
2. For grants executed by one or more of the authors, "all of a particular author's rights . . . covered by the terminated grant revert . . . to that author," or, if that author is dead, to the persons owning that author's "termination interest," "including those owners who did not join in signing the notice of termination."

The reversion of rights[35] is subject to the following limitations:[36]

1. A derivative work prepared under authority of the grant before its termination may continue to be utilized under the terms of the grant after its termination.[37]
2. The "future rights" "that will revert upon termination" become "vested" on the date the "notice of termination" has been "served."[38]

---

35. "Reversion of rights" is a vestige of the pre-"termination interests" terminology of the 1976 Act.
36. 17 U.S.C.A. § 304(c)(6).
37. 17 U.S.C.A. § 304(c)(6)(A). This privilege does not extend to the preparation after the termination of other derivative works based upon the copyrighted work covered by the terminated grant. Section 304(c)(6)(A) was cited to the effect that a derivative work may be utilized during a renewal term even without a grant from the renewal claimant. Rohauer v. Killian Shows, Inc. 551 F.2d 484 (2d Cir.) (pre-1976 law), *cert. denied*, 431 U.S. 948 (1977). This view was rejected in Stewart v. Abend, 110 S. Ct. 1750 (1990) (5–1–3). *See* Mills Music, Inc. v. Snyder, 405 U.S. 638 (1985)(holding that derivative-work exception to termination provisions preserves music publisher's contractual right to share in royalties on such works). *See also* Abrams, WHO'S SORRY NOW? TERMINATION RIGHTS AND THE DERIVATIVE WORKS EXCEPTION, 62 U. DET. L. REV. 181 (1985).
38. 17 U.S.C.A. § 304(c)(6)(B).

3. Where the author's rights revert to two or more persons, the vesting is in the aforementioned proportionate shares.[39]
4. A further grant, or agreement to make a further grant, of any right covered by a terminated grant is valid only if made after the "effective date of the termination."[40]
5. Termination of a grant affects only those rights covered by the grant, and in no way affects rights arising under any other federal, state, or foreign laws.[41]
6. Unless and until termination is effected, the grant, "if it does not provide otherwise," continues in effect for the remainder of the extended renewal term.[42]

The only United States Supreme Court termination case to date held, five to four, that termination of an author's

---

39. 17 U.S.C.A. § 304(c)(6)(C). *See* text accompanying notes 12, 13 *supra*. A further grant, or agreement to make a further grant, of a particular author's share with respect to any right covered by a terminated grant is valid only if signed by the same number and proportion of the owners in whom the right has vested as are required to terminate the grant. Such further grant or agreement is effective with respect to all of the persons in whom the right it covers has vested, including those who did not join in signing it. If any person dies after rights under a terminated grant have vested in that person, that person's legal representatives, legatees, or heirs at law represent that person. Where the extended term reverts to joint authors or to a class of renewal beneficiaries who have joined in executing a grant, their rights would be governed by the general rules of tenancy in common; each co-owner would have an independent right to sell that co-owner's share, or to use or license the work subject to an accounting. 1976 House Report 141–42.
40. 17 U.S.C.A. § 304(c)(6)(D). Excepted is an agreement for such a further grant made between the author and or any of the persons provided by the first sentence of § 304(c)(6) or between the persons provided by § 304(c)(6)(C) and the original grantee or such grantee's successor in title, after the notice of termination has been served.
41. 17 U.S.C.A. § 304(c)(6)(E).
42. 17 U.S.C.A. § 304(c)(6)(F).

contract with a publisher did not affect the publisher's negotiated license with a recording company and right to royalties under that license leaving little for the author and successors to enjoy after termination.[43]

43. Mills Music, Inc. v. Snyder, 405 U.S. 638 (1985)(5-4)(royalties payable on continuing use of derivative work payable to party who issued license to prepare derivative work from underlying copyright even after licensor's interest in copyright had been terminated by author). Bills have been introduced to provide that all rights to enforce contracts and to receive royalties for continued use of a derivative work shall become the property of the person to whom the copyright reverts after termination of the grant.

17. Exclusive Rights of Copyright

Copyright comprises a bundle of cumulative and somewhat overlapping exclusive rights—five in number[1]—

1. 17 U.S.C.A. § 106(a). Questions of scope of exclusive rights and infringement, like preemption and copyright subject matter, are facets of the same problem. A literal reading of § 201(d)(2) implies that copyright may encompass more than the rights enumerated in § 106. Section 201(d)(2) discusses, *inter alia:* "Any of the exclusive rights comprised in a copyright, including . . . any of the rights specified by section 106." Section 101 defines "including" as "illustrative and not limitative." The copyright, therefore, may encompass rights other than those specified in § 106. There is nothing, however, in the law or legislative history that indicates that § 106 is less than an exhaustive list of the entire "bundle of rights" encompassed within a copyright. 1976 House Report 61. With the statutory broadening of copyrightable subject matter, there has been statutory enlarging of the exclusive rights encompassed by copyright. For example, the 1790 Act specified printing, publishing, and vending; public performance rights were added in 1856; recording rights, in 1909; public display rights, in 1976.

   The 1909 Act § 1, as amended, conferred on all classes of copyrighted works the exclusive right "To print, reprint, publish, copy, and vend." 1909 Act § 1(a). Additional exclusive rights depended upon class of work (not following the section 5 classification of works for registration):

   1. Literary works: Translation; making another version (§ 1[b]);
   2. Nondramatic work: Dramatizing (§ 1[b]);
   3. Drama: Converting into novel or other Nondramatic work (§ 1[b]);
   4. Musical work: Arranging or adapting (§ 1[b]);

subject to certain qualifications.[2] Each exclusive right may be subdivided, transferred, and owned separately, and the owner of any particular exclusive right is entitled, to the extent of that right, to all of the protection and remedies accorded the "copyright owner."[3] The symmetry of these provisions has been affected by the omnibus copyright riders to the Judicial Improvements Act of 1990, enacted on December 1, 1990. The riders included the Visual Artists Rights Act, the Architectural Works Copyright Protection Act, and the Computer Software Rental Act, effective as of varying dates, for differing durations.[4]

---

5. Model or design for work of art: Completing, executing, or finishing (§ 1[b]);
6. [As amended, eff. Jan. 1, 1953]: Lecture, sermon, address, or similar production, or other nondramatic literary work: Delivering, authorizing delivery, reading, or presenting in public for profit; making or procuring the making of any transcription or record, playing or performing it in public for profit, exhibiting, representing, producing, or reproducing in any manner or by any method whatsoever (§ 1[c]);
7. Drama: Performing or representing publicly (§ 1[d]);
8. Dramatic work not reproduced in copies for sale: Vending any manuscript or record whatsoever; making or procuring the making of any transcription or record; exhibiting, performing, representing, producing, or reproducing in any manner or by any method whatsoever (§ 1[d]);
9. Musical composition: Performing publicly for profit; making any arrangement or any form of record (subject to reciprocity by nation of foreign author or composer, and subject to mechanical reproduction compulsory license and to exemption for coin-operated machines ["juke box exemption"] (§ 1[e]);
10. (As amended, eff. Feb. 15, 1972) Sound recording: Reproducing and distributing to the public by sale or other transfer of ownership, or by rental, lease, or lending reproductions—exclusive right limited to duplicating actual sounds ("dubbing" only, not imitation or simulation) (§ 1[f]).

2. 17 U.S.C.A. §§ 107–118. *See* text accompanying notes 8–37 *infra*.
3. 17 U.S.C.A. § 201(d)(2). *See* text accompanying chapter 28, notes 8–10, *infra*.
4. Pub. L. 101-650, 104 Stat. 5089 (Dec. 1, 1990).

The first three exclusive rights, which comprise all of the rights except those of public performance and public display, extend to every kind of copyrighted work. Violation of any of the exclusive rights, as qualified, constitutes infringement of copyright.[5] A single infringing act may violate one, some, or all of the rights.

17.1 Exclusive Rights

The "owner of copyright,"[6] under § 106, has the exclusive rights "to do and to authorize"[7] any of the following:[8]

1. *Reproduction:* To reproduce the copyrighted work in copies or phonorecords;
2. *Adaptation:* To prepare "derivative works based upon" the copyrighted work;
3. *Public distribution:* To distribute copies or phonorecords of the copyrighted work to the public by sale or other transfer of ownership, or by rental, lease, or lending;
4. *Public performance:* In the case of literary, musical, dramatic, and choreographic works, pantomimes, and motion pictures and other audiovisual works, to perform the copyrighted work publicly;
5. *Public display:* In the case of literary, musical, dramatic, and choreographic works, pantomimes, and

---

5. 17 U.S.C.A. § 501(a).
6. "Owner of copyright" is not a defined term. *See* chapter 7, note 51 *supra*.
7. 17 U.S.C.A. § 106. Use of the phrase "to authorize" is intended to avoid any questions as to the liability of contributory infringers. 1976 House Report 61. *See* Campbell v. Trustees of Stanford Univ., 817 F.2d 499 (9th Cir. 1987) (transfer of exclusive license in breach of contract held violative of copyright).
8. 17 U.S.C.A. § 106; Fabe, The *Fine Artist's Right to the Reproduction of His Original Work*, 23 COPYRIGHT L. SYMP. (ASCAP) 81 (1977).

pictorial, graphic, or sculptural works, including the individual images of a motion picture or other audiovisual work, to display the copyrighted work publicly.

17.1[1] Reproduction

The first of the exclusive rights is "to reproduce the copyrighted work in copies or phonorecords."[9] The term "reproduce" is not defined, but presumably has the same meaning as under the 1909 Act.[10] Exception is provided for the reproduction of copyrighted sound recordings.[11] The term "copies" and "phonorecords" are mutually exclusive.

The term, "copies," is defined as "material objects, other than phonorecords," in which a work is "fixed"[12] by any method now known or later developed, and from which the

---

9. 17 U.S.C.A. § 106(a). The plural includes the singular. 1 U.S.C.A. § 1. The exclusive rights of reproduction, besides being limited by the right of fair use (§ 107), are also limited by §§ 108, 111(e), 112, 113, 114(b), 115(a), 117, 118, and 119. These are discussed in chapters 18, 22, 24, 25, and 26 *infra*. The exclusive rights to reproduce a work in phonorecords and to distribute phonorecords do not extend to any nondramatic musical work copyrighted before July 1, 1909. Transitional and Supplementary Provisions sec. 103. The law respecting computer use was frozen from December 31, 1977, to December 12, 1980. *Id.* § 117. *See* note 53 *infra*.
10. Reproduction could be in whole or in any substantial part, and by exact duplication ("literal") or simulation ("nonliteral"). Wide departures or variations would still be an infringement as long as the author's "expression" rather than merely the author's "ideas" were taken. 1976 House Report 61. *See* Horgan v. Macmillan, Inc., 789 F.2d 157 (2d Cir. 1986) (use in book of still photographs of ballet performance not fair use of choreographic work if substantial similarity even though staged performance could not be recreated from photographs).
11. 17 U.S.C.A. § 114.
12. "Fixed" is defined in 17 U.S.C.A. § 101. The transitory showing of an image on a screen or cathode ray tube would not constitute fixation.

work "can be perceived, reproduced, or otherwise communicated, either directly or with the aid of a machine or device."[13]

The term, "phonorecords," is defined as "material objects in which sounds, other than those accompanying a motion picture or other audiovisual work, are fixed by any method now known or later developed," and from which the "sounds can be perceived, reproduced, or otherwise communicated, either directly, or with the aid of a machine or device."[14]

17.1[2] Preparation of Derivative Work

The second of the exclusive rights is "to prepare derivative works based upon the copyrighted work."[15]

The term "derivative work" is defined as a work "based upon" one or more preexisting works, such as a "translation, musical arrangement, dramatization, fictionalization, motion picture version, sound recording, art reproduction, abridgment, condensation, or any other form in which a work may be recast, transformed, or adapted," including a "work consisting of editorial revisions, annotations, elabora-

---

13. 17 U.S.C.A. § 101. Machine or device is broadly defined. See definitions of "device," "machine," or "process" (one now known or later developed).
14. 17 U.S.C.A. § 101.
15. 17 U.S.C.A. § 106(2). The Berne Convention recognizes the "exclusive right of authorizing the reproduction . . . in any manner or form" (art. 9(1)), and the "exclusive right of authorizing adaptations, arrangements and other alterations of their works" (art. 12). The exclusive rights to prepare derivative works, besides being limited by the right of fair use (§ 107), are also limited by §§ 108, 112, 113(a), 114(b), 115(a)(2), 117, 118, and 119. These are discussed in chapters 18, 19, 21, 22, and 24 *infra*. *See* Bobbs-Merrill Co. v. New Am. Library, Copyright L. Rep. (CCH) ¶ 25,752 (S.D.N.Y. 1985) (selected excerpts from *Joy of Cooking* not within exclusive license to condense); Note, 73 MINN. L. REV. 1921 (1989).

tions, or other modifications which, as a whole, represent an original work of authorship."[16]

This exclusive right overlaps the exclusive right of reproduction, but is broader in the sense that reproduction requires fixation in copies or phonorecords, whereas preparation of a derivative work may be an infringement even though nothing is ever fixed in tangible form.[17]

Adaptation for use in information storage and retrieval systems was governed by pre-1978 law until December 12, 1980.[18]

17.1[3] Public Distribution

The third of the exclusive rights is "to distribute copies or phonorecords of the copyrighted work to the public by sale or other transfer of ownership, or by rental, lease, or lending."[19]

---

16. 17 U.S.C.A. § 101. Quaere, whether protection of derivative rights should be broader than unauthorized copying, and whether infringing derivative works need satisfy requirements for statutory copyright. Lone Ranger Television, Inc. v. Program Radio Corp., 740 F.2d 718 (9th Cir. 1984) (under 1909 Act); Mirage Editions, Inc. v. Albuquerque A.R.T. Co., 856 F.2d 1341 (9th Cir. 1988) (removing illustrations from book and mounting them on tiles with transparent covering held unlawful preparation of derivative work based upon copyrighted work; derivative work includes "any other form in which a work may be recast"; "first-sale doctrine" inapplicable where derivative work made). Quaere, whether mounted tile amounted to sufficient authorship for derivative work. *See* Paramount Pictures Corp. v. Video Broadcasting Sys. Inc., 724 F. Supp. 808 (D. Kan. 1989) (unauthorized insertion of advertisements in videocassettes preceding copyrighted motion picture held not infringement). *See* chapter 5, note 11 *supra*.
17. 1976 House Report 62. Lacking fixation, a derivative work would not be copyrightable.
18. 17 U.S.C.A. § 117, as amended by Pub. L. No. 96-517, 94 Stat. 3015 (1980). *See* note 53 *infra*.
19. 17 U.S.C.A. § 106(3); Kernochan, *The Distribution Right in the United States of America: Review and Reflections*, 42 VAND. L. REV. 1407 (1989). The exclusive rights of public distribution, besides be-

The statute does not define "distribute," but does define "publication" as the "distribution of copies or phonorecords of a work to the public by sale or other transfer of ownership, or by rental, lease, or lending," including the "offering to distribute copies or phonorecords to a group of persons for purposes of further distribution, public performance, or public display." A public performance or display does not "of itself" constitute publication.[20]

The copyright owner's rights of public distribution cease with respect to a particular copy or phonorecord once one has parted with ownership[21] but not if one has parted with possession alone.[22]

---

ing limited by the right of fair use (§ 107), are also limited by §§ 108, 109(a), 109(c), 112(c), 113(b), 113(c), 114(b), 115(a), 117, 118, and 119. These are discussed in chapters 8 *supra* and 18, 19, 21, 22, and 24 *infra*. *See* Obolensky v. G.P. Putnam's Sons, 628 F. Supp. 1552 (S.D.N.Y. 1986) (trade publications erroneously listing plaintiff's book as defendant's publication held not to infringe exclusive rights of distribution).

20. 17 U.S.C.A. § 101.

21. 17 U.S.C.A. § 109(a). Copyright ownership is distinct from ownership of any material object in which the work is embodied—copy or phonorecord. 17 U.S.C.A. § 202. The "first-sale doctrine," based on such distinction, is discussed in chapter 7, note 2 *supra*. *See also* Seiman, *A Look at the Public Lending Right*, 30 COPYRIGHT L. SYMP. (ASCAP) 71 (1983); Note, 63 N.Y.U. L. REV. 878 (1988). Sending copies of videotapes for nonpublic viewing is permissible. *See* Columbia Pictures Indus., Inc. v. Professional Real Estate Investors, Inc. 866 F.2d 278 (9th Cir. 1989) (hotels providing videodisc players and renting discs to guests for viewing in their rooms held permissible nonpublic performance). *Cf.* Red Baron-Franklin Park, Inc. v. Tarto Corp., 883 F.2d 275 (4th Cir. 1989) (video arcade owner's use of copyrighted circuit boards in coin-operated video machine held public performance; first-sale doctrine relevent to distribution and not public performance right). For discussion of the Record Rental Amendment Act of 1984, see Horowitz, *The Record Rental Amendment of 1984: A Case Study in the Effort to Adopt Copyright Law to New Technology*, 12 COLUM.-V.L.A. J. L. & ARTS 31 (1987). *See* Nolan, *All Rights Not Reserved After the First Sale*, 23 BULL. COPYRIGHT SOC'Y 76 (1975).

22. 17 U.S.C.A. § 109(c). The burden of showing unlawful possession in a criminal copyright infringement proceeding is on the government.

17.1[4] Public Performance

The fourth of the exclusive rights, unlike the first three exclusive rights, is limited to certain classes of works, namely, five of the seven categories of copyrighted works:[23] literary, musical, dramatic, choreographic works and pantomimes, and motion pictures and other audivisual works.[24] Excluded are pictorial, graphic and sculptural works,[25] and sound recordings.[26]

The fourth of the exclusive rights, in the case of the five specified categories of works, is "to perform the copyrighted work publicly."[27]

In a civil copyright infringement action, the defendant is required to establish either authorization from the copyright holder or title acquired through a first sale. Possession alone is not probative of title, because one in possession acquires no better title than one's transferor. American Int'l Pictures, Inc. v. Foreman, 576 F.2d 661 (5th Cir. 1978). *See* note 44 *infra*. *See also* United States v. Moore, 604 F.2d 1228 (9th Cir. 1979) (burden of proving absence of "first sale" may be established by circumstantial evidence).

23. 17 U.S.C.A. §§ 106(2), 102.
24. *Id.* The 1976 Act expanded the exclusive right of public performance to include not only rnotion pictures, including works recorded on film, video tape, and video disks, but also such audiovisual works as filmstrips and sets of slides. 1976 House Report 63.
25. *See* text accompanying chapter 5, notes 21, 22, *supra*.
26. *See* text accompanying chapter 5, notes 26–28, *supra*. Any right of performance in sound recordings is expressly negatived. 17 U.S.C.A. § 114(a). The exclusive right to perform publicly, by means of a phonorecord, is expressly not limited or impaired by section 114. § 114(c).
27. 17 U.S.C.A. § 106(4). This represents a change so far as musical and nondramatic literary works are concerned. Under the 1909 Act, the performance right was public performance "for profit." 1909 Act § 1(e); Varmer, *Limitations on Performing Rights* (1958), *reprinted in* 2 Studies on Copyright—Arthur Fisher Memorial Edition 835 (1963). The "for profit" rationale of Herbert v. Shanley, 242 U.S. 591 (1917), thus is no longer relevant. The new law eliminated the "for profit" limitation, but specifically exempted some educational nonprofit uses. 1976 House Report 62-63; Almo Music Corp. v. 77 East

To "perform" a work is defined to mean "to recite, render, play, dance, or act it, either directly or by means of any device or process or, in the case of a motion picture or other audiovisual work, to show its images in any sequence or to make the sounds accompanying it audible."[28]

To perform "publicly" means to perform a work "at a place open to the public or at any place where a substantial number of persons outside of a normal circle of a family and its social acquaintances is gathered," or to "transmit" or otherwise communicate a performance of the work to such place "by means of any device or process, whether the members of the public, capable of receiving it receive it in

---

Adams, Inc., 647 F. Supp. 123 (N.D. Ill. 1986) (complaint under 1976 Act need not allege performance "for profit"); LaSalle Music Publishers, Inc. v. Highfill, 622 F. Supp. 168 (W.D. Mo. 1985); Cramer, *Performance of Copyrighted Music*, 6 A.P.L.A. Q.J. 41 (1978). The exclusive rights of public performance, besides being limited by the right of fair use (§ 107), are also limited by §§ 110, 111, 114(a), 114(c), 116, 117, 118, and 119. These are discussed in chapters 18, 20, and 23–26 *infra*.

28. 17 U.S.C.A. § 101. The broad statutory definitions of "performance," "to perform" or display a work "publicly," and to "transmit" (§ 101) overrule Twentieth Century Music Corp. v. Aiken, 422 U.S. 151 (1975); Teleprompter Corp. v. C.B.S., Inc., 415 U.S. 394 (1974); and Fortnightly Corp. v. United Artists Television, Inc., 392 U.S. 390 (1968); and codify Buck v. Jewell-LaSalle Realty Co., 283 U.S. 191 (1931). 1976 House Report 87-88. Performance includes not only the initial rendition or showing, but also any transmission, simultaneous or from records, *e.g.*, singing or playing music; transmission of the performance by a network or local broadcaster; retransmission by a cable television system; playing of a phonorecord embodying the performance; communication of the performance by turning on a receiving set; reading a literary work aloud; dancing a ballet or other choreographic work; acting out a dramatic work or pantomime; showing images in any sequence of a motion picture or other audiovisual work; or making audible sound accompanying it. *Id.* 63–64. "To 'transmit' a performance" means "to communicate it by any device or process whereby images or sounds are received beyond the place from which they are sent." 17 U.S.C.A. § 101.

the same place or in separate places and at the same time or at different times"[29]

---

29. 17 U.S.C.A. § 101. "Public" includes quasipublic places, e.g., clubs, lodges, factories, camps, hotels, schools, and even prisons and nursing homes. *See* Columbia Pictures Indus., Inc. v. Professional Real Estate Investors, Inc., 866 F.2d 278 (9th Cir. 1989) (hotel guest rooms not "public-place"; therefore, hotel's rental of videodiscs for viewing on hotel-provided video equipment in guest rooms not infringement); Columbia Pictures Indus., Inc. v. Aveco, Inc., 800 F.2d 59 (3d Cir. 1986) (screenings of videocassettes in private viewing rooms of video rental store held public performance because rooms available for rental by public); Lodge Hall Music, Inc. v. Waco Wrangler Club, Inc., 831 F.2d 77 (5th Cir. 1987) (playing recorded music in bar or music club infringing public performance); Merrill v. Country Stores, Inc., 669 F. Supp. 1164 (D.N.H. 1987) (transmission of radio broadcast of music in workplace for benefit of employees held public performance); Home Box Office, Inc. v. Corinth Motel, Inc., 647 F. Supp. 1186 (N.D. Miss. 1986) (authorized reception on motel satellite dishes for guests held infringing secondary transmission); ESPN v. Edinburgh Community Hotel, 623 F. Supp. 647 (S.D. Tex. 1985); 47 U.S.C.A. § 705(a) (not "private viewing" under Federal Communications Act § 705[c][4]); CAL. OP. ATT'Y GEN. NO. 81-503 (Feb. 2, 1982) (showing of videocassette tapes of copyrighted movies to prisoners held to constitute public performance; "public place" not requisite element; no fair use since not "productive use"). Nonlegislative licensing agreements at nominal fees might be negotiated.

"Cavalcade rights" encompass all rights in each composition; "grand rights" cover dramatic performing rights; "small rights" are *non*dramatic performing rights, e.g., dialogue, scenery, costumes, plot, story line.

Private performing-rights societies largely license and police the nondramatic public performance of musical works in their repertories. The three American performing-rights societies are American Society of Composers, Authors, and Publishers (ASCAP), Broadcast Music, Inc. (BMI), and SESAC, Inc. (SESAC). *See* Robert Stigwood Group, Ltd. v. Sperber, 346 F. Supp. 376 (D. Conn. 1972), *aff'd*, 530 F.2d 1096 (2d Cir. 1973) (holding concert of nearly all songs from "Jesus Christ, Superstar" rock opera sung sequentially by singers in respective roles to be dramatico-musical performance outside ASCAP license), *cert. denied*, 429 U.S. 848 (1976); Rice v. American Program Bureau, 446 F.2d 685 (2d Cir. 1971) (2-1) (nondramatic performing rights license held not to cover performance of "Jesus Christ, Superstar" in entirety or with dialog, pantomime, dance, costumes, or scenery).

No right of performance applies to sound recordings.[30] However, the Register of Copyrights has recommended to Congress that performance rights in sound recordings be provided for performers and copyright owners.[31]

See 17 U.S.C.A. § 116(e)(3); Korman, *Performing Rights in Musical Compositions*, 25 BULL. COPYRIGHT SOC'Y 233 (1978); Finkelstein, *The Role of ASCAP in Licensing the Right to Perform Copyrighted Musical Works*, 17 IDEA 15 (Fall 1975); Korman & Koenigsberg, *Performing Rights in Music and Performing Rights Societies*, 33 J. COPYRIGHT SOC'Y 332 (1986).

Nearly all of the current antitrust cases in the copyright field involve ASCAP or BMI, both of which operate under consent decrees and judicial monitoring. Buffalo Broadcasting Co. v. ASCAP, 744 F.2d 917 (2d Cir. 1984)(upholding blanket licenses to local television stations), *cert. denied*, 469 U.S. 1211 (1985); Broadcast Music, Inc. v. Columbia Broadcasting Sys., Inc., 441 U.S. 1 (1979)(issuance of blanket performance rights by performing societies to television networks held not price-fixing per se under antitrust laws), *after remand sub nom.* CBS, Inc. v. ASCAP, 620 F.2d 930 (2d Cir. 1980)(finding no unreasonable restraint of trade), *cert. denied*, 450 U.S. 970 (1981). Cases have consistently held that the performing rights societies need not supply their repertory lists. Famous Music Corp. v. Bay State Harness Horse Racing & Breeding Ass'n, 554 F.2d 1213 (1st Cir. 1977). For discussion of ASCAP, BMI, and SESAC and antitrust consent decrees, see A. LATMAN, R. GORMAN & J. GINSBURG, COPYRIGHT FOR THE NINETIES 569–78 (3d ed. 1989).

30. 17 U.S.C.A. §§ 106(4), 114(a); Meyers, *Sound Recordings and the New Copyright Act*, 22 N.Y.L. SCH. L. REV. 573 (1977); Lang, *Performance and the Right of the Performing Artist*, 21 ASCAP COPYRIGHT L. SYMP. 69 (1974).

31. On January 3, 1978, the Register of Copyrights submitted to Congress the required report, which recommended legislation to provide performance rights for performers and copyright owners. Performing rights in the recording itself in favor of the performer or recorder or both should be distinguished from the rights to perform the underlying work (e.g., literary, dramatic, or musical work) in favor of the owner of the latter. 17 U.S.C.A. § 114(d); 43 Fed. Reg. 1,655 (Jan. 11, 1978), 11,773 (Mar. 21, 1978)(addenda to report), 12,763 (Mar. 27, 1978)(addenda to report). Included was a draft bill, which was essentially a revision of the then pending Performance Rights Amendment of 1977, H.R. 6063, 95th Cong., 1st Sess. (Apr. 5, 1977). The bill would have created another compulsory license with royalty rates to be re-examined by the Copyright Royalty Tribunal, and royalties to

17.1[5] Public Display

The fifth of the exclusive rights, unlike the first three exclusive rights, is also limited, namely, to five and partially to six of the seven categories of copyrighted works:[32] literary, musical, dramatic, choreographic works and pantomimes, and pictorial, graphic, or sculptural works, including the individual images of a motion picture or other audiovisual work.[33] Excluded are sound recordings and motion pictures and other audiovisual works other than individual images therefrom.[34]

The fifth of the exclusive rights, in the case of the five-plus specified categories of works, is "to display the copyrighted work publicly."[35]

To "display" a work is defined to mean "to show a copy of it, either directly or by means of a film, slide, television image, or any other device or process or, in the case of a motion picture or other audiovisual work, to show individual images nonsequentially."[36]

---

be collected by the Copyright Office and distributed by the Tribunal. Levine & Meyer, *Unfinished Business—Copyright Issues Unresolved by the Act of 1976*, 6 A.P.L.A. Q.J. 61, 71 (1978). Similar bills were introduced in but not passed by subsequent Congresses. Use of the terms "performance rights," "performing rights," and "performers' rights" is confusing. *See* Bard & Kurlantzick, *A Public Performance Right in Recordings: How to Alter the Copyright System Without Improving It*, 43 GEO. WASH. L. REV. 152 (1974).

32. 17 U.S.C.A. §§ 106(5), 102.
33. 17 U.S.C.A. §§ 106(5), 102. 1976 House Report 64–65.
34. *Id.*
35. *Id.* This is the first statutory recognition of the exclusive right to show a copyrighted work or an image of it to the public. The exclusive rights of public display, besides being limited by the right of fair use (§ 107), are also limited by §§ 109(b), 109(c), 110(1), 110(2), 110(3), 110(5), 111, 113(b), 113(c), 117, 118, and 119. These are discussed in chapters 18, 20, 24, 25, and 26 *infra.*
36. 17 U.S.C.A. § 101. "Display" would include, besides direct showings of a copy of a work, the projection of an image on a screen or other surface by any method, the transmission of an image by electronic or

The definition of "publicly" was previously described in connection with public performance.[37]

17.2 "Owner of Copyright"

The statute grants the five exclusive rights to "the owner of copyright"[38] a term not defined in the statute. However, the term "copyright owner" is defined, with respect to any one of the exclusive rights comprised in a copyright, to refer to the owner of that particular right.[39] An infringer of the copyright is anyone who violates any of the exclusive rights of the "copyright owner" or author as provided in section 106A.[40]

17.3 Qualifications on Scope of Exclusive Rights

The five exclusive rights are subject to thirteen qualifying provisions.[41] Seven of the qualifying provisions are captioned "Limitations on Exclusive Rights"; the other six are entitled "Scope of Exclusive Rights."

---

other means, and the showing of an image on a cathode ray tube, or similar viewing apparatus, connected with any sort of information storage and retrieval system. 1976 House Report 64; Broderbund Software v. Unison World, 231 U.S.P.Q. (BNA) 700 (N.D. Cal. 1986). The law respecting uses in conjunction with computers or similar information systems was frozen between December 31, 1977, and December 12, 1980. 17 U.S.C.A. § 117. *See* note 53 *infra*.

37. 17 U.S.C.A. § 101. *See* text accompanying notes 23–31 *supra*. For discussion of whether public display constituted publication divestiture of common-law copyright, *see* American Tobacco Co. v. Werckmeister, 207 U.S. 284 (1907).
38. 17 U.S.C.A. § 106. "Owner of copyright" is not defined. *See* chapter 7, note 51 *supra*.
39. 17 U.S.C.A. § 101.
40. 17 U.S.C.A. § 501(a) (since 1990 "anyone" includes State).
41. 17 U.S.C.A. § 106.

17.3[1] Limitations on Exclusive Rights

The seven limitations on exclusive rights relate to:

1. Fair use;[42]
2. Reproduction by libraries and archives;[43]
3. Effect of transfer of particular copy or phonorecord;[44]
4. Exemption of certain performances and displays;[45]
5. Secondary transmissions;[46]
6. Ephemeral recordings;[47]
7. Secondary transmissions by satellite carriers of superstations and network stations for private home viewing.[48]

---

42. *See* chapter 18 *infra*.
43. *See* chapter 19 *infra*.
44. Notwithstanding the exclusive rights of public distribution, the owner of a lawfully made copy or phonorecord or licensee may sell or otherwise dispose of the possession of that copy or phonorecord. 17 U.S.C.A. § 109(a). Notwithstanding the exclusive rights of public display, the owner of a lawfully made copy or licensee may publicly display the copy, either directly or by the projection of no more than one image at a time, to viewers present where the copy is located. § 109(c). These privileges do not extend to any person who has acquired possession of the copy or phonorecord from the copyright owner by rental, lease, loan, or otherwise, without acquiring ownership of it. § 109(d). *See* notes 21, 22 *supra*. *See also* chapter 7, note 2, *supra*, for discussion of "first-sale doctrine").

    The owner of a particular phonorecord may not, however, dispose of the possession of that phonorecord for commercial advantage by rental, lease, or lending, except a nonproft library or educational institution for nonprofit purposes. 17 U.S.C.A. § 109(b)(1); Record Rental Amendment of 1984, Pub. L. 98–450, 98 Stat. 1727 (Oct. 4, 1984). "Antitrust laws" are not affected by that provision. 17 U.S.C.A. § 109(b)(2). The usual remedies, except criminal penalties, apply to infringing rentals, leasings, or lendings. § 109(b)(4). The provision is not applicable to a phonorecord acquired before October 4, 1984, or after October 4, 1997. Pub. L. No. 98-450, § 4, 98 Stat. 1728 (1984).
45. *See* chapter 20 *infra*.
46. *See* chapter 25 *infra*.
47. *See* chapter 21 *infra*.
48. *See* chapter 26 *infra*.

17.3[2] Scope of Exclusive Rights

These eight qualifying provisions relate to:

1. Pictorial, graphic, and sculptural works;[49]

---

49. The exclusive right to reproduce a pictorial, graphic, or sculptural work includes the right to reproduce the work in or on any kind of article, whether useful or otherwise. 17 U.S.C.A. § 113(a). However, the rights in a work portraying a "useful article" (for definition, *see* 17 U.S.C.A. § 101) as such are no greater or lesser with respect to the making, distribution, or display of the useful article so portrayed than those under the 1909 Act. 17 U.S.C.A. § 113(b).

Architectural plans involve a sophisticated distinction between copyrights ("original" works of "authorship") and patents ("novel" "utilitarian" concepts). A structure, no matter how original, unless itself a work of art (e.g., sculpture), prior to 1990 was not protectable. *See* chapter 5, note 22, *supra*. Litigation involving such plans could be complicated. M.G.B. Homes, Inc. v. Ameron Homes, Inc., 903 F.2d 1486 (11th Cir. 1990) (ownership). Unauthorized copying of copyrightable elements may infringe copyright, but building a structure based on the plans traditionally were not within the exclusive rights afforded to such plans. Under the 1976 Act, protection of architectural plans was frozen as of December 31, 1977. 17 U.S.C.A. § 113(b). Congressional reports indicate no intent to enlarge rights under the 1909 Act.

The Berne Act inserted "including architectural plans" in the definition of "pictorial, graphic, and sculptural works" in 17 U.S.C.A. § 101, but this insertion did not affect their copyrightability or enlarge their protection. The Berne Convention (art. 9[1]) generally prescribes "reproduction" "in" any form or manner," and then (art. 9[2]) allows each adhering country to permit reproduction "in certain special cases." The Copyright Office proposed amendment of the Copyright Act to provide greater protection for architectural works. Copyright Office Report, COPYRIGHT IN WORKS OF ARCHITECTURE, 1989 CCH COPYRIGHT L. REP. ¶ 20,546 (June 19, 1989).

The "Architecture Works Copyright Protection Act," enacted as a rider to the Judicial Improvements Act of 1990, on December 1, 1990, broadly defines "architectural work" as:

> the design of a building as embodied in any tangible medium of expression, including a building, architectural plans, or drawings. The work includes the overall form as well as the arrangement and composition of spaces and elements in the design, but does not include individual standard features. (17 U.S.C.A. § 101.)

The 1990 legislation also adds "architectural works" to the seven pre-1990 "categories" of works of authorship. 17 U.S.C.A. § 102(a)(8).

The 1990 legislation, by creating a new category for "architectural works," purported to differentiate them from "pictorial, graphic, and sculptural works," and to avoid the limitation in the statutory definition of the latter that their "artistic craftsmanship" can be "identified separately from, and are capable of existing independently of," their "utilitarian aspects."

The added section 120 (captioned "Scope of exclusive rights in architectural works") is negative. It provides that a copyright in a "constructed" architectural work "does not include the right to prevent the making, distributing, or public display" of "pictorial representations" of the work, if the "building in which the work is embodied" is "located in or ordinarily visible from a public place." 17 U.S.C.A. § 120(a). Owners of buildings, notwithstanding § 106(a), may alter or destroy their buildings. 17 U.S.C.A. § 120(b).

The 1990 legislation, effective December 1, 1990, is applicable to any "architectural work" created on or after December 1, 1990. For works "unreconstructed but embodied in unpublished plans," protection will "terminate on December 31, 2002," unless the work is constructed by that date. Pub. L. 101-650, § 706 (Dec. 1, 1990).

Expressly not preempted are rights or remedies under state common law or statutes with respect to "state and local landmarks, historic preservation, zoning, or building codes, relating to architectural works." Pub. L. 101-650, § 301(b)(4).

Representative of the conventional approach is Dematriades v. Kaufman, 680 F. Supp. 658 (S.D.N.Y. 1988) (architectural plans to depict "useful articles" subject to section 113(b) limitations or use under pre–1978 law; construction of home based on plans not infringement; further copying of plans *qua* plans enjoined and impoundment of copies ordered). *See* Shipley, *Copyright Protection for Architectural Works*, 37 S. C. L. REV. 393 (1986); Note, 70 CORNELL L. REV. 81 (1984). Some lower federal courts have recently expanded the exclusive rights and remedies for copying plans, e.g., to enjoin building a structure based thereon or enhancing damages based thereon. Intown Enters., Inc. v. Barnes, 721 F. Supp. 1269 (N.D. Ga. 1989) (losses from using infringing plans to build house included in damages); (Arthur Ruttenberg Corp. v. Dawney, 647 F. Supp. 1214 (M.D. Fla. 1986) (willful copying of architectural plans and construction of house based thereon; $134,750 profits from sale of house, $10,000 attorneys' fees, and $1,002 costs awarded). *Cf.* Ga–On Homes, Inc. v. Spitzer Homes, Inc., 178 U.S.P.Q. (BNA) 183 (M.D. Fla. 1973) (case of first impression in district; oral opinion that copying of plans is gist of claim, and that design concept from peculiar arrangement of elements, which is appealing and salable product, can be copyrighted and may not be copied from memory, after visitation and possession

2. Sound recordings;[50]
3. Compulsory license for making and distributing phonorecords of nondramatic musical works;[51]

---

of plans, in building home), *aff'd mem.*, 492 F.2d 1241 (5th Cir. 1974). *See* Frankel Org. v. Tegman, 367 F. Supp. 1051 (E.D. Mich. 1973) ("A person should . . . be able to prevent another from copying copyrighted houseplans and using them to build the house."). Also in the case of a work lawfully produced in useful articles offered for sale or other distribution to the public, there is no right to prevent the making, distribution, or display of pictures or photographs of such articles in connection with advertisements or commentaries related to the distribution or display of such articles, or in connection with news reports. § 113(c). *See* Brenner, *A Two-Phase Approach to Copyrighting the Fine Arts*, 24 BULL. COPYRIGHT SOC'Y 85 (1976).

50. 17 U.S.C.A. § 114. For sound recordings, the exclusive rights are those of reproduction, adaptation, and public distribution, but not public performance. 17 U.S.C.A. §§ 114(a), 106(1)–(4). Reproduction rights are limited to the right to duplicate the sound recording in the form of phonorecords, or of copies of motion pictures and other audiovisual works, that directly or indirectly recapture the actual sounds fixed in the recording. Adaptation rights are limited to the right to prepare a derivative work in which the actual sounds fixed in the sound recording are rearranged, remixed, or otherwise altered in sequence or quality. Neither the exclusive rights of reproduction nor those of adaptation extend to the making or duplication of another sound recording that consists entirely of an independent fixation of other sounds, even though such sounds imitate or simulate those in the copyrighted sound recording. None of the exclusive rights apply to sound recordings included in educational television and radio programs (as defined in 47 U.S.C.A. § 397) distributed or transmitted by or through "public broadcasting entities" (*see* 17 U.S.C.A. § 118(g)), provided that the copies or phonorecords of such programs are not commercially distributed by or through broadcasting entities to the general public. 17 U.S.C.A. § 114(b). Prior to February 15, 1972, sound recordings were not protected by copyright. See chapter 5, note 26 *supra*. *See* Ringer, *The Unauthorized Duplication of Sound Recordings* (1957), *reprinted in* 1 STUDIES ON COPYRIGHT—ARTHUR FISHER MEMORIAL EDITION 117 (1963). Federal preemption of the protection of sound recordings fixed before February 15, 1972, is being delayed until February 15, 2047. *See* Sparkman, *Tape Pirates: The New "Buck"aneer$*, 21 COPYRIGHT L. SYMP. (ASCAP) 98 (1974).

51. *See* chapter 22 *infra*.

4. Public performances by means of coin-operated phonorecord players;[52]
5. Use in conjunction with computers and similar information systems;[53]

---

52. *See* chapter 23 *infra.*
53. No greater or lesser rights were afforded by the 1976 Act with respect to the use of copyrighted works in conjunction with automatic systems capable of storing, processing, retrieving, or transferring information, or in conjunction with any similar device, machine, or process, than under the 1909 Act. 1976 Act § 117. Regardless of the applicable law—1909 Act or state statutory or common law—any infringement action would be a federal action. Only the exclusive rights were frozen as of December 31, 1977. Otherwise, the provisions of the 1976 Act applied to computer programs, such as their copyrightability, ownership, duration, and formalities. 1976 House Report 116; Vault Corp. v. Quaid Software, Ltd., 847 F.2d 255 (5th Cir. 1988) (use of anticopying software in computer not infringement under section 117(1) since defendant was rightful possessor of copied software). Ramey, *A Copyright Labyrinth: Information Storage and Retrieval Systems,* 17 COPYRIGHT L. SYMP. (ASCAP) 1 (1969). Findings and recommendations for future legislation were left to the National Commission on New Technological Uses of Copyrighted Works (CONTU). NATIONAL COMM'N ON NEW TECHNOLOGICAL USES OF COPYRIGHTED WORKS, FINAL REPORT (July 31, 1978). The final report of CONTU, dated July 31, 1978, recommended statutory amendments (with partial dissent by Commissioner John Hersey): (1) to delete 1976 Act § 117, thereby making 17 U.S.C.A. applicable to all computer uses of copyrighted programs, data bases, and other copyrighted works fixed in computers; (2) to provide explicitly that computer programs, to the extent that they embody an author's original creation, are proper subject matter of copyright; and (3) to provide assurance that rightful possessors of copies of computer programs may use or adapt the copies for their use. Works created by the use of computers, to the extent that they are original works of authorship, should be afforded copyright protection, but no amendment was deemed necessary. Recommended were appropriate regulations regarding the affixation of notice and registration and deposit of works of authorship used in conjunction with computers, and periodic review of the recommendations, with special consideration of the impact of the legislation on competition and consumer prices in the computer and information industries and the effect on cultural values of including computer programs within the ambit of copyright.

In 1980, 1976 Act § 117 was replaced by a new § 117, which embodied the CONTU recommendations to clarify the law of copyrights of computer software, and a definition was added to § 101 of "computer program":

> A "computer program" is a set of statements or instructions to be used directly or indirectly in a computer in order to bring about a certain result.

Section 117 now provides that, notwithstanding § 106, it is not an infringement for the owner of a copy of a computer program to make or authorize the making of another copy or adaptation of the computer program under specified conditions. No preemption of state law protection of computer software, especially unfair competition and trade secret laws, was intended. Dickerman Assocs. v. Tiverton Bottled Gas Co., 222 U.S.P.Q.(BNA) 529 (D. Mass. 1984)(unauthorized copying of computer program found misappropriation of trade secrets). *Compare* Whelan Assocs. v. Jaslow Dental Laboratory, Inc., 797 F.2d 1222 (3d Cir. 1986)(computer program's structure, sequence, and organization, as well as literal code, protectible), *cert. denied*, 107 S. Ct. 877 (1987) *with* Plains Cotton Coop. Ass'n v. Goodpasture Computer Serv., 807 F.2d 1256 (5th Cir. 1987); Apple Computer, Inc. v. Formula Int'l, Inc., 725 F.2d 521 (9th Cir. 1984)(operating system computer programs embodied in "ROMs" held copyrightable); Apple Computer, Inc. v. Franklin Computer Corp., 714 F.2d 1240 (3d Cir. 1983)(computer program, whether in source or object code, embodied in ROM chip copyrightable), *cert. dismissed*, 464 U.S. 1033 (1984); Williams Elecs., Inc. v. Artic Int'l, Inc., 685 F.2d 870 (3d Cir. 1982)(computer program expressed in object code and stored only in ROM copyrightable); Rand McNally & Co. v. Fleet Management Sys., Inc., 591 F. Supp. 726 (N.D. Ill. 1983)(inputting of copyrighted data into computer database held infringement); Tandy Corp. v. Personal Micro Computers, Inc., 524 F. Supp. 171 (N.D. Cal. 1981)(duplication of computer chips held infringement of copyrighted computer programs); Synercon Technology, Inc. v. University Computing Co., 462 F. Supp. 1003 (N.D. Tex. 1978)(discussing (1) computer input, (2) storage of input by memory, (3) control unit receiving data from memory and giving instructions, (4) carrying out of commands, and (5) output); Copyright Office Circular R65 (Copyright Registration for Automated Databases); S. MANDELL, COMPUTERS, DATA PROCESSING, AND THE LAW (1984); Symposium, 7 W. NEW ENG. L. REV. 397–790 (1985). For discussion of the special protection of "mask works" under the Semiconductor Chip Protection Act of 1984, *see* chapter 32 *infra*.

In 1990, the Computer Software Rental Amendment Act was enacted as a rider to the Judicial Improvements Act of 1990, on December 1, 1990. The legislation, in effect, added a "computer program (including any tape, disk, or other medium embodying such pro-

6. Use of certain works in connection with noncommercial broadcasting;[54]
7. Attribution and integrity of works of visual art;[55]
8. Architectural works.[56]

---

gram)" to exemption from the first-sale doctrine made for phonorecords under the Phonorecord Rental Amendment of 1984. The 1990 amendments, for a "lawfully made copy of a computer program," expressly allow transfers of possession by nonprofit educational institutions. The amendments do not apply to embodied computer programs that cannot be copied during "ordinary operation and use" or computer programs "designed for playing video games." 17 U.S.C.A. § 109(b)(1)(A). Public performances or displays of electronic audiovisual games in coin-operated equipment are governed by new section 109(e), which has only prospective application. Except for the audiovisual-games provision (Dec. 1, 1991–Oct. 1, 1995), the 1990 amendments became effective on December 1, 1990, and terminate on October 1, 1995.

The same principles applicable to computers generally have been applied to audiovisual games. M. Kramer Mfg. Co. v. Andrews, 783 F.2d 427 (4th Cir. 1986)(copyright in audiovisual game held to protect underlying computer program to extent of game's expression embodied therein); Midway Mfg. Co. v. Artic Int'l, Inc., 704 F.2d 1009 (7th Cir.) (video game protected as audiovisual work; distinctive set of images and sounds stored in circuit boards), *cert. denied*, 464 U.S. 823 (1983); Atari, Inc. v. North Am. Phillips Consumer Elecs. Corp., 672 F.2d 607 (7th Cir.) (protecting image-chase "Pac-Man" game against "K.C. Munchkin"; expression of principal characters emphasized; play mode varied by human intervention, but limited repetitive sequences of sight and sound constituted fixation), *cert. denied*, 450 U.S. 880 (1982); Stern Elecs., Inc. v. Kaufman, 669 F.2d 852 (2d Cir. 1982) (audiovisual display of electronic video game held copyrightable even though underlying computer program not copyrighted); Annot., 66 A.L.R. Fed. 490 (1982) (copyrightability of video games). See Red Baron–Franklin Park, Inc. v. Taito Corp., 883 F.2d 275 (4th Cir. 1989) (first-sale doctrine no defense for public performance of video game by arcade operator), *cert. denied*, 110 S. Ct. 869 (1990). *Cf.* 17 U.S.C.A. § 109(e) (until Oct. 1, 1995).

54. *See* chapter 24 *infra*.
55. Pub. L. 101-650, § 608 (Dec. 1, 1990).
56. Pub. L. 101-650, § 708 (Dec. 1, 1990).

17.4 Moral Rights

"Moral rights" *(droit moral)* are recognized in varying degrees under the Berne Union system, and may be perpetual in duration and inalienable. They are intended to safeguard the author's artistic reputation (noneconomic) as distinguished from the proprietary aspect (economic) of the copyright. They include the rights:

1. To be known as the author of the work;
2. To prevent others from being named as the author of the work;
3. To prevent others from falsely attributing to one the authorship of work that one has not in fact written;
4. To prevent others from making deforming changes in one's work;
5. To withdraw a published work from distribution if it no longer represents the views of the author;
6. To prevent others from using the work or the author's name in such a way as to reflect on the author's professional standing.[57]

---

57. R. LERNER & J. BRESLER, ART LAW: THE GUIDE FOR COLLECTORS, INVESTORS, DEALERS, AND ARTISTS 417–76 (1989); Strauss, *The Moral Right of the Author* (1959), *reprinted in* 2 STUDIES ON COPYRIGHT—ARTHUR FISHER MEMORIAL EDITION 963 (1963); Kwall, *Copyright and Moral Rights: Is an American Marriage Possible?* 38 VAND. L. REV. 1 (1985); Amarnick, *American Recognition of the Moral Right: Issues and Options*, 29 COPYRIGHT L. SYMP. (ASCAP) 31 (1983); Steilbich, *Moral Right of Ownership of Intellectual Property*, 6 MEM. ST. U.L. REV. 45 (1976); Roeder, *The Doctrine of Moral Right: A Study in the Law of Artists, Authors and Creators*, 53 HARV. L. REV. 554 (1940); Note, *Moral Rights and the Realistic Limits of Artistic Control*, 14 GOLDEN GATE U.L. REV. 447 (1984).

Colorization of older black-and-white films has raised moral rights issues. *See* Notes, 64 N.Y.U. L. REV. 628 (1989); 16 HOFSTRA L. REV. 503 (1988); 5 CARDOZO ARTS & ENT. L.J. 497 (1986). Colorized films

The Berne Act declared that it, with existing law, satisfied the "obligations of the United States in adhering to the Berne Convention and no further rights or interests shall be recognized or created for that purpose."[58] This declaration

---

on the National Film Registry must be so labeled. 55 Fed. Reg. 32,566 (Sept. 29, 1990).

Protection comparable to moral rights sometimes has been afforded under common-law principles of unfair competition (false attribution of authorship was analogized to passing off; nonattribution, to reverse passing off), defamation (problem of deceased author), invasion of privacy or the right of publicity, or breach of contract. Damick, *The Right of Personality: A Common-Law Basis for the Protection of the Moral Rights of Authors*, 23 GA. L. REV. 97 (1985); Hathaway, *American Law Analogues to the Paternity Element of the Doctrine of Moral Right: Is the Creative Artist in America Really Protected?*, 30 COPYRIGHT L. SYMP. (ASCAP) 121 (1983); Maslow, *Droit Moral and Sections 43(a) and 44(i) of the Lanham Act—A Judicial Shell Game?*, 48 GEO. WASH. L. REV. 377 (1980); Solomon, *Monty Python and the Lanham Act: In Search of the Moral Right*, 30 RUTGERS L. REV. 452 (1977); Treece, *American Law Analogues of the Author's "Moral Right,"* 16 AM. J. COMP. L. 487 (1968).

Some states have enacted statutes prohibiting mutilation or other invasions of moral rights in the fine arts, e.g., CAL. CIV. CODE § 987(a) (West Supp. 1988); N.Y. ARTS & CULT. AFF. LAW § 14.03 (McKinney 1988). In this respect, state or common law was expressly preserved. Berne Act § 3(b). *See* Engdahl, *Moral Rights in State Statutes: A Comparison of the California Art Preservation Act and the New York Artists' Authorship Act*, 34 COPYRIGHT L. SYMP. (ASCAP) 203 (1987); Damich, *The New York Artists Authorship Rights Act: A Comparative Critique*, 84 COLUM L. REV. 1733 (1984); Karlen, *Moral Rights in California*, 19 SAN DIEGO L. REV. 675 (1982). Quaere, as to the effect of federal preemption.

False attribution of authorship may violate the trademark law. 15 U.S.C.A. §§ 1125(a), 1126(i) (prohibition against false designation of origin); Smith v. Montoro, 648 F.2d 602 (9th Cir. 1981); Paramount Pictures Corp. v. Video Broadcasting Sys., Inc., 724 F. Supp. 808 (D. Kan. 1989) (insertion of lead-in advertisement to videocassettes held not violative of "moral rights" or preparation of derivative work); Joseph J. Legat Architects v. United States Dev. Corp., 625 F. Supp. 293 (N.D. Ill. 1985) (wrongful attribution of authorship held to infringe).

58. Berne Act § 2(3).

purportedly met the Convention's recognition of moral rights.[59] The Berne Act expressly states that the Convention provisions, the United States adherence thereto, and satisfaction of the United States obligations thereunder:

> do not expand or reduce any right of an author of a work, whether claimed under Federal, State, or the common law—
> (1) to claim authorship of the work; or
> (2) to object to any distortion, mutilation, or other modification of, or other derogatory action in relation to, the work that would prejudice the author's honor or reputation.[60]

Although this language parroted Berne Convention article 6 *bis*, it has been questioned whether the hodgepodge of some recent state statutes on moral rights and scattered court decisions applying various common-law principles and federal and state unfair competition and like statutes complied sufficiently with the Berne Union mandate. But then the Berne Union countries themselves afford varying degrees of protection for moral rights.

In any event, the Visual Artists Rights Act, as a copyright rider to the Judicial Improvements Act of 1990, added a lengthy definition of "work of visual art,"[61] and a new section 106A on "attribution and integrity" rights, effective June 1, 1991.[62]

---

59. Berne Convention art. 6 *bis*.
60. Berne Act § 3(b). *See Final Report of the Ad Hoc Working Group on U.S. Adherence to the Berne Convention*, 10 COLUM.–V.L.A. J.L. & ARTS 513, 547–57 (1986).
61. 17 U.S.C.A. § 101. The definition is expressed in both positive and negative terms. A "work of visual art" is limited to a work "existing in a single copy" or in a "limited edition of 200 copies or fewer" signed by (or for "fabricated sculptures" bearing the signature or "other identifying mark" of), and "consecutively numbered by," the author. Works expressly not included within the definition are, *inter alia*, motion pictures and works made for hire.
62. Pub. L. No. 101-533, §§ 603, 609 (Dec. 1, 1990).

The "attribution and integrity" rights apply to works of visual art:[63]

1. Created before June 1, 1991, but "title" to which has not, as of June 1, 1991, been transferred to another;
2. Created on or after June 1, 1991, but not to any "destruction, distortion, mutilation," or other proscribed "modification," which occurred before June 1, 1991.

The "author of a work of visual art" has the right:[64]

1. To claim authorship of the work;
2. To prevent the use of "his or her name" as the author of any work of visual art "he or she" did not create;
3. To prevent the use of "his or her name" as the author of any "distortion, mutilation, or other modification" "prejudicial to his or her honor or reputation";
4. Subject to specified limitations,[65] to prevent "intentional" *distortion, mutilation, or other modification,*[66] or to prevent any "intentional or grossly negligent" *destruction* of a work of "recognized stature."[67]

Several exceptions are enumerated.[68]

---

63. Pub. L. No. 101-533, § 610(b).
64. 17 U.S.C.A. § 106A (only "author," whether or not "author" is "copyright owner"; co-authors of joint work are co-owners of "attribution and integrity" rights).
65. 17 U.S.C.A. § 106A(c)(3).
66. 17 U.S.C.A. § 106A(a)(3)(A).
67. 17 U.S.C.A. § 106A(a)(3)(B).
68. 17 U.S.C.A. § 106A(c) (modification resulting from passage of time or inherent nature of materials; result of conservation or of public presentation, including lighting and placement, unless caused by gross negligence).

The duration of "attribution and integrity rights" is the life of the author.[69]

"Attribution and integrity" rights may not be "transferred," but may be "waived" by an express "written instrument signed by the author that meets the statutory requirements."[70]

Ownership of "attribution and integrity" rights is distinct from ownership of any copy or of a copyright or any exclusive right thereunder.[71]

There are rather complicated provisions on the removal of works of visual art from buildings.[72] A "system of records" is mandated in that connection.[73]

On or after June 1, 1991, the "attribution and integrity" rights are preemptive.[74]

Infringement actions for violators of "attribution and integrity" rights may be brought by the author.[75] Criminal penalties are expressly excluded.[76] Registration is not a prerequisite to suit and certain remedies.[77]

Studies and reports by the Register of Copyrights on waivers of "attribution and integrity" rights are mandated.[78] A Copyright Office study on "resale royalties" (*droit de suite*) also is mandated.[79]

---

69. 17 U.S.C.A. § 106A(d). For a joint work, the term is for the life of the last surviving author. All terms run to the end of the calendar year in which they would otherwise expire.
70. 17 U.S.C.A. § 106A(e)(1). Waiver by one co-author of joint work waives such rights for all. *Id.* Presumably waivers should be recorded to provide data for the Copyright Office study on waivers.
71. 17 U.S.C.A. § 106A(e)(2). Transfers of copyright or of a copy do not constitute waivers.
72. 17 U.S.C.A. § 113(d)(1), (2).
73. 17 U.S.C.A. § 113(d)(3).
74. 17 U.S.C.A. § 301(f).
75. 17 U.S.C.A. § 501(a).
76. 17 U.S.C.A. § 507(f).
77. 17 U.S.C.A. § 411(a).
78. Pub. L. No. 101-553, § 608(a) (Dec. 1, 1990).
79. Pub. L. No. 101-553, § 608(b) (effective Dec. 1, 1990). See note 81 *infra*.

Compliance with the first amendment is required![80]

17.5 Rights Not Recognized

Among the rights not recognized are:

1. *Droit de suite*
2. Performance rights

17.5[1] *Droit de Suite*

The *droit de suite*, recognized in only a few countries, is the right of an artist to "follow" or participate in the proceeds realized from the resale of the tangible embodiment of the work.[81]

---

80. Pub. L. No. 101-553, § 609.

81. Price *Governmental Policy and Economic Security for Artists: The Case of the* Droit de Suite, 77 YALE L.J. 1333 (1968); Plaissant, *The Protection of* Droit Moral *and* Droit de Suite, 11 COLUM.–V.L.A. J.L. & ARTS 157 (1986); Recht, *Has the* "Droit de Suite" *a Place in Copyright?*, 3 UNESCO COPYRIGHT BULL. (No. 1) 51 (1950) (answered in the negative). The *droit de suite* has been recognized in California in the 1976 Resale Royalties Act. Quaere, as to federal preemption. Ashley, *A Critical Comment on California* Droit de Suite, *Civil Code Section 986*, 29 HASTINGS L.J. 249 (1977); Comment, *The* Droit de Suite *Has Arrived, Can It Survive in California as It Has in Calais?*, 11 CREIGHTON L. REV. 529 (1977). Morseburg v. Balyon, 621 F.2d 972 (9th Cir.) (California Resale Royalties Act providing for art-proceeds right held not preempted by 1909 Act because both acts function harmoniously rather than discordantly), *cert. denied*, 449 U.S. 983 (1980). *See* chapter 4, note 28, *supra*, as to preemption of exclusive right of public distribution and nonpreemption of ownership of material objects in which copyrighted works are embodied. Federal legislation has been introduced to recognize the *droit de suite*. *Symposium, Artists' Rights, The Kennedy Proposal to Amend the Copyright Law*, 7 CARDOZO ARTS & ENT. L.J. 227 (1989). Quaere, as to whether the legislation is constitutional. The Visual Artists Rights Act of 1990 requires the Register of Copyrights, in consultation with the Chair of the National Endowment for the Arts and other

17.5[2] Performance Rights

Performance rights of artists, recorders, and broadcasters, known as "neighboring rights" or "related rights" because of their neighboring relationship to copyright, are recognized in a growing number of countries.[82] The Register of Copyrights has recommended that performance rights in sound recordings be accorded performers and copyright owners.[83]

"groups," to conduct a "study" on the "feasibility" of implementing a *droit de suite*, and to report to Congress no later than June 1, 1992. Pub. L. No. 101-553, §§ 608, 610(c) (Dec. 1, 1990). Public domain fees for the National Endowment for the Arts have been proposed.

82. Hayes, *Performance Rights in Sound Recordings: How Far to the Horizon?*, 27 COPYRIGHT L. SYMP. (ASCAP) 113 (1982); Lang, Performance and the Right of the Performing Artist, 21 COPYRIGHT L. SYMP. (ASCAP) 69 (1974); Phillips, *Related Rights and American Copyright Law: Compatible or Incompatible?*, 10 COPYRIGHT L. SYMP. (ASCAP) 219 (1959). The Rome Convention of 1961, which has not been ratified by the United States, dealt with so-called neighboring or related rights.
83. *See* note 31 *supra*.

18. Fair Use

A scholar builds on the work of predecessors.
A dwarf standing on the shoulders of a giant can see farther than the giant himself.[1]

Fair use is often defined as the "privilege in others than the owner to use the copyrighted material in a reasonable manner" without consent, "notwithstanding the monopoly granted to the owner."[2]

The 1976 Act was the first statutory recognition of the fair use doctrine,[3] although it had been judicially recognized under federal copyright statutes at least since 1841. As Mr. Justice Story stated:[4]

---

1. Chafee, *Reflections on the Law of Copyright*. 45 COLUM. L. REV. 508, 511 (1945). The quotation itself is an example of fair use in making derivative works or works using material authored by others. The idea in more or less similar expression is found in earlier writings, at least as far back as Lucan (A.D. 39–65).
2. Rosemont Enters. v. Random House, Inc., 366 F.2d 303, 306 (2d Cir. 1966), *cert. denied,* 385 U.S. 1009 (1967). A copyright purist might well object to calling copyright a "monopoly." Fair use has been characterized as an equitable rule of reason based on the user's acting fairly and in good faith. Weissmann v. Freeman, 868 F.2d 1113 (2d Cir. 1989).
3. 17 U.S.C.A. § 107. *Compare* 1976 House Report 65–74 *with* 1975 Senate Report 61–67. The differing interpretations of the same or similar statutory fair use language are detailed in Copyright Office Circular R21 (Reproduction of Copyrighted Works by Educators and Libraries).
4. Folson v. Marsh, 9 F. Cas. 342, 348 (C.C.D. Mass. 1841) (No. 4,901)

> In short we must often, in deciding questions of this sort, look to the nature and objects of the selections made, the quantity and value of materials used, and the degree to which the use may prejudice the sale, or diminish the profits, or supersede the objects, of the original work.

Whether or not the doctrine applied to common-law copyright has been irrelevant since January 1, 1978, when all copyrights became federal statutory copyrights. Courts may allow broader fair use for published than for unpublished works,[5] for factual than for fictional works,[6] and for paro-

---

(Story, J.) ("justifiable use"; terms "fair use" apparently first used in 1865). The doctrine is essentially a rule of reason. Not until 1984 did the United States Supreme Court consider the doctrine of fair use, and then by a five–four divided Court after reargument. *See* text accompanying notes 62–74, *infra.*

5. New Era Publications Int'l v. Henry Holt & Co., 873 F.2d 576 (2d Cir. 1989) (under second factor, fact that used work is unpublished favors plaintiff), *petition for reh'g en banc denied*, 884 F.2d 659 (2d Cir. 1989) (7–5) (fair use of unpublished work rare; concurring opinion: copying for accurate portrayal may be fair use), *cert. denied*, 110 S. Ct. 1168 (1990); Salinger v. Random House, Inc., 650 F. Supp. 413 (S.D.N.Y. 1986)(fair use applicable to unpublished works, although sparingly to protect author's artistic reputation and control over initial presentation), *rev'd*, 811 F.2d 90 (2d Cir.) (quotation from unpublished letters in biography without consent of their author, who was subject of biography; quoting or closely paraphrasing at least one-third of seventy-seven letters and 10 percent of forty-two other letters found excessive), *cert. denied*, 484 U.S. 890 (1987); Haberman v. Hustler Magazine, 626 F. Supp. 201 (D. Mass. 1986). *See also* Harper & Row, Publishers, Inc. v. Nation Enters., 471 U.S. 539, 553–55 (1985) ("under ordinary circumstances" right of first publication outweighs fair use defense); Association of Am. Medical Colleges v. Mikaelian, 571 F. Supp. 144 (E.D. Pa. 1983), *aff'd without opinion*, 734 F.2d 3 (3d Cir. 1984). Bills have been introduced to expand the fair use of unpublished works.
6. Factual works are subject to broader fair use than are fictional works; fictional works may make fair use of factual works, but no more individualized expression than necessary to state the facts. Narell v. Freeman, 872 F.2d 907 (9th Cir. 1989) (novelist's use of historical facts quoted or paraphrased from plaintiff's work held fair use; two works not substantially similar under extrinsic test; nor total concept and feel of works under intrinsic test); Hoehling v. Universal City Studios, Inc., 618 F.2d 972, 978 (2d Cir.) *(Who Destroyed the Hindenburg?)*

("broad latitude must be granted to subsequent authors who make use of historical subject matter, including theories or plots"), *cert. denied*, 449 U.S. 841 (1980). Fair use narrows as to the use of a compilation after the facts have been collected, selected, and arranged in the compilation. United Tel. Co. v. Johnson Publishing Co., 855 F.2d 604 (8th Cir. 1988) (no new canvas by defendant of new listings); Southern Bell Tel. & Tel. Co. v. Associated Tel. Directories, 756 F.2d 801 (11th Cir. 1985). Use for verification after independent collection of data can be fair use. Central Tel. Co. v. Johnson Publishing Co., 526 F. Supp. 838 (D. Colo. 1981)(converse sequence not fair use). Francione, *The Standards for Copyright Infringement, and Fair Use of Factual Works*, 134 U. PA. L. REV. 519 (1986).

Biographies have presented fair use problems. Harper & Row, Publishers, Inc. v. Nation Enters., note 5 *supra*; New Era Publications Int'l v. Carol Publishing Group, 14 U.S.P.Q. (BNA) 2030 (2d Cir. 1990) (use of quotations from published writings of Scientology Church founder in critical biography held fair use); Iowa State Univ. Research Found. v. American Broadcasting Cos., 621 F.2d 57 (2d Cir. 1980) (use of three short segments from biographical film in television network presentation in part for commercial exploitation held unlawful appropriation of expression of factual information); Wright v. Warner Books, Inc., Copyright L. Rep. (CCH) ¶ 26,634 (S.D.N.Y. 1990) (fair use; no adverse market effect; biographer's use of quotations and paraphrases from published (some out-of-print) and unpublished works minimal and primarily for informational purposes); Craft v. Kobler, 667 F. Supp. 120 (S.D.N.Y. 1987) (reproduction of words of composer in biography too numerous and with too little instructional justification to constitute fair use); Radji v. Khakbaz, 607 F. Supp. 1296 (D.D.C. 1985). Among the problems is the use in biographies of reports of interviews with others. Maxtone-Graham v. Burtchaell, 631 F. Supp. 1432 (S.D.N.Y.), *aff'd*, 803 F.2d 1253 (2d Cir. 1986); Sicrol v. Newsweek Magazine, 503 F. Supp. 146 (D. Colo 1980)(where assignment received from interviewer).

The use of copyrighted questions, even of a few out of thousands, has been held excessive, sometimes on the ground that such use rendered the questions worthless. Educational Testing Servs. v. Katzman, 793 F.2d 533 (3d Cir. 1986); Association of Am. Medical Colleges v. Mikaelian, note 5 *supra;* Rubin v. Boston Magazine Co., 645 F.2d 80 (1st Cir. 1981). On the use of materials from current events, *compare* Italian Book Corp. v. American Broadcasting Cos., 458 F. Supp. 65 (S.D.N.Y. 1978) (telecast of music played in parade held fair use) *with* New Boston Television, Inc. v. Entertainment Sports Programming Networks, Inc., 215 U.S.P.Q. (BNA) 755 (D. Mass. 1981)(videotaping of highlights of baseball games for use in news telecasts held use of expression beyond fair use). *See* Georgia Television Co. v. News Clips of Atlanta, Inc., 718 F. Supp. 939 (N.D. Ga. 1989) (videotaping of

dies than for other reproductions.[7] Because of the fair use doctrine, it can be argued that the parameters of freedom of expression under the first amendment are coextensive with those of fair use.[8] This view is buttressed by the idea-expression dichotomy. Verbatim quotation may be justifiable for more accurate reporting.[9]

18.1 In General

The 1976 Act[10] merely attempted to restate the judicially evolved doctrine with "no disposition to freeze" and "not to

---

television news broadcasts for sale of clippings more than personal noncommercial use preliminarily enjoined; no impoundment but $125,000 security bond ordered).

Use of data from maps has been litigated. *Compare* Rand McNally & Co. v. Fleet Management Sys., Inc., 600 F. Supp. 933 (N.D. Ill. 1984)(computerizing highway mileage not fair use) *with* Key Maps, Inc. v. Pruitt, 470 F. Supp. 33 (S.D. Tex. 1978) (county fire marshall's map based on thoroughfare map fair use).

Use of film clips or tapes may depend on amount and purpose. Roy Export Co. Establishment v. Columbia Broadcasting Sys., Inc., 672 F.2d 1095 (2d Cir. 1982)(use of entire film clip compilation as part of telecast on Charles Chaplin's death held beyond fair use), *cert. denied*, 459 U.S. 826 (1982); Bruzzone v. Miller Brewing Co., 202 U.S.P.Q. (BNA) 809 (N.D. Cal. 1979)(videotaping and use of television for market research on audience reaction held fair use); Keep Thomson Governor Comm. v. Citizens for Gallen Comm., 457 F. Supp. 957 (D.N.H. 1978)(use of fifteen-second segment from political candidate's theme song held fair use).

7. *See* note 15 *infra*.
8. Complementing the fair use doctrine is the idea-expression dichatomy. *See* New Era Publications Int'l v. Henry Holt & Co., 873 F.2d 576 (2d Cir. 1989) (denial of permanent injunction because of laches affirmed; dictum that second factor militated against fair use of unpublished work and that copyright law concepts of ideas vs. expression and fair use adequately recognized first amendment concerns; concurring opinion expressed first amendment concerns but agreed that noninjunctive remedies offered sound balance), *cert. denied*, 110 S. Ct. 1168 (1990); Patterson, *Free Speech, Copyright, and Fair Use*, 40 VAND. L. REV. 1 (1987); Roy Export Co. Establishment v. Columbia Broadcasting Sys., Inc., note 6 *supra* (refusing to recognize that first amendment permitted use beyond fair use).
9. Consumers Union v. General Signal Corp., 724 F.2d 1044 (2d Cir.

change, narrow, or enlarge it in any way."[11] The doctrine is a means of balancing the exclusive rights of the copyright holder with the public interest in the dissemination of information.[12]

When a "use"[13] is "fair," there is no "infringement of copyright."[14] This raises the question of who has the burden of proving that the use is fair or not fair. Most courts have held that the party asserting the fair use exception carries the burden of persuasion since the exception is an affirmative defense.[15]

The statute provides no definitions of fair use, but sug-

1983) (2–1), *cert. denied,* 105 S. Ct. 100 (1984); Haberman v. Hustler Magazine, 626 F. Supp. 201 (D. Mass. 1986).

10. 17 U.S.C.A. § 107; L. SELTZER, EXEMPTIONS AND FAIR USE OF COPYRIGHT (1978); Seidel, *The Doctrine of Fair Use and 17 U.S.C. Sections 102, 107 and 108,* 6 A.P.L.A. Q.J. 31 (1978); Freid, *Fair Use and the New Act,* 22 N.Y.L. SCH. L. REV. 497 (1977); Annot., 23 A.L.R.3d 139 (1969).

11. 1976 House Report 66; Latman, *Fair Use of Copyrighted Works* (1958), *reprinted in* 2 STUDIES ON COPYRIGHT—ARTHUR FISHER MEMORIAL EDITION 871 (1963); Leval, *Toward a Fair Use Standard,* 103 HARV. L. REV. 1105 (1990); Weinreb, Fair's Fair: A Comment on the Fair Use Doctrine, 103 HARV. L. REV. 1137 (1990); Miner, *Exploiting Stolen Text: Fair Use or Foul Play?* 37 J. COPYRIGHT SOC'Y 1 (1989); Newman, *Not the End of History: The Second Circuit Struggles with Fair Use,* 37 J. COPYRIGHT SOC'Y 12 (1989); Leval, *Fair Use or Foul?,* 36 J. COPYRIGHT SOC'Y 167 (1989); Fisher, *Reconstructing the Fair Use Doctrine,* 101 HARV. L. REV. 1659 (1988); Lawrence, *Fair Use: Evidence of Change in a Traditional Doctrine,* 27 COPYRIGHT L. SYMP. (ASCAP) 71 (1982).

12. Iowa State Univ. Research Found. v. American Broadcasting Cos., 621 F.2d 57, 60 (2d Cir. 1980)(fair use doctrine "permits courts to avoid rigid application of the copyright statute when, on occasion, it would stifle the very creativity which that law is designed to foster"); Meeropol v. Nizer, 560 F.2d 1061 (2d Cir. 1977), *cert. denied,* 434 U.S. 1013 (1978).

13. "Use" is neither defined nor included in the statutory enumeration of rights. Presumably, use refers to any of the bundle of rights, as indicated by the phrase "use by reproduction . . . or by any other means." 17 U.S.C.A. § 107.

14. 17 U.S.C.A. § 107; Harper & Row, Publishers, Inc. v. Nation Enters., note 5 *supra.*

15. Meeropol v. Nizer, note 12 *supra* (mixed questions of law and fact).

gests criteria. Whether a use is fair depends upon:

1. The "purpose" of the use
2. At least four "factors"

18.2 Purposes

Use can be "fair" for "purposes" "such as"[16] criticism,

---

16. "Such as" is defined as "illustrative and not limitative." 17 U.S.C.A. § 101. *See* Nimmer, *Reflections on the Problem of Parody—Infringement*, 17 COPYRIGHT L. SYMP. (ASCAP) 133 (1969). Permission to prepare and use a parody obviously is difficult to obtain from the copyright holder. The only parody case to reach the United State Supreme Court was affirmed by a Court divided four-four. Benny v. Loew's, Inc., 239 F.2d 532 (9th Cir. 1956), *aff'd by equally divided Court per curiam*, 356 U.S. 43 (1958)("Autolite's" tracking of parodied "Gas Light" in locale, period, setting, characters, story points, incidents, climax, and much dialog held substantial taking beyond fair use); Fisher v. Dees, 794 F.2d 431 (9th Cir. 1986) ("When Sunny Gets Blue" parodied as "When Sonny Sniffs Glue"); (parody may exceed conjuring up original when necessary to accomplish parodic purpose; effect on demand for original critical: "Biting criticism suppresses demand; copyright infringement usurps it"); MCA v. Wilson, 677 F.2d 180 (2d Cir. 1981) (2–1) ("dirty lyrics" for "Boogie Woogie Bugle Boy" neither parody nor humorous commentary fair use); Warner Bros. v. American Broadcasting Cos., 654 F.2d 204 (2d Cir. 1981)("The Greatest American Hero" parody of "Superman" held fair use; no more used than to recall or conjure up subject); Elsmere Music, Inc. v. National Broadcasting Co., 623 F.2d 252 (2d Cir. 1980) (song "I Love Sodom" publicly performed to music of "I Love New York" held parody and fair use); Dallas Cowboy Cheerleaders, Inc. v. Scoreboard Posters, Inc., 600 F.2d 1184 (5th Cir. 1979)(partially nude cheerleaders poster held not parody or fair use of poster); Walt Disney Prods. v. Air Pirates, 581 F.2d 751 (9th Cir. 1978), *cert. denied*, 439 U.S. 1132 (1979)(parody of personalities of readily identifiable characters in unwholesome manner held not fair use because more copied than necessary to recall or conjure up object of satire); Berlin v. E.C. Publications, Inc., 329 F.2d 541 (2d Cir.)(test: whether parodist appropriated greater amount of original work than necessary to "recall or conjure up" object of satire), *cert. denied*, 379 U.S. 822 (1964); Tin Pan Apple, Inc. v. Miller Brewing Co., 537 F. Supp. 826 (S.D.N.Y. 1990) (television commercial held not fair use parody of Fat Boys, who had refused to do commercial); Steinberg v. Columbia Pictures Indus., 663 F. Supp. 706 (S.D.N.Y. 1987) (plaintiff's famous *New*

comment, news reporting, teaching (including multiple copies for classroom use),[17] scholarship, or research.[18]

Yorker cover illustration of New Yorker's parochial view of world held infringed by defendant's promotional poster for motion picture *Moscow on the Hudson*); DC Comics, Inc. v. Unlimited Monkey Business, Inc., 598 F. Supp. 110 (N.D. Ga. 1984)(singing telegrams using elements of "Superman" and "Wonder Woman" characters in creating "Super Stud" and "Wonder Wench," including most recognizable expressions, to tarnish images held not fair use); Bisceglia, *Parody and Copyright Protection: Turning the Balancing Act into a Juggling Act*, 34 COPYRIGHT L. SYMP. (ASCAP) 1 (1987); Clemmons, *Author v. Parodist: Striking a Compromise*, 33 COPYRIGHT L. SYMP. (ASCAP) 35 (1987); Bernstein, *Parody and Fair Use in Copyright Law*, 31 COPYRIGHT L. SYMP. (ASCAP) 1 (1984); Comment, *Parody, Copyrights and the First Amendment*, 10 U.S.F. L. REV. 564 (1976); Annot., 75 A.L.R. Fed. 822 (1985).

17. The phrase "including multiple copies for classroom use," added by the House substitute bill, recognized that, "under the proper circumstances of fairness," the doctrine of fair use could be applied to reproductions of multiple copies for the members of a class. 1976 House Report 66. A proposed specific exemption freeing certain reproductions of copyrighted works for "educational and scholarly purposes" from copyright control was rejected. *Id.* 66–67.

18. 17 U.S.C.A. § 107. *But see* Sony Corp. v. Universal City Studios, Inc., *infra* note 63 (fair use found, 5 to 4, where none of such uses). Such uses have been called "productive" rather than ordinary." For a more detailed list, *see* 1976 House Report 65:

> The examples enumerated at page 24 of the Register's 1961 Report, while by no means exhaustive, give some idea of the sort of activities the courts might regard as fair use under the circumstances: "quotation of excerpts in a review or criticism for purposes of illustration or comment; quotation of short passages in a scholarly or technical work, for illustration or clarification of the author's observations; use in a parody of some of the content of the work parodied; summary of an address or article, with brief quotations, in a news report; reproduction by a library of a portion of a work to replace part of a damaged copy; reproduction by a teacher or student of a small part of a work to illustrate a lesson; reproduction of a work in legislative or judicial proceedings or reports; incidental and fortuitous reproduction, in a newsreel or broadcast, of a work located in the scene of an event being reported.

Purpose not inherently productive or creative does not rule out fair

18.3 Factors

In determining whether the use "in any particular case"[19] is a fair use, the "factors" to be considered shall "include":[20]

---

use without consideration of the four factors. Pacific & S. Co. v. Duncan, 744 F.2d 1490 (11th Cir. 1984), *cert. denied*, 471 U.S. 1004 (1985). For discussion of productive use, compare majority and minority opinions in Sony Corp. v. Universal City Studios, Inc., note 63 *infra*. Public interest broadens fair use. Maxtone-Graham v. Burtchaell, 631 F. Supp. 1432 (S.D.N.Y.) (public interest in abortion held to broaden fair use as applied to extensive quotations of interviews; only 4.3 percent of words used, and plaintiff's work was about to go out of print), *aff'd*, 803 F.2d 1253 (2d Cir. 1986); Time, Inc. v. Bernard Geis Assocs., 293 F. Supp. 130 (S.D.N.Y. 1968)(use of charcoal drawings of some Kennedy assassination motion picture frames in serious study of event held fair use; no competition; great public interest; no injury).

19. 17 U.S.C.A. § 107 (allowing the courts "to adapt the doctrine to particular situations on a case-by-case basis"). *See* 1976 House Report 66:

    [T]he endless variety of situations and combinations of circumstances that can arise in particular cases precludes the formulation of exact rules in the statute. The bill endorses the purpose and general scope of the judicial doctrine of fair use, but there is no disposition to freeze the doctrine in the statute, especially during a period of rapid technological change.

20. 17 U.S.C.A. § 107. "Including" is defined as illustrative and not limitative. 17 U.S.C.A. § 101. However, "normally these four factors would govern the analysis." Triangle Publications, Inc. v. Knight-Ridder Newspapers, Inc. 626 F.2d 1171, 1175, n. 10 (5th Cir. 1980). The considerations behind the four "factors," often called "criteria," are discussed in 1975 Senate Report 63–65; H.R. REP. NO. 2237, 89th Cong., 2d Sess. 32–35 (1966). *See* Meeropol v. Nizer, 560 F.2d 1051 (2d Cir. 1977) (mentioning four factors). Acknowledgment of the copyright work may be relevant. Marais v. Rowley, Norell & Freeman, 872 F.2d 907 (9th Cir. 1989) (failure to acknowledge source weakens fair use, even though acknowledgment no defense). Under pre-1978 case law, a credit line was no defense, Henry Holt & Co. v. Liggett & Myers Tobacco Co., 23 F. Supp. 302 (E.D. Pa. 1938), and was afforded opposite effects by the courts. *Compare* Warren v. White & Wyckoff Mfg. Co., 39 F.2d 922, 923 (S.D.N.Y. 1930) (where court in awarding substantial damages emphasized that "deliberate" copying in calendars of some 300–400 words from book was "without even

1. The "purpose" and "character" of the use, including whether such use is of a "commercial nature" or is "for nonprofit educational purposes";
2. The "nature" of the copyrighted work;
3. The "amount and substantiality of the portion used" in relation to the copyrighted work as a whole;
4. The effect of the use upon the "potential market for or value of" the copyrighted work.

18.3[1] Purpose and Character of Use

This first "factor" repeats "purpose,"[21] adding "character," of the use, "including"[22] whether the use is of a "commercial nature" or "for nonprofit educational purposes."[23] While this factor is not conclusive, "commercial" versus "non-profit" use, especially "commercial" versus "nonprofit educational" use, can be determinative.[24]

---

the gesture of 'by your leave' implied in quotation marks and an acknowledgment of the source") *with* Chicago Record-Herald Co. v. Tribune Ass'n, 275 F. 797, 799 (7th Cir. 1921) ("Far from there being any exculpatory virtue in this [credit], it would tend rather to convey to the reading public the false impression that authority to appropriate the extracts from the copyrighted article had been duly secured by the offending publisher."). The judicial trend has been to consider the first and fourth factors as primary and the second and third as "additional" factors. Sony Corp. of Am. v. Universal City Studios, Inc., note 63 *infra;* Harper & Row, Publishers, Inc. v. Nation Enters., note 5 *supra;* Freid, *Fair Use and the New Act*, 22 N.Y.L. SCH. L. REV. 497, 499 (1977); Note, *Copyright Fair Use—Case Law and Legislation*, 1969 DUKE L.J. 73, 88–94.

21. *See* chapter 5, note 10 *supra*.
22. *See* note 11 *supra*.
23. 17 U.S.C.A. § 107(1) (added by House substitute bill). Marcus v. Rowley, 695 F.2d 1171 (9th Cir. 1983) (nonprofit educational use not necessarily fair use); *Compare* Copyright Permissions: A Guide for Noncommercial Use from the Association of American Publishers 1 (Association of American Publishers) (fact that duplication is for non-proft use has no bearing on question of fair use) *with* Shaw, *Publication and Distribution of Scientific Literature*, 17 COLL. & RESEARCH LIBRARIES 294–301 (1956)(private use is completely outside scope and intent of restriction by copyright).
24. The question may be who ultimately benefits from such use. Mone-

18.3[2] Nature of Copyrighted Work

This second factor[25] is without legislative history and is the vaguest of the four factors. It is corollary to the first factor: "the purpose and character of the use." Distinctions between unpublished and published works and between factual and fictional works have been made; also whether the copyrighted work is out of print.

18.3[3] Amount and Substantiality of Portion Used

Usually, copying of an entire work is not "fair use, but to conclude that such use cannot be fair use is an overgenera-

---

tary gain is not the sole criterion of the first factor; recognition among one's peers and authorship credit may be important, especially in academic areas to support promotion, advancement, and tenure. Gordon, *Fair Use as Market Failure: A Structural Analysis of the* Betamax *Case and Its Predecessors*, 82 COLUM. L. REV. 1600, 1630 (1982). *See* Harper & Row, Publishers, Inc. v. Nation Enters., note 5 *supra* (test: does user stand to profit without paying customary price?); Sony Corp. of Am. v. Universal City Studios, Inc., note 67 *infra* (commercial use presumptively unfair; fair use need not be productive use). As one court put it, "chiseling" for personal profit is not fair use. Wainwright Sec. Inc. v. Wall Street Transcript Corp., 558 F.2d 91 (2d Cir. 1977), *cert. denied*, 434 U.S. 1014 (1978). *See also* Hustler Magazine, Inc. v. Moral Majority, Inc., 796 F.2d 1148 (9th Cir. 1986)(2–1); Bremer v. Hustler Magazine, 749 F.2d 527 (9th Cir. 1984); Consumers Union v. General Signal Corp., 730 F.2d 47 (2d Cir. 1983) (2–1), *cert. denied*, 469 U.S. 823 (1984); Triangle Publications, Inc. v. Knight-Ridder Newspapers, Inc., 626 F.2d 1171 (5th Cir. 1980); Dow Jones & Co. v. Board of Trade, 546 F. Supp. 113 (S.D.N.Y. 1982); Encyclopaedia Britannica Educ. Corp. v. Crooks, 542 F. Supp. 1156 (W.D.N.Y. 1982); Time, Inc. v. Bernard Geis Assocs., 293 F. Supp. 130 (S.D.N.Y. 1968).

25. 17 U.S.C.A. § 107(2). The second factor suggests that articles of a scholarly nature of limited circulation and compilations of information in the public domain are more inclined to fair use. *See* New York Times Co. v. Roxbury Data Interface, Inc., 434 F. Supp. 217, 221 (D.N.J. 1977).

lization."[26] Qualitative is more important than quantitative. The statutory language is "in relation to the copyrighted

---

26. 17 U.S.C.A. § 107(d); Sony Corp. of Am. v. Universal City Studios, Inc., notes 63–69 *infra*; Hustler Magazine, Inc. v. Moral Majority, Inc., 796 F.2d 1148 (9th Cir. 1986) (2–1) (copying of entire work raising $1 million to refute parody attack on user held fair use). Educational Testing Servs. v. Katzman, 793 F.2d 533 (3d Cir. 1986); Diamond v. American Law Publishing Co., 745 F.2d 142 (2d Cir. 1984); Iowa State Univ. Research Found. v. American Broadcasting Cos., 621 F.2d 57 (2d Cir. 1980); Schroeder v. William Morrow & Co., 566 F.2d 3 (7th Cir. 1977); Whitol v. Crow, 309 F.2d 777, 780 (8th Cir. 1962); Maxtone-Graham v. Burtchaell, 803 F.2d 1253 (2d Cir. 1986); Jackson v. MPI Home Video, 694 F. Supp. 483 (N.D. Ill. 1988) (videotape of television news coverage of entire speech at national political convention not fair use); Schumann v. Albuquerque Corp., 664 F. Supp. 473 (D.N.M. 1987) (broadcast of entire songs in remote spots covering fiesta held not fair use). For cases under pre-1978 law, *see* Colonial Book Co. v. Amsco School Publications, Inc., 41 F. Supp. 156 (S.D.N.Y. 1941), *aff'd per curiam*, 142 F.2d 362 (2d Cir. 1944) (11 out of defendant's 254 pages held infringement); Perkins Marine Lamp & Hardware Corp. v. Goodwin-Stanley Corp., 86 F. Supp. 630 (E.D.N.Y. 1949) (20 out of plaintiff's 137 cuts held infringement); Boosey v. Empire Music Co., 224 F. 646 (S.D.N.Y. 1915) (five words and accompanying musical phrase held infringement); Macmillan Co. v. King, 223 F. 862 (D. Mass. 1914) (thirty-page mimeographed outline of 1100-page book held infringement); Da Prato Statuary Co. v. Giuliani Statuary Co., 189 F. 90 (D. Minn. 1911) (11 out of plaintiff's 2,813 and defendant's 393 cuts held infringement). There was no legal basis for the occasionally encountered view that a maximum of a certain number of words—usually ranging from fifty to 300—from a copyrighted publication may be used without permission if full credit is given to the author and publisher. *But see* text accompanying notes 30–38 *infra*. "The right to quote poetry is more circumscribed than the right to quote prose, although no one can say how many lines exactly may be taken. Depending upon the poem, the limit of fair use may be two lines, twenty lines, or two hundred; the latter instance, however, would demand an epic." Price, *Quotation of Copyrighted Material and the Doctrine of Fair Use*, 41 JOURNALISM Q. 37, 41 (1944).

The publication of words of a song without music in a magazine as background or related material for fictional or nonfictional material has been uniformly held to be within the doctrine of fair use. Kriger

work as a whole." Although not expressed, the amount and substantiality of the portion of the copyrighted work used in relation to the alleged infringing work may be relevant, as are the independent labor avoided and benefit achieved from the copyright owner's research, labor, and skill.

18.3[4] Economic Effect of Use

This fourth factor, "the effect of the use upon the potential market for or value of the copyrighted work,"[27] "is undoubtedly the single most important element of fair use."[28]

---

v. MacFadden Publications, Inc., 43 F. Supp. 170 (S.D.N.Y. 1941) (chorus); Karll v. Curtis Publishing Co., 39 F. Supp. 836 (E.D. Wis. 1941) (eight lines of chorus), *noted in* 15 S. CAL. L. REV. 249 (1942); Broadway Music Corp. v. F-R Publishing Corp., 31 F. Supp. 817 (S.D.N.Y. 1940) (whole song; about one-half of magazine article); Shapiro, Bernstein & Co. v. P.F. Collier & Son, 26 U.S.P.Q. (BNA) 40 (S.D.N.Y. 1934) (ten out of eighteen lines of first chorus, in snatches). *But see* Sayers v. Spaeth, 20 Copy. Off. Bull. 625 (S.D.N.Y. 1932) (words of entire song and melody of one line of music in history of popular songs held infringement); *see also* Boosey v. Empire Music Co., 224 F. 646 (S.D.N.Y. 1915) (five words and accompanying music of song in later song held infringement); Allen v. Walt Disney Prods., Ltd., 41 F. Supp. 134 (S.D.N.Y. 1941) (music of chorus in other song deemed infringement). The photograph of a person incidentally reading a current magazine in which the copyrighted cover was reproduced as a matter of background is probably fair use.

27. 17 U.S.C.A. § 107(4); Horgan v. Macmillan, Inc., 789 F.2d 157 (2d Cir. 1986)(use in book of still photographs of ballet performance not fair use of choreographic work if substantial similarity even though staged performances could not be recreated from photographs); Standard & Poor's Corp. v. Commodity Exch., Inc., 683 F.2d 704 (2d Cir. 1982)(Comex enjoined from trading futures contracts based on plaintiff's "500" index, whose use had been leased to competing exchange); Dow Jones & Co. v. Board of Trade, 546 F. Supp. 113 (S.D.N.Y. 1982)(Dow Jones stock market index in rulebook or submissions to Commodity Futures Trading Commission held fair use).

28. Harper & Row, Publishers, Inc. v. Nation Enters., note 5 *supra;* Sony Corp. of Am. v. Universal City Studios, Inc., notes 70–74 *infra*. The "newsworthiness" of an event has consistently been held to be no defense when the use is commercial and when describing the event

Where the use is commercial, there is a presumption of unfair exploitation. The defendant bears the burden of rebutting that presumption. Where the use is noncommercial, however, the plaintiff bears the burden of proving that the particular use is harmful, or that if it should become widespread, it would adversely affect the potential market for the copyrighted work. Actual present harm need not be shown.

Some slight detrimental economic effect is probably permissible, as long as the other three factors favor "fair use."

An earlier case had suggested that actual (rather than probable) effect was the standard for judging the impact of the copying upon the potential market.[29]

---

does not require the use of the copyrighted work. Harper & Row, Publishers, Inc. v. Nation Enters. *supra* (nature of copyright interest at stake—right of first publication—was regarded as so valuable that its usurpation was, virtually by definition, unfair use). *See also* Roy Export Co. Establishment v. Columbia Broadcasting Sys., Inc., 672 F.2d 1095 (2d Cir. 1982), *cert. denied*, 459 U.S. 826 (1982); Hustler Magazine, Inc. v. Moral Majority, Inc., 796 F.2d 1148 (9th Cir. 1986) (2–1) (use of copyrighted parody of user, although presumptively unfair because designed to raise money, held fair because motivated to refute parody's personal attack on user, thereby rebutting presumption); Consumer's Union v. General Signal Corp., 724 F.2d 1044 (2d Cir. 1983) (2–1) (manufacturer's use of Consumer's Union ratings and comments, with appropriate disclaimer, in televised advertising held fair use; commercial use per se not beyond fair use; verbatim quotation more justified when required for accurate reporting; greater leniency where original work more factual than creative), *cert. denied*, 469 U.S. 823 (1984). A parody that damages the integrity of the original work may cause commercial harm. Walt Disney Prods. v. Air Pirates, 581 F.2d 751 (9th Cir. 1978); Georgia Television Co. v. TV News Clips of Atlanta, Inc., 718 F. Supp. 939 (N.D. Ga. 1989) (videotaping of telecasts for sale to interested individuals and businesses preliminarily enjoined; *compare* personal noncommercial use).

29. Williams & Wilkins Co. v. United States, 487 F.2d 1345 (Ct. Cl. 1973), *aff'd by an equally divided court*, 420 U.S. 376 (1975).

18.4 Guidelines

The vagueness of "fair use" prompted various interested groups to meet and attempt to set guidelines concerning classroom copying, educational uses of music, and classroom use of off-the-air tapes of radio and television broadcasts. Initially, agreement was reached in the first two areas.[30]

---

30. The guidelines constitute "the minimum and not the maximum standards of educational fair use." 1976 House Report 70. The parties recognized that conditions may change in the future, possibly rendering the guidelines either too broad or too narrow. *Id.* at 68, 70. Further, the parties made clear that where the general concept of "fair use" allowed greater leeway in copying than did the guidelines, then "fair use" would govern. *Id.* at 68, 70–71. The guidelines were called "a reasonable interpretation of the minimum standards of fair use." *Id.* at 72. The report also indicated that the guidelines would give teachers a greater degree of certainty and protection. *Id.* The Conference Report accepted the books and periodicals and music fair use guidelines and endorsed the concept of "teacher" as "broad enough to include instructional specialists working in consultation with actual instructors." 122 CONG. REC. H10,875 (daily ed. Sept. 22, 1976); Conference Report 70. Strong dissent against the guidelines, as unduly restrictive, was registered by the Association of American Law Schools and the American Association of University Professors. *But see* Marcus v. Rowley, 695 F.2d 1171, 1178 (9th Cir. 1983); (nonprofit educational use not necessarily fair use); Encyclopaedia Britannica Educ. Corp. v. Crooks, 558 F. Supp. 1247 (W.D.N.Y. 1983)(off-the-air videotaping and distribution to public schools of publicly televised motion picture films by BOCES, a nonprofit corporation providing educational services to some 100 schools in a county, held not fair use); Whitol v. Crow, 309 F.2d 777 (8th Cir. 1962)(choral instructor and church where instructor was organist—but not public school where instructor was teacher because of eleventh amendment—held liable for preparing choral arrangement (in forty-eight copies) of two versions of entire religious song where original twenty-four copies had been acquired by school, but found unsuitable for choir use, and performed once in church and school; held not fair use); Macmillan Co. v. King, 223 F. 862 (D. Mass. 1914) (preparation and use of some sixty one-page memoranda abridged and paraphrased from part of a 1,100-page textbook for tutoring sessions held infringement).

18.4[1] Classroom Copying of Books and Periodicals

The guidelines for classroom copying in not-for-profit educational institutions with respect to books and periodicals were prepared by representatives of the Ad Hoc Committee of Educational Institutions and Organizations on Copyright Law Revision, the Authors League of America, Inc., and the Association of American Publishers, Inc. Although not binding, the guidelines may significantly influence courts, and have the practical impact of statutory provisions.[31]

18.4[1][a] Single Copies

A teacher may reproduce a *single* copy, subject to "prohibitions," for research or teaching purposes, of:[32]

1. A chapter from a book;
2. An article from a periodical or newspaper;
3. A short story, short essay, or short poem, whether or not from a collective work;
4. A chart, graph, diagram, drawing, cartoon, or picture from a book, periodical, or newspaper.

18.4[1][b] Multiple Copies

A teacher may make *multiple* copies[33] for classroom use if the copying meets certain tests for brevity,[34] spontaneity,[35]

31. Marcus v. Rowley, 695 F.2d 1171, 1178 (9th Cir. 1983).
32. 1976 House Report 68.
33. The teacher may not make more than one copy per pupil in a course. *Id.*
34. "Brevity" is defined

1. Poetry: a. Complete poem if less than 250 words and if printed on not more than two pages
   b. Excerpt of not more than 250 words
2. Prose: a. Complete article, story, or essay of less than 2,500 words
   b. Excerpt of not more than 1,000 words or 10 per-

and cumulative effect.[36] Each copy must also include a notice of copyright.[37]

18.4[1][c] Prohibitions

Prohibitions applicable to both single and multiple copying are:[38]

---

cent of work, whichever is less, but in any event a minimum of 500 words

3. Illustration: One chart, graph, diagram, drawing, cartoon, or picture per book or per periodical issue
4. "Special" works: Excerpt of not more than two published pages and not more than 10 percent of words found in text

1976 House Report 68–69.

35. "Spontaneity" is defined:

1. The copying must be at the instance and inspiration of the individual teacher
2. The inspiration and decision to use the work and the maximum teaching effectiveness must be so close in time that it would be unreasonable to expect a timely reply to a request for permission

1976 House Report at 69; Marcus v. Rowley, 695 F.2d 1171 (9th Cir. 1983)(no spontaneity where teacher used materials for three successive school years). *See also* Encyclopaedia Britannica Educ. Corp. v. Crooks, 542 F. Supp. 1156 (W.D.N.Y. 1982).

36. "Cumulative effect" is defined

1. The copying is for only one course in the school
2. Not more than one short poem, article, story, essay or two excerpts may be copied from the same author, nor more than three from the same collective work or periodical volume during one class term
3. Multiple copying is limited to no more than nine instances for one course during one class term

The last two limitations do not apply to current news periodicals and newspapers and current news sections of other periodicals. 1976 House Report 69.

37. 1976 House Report at 68.
38. *Id.* at 69–70.

1. The copies may not be used for anthologies, compilations, or collective works.
2. "Consumable" materials, such as workbooks, tests, and answer sheets, may not be copied.
3. Copying may not be used to substitute for purchasing, be "directed by higher authority," or be repeated "with respect to the same item by the same teacher from term to term."
4. The student may not be charged more than the actual costs of the photocopying.

18.4[2] Educational Uses of Music

The guidelines for educational uses of music were prepared by representatives of the Music Publishers' Association of the United States, Inc., the Music Teachers National Association, the Music Education National Conference, the National Association of Schools of Music, and the Ad Hoc Committee on Copyright Law Revision.

18.4[2][a] Permissible Uses

Five permissible uses are enumerated:[39]

1. Emergency copying to replace purchased copies not available "for an imminent performance," provided purchased replacement copies are substituted "in due course."
2. "For academic purposes" other than performance, single or multiple copies, not to exceed one copy per pupil, may be made of excerpts of no more than 10 percent of the whole work, provided that the ex-

39. *Id.* at 71.

cerpts do not constitute a "performable unit"[40] (as revised).[41]

3. Purchased printed copies may be edited or simplified provided that the "fundamental character" of the work is not distorted or any lyrics altered or added.
4. A single copy of recordings of performances by students may be made for evaluation or rehearsal purposes and may be retained by the educational institution or individual teacher.
5. A single copy of a sound recording of copyrighted music may be made from sound recordings owned by an educational institution or an individual teacher for the purpose of constructing aural exercises or examinations and may be retained by the educational institution or individual teacher.[42]

18.4[2][b] Prohibitions

The applicable prohibitions are:[43]

1. The copies may not be used as substitutes for anthologies, compilations, or collective works.
2. "Consumable" materials, such as workbooks, exercises, tests, and answer sheets, may not be copied.

---

40. *Id.* Examples of a "performable unit" are a section, movement, or aria.
41. The guidelines in the House subcommittee report had two separate paragraphs, one dealing with multiple copies and a second dealing with single copies. Single copies were permitted "for academic purposes" solely for the purpose of scholarly research or in preparation to teach a class, when the work was out of print, confirmed by the "copyright proprietor," or unavailable except in a larger work. 1976 House Report 71. *See* 122 CONG. REC. H10875 (daily ed. Sept. 22, 1976).
42. 1976 House Report 71 (pertaining only to copyright in music itself and to any copyright that may exist in sound recording).
43. *Id.*

3. No other copying for the purpose of performance, except as in first permissible use.
4. No other copying for the purpose of substituting for the purchase of music, except as in first and second permissible uses.
5. No copying without inclusion of the copyright notice that appears on the printed copy.

18.4[3] Classroom Use of Off-the-Air Tapes

In 1981, guidelines for off-the-air taping of copyrighted works for educational use were adopted and published in the *Congressional Record*.[44] These guidelines would permit off-the-air taping for relevant teaching activities during the first ten school days after the taping, and only if the tapes were erased after forty-five calendar days.

18.5 Certain Other Uses

To counteract the emphasis on classroom teaching activities, the legislative history deals with other uses under the doctrine of fair use. For example, educational broadcasting not covered by section 110(2), 112, or 118 could be considered fair use under the appropriate circumstances,[45] as

---

44. Cong. Rec. E4750 (daily ed. Oct. 14, 1981). The 1981 guidelines were not followed in Encyclopaedia Britannica Educ. Corp. v. Crooks, 558 F. Supp. 1247 (W.D.N.Y. 1983). The court focused on 17 U.S.C.A. § 107(4) (effect of use on potential market), and emphasized that the works copied from the air were available for short-term rental, and that licensing agreements permitting duplication were available.
45. In these cases the factors to be weighed in applying the criteria of § 107 would include whether the performers, producers, directors, and others responsible for the broadcast were paid, the size and nature of the audience, the size and number of the excerpts taken and, in the case of recordings made for broadcast, the number of copies reproduced and the extent of their reuse or exchange. 1976 House Report 72. Use of "motion pictures and other audiovisual works" would receive narrower fair use treatment. *Id.* at 72–73.

could the making of works in special forms for the blind.[46] Other potential "fair" uses are the preservation of old films,[47] the refutation of unfair criticism,[48] and the publication of copyrighted works in congressional hearings and documents.[49] The House Report also mentions reproduction of newsletters, suggesting that the scope of fair use would be narrow here because of the "commercial nature of the user."[50] The work of calligraphers is also mentioned.[51] This list merely illustrates that the "fair use" doctrine is relevant to any use of a copyrighted work.

The final Senate and House subcommittee reports contain much soothing language concerning fair use, sometimes interpreting the same statutory language substantially differently.[52]

---

46. The 1976 House Report states: "(T)he making of a single copy or phonorecord by an individual as a free service for a blind persons (sic) would properly be considered a fair use under section 107." *Id.* at 73. *See* text accompanying chapter 30, notes 92–95, *infra*.
47. The primary purpose here is to "preserve this irreplaceable contribution to our cultural life" through archival preservation. 1976 House Report 73.
48. The victim of such criticism could copy parts of the criticizing work "to permit understandable comment on the statements made in the work." 1976 House Report 73.
49. Factors here include the length of the work published, the number of copies authorized, and the relevance of the work "to a matter of legitimate legislative concern." 1976 House Report 73.
50. Newsletters generally have a limited circulation and are easily copied. Therefore, even a small amount of reproduction could have a significant impact upon the potential market for the newsletters. 1976 House Report 73–74.
51. > [A] single copy reproduction of an excerpt from a copyrighted work by a calligrapher for a single client does not represent an infringement of copyright. Likewise, a single reproduction of excerpts from a copyrighted work by a student calligrapher or teacher in a learning situation would be a fair use of the copyrighted work.

    1976 House Report 74.
52. *See* note 1 *supra*.

The right of fair use, as codified by the 1976 statute, is not in any way affected by the specific statutory provisions permitting limited reproduction and distribution by libraries and archives.[53]

Off-the-air recording problems were not resolved by the statute. Nothing in the statute was intended to change the law on off-the-air taping for nonprofit classroom use of copyrighted audiovisual works incorporated in radio and television broadcasts.[54] Arguably, no restraints were intended on home recording, from broadcasts or from tapes of records, of recorded performances, "for private use and with no purpose of reproducing or otherwise capitalizing commercially on it." This view was confirmed by the United States Supreme Court, five to four, in 1984.[55]

---

53. 17 U.S.C.A § 108(f)(4). *See* chapter 19 *infra*. Williams & Wilkins Co. v. United States, note 29 *supra*, offers little guidance. *See* 1975 Senate Report 71:

> Indeed, the opinion of the Court of Claims said the Court was engaged in "a 'holding operation' in the interim period before Congress enacted its preferred solution."
>
> While the several opinions in the *Wilkins* case have given the Congress little guidance as to the current state of the law on fair use, these opinions provide additional support for the balanced resolution of the photocopying issue adopted by the Senate last year in S. 1361 and preserved in section 108 of this legislation. As the Court of Claims opinion succinctly stated "there is much to be said on all sides."

Arguably, libraries and archives should be able to assert their patrons' rights of fair use beyond § 108 and the guidelines thereunder.

54. Sony Corp. of Am. v. Universal City Studios, Inc., *infra* notes 63–69; 1976 House Report 71–72 (expressing belief that "fair use doctrine has some application in this area" and recommending development of detailed guidelines).

55. *See* H.R. REP. No. 92-487, 92d Cong., 1st Sess. 7 (1971)(accompanying 1971 Sony Corp. of Am. v. Universal City Studios, Inc., *infra* note 68; sound recording amendment); Holland, *The Audiovisual Package: Handle with Care*, 22 BULL. COPYRIGHT SOC'Y 104, 122–26 (1974).

18.6 Remission of Statutory Damages

When an infringer believed and had reasonable grounds for believing that the use of the copyrighted work was a fair use, statutory damages may not be awarded against an employee or agent of a nonprofit educational institution, library, or archives acting within the scope of employment, or against such institution, library, or archives itself.[56]

18.7 Future Prospects

"Fair use," especially with respect to educational uses and library photocopying, received inordinate congressional attention,[57] and has been the subject of tremendous commentary.[58]

---

56. 17 U.S.C.A. § 504(c)(2). The burden of proof with respect to the defendants good faith is intended to rest on the plaintiff. 1976 House Report 163. Quaere, as to reasonableness. Compare the statutory burdens of proving willfulness and innocence.

57. *See* note 1 *supra*.

58. In addition to other references in this chapter: Schwartz & Hogan, *Copyright Law and the Academic Community: Issues Affecting Teachers Researchers, Students, and Libraries*, 17 U.C.D. L. REV. 1147 (1984); Lieb, *Library Photocopying Under the 1976 Copyright Law*, 25 BULL. COPYRIGHT SOC'Y 243 (1978); *Symposium—Copyright and Educational Media*, 7 PERFORMING ARTS REV. 1 (1977); Seltzer, *Exemptions and Fair Use in Copyright: The Exclusive Rights Tensions in the New Copyright Act*, 24 BULL. COPYRIGHT SOC'Y 215 (1977); Cardozo, *To Copy or Not to Copy for Teaching and Scholarship: What Shall I Tell My Client?*, 4 J. COLL. & U. L. 59 (Winter 1976–77); Smith, *The New Copyright Law: What You Can and Can't Do*, 8 EDUC. & IND. TELEVISION 22 (Nov. 1976); Rosenfeld, *The Constitutional Dimensions of Fair Use in Copyright Law*, 50 NOTRE DAME LAW. 790 (1975); Rosenfeld, *Customary Use as Fair Use in Copyright Law*, 25 BUFFALO L. REV. 119 (1975); Stevenson, *Doctrine of Fair Use as It Affects Libraries*, 68 L. LIB. J. 254 (1975); Weinberg, *The Photocopying Revolution and the Copyright Crisis*, 38 PUB. INTEREST 99 (Winter 1975).

Some of the compromises were very delicate,[59] and there were warnings of a "cauldron of litigation brewing as to true application of fair use."[60]

A private Copyright Clearance Center has been established to collect fees from photocopiers and divide the proceeds among copyright owners.[61]

---

59. *Flareup at the Fair Use Frontier,* 103 LIB. J. 601 (1978). *Compare* ASSOCIATION OF AMERICAN PUBLISHERS, INC. & AUTHORS LEAGUE OF AMERICA, INC., PHOTOCOPYING BY ACADEMIC, PUBLIC AND NONPROFIT RESEARCH LIBRARIES (1978); ASSOCIATION OF AMERICAN PUBLISHERS, INC. & AUTHORS LEAGUE OF AMERICA, INC., A STATEMENT OF POSITION WITH RESPECT TO THE PHOTOCOPYING OF JOURNAL ARTICLES AND OTHER SHORT WORKS BY CORPORATE LIBRARIES UNDER THE NEW COPYRIGHT LAW, AND ANSWERS TO SOME QUESTIONS FREQUENTLY ASKED (1978); ASSOCIATION OF AMERICAN PUBLISHERS, INC., EXPLAINING THE NEW COPYRIGHT LAW: A GUIDE TO LEGITIMATE PHOTOCOPYING OF COPYRIGHTED MATERIALS (1977) *with* MEDICAL LIBRARY ASS'N, THE COPYRIGHT LAW AND THE HEALTH SCIENCES LIBRARIAN (1978); SPECIAL LIBRARIES ASS'N, LIBRARY PHOTOCOPYING AND THE U.S. COPYRIGHT LAW OF 1976: AN OVERVIEW FOR LIBRARIANS AND THEIR COUNSEL (1977); ASSOCIATION FOR EDUCATIONAL COMMUNICATIONS AND TECHNOLOGY, COPYRIGHT AND EDUCATIONAL MEDIA: A GUIDE TO FAIR USE AND PERMISSIONS PROCEDURE (1977); AMERICAN LIBRARY ASS'N, LIBRARIES AND COPYRIGHT: A SUMMARY OF THE ARGUMENTS FOR LIBRARY PHOTOCOPYING (rev. ed. 1976); *Librarian's Guide to the New Copyright Law,* 38 WASHINGTON NEWSLETTER NO. 13, 1 (Nov. 15, 1976). Previous dissent had been recorded by the Association of American Law Schools and the American Association of University Professors.
60. Selkirk, *Fair Use and the Copyright Act of 1976,* 49 N.Y. ST. B.J. 558, 567 (1977).
61. Copyright Clearance Center, Inc., sponsored by Association of American Publishers, Inc., chartered July 1978. *See* AAP/TSM COPYRIGHT CLEARANCE CENTER TASK FORCE, A HANDBOOK FOR SERIAL PUBLISHERS: PROCEDURES FOR USING THE PROGRAMS OF THE COPYRIGHT CLEARANCE CENTER, INC. (1977). *See* chapter 19, notes 65, 66, *infra.* The C.C.C. currently has some 1.5 million titles, including 350,000 U.S.S.R. titles, in its repertoire, representing the works of more than 8,000 domestic and international publishers. Its Annual Authorizations Service provides permission for more than 100 corporations and another 400 subsidiary companies to photocopy for internal use for annual fees, which include royalties to the rightsholders. The Antitrust Division of the Department of Justice has stated that it has no present intention of challenging the organization or operation of the Center under the antitrust laws.

18.8 United States Supreme Court Cases

Not until 1984 did the United States Supreme Court address the issue of fair use.[62] After reargument, the Court divided five to four. The case was *Sony Corp. of America v. Universal City Studios, Inc.*[63] The owners of televised motion pictures sued the alleged direct infringer,[64] who taped them off the air for private use, and several alleged contributory infringers,[65] especially Sony Corp., which manufactured and distributed the videocassette recorder used in the taping.[66]

A majority of the Court[67] accepted the findings of the trial court[68] and concluded that the private "noncommercial" taping at home for "timeshifting" purposes, even if unauthorized, consituted fair use, and that, even if the taping exceeded fair use, Sony was not a contributory infringer. According to the majority, commercial or profit-making use was presumptively unfair, in contrast to noncommercial,

62. There were two earlier cases where the Court was equally divided with no opinions. Williams & Wilkins Co. v. United States, 487 F.2d 1345 (Ct Cl. 1973), *aff'd*, 420 U.S. 376 (1975) (photocopying of medical journals); Benny v. Loew's, Inc. 239 F.2d 532 (9th Cir. 1956), *aff'd sub nom.* CBS, Inc. v. Loew's, Inc., 356 U.S. 43 (1958)(parody).
63. Sony Corp. of Am. v. Universal City Studios, Inc., 464 U.S. 417 (1984)(5–4). The structure of the majority and dissenting opinions suggests that each started out as the opinion of the Court; each is of twenty-three-page length.
64. Although named as a defendant, the individual taper was not a party against whom relief was sought.
65. For discussion of contributory infringement, *see* text accompanying chapter 27, notes 20–22, *infra*.
66. The Court referred to the defendants collectively as Sony. Quaere, as to whether Sony Corporation's manufacture of digital audio tape recorders capable of producing flawless copies of compact discs may constitute contributory infringement.
67. Stevens, J.; Burger, C.J.; Brennan, White, and O'Connor, JJ., concurring.
68. Universal City Studios v. Sony Corp. of Am., 480 F. Supp. 429 (C.D. Cal. 1979), *rev'd*, 659 F.2d 963 (9th Cir. 1981).

nonprofit activity, which was presumptively fair. Where the use is noncommercial, proof of actual or potential harm is required. Such harm was not shown. Further, fair use need not be productive use.

The dissent[69] argued that no statutory authorization existed for the making of one complete copy for personal private use, as shown by various statutory references to single copies and nonpublic use. Fair use was to promote scholarship, education, and other socially "productive" activities. "Time-shifting," while convenient, was meant only for the personal enjoyment of the taper, with no benefit to anyone else. Where the use was unproductive, only potential for harm need be proven: in this case, loss of revenues from theaters, rental or sale of videocassettes, and reruns.

A second Supreme Court case followed in 1985. The Court split six to three in *Harper & Row, Publishers, Inc. v. Nation Enterprises.*[70] There, the defendant temporarily gained unauthorized possession of the unpublished memoirs written by former President Ford and prepared a 2,250-word excerpt, dealing primarily with the pardon of former President Nixon. The defendant, without any independent research, comment, or criticism, published its version in the *Nation* before authorized magazine serialization and publication in book form. As a result, the magazine that had the first publication rights did not publish the material and did not pay for those rights.

The trial court found infringement.[71] This was reversed by

69. Blackmun, J., joined by Marshall, Powell, and Rehnquist, JJ.

70. Harper & Row, Publishers, Inc. v. Nation Enters., 471 U.S. 539 (1985)(6–3). *See also* Salinger v. Random House, 811 F.2d 90 (2d Cir.), *cert. denied*, 108 S. Ct. 213 (1987); Brennan, Harper & Row v. The Nation, Inc.: *Copyrightability and Fair Use*, 33 J. COPYRIGHT SOC'Y 368 (1986); Kernochan, *Protection of Unpublished Works in the United States Before and After the* Nation *Case*, 33 J. COPYRIGHT SOC'Y 322 (1986).

71. Harper & Row, Publishers, Inc. v. Nation Enters., 557 F. Supp. 1067 (S.D.N.Y. 1983).

the court of appeals, two to one.[72] The appellate court, dissecting the defendant's excerpt, concluded that only some 300 words were covered by copyright—the rest being factual or statements of third parties—and that use thereof as news was fair use. Even though the work was factual and of historic importance, the valuable right of first publication had been adversely affected; the purposes were not nonprofit; the portraiture of public figures and use of subjective descriptions involved more than factual reporting of a newsworthy event.[73] The dissent[74] followed the reasoning of the majority of the court of appeals.

72. Harper & Row Publishers, Inc. v. Nation Enters., 723 F.2d 195 (2d Cir. 1983)(2–1).
73. O'Connor, J.; Burger, C.J., Rehnquist, Blackmun, Powell, and Stevens, JJ., concurring.
74. Brennan, J., joined by White and Marshall, JJ.

19. Reproduction and Distribution by Libraries and Archives

The reproduction or distribution of a copy or phonorecord by a library or archives is not an infringement of copyright if:

1. Within the fair use provisions[1]
2. Within the specific libraries and archives provisions[2]

---

1. 17 U.S.C.A. § 108(f)(4) (right of fair use not affected by libraries-and-archives provisions); *id.* § 108(f)(2) (reproduction or distribution under latter provisions not infringement notwithstanding fair use provisions). For discussion of fair use, *see* chapter 18 *supra.*
2. 17 U.S.C.A. § 108 (notwithstanding fair use provisions); L. SELTZER, EXEMPTIONS AND FAIR USE OF COPYRIGHT (1978); ASSOCIATION OF AMERICAN PUBLISHERS, INC., EXPLAINING THE NEW COPYRIGHT LAW: A GUIDE TO LEGITIMATE PHOTOCOPYING OF COPYRIGHTED MATERIALS (1977); ASSOCIATION OF AMERICAN PUBLISHERS, INC. & AUTHORS LEAGUE OF AMERICA, INC., PHOTOCOPYING BY ACADEMIC, PUBLIC AND NONPROFIT RESEARCH LIBRARIES (1978); SPECIAL LIBRARIES ASS'N, LIBRARY PHOTOCOPYING AND THE U.S. COPYRIGHT LAW OF 1976: AN OVERVIEW FOR LIBRARIANS AND THEIR COUNSEL (1978); MEDICAL LIBRARY ASS'N, THE COPYRIGHT LAW AND THE HEALTH SCIENCES LIBRARIAN (1978). The different interpretations on library and archives reproduction and distribution are detailed in Copyright Office Circular R21 (Reproduction of Copyrighted Works by Educators and Librarians). *See* chapter 18, note 1, *supra. See also* Adams, Reprography, 11 COLUM.-VLA J.L. & ARTS 195 (1986); Young, *Copyright and the New Technologies—The Case of Library Photocopying*, 28 COPYRIGHT L. SYMP. (ASCAP) 51 (1982); Stedman, *Academic Library Reserves: Photocopying and the Copyright Law*, 64 A.A.U.P. BULL. 142

19.1 In General

The rights of reproduction and distribution[3] under the libraries-and-archives provisions do not apply, with minor exceptions,[4] to musical works, pictorial, graphic, or sculptural works, and motion pictures or other audiovisual works other than "audiovisual works dealing with news."[5]

19.2 Conditions

The rights of reproduction and distribution of a library or archives, or any of its employees acting within the scope of their employment, are limited to "no more than one copy or phonorecord of a work"[6] and are subject to three specified overall conditions:[7]

(1978); Treece, *Library Photocopying*, 24 U.C.L.A. L. REV. 1025 (1977); Varmer, *Photoduplication of Copyrighted Material by Libraries* (1959), *reprinted in* 2 STUDIES ON COPYRIGHT—ARTHUR FISHER MEMORIAL EDITION 813 (1963).

3. 17 U.S.C.A. § 108. The caption reference to reproduction, with no mention of distribution, is misleading. Public distribution, the third exclusive right, as well as reproduction, the first exclusive right (17 U.S.C.A. § 106(1), (3)), are coupled and coextensive under the libraries and archives provisions. This suggests that a library or archive may not distribute publicly beyond its rights of public distribution under § 108 or its patron's rights of fair use under § 107. Arguably, libraries and archives may reproduce and distribute, beyond the libraries-and-archives provisions, under the rights of fair use of their patrons. 1976 House Report 77–78.
4. Except for "archives exemption" (17 U.S.C.A. § 108(b)) and "replacement exemption" (§ 108(c)), and pictorial or graphic works published as illustrations, diagrams, or similar adjuncts to works of which copies or phonorecords are reproduced or distributed in accordance with the "articles and small excerpts" exemption (§ 108(d)), and "unobtainable copy exemption" (§ 108(e)).
5. 17 U.S.C.A. § 108(h). *See* § 108(f)(3) ("audiovisual news program"), *infra* notes 55 and 56. Works excepted from § 108 are subject to fair use under § 107. 1976 House Report 78.
6. 17 U.S.C.A. § 108(a) ("or to distribute such copy or phonorecord").
7. 17 U.S.C.A. § 108(a). The paragraph introducing the three specified

1. The making must be "without any purpose of direct or indirect commercial advantage."[8]
2. The collections of the library or archives must be open to the public or available not only to affiliated researchers but also to other persons "doing research in a specialized field."[9]
3. The reproduction or distribution must include a "notice of copyright."[10]

19.2[1] Single Copy or Phonorecord

The subsequent subsections refer to "a" copy or phonorecord[11] and to the "isolated and unrelated reproduction or distribution of a single copy or phonorecord of the same material on separate occasions."[12] Thus, this limitation should be construed as "no more than one copy or phonorecord" *at a time.*

19.2[2] No Commercial Advantage

Forbidden is "any purpose of direct or indirect commercial advantage."[13] Thus, a purely commercial enterprise

---

overall "conditions" specifies "no more than one copy or phonorecord of a work."

8. 17 U.S.C.A. § 108(a)(1). "CONTU" in its final report, dated July 31, 1978, recommended that the 1976 Act be amended to provide specific guidance for situations where photocopying is done by commercial organizations on demand and for profit. There has been no implementation of this recommendation.
9. 17 U.S.C.A. § 108(a)(2).
10. 17 U.S.C.A. § 108(a)(3). Four notices are prescribed in § 108: (1) notice of copyright (§ 108(a)(3)); (2) warning of copyright per regulations (§ 108(d)(2)); (3) warning of copyright per regulations (§ 108(e)(2)); (4) notice that making of copy may be subject to copyright law (§ 108(f)(1)). Concerning the first and fourth notices, Copyright Office regulations are not authorized.
11. 17 U.S.C.A. § 108(b), (e).
12. 17 U.S.C.A. § 108(g).
13. 17 U.S.C.A. § 108(a)(1).

could not establish a collection of copyrighted works, call itself a library or archive, and engage in for-profit reproduction and distribution of photocopies.[14]

The phrase "indirect commercial advantage" raises problems, especially as to the status of photocopying done by or for libraries or archival collections within industrial, profit-making, or proprietary institutions (such as the research and development departments of chemical, pharmaceutical, automobile, and oil corporations; the library of a proprietary hospital; or the collections owned by a law or medical partnership).[15] The conference committee attempted to provide an answer:[16]

> As long as the library or archives (within an industrial, profit-making, or proprietary institution) meets the criteria in section 108(a) and the other requirements of the section, including the prohibitions against multiple and systematic copying in subsection (g), the conferees consider that the isolated, spontaneous making of single photocopies by a library or archives in a for-profit organization without any commercial motivation, or participation by such a library or archives in interlibrary arrangements, would come within the scope of section 108.

By this reasoning a library in a profit-making institution could not systematically use a single subscription or copy to supply multiple copies or use multiple copies gained by "interlibrary arrangements" to supply employees of the institution with material relevant to their work—this would involve "commercial motivation." However, such a library may allow isolated, spontaneous making of single photocopies without any systematic effort to substitute photocopying for subscriptions or purchases, even though the

14. 1976 House Report 74. Copying or distribution by a commercial enterprise for a nonprofit organization would not be exempt.

15. *Id.*

16. Conference Report 72-74.

copies are furnished to the employees of the organization for use in their work.[17] Interlibrary arrangements would also be exempt, as long as they are not "systematic."[18] The "advantage" referred to must attach to the immediate commercial motivation behind the reproduction or distribution itself, rather than to the ultimate profit-making motivation behind the enterprise in which the library is located.[19]

19.2[3] Open Library

Libraries and archives, to be eligible for the exemption, must have their collections:[20]

1. Open to the public;
2. Available not only to researchers affiliated with the library or archives or with the institution of which it is a part, but also to other persons "doing research in a specialized field."

19.2[4] "Notice of Copyright"

A "notice of copyright"[21] is required to be included in "the reproduction or distribution of the work."[22]

17. 1976 House Report 75. A library in a profit-making organization could not evade these obligations by installing reproducing equipment on its premises for unsupervised use by the organization's staff.
18. *Id.*
19. *Id.*
20. 17 U.S.C.A. § 108(a)(2).
21. 17 U.S.C.A. § 108(a)(3). The form of "notice of copyright" is not prescribed by the statute or regulations. *See* note 10 *supra*. *Cf.* 17 U.S.C.A. §§ 401(b), 402(b) ("form of notice" as provided by those sections). Quaere, as to how specific the notice must be, and whether a general stamp stating that the work is copyrighted would suffice.
22. 17 U.S.C.A. § 108(a)(3).

19.3 Permissible Reproduction and Distribution

If the four conditions are satisfied, reproduction and distribution are permitted in four situations:

1. For the preservation and security of a copy or phonorecord of an *unpublished* work;
2. For the replacement of a damaged, lost, or stolen copy or phonorecord of a *published* work;
3. For a copy of no more than one contribution to a collective work, or copy or phonorecord of a small part of any other copyrighted work;
4. For a copy or phonorecord of an entire or substantial part of an unobtainable work.

19.3[1] Four Situations

19.3[1][a] For Preservation and Security of Unpublished Works

This so-called "archival exemption" applies only to *unpublished* works but they may be of any type. The duplication "in facsimile form"[23] of "a" copy or phonorecord "solely for purposes of preservation and security or for deposit for research use in another library or archives"[24] is permitted. However, the copy or phonorecord being reproduced must be "currently in the collections" of the reproducing library or archive.[25]

23. 17 U.S.C.A. § 108(b). A repository could make photocopies of manuscripts by microfilm or electrostatic process, but could not reproduce the work in "machine-readable" language for storage in an information system. 1976 House Report 75.
24. 17 U.S.C.A. § 108(b).
25. *Id.*

19.3[1][b] For Replacement of Published Works

This so-called "replacement exemption" applies to any type of *published* works. The duplication "in facsimile form"[26] "solely for the purpose of replacement" of "a" copy or phonorecord that is "damaged, deteriorating, lost, or stolen" is permitted if the library or archive has, "after a reasonable effort," determined that an unused replacement cannot be obtained at a fair price.[27] Although "reasonable effort" will vary according to circumstances,[28] it will "always require recourse to commonly known trade sources in the United States," and "in the normal situation also to the publisher or other copyright owner . . . or an authorized reproducing service.[29]

19.3[1][c] Articles and Small Excerpts

Unlike the "preservation" and "replacement" exemptions, which permit duplication of the entire work of any type, this exemption applies only to "a" copy of no more than "one article or other contribution to a copyrighted collection or periodical issue" or to "a" copy or phonorecord of a "small part of any other copyrighted work."[30] The reproduced work may be in the collection of the library or archives where the user makes his request or in the collection of another library or archives. Two conditions must be met:[31]

26. 17 U.S.C.A. § 108(c). *See* note 23 *supra*.
27. 17 U.S.C.A. § 108(c). The copies or phonorecords being reproduced need not be currently in the collections of the reproducing library or archives.
28. 1976 House Report 75–76.
29. *Id.* at 76. The copyright owner need not be consulted if not at the address listed on the copyright registration.
30. 17 U.S.C.A. § 108(d).
31. *Id.*

1. The copy or phonorecord must become the property of the user, and the library or archives must have had no "notice" that it would be used "for any purpose other than private study, scholarship, or research."[32]
2. The library or archives must "display prominently" at the place where orders are accepted and include in its order form a "warning of copyright"[33] as prescribed by the Register of Copyrights.[34]

19.3[1][d] Unobtainable Works

This exemption applies to the entire work or to a substantial part of it. The reproduced work may be in the collection of the library or archive where the user makes the

---

32. 17 U.S.C.A. § 108(d)(1). What constitutes "notice" is not made clear in either the House or Conference Report. The "user" may be either a private party or "another library pursuant to an interlibrary loan." 1976 House Report 76.

33. 17 U.S.C.A. § 108(d)(2). As required, the Register of Copyrights has prescribed by regulation the definition, contents, form, and manner of use of the "warning of copyright." Verbatim adherence is required:

NOTICE
WARNING CONCERNING
COPYRIGHT REGISTRATIONS

The copyright law of the United States (Title 17, United States Code) governs the making of photocopies or other reproductions of copyrighted material.

Under certain conditions specified in the law, libraries and archives are authorized to furnish a photocopy or other reproduction. One of these specifed conditions is that the photocopy or reproduction is not to be "used for any purpose other than private study, scholarship, or research." If a user makes a request for, or later uses, a photocopy or reproduction for purposes in excess of "fair use," that user may be liable for copyright infringement.

This institution reserves the right to refuse to accept a copying order if, in its judgment, fulfillment of the order would involve violation of copyright law.

34. 17 U.S.C.A. § 108(d)(2); 37 C.F.R. § 201.14.

request or in the collection of another library or archives. The library or archives must first determine "on the basis of a reasonable investigation"[35] that a copy or phonorecord cannot be obtained at a fair price. The same two conditions applicable to the "articles and small excerpts" exemption[36] apply to this exemption.[37]

19.3[2] "Isolated and Unrelated" Versus "Related or Concerted" or "Systematic"

The rights of reproduction and distribution extend to the "isolated and unrelated" reproduction or distribution of a "single" copy or phonorecord "of the same material on separate occasions," but not where the library or archive, or its employees:[38]

1. Is "aware" of "related or concerted" reproduction or distribution;
2. Engages in "systematic" reproduction or distribution of articles or small excerpts.

19.3[2][a] Awareness of "Related or Concerted" Reproduction or Distribution

Not permitted is reproduction or distribution when the library or archives, or its employee, is "aware" or has "substantial reason to believe"[39] that it is engaging in the "related or concerted"[40] reproduction or distribution of

35. 17 U.S.C.A. § 108(e). "Reasonable investigation" in § 108(e) has a similar meaning to "reasonable efforts" in § 108(c). *See* note 28 *supra*.
36. 17 U.S.C.A. § 108(d)(1), (2). *See* text accompanying notes 31–34 *supra*.
37. 17 U.S.C.A. § 108(e)(1), (2).
38. 17 U.S.C.A. § 108(g).
39. 17 U.S.C.A. § 108(g)(1). The phrase "aware or has substantial reason to believe" is neither defined in the law nor clarified in the reports.
40. 17 U.S.C.A. § 108(g)(1). The phrase "related or concerted" is neither defined nor discussed meaningfully.

multiple copies or phonorecords of the same material, whether made on one occasion or over a period of time, and whether intended for aggregate use by one or more individuals or for separate use by the individual members of a group.[41]

19.3[2][b] "Systematic" Reproduction or Distribution of Articles or Small Excerpts

Not permitted is "systematic" reproduction or distribution of single or multiple copies or phonorecords of articles or other contributions to a copyrighted collection or periodical issue, or of a small part of any other copyrighted work.[42] The library or archive, however, is not prevented from participating in "interlibrary arrangements"[43] that do not have "as their purpose or effect" that the receiving library or archive does so in "such aggregate quantities as to substitute for a subscription to or purchase of such work."[44]

Construing the statutory phrase "such aggregate quantities as to substitute for a subscription to or purchase of such work" are guidelines prepared by the National Commission on New Technological Uses of Copyrighted Works (CONTU)[45] and accepted by the conference committee as a "reasonable interpretation" in the most common situations in which they applied.[46]

---

41. *Id.*
42. 17 U.S.C.A. § 108(g)(2).
43. *Id.* "Interlibrary arrangements" is more accurate than the older term "interlibrary loans." Ensign, *Copyright Considerations for Telefacsimile Transmission of Documents in Interlibrary Loan Transactions*, 81 LAW LIBR. J. 805 (1989).
44. *Id.* Any copying done by institutions established to serve as a central source of photocopies through interlibrary arrangements would require clearance.
45. The guidelines are reprinted in the Conference Report, at 72–73.
46. *Id.* at 71. The conference committee qualified its approval of the guidelines:

Not permitted under the guidelines are a total of six or more copies[47] within any calendar year of articles from any given periodical (as opposed to any given issue of a periodical) published within five years prior to the request.[48] Also not permitted are a total of six or more copies or phonorecords within any calendar year of small parts of other copyrighted works during the entire period while such material is protected by copyright. Any request must be accompanied by a representation by the requesting entity that the request was being made in conformity with the guidelines. Records of requests are required to be maintained by the requesting entity.[49]

In its final report on photocopying, CONTU recommended no change in the guidelines.[50] A subsequent review, recommended by CONTU, resulted in no changes.

> [They] are not intended as, and cannot be considered, explicit rules or directions governing any and all cases, now or in the future. It is recognized that their purpose is to provide guidance in the most commonly-encountered interlibrary photocopying situations, that they are not intended to be limiting or determinative in themselves or with respect to other situations, and that they deal with an evolving situation that will undoubtedly require their continuous reevaluation and adjustment.

The guidelines have been called "guidelines to the proviso to the exception to the exemption." Latman, *The New Copyright Law,* A.P.L.A. BULL. 648, 671 (1976).

47. This was considered "the most frequently encountered interlibrary case." Conference Report 71. It has been suggested that the CONTU interlibrary "rule of five" be applicable to on-the-premises library copying by the library for its own patrons.
48. CONTU left the relationship of 17 U.S.C.A. § 108(g)(2) to issues of periodicals more than five years old "to future interpretations." Conference Report 72.
49. *Id.* at 73.
50. CONTU, in its final report, dated July 31, 1978, did recommend specific statutory guidance for commercial photocopying. *See* note 8 *supra*.

19.4 Unaffected by Library and Archives Provisions

Unaffected by the library and archives provisions are:[51]

1. Liability for unsupervised use of reproducing equipment located on the premises;
2. Liability of the user of such equipment or requester of a copy or phonorecord of articles or small excerpts for such act or for later use exceeding fair use;
3. Use of "audiovisual news programs;"
4. Right of fair use or any contractual obligation.

19.4[1] Liability for Unsupervised Use of Reproducing Equipment Located on Premises

Liability for copyright infringement is not "imposed" by the libraries-and-archives provisions upon a library or archives or its employees for the unsupervised use of reproducing equipment located on the premises,[52] provided that such equipment "displays a notice that the making of a copy may be subject to the copyright law."[53]

19.4[2] Liability of User of Reproducing Equipment or Requester of Copies or Phonorecords

Liability for copyright infringement of a person who uses the reproducing equipment in a library or archive or who requests copies or phonorecords of articles or other contributions to a copyrighted collection or periodical issue or of

51. 17 U.S.C.A. § 108(f).
52. 17 U.S.C.A. § 108(f)(1). Nothing in § 108 "imposes" any liability. Arguably, § 108(f)(1) exculpates libraries and archives and their employees from such possible liabilities. Quaere, as to their liabilities absent the required notice. This exemption is not available to an industry-related library or to the industry itself. 1976 House Report 75.
53. 17 U.S.C.A. § 108(f)(1). *See* note 10 *supra*.

a small part of any other copyrighted work for any such act, or for any later use of such copy or phonorecord, if it exceeds fair use, is not excused by the libraries-and-archives provisions.[54]

19.4[3] Use of "Audiovisual News Programs"

The reproduction and distribution "by lending"[55] of a "limited number" of copies and excerpts by a library or archives of an "audiovisual news program" are not limited by the libraries and archives provisions.[56]

19.4[4] Right of Fair Use or Any Contractual Obligation

The right of fair use as provided by the fair-use provision[57] is not "in any way" affected by the libraries-and-archives provisions.[58] Nor are any contractual provisions

54. 17 U.S.C.A. § 108(f)(2). Such a copy is not "lawfully made" for purposes of other sections of the law.
55. 17 U.S.C.A. § 108(f)(3). The distribution is limited to "lending," to prevent the recipient from performing, copying, or selling the taped broadcast. 1976 House Report 77.
56. 17 U.S.C.A. § 108(f)(3). *Cf.* § 108(h) ("other than an audiovisual work dealing with news"). This exemption is to allow libraries and archives to make off-the-air videotape recordings of daily network newscasts for limited distribution to scholars and researchers. *Compare* 1976 House Report 77 ("daily newscasts of the national television networks, which report the major events of the day," excluding documentaries, magazine-type and other public affairs programs "dealing with subjects of general interest to the viewing public") *with* Conference Report 73 ("local, regional, or network newscasts, interviews concerning current news events, and on-the-spot coverage of news events").
57. 17 U.S.C.A. § 107. *See* chapter 18 *supra*.
58. 17 U.S.C.A. § 108(f)(4). Hence the fair use doctrine is applicable "to a wide variety of situations involving photocopying or other reproduction by a library of copyrighted material in its collections, where the user requests the reproduction for legitimate scholarly or research purposes." 1976 House Report 78–79. Fair use can be broader than the reproduction and distribution exempted by § 108 and vice versa.

assumed at any time by the library or archive when it obtained a copy or phonorecord of a work in its collections.[59]

19.5 Nonremission of Statutory Damages

Reproduction and distribution, purportedly under the libraries-and-archives provisions, but not exempt thereunder, are not eligible for remission of statutory damages, as in the case of infringing uses reasonably believed to be within the provisions of fair use.[60]

19.6 Reports of Register of Copyrights

By January 1, 1983, and at five-year intervals thereafter, the Register of Copyrights is required to submit to Congress a report setting forth the extent to which the libraries-and-archives provisions have achieved the intended statutory balancing of the rights of creators and the needs of users, describing any problems that may have arisen, and presenting any warranted legislative or other recommendations.[61] CONTU had recommended that its guidelines be reviewed not later than January 1, 1983, as part of the review by the Register of Copyrights.[62]

---

59. 17 U.S.C.A. § 108(f)(4). This provision is intended to apply to situations where someone sells or donates a work to a library with the express condition that the work will not be reproduced. 1976 House Report 77.
60. Unlike the remission of statutory damages for infringements in the reasonable belief that the use was fair use. *See* chapter 18, note 56, *supra*.
61. 17 U.S.C.A. § 108(i). The special study was prepared under a contract with King Reese Inc. (King Report). The several recommendations made as a result by the Copyright Office have not been enacted.
62. Conference Report 73. CONTU, in its final report, dated July 31, 1978, had recommended that the Register of Copyrights begin immediately to plan and implement a study of the overall impact of all

19.7 Future Prospects

Library and archives photocopying had been a highly controversial subject.[63] So far, the threat of growing disputes between publishers and authors, on the one hand, and librarians and educators, on the other,[64] has not materialized.

A private Copyright Clearance Center (CCC) was established in 1978 to collect fees from photocopiers and to divide the proceeds among copyright owners.[65] In 1984, the Center began to issue blanket licenses under a contract fee based on statistical samples for perodicals and journals ("Annual Authorization Service"). As a result, increased numbers of corporations have subscribed. The Center has been denied tax-exempt status.[66]

---

photoduplication practices on both proprietors' rights and the public's access to published information.

63. *See* chapter 18, notes 59, 60 *supra*. The invention of copyproof paper and ink may serve as a deterrent to copying.
64. *See* chapter 18, note 59 *supra*.
65. *See* chapter 18, note 61 *supra*.
66. Copyright Clearance Center Inc. v. Commissioner, ___ T.C. ___ (1982) (donative intent and lack of primary purpose of furthering economic interest of publishers not established).

20. Exempted Performances and Displays

Ten exemptions from the exclusive rights of public performance and display are provided in the specific performances-and-displays provisions.[1]

Under the 1909 Act, the exclusive rights of performance were limited to "public" performance[2] and in the case of nondramatic literary[3] and musical works[4] to "public" performance "for profit."[5] No exclusive right of "display" was expressed in the 1909 Act.[6] Also, the concept of "performance" was narrowly construed by the courts.[7] Besides

1. 17 U.S.C.A. § 110; Symposium, *Copyright and Educational Media*, 7 PERFORMING ARTS REV. (No. 1) 1 *et seq.* (1977); Korman, *Performance Rights in Music Under Sections 110 and 118 of the 1976 Copyright Act*, 22 N.Y.L. SCH. L. REV. 521 (1977).
2. 1909 Act § 1(d) (drama).
3. 1909 Act § 1(c).
4. 1909 Act § 1(e).
5. *See* Varmer, *Limitations on Performing Rights* (1958), *reprinted in* 2 STUDIES ON COPYRIGHT—ARTHUR FISHER MEMORIAL EDITION (1963).
6. *See* text accompanying chapter 17, notes 32–37, *supra*. To "display" a work means to show a copy of it, either directly or by means of a film, slide, television image, or any other device or process or, in the case of a motion picture or other audiovisual work, to show individual images nonsequentially. 17 U.S.C.A. § 101. For definition of "to perform or display a work 'publicly'," *see* note 10 *infra*.
7. Twentieth Century Music Corp. v. Aiken, 422 U.S. 151 (1975); Teleprompter Corp. v. CBS, Inc., 415 U.S. 394 (1974); Fortnightly Corp. v. United Artists, 392 U.S. 390 (1968).

eliminating the "for profit" limitation for nondramatic literary and musical works,[8] the 1976 Act broadly defined "perform"[9] and "to perform or display a work 'publicly.' "[10] To provide some balance for these enhanced rights, the 1976 Act specified that certain performances and displays "were not infringements of copyright."[11]

The ten exemptions relate to:

1. Face-to-face teaching activities;
2. Instructional broadcasting;
3. Religious services;

---

8. 17 U.S.C.A. § 106(4). *See* text accompanying chapter 17, notes 23–31, *supra*.
9. 17 U.S.C.A. § 101 ("to recite, render, play, dance, or act it, either directly or by means of any device or process or, in the case of a motion picture or other audiovisual work, to show its images in any sequence or to make the sounds accompanying it audible").
10. 17 U.S.C.A. § 101 ("at a place open to the public or at any place where a substantial number of persons outside of a normal circle of a family or its social acquaintances is gathered," or "to transmit or otherwise communicate" it to such a place or to the public, by means of any device or process, whether the members of the public capable of receiving the performance or display receive it in the same place or in separate places and at the same time or at different times." *Id.* § 101. "Transmit" means to "communicate" by any device or process "whereby images or sounds are received beyond the place from which they are sent." *Id.* § 101. *See* Columbia Pictures Indus., Inc. v. Redd Horne, Inc., 749 F.2d 154 (3d Cir. 1984); Columbia Pictures Indus., Inc. v. Aveco, Inc., 800 F.2d 393 (3d Cir. 1986) (exhibition of copyrighted motion pictures in rented four-person private screening rooms in videocassette rental store held public performance; store open to public; viewing rooms considered mini-movie theaters); Hinton v. Mainlands of Tamarac, 611 F. Supp. 494 (S.D. Fla. 1985)(condominium association's presentation of musical in its clubhouse held public performance, not subject to "family exception"); National Football League v. McBee & Bruno's, 621 F. Supp. 880 (E.D. Mo. 1985)(performance for three friends while bar not in use held not public), *aff'd*, 792 F.2d 726 (8th Cir. 1986).
11. 17 U.S.C.A. § 110; F.E.L. Publications, Ltd. v. Catholic Bishop, 754 F.2d 216 (7th Cir.)(reproduction of copies for exempted performance held actionable), *cert. denied*, 106 S. Ct. 79 (1985).

4. Certain other nonprofit performances;
5. Public reception by single receiving apparatus;
6. Agricultural fairs;
7. Retail sale of copies or phonorecords;
8. Transmission to blind or deaf audiences of nondramatic literary works;
9. Single transmission to blind audiences of dramatic literary works published at least ten years earlier;
10. Certain performances by nonprofit veterans' or fraternal organizations of nondramatic literary or musical works.

20.1 Face-to-Face Teaching Activities

The first exemption applies to *untransmitted* performances and displays of all classes of works, with an added requirement that "lawfully made" copies of motion pictures or other audiovisual works be used. It covers instructional activities other than educational broadcasting.

Exempted is the performance or display of a work "by instructors or pupils" in the course of "face-to-face teaching activities" of a nonprofit educational institution in a "classroom or similar place devoted to instruction." However, in the case of a motion picture or other audiovisual work, the performance, or the display of individual images, may not be given by means of a copy that is not "lawfully made" if the person responsible for the performance knew or had reason to believe that the copy was not lawfully made.[12]

20.1[1] "Instructors or Pupils"

"Instructors" would include guest lecturers if their instructional activities remained confined to classroom situa-

12. 17 U.S.C.A. § 110(a). Ineligible are for-proft institutions like dance studios and language schools.

tions, but would exclude performances by actors, singers, or instrumentalists brought in from outside the school to put on a program.[13] "Pupils" are limited to "enrolled members of a class."[14]

20.1[2] "Face-to-Face Teaching Activities"

Instructor and pupils need not be able to see each other, but they must be simultaneously present in the same general place, thus limiting the exemption to instructional performances and displays that are not "transmitted."[15] The teaching activities may be quite varied, but would not include "performances or displays, whatever their cultural value or intellectual appeal, that are given for the recreation or entertainment of any part of their audience."[16]

20.1[3] "Classroom or Similar Place Devoted to Instruction"

Excluded are places where "the audience is not confined to the members of a particular class."[17] A "similar place" is required to be used "as a classroom for systematic instructional activities," such as a studio, workshop, gymnasium, training field, library, auditorium stage, or an auditorium itself.[18]

---

13. 1976 House Report 82.
14. *Id.*
15. 1976 House Report at 81 ("intended to exclude broadcasting or other transmissions from an outside location into classrooms, whether radio or television and whether open or closed circuit").
16. *Id.*
17. 1976 House Report at 82. Thus excluded from the exemption would be performances "in an auditorium or stadium during a school assembly, graduation ceremony, class play, or sporting event." *Id.* However, the fourth exemption might apply. *See* text accompanying notes 31–35 *infra*.
18. *Id.*

20.1[4] Examples of Permissible Activities

Instructors or pupils may read aloud from copyrighted text material, act out a drama, sing or play a musical work, perform a motion picture or filmstrip, or display text or pictorial material to the class by means of a projector.[19] Not sanctioned is the unauthorized reproduction of copies or phonorecords for the purpose of classroom performance or display.[20]

20.1[5] "Lawfully Made" Requirement

Performances or displays of motion pictures or other audiovisual works are not exempt if the copies are not "lawfully made" and the person responsible for the performance or display knew or had reason to believe that they were not lawfully made.[21]

20.2 Instructional Broadcasting

The second exemption applies to *transmitted* performances of nondramatic literary and musical works,[22] and

19. *Id.* Exemption is also possible under 17 U.S.C.A. § 109(b).
20. 1976 House Report 82.
21. 17 U.S.C.A. § 110(1). This special exception to the exemption would not apply to performances from lawfully made copies, even if the copies were acquired from someone who had stolen or converted them, or if the performances were in violation of an agreement. However, there might be a cause of action for unauthorized distribution or for breach of contract. 1976 House Report 82.
22. 17 U.S.C.A. § 110(2). Thus, performances of dramatic works or dramatico-musical works, or sequential showings of motion pictures or other audiovisual works would require the copyright owner's permission. The exemption, being for performances and displays, does not include the making of dramatizations, adaptations, or other derivative works. *See* 1976 House Report 83. *See* Billings, *Off-the-Air Videorecording, Face-to-Face Teaching, and the 1976 Copyright Act*, 4 N. Ky. L. Rev. 225 (1977).

displays of works without limitation as to class of work. Exempted is the performance of a nondramatic literary or musical work or display of a work, by or in the course of transmission, if:

1. The performance or display is a "regular part of the systematic instructional activities" of a governmental body or a nonprofit educational institution.[23]
2. The performance or display is "directly related and of material assistance to the teaching content" of the transmission.[24]
3. The transmission is made "primarily" for:[25]

    - Reception in "classrooms or similar places normally devoted to instruction."[26]
    - Reception by persons to whom the transmission is directed because their disabilities or other special circumstances prevent their attendance in classrooms or similar places normally devoted to instruction.[27]

---

23. 17 U.S.C.A. § 110(2)(A). "Systematic instructional activities" are the "general equivalent of 'curriculums' " although not necessarily "related to specific course work." 1976 House Report 83. Use of commercial transmission facilities, such as a cable service, does not affect the exemption so long as the actual performance or display was for nonprofit purposes. *Id.*
24. 17 U.S.C.A. § 110(2)(B).
25. 17 U.S.C.A. § 110(2)(B). "Primarily" rather than "solely" is the test. Primary purpose of a program is determined by such factors as subject matter, content, and time of transmission. 1976 House Report 83. A transmission could still be exempt even though it is capable of reception by the public at large. *Id.*
26. 17 U.S.C.A. § 110(2)(C)(i). For meaning of "classrooms or similar places normally devoted to instruction," *see* text accompanying notes 17 and 18 *supra*.
27. 17 U.S.C.A. § 110(2)(C)(ii). Some examples are "preschool children, displaced workers, and shut-ins." 1976 House Report 84. Television courses designed to provide college credit, called "telecourses," could

- Reception by officers or employees of governmental bodies as part of their official duties or employment.[28]

The instructional broadcasting exemption and the face-to-face teaching activities exemption are intended to cover all of the various methods of performances and displays in the course of systematic instruction.

20.3 Religious Services

The third exemption is of performances of nondramatic literary or musical works or of "dramatico-musical" works "of a religious nature,"[29] or display of works without limitation as to class, "in the course of services at a place of worship or other religious assembly."[30]

---

also be exempt, since they "are aimed at undergraduate and graduate students in earnest pursuit of higher educational degrees who are unable to attend daytime classes because of daytime employment, distance from campus, or some other intervening reason." *Id.*

28. 17 U.S.C.A. § 110(2)(C)(iii).
29. 17 U.S.C.A. § 110(3). Performances of "dramatic" sacred music, such as oratorios, cantatas, musical settings of the mass, and choral services, would be exempt, while religious performances of "secular operas, musical plays, motion pictures, and the like," even if they have an underlying religious or philosophical theme, would not be exempt. 1976 House Report 84.
30. 17 U.S.C.A. § 110(3). Not exempt would be the sequential showing of motion pictures and other audiovisual works. The phrase "in course of services" excludes activities "that are for social, educational, fund raising, or entertainment purposes." 1976 House Report 84. The phrase "at a place of worship or other religious assembly" excludes "religious broadcasts to the public at large," but would include services being conducted before a religious gathering in places such as auditoriums, outdoor theaters, and the like. *Id.*

20.4 Certain Other Nonprofit Performances

The fourth exemption is of performances of nondramatic literary or musical works "otherwise than in transmission to the public":[31]

1. Without "any purpose of direct or indirect commercial advantage."[32]
2. Without payment of "any fee or other compensation for the performance to any of its performers, promoters, or organizers if":[33]

   - There is no "direct or indirect admission charge."[34]
   - The proceeds, after deducting the reasonable costs of producing the performance, are "used exclusively for educational, religious, or charitable purposes, and not for private financial gain," except where the "copyright owner" has served the prescribed "notice of objection to the performance."[35]

---

31. *See* 1976 House Report 85–86. Performances must be given directly in the presence of an audience, whether by living performers, playing of phonorecords, or operation of a receiving apparatus.
32. 17 U.S.C.A. § 110(4). *But cf.* note 48 *infra*.
33. 17 U.S.C.A. § 110(4). Payments for salaries to performers, directors, or producers for "duties encompassing the performance" are permissible. Examples would be performances by a school orchestra conducted by a music teacher receiving an annual salary or performances by service bands whose members and conductors perform as part of their assigned duties and who receive armed forces pay. 1976 House Report 85. The use of one or more paid professionals to bolster a weak section or to perform as soloists would destroy the exemption.
34. 17 U.S.C.A. § 110(4)(A); Fourth Floor Music v. Highfill, 622 F. Supp. 168 (M.D. Mo. 1985)(public performance with "donations" for admission and "gas money" for performers held not within § 110(4) exemptions).
35. 17 U.S.C.A. § 110(4)(A) (to avoid owners' being compelled to contribute involuntarily to fund-raising activities of causes they do not favor). The "notice of objection" must be in writing and signed by the

20.5 Public Reception by Single Receiving Apparatus

The fifth exemption is of communications of transmissions embodying performances or displays of works, without limitation as to class of work, by "public reception" of the transmission "on a single receiving apparatus of a kind commonly used in private homes"[36] unless:

"copyright owner" or such owner's duly authorized agent; shall be served on the "person responsible for the performance" at least seven days before the date of the performance stating the "reasons for the objection"; and shall comply, in form, content, and manner of service prescribed by regulations of the Register of Copyrights. *See* 37 C.F.R. § 201.13.

36. 17 U.S.C.A. § 110(5). Exempted would be "small commercial establishments whose proprietors merely bring onto their premises standard radio or television equipment and turn it on for their customers' enjoyment," but not proprietors who have a "commercial 'sound system' " installed or convert a "standard home receiving apparatus (by augmenting it with sophisticated or extensive amplification equipment) into the equivalent of a commercial sound system." 1976 House Report 87.

> Factors to consider in the particular case include the size, physical arrangement, and noise level of the areas within the establishment where the transmissions are made audible or visible, and the extent to which the receiving apparatus is altered or augmented for the purpose of improving the aural or visual quality of the performance for individual members of the public using those areas.

Id. Shipley, *Copyright Law and Your Neighborhood Bar and Grill: Recent Developments in Performance Rights and the Section 110(5) Exemption*, 29 ARIZ. L. REV. 475 (1987).

Columbia Pictures Indus., Inc. v. Professional Real Estate Investors, Inc. 866 F.2d 278 (9th Cir. 1989) (motel rental of videocassettes to guests for viewing in private guest rooms on VCR-equipped television sets held no infringement); International Korwin Corp. v. Kowalczyk, 665 F. Supp. 652 (N.D. Ill. 1987), *aff'd*, 855 F.2d 375 (7th Cir. 1988) (expert testimony of commercially typical amplified receivers); Columbia Pictures Indus., Inc. v. Aveco, Inc., 800 F.2d 59 (3d Cir. 1986) (rental of some thirty viewing rooms for rented or other video cassettes to individual customers (with members of family or social acquaintances) who played cassettes held unauthorized public performances—places "open to the public"). Broadcast Music, Inc. v.

1. A direct charge is made to see or hear the transmission.
2. The transmission thus received is further transmitted to the public.

United States Shoe Corp., 678 F.2d 816 (9th Cir. 1982)(use by apparel stores of commercial monaural system with widely separated speakers not commonly used in private homes not exempt); Robert Stigwood Group Ltd. v. O'Reilly, 530 F.2d 1096 (2d Cir.), *cert. denied,* 429 U.S. 848 (1976); Sailor Music v. Gap Stores, Inc.. 668 F.2d 84 (2d Cir. 1981)(2,796-square-foot chain store transmitting radio music programs by receivers connected to loudspeakers held not within § 106 exemption), *cert. denied,* 456 U.S. 945 (1982); Rogers v. Eighty-Four Lumber Co., 617 F. Supp. 1021 (W.D. Pa. 1985)(§ 110(5) exemption held inapplicable to lumber chain store using radio receiver and separate amplifiers wired to two to five speakers within stores and one to three speakers mounted outside stores to muffle industrial noise, with public address system, where stores' public spaces exceeded 10,000 square feet each; $122,550 [$2,500 for each of forty-nine infringements, plus costs and attorneys' fees]); Merrill v. Bill Miller's Bar B-Q Enters., Inc., 688 F. Supp. 1172 (W.D. Tex. 1988) (equipment exceeded "homestyle" apparatus, and sufficient size to justify subscription to commercial background music service). Laminations Music v. P&X Markets, Inc., Copyright L. Rep. (CCH) ¶ 25, 790 (N.D. Cal. 1985)(transmission of radio broadcasts by small grocery store chain via six to ten ceiling speakers over 10,000 to 14,500 square feet held public performance beyond section 110(5) private-home exemption); Springsteen v. Plaza Roller Dome, Inc., 602 F. Supp. 1113 (D.N.C. 1985)(use of home-type receiver and six barely audible speakers by seasonal miniature golf course with modest income held exempt). Quaere, as to viewing of videotapes in recreational rooms of nursing homes and prisons, performance via loud radio carried along beach or for telephone callers on hold.

The "outer limit" of the exemption has been stated to be the fact situation of Twentieth Century Music Corp. v. Aiken, 422 U.S. 151 (1975)(small commercial establishment using home receiver with four ordinary loudspeakers grouped within relatively narrow circumference from set). The *Aiken* case's narrow construction of "performance," however, has been "completely overturned" in favor of the pre-*Aiken* interpretation of Buck v. Jewell-LaSalle Realty Co., 283 U.S. 191 (1931), by the 1976 Act's definition of "performance." *See* notes 9, 10 *supra*. The fifth exemption has "nothing to do with cable television systems and the exemption would be denied in any case where the audience is charged directly to see or hear the transmission." 1976 House Report 86.

20.6 Agricultural Fairs

The sixth exemption applies to the performances of non-dramatic musical works, exempting their performances "by a governmental body or a nonprofit agricultural or horticultural organization, in the course of an annual agricultural or horticultural fair or exhibition conducted by such body or organization."[37] The exemption extends to any liability for copyright infringement that would otherwise be imposed on such body or organization, "under doctrines of vicarious liability or related infringement," for a performance by a concessionnaire, business establishment, or other person at such fair or exhibition, but does not excuse any such person from liability for the performance.[38]

20.7 Retail Sale of Copies or Phonorecords

The seventh exemption permits the performances of non-dramatic musical works by vending establishments open to the public at large:[39]

1. Without any direct or indirect admission charge;
2. When the sole purpose of the performance is to promote the retail sale of copies or phonorecords of the work;
3. When the performance is not transmitted beyond the place where the establishment is located and is within the immediate area where the sale is occurring.

---

37. 17 U.S.C.A. § 110(6); Mills Music, Inc. v. Arizona, 187 U.S.P.Q. (BNA) 22 (D. Ariz. 1975).
38. 17 U.S.C.A. § 110(6). N.B.: reference to "vicarious liability or related infringement."
39. 17 U.S.C.A. § 110(7).

20.8 Transmission to Blind or Deaf Audiences of Nondramatic Literary Works

The eighth exemption is limited to nondramatic literary works, permitting their performances "by or in the course" of a transmission "designed for and primarily directed to" the blind, the deaf, or other handicapped persons whose sight or hearing is impaired.[40] The performance may not involve "any purpose of direct or indirect commercial advantage,"[41] and the transmission must be made "through the facilities" of:[42]

1. A government body
2. A noncommercial educational broadcast station[43]
3. A "radio subcarrier authorization"[44]
4. A "cable system"[45]

20.9 Single Transmission to Blind Audiences of Dramatic Literary Works Published at Least Ten Years Earlier

The ninth exemption applies to dramatic literary works published at least ten years before the date of the performance, permitting their performance "on a single occasion" "by or in the course" of a transmission "specifically designed for and primarily directed to" blind or other handicapped persons unable to read normal printed material. The

40. 17 U.S.C.A. § 110(8).
41. *Id.*
42. *Id.*
43. 17 U.S.C.A. § 110(8)(ii). The term "noncommercial educational broadcast station" is defined in 47 U.S.C.A. § 397.
44. 17 U.S.C.A. § 110(8)(iii). The term "radio subcarrier authorization" is defined in 47 C.F.R. §§ 73.293–295, 73.593–595.
45. 17 U.S.C.A. § 110(8)(iv). The term "cable system" is defined in § 111(f). See chapter 25, note 11, *infra*.

performance may not involve "any purpose of direct or indirect commercial advantage" and its transmission must be made through the facilities of a "radio subcarrier authorization."[46] The exemption does not apply to more than one performance of the same work by the same performers or under the auspices of the same organization.[47]

20.10 Certain Performances by Nonprofit Veterans' or Fraternal Organizations of Nondramatic Literary or Musical Works

The tenth exemption permits the performance of nondramatic literary or musical works:[48]

1. In the course of a "social function";
2. Organized and promoted by a:
   - "Nonprofit veterans' organization"; or
   - "Nonprofit fraternal organization";
3. To which the "general public" is not invited, but not including the "invitees of the organization"; and
4. If the proceeds from the performance, after deducting the "reasonable costs" of producing the performance, are used "exclusively" for "charitable purposes" and not for "financial gain."

Social functions for any college or university fraternity or sorority are not included unless the social function is held "solely" to raise funds for a "specific charitable purpose."

---

46. 17 U.S.C.A. § 110(9). *See* note 44 *supra*.
47. *Id.*
48. 17 U.S.C.A. § 110(10), added by Pub. L. No. 97-366, § 3, 96 Stat. 1759 (Oct. 25 1982) (notwithstanding § 110(4)).

21. Exempted Ephemeral Recordings

21.1 Specific Ephemeral Recordings Exemptions

"Ephemeral recordings" are accorded limited exemptions from the exclusive rights of reproduction.[1] The term "ephemeral recordings," which is not defined in the statute, means copies or phonorecords of a work made for purposes of later transmission by a broadcasting organization legally entitled to transmit the work. Such limited exemption is needed because of the practical exigencies of broadcasting.[2]

Four exemptions are provided for:

1. Recordings for licensed transmissions;
2. Recordings for instructional transmissions;
3. Recordings for religious transmissions;
4. Recordings for transmission to handicapped audiences.

21.1[1] Recordings for Licensed Transmissions

The first exemption applies to all classes of works except motion pictures and other audiovisual works. Exempted is

1. 17 U.S.C.A. § 112.
2. 1976 House Report 101. "Ephemeral" refers to the limited permissible retention of the recordings for other than archival preservation or security purposes (six months, one year, seven years), rather than to their "transitory" as distinguished from their "fixed" nature.

the making of "no more than one copy or phonorecord" of a "particular transmission program"[3] embodying the performance or display of the work by a "transmitting organization"[4] "entitled to transmit" to the public a performance or display of the work.[5]

Three limitations are imposed:

1. The copy or phonorecord may be retained and used "solely by the transmitting organization that made it," and no further copies or phonorecords may be reproduced from it.[6]
2. The copy or phonorecord may be used "solely for

---

3. "Transmission program" is defined as "a body of material that, as an aggregate, has been produced for the sole purpose of transmission to the public in sequence and as a unit." 17 U.S.C.A. § 101. The same work may be used in different "transmission programs."
4. 17 U.S.C.A. § 112(a). "Transmitting organization" covers a "broadcasting network, or a local broadcaster or individual transmitter." 1976 House Report 102.
5. 17 U.S.C.A. § 112(a). Transmission may be entitled "under a license (negotiated or compulsory) or transfer of the copyright or under the limitation on exclusive rights in sound recordings specified by" § 114(a). Sound recordings have no exclusive performing rights. *See* text accompanying chapter 17, notes 30–31, *supra*. All types of public transmission are permissible: commercial radio and television broadcasts, public radio and television broadcasts not exempted under the instructional broadcasting performances and displays exemption, pay-TV, closed circuit, background music, and so forth. 1976 House Report 102.
6. 17 U.S.C.A. § 112(a)(1). A transmitting organization would have no privilege of exchanging ephemeral recordings with other transmitters or of allowing them to duplicate their own ephemeral recordings from the copy or phonorecord it has made. A transmitting organization is not prevented from having an ephemeral recording made by means of facilities other than its own, although it would not be permissible for a person or organization other than a transmitting organization to make a recording on its own initiative, for possible sale or lease to a broadcaster. The privilege would extend to copies or phonorecords made in advance for later broadcast, as well as recordings of a program made during transmission and intended for deferred transmission or preservation. 1976 House Report 102–03.

the transmitting organization's own transmissions within its local service area, or for purposes of archival preservation or security."[7]

3. Unless "preserved exclusively for archival purposes," the copy or phonorecord must be destroyed within six months from the date the transmission program was first transmitted to the public.[8]

21.1[2] Recordings for Instructional Transmissions

The second exemption applies, because of its cross-reference to the instructional broadcasting performance-and-display exemption, to the transmitted performances of nondramatic literary and musical works and displays of works.[9] Exempted is the making of "no more than thirty copies or phonorecords" of a "particular transmission program"[10] embodying the performance or display by a "governmental body or other nonprofit organization" "entitled to transmit" the performance or display.[11]

Two limitations are imposed:

---

7. 17 U.S.C.A. § 112(a)(2). "Local service area" is defined in *id.* § 111(f).
8. 17 U.S.C.A. § 112(a)(3). Within the six-month period, the copies or phonorecords may be reissued in any number of transmissions.
9. 17 U.S.C.A. § 112(b) (or under limitations on exclusive rights in sound recordings). *See* note 11 *infra*.
10. 17 U.S.C.A. § 112(b). *See* note 3 *supra*.
11. 17 U.S.C.A. § 112(b). Transmission may be entitled under the instructional broadcasting performances and displays exemption applicable to nondramatic literary and musical works (*see* text accompanying chapter 20, notes 22–28, *supra*) or under the limitations on exclusive rights in sound recordings specified by § 114(a). *Id.* Sound recordings have no exclusive performing rights. *See* text accompanying chapter 17, notes 30–31, *supra*. Among the classes of works not included in the exemption are motion pictures and other audiovisual works. Exchanges of recordings among instructional broadcasters are permitted. Nonexempted are copies or phonorecords made for educational broadcasts of a general cultural nature, or for transmission as part of an information storage and retrieval system. 1976 House Report 103.

1. No further copies or phonorecords may be reproduced from the copies or phonorecords under the exemption.[12]
2. Except for one copy or phonorecord that may be "preserved exclusively for archival purposes," the copies or phonorecords must be destroyed within seven years from the date that the transmission program was first transmitted to the public.[13]

21.1[3] Recordings for Religious Transmissions

The third exemption applies to nondramatic musical works "of a religious nature."[14] Exempted is the making "for distribution" of "no more than one copy or phonorecord" for each specified "transmitting organization"[15] of a "particular transmission program"[16] embodying a performance of the work or a sound recording thereof.[17]

Three limitations are imposed:

1. There may be no direct or indirect charge for making or distributing any such copies or phonorecords.[18]
2. None of such copies or phonorecords may be used for any performance other than "a single transmis-

---

12. 17 U.S.C.A. § 112(b)(1). Neither by the nonprofit organization that made them nor by anyone else. However, if others duplicated additional copies or phonographs without some participation by the nonproft organization, it would not be liable for the infringement and the unauthorized copies or phonorecords would not count against the organization's total of thirty. 1976 House Report 104.
13. 17 U.S.C.A. § 112(b)(2). Within the seven-year period, the copies or phonorecords may be reused in any number of transmissions.
14. 17 U.S.C.A. § 112(c).
15. 17 U.S.C.A. § 112(c). Exchanges are permitted under the "for distribution" phrase.
16. 17 U.S.C.A. § 112(c). *See* note 3 *supra*.
17. 17 U.S.C.A. § 112(c).
18. 17 U.S.C.A. § 112(c)(1).

sion to the public"[19] by a "transmitting organization"[20] "entitled to transmit" to the public a performance of the work.[21]

3. Except for one copy or phonorecord that may be "preserved exclusively for archival purposes," the copies or phonorecords must all be destroyed within one year from the date the transmission program was first transmitted to the public.[22]

21.1[4] Recordings for Transmissions to Handicapped Persons

The fourth exemption applies, because of its cross-reference to the eighth performance exemption, to nondramatic literary and musical works.[23] Exempted is the making of "no more than ten copies or phonorecords" embodying the performance by a "governmental body or other nonprofit organization" "entitled to transmit" a performance under the eighth performance exemption.[24] Such organization may permit the use of any such copy or phonorecord by any "governmental body or nonprofit organization" "entitled to transmit" a performance under such eighth performance exemption.[25]

Three limitations are imposed:

---

19. 17 U.S.C.A. § 112(c)(2). The limitation of "single transmission" by a "transmitting organization" does not apply to the other exemptions. *See* notes 8 and 13 *supra* and note 27 *infra*.
20. 17 U.S.C.A. § 112(c)(2).
21. *Id.* Transmission may be entitled "under a license (negotiated or compulsory) or transfer of the copyright."
22. 17 U.S.C.A. § 112(c)(3).
23. 17 U.S.C.A. § 112(d). *See* note 24 *infra*.
24. 17 U.S.C.A. § 112(d). The eighth performance exemption (§ 110(h)) relates to transmissions to sight- and hearing-handicapped audiences of nondramatic literary works. *See* text accompanying chapter 20, notes 40–45, *supra*.
25. 17 U.S.C.A. § 112(d). Exchanges of recordings are not permitted.

1. Any such copy or phonorecord may be retained and used "solely by the organization that made it, or by a governmental body or nonprofit organization" entitled to transmit a performance under the eighth performance exemption, and no further copies or phonorecords may be reproduced from it.[26]
2. Any such copy or phonorecord may be used "solely for transmissions authorized" under the eighth performance exemption, or "for purposes of archival preservation or security."[27]
3. The "governmental body or nonprofit organization permitting any use of any such copy or phonorecord by any governmental body or nonprofit organization under the fourth ephemeral recordings exemption[28] may "not make any charge for such use."[29]

21.2 Copyright Status of Ephemeral Recordings

Transmission programs embodied in copies or phonorecords made under the ephemeral recordings exemptions are not subject to protection as derivative works[30] except with the "express consent" of the "owner of copyright"[31] in the preexisting works employed in the programs.[32]

---

26. 17 U.S.C.A. § 112(d)(1).
27. 17 U.S.C.A. § 112(d)(2). Indefinite retention and use are permitted.
28. 17 U.S.C.A. § 112(d)(3). The fourth ephemeral recordings exemption (§ 110(d)) relates to certain nonprofit performances of undramatic literary and musical works. *See* text accompanying chapter 20, notes 31–35, *supra.*
29. *Id.*
30. 17 U.S.C.A. § 112(e).
31. *Id.* "Owner of copyright," unlike "copyright owner," is not defined. *See* chapter 7, note 51, *supra.*
32. 17 U.S.C.A. § 112(e).

22. Compulsory Musical Recording License

Retained in the 1976 Act[1] with some modifications is the 1909 Act compulsory license subjecting the then newly recognized recording rights in "musical compositions" to licensing by others if the owner recorded or authorized recording of the composition.[2] This compulsory license is a

1. 17 U.S.C.A. § 115 (limiting exclusive rights of reproduction and distribution); Manchester, *Legalized Piracy: The Compulsory Licensing of Phonorecords under the Copyright Revision Act of 1976*, 19 IDEA 149 (1978); Copyright Office Circular R73 (Compulsory License for Making and Distributing Phonorecords).
2. 1909 Act § 1(e) ("parts of instruments serving to reproduce mechanically the musical work"; "mechanical reproductions"). Compare "musical compositions" with "dramatic or dramatico-musical compositions." *Id.* § 5(d), (e). Dramatico-musical works were not subject to the compulsory license. Nor were works under common-law copyright. *See* Henn, *The Compulsory License Provisions of the United States Copyright Law* (1956), *reprinted in* 2 STUDIES ON COPYRIGHT—ARTHUR FISHER MEMORIAL EDITION 877 (1963); Blaisdell, *Economic Aspects of the Compulsory License in the Copyright Law* (1958), *reprinted in* 2 STUDIES ON COPYRIGHT—ARTHUR FISHER MEMORIAL EDITION 937 (1963). Whether foreign works were entitled to musical recording rights in the United States under the 1909 Act depended upon Presidential proclamations specifically declaring mechanical rights reciprocity. No new compulsory license is required for persons having a compulsory license under the 1909 Act to continue to make and distribute "parts embodying the same mechanical reproduction." However, such parts made on or after January 1, 1978, constitute "phonorecords" and are otherwise subject to 17 U.S.C.A. § 115. Transitional and Supplementary Provisions sec. 106.

limitation on the exclusive rights of reproduction and distribution of phonorecords of nondramatic musical works, and is one of four compulsory licenses in the 1976 Act,[3] with others having been since imposed or proposed.[4]

22.1 Scope of Compulsory License

The compulsory license "to make and to distribute" phonorecords of "nondramatic musical works"[5] becomes available once phonorecords of the work have been "distributed to the public in the United States" under the authority of the "copyright owner."[6] The licensee's "primary purpose in making phonorecords" must be "to distribute them to the public for private use."[7]

Not subject to compulsory license is duplication of a sound recording "fixed" by another unless:[8]

1. The sound recording was fixed lawfully;[9]

---

3. Compulsory coin-operated phonorecord players license (currently suspended), chapter 23 *infra;* compulsory noncommercial broadcasting license, chapter 24 *infra;* and compulsory CTV secondary transmission license, chapter 25 *infra. See* Goldstein, *Preempted State Doctrines, Involuntary Transfers and Compulsory Licenses: Testing the Limits of Copyright,* 24 U.C.L.A. L. REV. 1107, 1127–39 (1977).
4. E.g., "Statutory" transmission by satellite carriers for private home viewing license (*see* chapter 26 *infra*); Compulsory license with respect to performance rights of performers, producers, and other copyright owners of sound recordings (*see* chapter 18, note 31 *supra*).
5. "Musical works, including any accompanying words" as distinguished from "dramatic works, including any accompanying music." 17 U.S.C.A. § 102(a)(2), (3). *See* note 2 *supra.*
6. 17 U.S.C.A. § 115(a)(1). "Copyright owner" is defined as referring, with respect to any one of the exclusive rights comprised in a copyright, to the owner of that particular right. *Id.* § 101.
7. 17 U.S.C.A. § 115(a)(1). This prevents broadcasters, jukebox operators, and background music services from taking advantage of the compulsory licensing provision. 1976 House Report 108.
8. 17 U.S.C.A. § 115(a)(1). *See* note 10 *infra.*
9. 17 U.S.C.A. § 115(a)(1). "Fixed" is defined in 17 U.S.C.A. § 101.

2. The making of the phonorecords was authorized by the "owner of copyright"[10] in the sound recording or, if the sound recording was fixed before February 15, 1972, by any person who fixed the sound recording pursuant to an "express license" from the "owner of the copyright" in the musical work or pursuant to a valid compulsory license for use of the work in a sound recording.

22.2 Notice of Intention to Obtain Compulsory License

To obtain a compulsory license, a "notice of intention"[11] to do so must be served on the "copyright owner"[12] before

---

10. 17 U.S.C.A. § 115(a)(1). A person is not entitled to a compulsory license for the purpose of making an unauthorized duplication of a musical sound recording originally developed and produced by another. 1976 House Report 108. "Owner of copyright," unlike "copyright owner," is not defined. *See* chapter 7, note 51, *supra*. *See* Harris v. Emus Records Corp., 734 F.2d 1329 (9th Cir. 1984)(compulsory license not applicable to duplication of existing recording); Heilman v. Bell, 583 F.2d 373 (7th Cir. 1978), (duplication of original recordings held not "similar use" under 1909 Act), *cert. denied*, 440 U.S. 959 (1979); Fame Publishing Co. v. Alabama Custom Tape, Inc., 507 F.2d 667 (5th Cir. 1975)(2–1)(not "similar use"); Jondora Music Publishing Co. v. Melody Recordings, Inc., 506 F.2d 392 (6th Cir. 1974)(2–1)("similar use" in 1909 Act § 1(3) held not to permit copying of authorized sound recording itself). *Cf.* 17 U.S.C.A. § 115(a)(1); Edward B. Marks Music Corp. v. Colorado Magnetics, Inc., 497 F.2d 285 (10th Cir. 1974)(5–2)(not "similar use"); Duchess Music Corp. v. Stern, 458 F.2d 1305 (9th Cir. 1972)(2–1).
11. 17 U.S.C.A. § 115(b)(1). Regulations prescribe the form, content, and manner of service of such notice. 37 C.F.R. § 201.18.
12. 17 U.S.C.A. § 115(b)(1). Copies of notices served on the "copyright owner" need not be filed in the Copyright Office. The 1909 Act nomenclature was "Notice of Intention to Use." Eliminated was the 1909 Act requirement of a "Notice of use." (form U); Copyright Office Circular R51. Registration and recordation of any transfer identifies the copyright owner entitled to any royalties.

or within thirty days after making, and before distributing, any phonorecord of the work.[13] If the registration or other public records of the Copyright Office do not identify the copyright owner and include an address at which notice can be served, filing of the notice in the Copyright Office is sufficient.[14]

Failure to serve or file forecloses the possibility of a compulsory license and, absent a negotiated license, renders the making and distribution of phonorecords actionable as acts of infringement "fully subject" to the remedies for infringement.[15]

22.3 Arrangements

Included in the compulsory license is the "privilege of making a musical arrangement" of the work "to the extent necessary to conform it to the style or manner of interpretation of the performance involved."[16] However, the arrangement may not change "the basic melody or fundamental character" of the work,[17] and shall not be subject to protection as a "derivative work,"[18] except with the "express consent" of the "copyright owner."[19]

22.4 Royalties Payable Under Compulsory License

The "copyright owner" is entitled to receive royalties only for phonorecords made and distributed after being

---

13. 17 U.S.C.A. § 115(b)(2).
14. 17 U.S.C.A. § 115(b)(2). The filing fee is $12. 17 U.S.C.A. § 708(a)(5).
15. 17 U.S.C.A. § 115(b)(2).
16. 17 U.S.C.A. § 115(a)(2) (in effect pro tanto limitation on exclusive right of adaptation).
17. 17 U.S.C.A. § 115(a)(2). The music may not be "perverted, distorted, or travestied." 1976 House Report 109.
18. *See* text accompanying chapter 5, notes 31–37, *supra*.
19. 1976 House Report 109. See note 6 *supra*.

identified in the registration or other public records of the Copyright Office.[20]

Royalties are payable for every phonorecord "made and distributed,"[21] compared to for each "part manufactured" under the 1909 Act.[22] A phonorecord is considered "distributed," if the person exercising the compulsory license has "voluntarily and permanently parted with its possession."[23]

The royalty rate for each work embodied in the record initially was the larger of:[24]

1. Two and three-fourths cents;
2. One-half of one cent per minute of playing time or fraction thereof.

Since 1990, the royalty rate is the larger of 5.7 cents or 1.1 cent per minute of playing time or fraction thereof.[25]

Included in the compulsory license is the right of the maker to distribute or authorize distribution of the phonorec-

---

20. 17 U.S.C.A. § 115(c)(1) (but not for any phonorecords previously made or distributed).
21. 17 U.S.C.A. § 115(c)(2). A maker, not involved in the distribution, would be jointly and severally liable for infringement. 1976 House Report 110.
22. 1909 Act § 1(e). The record producer need not pay a royalty for phonorecords "which merely go into inventory, which may later be destroyed, and from which the record producer gains no economic benefit." 1976 House Report 110.
23. 17 U.S.C.A. § 115(c)(2).
24. 17 U.S.C.A. § 115(c)(2) (up from "2 cents on each such part manufactured" under the 1909 Act). The royalty rates are subject to adjustment by petition by "any owner or user" filed with the Copyright Royalty Tribunal as provided in 17 U.S.C.A. §§ 801(b)(1), 804(a)(2)(B). On November 1, biennially, the rates are adjusted based on the percent change in the Consumer Price Index. 37 C.F.R. §§ 307.1–307.3. *See* chapter 31 *infra*. Quaere, as to the construction of negotiated licenses that incorporate by reference the statutory compulsory license rates.
25. *See* 37 C.F.R. § 307.3 (providing for adjustments). Adjusted royalty rates are published in the Federal Register.

ord by rental, lease, or lending. In addition to the aforementioned royalty, the compulsory licensee shall pay a proportionate royalty for every act of distribution by or in the nature of rental, lease, or lending by or under the authority of the compulsory licensee.[26]

Monthly royalty payments, each under oath and in compliance with regulations,[27] must be made on or before the twentieth day of each month for the preceding month. Detailed cumulative annual statements of account, certified by a certified public accountant, as prescribed by regulations,[28] shall be filed for every compulsory license.[29] Such regulations covering both the monthly and annual statements of account shall prescribe the form, content, and manner of certification with respect to the number of records made and the number distributed.[30]

If the "copyright owner" does not receive the monthly payments and the monthly and annual statements of account when due, the owner may give written notice to the licensee that, unless the default is remedied within thirty days from the date of the notice, the compulsory license will be automatically terminated. Such termination renders either the making or the distribution, or both, of all phonorecords for which the royalty has not been paid, actionable as acts of infringement "fully subject" to the remedies for infringement.[31]

---

26. 17 U.S.C.A. § 115(c)(3), added by Record Rental Amendment of 1984, Pub. L. No. 98–450, § 3, 98 Stat. 1727 (Oct. 4, 1984). The distribution royalty will be a proportion of the revenue received by the compulsory licensee from every such act of distribution equal to the proportion of the revenue received by the compulsory licensee from distribution under § 115(c)(2).
27. *See* 37 C.F.R. § 201.19.
28. *Id.*
29. 17 U.S.C.A. § 115(c)(3).
30. *See* 37 C.F.R. § 201.19.
31. 17 U.S.C.A. § 115(c)(5).

22.5 Effect on Recording License of Termination

Termination of an author's book publishing grant with subsidiary recording rights does not terminate negotiated recording licenses and the right of the book publisher to share in the royalties from the distribution of the recordings.[32]

---

32. *See* chapter 16, note 43, *supra*.

23. Compulsory Coin-Operated Phonorecord Players License (Suspended as of August 9, 1990, from January 1, 1990, to December 31, 1999, or Until Termination of Negotiated License)

23.1 Limitation of Exclusive Rights of Public Performance of Nondramatic Musical Works

The exclusive rights of public performance of nondramatic musical works[1] prior to 1990 was limited by the compulsory "coin-operated phonorecord players"[2] license provided in section 116, as qualified by the negotiated license provisions of section 116A added as of March 1, 1989.[3]

As of August 9, 1990, the "jukebox" compulsory license fee was suspended by the Copyright Royalty Tribunal from January 1, 1990, to December 31, 1999, or until termination of the license agreement between the Amusement and Mu-

1. 17 U.S.C.A. § 106(4). Under the 1909 Act, the exclusive rights were to perform nondramatic musical works publicly *"for profit."* *See* chapter 17, note 27, *supra*.
2. The term "coin-operated phonorecord player" is defined. *See* text accompanying notes 16–20 *infra*. The 1909 Act used the term "coin-operated machines," without definition, and provided that the "reproduction or rendition of a musical composition by or upon coin-operated machines shall not be deemed a public performance for profit unless a fee is charged for admission to the place where such reproduction or rendition occurs." 1909 Act § 1(e). For a brief discussion of the arguments for and against the so-called jukebox exemption, *see* 1976 House Report 112–13.
3. 17 U.S.C.A. § 116; Copyright Office Circular R70. For discussion of 17 U.S.C.A. § 116A (negotiated licenses for public performances by means of coin-operated phonorecord players), *see* text accompanying notes 41–48 *infra*.

sic Operators Associations and the music performing-rights societies. A copy of the negotiated agreement was filed with the Tribunal.[4]

Previously, for public performances on "coin-operated phonorecord players" (the "juke box exemption" having been eliminated), there was no liability on the part of:[5]

1. The proprietor of the establishment in which the public performance took place unless:[6]
   - That proprietor was the "operator"[7] of the phonorecord player;
   - That proprietor refused or failed, within one month after receiving a request,[8] at a time during which the required certificate was not affixed to the phonorecord player,[9] by the "copyright owner,"[10] to make full disclosure[11] of the identity of the "operator" of the phonorecord player;

---

4. *See* Copyright L. Rep. (CCH) ¶ 16,677 (text of license), ¶ 20,571 (Tribunal notice). The 1990 rates were $275 for the first jukebox, $55 for each of the second through tenth jukeboxes, and $48 for each additional jukebox. For 1991 through 1994, fees are reduced, e.g., $48 fee reduced to $47; 1992 maximum $45. Beginning in 1993, base rate will be adjusted to percentage increase in the Consumer Price Index from October 1, 1991, to October 1, 1992. Fees will be on an annual basis without proration.
5. 17 U.S.C.A. § 116(a).
6. 17 U.S.C.A. § 116(a)(1).
7. 17 U.S.C.A. § 116(a)(1)(A). The term "operator" is defined to include joint operators. *Id.* § 116(e)(2). *See* text accompanying notes 21–24 *infra.*
8. 17 U.S.C.A. § 116(a)(1)(B).
9. 17 U.S.C.A. § 116(a)(1)(B). The request must be by registered or certified mail.
10. The term "copyright owner" is defined as referring, with respect to any one of the exclusive rights comprised in a copyright, to the owner of that particular right. *Id.* § 101.
11. 17 U.S.C.A. § 116(a)(1)(B). The disclosure must be by registered or certified mail.

2. The "operator" of the "coin-operated phonorecord player" who had obtained a compulsory license to perform the work publicly on "that phonorecord player."[12]

23.2 Obtaining Compulsory License

An "operator" of a "coin-operated phonorecord player" could, until 1990, have obtained annually a compulsory license to perform the work publicly on "that phonorecord player" by filing in the Copyright Office the required application,[13] affixing the prescribed certificate,[14] and depositing

---

12. 17 U.S.C.A. § 116(a)(2). A separate certification for each phonorecord player is issuable within twenty days after receipt by the Register of Copyrights of the required application and royalty fee. *Id.* § 116(b)(1)(B). The certificate consists of two parts, each 1″ × 3″ in size, and contains the name and address of the operator, identification of the particular coin-operated phonorecord player, date of expiration of the license, date of issuance of the certificate, and requirements of affixation. Certificates issued upon payment of the $4 fee are valid after July 1 of the year of issuance. The certificate is mailed to the operator whose name and address appear on the application.
13. *Id.* § 116(b)(1). The application, with royalty fees, is required to be filed before or within one month after performances are made available on a particular phonorecord player and during the month of January in each succeeding year that such performances are made available on that particular phonorecord player, in accordance with regulations prescribed by the Register of Copyrights after consultation with the Copyright Royalty Tribunal. Form JB and information concerning the compulsory license are available from: Licensing Division, Copyright Office, Library of Congress, Washington, D.C. 20557. 37 C.F.R. § 201.16; Copyright Office Form JB; Copyright Office Circulars R70, R75. The application must state the name and address of the "operator" and the manufacturer and serial number or other explicit identification of the phonorecord player. Within twenty days of receipt of the required application and royalty fee, the Register of Copyrights is required to issue to the applicant a certificate for the phonorecord player. 17 U.S.C.A. § 116(b)(1)(B).
14. 17 U.S.C.A. § 116(b)(1)(B), (C). The "operator," on or before March 1

the statutory royalties for the particular phonorecord player with the Register of Copyrights.[15]

23.3 Definitions

Statutorily defined are the terms:

1. "Coin-operated phonorecord player"

---

of the year in which the certificate is issued, or within ten days after the date of issue of the certificate, whichever is later, shall "affix to the particular phonorecord player," "in a position where it can be readily examined by the public" the certificate issued by the Register of Copyrights of the latest application made by that operator with respect to that phonorecord player. The certificate may be placed on the record selection (title strip) panel, but if so both parts must be clearly visible. Copyright Office Circular R70. When a jukebox operator discovers that the certificate for a particular machine has been misplaced, discarded, stolen, obliterated, or otherwise lost or destroyed, that operator should write immediately to the Copyright Office requesting a replacement. Then, as soon as the replacement certificate is issued, the operator should affix it to the machine in a position where the public can readily examine it.

The Copyright Office does not provide printed forms for operators to use in requesting replacement certificates. Under the regulations, a request must be in the form of an affidavit or statement (preferably typewritten), which must contain certain specified information and must be accompanied by a prescribed fee payable to the Register of Copyrights in the form of a certified check, cashier's check, or money order. A replacement certificate cannot be issued unless and until the necessary fee has been received.

For accounting reasons, requests and fees for replacement certificates should *not* be sent to the Copyright Office's Licensing Division (ZIP Code 20557). Instead, they should be addressed to: Copyright Office, Library of Congress, Washington, D.C. 20559. The affidavit or statement should be mailed together in the same envelope. Copyright Office Circular R71 (Replacement Certificates). *See* 37 C.F.R. § 201.16.

15. 17 U.S.C.A. § 116(b)(1)(A). *See* text accompanying notes 26–28 *infra*.

2. "Operator"
3. "Performing rights society"

23.3[1] "Coin-Operated Phonorecord Player"

A "coin-operated phonorecord player" is a "machine or device":[16]

1. Employed "solely for the performance" of nondramatic musical works by means of phonorecords "upon being activated by insertion of coins, currency, tokens, or other monetary units or their equivalent";[17]
2. Located in an establishment making "no direct or indirect charge for admission";[18]
3. Accompanied by a "list of the titles of all the musical works available for performance on it";[19]
4. Affording a "choice of works available for performance" and permitting the choice "to be made by

---

16. 17 U.S.C.A. § 116(e). "Machine" or "device" is "one now known or later developed." *Id.* § 101.
17. 17 U.S.C.A. § 116(e)(1)(A). Not included are coin-operated radio or television sets, as well as jukebox-like devices that perform musical motion pictures.
18. 17 U.S.C.A. § 116(e)(1)(B). No license would issue for machines in establishments that impose cover or minimum charges or in clubs that are open to the public, but require membership fees for admission. MCA, Inc. v. Parks, 796 F.2d 200 (6th Cir. 1986)(skating fee held indirect charge for admission); BGO Music Inc. v. Pee Bee Invs., Inc., 785 F.2d 304 (4th Cir. 1986); Stewart v. Southern Music Distrib. Co., 503 F. Supp. 258 (M.D. Fla. 1980)(operator contributorily infringes if admission charge imposed); *accord* Blendingwell Music, Inc. v. Moor-Law, Inc., 612 F. Supp. 474 (D. Del. 1985)(where charge meant for live music rather than jukebox).
19. 17 U.S.C.A. § 116(e)(1)(C). The list must be "affixed to the phonorecord player" or "posted in the establishment in a prominent position where it can be readily examined by the public." *Id.* A list available only upon request would not satisfy this condition.

> the patrons of the establishment in which it is located."[20]

23.3[2] "Operator"

An "operator" is any person "who, alone or jointly with others":[21]

1. Owns a "coin-operated phonorecord player";[22]
2. Has the "power" to make a "coin-operated phonorecord player" "available for placement in an establishment for purposes of public performance";[23]
3. Has the "power" to exercise "primary control" over the selection of the musical works made available for public performance on a "coin-operated phonorecord player."[24]

23.3[3] "Performing Rights Society"

A "performing rights society" is an association or corporation that licenses the "public performance of nondramatic musical works" on behalf of the "copyright owners," such as the American Society of Composers, Authors and Publishers (ASCAP), Broadcast Music, Inc. (BMI), and SESAC, Inc. (SESAC).[25]

---

20. 17 U.S.C.A. § 116(e)(1)(D). A situation where someone other than patrons of the establishment makes selections (such as a disc jockey in a discotheque) clearly falls outside the definition. Similarly, a machine that merely provides continuous music without affording any choice over specific compositions at a particular time would also run afoul of the definition.
21. 17 U.S.C.A. § 116(e)(2).
22. 17 U.S.C.A. § 116(e)(2)(A).
23. 17 U.S.C.A. § 116(e)(2)(B).
24. 17 U.S.C.A. § 116(e)(2)(C).
25. 17 U.S.C.A. § 116(e)(3). *See* ACEMLA v. Copyright Royalty Tribunal, 763 F.2d 101 (2d Cir. 1985)(denial of proof of entitlement). *See* chapter 17, note 29, *supra*.

23.4 Royalty Rates

The initial statutory royalty fee, required to be deposited with the Register of Copyrights, was $8 per calendar year[26] for a particular phonorecord player.[27] Royalty rates are subject to adjustment by petition by "any owner or user" filed with the Copyright Royalty Tribunal in 1990 and in each subsequent tenth calendar year, and at any time within one year after negotiated licenses under section 116A are terminated or expire and are not replaced by subsequent agreements.[28] By 1990, when the annual fee was suspended, the fee had been increased to $63.

23.5 Distribution of Royalties

All royalty fees deposited with the Register of Copyrights, after deducting the reasonable costs incurred by the Copy-

26. 17 U.S.C.A. § 116(b)(1)(A). Since 1987 the fee has been $63 subject to cost-of-living adjustment. 37 C.F.R. § 306.3. For performances available on a particular phonorecord player after July 1 of any year, the royalty fee for the remainder of that year is one-half of the annual rate subject to adjustment. 17 U.S.C.A. § 116(b)(1)(A). Such fees were suspended by the Tribunal as of January 1, 1990.

27. 17 U.S.C.A. § 116(b)(1)(A). Along with the application on form JB, the operator is required to send a full payment of the royalty fee for all of the jukeboxes listed on the form. The total amount of royalties payable is computed by multiplying the total number of phonorecord players listed on the form by the statutory royalty fee. Phonorecord players covered by full-year fees should not be mixed with phonorecord players covered by half-year fees on the same application.

Remittances accompanying form JB must be in the form of a certified check, cashier's check, or money order, payable to: Register of Copyrights. The Copyright Office will not issue a certificate for affixation to a jukebox until it has received an acceptable remittance covering the royalty fee for that player.

28. 17 U.S.C.A. § 804(a)(2)(C); 37 C.F.R. §§ 306.1–306.3. See chapter 31 *infra*.

right Office, shall be deposited in the Treasury of the United States,[29] for later distribution "with interest" by the Copyright Royalty Tribunal.[30] Each January, "every person claiming to be entitled to compulsory license fees" for performances during the preceding twelve-month period shall file a claim with the Copyright Royalty Tribunal in accordance with its regulations.[31] The claim shall include "an agreement to accept as final, except as provided in section 810," the determination of the Copyright Royalty Tribunal in any controversy concerning the distribution of deposited royalty fees "to which the claimant is a party."[32]

An antitrust exemption is provided for claimants who:[33]

1. Agree among themselves as to the proportionate division of compulsory licensing fees among them;
2. Lump their claims together and file them jointly or as a single claim;
3. Designate a common agent to receive payment on their behalf.

After October 1 of each year, the Copyright Royalty Tribunal is required to determine whether there exists a "controversy" concerning the distribution of deposited royalty fees. If the Tribunal determines that no such controversy exists, it shall, after deducting its reasonable administrative costs,

29. 17 U.S.C.A. § 116(c)(1) ("in such manner as the Secretary of the Treasury directs"). All funds held by the Secretary of the Treasury shall be invested in interest-bearing United States securities.
30. 17 U.S.C.A. § 116(c)(1) The Register of Copyrights is required to submit to the Copyright Royalty Tribunal, on an annual basis, a detailed statement of account covering all fees received for the relevant period.
31. 17 U.S.C.A. § 116(c)(2); 37 C.F.R. §§ 305.1–305.5.
32. 17 U.S.C.A. § 116(c)(2). Information concerning royalty distributions is available from: Copyright Royalty Tribunal, 1111-20th Street, N.W., Suite 450, Washington, D.C. 20036.
33. *Id.*

distribute such fees to the "copyright owners" entitled, or to their designated agents. If it finds that such a controversy exists, it shall conduct a proceeding to determine the distribution.[34]

Fees to be distributed should be divided as follows:[35]

1. To every "copyright owner" not affiliated with a "performing rights society," the pro rata share of the fees to be distributed to which such "copyright owner" proves entitlement;
2. To the "performing rights societies," the remainder of the fees to be distributed in such pro rata shares as they shall by agreement stipulate among themselves,[36] or, if they fail to agree, the pro rata share to which such "performing rights societies" prove entitlement;
3. Withholding from distribution by the Copyright Royalty Tribunal, during the pendency of any proceeding, "an amount sufficient to satisfy all claims with respect to which a controversy exists," with the Tribunal having discretion to proceed to distribute "any amounts that are not in controversy."

The Copyright Royalty Tribunal is required to promulgate regulations under which "persons who can reasonably be expected to have claims" may, during the year in which performances take place, "without expense to or harassment of operators or proprietors of establishments in which phonorecord players are located," have:[37]

---

34. 17 U.S.C.A. § 116(c)(3). *See* chapter 31 *infra*.
35. 17 U.S.C.A. § 116(c)(4); ACEMLA v. Copyright Royalty Tribunal, 809 F.2d 926 (D.C. Cir. 1987).
36. For antitrust exemption, *see* text accompanying note 33 *supra*.
37. 17 U.S.C.A. § 116(c)(5); 37 C.F.R. §§ 303.1–303.2; 43 Fed. Reg. 53,795 (Nov. 17, 1978). For denial of access permitted under the regulations prescribed by the Copyright Royalty Tribunal, any person may bring

1. Access to such establishments and to the phonorecord players located therein;
2. Opportunity to obtain information "as may be reasonably necessary to determine, by sampling procedures or otherwise, the proportion of contribution of the musical works of each such person to the earnings of the phonorecord players for which fees shall have been deposited."

23.6 Liabilities and Criminal Penalties

Failure to file the application, to affix the certificate, or to pay the royalty required renders each public performance actionable as an act of infringement[38] and "fully subject to the remedies" for infringement.[39]

Criminal fines of not more than $2,500 may be imposed on any person who "knowingly":[40]

1. Makes a false representation of a "material fact" in an application;

---

an action in the United States District Court for the District of Columbia for the cancellation of the compulsory license of the phonorecord player to which such access has been denied, and the court shall have the power to declare the compulsory license thereof invalid from the date of issue thereof.

38. 17 U.S.C.A. § 116(b)(2). *See* note 14 *supra*. Such liability is on the "operator" and not on the "proprietor of the establishment" unless the "proprietor" is the "operator" or fails to make full disclosure of the identity of the "operator." *Id.* § 116(a); Broadcast Music, Inc. v. Xanthas, Inc., 855 F.2d 233 (5th Cir. 1988) (problem of proof of ownership of jukeboxes). *See* text accompanying notes 5–12 *supra*.
39. 17 U.S.C.A. § 116(b)(2). *See* chapter 28 *infra*, *see also* Broadcast Music, Inc. v. Dugas Music Serv., Copyright L. Rep. (CCH) ¶ 26,003 (D. Mass. 1986)(affixation of certificate *inside* jukebox held infringement).
40. 17 U.S.C.A. § 116(d).

2. Alters a certificate;
3. Affixes a certificate to a phonorecord player other than the one it covers.

23.7 Negotiated Licenses

The Berne Act qualified section 116 (compulsory licenses) by a new section 116A, captioned "negotiated licenses for public performances by means of coin-operated phonorecord players."[41] "Compulsory licenses for" was inserted before "Public" in the heading of section 116.[42] The application of the compulsory license was limited to phonorecords "the performance of which is subject to this section as provided in section 116A."[43] The definitions in section 116(e) are applicable also to section 116A.[44]

Negotiated licenses are to be given effect "in lieu of any otherwise applicable determination by the Copyright Royalty Tribunal."[45] Periodically, beginning one year after March 1, 1989, the Tribunal must determine whether or not negotiated licenses are in effect "so as to provide permission to use a quantity of musical works not substantially smaller than the quantity of such works performed on coin-operated phonorecord players during the one-year period ending on" March 1, 1989, the Tribunal's rate-making activity for coin-operated phonorecord players being suspended during the year. Only if the determination is negative do the

41. Berne Act § 4(a)(4); 17 U.S.C.A. § 116A (effective Mar. 1, 1989). Martin, *The Berne Convention and the U.S. Compulsory License for Jukeboxes: Why the Song Could Not Remain the Same*, 37 J. COPYRIGHT SOC'Y 262 (1990).
42. Berne Act § 4(b).
43. Berne Act § 4(b)(1)(B); 17 U.S.C.A. § 116.
44. Berne Act § 4(b)(1)(C); 17 U.S.C.A. § 116(e). For definitions, see notes 16, 21, 25 *supra*.
45. Berne Act § 4(a)(4); 17 U.S.C.A. § 116A(d).

compulsory license provisions apply, but then only to musical works that are not the subject of negotiated licenses. Negotiable licenses are given effect "in lieu of any otherwise applicable determination" by the Tribunal.[46] Meanwhile, compulsory licenses in effect prior to March 1, 1989 "shall remain in force."[47] Besides having to determine the extent of negotiable licenses, the Tribunal, by its chairman, is involved in the timing and location of negotiation schedules.[48]

---

46. *Id.*
47. Berne Act § 4(a)(4); 17 U.S.C.A. § 116(g).
48. Berne Act § 4(a)(4); 17 U.S.C.A. § 116(e).

24. Compulsory Noncommercial Broadcasting License

The compulsory noncommercial broadcasting license provisions[1] limit the exclusive rights of public performance and display, adaptation, reproduction, and public distribution of:

1. *Published* nondramatic musical works[2]
2. *Published* pictorial, graphic, and sculptural works[3]

In effect, public broadcasters are permitted to use such types of works without seeking individual permissions and at predetermined fees set either through voluntary negotia-

---

1. 17 U.S.C.A. § 118; 37 C.F.R. §§ 304.1–304.13. *See* Korman, *Performance Rights in Music Under Sections 110 and 118 of the 1976 Copyright Act,* 22 N.Y.L. SCH. L. REV. 521 (1977). This compulsory license is to be distinguished from the other three in the 1976 Act: (1) musical recording, (2) coin-operated phonorecord players, and (3) cable television secondary transmissions, and from the proposed compulsory performance rights license, and other new or proposed compulsory licenses.
2. 17 U.S.C.A. § 118(b). Concerning negotiation of licenses for nondramatic literary works, *see* text accompanying notes 56–60 *infra*.
3. 17 U.S.C.A. § 118(b). Excluded are unpublished works of all classes, and other classes of published works, such as nondramatic literary works, plays, operas, ballets, and other stage presentations, and motion picture television programs, documentary films, and audiovisual works.

tions or by the Copyright Royalty Tribunal. The provisions are limited to such types of works and do not extend to other works included in the transmission program.

24.1 Scope of Compulsory License

Subject to the terms of "any voluntary license agreements that have been negotiated,"[4] a "public broadcasting entity"[5] has a compulsory license to engage in the following "activities":[6]

1. Performance or display "by or in the course of a transmission"[7] made by a "noncommercial educational broadcast station";[8]
2. Production of a "transmission program," and reproduction and distribution of copies or phonorecords thereof, "where such production, reproduction, or distribution is made for a nonprofit institution or organization solely for the purpose of transmissions" made by a "noncommercial educational broadcast station";[9]
3. Making of reproductions "by a governmental body or a nonprofit institution of a transmission program simultaneously with its transmission" by a "noncom-

4. 17 U.S.C.A. § 118(d). *See* text accompanying notes 52–55 *infra*.
5. 17 U.S.C.A. § 118(d). "Public broadcasting entity" is defined to mean a "noncommercial educational broadcast station," as defined in 48 U.S.C. § 397, and any nonprofit institution or organization engaged in the "activities" described in 17 U.S.C.A. § 118(d)(2). *Id.* § 118(g).
6. 17 U.S.C.A. § 118(d). "Interconnection" activities serving as a technical adjunct to such transmissions, such as the use of satellites or microwave equipment, are intended to be included within the specified "activities." 1976 House Report 119.
7. 17 U.S.C.A. § 118(d)(1). For meaning of "noncommercial educational broadcast station," *see* note 5 *supra*.
8. 17 U.S.C.A. § 118(d)(1).
9. 17 U.S.C.A. § 118(d)(2).

mercial educational broadcast station" and the "performance or display of the contents of such program under the conditions specified" in the "face-to-face teaching activities" performance-or-displays exemption,[10] "but only if" the reproductions are:[11]

- Used for performances or displays for a period of no more than seven days from the date of transmission;
- Destroyed during or at the end of such period.[12]

24.2 Royalty Payments Under Compulsory License

24.2[1] Initial Terms and Rates

The initial reasonable terms and royalty rates under this compulsory license, unlike the other compulsory licenses, were left to the Copyright Royalty Tribunal to determine.[13] The initial determination was for the period beginning on June 8, 1978,[14] and ending on December 31, 1982.[15] The 1990–91/1992 schedules of rates and terms are, respectively:[16]

---

10. 17 U.S.C.A. § 110(1). *See* text accompanying chapter 20, note 12, *supra*.
11. 17 U.S.C.A. § 118(d)(3). The seven-day limitation and destruction requirement "applies" only to the third "activities."
12. 17 U.S.C.A. § 118(d)(3) See text accompanying notes 45–47 *infra*.
13. 17 U.S.C.A. §§ 118(b), 801(b). *See* chapter 31 *infra*.
14. 17 U.S.C.A. § 118(b)(3). June 8, 1978 was six months after the publication of the required notice in the *Federal Register* on December 8, 1977. *Id.* § 118(b).
15. 17 U.S.C.A. § 118(b).
16. 37 C.F.R. §§ 304.1 *et seq.* (3–2, with minority favoring revenue, rather than flat-rate, method for musical works). The Copyright Royalty Tribunal decided that at one-year intervals, beginning August 1, 1979, a revised schedule of rates would become effective to reflect the change in the cost of living as determined by the Consumer Price Index. *Id.* § 304.10.

1. Published nondramatic musical compositions:[17]
   a. Performances by Public Broadcasting Service (PBS), National Public Radio (NPR), and their respective stations[18] of all compositions not subject to negotiated[19] licenses:[20]
      i. In "feature presentation" of:[21]
         PBS, $175/$184;
         PBS station, $15/$16;
         NPR, $17.75/$18.70;
         NPR station, $1.25/$1.30.
      ii. As "background or theme music" in:[22]
         PBS program, $44.35/$46.70;
         PBS station's program, $3.15/$3.30;
         NPR program, $4.30/$4.50;
         NPR station's program, $0.45/$0.50.
   b. Performances by "public broadcasting entities" licensed to colleges and universities, or other nonprofit educational institutions not affiliated with NPR for:[23]
      i. All compositions in ASCAP repertory, $173 annually;
      ii. All compositions in BMI repertory, $173 annually;

17. 37 C.F.R. §§ 304.4–.6.
18. *Id.*
19. 37 C.F.R. § 304.3 relating to performance of ASCAP musical compositions has been deleted ($1.25 million payable to ASCAP). BMI and SESAC had negotiated their agreements with PBS and NPR.
20. 37 C.F.R. § 304.4(a) (with series theme music rates being double the single program rate for the entire series). This is payable in two equal installments on July 31 and December 31 of each calendar year. The basic rate is adjusted in specified ways with each new affiliation or disaffiliation of a station.
21. *Id.*
22. *Id.*
23. 37 C.F.R. §§ 304.5(c), 304.2.

iii. All compositions in SESAC repertory, $41 annually;

iv. Any other compositions, $1.

c. Performances by other "public broadcasting entities" (for 1990/1991/1992):[24]

i. All compositions in ASCAP repertory, $250/$265/$280 annually;

ii. All compositions in BMI repertory, $250/$265/$280 annually;

iii. All compositions in SESAC repertory, $54/$57/$60 annually;

iv. Any other compositions, $1.

d. Recording[25] "on and for" the radio and television programs of "public broadcasting entities,"[26] and making, reproducing, and distributing copies and phonorecords "solely for the purpose of transmission by public broadcasting entities" (for 1990–91/1992):[27]

i. In PBS "distributed program:"

"Feature," $87.70/$92.05;

"Feature (concert)"[28] (per minute), $26.35/$27.75;

"Background" $44.35/$46.70;

"Theme":

24. 37 C.F.R. §§ 304.6(a), (c), 304.2.

25. 37 C.F.R. § 304.7(a).

26. 37 C.F.R. §§ 304.2, 304.7(a) ("whether or not in synchronization or timed relationship with the visual or aural content").

27. 37 C.F.R. §§ 304.7(a), 304.7(b). The schedule of fees covers broadcast use for a period of three years following the first broadcast. *Id.* § 304.7(b)(5). Reduced payments are prescribed for succeeding broadcast use periods.

28. 37 C.F.R. § 304.7(b). A "concert" feature is deemed to be the nondramatic presentation of all or part of a symphony, concerto, or other series work originally written for concert or opera performance. *Id.* § 304.7(b)(3).

"Single program" or "first series program," $44.35/$46.70;
"Other series program," $18/$18.95.

ii. Other than in PBS-distributed television program:[29]
"Feature," $7.30/$7.95;
"Feature (concert)" (per minute), $1.90/$2;
"Background," $3.15/$3.30;
"Theme":
"Single program" or "first series program," $3.15/$3.30;
"Other series program," $1.25/$1.30.

iii. In NPR "produced program" (per composition):[30]
"Feature," $9.50/$10;
"Feature (concert)" (per half-hour), $14/$15;
"Background," $4.75/$5;
"Theme":
"Single program" or "first series program," $4.75/$5;
"Other series program," $1.90/$2.

iv. Other than in NPR-produced radio program:[31]
"Feature," $0.60;
"Feature (concert)" (per half-hour), $1.20;
"Background and theme," $0.30.

2. Published pictorial, graphic, and sculptural works (for use by "public broadcasting entities" for permissible "activities," including making of reproductions):[32]
a. In PBS-distributed program:

29. 37 C.F.R. § 304.7(b)(1).
30. 37 C.F.R. § 304.7(b)(2).
31. 37 C.F.R. § 304.7(b)(4).
32. 37 C.F.R. § 304.8.

"Featured display,"[33] $58/$61;
"Background and montage display,"[34] $28.25/$29.75;
"Program identification" or "thematic use,"[35] $114.25/$120.25;
Display of "art reproduction copyrighted separately from the work of fine art from which the work was reproduced,"[36] $37.50/$39.50.

b. In other than PBS-distributed programs:
"Featured display," $37.50/$39.50;
"Background and montage display," $19.25/$20.25;
"Program identification" or "thematic use," $76.75/$80.75;
Display of "art reproduction copyrighted separately from the work of fine art from which the work was reproduced," $19.25/$20.25.

With respect to the period from January 1 to June 8, 1978, the "owners of copyright" or "public broadcasting entities" were not afforded "any greater or lesser rights" with respect to the "activities specified"[37] as applied to the "works specified"[38] than "those afforded under the law in effect on De-

33. "Featured display" means a full-screen or substantially full-screen display for more than three seconds. Any other display would be a "background or montage display." 37 C.F.R. § 304.8(b)(2).
34. "Background or montage display" is a display other than a "featured display." *See* note 33 *supra*.
35. "Thematic use" is the utilization of the work of one or more artists where the works constitute the central scheme of the program or convey a story line. 37 C.F.R. § 304.8(b)(3).
36. "Display of an art reproduction copyrighted separately from the work of fine art from which the work was reproduced" means a transparency or other reproduction of an underlying work of fine arts. 37 C.F.R. § 304.8(b)(4).
37. 17 U.S.C.A. § 118(b)(4).
38. *Id.*

cember 31, 1977, as held applicable and construed by a court in an action" brought under the 1976 Act.[39]

24.2[2] Adjustments of Terms and Rates

The initial procedure for determining the reasonable terms and royalty rates is required to be repeated between June 30 and December 31, 1982, and at five-year intervals thereafter, in accordance with regulations prescribed by the Copyright Royalty Tribunal.[40] Annual cost-of-living adjustments also are made.

24.2[3] Payment of Royalties

Unlike the scheme for the compulsory coin-operated phonorecord players licenses, where the "operators" pay the annual royalty fees to the Copyright Office for later distribution by the Copyright Royalty Tribunal to copyright owners, the Tribunal neither collects nor distributes the proceeds. Rather, the Tribunal devises terms as to acceptable methods for the payment of royalty fees by public broadcasters to copyright owners.[41]

Accordingly, the Tribunal has established requirements by which "copyright owners" may receive reasonable notice of the use of their works. It has established recordkeeping requirements for public broadcasters to facilitate identification, calculation, allocation, and payment of claims and royalties.[42] In some cases, especially in the area of pictorial,

---

39. *Id.*

40. 17 U.S.C.A. §§ 118(c), 801(b)(1). The Copyright Royalty Tribunal decided that at one-year intervals, beginning August 1, 1979, a revised schedule of rates would become effective to reflect the change in the cost of living as determined by the Consumers Price Index. 37 C.F.R. § 304.10.

41. 1976 House Report 118–19.

42. 17 U.S.C.A. § 118(b)(3); 37 C.F.R. §§ 304.4(c), 304.5(e), 304.6(e), 304.7(d), 304.7(e), 304.8(d), 304.8(e), 304.9.

graphic, and sculptural works, no one may know the whereabouts of a particular "copyright owner," and such owner may never appear to claim payment of royalties. The Tribunal's terms therefore:

1. Specify the nature of a public broadcaster's duty to locate the owner, or to set aside or otherwise assure payment of appropriate royalties should the owner appear and make a claim.[43]
2. Provide for the specific termination of any period during which the public broadcaster must set aside payments.[44]

24.3 Liabilities

Infringement by noncommercial broadcasts is subject to the usual remedies,[45] qualified by specific provisions for:

1. Remission of statutory damages for innocent infringements;
2. Liabilities for nondestruction of reproductions within seven days.

24.3[1] Remission of Statutory Damages

When an infringer believed and had reasonable grounds for believing that the use of the copyrighted work was a "fair use," statutory damages may not be awarded against a "public broadcasting entity" or against a person who, as a "regular part of the nonprofit activities of a public broad-

43. 37 C.F.R. §§ 304.4(c), 304.5(e), 304.6(e), 304.7(d), 304.7(e), 304.8(d), 304.8(e), 304.9.
44. 37 C.F.R. § 304.9 (three years from date of required payment).
45. 17 U.S.C.A. §§ 502–506. *See* chapter 28 *infra*.

casting entity" performed or reproduced a "transmission program" embodying a performance.[46]

24.3[2] Liabilities for Nondestruction of Reproductions Within Seven Days

A public broadcaster who has made a reproduction and has distributed it to an institution can avoid liability for the failure to destroy the reproduction within the required seven days[47] by notifying the receiving institution of the destruction requirement. Thereafter, only the receiving institution may be held liable as an infringer for failure to obey the destruction requirement.[48] The Copyright Royalty Tribunal has established standards for adequate notice under this provision.[49]

24.4 Negotiated Noncommercial Broadcasting Licenses

Specific provisions apply to negotiated licenses concerning the noncommercial broadcasting of:

1. Published nondramatic musical works, and published pictorial, graphic, and sculptural works (works subject to the compulsory license provision);[50]
2. Nondramatic literary works (works not subject to the compulsory license provision).[51]

---

46. 17 U.S.C.A. § 504(c)(2). The burden of proof with respect to the defendant's good faith should rest on the plaintiff. 1976 House Report 163. Compare the statutory burdens of proving willfulness and innocence.
47. 17 U.S.C.A. § 118(d)(3).
48. *Id.*
49. 17 U.S.C.A. § 118(d)(3), 37 C.F.R. § 304.11.
50. 17 U.S.C.A. § 118(b).
51. 17 U.S.C.A. § 118(e).

24.4[1] Negotiated Licenses for Published Nondramatic Musical Works, and Published Pictorial, Graphic, and Sculptural Works

Public broadcasters and copyright owners have the opportunity to vary the Tribunal's terms and rates. "License agreements voluntarily negotiated at any time"[52] are to be given effect in lieu of any determination by the Tribunal.[53] Such agreements and designations of common agents are exempted from the antitrust laws.[54]

Copies of such agreements are required to be filed in the Copyright Office within thirty days of execution in accordance with regulations prescribed by the Register of Copyrights.[55]

24.4[2] Negotiated Licenses for Nondramatic Literary Works

Since the compulsory license provisions apply only to published nondramatic musical works and published pictorial, graphic, and sculptural works,[56] they do not include nondramatic literary works.[57] However, negotiated agreements on terms and rates of royalty payments for the use of nondramatic literary works, whether published or unpublished, are encouraged by exempting such agreements from liability under the antitrust laws.[58]

---

52. 17 U.S.C.A. § 118(b)(2). "At any time" permits negotiation before, during, or after determinations by the Tribunal.
53. 17 U.S.C.A. § 118(b)(2).
54. 17 U.S.C.A. § 118(b).
55. 17 U.S.C.A. § 118(b)(2); 37 C.F.R. § 201.9.
56. *See* notes 2, 3 *supra*.
57. *See* note 2 *supra*.
58. 17 U.S.C.A. § 118(e)(1). Copying of other public and instructional television programs is the subject of a joint policy developed by PBS, Agency for Instructional Television (AIT), Public Television Library (PTL), and Great Plains National Instructional Television Library (GPNITL). The joint policy is to permit automatically, within certain

Any such terms and rates of royalty payments are effective, upon filing in the Copyright Office, in accordance with regulations prescribed by the Register of Copyrights.[59]

The Register of Copyrights was required to report to Congress on January 3, 1980, on the extent of voluntary licensing arrangements reached for the use of nondramatic literary works, on any problems that may have arisen, and on any legislative or other recommendations.[60]

24.5 Unaffected by Compulsory Noncommercial Broadcasting License Provisions

The compulsory noncommercial broadcasting license provisions do not permit, "beyond the limits of fair use,"[61] the following activities:[62]

1. Unauthorized dramatization of a nondramatic musical work;
2. Production of a "transmission program" drawn to any "substantial extent" from a published "compilation" of pictorial, graphic, or sculptural works;
3. Unauthorized use of any portion of an audiovisual work.

---

limitations, off-the-air recording by schools of "public and instructional television programs distributed by them" and retention of such recordings for seven days. It is their intent to publish lists of those programs that schools can copy under this policy.

59. 17 U.S.C.A. § 118(e)(1); 37 C.F.R. § 201.9.

60. 17 U.S.C.A. § 118(e)(2). The Copyright Royalty Tribunal reported on its experience under the compulsory noncommercial broadcasting license provisions on January 3, 1980.

61. 17 U.S.C.A. § 118(f). *See* chapter 29 *supra*.

62. *Id.*

25. Compulsory Cable Television Secondary Transmission License

Limiting the exclusive rights of public performance and display are the compulsory cable television secondary transmission license provisions.[1]

1. 17 U.S.C.A. § 111. The compulsory cable television secondary transmission license provisions should be distinguished from the three other 1976 Act compulsory license provisions: (1) musical recording, (2) coin-operated phonorecord players, and (3) noncommercial broadcasting. *See* chapters 22–24 *supra*. Other compulsory license provisions have been imposed or suggested, e.g., "statutory license for secondary transmission by satellite carriers for private home viewing," 17 U.S.C.A. § 119, discussed in chapter 26 *infra*; compulsory licenses have been suggested for, inter alia, video cassette recorders, for rentals of works, for the proposed performers' and other owners' rights in sound recordings. *See* chapter 17, note 31, *supra*. The provisions are not limited to cable television systems, but also relate to apartment house and hotel systems, wired instructional systems, common carriers, nonprofit "boosters" and translators, and secondary transmissions of primary transmissions to controlled groups. 1976 House Report 88. *See* Greene, *The Cable Television Provisions of the Revised Copyright Act*, 27 CATH. U.L. REV. 263 (1978); Olsson, *Teleprompter v. CBS, and the United States Copyright Act of 1976*, 28 EBU REV. 51 (July 1977); Kachigian, *The New Copyright Law and Cable Television, Interpretation and Implications*, 7 PERFORMING ARTS REV. 176 (1977); Meyer, *The Feat of Houdini or How the New Act Disentangles the CATV Copyright Knot*, 22 N.Y.L. SCH. L. REV. 545 (1977); Botein, *New Copyright Act and Cable Television—A Signal of Change*, 24 BULL. COPYRIGHT SOC'Y 1 (1976). For discussion of satellite cable programming under the Cable Communications Policy Act of 1984, see chapter 33 *infra*. Section 111(d) and (f) was revised in 1986. Pub. L. No. 99-397, 100

Under the 1909 Act, retransmissions of over-the-air broadcast signals had been held not to constitute "publication" and, therefore, not copyright infringement.[2] Also, cable television[3] was held to be subject to regulation by the Federal Communications Commission.[4] Section 111 is coordinated with FCC policies, and reads like FCC regulations.

The 1976 Act broadened the definition of "performance"[5] eliminated the "for profit" limitation on performing rights for music and other nondramatic works,[6] expressly provided for exclusive rights of public display,[7] and defined "to perform or display a work 'publicly' "[8] to include every transmission or other communication of a "performance" or "display" "to the public, by means of any device or process, whether the members of the public capable of receiving the performance or display receive it in the same place or in separate places and at the same time or at different times."[9]

Stat. 848 (Aug. 27, 1986). *See* Jennings, *Cables and Satellites*, 11 COLUM.-V.L.A. L. & ARTS 129 (1986). The Satellite Home Viewer Act of 1988 (eff. Jan. 1, 1989) is discussed in chapter 26 *infra*.

2. Teleprompter Corp. v. Columbia Broadcasting Sys., Inc., 415 U.S. 394 (1974)(distant signals); Fortnightly Corp. v. United Artists Television, Inc., 392 U.S. 390 (1968)(local signals). The opinions in both cases suggested congressional action.
3. The earlier term, reflecting the then technology, was "community antenna television" (CATV).
4. United States v. Southwestern Cable Co., 392 U.S. 157 (1968). The 1976 Act left "communications policy" to the Federal Communications Commission. 1976 House Report 89. United Video, Inc. v. FCC, 890 F.2d 1173 (D.C. Cir. 1989) (reinstatement of FCC syndicated exclusivity (syndex) rules upheld; coexistence of communications and copyright systems).
5. 17 U.S.C.A. § 101; 1976 House Report 63. *See* text accompanying chapter 17, notes 23–31, *supra*.
6. 17 U.S.C.A. § 106(4). *See* chapter 17, note 27, *supra*.
7. 17 U.S.C.A. § 106(5). *See* text accompanying chapter 7, notes 32–37, *supra*.
8. 17 U.S.C.A. § 101; David v. Showtime/The Movie Channel, Inc., 697 F. Supp. 752 (S.D.N.Y. 1988) (cable channel operators held to perform publicly).
9. *Id.*

The compulsory license provisions are the longest and most complex section in the statute.[10] The provisions rest on the premise that cable operators *should* pay royalty fees to copyright owners for the retransmission of their works.

A "cable system"[11] picks up a broadcast station's "primary transmission"[12] from the air waves, and relays it as a "secondary transmission"[13] to its subscribers via a network of cables. Because it would be too impractical to require that

10. Ten pages out of sixty-two pages, and one section out of eighty-eight sections. The 1976 House Report, at 88–101, consumes thirteen pages out of a total of 139 pages.

11. "Cable system" is defined as a facility that in whole or in part receives signals of one or more television broadcast stations licensed by the Federal Communications Commission and makes secondary transmissions of such signals to subscribing members of the public who pay for such service. A closed circuit wire system that only originates programs and does not carry television broadcast signals would not come within the definition. Further, the definition provides that, in determining the applicable royalty fee and system classification, cable systems in contiguous communities under common ownership or control or operating from one headend are considered as one system. 17 U.S.C.A. § 111(f); 1976 House Report 99.

12. "Primary transmission" is defined as a transmission made to the public by the transmitting facility whose signals are being received and further transmitted by the secondary transmission service, regardless of where or when the performance or display was first transmitted. 17 U.S.C.A. § 111(f). Additional language concerning low-power television stations was added in 1986. Pub. L. No. 99-397, 100 Stat. 848 (Aug. 27, 1986).

13. "Secondary transmission" is defined as the further transmitting of a primary transmission simultaneously with the primary transmission, or nonsimultaneously with the primary transmission if by a "cable system" not located in whole or in part within the boundary of the forty-eight contiguous states, Hawaii, or Puerto Rico. However, a nonsimultaneous further transmission by a cable system located in Hawaii of a primary transmission is deemed to be a secondary transmission if the carriage of the television broadcast signal comprising such further transmission is permissible under the rules, regulations, or authorizations of the Federal Communications Commission. 17 U.S.C.A. § 111(f); 37 C.F.R. § 201.12. The definition was incorporated by reference in the Satellite Home Viewer Act of 1988, discussed in chapter 26 *infra*.

every cable system negotiate for every "secondary transmission" of a copyrighted work, the statute provides compulsory licenses whereby the cable systems pay certain royalties to the Register of Copyrights for later distribution, with interest, to the copyright owners by the Copyright Royalty Tribunal.

25.1 Basic Approach

The basic approach of the compulsory license provisions is that every retransmission of a copyrighted work originally transmitted over the air waves is a "public performance"[14] of the work, and therefore, unless specifically authorized by the copyright owner, an infringement, unless:

1. The retransmission falls within one of four enumerated exemptions.
2. The "cable operator" secures and acts under a compulsory license.

25.2 Four Exemptions

The four exemptions are:[15]

The effect of this definition is to permit certain cable systems in offshore areas, but not including cable systems in the offshore area of Puerto Rico and to a limited extent only in Hawaii, to tape programs and retransmit them to subscribers under the compulsory license. Puerto Rico was excluded at the request of the governor of Puerto Rico, who stated that the particular television broadcasting problems that the definition seeks to solve for cable systems in other noncontiguous areas do not exist in Puerto Rico. 1976 House Report 99.

See National Cable Television Ass'n v. Copyright Royalty Tribunal, 689 F.2d 1077 (D.C. Cir: 1982); Cablevision Co. v. Motion Picture Ass'n, 641 F. Supp. 1154 (D.D.C. 1986).

14. *See* notes 2, 5–9 *supra*.
15. 17 U.S.C.A. § 111(a).

1. Relaying to private lodgings of guests or residents without any direct charge;
2. Secondary transmissions within "instructional broadcasting" exemption;
3. Secondary transmissions by passive carriers;
4. Nonprofit secondary transmissions.

25.2[1] Relaying to Private Lodgings of Guests and Residents Without Any Direct Charge

Exempted under this exemption are secondary transmissions not made by a "cable system" and consisting "entirely of the relaying by the management of a hotel, apartment house, or similar establishment," of a transmission "to the private lodgings of guests or residents," provided "no direct charge is made to see or hear the secondary transmission."[16]

If the secondary transmission consists of anything other than the mere relay of ordinary broadcasts, the exemption does not apply. Thus, any change in the signal relayed, such as the cutting out of advertising or the running in of new commercials, would subject the secondary transmitter to infringement liability.[17] In addition, "private lodgings" means rooms used as living quarters or for private parties, and does not include dining rooms, meeting halls, theatres, ballrooms, or similar places outside the normal circle of a family and its social acquaintances.[18] Obviously, the mere playing of an ordinary radio or television set in a private hotel room does not constitute an infringement.[19]

---

16. 17 U.S.C.A. § 111(a)(1). The signals must be transmitted by a broadcast station licensed by the Federal Communications Commission within the "local service area" of such station. "Local service area" is defined in 17 U.S.C.A. § 111(f).
17. 1976 House Report 91.
18. *Id.*
19. 1976 House Report at 92.

25.2[2] Secondary Transmissions Within "Instructional Broadcasting" Exemption

The second exemption is for secondary transmissions made "solely for the purpose" and "under the conditions specified" in the "instructional broadcasting" exemption.[20]

25.2[3] Secondary Transmissions by Passive Carriers

The third exemption extends to secondary transmitters that act solely as passive carriers. For a carrier to be passive, it must have no "direct or indirect control over the content or selection of the primary transmission or over the particular recipients of the secondary transmission," and its activities with respect to the secondary transmission must "consist solely of providing wires, cables, or other communications channels for the use of others."[21] This exemption does not apply to a cable television system.

---

20. 17 U.S.C.A. §§ 111(a)(2), 110(2).

21. 17 U.S.C.A. § 111(a)(3). The exemption extends only to the activities of that carrier, and does not exempt from liability the activities of others with respect to their own primary or secondary transmissions.

> . . .To qualify for the exemption, five elements must be established:
>
> 1. There must be a "secondary transmission of a primary transmission"
> 2. made by a "carrier"
> 3. that has "no direct or indirect control over the content or selection of the primary transmission"
> 4. that has no "direct or indirect control over the . . . particular recipients of the secondary transmission"
> 5. "whose activities with respect to the secondary transmission consist solely of providing wires, cables, or other communications channels for the use of others"

Hubbard Broadcasting Co. v. Southern Satellite Sys., Inc., 777 F.2d 393, 401 (8th Cir. 1985), *cert. denied*, 479 U.S. 1005 (1986); *see also* WGN Continental Broadcasting Co. v. United Video, Inc., 685 F.2d 218 (7th Cir. 1982)(passive-carrier exemption no defense to television station that deleted teletext information from news program); Notes, 13 RUTGERS COMPUTER & TECH. L. J. 519 (1987); 19 WAKE FOREST L. REV. 197 (1983); Annot., 66 A.L.R. Fed. 933 (1986).

25.2[4] Nonprofit Secondary Transmissions

Exempted by the fourth exemption are secondary transmissions not made by a "cable system," but made by a governmental body or other nonprofit organization without "any purpose of direct or indirect commercial advantage" and without charge to recipients "other than assessments necessary to defray the actual and reasonable costs of maintaining and operating the secondary transmission service."[22]

25.3 Compulsory License

To enjoy a compulsory license, a "cable system" must comply with:

1. Filing requirements
2. Reporting requirements

25.3[1] Former Filing Requirements

Prior to August 27, 1986, a "cable system," at least one month before its operations began,[23] had to file with the Copyright Office an Initial Notice of Identity and Signal Carriage Complement.[24] Signals "regularly carried" were those signals that the Federal Communications Commission had specifically authorized the cable system to carry, and that the system actually carried on a regular basis.[25] Whenever the recorded information changed, the cable system had to file the change within thirty days in a supplemental notice.[26]

---

22. 17 U.S.C.A. § 111(a)(4).
23. Former 17 U.S.C.A. § 111(d)(1) (eliminated by Pub. L. No. 99–397, 100 Stat. 848 [Aug. 27, 1986]).
24. *Id.* As prescribed by the Register of Copyrights after consultation with the Copyright Royalty Tribunal. Former 37 C.F.R. § 201.11.
25. 1976 House Report 95.
26. Former 17 U.S.C.A. § 111(d)(1).

25.3[2] Reporting Requirements

The "cable system" is required to file semiannual statements of account and such other data prescribed by the Register of Copyrights after consultation with the Copyright Royalty Tribunal.[27]

25.3[3] Limitations on Compulsory License

The compulsory license permits the "cable system" to carry over-the-air broadcast signals coming from stations licensed by the Federal Communications Commission (or analogous governmental authorities in Canada or Mexico), as long as Federal Communications Commission rules and regulations permit the cable system to carry those signals as secondary transmissions.[28] Thus, the compulsory license does not apply to the carriage of any nonbroadcast primary transmissions, such as programs originated by a cable system or a cable network.[29]

In addition, the "cable system" may not violate five limitations:[30]

1. "Secondary transmission" to public of "primary transmission" to "controlled group";
2. "Willful or repeated" nonpermissible secondary transmissions;
3. Intentional alteration of content of programming;
4. Canadian and Mexican television signals;
5. Nonsimultaneous secondary transmissions.

27. 17 U.S.C.A. § 111(d)(1)(A); 37 C.F.R. § 201.17. The semiannual statements of account must be filed on printed forms supplied by the Licensing Division of the Copyright Office (forms SA1–2, SA 3, SC). The form to be used depends on the "gross receipts for secondary transmissions."
28. 1976 House Report 93.
29. *Id.*
30. 17 U.S.C.A. § 111(b), (c)(2)–(4).

25.3[3][a] "Secondary Transmission" to Public of "Primary Transmission" to "Controlled Group"

Not permitted are secondary transmissions of primary transmissions "not made for reception by the public at large," but "controlled and limited to reception by particular members of the public."[31] Examples of transmission not intended for the general public are background music services such as "MUZAK," closed circuit broadcasts to theatres, pay television (STV), and pay cable.[32]

25.3[3][b] "Willful or Repeated" Nonpermissible Secondary Transmissions

Also not within the compulsory license are "willful or repeated" secondary transmissions of a primary transmission when the carriage of signals is not permissible under Federal Communications Commission rules and regulations.[33] "Repeated" does not mean merely "more than once"; rather, it denotes a degree of aggravated negligence that borders on willfulness.[34]

25.3[3][c] Intentional Alteration of Content of Programming

The "cable system" may not intentionally alter the content of the retransmitted program, or change, delete, or aug-

31. 17 U.S.C.A. § 111(b). Excepted from the limitation are secondary transmissions if: (1) the primary transmission is by a licensed broadcast station; (2) the carriage of the signals comprising the secondary transmission is required by the Federal Communications Commission; and (3) the signal of the primary transmitter is not altered or changed in any way by the secondary transmitter. 17 U.S.C.A. § 111(b)(1)–(3).
32. 1976 House Report 92.
33. 17 U.S.C.A. § 111(c)(2); 37 C.F.R. § 201.11. The cable system must have deposited the required statement of account and royalty fee.
34. 1976 House Report 93.

ment commercial advertising or station announcements transmitted by the originating station.[35] Either the originating broadcast station or any broadcast station in the "local station area" where the altered retransmission took place may sue the cable system for infringement.[36] This in effect precludes a cable operator from negotiating directly with a copyright owner because the cable operator decides that the economic benefits of commercial substitution or the like are significant enough to forgo the compulsory license. Once a court finds an infringing alteration, it may deprive the cable system of its compulsory license for up to thirty days.[37]

25.3[3][d] Canadian and Mexican Television Signals

Not covered by the compulsory license are the retransmissions by most cable systems of Canadian and Mexican signals.[38]

---

35. 17 U.S.C.A. § 111(c)(3). Permitted is very limited alteration of commercial advertisements performed by those engaged in television commercial advertising market research.
36. 17 U.S.C.A. § 501(c), (d). *See* chapter 28, note 34 *infra*.
37. 17 U.S.C.A. § 510. *See* text accompanying chapter 28, notes 33–36, *infra*.
38. 17 U.S.C.A. § 111(c)(4). With respect to Canadian signals, the compulsory license applies to an area located 150 miles from the United States-Canadian border, or south from the border to the 42nd parallel of latitude, whichever distance is greater. Thus the cities of Detroit, Pittsburgh, Cleveland, Green Bay, and Seattle would be included within the compulsory license area, while such cities as New York, Philadelphia, Chicago, and San Francisco would be located outside the area. With respect to Mexican signals, the compulsory license applies only in the area in which such signals may be received by means of "direct interception of a free space radio wave." The compulsory license also applies to the carriage of signals by cable systems "specifically authorized" to do so by the Federal Communications Commission as of April 15, 1976. 1976 House Report 94–95.

25.3[3][e] Nonsimultaneous Secondary Transmissions

Nonsimultaneous secondary transmissions are not permitted,[39] subject to a very elaborate exception[40] with detailed provisions controlling the videotapes.[41]

25.3[4] Royalty Payments

25.3[4][a] Initial Rates

There is a complex formula for determining the amount of royalties of a "cable system" under the compulsory license. Usually the fee is a specified percentage of the cable system's gross receipts from subscribers for the period covered by the statement of account.[42] For the computation of royalty fees, "gross receipts" includes only amounts received from cable subscribers for the basic service of providing secondary transmissions from primary broadcast transmitters. Other receipts from subscribers, such as those for pay-cable services or installation charges, are not included.[43]

The statutory royalty percentage varies depending on the amount of distant, nonnetwork programming carried by the cable system, measured by units called "distant signal equivalents."[44] To determine how many "distant signal

---

39. 17 U.S.C.A. § 111(e). Recording a program off the air and later transmitting the program from the videotape or record to the public is permitted only by cable systems outside the continental United States (not including Puerto Rico and, with limited exceptions, Hawaii). This is because the off-the-air signals are generally not available in the offshore areas. 1976 House Report 91.
40. 17 U.S.C.A. § 111(e)(1)(A)–(F).
41. 17 U.S.C.A. § 111(e)(1)(C)–(E), (2); 37 C.F.R. § 201.12; 1976 House Report 98.
42. 17 U.S.C.A. § 111(d)(1)(B).
43. 1976 House Report 96.
44. "Distant signal equivalent" is defined as the value assigned to the secondary transmission of any nonnetwork television programming

equivalents" a cable system has, one adds certain values assigned to the actual number of distant television stations carried by the system. The actual dollar value of the royalty fee comes from applying a regressive percentage scale based on the number of distant signal equivalents to the system's "gross receipts."

For example, the royalty fee, subject to additional percents, for the first "distant signal equivalent" is .00893 percent of the cable system's gross subscriber revenues.[45] For each of the second, third, and fourth "distant signal equivalents," the royalty fee is .00563 percent,[46] and for each additional "distant signal equivalent," .00265 percent.[47]

There are smaller fees for cable systems with semiannual gross receipts of $146,000 or less and for those with more than $146,000 but less than $292,000.[48]

25.3[4][b] Adjustment of Rates

The Copyright Royalty Tribunal is empowered to adjust the initial royalty rates during 1985 and in each subsequent fifth calendar year,[49] or upon petitions of any owner or user based on statutory standards and conditions.[50]

---

carried by a cable system in whole or in part beyond the "local service area" of the primary transmitter of such programming. 17 U.S.C.A. § 111(f); 1976 House Report 100.

45. 17 U.S.C.A. § 111(d)(2)(B)(i), (ii); 37 C.F.R. § 308.2(a), (d), 1976 House Report 96–97.
46. 17 U.S.C.A. § 111(d)(1)(B)(iii).
47. 17 U.S.C.A. § 111(d)(1)(B)(iv).
48. 17 U.S.C.A. § 111(d)(1)(C), (D).
49. 17 U.S.C.A. § 804(a)(1)(A). The petitioner may be "any owner or user of a copyrighted work" whose royalty rates are specified by statute or established by the Copyright Royalty Tribunal with "a significant interest in the royalty rate." 17 U.S.C.A. § 804(a)(2).
50. 17 U.S.C.A. § 801(b)(2). Semiannual adjustments are computed. 37 C.F.R. § 308.2(b). Explicit limitations were placed on the factors the Tribunal can consider in making its periodic rate revisions, but rate adjustments can be made at any time if the Federal Communications

25.3[5] Distribution to Copyright Owners

Royalty fees are payable to the Register of Copyrights, who, "after deducting the reasonable costs" incurred by the Copyright Office, is required to deposit them in the Treasury of the United States, which is required to invest the funds in interest-bearing United States securities.[51]

The copyright owners only of the following works are entitled to royalties:[52]

1. Works included in a cable system's secondary transmission of a primary transmission of a distant nonnetwork television station;[53]
2. Works included in a secondary transmission identified in a "special statement of account;"[54]
3. Works included in distant nonnetwork programming consisting exclusively of aural signals.[55]

In effect, no copyright owner may claim a royalty fee for

Commission amends its rules and regulations governing the carriage of distant signals or its rules and regulations dealing with syndicated and sports program exclusivity. 1976 House Report 176. *See* chapter 31 *infra*.

51. 17 U.S.C.A. § 111(d)(3) (also requiring semiannual filing of statement of account by Copyright Offce with Copyright Royalty Tribunal); 37 C.F.R. § 201.17.
52. 17 U.S.C.A. § 111(d)(3); Barris Indus. v. Worldvision Enters., Inc., 875 F.2d 1446 (9th Cir. 1989) (license agreements for division of royalties between creator and distributor of "The Newlywed Game" construed not to apply to statutory cable royalties).
53. 17 U.S.C.A. § 111(d)(3)(A) (beyond "local service area" of "primary transmitter").
54. 17 U.S.C.A. § 111(d)(3)(B). A "special statement of account" is required for any nonnetwork television programming carried by a cable system beyond the "local service area" of the primary transmitter. 17 U.S.C.A. § 111(d)(1)(A).
55. 17 U.S.C.A. § 111(d)(3)(C) (beyond "local service area" of "primary transmitter").

the secondary transmission of "local"[56] or "network" programs.[57]

Detailed procedures for annual distribution of royalty fees are provided.[58] The distribution is by the Copyright Royalty Tribunal, which determines, where controversy exists, the distribution.[59] "Reasonable administrative costs" are deductible by the Tribunal.[60]

25.4 Liabilities for Infringing Secondary Transmissions

Liabilities for infringing secondary transmissions include not only the full remedies for copyright infringement,[61] but

56. It was believed that the retransmission of "local" signals, those already available over the air in the cable system's community, did not economically injure copyright owners, since they received compensation for use of their programs in the local markets under their broadcast licenses. 1976 House Report 90.
57. It was believed that the retransmission of network programming, whether local or distant, would not injure the copyright owner, since the owner receives adequate compensation under the owner's contract with the network with payment generally based on reaching all markets served by the network by any means. 1976 House Report 90.
58. 17 U.S.C.A. § 111(d)(4); 37 C.F.R. §§ 302.1–302.10. An antitrust exemption enables claimants to agree among themselves as to the proportionate division of compulsory licensing fees among them, to lump their claims together and to file them jointly or as a single claim, or to designate a common agent to receive payment on their behalf.
59. 17 U.S.C.A. §§ 111(d)(4), 801(b)(3); ACEMLA v. Copyright Royalty Tribunal, 854 F.2d 10 (2d Cir. 1988) (ASCAP, BMI, and SESAC entitled to lion's share of 1985 cable television royalty fund attributable to Spanish-language music); NBC v. Copyright Royalty Tribunal, 848 F.2d 1289 (D.C. Cir. 1988) (syndicate entitled to full litigation of contractual issues of licensing rights).
60. 17 U.S.C.A. §§ 111(d)(4)(B), 807.
61. 17 U.S.C.A. §§ 502–506, 509. *See* chapter 28 *infra*. More limited remedies are provided for distant-signal transmitters and other local stations with standing to sue. 17 U.S.C.A. § 501(d). *See* chapter 28, note 34 *infra*.

also an additional remedy of suspension for not more than thirty days of a compulsory license for one or more distant signals carried by the infringing cable system.[62]

62. 17 U.S.C.A. § 510. *See* text accompanying chapter 28, notes 33–36, *infra*.

26. "Statutory" Secondary Transmission by Satellite Carriers for Private Home Viewing License

26.1 Satellite Home Viewer Act of 1988

26.1[1] Overview of Section 119

The Satellite Home Viewer Act of 1988,[1] adding a new section 119 to the Copyright Act, further limited the exclusive rights of public performance and display. It set temporary royalty fees for "statutory" licenses to make "secondary transmissions." The fees may be set by voluntary negotiation or, if necessary, compulsory arbitration. There is provision for review by the Copyright Royalty Tribunal and judicial review.

26.1[2] Exclusivity and Expiration of Section 119

The Satellite Home Viewer Act is expressly exclusive with respect to secondary transmissions without the consent of the copyright owner by a satellite carrier for private home viewing of programming contained in a primary

---

1. Pub. L. No. 100–667, tit. II, § 202, 102 Stat. 3949 (Nov. 16, 1988) (codified at 17 U.S.C. § 119) (effective Jan. 1, 1989); 37 C.F.R. §§ 309.1 *et seq.*

transmission of a network station,[2] and, without extension, will expire on December 31, 1994.[3]

26.2 Applicability of "Statutory" License

26.2[1] Secondary Transmissions by Satellite Carriers

Subject to "statutory" licensing under section 119 are "secondary transmissions"[4] by "satellite carriers"[5] of a "primary transmission"[6] made by a "superstation"[7] or "network station"[8] embodying a performance or display of a work if that secondary transmission is:[9]

---

2. 17 U.S.C.A. § 119(e). No provisions of any law (other than section 119) "shall be construed to contain any authorization, exemption, or license through which secondary transmissions by satellite carrier for private home viewing of programming contained in a primary transmission made by a superstation or a network station may be made without obtaining the consent of the copyright owner." Quaere, as to effect of section 119 on the "satellite cable programming" for "private viewing" provisions of the Cable Communications Policy Act of 1984. *See* chapter 33 *infra*.
3. Pub. L. No. 100–667, tit. II, § 207, 102 Stat. 3960 (Nov. 16, 1989): "This title and the amendments made by this title (other than the amendments made by section 205 [amending 47 U.S.C. § 605]) cease to be effective on December 31, 1994."
4. "Secondary transmission" has the meaning given that term in 17 U.S.C.A. § 111(f). 17 U.S.C.A. § 119(d)(7). *See* chapter 25, note 13, *supra*.
5. "Satellite carrier" is defined in 17 U.S.C.A § 119(d)(6).
6. "Primary transmission" has the meaning given that term in 17 U.S.C.A. § 111(f). 17 U.S.C.A. § 119(d)(4). *See* chapter 25, note 12, *supra*.
7. "[S]uperstation means a television broadcast station, other than a network station, licensed by the Federal Communications Commission that is secondarily transmitted by a satellite carrier." 17 U.S.C.A. 119(d)(9).
8. "Network station" has the meaning given that term in 17 U.S.C.A. § 111 (f), and includes any translator station or terrestrial satellite station that rebroadcasts all or substantially all of the programming broadcast by a network station. 17 U.S.C.A. § 119(d)(2).
9. 17 U.S.C.A. § 119(a).

1. To the public for "private home viewing"[10] and the carrier makes a direct or indirect charge for each retransmission service to each receiving household;[11] or
2. To a "distributor"[12] that has contracted with the carrier for direct or indirect delivery of a secondary transmission made by a superstation to the public for private home viewing.[13]

The statutory license for secondary transmissions of primary transmissions made to network stations is limited to secondary transmissions to persons who reside in "unserved households."[14]

26.2[2] Submission of Subscriber Lists to Networks

Up-to-date "subscriber"[15] information must be submitted by the satellite carrier to the network if the network files

---

10. 17 U.S.C.A. § 119(a)(1), (2)(A). "Private home viewing" means the viewing, for "private use in a household" by means of satellite reception equipment, operated by an individual in that household that serves only that household, of a secondary transmission delivered by a secondary carrier of a primary transmission of a television station licensed by the FCC. 17 U.S.C.A. § 119(d)(5).
11. 17 U.S.C.A. § 119(a)(1), (2)(A).
12. 17 U.S.C.A. § 119(a)(1). "Distribution" is defined in 17 U.S.C.A. § 119(d)(1).
13. 17 U.S.C.A. § 119(a)(1).
14. 17 U.S.C.A. § 119(a)(2)(B). "Unserved household," with respect to a particular television network, means a household that cannot receive with a conventional outdoor rooftop receiving antenna an over-the-air signal of certain intensity of a "primary network station" affiliated with that network, and has not, before subscribing, subscribed to a cable system that provides the signal of a "primary network station" affiliated with that network. 17 U.S.C.A. § 119(d)(10). "Primary network station" is defined in 17 U.S.C.A. § 119(d)(3) for this purpose.
15. 17 U.S.C.A. § 119(a)(2)(C). "Subscriber" means an individual who receives a secondary transmission service for private home viewing by means of a secondary transmission from a satellite carrier and

with the Register of Copyrights a document identifying the person to whom such submissions are to be made.[16] Those documents are open to public inspection.[17]

26.3 Determination of Royalty Fees

26.3[1] Statement of Account and Initial Fees

Satellite carriers whose secondary transmissions are subject to statutory licensing must, every six months, deposit:[18]

1. A statement of account specifying all superstations and network stations whose signals were transmitted during that period to subscribers for private home viewing;[19]
2. A royalty fee for the period computed by:
   - Multiplying the total number of subscribers receiving each secondary transmission of a superstation during each calendar month by twelve cents;[20]
   - Multiplying the number of subscribers receiving each secondary transmission of a network station during each calendar month by three cents;[21]
   - Adding together the two totals so computed.[22]

This royalty fee will be effective until December 31, 1992, unless a royalty fee is established by voluntary negotiation or compulsory arbitration. After December 31, 1992, the fee

---

pays a fee for the service, directly or indirectly, to the satellite carrier or distributor. 17 U.S.C.A. § 119(D)(8).

16. 17 U.S.C.A. § 119(a)(2)(C).
17. *Id.*
18. 17 U.S.C.A. § 119(b)(1).
19. 17 U.S.C.A. § 119(b)(1)(A).
20. 17 U.S.C.A. § 119(b)(1)(A)(i).
21. 17 U.S.C.A. § 119(b)(1)(A)(ii).
22. 17 U.S.C.A. § 119(b)(1)(A)(iii).

will be determined in accordance with such negotiation or arbitration.[23]

26.3[2] Voluntary Negotiation

Voluntary negotiation procedures are prescribed.[24] Voluntary negotiation agreements are binding upon all satellite carriers, distributors, and copyright owners that are parties thereto.[25] The agreements must be filed with the Register of Copyrights,[26] and will remain in effect until December 31, 1994.[27]

26.3[3] Compulsory Arbitration

Compulsory arbitration is prescribed to determine a reasonable royalty fee by satellite carriers who are not parties to a voluntary agreement filed with the Copyright Office.[28] The arbitrators selected will constitute an "Arbitration Panel,"[29] and act on the basis of a full documented written record. The parties to the proceeding bear its entire cost.[30]

26.3[4] Factors for Determining Fees

The Arbitration panel will consider:[31]

1. Approximate average cost to a cable system for the right to secondarily transmit to the public a primary transmission made by a broadcast station;

23. 17 U.S.C.A. § 119(c).
24. 17 U.S.C.A. § 119(c)(2)(A), (B).
25. 17 U.S.C.A. § 119(c)(2)(C).
26. *Id.*
27. 17 U.S.C.A. § 119(c)(2)(D). *See* note 3 *supra*.
28. 17 U.S.C.A. § 119(c)(3).
29. 17 U.S.C.A. § 119(c)(3)(B).
30. 17 U.S.C.A. § 119(c)(3)(C).
31. 17 U.S.C.A. § 119(c)(3)(D).

2. The fee established under any voluntary agreement filed with the Copyright Office;
3. The last fee proposed by the parties before the arbitration proceedings.

The fee will be calculated to achieve the following objectives:[32]

1. To maximize the availability of creative works to the public;[33]
2. To afford the copyright owner a fair return on the creative work and the copyright user a fair return under existing economic conditions;[34]
3. To reflect the relative roles of the copyright owner and the copyright user in the product made available to the public with respect to relative creative contribution, technological contribution, capital investment, cost, risk, and contribution to the opening of new markets for creative expression and media for their communication;[35]
4. To minimize any disruptive impact on the structure of the industries involved and on generally prevailing industry practices.[36]

26.3[5] Report to and Action by Copyright Royalty Tribunal

The determination concerning the royalty fee must be reported to the Copyright Royalty Tribunal, which will adopt or reject the determination of the Arbitration Panel. If the

32. *Id.*
33. 17 U.S.C.A. § 119(c)(3)(D)(i).
34. 17 U.S.C.A. § 119(c)(3)(D)(ii).
35. 17 U.S.C.A. § 119(c)(3)(D)(iii).
36. 17 U.S.C.A. § 119(c)(3)(D)(iv).

Tribunal rejects the Panel's determination, it will determine the royalty fee.[37]

26.3[6] Effectiveness of Fee So Determined

The fee so determined becomes effective upon publication in the *Federal Register*, and remains in effect until modified by judicial review[38] or until December 31, 1994[39] and will be binding on all satellite carriers, distributors, and copyright owners who are not parties to a voluntary agreement filed with the Copyright Office.[40]

26.4 Acts by Satellite Carrier Actionable as Infringement

Actionable as an act of infringement by a satellite carrier are:[41]

1. "Noncompliance with reporting and payment requirements" by satellite carrier;[42]
2. "Willful alterations" of primary transmission by satellite carrier;[43]
3. Willful or repeated "individual violations"[44] or "pattern of violations"[45] by satellite carrier of territorial

---

37. 17 U.S.C.A. § 119(c)(3)(F).
38. 17 U.S.C.A. § 119(c)(4).
39. 17 U.S.C.A. § 119(c)(2)(D). *See* note 3 *supra.*
40. 17 U.S.C.A. § 119(c)(2)(C).
41. *See* chapter 27 *infra* (Infringement).
42. 17 U.S.C.A. § 119(a)(3).
43. 17 U.S.C.A. § 119(a)(4).
44. 17 U.S.C.A. § 119(a)(5)(A)(i), (ii). Prompt corrective action can reduce statutory damages to $5 per ineligible subscriber per month.
45. 17 U.S.C.A. § 119(a)(5)(B). There may be statutory damages up to $250,000 for each six-month period during which the pattern or practice was carried out.

or statutory licenses for network stations;[46]

4. Unlawful discrimination by satellite carrier against distributor.[47]

---

46. 17 U.S.C.A. § 119(a)(5). Not subject to this provision are secondary transmissions by a satellite carrier to persons who subscribed to receive such secondary transmissions from the satellite carrier or a distributor before November 16, 1988. 17 U.S.C.A. § 119(a)(5)(C).
47. 17 U.S.C.A § 119(a)(6).

27. Infringement

Copyright infringement is:[1]

1. 17 U.S.C.A. § 501(a); Copyright infringement under the Copyright Law requires some act in the United States, direct or contributory, in violation of an exclusive right of copyright. *See* chapter 17 *supra*. Update Art, Inc. v. Modin Publishing, Ltd., 843 F.2d 67 (2d Cir. 1988) ($500,000 damages for unauthorized reproduction abroad where predicate infringement occurred in United States); Peter Star Prods. v. Twin Continental Films, 783 F.2d 1440 (9th Cir. 1986) (*authorization* in United States to commit infringing acts abroad held infringement in United States—"to do or to authorize" in 17 U.S.C.A. § 106). Infringement is unauthorized "substantial" (excessive) copying in violation of an exclusive right of "protectible" elements ("expression") of copyrighted ("copyrightable") subject matter. Not all expression is protectible; nor are all similarities "substantial." Where there is merger of idea and expression, there is no infringement. *E.g.*, Frybarger v. IBM, 812 F.2d 525 (9th Cir. 1987) (video game not infringement; only similarities were indispensable expression of same ideas and not virtually identical). *See* Stillman v. Leo Burnett Co., 720 F. Supp. 1353 (N.D. Ill. 1989) (perceptive analysis of semantic problems in using same word for different purposes; e.g., "copying" to help prove access or to establish infringement of protectible expression and "substantial similarity" to help prove access [and copying] or such infringement; however, summary judgment for defendants denied on synergism theory—whole is greater than parts). Materials prepared in the process of production may constitute fixation and infringing copies. Walt Disney Prods. v. Filmation Assocs., 628 F. Supp. 871 (C.D. Cal. 1986); Libott, *Infringement and Remedies Under the Copyright Act of 1976*, 25 BULL. COPYRIGHT SOC'Y 237 (1978); Wasserstrom, *An Analysis of the Infringe-*

1. The violation of any of the exclusive rights of the "copyright owner" or of the "attribution and integrity" rights of the "author,"[2] by "anyone";[3]
2. The importation of copies or phonorecords into the United States in violation of the importation restrictions;[4] or
3. Acts actionable as infringements under section 119.[5]

Fair use is not an infringement of copyright;[6] nor are the other exempted uses.[7] The Berne Act expressly provided that 17 U.S.C. controls, and that rights "shall not be enforceable" in any action brought under the "provisions of the Berne Convention itself."[8]

---

ment Sections in the Copyright Code and Chapter 5 of S. 22, 22 N.Y.L. SCH. L. REV. 271 (1977). Questions of infringement are closely interrelated with preemption, copyright subject matter, and scope of exclusive rights.

See Warner Bros. v. American Broadcasting Co., 720 F.2d 231 (2d Cir. 1983) ("The Greatest American Hero" spoof of "Superman" held not substantially similar as matter of law); Kamar Int'l, Inc. v. Russ Berrie & Co., 657 F.2d 1059 (9th Cir. 1981) (once plaintiff demonstrates access and substantial similarity, burden shifts to defendant to prove independent creation); Leeds Music Ltd. v. Robin, 358 F. Supp. 650 (S.D. Ohio 1973) (upholding copyrights for rock opera "Jesus Christ Superstar," since parallelisms with earlier copyrighted work could have come from common source, the Bible; mandatory costs kept minimal; attorney's fees denied). Similarity is the ultimate test of infringement, compared to originality for copyright ability. For discussion of proof of infringement, *see* text accompanying notes 22–28 *infra*. *See also* Houts v. Universal City Studios, Inc., 603 F. Supp. 26 (C.D. Cal. 1984) (doctrine of copyright estoppel applicable where fictional work represented as factual).

2. 17 U.S.C.A. § 501(a) (as amended Dec. 1, 1990). *See* chapter 17 *supra*.
3. "Anyone," as used in § 501(a), includes any state, any state instrumentality, and any officer or employee of a state acting in "his or her official capacity." 17 U.S.C.A. § 501(a). See chapter 28, note 37, *infra*.
4. 17 U.S.C.A. § 501(a). *See* chapter 29 *infra*.
5. *See* text accompanying chapter 26, notes 41–47, *supra*.
6. 17 U.S.C.A. § 107. *See* text accompanying chapter 18, notes 13–15, *supra*.
7. 17 U.S.C.A. §§ 108–116, 118. *See* chapters 19–26 *supra*.
8. Berne Act §§ 2, 3.

27.1 Standing to Sue

The "legal or beneficial owner of an exclusive right under a copyright"[9] may institute an action for "any infringement

9. 17 U.S.C.A. § 501(b). The term "legal or beneficial owner of an exclusive right under a copyright" is not defined. *But see* 1976 House Report 159 ("beneficial owner" would include, for example, author who had parted with legal title to copyright in exchange for percentage royalties based on sales or license fees). The term "copyright owner" is defined as referring, with respect to any one of the exclusive rights comprised in a copyright, to the owner of that particular right. § 101. Compare the undefined term "owner of copyright." *See* chapter 7, note 51, *supra*.

Under the 1909 Act, the "copyright proprietor" was an indispensable party to a copyright infringement action. If the proprietor did not voluntarily join as plaintiff, an exclusive licensee could join the proprietor as defendant, if amenable to process, or as involuntary plaintiff. Independent Wireless Tel. Co. v. Radio Corp. of Am., 269 U.S. 459 (1926); Waterman v. MacKenzie, 138 U.S. 252 (1891); *Cf.* M.G.B. Homes, Inc. v. Ameron Homes, Inc., 903 F.2d 1486 (11th Cir. 1990) (judgment for more than $1.2 million reversed for plaintiff's nonownership of copyright in advertising flyer as author of work made for hire or as co-author of joint work). Falloway Prods., Inc. v. Maurer, 603 F.2d 72 (9th Cir. 1979). *See* Motta v. Samuel Weiser, Inc., 768 F.2d 481 (1st Cir. 1985)(member of unincorporated cult association without standing to sue for infringement of works of cult founder); Oddo v. Ries, 743 F.2d 630 (9th Cir. 1984) (partner as co-owner of partnership copyrights); Cortner v. Israel, 732 F.2d 267 (2d Cir. 1984)(transferors of legal title, retaining rights to royalties, held to have standing to sue as beneficial owners); Hulex Music v. Santy, 698 F. Supp. 1024 (D.N.H. 1988) (licensing agent, who was not legal or beneficial owner, without standing to sue for infringement); Moran v. London Records, Ltd., 642 F. Supp. 1023 (N.D. Ill. 1986) (performer of commercial without any interest in commercial except limitation to commercial use and royalties based on use held not beneficial owner with standing to sue for infringement); Wales Indus., Inc. v. Hasbro Bradley, Inc., 612 F. Supp. 510 (S.D.N.Y. 1985)(exclusive licensee for three years held transferee with standing to sue); Wildlife Int'l, Inc. v. Clements, 782 F. Supp. 1044 (S.D.N.Y. 1984)(transferee entitled to receive royalties held beneficial owner with standing to sue without then-required recordation since ownership by virtue of transfer not claimed); BMI v. CBS, 221 U.S.P.Q. (BNA) 246 (S.D.N.Y. 1983) (nonexclusive licensee without standing to sue; issue apparently not raised in prior cases; suggestion that BMI move for class certification under FED. R. CIV. P. 23). For a

of that particular right"[10] committed while so owned.[11]

For actionable secondary transmissions by cable systems, there are more specific provisions on standing to sue.[12]

---

case where the author allegedly infringed a work written by the author, see Fantasy, Inc. v. Fogerty, 664 F. Supp. 1345 (N.D. Cal. 1987) (defendant, beneficial owner entitled to royalties from song written by defendant and assigned to plaintiff, held suable by legal owner because later song by defendant infringed copyright in music of earlier song; immunity of co-owners from suit by co-owner for infringement irrelevant). SBK Catalogue Partnership v. Orion Pictures Corp., 723 F. Supp. 1053 (D.N.J. 1989) (composers of song liable for own alleged infringement of song; their standing to sue as beneficial owners (royalties) no defense).

10. 17 U.S.C.A. § 501(b). For discussion of divisibility of copyright, *see* text accompanying chapter 7, notes 42–52, *supra.* Section 501(b) attempts to safeguard the rights of all copyright owners and to avoid a multiplicity of suits. It enables the owner of a particular right to bring an infringement action in that owner's name alone, while at the same time ensuring to the extent possible that the other owners whose rights may be affected are notified and given a chance to join the action. 1976 House Report 158-59.

11. 17 U.S.C.A. § 501(b). The court may, in its discretion, require the complainant to serve written notice of the action with a copy of the complaint upon "any person shown, by the records of the Copyright Office or otherwise, to have or claim an interest in the copyright." However, the court is mandated to require that such notice be served upon any person whose "interest" is likely to be affected by a decision in the case. As under the Federal Rules of Civil Procedure, the court has discretion to require the joinder of "any person having or claiming an interest in the copyright," but, if any such person wishes to become a party, the court must permit the person's intervention. Section 501(b) is intended to allow a court to permit or compel joinder of the owners of rights in works upon which a derivative work is based. 1976 House Report 159.

12. 17 U.S.C.A. § 501(c). If actionable under § 111(c), a television broadcast station holding a copyright or other license to transmit or perform the same version is treated as "a legal or beneficial owner" if such transmission occurred within the local service area of that television station. § 501(c). If actionable pursuant to § 111(c)(3), those with standing to sue are: (1) the primary transmitter whose transmission has been altered by the cable system; and (2) any broadcast station within whose local service area the secondary transmission occurs. *Id.* § 501(d). *See id.* § 510.

27.2 Conditions Precedent to Suit

Compliance with the registration requirement (inapplicable since March 1, 1989, for "Berne Convention works" whose "country of origin" is *not* the United States) must be before institution of the action, but not before the infringement.[13] For *all* works since March 1, 1989, recordation of instruments of transfer has not been prerequisite to an infringement suit by a transferee.[14]

27.3 Innocent Infringers

Innocence generally is no defense to an action for copyright infringement.[15] There are some exceptions:

1. When a copyright notice has been omitted from an authorized copy or phonorecords before March 1, 1989, any person who innocently infringes in reliance upon such omission incurs no liability for actual or statutory damages for any infringing acts committed before receiving actual notice that registration of the work has been made, if such person proves that such person was misled by the omission of the notice; the court may allow or disallow recov-

---

13. 17 U.S.C.A. §§ 501(b), 411. *See* text accompanying chapter 12, notes 39–46, *supra*.
14. 17 U.S.C.A. §§ 501(b), 205(d). *See* text accompanying chapter 9, notes 11–12, *supra*.
15. *See* Latman & Tager, *Liability of Innocent Infringers of Copyrights* (1958), *reprinted in* 2 STUDIES ON COPYRIGHT—ARTHUR FISHER MEMORIAL EDITION 1045 (1963). Since March 1, 1989, if the specified copyright notice appears on the published copy or phonorecord to which a defendant in a copyright infringement suit had access, no weight shall be given to such defendant's interposition of a defense based on innocent infringement in mitigation of actual or statutory damages, except as provided in the last sentence of section 504(c)(2). Berne Act § 7(a)(4), (b)(4); 17 U.S.C.A. § 401(a)(4), (b)(4).

ery of any of the infringer's profits "attributable to the infringement," and may enjoin the continuation of the infringing undertaking or may require, as a condition for permitting the continuation of the infringing undertaking, that the infringer pay the "copyright owner" a reasonable license fee in an amount and on terms fixed by the court.[16]

2. When there is an error in name in the copyright notice on copies or phonorecords publicly distributed by authority of the "copyright owner," any person who innocently infringes has a complete defense if such person proves that such person was misled by the notice and began the undertaking in good faith under a purported transfer or license from the person named therein, unless before the undertaking was begun:[17]
   - Registration of the work had been made in the name of the "owner of copyright."
   - A document executed by the person named in the copyright notice and showing the "ownership of the copyright" had been recorded.
3. Reduction of statutory damages to not less than $200 when the infringer sustains the burden of proving, and the court finds, that such infringer was not aware, and had no reason to believe, that the acts constituted infringement.[18]
4. Remission of statutory damages when an infringer believed and had reasonable grounds to believe that the use was a fair use, if the infringer was:[19]

---

16. 17 U.S.C.A. § 405(b), as amended by Berne Act § 7(e)(2). The Berne Act made notice permissive as of March 1, 1989. *See* chapter 10 *supra*.
17. 17 U.S.C.A. § 406(a).
18. 17 U.S.C.A. § 504(c)(2), as amended by Berne Act § 10(b)(2)(B). *See* 1976 House Report 163. *See also* chapter 18, note 42, *supra*.
19. 17 U.S.C.A. Act § 504(c)(2).

- An employee or agent of a nonprofit educational institution, library, or archive acting within the scope of employment, or such institution, library, or archive itself.
- A "public broadcasting entity" that, or a person who, as a regular part of the nonprofit activities of a "public broadcasting entity," infringed by performing a published nondramatic literary work or by reproducing a transmission program embodying a performance of such a work.

27.4 Contributory Infringers

Contributory infringement[20] is defined as a violation of any of the exclusive rights,[21] which includes *authorizing*[22] as well as using.

---

20. *See* 1976 House Report 159:

> A well-established principle of copyright law is that a person who violates any of the exclusive rights of the copyright owner is an infringer, including persons who can be considered related or vicarious infringers. To be held a related or vicarious infringer in the case of performing rights, a defendant must either actively operate or supervise the operation of the place wherein the performances occur, or control the content of the infringing program, and expect commercial gain from the operation and either direct or indirect benefit from the infringing performance.

Obviously, there can be no contributory infringement absent direct infringement. Demetriades v. Kaufmann, 680 F. Supp. 658 (S.D.N.Y. 1988) (copyright protection for architectural plans did not extend to defendant's construction of home based on plans). Assisting a customer in using cassette tape recording would be direct infringement. RCA/Ariola Int'l, Inc. v. Thomas & Grayston Co., 845 F.2d 773 (8th Cir. 1988). For distinction between vicarious liability ("respondeat superior") and contributory infringement ("enterprise liability"), *see* Demetriades v. Kaufmann, 690 F. Supp. 289 (S.D.N.Y. 1988). *See also* RCA/Ariola Int'l, Inc. v. Thomas & Grayston Co., 845 F.2d 773 (8th Cir. 1988) (major shareholder vicariously liable; retailers ordered to control use on Rezound cassette duplicating machine); Casella v. Morris, 820 F.2d 362 (11th Cir. 1987) (50 percent shareholder contributory infringer); Little Mole Music v. Spike Inv., Inc., 720 F. Supp. 751 (W.D. Mo. 1989) (joint and several liability for direct or vicarious infringers, latter for control and financial interest); Barnaby Music Corp. v. Catoctin Broadcasting Corp., [1988 Binder] Copyright L. Rep. (CCH) ¶ 26,335 (W.D.N.Y. 1988) (radio station manager liable for infringing public performance; defendants liable for $11,250 [$1,250 × 9 infringements], $300 costs, and $6,220 attorneys' fees, where license fees would have been $4,800). Some lower courts have found infringement by dance hall owners, etc., who leased their premises to musicians who infringed, even in contravention of express instructions, on theories of "control" and in recognition of the difficulty of obtaining adequate redress from traveling musicians. As to requisite control by any contributory infringer, *compare* Famous Music Corp. v. Bay State Harness Horse Racing & Breeding Ass'n, 554 F.2d 1213 (1st Cir. 1977)("dance hall case") *with* Deutsch v. Arnold, 98 F.2d 686 (2d Cir. 1938)(landlord-tenant case). A device does not contribute to infringement if capable of substantial noninfringing use, such as private noncommercial time-shifting of television programs in the home. Sony Corp. of Am. v. Universal City Studios, Inc., 464 U.S. 417 (1984)(5–4). Justice Blackmun in dissent stated, "if a *significant* portion of the product's use is *noninfringing,* the manufacturers and sellers cannot be held contributorily liable for the product's infringing uses. . . . (I)f no one would buy the product for noninfringing purposes alone, it is clear . . . that liability is appropriately imposed. . . ." *Id.* at 491. The "staple article of commerce" doctrine of patent law was, therefore, not applicable. *Id.* No one would buy a VCR with a tuner for noninfringing purposes alone. *Id.* at 492. *See* Cable/Home Communication Corp. v. Network Prods., Inc. 900 F.2d 829 (11th Cir. 1990) (promotion of devices to descramble scrambled copyrighted satellite transmissions held contributory infringement; award of $20,000 statutory damages and $45,000 attorneys' fees and costs); Vault Corp. v. Quaid Software, Ltd., 847 F.2d 255 (5th Cir. 1988) (no contributory infringement by producer of anticopying software program capable of substantial noninfringing use—archival copy exception); Oddi, *Contributory Copyright Infringement: The Tort and Technological Tensions,* 64 NOTRE DAME LAW. 47 (1989). Contributory infringement actions are pending against manufacturers of digital audio tape (DAT) recorders and tapes. Legislation has been introduced to require that all DAT recorders sold in the United States be unable to make all but initial taped copies of compact disks.

21. 17 U.S.C.A. § 501(a).
22. 17 U.S.C.A. § 106. A proposed exemption of proprietors of establishments from liability for infringement committed by an independent contractor was not enacted. *See* note 18 *supra.* Hal Roach Studios, Inc. v. Richard Feiner & Co., Copyright L. Rep. (CCH) ¶ 25,709

27.5 Jurisdiction over Copyright Infringement Actions

Original jurisdiction over civil copyright infringement actions arising under the copyright laws of the United States is conferred exclusively on the United States district courts, exclusive of the courts of the states.[23]

27.6 Infringement

Infringement is the substantial unauthorized[24] copying of

(S.D.N.Y. 1984)(licensor held to have infringed vicariously exclusive licensee's rights by authorizing use by recording company).

23. 28 U.S.C.A. § 1338(a). Official Form 17 is for a copyright infringement complaint. Attachment of copies of the plaintiff's and defendant's works is optional. Case where only issue is of actual ownership, where remedies under copyright law are sought, is one "arising under" 28 U.S.C.A. § 1338(a). Vestron, Inc. v. Home Box Office, Inc., 839 F.2d 1380 (9th Cir. 1988); Topolos v. Caldeway, 698 F.2d 991 (9th Cir. 1983) (distinguishing copyright cases where contract issues are sole questions and where contract issues are merely threshold questions). *See also* Arthur Young & Co. v. Richmond, Copyright L. Rep. (CCH) ¶ 26,529 (4th Cir. 1990) (federal court jurisdiction over complaint alleging copyright claims not lost because of difficulty and centrality of state law claims); Borden v. Katzman, 881 F.2d 1035 (11th Cir. 1990) (claim of right to publish under implied agreement of confidentiality held to raise only state law issues).

    On appeal, factual questions are reviewed under the "clearly erroneous" standard, greater review is made of mixed questions of law and fact. Whimsicality, Inc. v. Rubie's Costumes Co., 891 F.2d 452 (2d Cir. 1989) (fraud on Copyright Office). Arbitration of copyright issues is not inconsistent with exclusive jurisdiction of the federal courts in copyright cases. Saturday Evening Post Co. v. Rumbleseat Press, Inc., 816 F.2d 1191 (7th Cir. 1987). *See* chapter 28, notes 37, 38, *infra*. *See* note 1 *supra*.

24. *See* chapters 18–26 *supra*, for exemptions and limitations. The certificate of registration, if timely filed, provides prima facie evidence of the facts stated therein, with the burden on the defendant to overcome such presumptive validity. Upon proof of contrary facts, the burden shifts to the plaintiff. For "Fraud on the Copyright Office," *see* chapter 12, note 47 *supra*. The initial burden of showing access and copying also is on the plaintiff. Copyright infringement requires

protected material[25] from a copyrighted work. Copying[26] is crucial to infringement; independent creation, therefore, is not unlawful. Access[27] and copying are the material elements.

---

showing, with or without the aid of presumptions, that the plaintiff owns the rights allegedly infringed, that the defendant had access, and that there is substantial similarity in protectible expression. Cooking Sys. & Flexibles, Inc. v. Stuart Radiator, Inc., 777 F.2d 485 (9th Cir. 1985). *See* Universal City Studios, Inc. v. Casey & Casey Inc., 622 F. Supp. 201 (S.D. Fla. 1985)(no substantial similarity between "Miami Vice" serious dramatic characters and comic figures in "Miami Mice").

25. *See* chapters 4 and 5 *supra*.
26. Copying may be "comprehensive nonliteral similarity" (fundamental essence or structure of substantial part) or "fragmented literal similarity" (substantial instances of literal similarity). Where there are common sources for derivative works, questions often arise as to whether the later derivative work infringed the copyright of the earlier derivative work. As Holmes, J., wrote: "Others are free to copy the original. They are not free to copy the copy." Bleistein v. Donaldson Lithographing Co., 188 U.S. 239 (1903). Use for verification where there was independent research may not be infringement. Contrariwise, compiler's use of plaintiff's work as basis for further compilation supports finding of infringement. Illinois Bell Tel. Co. v. Haines & Co., 905 F.2d 1081 (7th Cir. 1990) (summary judgment against defendant for rearranging white pages from alphabetical by name of telephone customer to alphabetical by street address). The Supreme Court has granted certiorari for Rural Tel. Serv. Co. v. Feist Publications (10th Cir. 1990) (unpublished opinion; copying from white pages without prior independent survey). Werlin v. Reader's Digest Ass'n, 528 F. Supp. 451 (S.D.N.Y. 1981). *See also* Original Appalachian Artworks, Inc. v. Toy Loft, Inc., 684 F.2d 821 (8th Cir. 1982)(proof of access and substantial similarity held to raise only presumption of copying rebuttable by defendants evidence of independent creations); John L. Perry Studios, Inc. v. Wernick, 597 F.2d 1398 (9th Cir. 1979) (burden of persuasion to show independent creation after plaintiff establishes prima facie case).
27. Access may be proven by direct or circumstantial evidence. Substantial similarities create an inference of access rebuttable by convincing evidence to the contrary. Access may be direct or indirect; Universal City Studios, Inc. v. Casey & Casey, Inc., 622 F. Supp. 201 (D. Fla. 1985). *See also* Walker v. Time-Life Films, Inc., 784 F.2d 44 (2d Cir.

Some courts have developed a two-part test:[28]

1986) (copying inferred where access and substantial similarities). Striking similarities alone are not sufficient to establish access; inference of access must be reasonable. Selle v. Gibbs, 741 F.2d 896 (7th Cir. 1984). Similarities may result from coincidence, independent authorship, or common source. Evidence of independent creation may rebut inference of copying. Keeler Brass Co. v. Continental Brass Co., 862 F.2d 1063 (4th Cir. 1988) (independent creation not affirmative defense; burden of proving infringement on plaintiff). Findings of access and substantial similarity are factual, i.e., reviewable for clear error. Data E. USA, Inc. v. Epyx, Inc., 862 F.2d 204 (9th Cir. 1988) (reversing trial court's finding of infringement because based on unprotectible expression).

28. The two-part "extrinsic"-"intrinsic" test is derived from Arnstein v. Porter, 154 F.2d 464 (2d Cir. 1946):

    1. Similarities sufficient to prove copying (analysis [dissection] is relevant; expert testimony admissible)
    2. Unlawful copying (ordinary lay observer or hearer)

    For resolution of whether there has been substantial unauthorized infringing use, one possibly should follow more closely the language of the preemption provisions of section 301 (*see* chapter 4 *supra*) ("legal or equitable rights [or remedies] with respect to" works of authorship). *See* Concrete Mach. Co. v. Classic Lawn Ornaments, Inc., 843 F.2d 600 (1st Cir. 1988) (two-step analysis of infringement: [1] dissection of similarities to substantiate copying and [2] decision whether copying amounted to unlawful appropriation of protectible expression; similarities between plaintiff's and prior works relevant only where originality of plaintiff's work challenged). "Indispensable expression" is protected only against virtually identical copying. Rachel v. Banana Republic, Inc., 831 F.2d 1503 (9th Cir. 1987). *Compare* Illinois Bell Tel. Co. v. Haines, *supra* note 25. The "ordinary lay observer" test for unlawful copying is undergoing refinements. *See* Dawson v. Hinshaw Music, Inc., 905 F.2d 731 (4th Cir. 1990) ("intended-audience" test) (*cert. pending*).

    Quaere, whether concepts of prima facie case, presumptions, burden of proof, and burden of going forward with the evidence do more than complicate matters. "Extrinsic" and "intrinsic" tests, respective functions of judge and jury, scope and standard of appellate review create false impressions of certainty and predictability. Has there been more than "fair use" by the defendant of "protectible" elements of the plaintiff's copyrighted work? This is a mixed question of law and fact, but can be resolved by a jury with simple but adequate court instructions or by a judge absent a jury. The

1. Is there substantial similarity as to the general ideas in the two works, i.e., copying—the so-called *extrinsic* test, on which expert testimony is admissible.

"extrinsic"-"intrinsic" tests seem only to obfuscate already complicated matters. *Compare* Harper House, Inc. v. Thomas Nelson, Inc., 889 F.2d 197 (9th Cir. 1989) (jury verdict for $6 million vacated for inadequate jury instructions on distinction between protectible and nonprotectible utilitarian elements; "total impact and effect" [or "total concept and feel"] test insufficient) *with* Roula v. Russ Berrie & Co., 886 F.2d 931 (7th Cir. 1989) (affirming single $4.3 million award for copyright infringement and trade dress infringement; compilation of nonprotectible [size, color, shape, stripes, etc.] elements held sufficient original authorship under "total concept and feel" test, even though messages of greeting cards were not copied), *cert. denied*, 110 S. Ct. 1124 (1990). Increasingly, appellate courts are reversing trial courts' (judge's or jury's) failure to find infringement by failing to distinguish protectible from nonprotectible matters. *See, e.g.*, Olson v. NBC, 855 F.2d 1446 (9th Cir. 1988) (rejecting jury's verdict erroneously based on "total concept and feel" test instead of trial court's application of extrinsic and intrinsic tests); Aliotti v. R. Dakin & Co., 831 F.2d 898 (9th Cir. 1987) (no substantial similarity of protectible expression; similarity of expression only where "total concept and feel" of works substantially similiar; "intrinsic" test permits analytic dissection of similarities to determine if they arise from protectible expression; analysis of dissimilarities would distract); Worth v. Selchow & Richter Co., 827 F.2d 569 (9th Cir. 1987) (defendant's "Trivial Pursuit" game held not to infringe plaintiff's trivia encyclopedia used as source of facts [22 percent of defendant's questions; 32 percent of plaintiff's factual entries]; not substantially similar in expression; directory cases distinguished; arrangement and selection different; "mood" and "concept and feel" different). The similarities not the differences are paramount. Atari, Inc. v. North Am. Philips Consumer Elecs. Corp., 672 F. 2d 607 (7th Cir.) ("Pac-Man"), *cert. denied*, 459 U.S. 580 (1982). Common errors or superfluous material can be persuasive. Some cases refer to "total concept and feel." Walker v. Time-Life Films, Inc., 784 F.2d 44 (2d Cir. 1986); Berkic v. Crichton, 761 F.2d 1289 (9th Cir 1985); Sid & Marty Krofft Television v. McDonald's Corp., 562 F.2d 1170 (9th Cir. 1977); *cf.* Shaw v. Lindheim, 908 F.2d 531 (9th Cir. 1990) (denial of summary judgment on issue of substantial similarity of protected expression under intrinsic test where there is substantial similarity of unprotectible expression under extrinsic test); Whelan Assocs. v. Jaslow Dental Laboratory, 797 F. 2d 1222 (3d Cir. 1986), *cert. denied*, 107 S. Ct. 877 (1987) (single inquiry in computer programs case, based on both lay and expert testimony).

2. Is there substantial similarity in expression so as to constitute infringement, i.e., illicit copying—the so-called *intrinsic* test, a question of fact for the ordinary lay observer.

Infringement decisions are ad hoc, and often determination is a matter of degree.[29]

Since copyright is territorial in effect, sufficient infringing acts must occur in the United States.[30]

27.7 Remedies for Infringement

For copyright infringement, there is an arsenal of remedies.[31]

27.8 Liabilities of States

States and their instrumentalities, officers, and employees, since 1990, expressly are not "immune under the Eleventh Amendment" or "under any other doctrine of sovereign immunity" from suit in federal court by "any person," including any governmental or nongovernmental entity for a violation of any of the exclusive rights of a copyright owner. Civil remedies are all inclusive.[32]

---

29. Durham Indus., Inc. v. Tony Corp., 630 F.2d 905 (2d Cir. 1980). On fair use, see chapter 18, note 26 *supra*.
30. *See* note 1 *supra* and chapter 34, note 50 *infra*.
31. *See* chapter 28 *infra*.
32. 17 U.S.C.A. § 511(a), (b). Previously, the cases on the immunities of states and their instrumentalities and employees had been in disarray. *See* COPYRIGHT OFFICE REPORT: COPYRIGHT LIABILITY OF STATES AND THE ELEVENTH AMENDMENT (June 1988).

28. Remedies

28.1 Civil Remedies

Civil remedies for copyright infringement include:[1]

1. 17 U.S.C.A. §§ 501–505; The remedies awarded should not exceed the scope of protection under the copyright laws. *See* chapter 17 *supra*. In awarding relief for violation of one exclusive right, courts should not exceed the limitations on other exclusive rights by awards that compensate for consequences lawful under such limitations, e.g., equitable or legal relief for building from copied copyrighted plans. *E.g.*, Robert R. Jones Assocs. v. Nino Homes, 858 F.2d 274 (6th Cir. 1988) (pre-Dec. 1, 1990 law). *See* chapter 17, note 49 *supra*. Libott, *Infringement and Remedies Under the Copyright Act of 1976*, 25 BULL. COPYRIGHT SOC'Y 237 (1978). For discussion of remedies under the 1909 Act, *see* Strauss, *The Damage Provisions of the Copyright Law* (1956), *reprinted in* 2 STUDIES ON COPYRIGHT LAW—ARTHUR FISCHER MEMORIAL EDITION 995 (1963); Brown, *The Operation of the Damage Provisions of the Copyright Law: An Exploratory Study* (1958), *reprinted in* 2 STUDIES ON COPYRIGHT LAW—ARTHUR FISHER MEMORIAL EDITION 1067 (1963); Strauss, *Remedies Other Than Damages for Copyright Infringement* (1959), *reprinted in* 2 STUDIES ON COPYRIGHT LAW—ARTHUR FISHER MEMORIAL EDITION 1029 (1963). The "legal or beneficial owner of an exclusive right under a copyright" has standing to sue for "any infringement of that particular right" committed while so owned. 17 U.S.C.A. § 501(b). Joinder of others might be required. *See* chapter 27, notes 9–12 *supra*. Several class or multiplaintiff actions were brought against copy centers, a university, and some faculty. The actions against the university and faculty were settled. Addison-Wesley Publishing Co. v. New York Univ. (1982–83); American Geophysical Union v. Texaco, Inc. (1985) (class action against corporate photocopier); Ba-

1. Temporary injunction;
2. Final injunction;
3. Actual damages of the copyright owner;
4. Profits of the infringer;
5. Statutory damages;
6. Impounding and disposition of infringing articles;
7. Allowance of costs;
8. Award of reasonable attorney's fee;
9. Importation restrictions;
10. Suspension of compulsory cable television secondary transmission license.

28.1[1] Temporary or Final Injunction

A temporary[2] or final[3] injunction "may," except against the federal government,[4] be granted on such terms as the

---

sic Books, Inc. v. Gnomon Corp. (against commercial photocopying firm). Infringement has been rampant in university and college communities, especially by editors of anthologies and their photocopiers. *See also* Blue Pearl Music Corp. v. Bradford, 728 F.2d 603 (3d Cir. 1984) (infringer could not be ordered to recreate work on pain of contempt because owner had lost all copies of work). *See* chapter 13 *supra*. For remedies for infringement of mask works, *see* chapter 32 *infra*.

2. Or "preliminary" or "interlocutory" injunction ("irreparable harm" presumed). The traditional criteria for injunctive relief include:

    1. Prima facie showing of infringement
    2. Likelihood of success on the merits
    3. Presumption of irreparable harm
    4. Balancing of hardships

    See Keeler Brass v. Continental Brass, 862 F.2d 1063 (4th Cir. 1988). Hasbro Bradley, Inc. v. Sparkle Toys, Inc., 780 F.2d 189 (2d Cir. 1985)(irreparable harm ordinarily presumed to support preliminary injunction for copyright infringement; likelihood of success on the merits). Laches is a basis for denying equitable relief, Cuddle Wit, Inc. v. Chan, Copyright L. Rep. (CCH) ¶ 26,507 (S.D.N.Y. 1989). Other equitable defenses include unclean hands (e.g., failure of full disclosure to Copyright Office) which may constitute fraud on the Copyright Office (see note 49 *infra*); New Era Publications Int'l v. Henry Holt &

court may deem reasonable to prevent or restrain copyright infringement.[5]

Any such injunction may be served anywhere in the United States on the person enjoined, shall be operative throughout the United States, and shall be enforceable, by proceedings in contempt or otherwise, by any United States court having jurisdiction of that person.[6]

28.1[2] Actual Damages of Copyright Owner

An infringer is liable for the copyright owner's "actual damages."[7] Along with damages, there may be recovery of

---

Co., 873 F.2d 576 (2d Cir. 1989) (2–1). Noninjunctive relief may best balance copyright and the first amendment. Denial of injunctive relief has been compared to a judicially crafted compulsory license. *See* note, 10 COLUM.-V.L.A. L. & ARTS 277 (1986).

3. Or "permanent" injunction. Past infringement and substantial likelihood of future infringements normally would justify a permanent injunction.
4. 17 U.S.C.A. § 502(a); 28 U.S.C.A. § 1498.
5. *Id.*; Apple Barrel Prods., Inc. v. Beard, 730 F.2d 384 (5th Cir. 1984) (balancing of hardships held to justify denial of injunction).
6. 17 U.S.C.A. § 502(b); FED. R. CIV. P. 65. The clerk of the court granting the injunction shall, when requested by any other court in which enforcement of the injunction is sought, transmit promptly to the other court a certified copy of all the papers in the case on file in such clerk's office.
7. 17 U.S.C.A. § 504(a)(1). The term "actual damages" is not defined in the statute. Manufacturers Technologies, Inc. v. Cams, Inc., 728 F. Supp. 75 (D. Conn. 1989) (award of $348,600 actual damages and $4,600 additional profits beyond actual damages). Punitive damages are not awarded for copyright infringement. Cormack v. Sunshine Food Stores, Inc., 675 F. Supp. 374 (E.D. Mich. 1987). Quaere, as to the recovery of prejudgment interest. *Compare* Frank Music Corp. v. Metro-Goldwyn-Mayer, Inc., 886 F.2d 1545 (9th Cir. 1989) (1909 Act) (interest awarded) *with* Robert R. Jones Assocs. v. Nino Homes, 858 F.2d 274 (6th Cir. 1988) (improper in addition to lost profits). The plaintiff must prove actual damages. *See* text accompanying note 13 *infra*. Cream Records, Inc. v. Joseph Schlitz Brewing Co., 754 F.2d 862 (9th Cir. 1985)(use of small portion of song in commercial found to have destroyed value of song for licensing purposes); Deltak, Inc. v.

"any additional profits of the infringer."[8] "Instead" of actual damages and profits, at the election of the copyright owner, statutory damages, subject to certain limitations, shall be awarded.[9]

28.1[3] Profits of Infringer

An infringer is liable for any profits of the infringer in addition to the copyright owner's actual damages.[10] At the election of the copyright owner, statutory damages may be awarded instead of actual damages and profits.[11] The recoverable profits of the infringer are the profits "attributable to

---

Advanced Sys., Inc., 767 F.2d 357 (7th Cir. 1986) (issue on appeal limited to actual damages; no monetary recovery because actual damages and profits not proven and statutory damages barred by lack of timely registration); Streeter v. Rolfe, 491 F. Supp. 416 (D. La. 1980)(no monetary recovery where no profits or actual damages). Punitive damages are not available in statutory, as distinguished from pre–1978 common-law, copyright infringement actions. Oboler v. Guldin, 714 F.2d 211 (2d Cir. 1983); Roy Export Co. Establishment v. Columbia Broadcasting Sys., Inc., 672 F.2d 1095 (2d Cir.), *cert. denied*, 459 U.S. 826 (1982).

8. 17 U.S.C.A. § 504(a)(1).
9. 17 U.S.C.A. § 504(c)(1). The two basic aims of the damages and profits section are reciprocal and correlative: (1) to give the courts specific unambiguous directions concerning monetary awards, thus avoiding the confusion and uncertainty that have marked the 1909 Act on the subject and, at the same time, (2) to provide the courts with reasonable latitude to adjust recovery to the circumstances of the case, thus avoiding some of the artificial or overly technical awards resulting from the language of the 1909 Act. 1976 House Report 161. Copyright infringers, as joint tortfeasors, usually are jointly and severally liable for damages, but severally liable for profits. Frank Music Corp. v. Metro-Goldwyn-Mayer, Inc., 722 F.2d 505 (9th Cir. 1985) (under 1909 Act). Infringements by agents may render their employers vicariously liable on principles of agency law. United States v. Shabazz, 724 F.2d 1536 (5th Cir. 1984); Van Halen Music v. Palmer, 626 F. Supp. 1163 (W.D. Ark. 1986). So also may shareholders' governing and controlling infringing conduct. Milene Music, Inc. v. Gotauco, 551 F. Supp. 1288 (D.R.I. 1982).
10. 17 U.S.C.A. § 504(a)(1).
11. 17 U.S.C.A. § 504(c)(1).

the infringement" and "not taken into account in computing the actual damages."[12]

In establishing the infringer's profits, the copyright owner is required to present proof only of the infringer's gross revenue, and the infringer is required to prove the "deductible expenses and the elements of profit attributable to factors other than the copyrighted work."[13]

---

12. 17 U.S.C.A. § 504(b). Section 504(b) recognizes the different purposes served by awards of damages and profits. Damages are awarded to compensate the copyright owner for losses from the infringement, and profits are awarded to prevent the infringer from unfairly benefiting from a wrongful act. Where the defendant's profits are nothing more than a measure of the damages suffered by the copyright owner, it would be inappropriate to award damages and profits cumulatively, since in effect they amount to the same thing. However, in cases where the copyright owner has suffered damages not reflected in the infringer's profits, or where there have been profits attributable to the copyrighted work, but not used as a measure of damages, both may be awarded. 1976 House Report 161. *See* Business Trends Analysts, Inc. v. Freedonia Group, 887 F.2d 399 (2d Cir. 1989) (dictum that enhanced good will and market recognition recognizable under section 504[b]). Sygma Photo News, Inc. v. High Soc'y Magazine, Inc. 778 F.2d 89 (2d Cir. 1985)(no more than 50 percent of profits reasonably attributable to infringement of photograph used on cover; no damages for 48 percent of copies unsold; allowable damages and deductions from profits); Abeshouse v. Ultragraphics, Inc., 754 F.2d 467 (2d Cir. 1985) (plaintiff entitled to recover actual damages plus defendants' profits not taken into account in computing damages); Kamar Int'l, Inc. v. Russ Berrie & Co., 752 F.2d 1326 (9th Cir. 1984) (deductible overhead expenses). *Compare* Cream Records, Inc. v. Joseph Schlitz Brewing Co., 754 F.2d 862 (9th Cir. 1985) *with* Sid & Marty Krofft Television Prods., Inc., v. McDonald's Corp., 221 U.S.P.Q. (BNA) 114 (S.D. Cal. 1983)(burden of proving portion of profits not related to infringement).
13. 17 U.S.C.A. §504(b). Gaste v. Kaiserman, 863 F.2d 1061 (2d Cir. 1988) (burden of proving apportionment of profits from infringing and non-infringing elements on defendant); Konor Enters. v. Eagle Publications, 878 F.2d 138 (4th Cir. 1989); Cream Records, Inc. v. Joseph Schlitz Brewing Co. 754 F.2d 826 (9th Cir. 1985). *But see* Blackman v. Hustler Magazine, 800 F.2d 1160 (D.C. Cir. 1986) (award of gross profits without deduction). *Cf.* note 7 *supra*. *See* Sheldon v. Metro-Goldwyn Pictures Corp., 309 U.S. 390 (1940); Frank Music Corp. v. Metro-Goldwyn Mayer, Inc., 886 F.2d 1545 (9th Cir. 1989) (de novo

28.1[4] Statutory Damages

Instead of actual damages and profits, the copyright owner "may elect," at any time before final judgment is rendered, to recover an award of statutory damages.[14]

Such election is "for all infringements involved in the action," with respect to any one work,[15] for which any one infringer is liable individually, or for which any two or more infringers are liable jointly and severally.[16]

The award of statutory damages ordinarily must be from $500 to $20,000, "as the court considers just."[17] For "willful

---

apportionment by appellate court), *cert. denied*, 110 S. Ct. 1231 (1990).

14. 17 U.S.C.A. § 504(c)(1); RSO Records, Inc. v. Peri, 596 F. Supp. 849 (S.D.N.Y. 1984) (deferral of election allowed pending court's determination of actual damages and profits, compared to statutory damages, where plaintiff requested award of greater of two). *See* Frank Music Corp. v. Metro-Goldwyn-Mayer, Inc., 886 F.2d 1545 (9th Cir. 1989), *cert. denied*, 110 S. Ct. 1231 (1990); Warner Bros. v. Multinational Prods. Corp., [1986 Binder] Copyright L. Rep. (CCH) ¶ 26,039 (S.D.N.Y. 1986) ($22,500 statutory damages and $26,750 costs and attorney's fees). Under 1909 Act, *see* F. W. Woolworth v. Contemporary Arts, Inc., 344 U.S. 228 (1952). *Cf.* Kleier Advertising Co. v. James Miller Chevrolet, Inc., 722 F. Supp. 1544 (N.D. Ill. 1989) (election between actual damages and profits not required).
15. 17 U.S.C.A. § 504(c)(1). For such purposes, all the parts of a compilation or derivative work constitute one work. The minimum-maximum amounts may be multiplied where multiple works are involved in the suit, but not with respect to multiple copyrights, multiple owners, multiple exclusive rights, or multiple registrations. 1976 House Report 162. Walt Disney Co. v. Powell, 897 F.2d 565 (D.C. Cir. 1990).
16. 17 U.S.C.A. § 504(c)(1), as amended by Berne Act § 10. A single amount is recoverable no matter how many acts of infringement are involved in the action, and regardless of whether the acts were separate, isolated, or incurred in a related series. 1976 House Report 162. The 1909 Act based statutory damages on infringements. 1909 Act § 101(b).
17. 17 U.S.C.A. § 504(c)(1). While the court may exercise discretion within the $250–$10,000 range, it cannot, unless within one of the statutory exceptions *(see infra)*, award less than $500 or more than $20,000 if the copyright owner has elected to recover statutory dam-

infringement," the maximum is $100,000; for "innocent infringement," the minimum is $200.

When the copyright owner sustains the burden of proving, and the court finds, that infringement was committed "willfully," the court in its discretion may increase the award to up to $100,000.[18]

---

ages. The current statutory damage awards were doubled by the Berne Act section 106. The 1909 Act range was $250–$5,000 with a schedule. 1909 Act § 101(b). The court may take into account evidence concerning actual damages and profits in awarding statutory damages within the permissible range. 1976 House Report 161. Increased statutory damages under the Berne Act apply to causes of action after March 1, 1989.

See Douglas v. Cunningham, 294 U.S. 207 (1935)(scope of appellate court review). The reference to "court" raises questions as to the right to a jury trial. Even in an action seeking only an injunction and minimum statutory damages, such a right has been found. Gnassos Music v. Mitken, Inc., 653 F.2d 117 (4th Cir. 1981). Jury trial has been denied on the issue of statutory damages on the ground of their "equitable" nature. Twentieth Century Music Corp. v. Firth, 645 F.2d 6 (5th Cir. 1981); Raydiola Music v. Revelation Rob, Inc., 729 F. Supp. 369 (D. Del. 1990) (denial of jury trial where only injunction and statutory damages sought). Right of trial by jury in "Suits at common law, where the value in controversy shall exceed twenty dollars" is preserved by U.S. CONST. amend. VII. In this post-common-law-copyright era, to what extent is jury trial required or desirable? *See* Patry, *The Right to a Jury in Copyright Cases*, 29 J. COPYRIGHT SOC'Y 139 (1981); note, 83 MICH. L. REV. 1950 (1985). Stumpff, *The Availability of Jury Trials in Copyright Infringement Cases: Limiting the Scope of the Seventh Amendment*, 83 MICH. L. REV. 1950 (1985); Annot., 64 A.L.R. Fed. 310 (1983). Minimum statutory damages have been awarded where actual damages were nominal or substantially less. Bly v. Banbury Books, Inc., 638 F. Supp. 983 (E.D. Pa. 1986); Rogers v. Eighty-Four Lumber Co., 623 F. Supp. 889 (W.D. Pa. 1985)($122,500 versus $77,805). Unimusic, Inc. v. Spanish Community Radio, Inc., [1987 Binder] Copyright L. Rep. (CCH) ¶ 26,091 (D.N.M. 1987) ($32,000 statutory damages award where ASCAP license fees would have been $20,000; permanent injunction; $5,100 in attorney's fees, costs, and expenses).

18. 17 U.S.C.A. § 504(c)(2). *See* Pye v. Mitchell, 574 F.2d 476 (9th Cir. 1978) (written release from copyright liability held actual notice of infringement). For willful infringement, maximum statutory damages

If the infringer sustains the burden of proving, and the court finds, that such infringer "was not aware and had no reason to believe" that the acts constituted infringement, the court in its discretion may reduce the award to not less than $200.[19]

No award of statutory damages shall be made for:

1. Any infringement of copyright in an unpublished work commenced before the effective date of its registration;[20]
2. Any infringement of copyright commenced after first publication of the work and before the effective date of its registration, unless such registration is made within three months after the first publication of the work;[21]
3. Any infringement of copyright by an infringer who "believed and had reasonable grounds for believing" that the use was a "fair use," if the infringer was:[22]

---

have reached $1.4 million where actual damages plus profits were $42,239. RSO Records, Inc. v. Peri, 596 F. Supp. 849 (S.D.N.Y. 1984); Fitzgerald Publishing Co. v. Baylor Publishing Co., 807 F. 2d 1110 (2d Cir. 1986)(copying with changed copyright notice held willful infringement justifying statutory damages up to $50,000 per infringement); Kamar Int'l, Inc. v. Russ Berrie & Co., 829 F.2d 783 (9th Cir. 1987) ($460,520 statutory damages); Fitzgerald Publishing Co. v. Baylor Publishing Co., *supra*, (willful infringers jointly and severally liable for statutory damages). Sections 504(c)(1) and (2) are silent as to joint and several liability. As to the punitive part of statutory damages (over $20,000), the less culpable defendant may have a claim against the more culpable defendant. Judgment for willful copyright infringement is not dischargeable in bankruptcy. 17 U.S.C.A. § 523(a)(6); BMI v. Elms, [1990 Binder] Copyright L. Rep. (CCH) (Bankr. E.D. La. 1990).

19. 17 U.S.C.A. § 504(c)(2).
20. 17 U.S.C.A. § 412(1); Streeter v. Rolfe, 491 F. Supp. 416 (D. La. 1980)(no grace period for unpublished works).
21. 17 U.S.C.A. § 412(2).
22. 17 U.S.C.A. § 504(c)(2). The burden of proof with respect to the defendant's good faith is intended to rest on the plaintiff. 1976 House Report 163.

- An employee or agent of a nonprofit educational institution, library, or archive acting within the scope of employment who, or such institution, library, or archive itself that, infringed by reproducing the work in copies or phonorecords.
- A "public broadcasting entity" that, or a person who, as a regular part of the nonprofit activities of a "public broadcasting entity," infringed by performing a published nondramatic literary work or by reproducing a "transmission program" embodying a performance of such a work.

28.1[5] Impounding and Disposition of Infringing Articles

At any time while an action is pending, the court may order the "impounding," on such terms as it may deem reasonable, of all copies or phonorecords "claimed" to have been made or used in violation of the copyright owner's exclusive rights, and of all plates, molds, matrices, masters, tapes, film negatives, or other articles by means of which such copies or phonorecords may be reproduced.[23]

As part of a final judgment or decree, the court may order the "destruction or other reasonable disposition" of all copies or phonorecords "found" to have been made or used in

---

23. 17 U.S.C.A. § 503(a); Owens, *Impoundment Procedures Under the Copyright Act: The Constitutional Infirmities*, 14 HOFSTRA L. REV. 211 (1985); Warner Bros. v. Dae Rim Trading, Inc., 877 F.2d 1120 (2d Cir. 1989) (ex parte impoundment order improper; search and seizure and "discovery" by copyright owner's attorneys and their agents not authorized by law). Midway Mfg. Co. v. Omni Video Games, Inc., 668 F.2d 70 (1st Cir. 1981); WPOW v. MRLJ Enters., 584 F. Supp. 132 (D.D.C. 1984)(requirements for impounding same as for preliminary injunction). The United States Supreme Court Copyright Rules, adopted without any express provisions therefor in the 1909 Act, dealt mainly with seizure. *See* Freedman v. Mangalick, Pat. Trademark & Copyright J. (BNA) No. 387, A1 (D.N.J. 1982)(impounding denied on basis of first amendment considerations and discretion of court), *aff'd without opinion*, 720 F.2d 662 (3d Cir.), *cert. denied*, 464 U.S. 939 (1983). *Cf.* 17 U.S.C.A. § 603(c).

violation of the copyright owner's exclusive rights, and of articles by means of which such copies or phonorecords may be reproduced.[24]

Seizure and forfeiture are also possible under the importation restrictions[25] and in cases of criminal infringement.[26]

28.1[6] Allowance of Costs

In any civil action, the court "in its discretion" may allow the recovery of full costs by or against any party other than the United States or an officer thereof.[27]

28.1[7] Award of Reasonable Attorney's Fee

Except as otherwise provided,[28] the court may award a "reasonable attorney's fee to the prevailing party as part of the costs."[29] No such award shall be made for:

---

24. 17 U.S.C.A. § 503(b). *Cf.* 17 U.S.C.A. § 603(c).
25. 17 U.S.C.A. § 603(c). *See* chapter 29 *infra.*
26. 17 U.S.C.A. § 509. *See* text accompanying notes 42–46 *infra.*
27. 17 U.S.C.A. § 505. Costs to the "prevailing party" were mandatory under the 1909 Act. 1909 Act § 116.
28. 17 U.S.C.A. § 412.
29. 17 U.S.C.A. § 505. The courts are divided on whether attorney's fees should be awarded as a matter of course or whether bad faith or frivolity on the part of the losing party must be shown. Most of the cases apply the same standard to "prevailing" plaintiffs and "prevailing" defendants, recognizing that an award for "a reasonable attorney's fee" (without recognizing that the term is singular) is discretionary ("may"). The Ninth Circuit, especially, and the Second Circuit impose a double standard: to prevailing plaintiffs regardless of defendant's bad faith; to prevailing defendants only on finding that action was brought in bad faith. Bibbero Sys., Inc. v. Colwell Sys., Inc., 893 F.2d 1104 (9th Cir. 1989) (double standard); Olson v. NBC, 855 F.2d 1446 (9th Cir. 1988); McCulloch v. Albert E. Price, Inc., 821 F.2d 316 (9th Cir. 1987); Whimsicality, Inc. v. Rubie's Costumes Co., 891 F.2d 452 (2d Cir. 1989); Diamond v. Am-Law Publishing Co., 745 F.2d 142 (2d Cir. 1984). *But see* Casella v. Morris, 320 F.2d 362 (11th Cir. 1987); Lieb v. Touchstone Indus., 788 F.2d 151 (3d Cir. 1986); Micromanipulator v. Bough, 779 F.2d 255 (5th Cir. 1985).

1. Any infringement of copyright in an unpublished work commenced before the effective date of its registration;[30]
2. Any infringement of copyright commenced after first publication of the work and before the effective date of its registration, unless such registration is made within three months after the first publication of the work.[31]

28.1[8] Importation Restrictions

Infringing copies and phonorecords may be denied importation into the United States.[32]

28.1[9] Suspension of Compulsory Cable Television Secondary Transmission License

The remedies for alteration of programming by a cable system in violation of section 111(c)(3)[33] may include, be-

---

Cf. Roulo v. Russ Berrie & Co., 886 F.2d 931 (7th cir. 1989) (attorney's fees award not warranted where substantial award of profits sufficient deterrence). For discussion of twelve factors in awarding attorney's fees under 1909 Act, *see* Johnson v. Georgia Highway Express, 488 F.2d 714 (5th Cir. 1974). The question of who is the "prevailing party" can be troublesome. There are sanctions against attorneys for raising frivolous claims. FED. R. CIV. P. 11; FED. R. APP. P. 38; Lloyd v. Schlag, 884 F.2d 409 (9th Cir. 1989); Hays v. Sony Corp. of Am., 847 F.2d 412 (7th Cir. 1988). Attorney's fees may far exceed any monetary recovery. Rockford Map Publishers, Inc. v. Directory Serv. Co., 768 F.2d 145 (7th Cir. 1985) (upholding award of $22,000 attorney's fees where relief granted was $250 statutory damages and injunction); Stanford Univ. v. Associated Business Assocs., 14 U.S.P.Q. 2d (BNA) 1326 (D. Kan. 1989) (upholding $107,000 attorney's fee and $7,000 statutory damages).

30. 17 U.S.C.A. § 412(1). Moore v. Columbia Pictures Indus., Copyright L. Rep. (CCH) ¶ 26,586 (D. Minn. 1990) (attorney's fees denied for failure to register unpublished work before infringement).
31. 17 U.S.C.A. § 412(2); Johnson v. University of Va., 606 F. Supp. 321 (W.D. Va. 1985).
32. 17 U.S.C.A. §§ 602–603. *See* chapter 29 *infra*.
33. *See* text accompanying chapter 25, notes 33–36, *supra*.

sides the other enumerated remedies,[34] deprivation for not more than thirty days of the "benefit of a compulsory license for one or more distant signals carried by such cable system."[35]

Such remedy is within the discretion of the court and is available in actions brought by television broadcast stations with standing to sue.[36]

28.2 Exclusive Civil Jurisdiction of Federal Courts

Original jurisdiction of any civil actions arising under the copyright laws of the United States is in the United States district courts,[37] exclusive of the courts of the states.[38]

---

34. 17 U.S.C.A. § 509(a). For regular copyright owners and local broadcaster-licensees, the full battery of remedies (§§ 502–505) is available. The two new classes of potential plaintiffs under § 501(d)—the distant-signal transmitter and other local stations—are limited to the following remedies: (1) discretionary injunctions, (2) discretionary costs and attorney's fees, (3) any actual damages the plaintiff can prove were attributable to the act of altering program content (§§ 502, 505). 1976 House Report 164.
35. 17 U.S.C.A. § 510(b). The term "distant signals" is intended to have a meaning consistent with the definition of "distant signal equivalent" in § 111. 1976 House Report 164. *See* chapter 25, note 44 *supra*.
36. 17 U.S.C.A. § 510(b). *See* chapter 27, note 12 *supra*.
37. 28 U.S.C.A. § 1338(a). The United States has waived its own sovereign immunity against claims of copyright infringement. 28 U.S.C.A. § 1498 (Court of Claims jurisdiction over copyright infringement action against United States). The Copyright Remedy Clarification Act of 1990 (effective Nov. 15, 1990), purported to eliminate state immunity. 17 U.S.C.A. §§ 501(a) (defining "anyone" to include "any State"), 571 (liability of states, instrumentalities of states, and state officials for infringement of copyright). *See* REPORT OF REGISTER OF COPYRIGHTS, *Copyright Liability of States and the Eleventh Amendment* (1988); Anderson Photography v. Radford Univ., 852 F.2d 114 (4th Cir. 1988) (states and officials in official capacity, but not in individual capacity, immune), *cert. denied*, 109 S. Ct. 1117 (1989); BV Eng's v. University of Cal., 858 F.2d 1394 (9th Cir. 1989) (state and its board of regents immune), *cert. denied*, 109 S. Ct. 1557 (1989); Lane v. First Nat'l Bank, 871 F.2d 166 (1st Cir. 1989) (state but

not officials immune); Note, 36 AM. U. L. REV. 163 (1986). The civil remedies against a state, since 1990, have been all-inclusive. 17 U.S.C.A. § 511(b).

Within one month after the filing of any copyright infringement action, the clerks of the courts of the United States are required to send written notification to the Register of Copyrights. Within one month after any final order or judgment, notification with a copy thereof, together with any written opinion, is required to be sent to the Register, who shall make the notifications part of the "public records" of the Copyright Office. 17 U.S.C.A. § 508; 43 Fed. Reg. 24,151 (June 2, 1978). The patent law contains comparable provisions. 35 U.S.C.A. § 290. The trial may be bifurcated on issues of infringement and remedies. FED. R. CIV. P. 42(b); Annot., 79 A.L.R. Fed. 532 (1986). Appeals are to the appropriate federal court of appeals, possibly including the United States Court of Appeals for the Federal Circuit. Atari, Inc. v. JS&A Group, Inc. 747 F.2d 1422 (Fed. Cir. 1984) (case based on patents and copyrights). *See* chapter 27, note 23 *supra*. *See* Zamba Enters. v. Club Magic, Inc., Copyright L. Rep. (CCH) ¶ 26,486 (S.D. Tex. 1989) (joinder of performing-rights society not proper); Shube's Mfg. Corp. v. Blake Bros. Int'l, Copyright L. Rep. (CCH) ¶ 26,535 (S.D.N.Y. 1990) (defendant corporate group sold infringing jewelry in state); Foster v. WNYC-TV, Copyright L. Rep. (CCH) ¶ 26,505 (S.D.N.Y. 1989) (no infringing acts by defendant within United States); AdVideo, Inc. v. Kimel Broadcast Group, Inc., 727 F. Supp. 1337 (N.D. Cal. 1989) (negotiating and signing contract held sufficient contact for personal jurisdiction and venue).

For copyright infringement under the laws of foreign countries (see chapter 34 *infra*), the federal courts may have jurisdiction, but not under 28 U.S.C.A. § 1338(a). Some other basis for federal court jurisdiction would be required, e.g., diversity of citizenship, including jurisdictional amount requirement, pendent jurisdiction, patent or trademark law. *See* London Film Prod. v. Intercontinental Communications, Inc., 580 F. Supp. 47 (S.D.N.Y. 1984), *noted in* 70 CORNELL L. REV. 1165 (1985). *See* chapter 34, note 50, *infra*. For discussion of consent and settlement judgments, and separate confidential agreements under seal, *see* James Films, Inc., v. Miller, 801 F.2d 578 (2d Cir. 1986).

38. Not every action predicated on rights derived from the Copyright Act is necessarily an action for copyright infringement, e.g., construction of contracts, royalties. The issues sometimes overlap, e.g., whether renewal expectancy has been assigned. S.O.S. Inc. v. Payday, Inc., 886 F.2d 1081 (9th cir. 1989) (scope of license in determining infringement matter of federal copyright, not state, law; licensee's employer not "joint author"); Effects Assocs., v. Cohen, 817 F.2d 72 (9th Cir. 1987) (federal court jurisdiction despite alleged breach of oral contract for use of work under state law); Saturday Evening Post Co. v.

28.3 Conditions Precedent to Civil Infringement Actions

Usually prerequisite to the institution of a copyright infringement action are:

1. Registration of copyright claim;
2. Recordation of transfer by person claiming "by virtue of a transfer" to be "owner of copyright or of any exclusive right."

28.3[1] Registration

Registration of the copyright claim, whether the work has been published or not, except for "Berne Convention works" whose "country of origin" is *not* the United States, is usually prerequisite to the institution of an action for copyright infringement.[39] However, suit may be instituted after registration on a claim that arose before registration.[40]

28.3[2] Recordation

Recordation of the "instrument of transfer" under which a person "claiming by virtue of a transfer to be the owner of copyright or of any exclusive right," prior to March 1, 1989, was prerequisite to the institution of the action. However, suit could have been instituted after recordation on a cause of action that arose before recordation.[41]

Rumbleseat Press, Inc., 816 F.2d 1191 (7th Cir. 1987) (federal court jurisdiction found, where arbitration of copyright infringement affirmed by court, under federal arbitration code, 9 U.S.C.A. § 9). *See* 3 M. NIMMER, COPYRIGHT § 12.01(A) (1978). *See* text accompanying chapter 15, notes 15–20, *supra.*

39. 17 U.S.C.A. § 411(a). *See* text accompanying chapter 12, notes 39–40, *supra.*

40. Registration after infringement might preclude an award of statutory damages or attorney's fees. 17 U.S.C.A. § 412. *See* text accompanying chapter 12, notes 36, 37, *supra.*

41. 17 U.S.C.A. § 205(d), deleted by Berne Act §§ 7(c), 5.

28.4 Criminal Offenses

"Criminal offenses" include:

1. "Criminal infringement";
2. Use of fraudulent copyright notice;
3. Fraudulent removal of copyright notice;
4. False representations in connection with copyright application.

28.4[1] Criminal Infringement

For infringing a copyright "willfully and for purposes of commercial advantage or private financial gain," a person "shall be punished as provided in 18 U.S.C. section 2319.[42]

For enumerated infringements of a sound recording[43] or of

42. 17 U.S.C.A. § 506(a). 18 U.S.C.A. § 2319 (Piracy and Counterfeiting Amendments Act of 1982), added by Pub. L. No. 97–180, 98 Stat. 71 (May 24, 1982), provides for fines of not more than $25,000 or imprisonment for not more than one year or both, and up to $250,000 or two to five years or both for specified repeated infringements of sound recordings or motion pictures or other audiovisual works. *See* United States v. Minor, 846 F.2d 1184 (9th Cir. 1988) (sentence for conspiracy to infringe may not exceed maximum punishment for infringement); United States v. Goss, 803 F.2d 638 (11th Cir. 1986) (analysis of elements of criminal infringement); Young, *Criminal Copyright Infringement and a Step Beyond*, 30 COPYRIGHT L. SYMP. (ASCAP) 157 (1983); Grumer, *Criminal Infringement of Copyright*, 10 J. BEVERLY HILLS B.A. 62 (1976); Gawthrop, *An Inquiry into Criminal Copyright Infringement*, 20 COPYRIGHT L. SYMP. (ASCAP) 154 (1972); United States v. Powell, 701 F.2d 70 (8th Cir. 1983)(indictment for criminal copyright infringement need not specifically allege that defendants knew first sale had not been made). The National Stolen Property Act, 18 U.S.C.A. § 2314, has been held not applicable to "bootleg" recordings, Dowling v. United States, 105 S. Ct. 3127 (1985)(6–3)(dissent, *id.* at 3140, held Act did not differentiate between tangible and intangible property), or to "piratical copies. Nunes v. United States, 630 F. Supp. 1048 (D. Hawaii 1986). *See* Association of Am. Medical Colleges v. Mikaelian, 571 F. Supp. 144 (E.D. Pa. 1983)(guilty plea to criminal infringement held to estop defendant in civil action).

43. For infringing rights afforded by 17 U.S.C.A. § 106(1)–(3)(repro-

a motion picture[44] the fine shall be not more than $50,000 or imprisonment for not more than one year, or both, for the first such offense, and not more than $100,000 or two years, or both, for any subsequent offense.[45]

When any person is convicted of criminal infringement, the court "in its judgment of conviction shall, in addition to the penalty therein prescribed" order the "forfeiture and destruction or other disposition" of all infringing copies or phonorecords and all implements, devices, or equipment used in the manufacture of such infringing copies or phonorecords.[46]

28.4[2] Use of Fraudulent Copyright Notice

Any person who, "with fraudulent intent," places on any article a notice of copyright or "words of the same purport" that such person "knows to be false, or who, with fraudulent intent," publicly distributes or imports for public distribution any article bearing such notice or words that such person knows to be false, "shall" be fined not more than $2,500.[47]

28.4[3] Fraudulent Removal of Copyright Notice

Any person who, "with fraudulent intent," removes or alters any notice of copyright appearing on a copy of a

---

duction, adaptation, public distribution). 17 U.S.C.A. § 506(a).

44. For infringing rights afforded by § 106(1), (3), or (4) (reproduction, public distribution, public performance), § 106A ("attribution and integrity" rights).
45. *Id.*
46. 17 U.S.C.A. §§ 506(b), 509; 28 C.F.R. § 0.55; 43 Fed. Reg. 6,228 (Feb. 14, 1978)(Department of Justice Order No. 766-78). Transitional and Supplementary Provisions sec. 111 amended the provisions of the Criminal Code dealing with counterfeit phonograph record labels (18 U.S.C.A. § 2318) to provide higher criminal penalties and to make the seizure and forfeiture provisions of § 509 applicable in such cases.
47. 17 U.S.C.A. § 506(c). *See* chapter 10, note 59 *supra.*

copyrighted work "shall" be fined not more than $2,500.[48]

28.4[4] False Representation in Connection with Copyright Application

Any person who "knowingly makes a false representation of a material fact" in the application for copyright registration, or in any written statement filed in connection with the application, "shall" be fined not more than $2,500.[49]

28.5 Statutes of Limitations

28.5[1] Criminal Proceedings

No criminal proceeding may be maintained unless commenced within three years after the "cause of action" arose.[50]

28.5[2] Civil Actions

No civil action may be maintained unless commenced within three years after the "claim" accrued.[51]

---

48. 17 U.S.C.A. § 506(d).
49. 17 U.S.C.A. § 506(e). For "fraud on the Copyright Office, *see* chapter 12, note 47, *supra*. Analogies of "patent misuse" have been applied to copyright as defense. Lasercomb Am., Inc. v. Reynolds, 911 F.2d 970 (4th Cir. 1990); Whimsicality, Inc. v. Rubie's Costumes Co., 891 F.2d 452 (2d Cir. 1989) (registration of fanciful costumes as "soft sculpture" to avoid useful article ineligibility held fraud on Copyright Office; copyrights invalid; attorney's fees awardable based on bad faith); Ashton-Tate Corp. v. Fox Software, Inc., Copyright L. Rep. (CCH) ¶ 26,679 (S.D. Cal. 1990) (failure to disclose material information in applications for registration of derivative works allegedly based on public domain material held fraud on Copyright Office and copyrights invalid).
50. 17 U.S.C.A. § 507(a).
51. 17 U.S.C.A. § 507(b); Taylor v. Meirick, 712 F.2d 1112 (7th Cir. 1983)(where efforts to prevent retail sales of infringing maps by defendant who had quit selling them were insufficient, wrong was controlling one and statute of limitations not tolled); Past Pluto

28.6 Preexisting Causes of Action or Claims

28.6[1] Infringement of Common-Law Copyright

Expressly not preempted are "any rights or remedies under the common law" with respect to causes of action "arising from undertakings commenced before January 1, 1978."[52]

28.6[2] Infringement of Statutory Copyright

28.6[2][a] Criminal

All "causes of action" that arose under the 1909 Act before January 1, 1978, shall be governed by the 1909 Act "as it existed when the cause of action arose."[53]

28.6[2][b] Civil

There is no comparable provision expressly relating to "claims." This is probably a drafting oversight, and claims that arose under the 1909 Act before January 1, 1978, should be governed by the 1909 Act "as it existed when the cause of action arose."

Prods. Corp. v. Dana, 627 F. Supp. 1435 (S.D.N.Y. 1986). In the case of a continuing infringement, the statute of limitations does not begin to run until the last wrongful act is over. Also, the cause of action may arise when the plaintiff knew or should have known of the infringement. Taylor v. Meirick, 712 F.2d 1112 (7th Cir. 1983). Damages have been held allowable only for the period of limitations. Hoste v. RCA, 654 F.2d 11 (6th Cir. 1981). *Compare* Taylor v. Meirick, *supra with* Gaste v. Kaiserman, 669 F. Supp. 583 (S.D.N.Y. 1987). Lack of diligence to the prejudice of the defendant may constitute laches, barring equitable remedies. *Cf.* Hoey v. Dexel Sys. Corp., 716 F. Supp. 222 (E.D. Va. 1989).

Whether infringements are single or continuing may affect statutory damages and attorney's fees, depending on whether registration was timely. Singh v. Famous Overseas, Inc., 680 F. Supp. 533 (E.D.N.Y. 1988). New York has enacted a statute of limitations to protect museums against adverse claims of ownership of art works in their possession. Quaere, as to preemption.

52. 17 U.S.C.A. § 301(b)(2).

53. Transitional and Supplementary Provisions sec. 112.

29. Importation Restrictions

The importation restrictions prohibit importation into the United States of:[1]

1. Infringing copies and phonorecords;[2]
2. Copies manufactured in violation of the manufacturing requirements, which lapsed July 1, 1986.[3]

29.1 Infringing Copies and Phonorecords

Importation into the United States, without the authority of the "owner of copyright,"[4] of copies or phonorecords acquired outside the United States[5] is an infringement of the exclusive right to distribute,[6] except:

---

1. Engel & McGrath, *Manufacturing Requirements: Importation Restrictions*, in 1 PLI, CURRENT DEVELOPMENTS IN COPYRIGHT LAW 1977, at 577 (1977). *See also* text accompanying chapter 32, note 43 *infra* (infringement of mask works). *Cf.* 1909 Act §§ 106, 107.
2. *See* chapter 17 *supra*.
3. *See* chapter 12 *supra*. The manufacturing requirements lapsed on July 1, 1986.
4. *See* text accompanying chapter 7, notes 6–59 *supra*.
5. "United States" is defined to include the several states, the District of Columbia, the Commonwealth of Puerto Rico, and the organized territories under the jurisdiction of the United States government. 17 U.S.C.A. § 101.
6. 17 U.S.C.A. § 501(a) (anyone who imports in violation of importation

1. Importation under the authority or for the use of the United States government or any "State"[7] or political subdivision of a state, other than for use in schools, or of any audiovisual work imported for purposes other than archival use;[8]
2. Importation, for the private use of the importer and not for distribution, by any person with respect to no more than one copy of any one work at any one time, or by any person arriving from outside the "United States"[9] with respect to copies or phonorecords forming part of such person's personal baggage;[10]
3. Importation by or for an organization operated for scholarly, educational, or religious purposes and not for private gain, with respect to no more than one copy of an audiovisual work solely for the archival purposes, and no more than five copies or phonorecords of any other work for its library lending or archival purposes, unless the importation is part of

---

restrictions is an infringer of copyright). *See* Sebastian Int'l, Inc. v. Consumer Contacts (PTY) Ltd., 847 F.2d 1093 (3d Cir. 1988) ("gray market" goods made in United States, shipped abroad, and imported); T. B. Harms Co. v. Jem Records, Inc., 655 F. Supp. 1575 (D.N.J. 1987) (album manufactured lawfully abroad); Hearst Corp. v. Stark, 639 F. Supp. 970 (N.D. Cal. 1986)(unauthorized importation of wholesale quantities of books held not subject to first-sale doctrine defense, which applies to "a particular" copy); Columbia Broadcasting Sys., Inc. v. Scorpio Music Distribs., Inc., 569 F. Supp. 50 (E.D. Pa. 1983) (first-sale doctrine held not to prevail over § 602's prohibition against unauthorized imports; § 109(a) grants first-sale protection to third-party buyer of copies legally manufactured and sold outside United States; language and legislative history clear).

7. "State" is defined to include the District of Columbia, the Commonwealth of Puerto Rico, and any territories to which the law is made applicable by Congress. 17 U.S.C.A. § 101.
8. 17 U.S.C.A. § 602(a)(1).
9. *Id.* For definition of "United States," *see* note 5 *supra*.
10. 17 U.S.C.A. § 602(a)(2).

an activity consisting of unlawful "systematic reproduction or distribution"[11] engaged in by such organization.[12]

Where the making of copies or phonorecords would have constituted an infringement of copyright if the 1976 Act had been applicable, their importation is prohibited. Where the copies or phonorecords were lawfully made, the United States Customs Service had no authority to prevent their importation unless the manufacturing requirements had been violated.[13]

29.2 Copies Manufactured in Violation of Manufacturing Requirements

Importation into the United States of copies manufactured in violation of the manufacturing requirements was prohibited. However, as of July 1, 1986,[14] the manufacturing requirements lapsed.[15]

29.3 Enforcement of Importation Restrictions

The Secretary of the Treasury is authorized to prescribe, by regulation, a procedure under which any person claiming an interest in the copyright in a particular work may, upon payment of a specified fee, be entitled to notification

11. 17 U.S.C.A. §§ 602(a)(3), 108(g)(2). *See* text accompanying chapter 19, notes 42–50, *supra*.
12. 17 U.S.C.A. § 602(a)(3).
13. 17 U.S.C.A. § 602(b) (not amended despite lapse of manufacturing requirements as of July 1, 1986). *See* Sebastian Int'l, Inc. v. Consumer Contact (PTY) Ltd., 847 F.2d 1093 (3d Cir. 1988) ("first-sale" doctrine applied to prevent injunctions against importation under section 602(a); labels not products protected by copyright).
14. 17 U.S.C.A. § 601(a).
15. *Id.* § 601(a). *See* chapter 13 *supra*.

by the Customs Service of the importation of articles that appear to be copies or phonorecords of the work.[16]

Regulations for the enforcement of the importation restrictions shall be made separately or jointly by the Secretary of the Treasury and the United States Postal Service.[17] The regulations may require, as a condition for the exclusion of articles, a court injunction or specified proof of valid copyright and violation of the importation restrictions, and the posting of a surety bond.[18]

29.4 Seizure and Disposition of Excluded Articles

Articles imported in violation of the importation restrictions are subject to seizure and forfeiture in the same manner as property imported in violation of the customs revenue laws. Forfeited articles shall be destroyed as directed by the Secretary of Treasury or the court, or may be returned to the country of export when it is shown to the satisfaction of the Secretary of the Treasury that the importer had no reasonable grounds for believing that the acts constituted a violation of law.[19]

---

16. 17 U.S.C.A. § 601(b); exclusion orders may be issued by the International Trade Commission. 19 U.S.C.A. §§ 1337 *et seq.* The Court of International Trade may have jurisdiction over suspected infringing imports. The Customs Service may lack authority to seize or deny entry to articles involved in contributory infringement. *See* 19 C.F.R. pt. 133.
17. 17 U.S.C.A. § 603(a).
18. 17 U.S.C.A. § 603(b); 19 C.F.R. §§ 133.31 *et seq.*
19. 17 U.S.C.A. § 603(c).

30. Copyright Office

All administrative functions and duties under the Copyright Act, with specified exceptions,[1] are the responsibility of the Register of Copyrights as director of the Copyright Office of the Library of Congress.[2]

1. For the functions of the Copyright Royalty Tribunal, established by the 1976 Act and initially appointed in 1977, *see* chapter 31 *infra*.
2. 17 U.S.C.A. §§ 701-710. The Library of Congress has administered copyright matters since 1870. Previously, copyright entries were made in the offices of the clerks of the United States district courts. From 1846 to 1865 a copy was required to be sent to the Smithsonian Institution and a copy to the Librarian of Congress. Deposits were kept in the Department of State from 1831 to 1859 and in the Patent Office of the Department of the Interior from 1859 to 1870. The Register of Copyrights, together with the subordinate officers and employees of the Copyright Office, are appointed by the Librarian of Congress, and act under the Librarian's general direction and supervision. 17 U.S.C.A. § 701(a). As of July 3, 1990, the salaries of the Register of Copyrights and Associate Registers (e.g., $90,000) were reclassified to make them comparable with salaries for their counterparts in the executive branch. The Register of Copyrights has been compensated as of July 3, 1990, at the rate of pay in effect for level IV of the Executive Schedule under 5 U.S.C.A. § 5315. 17 U.S.C.A. § 701(e) ($108,300).

   A cost-benefit of analysis of American copyright formalities concluded that: (1) some European systems have some formalities; (2) mandatory deposits build libraries; (3) notice requirements may substitute for any formalities that might be required by Universal Copyright Convention countries; and (4) survey respondents preferred the Ameri-

30.1 Copyright Office Functions

The role of the Copyright Office,[3] established in 1897, was substantially increased by the 1976 Act,[4] but decreased by the Berne Act.

Almost everything written by any person any place in the world, in any language or dialect, not in the public domain, is protectible under federal copyright laws automatically from "creation."[5]

---

can system. Quaere, as to the persuasiveness of these conclusions, especially since United States adherence to the Berne Convention in 1989. *See* chapter 1, notes 37–51, *supra* and chapter 34 *infra*.

3. The very frequent references in the statute are to the "Register of Copyrights," with lesser mention of the "Copyright Office." Most actions taken by the Register of Copyrights, essentially "ministerial" in nature, are subject to the Administrative Procedure Act of 1946. 17 U.S.C.A. § 701(d). *Cf.* Cablevision Sys. Dev. Co. v. Motion Picture Ass'n, 836 F.2d 599 (D.C. Cir.) (Copyright Office interpretation of 1976 Act, at least § 111, due judicial deference), *cert. denied*, 108 S. Ct. 2901 (1988).
4. As a result, the Copyright Office became "all tied up." *See* Copyright Office ML-206 (June 1978)("due to the unfamiliarity of the public with the new copyright forms" and "novelty of examining these applications and the distinctive problems they have brought to the surface"). Quaere, despite Copyright Office assurances, whether the concept of "effective date," *see* text accompanying notes 84, 85 *infra*, can prejudice rights of those who rely on the public records while Office actions are pending. The 1991–92 Copyright Office appropriations were $23 million, compared to some $12.5 million in 1978–79, which had almost doubled from 1975–76 and more than quadrupled from 1968–69. In 1989, the Copyright Office employees numbered 489, including four associate registers (legal affairs-general counsel, management, "special programs," "research programs"), assistant general counsel (and other lawyers), assistant register, five "policy planning advisers" ($75,000), administrative officers and six division chiefs. Some 43 percent of the cost of operating the Copyright Office is recovered from fees, and there are substantial additions to the collections of the Library of Congress—more than 790,000 pieces annually (one-third of total acquisitions)—doubled since 1977. 1909 Act § 202 frugally provided for "a Register of Copyrights and one Assistant Register of Copyrights" with "subordinate assistants."
5. 17 U.S.C.A. § 302(a). *See* chapter 14, note 17 *supra*.

Whether published or unpublished, works are subject to the execution,[6] recordation,[7] and registration[8] provisions. If published, the copyright notice[9] and deposit[10] provisions apply.

As of March 1, 1989, the Berne Act drastically reduced the role of the Copyright Office.

As mentioned, recordation requirements were eliminated as a condition precedent to infringement suit for all works after that date.[11] Copies or phonorecords distributed after that date did not have to bear copyright notices,[12] thereby eliminating the need to examine for notice. While registration is still prerequisite to infringement suit where the "country of origin" is the United States,[13] it is no longer required for other "Berne Convention works."[14] Deposit of copies or phonorecords for the Library of Congress is required of published works, whether or not they bear a copyright notice and regardless of "country of origin."[15]

30.2 Responsibilities of Register of Copyrights

Among the responsibilities of the Register of Copyrights are:

1. To establish regulations;

---

6. *See* chapter 8 *supra*.
7. *See* chapter 9 *supra*.
8. *See* chapter 12 *supra*.
9. *See* chapter 10 *supra*. Under the "rule of doubt," questions of validity of form and location of notice often were resolved in favor of the copyright claimant.
10. *See* chapter 11 *supra*.
11. Berne Act § 5, deleting former 17 U.S.C.A. § 205(d).
12. Berne Act § 7, amending 17 U.S.C.A. §§ 401–406.
13. Berne Act § 9, amending 17 U.S.C.A. §§ 411.
14. *Id.*
15. Berne Act § 8, amending 17 U.S.C.A. § 407(a).

2. To register copyright claims, including renewal claims;
3. To receive deposits for the Library of Congress and to enforce compliance with deposit requirements;
4. To record documents and statements;
5. To receive various filings;
6. To maintain records and files, open to public inspection;
7. To index Copyright Office records and files;
8. To make searches and to report thereon;
9. To issue certificates and receipts for deposit;
10. To license phonorecord players, to receive deposits of compulsory and "statutory" license royalty fees, and to account to the Copyright Royalty Tribunal;
11. To compile and publish periodic catalogs of all copyright registrations;
12. To furnish without charge application forms and general informational materials;
13. To compile obituary information;
14. To make specified reports, including annual reports to the Librarian of Congress;
15. To adopt the Copyright Office seal;
16. To maintain a system of deposit accounts.

30.2[1] To Establish Regulations

Besides general authorization "to establish regulations not inconsistent with law for the administration of the functions and duties made the responsibility" of the Register of Copyrights,[16] numerous specific regulations are mandated.[17]

16. 17 U.S.C.A. § 702.
17. 17 U.S.C.A. §§ 108(d)(2), (e)(2) (warning of copyright) (*cf.* § 108(a)(3), (f)(1)), 110(4)(B)(iii) (notice of objection to performance), 111(d)(1) (further information in connection with compulsory cable television secondary transmission license, after consultation with Copyright Royalty Tribunal), 115(b)(1) (form, content, and manner of service of

All regulations established by the Register of Copyrights are subject to the approval of the Librarian of Congress.[18]

---

notice of intention to obtain compulsory musical recording license), 115(c)(3) (detailed cumulative annual statements of account under compulsory musical recording license), 118(b)(2) (filing of voluntarily negotiated license agreements for noncommercial broadcasting of published nondramatic musical works and published pictorial, graphic, and sculptural works), 118(e)(1) (filing of voluntary licensing arrangements for noncommercial broadcasting of nondramatic literary works), § 119 (deposits of statements of account and other data concerning secondary transmissions for private home viewing), 203(a)(4)(B) (form, content, and manner of service of notice of termination), 302(c) (form and content of statement identifying one or more authors of anonymous or pseudonymous work), 302(d) (form and content of statement of date of death of author), 304(c)(4)(B) (form, content, and manner of service of notice of termination), 401(c) (examples of specific methods of affixation and positions of copyright notice on various types of works), 407(c) (exemptions of categories of material), 407(e) (acquisition, through deposit or otherwise, of copies or phonorecords of unpublished fixed and transmitted transmission programs for collections of Library of Congress, after consulting with Librarian of Congress), 408(b) (additional identifying material to accompany copies or phonorecords deposited for Library of Congress; use to satisfy deposit requirements of registration provision by § 407(e) acquisitions), 408(c) (administrative classification for purposes of deposit and registration and nature of required deposits), 408(d) (formal procedures for filing application for supplementary registration), 409 (forms of application for copyright registration), 411(b) (service of notice upon infringer and registration within three months after first transmission of work fixed simultaneously with transmission), 704(b) (selection by Library of Congress of deposits of unpublished works for its collection or for transfer to National Archives of United States or to federal records center), 710 (standardized forms and procedures for voluntary grants to Library of Congress of license to reproduce solely for use of blind and physically handicapped). *See also* 17 U.S.C.A. § 908 (regulations under Semiconductor Chip Protection Act of 1984).

18. 17 U.S.C.A. § 702. Regulations have been issued under the Privacy Act of 1974 and the Freedom of Information Act.

30.2[2] To Register Copyright Claims, Including Renewal Claims

Registration of copyright claims is more important under the current law[19] than under the 1909 Act for most subject matter of copyright, unpublished as well as published.[20] Failure to register promptly may have adverse effects.[21]

Renewal applications are still required for works subsisting in their first term of copyright on January 1, 1978.[22] Failure to make timely renewal results in loss of copyright after the first term.

Cancellation of improper registration is possible.

30.2[3] To Receive Deposits for Library of Congress and to Enforce Compliance with Deposit Requirements

Deposits of copies and phonorecords are required for the Library of Congress and for registration, but deposit for the former may satisfy the deposit requirements of the registration provision.[23]

Failure to deposit for the Library of Congress by the "owner of copyright or of the exclusive right of publication"[24] "within three months" after "written demand" of the

---

19. 17 U.S.C.A. §§ 408-412. Registration should be by the "owner of copyright or of any exclusive right." *See* chapter 12, note 5 *supra*. Supplemental registrations are possible. *See* text accompanying chapter 12, note 24, *supra*. *Cf* § 411(a) (option of Register of Copyrights to become party to infringement action with respect to issue of registrability). *See* chapter 12 *supra*.
20. 17 U.S.C.A. § 411(a). *See* chapter 12, note 4 *supra*.
21. *See* text accompanying chapter 12, notes 31–38 *supra*. Deposit and fee should accompany the application for registration. The Copyright Office no longer refunds payments when registration is not made.
22. 17 U.S.C.A. § 304(a). *See* text accompanying chapter 15, note 25 *supra*.
23. 17 U.S.C.A. § 407. *See* chapter 11 *supra*. The Copyright Office serves as a superannuated and superfluous intermediary for the Library of Congress.
24. 17 U.S.C.A. § 407(a). *See* chapter 11, note 4 *supra*.

Register of Copyrights,[25] subjects such persons to specified liabilities.[26]

30.2[4] To Record Documents and Statements

Any "transfer of copyright ownership" or other "document pertaining to copyright" may be recorded in the Copyright Office.[27] Recordation may afford constructive notice,[28] but since March 1, 1989, has not been prerequisite to an infringement suit,[29] and may affect priority between conflicting grants.[30] Required to be recorded are notices, including statements of identity, under compulsory cable television secondary transmission licenses, (since repealed),[31] and notices of termination.[32] Although the "recordation" provision uses the term "filed for recordation,"[33] there are numerous provisions requiring various "filings."

30.2[5] To Receive Various Filings

In addition to its recording responsibilities, the Copyright Office is the "filing" office for various statements, agreements, notices, and applications.[34]

---

25. 17 U.S.C.A. § 407(d). *See* text accompanying chapter 11, notes 10–14 *supra*.
26. *Id.*
27. 17 U.S.C.A. § 205(a). *See* chapter 9 *supra*.
28. *See* text accompanying chapter 9, note 10 *supra*.
29. *See* text accompanying chapter 9, notes 11–12 *supra*.
30. *See* text accompanying chapter 9, notes 13–19 *supra*.
31. Former 17 U.S.C.A. § 111(d)(1). *See* text accompanying chapter 25, notes 23–26 *supra*.
32. 17 U.S.C.A. §§ 203(a)(4)(A), 304(c)(4)(A). *See* text accompanying chapter 16, notes 13–17, 31–33 *supra*.
33. 17 U.S.C.A. § 205(a).
34. 17 U.S.C.A. §§ 111(d)(2) ("deposit" of semiannual statement of account under compulsory cable television secondary transmission license), 111(e)(2)(A) (written nonprofit contract for nonsimultaneous secondary transmissions by cable systems outside continental United States), 115(b)(1) (notice of intention to obtain compulsory musical

30.2[6] To Maintain Records and Files, Open to Public Inspection

The Register of Copyrights is required to provide and keep in the Copyright Office records of all deposits, registrations, recordations, and other actions taken under the statute.[35]

Also required are records of the disclosed names of authors of anonymous and pseudonymous works[36] and current records of information relating to the death of authors.[37]

The records and indexes, as well as the articles deposited in connection with "completed" copyright registrations and retained under Copyright Office control, are required to be open to public inspection.[38]

Copies may be made of any public records or indexes. Copies and additional certificates of copyright registration must be furnished upon request and payment of the specified fee.[39] Copies or reproductions of deposited articles re-

---

recording license where copyright owner not identified with address in Copyright Office public records), 116(b)(1)(A) (application for compulsory coin-operated phonorecord player license—suspended from Jan. 1, 1990), 118(b)(2) (voluntarily negotiated license agreements for noncommercial broadcasting of published nondramatic works and published pictorial, graphic, and sculptural works), 118(e)(1) (voluntarily negotiated license agreements for noncommercial broadcasting of nondramatic literary works), 119(b)(1) (deposits under Satellite Home Viewer Act of 1988); 508 (written notice of filing in federal courts of copyright infringement actions, any final order or judgment, together with any written opinion). Notifications of infringement actions have not been separately indexed since 1986; instead they are microfilmed alphabetically under the plaintiff's name. 51 Fed. Reg. 29,973 (Aug. 22, 1986).

35. 17 U.S.C.A. § 705(a). *See* chapters 9, 11, and 12 *supra*.
36. 17 U.S.C.A. § 302(c).
37. 17 U.S.C.A. § 302(d).
38. 17 U.S.C.A. § 705(b); National Conference of Bar Examiners v. Multistate Legal Studies, Inc., 692 F.2d 478 (7th Cir. 1982), *cert. denied*, 464 U.S. 814 (1983). *See* Copyright Office Circular R6 (Obtaining Copies of Copyright Office Records and Deposits).
39. 17 U.S.C.A. § 706(a).

tained under Copyright Office control may be authorized or furnished only under conditions specified by the Copyright Office regulations.[40]

30.2[7] To Index Copyright Office Records and Files

The Register of Copyrights is required to prepare indexes of all records of all deposits, registrations, recordations, and other actions taken under the statute.[41] Such indexes are open to public inspection[42] and may be copied,[43] and copies must be furnished upon request and payment of the specified fee.[44] Indexing may affect constructive notice resulting from recordation[45] and the identity of the copyright owner entitled to compulsory musical recording license royalties.[46]

30.2[8] To Make Searches and to Report Thereon

The Copyright Office is required to make searches of its public records, indexes, and deposits, and to furnish reports of the information disclosed, upon request and payment of the specified fee.[47]

---

40. 17 U.S.C.A. § 706(b).
41. 17 U.S.C.A. § 705(a). The Copyright Office card catalog, except for periodicals not yet on line, has been computerized for registrations made after January 1, 1978. There are some 41 million pre-1978 cards.
42. 17 U.S.C.A. § 705(b).
43. 17 U.S.C.A. § 706(a).
44. 17 U.S.C.A. § 706(b).
45. 17 U.S.C.A. § 205(c).
46. 17 U.S.C.A. § 115(c). Filing of notice of intention to obtain a compulsory musical recording license may be filed in the Copyright Office where its "public records" do not "identify" the "copyright owner" and include an address at which the notice can be served. 17 U.S.C.A. § 115(b)(1).
47. 17 U.S.C.A. § 705(c). *See* § 708(a)(7) ($20 per hour or fraction, including reports). Searches are not made (and are not necessary) to determine whether a similar work has already been copyrighted. Copyright Office Circular R4.

30.2[9] To Issue Certificates and Receipts for Deposit

The Register of Copyrights, upon registering a claim, is required to issue to the applicant a certificate of registration under the seal of the Copyright Office.[48] When requested by the depositor and payment of the prescribed fee, a receipt for the deposit of copies or phonorecords must be issued.[49] Recorded documents are required to be returned with a certificate of recordation.[50] Also required are the issuance of certificates for phonorecord players under compulsory license,[51] of certified reports to support the presumption of an author's death after seventy-five years after the year of first publication or 100 years from the year of creation, whichever expires first,[52] and of import statements for presentation to the United States Customs Service.[53]

30.2[10] To License Phonorecord Players, to Receive Deposits of Compulsory and "Statutory" License Royalty Fees, and to Account to Copyright Royalty Tribunal

The Register of Copyrights is required to license phonorecord players; to receive all fees deposited under compulsory cable television secondary transmission licenses,[54] compulsory coin-operated phonorecord player licenses,[55] and "statutory" transmission by satellite carriers for private home viewing licenses;[56] to deposit such funds, after deducting

48. 17 U.S.C.A. § 410(a).
49. 17 U.S.C.A. § 407(b).
50. 17 U.S.C.A. § 205(b).
51. 17 U.S.C.A. § 116(b)(1)(B). For obtaining replacement certificates, see Copyright Office Circular R71.
52. 17 U.S.C.A. § 302(e).
53. 17 U.S.C.A. § 601(b)(2).
54. 17 U.S.C.A. § 111(d)(2)(B) (semiannually).
55. 17 U.S.C.A. § 116(b) (initially $8 annually; $63 a year after 1987, subject to cost-of-living adjustment) (suspended from Jan. 1, 1990).
56. 17 U.S.C.A. § 119(b)(2), (3), (4).

the reasonable costs incurred by the Copyright Office, in the Treasury of the United States;[57] and to submit statements of account to the Copyright Royalty Tribunal.[58]

30.2[11] To Compile and Publish Periodic Catalogs of All Copyright Registrations

Catalogs of all copyright registrations are required to be compiled and published at periodic intervals by the Register of Copyrights. Such catalogs are to be divided into parts in accordance with the various classes of works.[59]

30.2[12] To Furnish Without Charge Application Forms and General Informational Material

Application forms for copyright registration and "general informational material in connection with the functions of the Copyright Office" are required to be furnished by the Register of Copyrights "free of charge upon request."[60] The Register of Copyrights also has the authority to publish compilations of information, bibliographies, and other material considered to be of value to the public.[61]

---

57. 17 U.S.C.A. §§ 111(d)(3), 116(c)(1).

58. 17 U.S.C.A. §§ 111(d)(3) (semiannually), 116(c)(1) (annually).

59. 17 U.S.C.A. § 707(a). The Register of Copyrights has discretion to determine, on the basis of practicability and usefulness, the form and frequency of publication of each particular part. *See* Dunne & Rogers, *The Catalog of Copyright Entries* (1960), *reprinted in* 1 STUDIES ON COPYRIGHT—ARTHUR FISHER MEMORIAL EDITION 451 (1963). *Cf.* 1909 Act § 210 (catalog admissible in any court as prima facie evidence of facts stated therein as regards any copyright registration).

60. 17 U.S.C.A. § 707(b). For list of available Copyright Office circulars, *see* appendix F *infra*.

61. *Id.* All publications of the Copyright Office are required to be furnished to depositary libraries as specified under 44 U.S.C.A. § 1905, and, aside from those furnished free of charge, are to be offered for sale to the public at prices based on the cost of reproduction and distribution. 17 U.S.C.A. § 707(c). *See* former Copyright Office Circulars R16 (Limitations on the information furnished by the Copyright

30.2[13] To Compile Obituary Information

The Register of Copyrights is required to maintain current records of information relating to the death of authors of copyrighted works, based on recorded statements[62] and, to the extent considered practicable, on data contained in any of the records of the Copyright Office or in other reference sources.[63] Such information may affect the presumption that an author died after seventy-five years from the year of first publication or 100 years from the year of creation, whichever expires first.[64]

30.2[14] To Make Specified Reports, Including Annual Reports, to Librarian of Congress

In addition to the annual report to the Librarian of Congress "of the work and accomplishments of the Copyright Office during the previous fiscal year,"[65] the 1976 Act required reports by the Register of Copyrights on reproductions by libraries and archives by January 1, 1983, and at five-year intervals thereafter,[66] and on the extent of voluntary licensing arrangements for noncommercial broadcasting of nondramatic literary works and its recommendations, by January 3, 1980.[67] Such reports were duly made. The required report and recommendations concerning performance rights for performers and copyright owners of sound

---

Office), R23 (The Copyright Card Catalog and the Online Files of the Copyright Office), R96 pt. 204 (Privacy Act: Policies and Procedures), R96 pt. 203 (Freedom of Information Act: Policies and Procedures).

62. *See* note 37 *supra*.
63. 17 U.S.C.A. § 302(d).
64. 17 U.S.C.A. § 302(e).
65. 17 U.S.C.A. § 701(c). The annual report of the Register of Copyrights is required to be published separately and as a part of the annual report of the Librarian of Congress.
66. 17 U.S.C.A. § 108(i).
67. 17 U.S.C.A. § 118(e)(2).

recordings, due on January 3, 1978,[68] were submitted to Congress.[69] No legislation has resulted.

In addition, the Register of Copyrights reviewed the impact of the elimination of the manufacturing clause by July 1, 1981.[70] The National Commission on New Technological Uses of Copyright Works (CONTU), in its final report, dated July 31, 1978, recommended that the Register of Copyrights, in conducting the required five-year review of photocopying practices,[71] should begin immediately to plan and implement a study of the overall impact of all photoduplication practices on both proprietors' rights and the public's access to published information.[72]

30.2[15] To Adopt Copyright Office Seal

As mandated by the 1976 Act, the Register of Copyrights adopted a seal, for use on and after January 1, 1978, to authenticate all certified documents issued by the Copyright Office.[73]

The new Copyright Office seal (a representation of the seal is shown below) is circular and consists of a stylized

---

68. 17 U.S.C.A. § 114(d).
69. *See* chapter 17, note 31 *supra*.
70. *See* chapter 13, note 2 *supra*.
71. *See* note 66 *supra*.
72. Also under consideration are problems relating to off-the-air videotaping. The Copyright Royalty Tribunal is also involved. *See* chapter 31, note 36 *infra*.
73. 17 U.S.C.A. § 701(b); 37 C.F.R. § 201(6)(b); 42 Fed. Reg. 64,747 (Dec. 28, 1977).

representation of the nib of a pen enclosed in a partial circle, which is encircled in turn by the words "United States Copyright Office" and "The Library of Congress."

30.2[16] To Maintain System of Deposit Accounts

Without any basis in the 1976 Act, the Copyright Office maintains a system of deposit accounts for the convenience of those who frequently use its services. The system allows an individual or firm to establish a deposit account in the Copyright Office and to make advance deposits into that account. Then, instead of sending separate remittances with applications and other requests for services, the deposit account holder can charge copyright fees against the balance in the account.[74]

Initial and other deposits must be at least $250, and there must be at least twelve transactions a year. The balance must be sufficient to cover all charges against the account. The Copyright Office sends holders periodic statements showing deposits, charges, and balances.[75]

If a deposit account has become depleted, the "effective date of registration" will not occur until the account has been replenished. Such delay could have serious consequences.[76]

30.3 Copyright Office Fees

After January 1, 1991, fees are payable to the Register of Copyrights, as follows:[77]

---

74. Copyright Office Circular R5 (with forms to establish deposit accounts).
75. *Id.*
76. *See* note 86 *infra*.
77. 17 U.S.C.A. § 708(a) (fees as of Jan. 3, 1991, were doubled); 37 C.F.R. § 201.6; Copyright Office Circular R4 (Payment and Refund of Copyright Office Fees). The fees are applicable to the United States Gov-

1. For registration (or supplementary registration) of copyright claim[78] (including certificate of registration)	$20
2. For registration of claim to renewal of subsisting copyright in its first term (including certificate of registration)	$12
3. For recordation of transfer of copyright ownership or other document pertaining to copyright (including certification):	
• Covering not more than one title	$20
• For additional titles, for each group of not more than ten titles	$10
4. For recordation of statement revealing identity of author of anonymous or pseudonymous work or of statement relating to death of author (including certification):	
• Covering not more than one title	$20
• For each additional title	$2
5. For additional certificates of registration[79]	$8

---

ernment and any of its agencies, employees, or officers, but the Register of Copyrights has discretion to waive the fee in occasional or isolated cases involving relatively small amounts. 17 U.S.C.A. § 708(b). The Register of Copyrights is required to deposit all fees in the Treasury of the United States in such manner as the Secretary of the Treasury directs. The Register may, in accordance with prescribed regulations, refund any sum paid by mistake or in excess of the required fee. However, before making a refund in any case involving a refusal to register a claim, the Register may deduct all or any part of the prescribed registration fee to cover the reasonable administrative costs of processing the claim. § 708(c).

Since 1982, the fee has been for the filing of an application for registration rather than the granting of the registration. Thus, the Copyright Office retains the fee in all registration cases, whether or not registration is actually made.

78. 17 U.S.C.A. § 708(a); Copyright Office Circular R8. *See* text accompanying chapter 12, notes 5–24 *supra*.

79. 17 U.S.C.A. § 708(a). The Register of Copyrights has discretion on the basis of their cost to fix the fees for preparing Copyright Office records, whether they are to be certified or not. 17 U.S.C.A. §

6. For other certificates (per hour or fraction thereof) $20
7. For making and reporting of searches and for related services (per hour or fraction thereof) ... $20
8. For filing notices of intention to make phonorecords under compulsory musical recording license $12
9. For receipt for deposit of copies and phonorecords for Library of Congress $4

The Register of Copyrights is authorized to fix additional fees, on the "basis of cost of providing the service" for "any other special services requiring a substantial amount of time or expense, and in 1995, and every subsequent fifth year, to increase fees to reflect cost-of-living changes."[80]

All remittances should be in the form of a check, money order, or bank draft, payable to the Register of Copyrights. The Copyright Office does not assume any responsibility for the loss of currency. Foreign remittances should be payable immediately in United States dollars.[81]

30.4 "Effective Date" of Copyright Office Actions

When the last day of a prescribed period falls on a Saturday, Sunday, holiday, or other nonbusiness day within the District of Columbia or the federal government, the action may be taken on the next succeeding business day, and is effective as of the date when the period expired.[82]

708(a)(9). Unless the number and year of registration are furnished to the Copyright Office, there is an additional charge of $10 for each hour or fraction required to locate the record.

80. 17 U.S.C.A. § 708(a)(11). There are additional charges for special handling ($200 per registration or recordation) 50 Fed. Reg. 46,206 (Nov. 8, 1985), 49 Fed. Reg. 39,741 (Oct. 10, 1984).

81. Copyright Office Circular R4. For deposit accounts, *see* text accompanying notes 74–76 *supra*.

82. 17 U.S.C.A. § 703.

In any case in which the Register of Copyrights determines, on the basis of such evidence as the Register may by regulation require, that a deposit, application, fee, or any other material to be delivered to the Copyright Office by a particular date, would have been received in the Copyright Office in due time except for a general disruption or suspension of postal or other transportation or communications services, the actual receipt of such material in the Copyright Office within one month after the date on which the Register determines that the disruption or suspension of such services has terminated, shall be considered timely.[83]

The "effective date of copyright registration" is the day on which an application, deposit, and fee, which are later determined by the Register of Copyrights or by a court of competent jurisdiction to be acceptable for registration, have all been received by the Copyright Office.[84] By analogy, the "effective date" of other Copyright Office actions would occur upon Copyright Office receipt of proper application or document and fee.[85]

Delay of the effective date can have serious consequences.[86]

---

83. 17 U.S.C.A. § 709.
84. 17 U.S.C.A. § 410(d).
85. E.g., termination notices, renewal applications, recordation of transfers of ownership and other documents pertaining to copyright, notices of intention to obtain compulsory musical recording license. There was some dispensation for tardiness in delayed payment of doubled fees effective January 3, 1991.
86. E.g., (1) renewal registration (where there are strict statutory deadlines); (2) cases where a court may limit the copyright owner's monetary recovery if the infringement started before the effective date of registration (unless for published works, registration was made within a grace period of three months following publication); and (3) recording assignments and other transfers (where there are time limits if the recordation is to be given the effect of "constructive notice" as against other transfers and licenses).

The Copyright Office no longer sends letters of reminder to applicants that after 120 days after an inquiry is sent without response, the file will be closed. *See* Copyright Office Circular R7c (The Effects

30.5 Retention and Disposition of Articles Deposited in Copyright Office

Upon their deposit in the Copyright Office, all copies, phonorecords, and identifying material, including those deposited in connection with claims that have been refused registration, are the property of the United States Government.[87]

In the case of published works, all copies, phonorecords, and identifying material deposited are available to the Library of Congress for its collections, or for exchange or transfer to any other library. In the case of unpublished works, the Library is entitled, under regulations that the Register of Copyrights shall prescribe, to select any deposits for its collections or for transfer to the National Archives of the United States or to a federal records center.[88]

The Register of Copyrights is authorized, for specific or general categories of works, to make a facsimile reproduction of all or any part of the material deposited, and to make such reproduction a part of the Copyright Office records of the registration, before transferring such material to the Library of Congress, or before destroying or otherwise disposing of such material.[89]

Deposits not selected by the Library, or identifying portions or reproductions of them, shall be retained under the control of the Copyright Office, including retention in government storage facilities, for the longest period considered practicable and desirable by the Register of Copyrights and the Librarian of Congress. After that period it is within the

---

of Not Replying Within 120 Days to Copyright Office Correspondence).

87. 17 U.S.C.A. § 704(a).

88. 17 U.S.C.A. § 704(b). For definition of federal records center, see 44 U.S.C.A. § 2901. *See also* 37 C.F.R. §§ 201.23, 202.23.

89. 17 U.S.C.A. § 704(c).

joint discretion of the Register and the Librarian to order their destruction or other disposition; but, in the case of unpublished works, no deposit shall be knowingly or intentionally destroyed or otherwise disposed of during its term of copyright unless a facsimile reproduction of the entire deposit has been made a part of the Copyright Office records.[90]

The depositor of copies, phonorecords, or identifying material, or the copyright owner of record, may request retention, under the control of the Copyright Office, of one or more of such articles for the full term of copyright in the work. The Register of Copyrights is required to prescribe, by regulation, the conditions under which such requests are to be made and granted, and to fix the fee to be charged if the request is granted.[91]

30.6 Reproduction of Copyrighted Works for Blind and Physically Handicapped

The Register of Copyrights has established by regulation, as required,[92] standardized forms and procedures by which, at the time applications covering certain specified categories of nondramatic literary works are submitted for registration, the copyright owner may voluntarily grant to the Library of Congress a license to reproduce the copyrighted work by means of Braille or similar tactile symbols, or by fixation of a reading of the work in a phonorecord, or both, and to distribute the resulting copies or phonorecords solely for the use of the blind and physically handicapped

90. 17 U.S.C.A. § 704(d).
91. 17 U.S.C.A. § 704(e); 37 C.F.R. § 202.23.
92. 17 U.S.C.A. § 710 (after consultation with the Chief of the Division for the Blind and Physically Handicapped and other appropriate officials of the Library of Congress).

and under limited conditions to be specified in the standardized forms.[93]

Granting a license[94] is entirely voluntary, and if a license is not granted, there is no effect on copyright registration. Such licenses are nonexclusive, and run from the effective date of registration for the copyright duration. They may be terminated by the copyright owner at any time by submitting a written statement of intent to terminate to the Division for the Blind and Physically Handicapped (DBPH), Library of Congress, Washington, D.C. 20542.[95]

30.7 Constitutional Aspects

Concern has been expressed as to the constitutionality of the increased role of the Copyright Office as a part of the legislative branch of the federal government.[96]

30.8 Future of Copyright Office

Whether the Copyright Office either, as now, within the Library of Congress or elsewhere in the government, will continue to exist is an open question.

---

93. 37 C.F.R. § 201.15.

94. Copyright Office Circular R63. Copyright Office form TX contains a space for granting the license. Special licensing agreements, different from the standardized procedure under 17 U.S.C.A. § 710, are possible.

95. 37 C.F.R. § 201.15. Termination becomes effective ninety days after the DBPH received the written statement, or at any later date set forth in the statement. Reproductions already made under the license before the effective date of termination may continue to be distributed and used after termination of the license. However, after the effective date of termination, the Library of Congress will be prohibited from reproducing any additional copies or phonorecords of the work, or both, without the consent of the copyright owner.

96. E. Brylawski, Outline of Some Matters Affecting the Copyright Office (1983); Brylawski, *The Copyright Office: A Constitutional Confrontation*, 44 Geo. Wash. L. Rev. 1 (1975). *But see* Eltra, Inc. v. Ringer, 579 F.2d 294 (4th Cir. 1978).

The Copyright Office has records of registrations, renewals, recordations, and filings, but lacks often critical data on copyright status and ownership. Indexing is less than ideal. Searches often raise more questions than they answer.

The Copyright Office has senior "policy planning advisors" to help to define its future role. Additional functions have been assumed: growing numbers of studies, educational programs for foreign copyright specialists (sometimes by way of reciprocity for foreign exchange programs), histories or other compendia of American copyright laws.[97]

97. A comprehensive 145-page report on "Copyright Liability of States and the Eleventh Amendment" (as of June 1988) was submitted by the Register of Copyrights. The copyright riders to the Judicial Improvements Act of 1990 authorized a "system of records" whereby any author of a "work of visual art" embodied in a "structure" may record "his" identity and address with the Copyright Office, and "separate records" for documents "designated as pertaining to computer software." Under the Visual Artists Rights Act of 1990, the Register of Copyrights is authorized to conduct a five-year study on the waiver of rights of attribution and integrity and an eighteen-month study, in consultation with the chair of the National Endowment of the Arts, of the feasibility of implementing a *droit de suite*. That latter provision requires wide-ranging consultations. Signed written instruments of waiver of rights of "attribution and integrity" presumably should be recorded in the Copyright Office to provide data for the Copyright Office study on waivers of such rights.

Under the Computer Software Rental Amendments Act of 1990, the Register of Copyrights is required within three years, and at times thereafter, to submit a report on whether the Act has achieved its "intended purpose of maintaining the integrity of the copyright system while providing nonprofit libraries the capability to fulfill their function." Consultation with representatives of copyright owners and librarians is mandated. Also, deposit of copies in the Library of Congress of "public domain computer software" is mentioned. In addition, the Copyright Office is preparing a study on digital audio broadcast and cable services and the effects on rights of performers and copyright owners of sound recordings. Possibly, the Copyright Office will become involved in proposing a governmentwide (military and civilian agencies) technical data regulation.

Budgetary constraints would suggest its abolition, as would American adherence to the Berne Union with its formality-free system. With decreased formalities, there are fewer functions left that the Library of Congress could not assimilate without duplication.

31. Copyright Royalty Tribunal

A Copyright Royalty Tribunal (CRT) was created by the 1976 Act.[1]

31.1 Composition and Compensation of Tribunal

The Tribunal[2] is composed of three[3] members appointed

1. 17 U.S.C.A. § 801(a); 37 C.F.R. §§ 301.1 *et seq.*; Brennan, *The Copyright Royalty Tribunal,* 25 BULL. COPYRIGHT SOC'Y 196 (1978); Brylawski, *The Copyright Royalty Tribunal,* 24 U.C.L.A. L. REV. 1265 (1977). The initial appointments were to be made as soon as possible after enactment (Oct. 19, 1976), and no later than six months following such date. 17 U.S.C.A. § 801(c). President Carter did not appoint the commissioners until September 26, 1977, or five months after the legislative deadline. 42 Fed. Reg. 49,435 (Sept. 27, 1977). Quaere, as to public funding for collecting royalties, even under compulsory licenses. Membership on the Tribunal is highly desirable. As of July 3, 1990, the number of commissioners was reduced from five to three, to serve until a successor is confirmed, and their salaries were raised to make them comparable with salaries for their counterparts in the executive branch.
2. The 1976 Senate bill had provided for the convening by the Register of Copyrights of an ad hoc panel of three members proposed by the American Arbitration Association to resolve any controversy concerning a specified royalty rate or distribution of royalty fees. S. 22, 94th Cong., 2d Sess. (Feb. 19, 1976). A version of arbitration was revived as of January 1, 1989, by the Satellite Home Viewer Act of 1988, but made subject to Tribunal review, adding one more level of administration.
3. The House substitute bill had provided for three members. The Con-

to seven-year staggered terms[4] by the President, with the advice and consent of the Senate.[5]

To assist in its work, the Tribunal has appointed a staff that is an administrative part of the Library of Congress, but that is responsible to the Tribunal,[6] and may procure temporary and intermittent services.[7]

31.2 Purposes of Tribunal

The purposes of the Tribunal are:

1. To fix initial terms and rates of royalty payments by public broadcasters under compulsory noncommercial broadcasting licenses;[8]
2. To review and to adjust periodically royalty rates under the four compulsory licenses:[9]

---

ference Report provides no explanation for enlarging the membership. There have been two vacancies for several years. A decrease to three authorized members has been enacted; proposed has been the restructure or abolition of the Tribunal. Each "commissioner" has a "confidential assistant." There also is a general counsel.

4. The House substitute bill had provided for five-year terms. No explanation for the increase to seven years is offered in the Conference Report.
5. 17 U.S.C.A. § 802(a). The first chairman, Thomas C. Brennan, with the longest tenure, had served as chief counsel of the Senate subcommittee with jurisdiction over copyright law revision. Compensation is at the highest rate now or hereafter prescribed for grade 18 of the General Schedule pay rates. 17 U.S.C.A. § 802(a); 5 U.S.C. § 5332. As of October 1, 1978, pay was $49,608 per year. 43 Fed. Reg. 46,824 (Oct. 11, 1978). The compensation of each member of the Tribunal was raised in 1990 to equal the rate of pay in effect for level V of the Executive Schedule under 5 U.S.C.A. § 5316 (currently $78,200 annually). Pub. L. No. 101-319, 104 Stat. 290 (July 3, 1990; effective July 3, 1990). The $500,000-per-year budget limitation for the Tribunal in the House substitute bill, Transitional and Supplementary Provisions, sec. 114, was deleted in conference with no explanation. The 1991 fiscal year appropriations for the Copyright Royalty Tribunal was $845,000.
6. 17 U.S.C.A. § 805(a).
7. 17 U.S.C.A. § 805(b); 5 U.S.C.A. § 3109.
8. 17 U.S.C.A. § 118(b); 37 C.F.R. §§ 304.1 *et seq.*

- Compulsory musical recording licenses (in 1987 and each subsequent tenth calendar year);[10]
- Compulsory coin-operated phonorecord players licenses (in 1990 and each subsequent tenth calendar year);[11]
- Compulsory noncommercial broadcasting licenses;[12]
- Compulsory cable television secondary transmission licenses (in 1980 and each subsequent fifth calendar year, or upon the petition of any person or user for reconsideration);[13]

3. To adopt or reject the Arbitration Panels' determinations of the royalty fees for "statutory" secondary transmission by satellite carriers for private home viewing licenses, and to determine the fee in case of rejection;[14]
4. To determine if sufficient negotiated licenses for public performance by means of coin-operated phonorecord players are in effect; and[15]
5. To distribute royalty fees under compulsory coin-operated phonorecord players licenses[16] compulsory cable television secondary transmission licenses,[17]

---

9. Diamond, *The Compulsory Licenses and the Copyright Royalty Tribunal*, 6 A.P.L.A. Q.J. 46 (1978); 37 C.F.R. §§ 301.60–301.69.
10. 17 U.S.C.A. §§ 801(b)(1), 804(a).
11. *Id.*
12. 17 U.S.C.A. §§ 118(c), 801(b)(2). Section 801(b)(2) was revised in 1986. Pub. L. No. 99-397, 100 Stat. 848 (Aug. 27, 1986). The Tribunal adjusts the royalty amounts on each August 1 according to the change in the cost of living as determined by the Consumer Price Index. 17 U.S.C.A. § 801(b)(2); 37 C.F.R. § 304.10.
13. 17 U.S.C.A. § 804(a),(b).
14. 17 U.S.C.A. § 119.
15. Berne Act § 4(a)(4).
16. 17 U.S.C.A. §§ 116(c), 801(b)(3).
17. 17 U.S.C.A. §§ 111(d)(5), 801(b)(3).

and "statutory" satellite secondary transmission licenses for private home viewing,[18] after settling any controversies over distribution.[19]

31.2[1] Fixing Initial Terms and Rates of Royalty Payments by Public Broadcasters Under Compulsory Noncommercial Broadcasting Licenses

The Tribunal, in establishing such terms and rates, considered the rates for comparable circumstances under voluntary negotiated license agreements,[20] and other factors based upon legislative history.[21]

31.2[2] Reviewing and Periodically Adjusting Royalty Rates Under Compulsory and "Statutory" Licenses

In adjusting the rates under compulsory musical recording licenses[22] and currently suspended compulsory coin-operated phonorecord players licenses,[23] and in reviewing determinations of "Arbitration Panels" of royalty fees under "statutory licenses" for satellite secondary transmission of "superstations" and "network stations" for "private home viewing."[24] Tribunal determinations must be calculated to achieve statutorily enumerated objectives.[25]

---

18. 17 U.S.C.A. § 119(b)(4). *See* chapter 23 *supra*.
19. 17 U.S.C.A. §§ 801(b)(3), 804.
20. *See* text accompanying chapter 23, notes 41–48, and chapter 24, notes 13–44 *supra*.
21. 17 U.S.C.A. § 118(b)(3); 43 Fed. Reg. 25,068 (June 8, 1978)(royalties reflecting "fair value" of materials used—1975 Senate Report 101; copyright owners should not be "required to subsidize public broadcasting"—1976 House Report 118; copyright owners should be assured of "reasonable compensation").
22. 17 U.S.C.A. § 801(b)(1); 37 C.F.R. §§ 307.1–307.3.
23. 17 U.S.C.A. § 801(b)(1); 37 C.F.R. §§ 306.1–306.3.
24. 17 U.S.C.A. § 119(c)(3)(F).
25. *Id.* The four objectives for §§ 115 and 116 rates are: (1) to maximize the availability of creative works to the public; (2) to afford the copyright owner a fair return for one's creative works and the copyright user a fair income under existing economic conditions; (3) to

For Tribunal determinations adjusting the rates under compulsory cable television secondary transmission licenses, there are four elaborate statutory provisions.[26]

In determining whether a return to a copyright owner under a compulsory coin-operated phonorecord players license is fair, appropriate weight shall be given to previously determined Tribunal rates and the rates contained in any negotiated license.[27] Provision was made for Tribunal ad interim royalty rates.[28]

31.2[3] Distributing Royalty Fees Under Compulsory Coin-Operated Phonorecord Players Licenses and Compulsory Cable Television Secondary Transmission Licenses, and "Statutory" Licenses for Satellite Secondary Transmissions for Private Home Viewing

Royalty fees deposited with the Register of Copyrights under compulsory coin-operated phonorecord players li-

---

reflect the relative roles of the copyright owner and the copyright user in the product made available to the public with respect to relative creative contribution, technological contribution, capital investment, cost, risk, and contribution to the opening of new markets for creative expression and media for their communication; and (4) to minimize any disruptive impact on the structure of the industries involved and on generally prevailing industry practices. In adjusting § 118 rates, the Tribunal may consider rates for comparable circumstances under voluntary license agreements. 17 U.S.C.A. § 118(c). It is also expected to consider both the general public interest in encouraging the growth and development of public broadcasting, and the "promotion of science and the useful arts" through the encouragement of musical and artistic creation. 1976 House Report 118.

26. 17 U.S.C.A. § 801(b)(2); 37 C.F.R. §§ 308.1–308.2. The controlling provisions for § 111 rate adjustments, subject to several detailed provisos and contingencies, are to reflect: (1) national monetary inflation or deflation, or (2) changes in average rates charged cable subscribers for basic service of providing secondary transmissions to maintain real constant dollar level of royalty fee per subscriber that existed as of October 19, 1976.

27. 17 U.S.C.A. § 801(b)(3)(i), added by Berne Act § 11(1).

28. 17 U.S.C.A. § 801(b)(3)(ii), added by Berne Act § 11(2).

censes,[29] compulsory cable television secondary transmission licenses,[30] and "statutory" satellite secondary transmission licenses for private home viewing,[31] after deduction by the Copyright Office of its reasonable costs,[32] are to be distributed by the Tribunal to the copyright owners whose works were used or their designated agents. In cases where controversy exists, the Tribunal, after deduction of its reasonable costs,[33] shall determine the distribution of such fees.[34]

Every final Tribunal determination shall be published in the *Federal Register*,[35] and may be appealed to the United States court of appeals, within thirty days after the publication in the *Federal Register*, by an aggrieved party.[36]

---

29. 17 U.S.C.A. § 116(b)(1)(A); 37 C.F.R. 201.16.
30. 17 U.S.C.A. § 111(d)(2) (semiannually); 37 C.F.R. § 201.17.
31. 17 U.S.C.A. § 119(b)(4).
32. 17 U.S.C.A. §§ 111(d)(3), 116(c)(1).
33. 17 U.S.C.A. §§ 111(d)(5)(B), 116(c)(3), 119(b)(4), 807.
34. 17 U.S.C.A. §§ 111(d)(5), 116(c)(3), 801(b)(3).
35. 17 U.S.C.A. § 803(b).
36. 17 U.S.C.A. § 809. Court decisions have involved review of both rate fixation, National Cable Television Ass'n v. Copyright Royalty Tribunal, 689 F.2d 1077 (D.C. Cir. 1982)(cable royalty rate); Amusement & Music Operators Ass'n v. Copyright Royalty Tribunal, 676 F.2d 1144 (7th Cir.), *cert. denied*, 459 U.S. 907 (1982)(jukebox royalty rate); Recording Indus. Ass'n v. Copyright Royalty Tribunal, 662 F.2d 1 (D.C. Cir. 1981)(phonorecord rates), and distribution among claimants. ACEMLA v. Copyright Royalty Tribunal, 854 F.2d 10 (2d Cir. 1988) (ASCAP, BMI, and SESAC held entitled to major portion of 1985 cable television royalty fund attributable to Spanish-language music); NBC v. Copyright Royalty Tribunal, 848 F.2d 1289 (D.C. Cir. 1988); National Ass'n of Broadcasters v. Copyright Royalty Tribunal, 809 F.2d 172 (2d Cir. 1986) (upholding cable royalty distributions based on three funds: basic, 3.75 percent, syndex); Christian Broadcasting Network, Inc. v. Copyright Royalty Tribunal, 772 F.2d 922 (D.C. Cir. 1985) ("unenviable mission of dividing up the booty"), *cert. denied*, 475 U.S. 1035 (1986); ACEMLA v. Copyright Royalty Tribunal, 763 F.2d 101 (2d Cir. 1985)(jukebox royalty distributions); Christian Broadcasting Network, Inc. v. Copyright Royalty Tribunal, 720 F.2d 1295 (D.C. Cir. 1983)(cable royalty distributions).

Before any funds are distributed pursuant to a final decision in a proceeding involving distribution of royalty fees, the Tribunal shall assess the reasonable costs of such proceeding.[37]

31.3 Regulations

The Tribunal is required to adopt regulations not inconsistent with law governing its procedure and methods of operation and, except as otherwise provided in the 1976 Act, is subject to the Administrative Procedure Act.[38]

31.4 Annual Report

Besides publishing reports of all final determinations, the Tribunal is required to make an annual report to the President and Congress concerning the Tribunal's work during the preceding fiscal year, including a detailed financial statement of account.[39]

31.5 Royalties

Cable television copyright royalty fees distributions have been lagging by one to three years, as have jukebox royalty fees. Meanwhile, tens of millions of dollars, after allowance of the Copyright Office administrative expenses, have been accumulating substantial interest.

---

37. 17 U.S.C.A. § 807.
38. 17 U.S.C.A. § 803(a). Specific Tribunal regulations are required by §§ 111(d)(5)(A), 116(c)(2), (5), 118(b)(3). Further, the Register of Copyrights is required to consult with the Tribunal concerning certain regulations. E.g. 17 U.S.C.A. §§ 111(d)(1), (2), 116(b)(1)(A). *See* 37 C.F.R. §§ 301.1 *et seq.*
39. 17 U.S.C.A. § 808. The Tribunal reported to Congress concerning § 118 on January 3, 1980.

Royalty rates are based on a cable system's gross receipts from basic services, with smaller cable systems paying a flat rate. The 1976 Act established the formula until 1980, with the Copyright Royalty Tribunal authorized to review the rate structure every five years thereafter. The Tribunal's first adjustment based on five-year consumer price index changes was judicially approved.[40]

31.6 Future of Tribunal

Abolition or at least restructuring of the Tribunal has been suggested, even by a former chairman, and the Tribunal has operated without its full authorized members. Collection of copyright royalties, even under compulsory licenses, should, in the opinion of some, be left to the private sector. Others have suggested more statutory emphasis on negotiated licenses and arbitration.

In 1981, the General Accounting Office recommended prompt distribution of royalties, copyright knowledgeability of commissioners, access to a general counsel, subpoena power, and funding to obtain objective expert opinion.

40. National Cable Television Ass'n v. Copyright Royalty Tribunal, 689 F.2d 1077 (D.C. Cir. 1982).

32. Semiconductor Chip Products

32.1 Semiconductor Chip Protection Act of 1984

In 1984, a new chapter 9 (§§ 901–914) was added.[1] Chapter 9, entitled, "Protection of Semiconductor Chip Products,"

1. Semiconductor Chip Protection Act of 1984, Pub. L. No. 98-620, 98 Stat. 3347 (Nov. 8, 1984) (effective for most purposes on Jan. 1, 1985; for purposes of limited protection to mask works marketed on or after Jan. 1, 1985, if registration was filed during 1985, on Jan. 1, 1984) (technically not part of copyright law). "Chip" is a nickname for an integrated circuit. In 1984, it was about one-fourth of an inch square, and could be a collection of some 250,000 transistors, used as microprocessors or for memory. Federal preemption is prescribed in § 912(c). *See* text accompanying notes 45, 46 *infra*. *See also* Copyright Office Circular R100 (Federal Statutory Protection for Mask Works); R. STERN, SEMICONDUCTOR CHIP PROTECTION (1986). Provisions due to lapse on November 9, 1987, have been extended to July 1, 1991. Pub. L. No. 100–159, 101 Stat. 899 (Nov. 9, 1987). Barker, *Copyright for Integrated Circuit Design: Will the 1976 Act Protect Against Chip Pirates?* 33 COPYRIGHT L. SYMP. (ASCAP) 37 (1987); Shih, *Semiconductor Chip Protection Act of 1984: Is Copyright Protection for Utilitarian Articles Desirable?* 7 COMPUTER L.J. 129 (1986); Stern, *Liability for Infringement of Mask Work Rights Under the Semiconductor Chip Protection Act*, 70 MINN. L. REV. 271 (1985); Kastenmeier & Remington, *Semiconductor Chip Protection Act of 1984: A Swamp or Firm Ground?* 70 MINN. L. REV. 417 (1985); Samuelson, *Creating a New Kind of Intellectual Property: Applying the Lessons of the Chip Law to Computer Programs*, 70 MINN. L. REV. 471 (1985); Brown, *Eligibility for Copyright Protection: The Search for Principled Standards*, 70 MINN. L. REV. 579

is a self-sufficient set of provisions, both structurally and substantively, from the rest of the law[2] because it deals with utilitarian or functional, rather than aesthetic, subject matter.[3]

Protected are "original" "*mask works*" "fixed" or embodied in "semiconductor chip products" for ten years from the earlier of the work's registration in the Copyright Office on first "commercial exploitation" anywhere in the world. Registration is required within two years after commercial exploitation.

32.1[1] "Mask Works"

Chapter 9, creates "mask works" as a new class of "copyrightable" subject matter, provides for a ten-year term of protection, limits the liability of innocent infringers, recognizes a reverse-engineering right, and does not use the word "copy." Such novel "industrial copyright" is sui generis, since the primary and often sole purpose of "mask works" is use in the manufacture of useful articles: semiconductor chip products.

(1985); Kidwell, *Software and Semiconductors: Why Are We Confused?* 70 MINN. L. REV. 533 (1985); Notes, 7 COMPUTER L.J. 245 (1986); 6 COMPUTER L.J. 543 (1986). The first reported case under the Act was Brooktree v. Advanced Micro Devices, Inc., 700 F. Supp. 491 (S.D. Cal. 1988) (defendant's work found to result from permissible reverse engineering).

2. S. REP. NO. 98-425, 98th Cong. 2d Sess. (1984); H.R. REP. NO. 98-781, 98th Cong., 2d Sess. Analogies, of course, may be drawn to other chapters, to the extent appropriate and feasible. *See* Copyright Office proposed 37 C.F.R. § 211.4; ML-333 (Final Regulations: Mask Work Protection; Implementation of the Semiconductor Chip Protection Act of 1984).
3. The design of a useful article, i.e., an article having an intrinsic utilitarian function that is not merely to portray the appearance of the article or to convey information, is considered a pictorial, graphic, or sculptural work only if, and only to the extent that, such design incorporates pictorial, graphic, or sculptural features that can be identified separately from, and are capable of existing independently of, the utilitarian aspects of the article. *See* 17 U.S.C.A. § 101 (definitions of "useful article" and "pictorial, graphic, and sculptural works") discussed in text accompanying chapter 5, notes 21–22 *supra*.

32.1[2] Definitions

"Semiconductor chip product" is defined as the final or intermediate form of any product:[4]

- Having two or more layers of metallic, insulating, or semiconductor material, deposited or otherwise placed on, or etched away or otherwise removed from, a piece of semiconductor material in accordance with a predetermined pattern;
- Intended to perform electronic circuitry functions.

"Mask work" is defined as a series of related images, however fixed or encoded:[5]

- Having or representing the predetermined, three-dimensional pattern of metallic, insulating, or semiconductor material present or removed from the layers of a semiconductor chip product;
- In which series the relation of the images to one another is that each image has the pattern of the surface of one form of the semiconductor chip product.

Other definitions for the purposes of chapter 9 include "any person,"[6] "fixed,"[7] "distribute,"[8] "commercially ex-

4. 17 U.S.C.A. § 901(a)(1) (Supp.).
5. 17 U.S.C.A. § 901(a)(2) (Supp.).
6. Includes any state, any instrumentality of a state, and any officer or employee of a state or instrumentality of a state acting in his or her official capacity. 17 U.S.C.A. § 910(a).
7. When the mask work's embodiment in the semiconductor chip product is sufficiently permanent or stable to permit the mask work to be perceived or reproduced from the product for a period of more than transitory duration. 17 U.S.C.A. § 901(a)(3). *See* definition of "fixed" in 17 U.S.C.A. § 101.
8. To sell, or to lease, bail, or otherwise transfer, or to offer to sell, lease, bail, or otherwise transfer. 17 U.S.C.A. § 901(a)(4) (Supp.).

ploit,"[9] "owner,"[10] "innocent purchaser,"[11] "notice of protection,"[12] and "infringing semiconductor chip product."[13] The distribution or importation of a product incorporating a semiconductor chip product as a part thereof is a distribution or importation of such semiconductor chip product.[14]

32.1[3] Protection

Protected are "original,"[15] "fixed,"[16] "*mask works*"[17] whose "author"[18] is eligible for protection on the basis of national-

9. To distribute to the public for commercial purposes a semiconductor chip product embodying the mask work; except that such term includes an offer to sell or transfer a semiconductor chip product only when the offer is in writing and occurs after the mask work is fixed in the semiconductor chip product. 17 U.S.C.A. § 901(a)(5). The concept of commercial exploitation is new. It is relevant, *inter alia*, as to duration of protection and when registration should be made.
10. The person who created the mask work, the legal representative of that person if that person is deceased or under a legal incapacity, or a party to whom all the rights of such person or representative are transferred in accordance with 17 U.S.C.A. § 903(b); except that, in the case of a work made within the scope of a person's employment, the owner is the employer for whom the person created the mask work or a party to whom all the rights of the employer are transferred in accordance with § 903(b). § 901(a)(6). Such definition is analogous to conventional copyright principles. *See* chapter 7 *supra*.
11. A person who purchased a semiconductor chip product in good faith and without having "notice of protection" with respect to the semiconductor chip products. 17 U.S.C.A. § 901(a)(7).
12. Actual knowledge that, or reasonable grounds to believe that, a mask work is protected. 17 U.S.C.A. § 901(a)(8).
13. A semiconductor chip product that is made, imported, or distributed in violation of the exclusive rights of the owners of a mask work. 17 U.S.C.A. § 901(a)(9).
14. 17 U.S.C.A. § 901(b).
15. 17 U.S.C.A. § 902(a)(1) (Supp.). *See* note 20 *infra*.
16. *Id. See* note 7 *supra*.
17. *Id. See* text accompanying note 5 *supra*.
18. *Id. See* note 10 *supra*.

ity of the author or the work.[19] Expressly not protected are mask works that are not original[20] or ideas, etc.[21]

32.1[3][a] Ownership, Transfer, Recording, Government Works

Chapter 9's provisions for ownership,[22] transfer or licensing,[23] and recording,[24] and for nonprotection of works prepared by a United States government officer or employee,[25] parallel analogous provisions in the copyright statute.

32.1[3][b] Duration

The duration of protection is for ten years from the earlier of the work's registration[26] or first "commercial exploita-

19. 17 U.S.C.A. § 902(a)(1), (2). Presidential proclamations (*see* text accompanying chapter 6, note 7 *supra*) applicable to mask works are to be requested by the Secretary of Commerce after consultation with the Secretary of State. Executive Order No. 12,504 (Jan. 13, 1985), 50 Fed. Reg. 4,849 (1985). Section 902 parallels 17 U.S.C.A. § 104.
20. 17 U.S.C.A. § 902(b). Not original or consisting of designs that are staple, commonplace, or familiar in the semiconductor industry, or variations of such designs, combined in a way that, considered as a whole, is not original. This concept is comparable to conventional "copyright" principles. The inventiveness (nonobviousness) required by the patent laws is not necessary.
21. 17 U.S.C.A. § 902(c). In no case does protection for a mask work extend to any idea, procedure, process, system, method of operation, concept, principle, or discovery, regardless of the form in which it is described, explained, illustrated, or embodied in such work. The language is identical to 17 U.S.C.A. § 102(b).
22. 17 U.S.C.A § 903(a). Generally similar to 17 U.S.C.A. § 201 and patent laws (35 U.S.C.A § 261).
23. 17 U.S.C.A. § 903(b). Inter vivos transfer by written instrument signed by owner or duly authorized owner.
24. 17 U.S.C.A. § 903(c). Including provisions for constructive notice and priorities in event of conflicting transfers.
25. 17 U.S.C.A. § 903(d). Generally similar to 17 U.S.C.A. § 105 (United States government works). *See* text accompanying chapter 6, notes 18–23, *supra*.
26. For registration, *see* 17 U.S.C.A. § 908 (Supp.), and text accompanying note 37 *infra*. *See also* Copyright Office Form MW.

tion"[27] anywhere in the world,[28] running to the end of the calendar year.[29]

32.1[4] Exclusive Rights

After an enumeration of the exclusive rights in mask works, there are two sets of limitations on such rights.

32.1[4][a] Enumeration

The exclusive rights enumerated are to do and to authorize any of the following:[30]

1. To reproduce the mask work by optical, electronic, or any other means;
2. To import or distribute a semiconductor chip in which the mask work is embodied;
3. To induce or knowingly cause another person to do any of the acts described in paragraphs (1) and (2).

32.1[4][b] Limitations

The first set of limitations permits use analogous to fair use[31] and the preparation by reverse engineering to produce

---

27. 17 U.S.C.A. § 908 (Supp.). *See* note 9 *supra*.
28. 17 U.S.C.A. § 908(a), (b).
29. 17 U.S.C.A. § 904(c), following language of 17 U.S.C.A. § 305.
30. 17 U.S.C.A. § 905 (Supp.). § 905(1) is similar to 17 U.S.C.A. § 106(1); 17 U.S.C.A. § 905(2) (Supp.) (importation and distribution), to 17 U.S.C.A. §§ 106(3), 602(a). Section 905(3) on contributory infringement has no express analogue in the copyright statute, but does in the patent laws, and attempts to follow existing case law, including Sony Corp. v. Universal City Studios, Inc. (*see* text accompanying chapter 27, notes 20–21, *supra*).
31. 17 U.S.C.A. § 906(a)(1) (Supp.). Solely for the purpose of teaching, analyzing, or evaluating the concepts or techniques embodied in the mask work or the circuitry, logic flow, or organization components used in the mask work.

a derivative work based on such use,[32] and restates the first-sale doctrine.[33]

The second set of limitations protects "innocent purchasers"[34] from liability.[35]

---

32. 17 U.S.C.A. § 906(a)(2) (Supp.). Performing analysis or evaluation described in § 906(a)(1), *supra* note 31, to incorporate results of such conduct in an *original mask* work which is made to be distributed. While the term "derivative work" is not used in § 906(a)(2), the analogy to compilations and derivative works is striking. *See* text accompanying chapter 5, notes 31–37, *supra*. To be able to demonstrate legitimate reverse engineering, as distinguished from chip piracy, documentary evidence of adequate originality to counterbalance substantial similarity in the derived work should be carefully preserved. H.R. REP. NO. 98-781, 98th Cong., 2d Sess. 26–27 (1984).
33. 17 U.S.C.A. § 906(b) (Supp.). Restating the first-sale doctrine that the owner of a particular semiconductor chip product made by the owner of the mask work, or by any person authorized by the owner of the mask work, may import, distribute, or otherwise dispose of or use, but not reproduce, that particular semiconductor chip product without the authority of the owner of the mask work. *See* United States v. Goss, 803 F.2d. 638 (11th Cir. 1986)(government held not to have rebutted defendant's evidence of lawful making and ownership of ROMs included in circuit boards under first-sale doctrine).
34. 17 U.S.C.A. § 907(a)(1) (Supp.). No liability with respect to importation or distribution of units of the infringing semiconductor chip product that occurs before the innocent purchaser has notice of protection with respect to the mask work embodied in the semiconductor chip product.
35. 17 U.S.C.A. § 907(a)(2), (b), (c), (d) (Supp.). Liability only for a reasonable royalty on each unit of the infringing semiconductor chip product that the innocent purchaser imports or distributes after having notice of protection with respect to the mask work embodied in the semiconductor chip product. Reasonable royalty is determined by the court in a civil action for infringement unless the parties resolve the issue by voluntary negotiation, mediation, or binding arbitration. Such immunity and limitation of remedies extend to any person who directly or indirectly purchases an infringing semiconductor chip product from an innocent purchaser before having notice of protection.

32.1[5] Registration

Application for registration of claims of protection *must* be made within two years after the date on which the mask work was first "commercially exploited" anywhere in the world.[36] Otherwise, protection terminates.[37] The provisions for registration of mask works differ from the registration provisions of the copyright statute.[38]

32.1[6] Notice of Protection

The mask work notice, which is optional but constitutes prima facie evidence of "notice of protection," consists of:[39]

1. The words "mask work", the symbol *M*, or the symbol Ⓜ (the letter M in a circle);
2. The name of the owner or owners of the mask work or an abbreviation by which the name is recognized or is generally known.

32.1[7] Infringement

Infringement is a violation of any of the rights of the owners.[40] Registration is prerequisite to a civil action for

---

36. 17 U.S.C.A. § 908 (Supp). Similar to 17 U.S.C.A. § 409. Section 908 has provisions similar to 17 U.S.C.A. § 410 for compelling registration which has been refused. Failure to register within three months is deemed refusal.
37. *See* notes 9, 34, 35 *supra*.
38. For discussion of registration of copyright claims, *see* chapter 12 *supra*.
39. 17 U.S.C.A. § 909 (Supp.). Specification of methods of affixation and positions as prescribed by Copyright Office regulations, but such specifications shall not be considered exhaustive. Affixation of notice expressly is not a condition of protection under chapter 9. For definition of "notice of protection," *see* note 11 *supra*. The "Ⓜ" symbol is to be contrasted with "©" for copyright, "℗" for sound recording, and "®" for federally registered trademark or other mark.
40. 17 U.S.C.A. § 910(a). Specifying "by conduct in or affecting commerce," by "any person," defined in 1990 as including any state or

infringement.[41] The statute of limitation is three years.[42]

32.1[8] Remedies

The remedies for infringement include temporary restraining orders, preliminary injunctions, permanent injunctions, actual damages, and profits (not taken into account in computing award of actual damages) or, by electing statutory damages, exclusion from importation.[43] Criminal sanctions are not available under chapter 9.

---

state instrumentality or employee. 17 U.S.C.A. § 910(a). Provisions clarifying their nonimmunity for infringement of a mask work were added in 1990, effective November 15, 1990. 17 U.S.C.A. § 911(g). Analogous in 17 U.S.C.A. § 501(a). Whether there is substantial similarity must be predicated upon the idea-expression dichotomy. Expression, when dictated by the idea, may not be protected. Morrissey v. Procter & Gamble Co., 379 F.2d 675, 678 (1st Cir. 1967). The 1984 legislation introduced the defense of reverse engineering and dealt further with innocent infringers. Brooktree v. Advanced Micro Devices, Inc., 705 F. Supp. 49 (S.D. Cal. 1989); Hart, *High Technology "Reverse Engineering": The Dual Standard*, 14 N. KY. L. REV. 237 (1987); Raskind, *Reverse Engineering, Unfair Competition, and Fair Use Under the Semiconductor Chip. Protection Act*, 70 MINN. L. REV. 395 (1985). Compilation and other fact-based-works copyright cases should provide analogous precedents. Infringement may be by "any person." "Any person," as used in § 910(a), includes any state, any state instrumentality, and any officer or employee of a state acting in "his or her official capacity." 17 U.S.C.A. § 910(a).

41. 17 U.S.C.A. § 910(b) (Supp.). For wrongful refusal of registration, the owner has remedies similar to those in 17 U.S.C.A. § 910. *See* chapter 12, note 28, *supra*. Section 910(d) is like 17 U.S.C.A. § 603. This registration requirement was not qualified by the Berne Act. *Cf.* chapter 12, note 40, *supra*.

42. 17 U.S.C.A. § 911(d) (Supp.). Similar to 17 U.S.C.A. § 507(b). Section 911(a) (temporary restraining orders and preliminary and permanent injunctions) is like 17 U.S.C.A. § 502(a); § 911(b) (damages and profits), like § 504(b); § 911(c) (statutory damages), with some exceptions, like § 504(c); § 911(d) (counsel fees), like § 500; § 911(f) (seizure and impoundment), like § 509. *See* note 43 *infra*. State sovereign immunity was expressly negatived by the Copyright Remedy Clarification Act of 1990. 17 U.S.C.A. §§ 910(a), 911(g)(1)(Supp.), like *id.* §§ 501(a), 511.

43. 17 U.S.C.A. §§ 910(c)(1), 911, 912(a) (Supp.). These provisions are

Nothing in chapter 9 shall affect any right or remedy under chapters 1 through 8 of the copyright law or under the patent laws (35 U.S.C. sections 1 *et seq.*)[44]

32.1[9] Preemption

The provisions of chapter 9 preempt the laws of any state to the extent those laws provide any rights or remedies with respect to a mask work that are equivalent to those rights or remedies provided by chapter 9 except that such preemption shall be effective only with respect to actions filed on or after January 1, 1986.[45] State or other federal laws respecting mask works first commercially exploited before July 1, 1983, are not affected.[46]

32.1[10] Transitional Provisions

Transitional provisions are contained in section 913 (international transitional provisions) and in section 914, the concluding sections of chapter 9.[47]

---

generally similar to 17 U.S.C.A. §§ 411(a), 501–503, 507(b), and 908(g), as mentioned in note 41 *supra*. The maximum statutory damages for mask works infringement are $250,000, compared to $20,000 ($100,000 if willful) for copyright infringement. Prejudgment relief is not included and there are no criminal penalties. Provisions concerning remedies in civil actions available to owners of mask works against states, their instrumentalities, officers, and employees, were included in 1990 to parallel those in the 1990 revision of § 511.

44. 17 U.S.C.A. § 912(c) (Supp.). Nonpreempted are state laws for breaches of contract, breaches of trust, trespass, conversion, and such deceptive trade practices as passing off and false misrepresentation. H.R. REP. NO. 98-781, 98th Cong., 2d Sess. 28–29 (May 15, 1984). Noteworthy is the omission in the report of "misappropriation" and the statement that "trade secrets" are not preempted. *See* text accompanying chapter 4, notes 8–17, *supra*. Mask works were not protected under the pre-existing copyright law.
45. 17 U.S.C.A. § 912(c).
46. 17 U.S.C.A. § 912(d).
47. 17 U.S.C.A. §§ 912, 914.

33. Satellite Cable Programming

The interception or receipt of any "satellite cable programming"[1] for "private viewing"[2] is the subject of the Cable Communications Policy Act of 1984[3] which amended the Communications Act of 1934[4] rather than the Copyright Act, which expressly was not affected by the amendment.[5]

---

1. "Satellite cable programming" is defined as meaning video programming that is transmitted via satellite and is primarily intended for the direct receipt by cable operators for their retransmission to cable subscribers. 47 U.S.C.A. § 705(c)(1). Satellites sometimes are called "dishes" or "earth stations."
2. "Private viewing" is defined as meaning the viewing for private use in an individual's dwelling unit by means of equipment, owned or operated by such individual, capable of receiving satellite cable programming directly from a satellite. 47 U.S.C.A. § 706(c)(4).
3. Pub. L. No. § 98-549, 99 Stat. 2779 (Oct. 30, 1984); 47 U.S.C.A. § 705. Nothing in 47 U.S.C.A. § 705(a) prevents any state, or political subdivision thereof, from enacting or enforcing any laws with respect to the importation, sale, manufacture, or distribution of equipment by any person with the intent of its use to assist in the prohibited interception or receipt of radio communications. 47 U.S.C.A. § 705(d)(6).
4. 47 U.S.C.A. §§ 151 *et seq.*
5. 47 U.S.C.A. § 705(e); Note, *Satellite/Dish Antenna Technology: A Copyright Owner's Dilemma*, 59 IND. L.J. 417 (1983–1984).

33.1 Cable Communications Policy Act of 1984

Subsection (a)[6] provides that no person not being entitled thereto shall receive or assist in receiving any interstate or foreign communication by radio and use such communication (or any information contained therein) for one's own benefit or for the benefit of another entitled thereto. Such prohibition is inapplicable to any radio communication broadcast or transmitted by amateurs or others "for the use of the general public."

33.1[1] Exemption

Such provision, however, does not apply if:

1. The programming involved is not "encrypted."[7]

---

6. 47 U.S.C.A. § 705(a); National Football League v. McBee & Bruno's, Inc., 792 F.2d 726 (8th Cir. 1986) (defendant restaurant's public displays of televised, "blacked-out" nearby football games by satellite dish antennae held not exempt, whether program was "clean feed" or "dirty feed" transmission; lower court's finding that satellite dishes were not "commonly found in private homes" not clearly erroneous); Programming Network, Inc. v. Edinbur Community Hotel, Inc., 623 F. Supp. 647 (S.D. Tex. 1985) (motel capturing signals through satellite dish antenna held to infringe public performance and display rights). For discussion of "passive carrier exemption," *see* chapter 25, note 21 *supra*. *See also* Hubbard Broadcasting, Inc. v. Southern Satellite Sys., Inc., 777 F.2d 393 (8th Cir. 1985) (communication commercial carrier retransmitting all programs of twenty-four-hour station without any changes held "passive carrier" despite its initial choice of station), *cert. denied*, 479 U.S. 1005 (1986); Movie Sys., Inc. v. Heller, 710 F.2d 492 (8th Cir. 1983) (microwave transmission not intended for use by any but paying subscribers held not for "use of the general public"); WGN Continental Broadcasting Co. v. United Video, Inc., 693 F.2d 622 (7th Cir. 1982) (satellite carrier's deletion of teletext and substitution of other material held modification disqualifying carrier for passive carrier exemption).
7. "Encrypt" is defined as meaning to transmit satellite cable programming in a form whereby the aural and visual characteristics (or both) are modified or altered for the purpose of preventing the unauthorized

2. A "market system"[8] either:
   - Is not established.[9]
   - Is established and the individual receiving such programming has obtained authorization for private viewing under that system.[10]

33.1[2] Penalties

Willful violations may entail fines of not more than $1,000 or imprisonment for not more than six months, or both, or more.[11]

33.1[3] Remedies

Remedies available to any person aggrieved by any violation are:[12]

---

receipt of such programming by persons without authorized equipment that is designed to eliminate the effects of such modification or alteration. 47 U.S.C.A. § 705(c)(3). *See* United States v. Westbrook, 502 F. Supp. 588 (E.D. Mich. 1980)(manufacturer of decoders of scrambled television signals held infringer, since broadcast not "for use of general public").

8. A "marketing system" requires the availability to the individual involved of authorization for private viewing under such system by a lawfully designated agent or agents. 47 U.S.C.A. § 705(b)(2). "Agent" is defined to include an employee. 47 U.S.C.A. § 705(c)(2).
9. 47 U.S.C.A. § 705(b)(2)(A).
10. 47 U.S.C.A. § 705(b)(2)(B).
11. 47 U.S.C.A. § 705(d)(1). If the willful violation is for purposes of "direct or indirect commercial advantage or private financial gain," it is subject to a fine of not more than $25,000 or imprisonment for not more than one year, or both, for the first conviction; $50,000 and two years for any subsequent conviction. 47 U.S.C.A. § 705(d)(2). "Private financial gain" does not include the gain resulting to any individual for the private use in such individual's dwelling unit of any programming for which the individual has not obtained authorization for that use. 47 U.S.C.A. § 705(c), (d)(2). The penalties are in addition to those prescribed under any other provision of title 47. 47 U.S.C.A. § 705(d)(5).
12. *Id.* § 705(d)(3) (in a United States district court or in any other court of competent jurisdiction); National Football League v. McBee &

1. Temporary or final injunctions;[13]
2. Damages;[14]
3. Full costs, including attorney's fees to any prevailing party.[15]

33.1[4] Contributory Infringement

Contributory infringers who import, manufacture, sell, or distribute equipment with the intent of its use to assist in

---

Bruno's, 621 F. Supp. 880, 890 (E.D. Mo. 1985)(construing aggrieved party to include copyright owners of programming as well as owners of satellite transmission)(citing pre-1984 cases), *aff'd*, 792 F.2d 726 (8th Cir. 1986); Movie Sys., Inc. v. Heller, 710 F.2d 492 (8th Cir. 1983); National Subscription Television v. S. & H. TV, 644 F.2d 820 (9th Cir. 1981); Chartwell Communications Group v. Westbrook, 637 F.2d 459 (6th Cir. 1980)(upholding implied private right of action under 47 U.S.C.A. § 705).

13. 47 U.S.C.A. § 705(d)(3)(B)(i) (on such terms as the court may deem reasonable to prevent or restrain violations).
14. 47 U.S.C.A. § 705(d)(3)(B)(ii). Damages awarded by any court shall be computed, at the election of the aggrieved party, either as:
    1. The actual damages suffered as a result of the violation and any profits of the violator that are attributable to the violations that are not taken into account in computing the actual damages (in determining the violator's profits, the party aggrieved shall be required to prove only the violator's gross revenue, and the violator shall be required to prove deductible expenses and the elements of profit attributable to factors other than the violation); or
    2. Statutory damages for each violation involved in the action in a sum of not less than $250 or more than $10,000, as the court considers just. § 705(d)(C)(i). When the court finds that the violation was committed willfully and for purpose of "direct or indirect commercial advantage or private financial gain," the court in its discretion may increase the award of damages, whether actual or statutory, by an amount of not more than $50,000. § 705(d)(C)(ii). *See* note 11 *supra*. When the court finds that the violator was not aware and had no reason to believe that the acts constituted a violation, the court in its discretion may reduce the award of damages to a sum of not less than $100. § 705(d)(C)(iii).
15. 47 U.S.C.A. § 705(3)(B)(iii).

any such activity are subject to the same penalties and remedies.[16]

33.2 Brussels Satellite Convention

In 1984, the United States ratified the Convention Relating to Distribution of Programme-Carrying Signals Transmitted by Satellite. Under the treaty, each party agrees to act to prevent unauthorized interception and distribution within its territory of program signals transmitted by satellite. Excepted are direct broadcast signals. No implementing United States legislation is required.

---

16. 47 U.S.C.A. § 705(4). *See* National Subscription Television v. S. & H. TV, 664 F.2d 820 (9th Cir. 1981)(makers and distributors of unauthorized decoding devices held violators).

34. Protection of American Works in Foreign Countries

Previous chapters have discussed copyright protection in the United States for eligible works, domestic and foreign.[1] This chapter discusses the converse: eligibility for protection in foreign countries of American works. The scope of protection depends on the foreign laws in the last analysis.

34.1 Application of National Laws

Most nations have enacted copyright laws, but they are not uniform and have no extraterritorial effect. The foreign laws, like American statutes and case law, are subject to frequent changes. There is no "world copyright." "Worldwide rights" is a misnomer.

Complications arise not only from frequent changes in domestic laws, but also from periodic revisions in multipartite conventions and bipartite treaties. The conventions and treaties usually are not self-executing and require implementation by domestic legislation. These changes generally

1. *See* chapter 6 *supra*. A work may be in the public domain in the United States and under subsisting copyrights in foreign countries. Infringing acts occurring outside the United States, at least with sufficient American contacts, may be actionable in American courts. See chapter 27, note 1 *supra*. *See also* P&D. Int'l v. Halsey Publishing Co., 672 F. Supp. 1429 (S.D. Fla. 1987) (territorial scope of copyright).

are not retroactive. The effect is kaleidoscopic, requiring everchanging, complex analyses.

National protection is afforded domestic works and *eligible* foreign works.[2]

34.2 Basis for Protection Abroad

Copyright protection abroad for American works generally is available under the following, which are *not* mutually exclusive:[3]

1. Berne Convention
2. Universal Copyright Convention
3. Pan American Copyright Conventions
4. Other reciprocal copyright relations

---

2. For current United States/foreign country copyright relations, see annotations to 17 U.S.C.A. § 104 (latest cumulative annual pocket part), Copyright Office Circulars R38a and R38c, and WIPO and UNESCO Publications. *See also* A. BOGSCH, *et al.*, COPYRIGHT LAWS AND TREATIES OF THE WORLD (1957-) (3 vols.) (Supps.), which covers the copyright laws of each country. For digests of such laws, see the appropriate volume of the latest edition of *Martindale-Hubbell Law Directory.*

   Protection of sound recordings is based on the UNESCO Convention for the Protection of Producers of Phonograms Against Unauthorized Duplication of Their Phonograms, dated October 29, 1971. The Convention entered into force with respect to the United States on March 10, 1974. Some forty countries have adhered to the Convention. The United States did not adhere to the Rome "Neighboring Rights" Convention of 1961, a UNESCO project. *See also* Sandison, *The Berne Union and the Universal Copyright Convention: The American Experience,* 11 COLUM.–V.L.A. J.L. & ARTS 89 (1986).

3. Leaffer, *International Copyright from an American Perspective,* 43 ARK. L. REV. 373 (1990). The conventions expressly provide that they do not preclude other bases for protection. *See, e.g,* UCC arts. X, XVII, XVIII, XIX, app. (Declaration Relating to Article XVII); Berne Convention art. 19 (greater national protection not precluded). As between different versions of any convention, the latest version adopted by the United States and the relevant foreign country applies.

34.2[1] Berne Convention (Paris Revision, 1971, as amended, 1979)

Since March 1, 1989, the United States has adhered to the Berne Convention,[4] thus becoming a "Berne Union country."[5]

---

4. "Berne Convention" is defined in Berne Act § 4(a)(1)(B) as the "Convention for the Protection of Literary and Artistic Works, signed at Berne, Switzerland, on September 9, 1886, and all acts, protocols, and revisions thereto." The Paris text, 1971, as amended in 1979, is the latest of several acts, protocols, and revisions. Ratified by the United States on October 31, 1988, it, with the Berne Act, became effective on March 1, 1989. The Berne Convention consists of several revisions: Paris (1896), Berlin (1908), Berne (1914), Rome (1928), Brussels (1948), Stockholm (1967). The Berne (also called International) Copyright Conventions eventually abolished formalities altogether for convention purposes, making protection automatic upon the creation of a work by an author who was a national of a Berne Union nation, independently of existence of protection in the country of origin; promoted the life of the author and fifty years thereafter as a minimum period for the full duration of copyright (permitting some reservations); fostered the so-called doctrine of moral rights; and covered works by non-Berne Union nations first (or simultaneously [within thirty days of one another]) published in a Berne Union nation. Such "simultaneous publication" was used by non-Berne Union authors as a "back door" to Berne Union protection, especially by American authors before United States adherence in 1989. Ginsberg & Kernochan, *One Hundred and Two Years Later the U. S. Joins the Berne Convention*, 13 COLUM.–V.L.A. J.L. & ARTS 1 (1988); S. RICKETSON, THE BERNE CONVENTION FOR THE PROTECTION OF LITERARY AND ARTISTIC WORKS: 1886–1986 (1987); *Conference Celebrating the Centenary of the Berne Convention*, 11 COLUM.–V.L.A. J.L. & ARTS 1–251 (1986).
5. The "Union" consists of countries to which the Convention applies. At present, the Berne or International Copyright Bureau is incorporated into the World Intellectual Property Organization (WIPO), with headquarters in Geneva, Switzerland. WIPO is a United Nations agency promoting "industrial property" (patents and other rights in technological inventions, rights in trademarks, industrial designs, appellations of origin, etc.) and "copyright and neighboring rights" (in literary, musical, and artistic works; in films, performances of performing artists, phonograms; etc.). Other western hemisphere Berne Union countries include Argentina, Bahamas, Barbados, Brazil, Canada, Chile, Colombia, Costa Rica, Mexico, Peru, Suriname, Trinidad & Tobago, Uruguay, and Venezuela.

34.2[1][a] Eligible Works

Berne Union protection applies to:[6]

1. Berne Union nationals, "for their works, whether published or not";[7]
2. Non-Berne Union nationals for their works first "published"[8] in a Berne Union country, or "simultaneously"[9] in a non-Berne Union country and a Berne Union country.[10]

Non-Berne Union authors having "their habitual residence" in a Berne Union country are "assimilated to nationals of that country."[11]

---

6. Berne Convention art. 3. *See also* Berne Convention art. 4 (cinematographic, architectural, and artistic works). *See* Berne Act § 4(a)(1). The Berne Convention states that any "sound or visual recording" will be considered a reproduction for its purposes. Berne Convention art. 9(3). Article 2(1) (protected works) includes "every production," but in its lengthy enumeration after "such as" does not specify sound recordings.
7. Berne Convention art. 3(1)(a) (nationality-of-author principle), implemented in Berne Act § 4(a)(1).
8. The expression "published works" means works published "with the consent of their authors" with sufficient copies available "to satisfy the reasonable requirements of the public." Not constituting publication are performances, recitations, broadcasts, and exhibitions. Berne Convention art. 3(3). *Cf.* 17 U.S.C.A. § 101 (definition of "publication").
9. Berne Convention art. 3(4), implemented in Berne Act § 4(a)(1). For so-called back door Berne Union protection for works of non-Berne Union authors by first or "simultaneous" "publication" in a Berne Union country, see note 4 *supra*. Berne Union versions and domestic laws varied as to simultaneity (on the same day; within fourteen or thirty days). Quaere, as to the substantive requirements of "publication," especially since the French text uses the word "*editees*."
10. Berne Convention art. 3(1)(b) (nationality-of-work principle), implemented in Berne Act § 4(a)(1). That principle, based on country of "publication," is not sufficient *alone* to protect unpublished works.
11. Berne Convention art. 3(2), implemented in Berne Act § 4(a)(1). A protocol referred to stateless persons and refugees. There are specific

34.2[1][b] Basic Protection

Works protectible under the Convention enjoy, in Berne Union countries "other than the country of origin,"[12] the rights that their respective laws grant to their nationals (known as reciprocal "national treatment"),[13] as well as the rights "specially granted" by the Convention.[14]

34.2[1][c] Freedom from Formalities

The "enjoyment and exercise" of the above rights "shall not be subject to any formality."[15]

---

provisions dealing with "Berne Convention work" status of "pictorial, graphic, or sculptural" or "architectural" works.

12. "Country of origin" is defined in the Berne Convention in rather complicated language. Berne Convention art. 5(4). *See* Berne Act § 4(a)(1).
13. Berne Convention art. 5(4). For parallel definition, see Berne Act § 4(a)(1)(C). "Reciprocal" means that aliens are protected in the home country. Protected foreign works usually enjoy national treatment plus any rights afforded by any applicable conventions or treaties. The Berne Convention has higher standards of protection than the Universal Copyright Convention (UCC). The domestic laws of Communist governments have tended to favor access over rights of copyright holders. Berne Convention art. 5(2), implemented by Berne Act § 4(a)(2). National treatment results in works' enjoying different bundles of rights in countries where protection ensues.
14. Berne Convention art. 5(1). "Specially granted" rights may be subject to various limitations by domestic legislation. Such rights include "moral rights." Berne Convention art. 6 *bis*. *Cf.* Berne Act § 3(b). *See* text accompanying chapter 17, notes 57–60, *supra*. The Berne Convention requires that a country before becoming "bound by" the Convention "be in a position under its domestic law to give effect to the provisions" of the Convention. Berne Convention art. 36(2). The Convention is not self-executing. Berne Act §§ 2, 3.
15. Berne Convention art. 5(2). This was implemented by relaxation of American formalities for American works (e.g., copyright notice made permissive; recordation of transfer as condition precedent to suit by transferee eliminated) and for "Berne Convention works whose country of origin is not the United States" (e.g., registration as condition precedent to suit).

34.2[1][d] Berne Union Countries

Depending on how counted, some eighty countries have adhered to the Berne Convention. The principal non-adherents are the Soviet Union and China, although both are expected to adhere.

34.2[2] Universal Copyright Convention[16]

Since September 16, 1955, the United States has adhered to the Universal Copyright Convention (UCC).[17]

34.2[2][a] Eligible Works

The UCC applies to:

1. Published works of "nationals" of "any Contracting State";[18]

---

16. Drafted under UNESCO auspices, the Convention was signed in Geneva, Switzerland, in 1952, and amended in Paris in 1971. The United States ratified the amended Convention as of July 10, 1974. The UCC started out as the "UNESCO Copyright Convention," but "UNESCO" became an unpopular term. The 1952 Geneva version became effective on September 16, 1955. The 1971 Paris revision became effective on July 10, 1974. Quaere, as to the protection of sound recordings, since they are not included in the classes of works described in UCC art. I. Since not "usually" perceivable, they could not be "published" works under the UCC definition of publication in article IV. *See* note 18 *infra*.
17. As of July 10, 1974, the United States ratified the 1971 Paris revision of the UCC. The UCC was the thirteenth major effort to promulgate a convention that would be "universal," if only in name. T. KUPFERMAN & M. FONER, eds., THE UNIVERSAL COPYRIGHT CONVENTION ANALYZED (1955). In fact, it is as "universal" as any multilateral international convention,, at least until the Soviet Union joins the Berne Union. *See* Henn, *The Quest for International Copyright Protection*, 39 CORNELL L.Q. 43 (1953).
18. UCC art. II(1) (nationality-of-author principle). "Publication," as used in the UCC, means the "reproduction in tangible form" and the "general distribution to the public" of "copies of a work from which it can be read or otherwise visually perceived." UCC art. IV.

2. Works "first published" "in that State";[19]
3. Unpublished works of nationals of "each Contracting State."[20]

34.2[2][b] Basic Protection

Published works enjoy in "each other Contracting State" the "same protection" accorded to works of "its nationals first published in its own territory,"[21] as well as the protection "specially granted" by the Convention.[22]

Unpublished works enjoy in "each other Contracting State" the "same protection" accorded to unpublished "works of its own nationals," as well as the protection "specially granted" by the Convention.[23]

Each Contracting State undertakes to provide for the "adequate and effective protection of the rights of authors and other copyright proprietors,"[24] including minimal translation rights.[25] The Convention expressly provides against its application to works "permanently in the public domain."[26]

34.2[2][c] Formalities

Any formalities required by domestic law "as a condition of copyright" are regarded "as satisfied" with respect to works "first published" outside of the Contracting State's territory and the "author is not one of its nationals" if all authorized published copies bear the "symbol © accompanied by the name of the copyright proprietor and the year of first publication placed in such manner and location as

19. UCC art. II(1) (nationality-of-work principle).
20. UCC art. II(2).
21. UCC art. II(3).
22. UCC art. II(1).
23. UCC art. II(2)
24. UCC art. I.
25. UCC art V.
26. UCC art. VII.

to give reasonable notice of claim to copyright."[27] Conditions precedent to suit and renewal requirements were not precluded.[28]

In each Contracting State there have to be "legal means" for protecting "without formalities" the "unpublished works" of nationals of other Contracting States.[29]

34.2[2][d] UCC Countries

Depending on how one counts them, some eighty countries have adhered to the UCC of 1952, with some forty-five of them adhering to the 1971 revision, with or without ratification of the protocols. The Soviet Union, but not China, has adhered. The United States, since its withdrawal from UNESCO in 1985, has not been involved in UCC meetings.

34.2[3] Pan American Copyright Conventions[30]

As of July 13, 1914, the United States ratified the Buenos Aires Copyright Convention of 1910.[31]

34.2[3][a] Eligible Works

Protectible under the Convention are works of "authors or their assigns, citizens or domiciled foreigners"[32] of a signatory country,[33] at least if published.[34]

---

27. UCC art. III(1). The three elements of the form of notice were very specific.
28. UCC art. III(2), (3).
29. UCC art. II(4). *See* note 33 *infra*.
30. Pan American began with the Montevideo Convention (1889), followed by Mexico City (1902), Rio de Janeiro (1906), Buenos Aires (1910), Havana (1928), Washington (1946). Of these six versions, the United States has ratified only two.
31. Replacing the Mexico City Convention of 1902, except with respect to El Salvador. Sound recordings are not mentioned.
32. Buenos Aires Convention art. 6th. It has been contended that both authors and assigns, if any, must be citizens or domiciled foreigners

34.2[3][b] Basic Protection

The copyright includes for its "author or assigns"[35] the "exclusive power of disposing of the same, of publishing, assigning, translating or authorizing its translation and reproducing it in any form whether wholly or in part."[36] The rights enjoyed are those that the "respective laws" of the signatory countries accord, "without those rights being allowed to exceed the term of protection granted in the country of origin."[37]

34.2[3][c] Formalities

The "acknowledgment of a copyright" obtained in one country, "in conformity with its laws," produces its "effects of full right, in all other States," without the necessity of complying with any other formality,[38] provided always that

---

of a signatory country. *See* Note, 69 HARV. L. REV. 1329, 1331 (1947).

33. The Convention is open to adherence only by western hemisphere republics.
34. Quaere, whether an unpublished work is protected. Literally, such protection is not precluded by the provisions of the Buenos Aires Convention.
35. *See* note 32 *supra.*
36. Buenos Aires Convention art. 4th. Quaere, as to the protection of translation rights.
37. Buenos Aires Convention art. 6th, 7th. "Country of origin" is deemed that of its first publication "in America," and if it shall have "appeared simultaneously" in several of the signatory countries, "that which fixes the shortest period of protection." The article 7th definition of "country of origin" literally relates to duration of protection. No minimum period of protection is prescribed.
38. Quaere, whether the required "acknowledgment of copyright" must be in the "country of origin," or that the work must be published in a signatory country by a national thereof. Presumably, once a copyright is acknowledged in any signatory country, in conformity with its laws, compliance with any other formality in any other signatory country (whether a condition precedent to securing or enforcing copyright or a condition subsequent) is not necessary for protection in the latter so long as the work carries a notice reserving the property right. Presumably, the United States form of statutory notice consti-

there appear in the work "a statement that indicates the reservation of the property right."[39]

34.2[3][d] Latin American Signatory Countries

Signatory countries, besides the United States, are Argentina, Bolivia, Brazil, Chile, Colombia, Costa Rica, Dominican Republic, Ecuador, Guatemala, Haiti, Honduras, Mexico, Nicaragua, Panama, Paraguay, Peru, and Uruguay. El Salvador/United States relations are subject to the Mexico City Convention of 1902. Nonsignatory countries include Cuba and Venezuela.[40]

34.2[4] Other Reciprocal Copyright Relations[41]

In addition to their protection under the Berne, Universal, and Pan American Conventions, American works are entitled to national treatment in many foreign countries, including countries adhering to those conventions, under the reciprocal copyright relations between those countries and the United States.

34.2[4][a] Eligible Works

Eligibility for national treatment may exist, as in France, regardless of reciprocity.[42] Many countries extend their pro-

---

tutes "a statement that indicates the reservation of the property right," but the more cautious procedure is to add "all rights reserved" and even to refer to the Pan American Copyright Conventions.

39. Buenos Aires Convention art. 3rd. Article 3rd does not use the terms "country of origin" or "publication."
40. *See* addendum to 17 U.S.C.A. § 104 (Supp.).
41. In a few countries, e. g., France (*see* note 42 *infra*), Luxembourg, and Portugal, reciprocity is not required, but their attitudes promote reciprocity.
42. French Decree of March 28, 1852, a landmark of international copyright progress. Quaere, as to its application to former French colonies. *See* Ginsburg, *French Copyright Law: A Comparative Overview,* 36 J. COPYRIGHT SOC'Y 269 (1989).

tection to works first (or, possibly, "simultaneously") published there, regardless of the nationality of the author.[43] Elsewhere, the basis is reciprocity. Reciprocity may be recognized as a basis for protection in the foreign domestic law itself, in a treaty or other bilateral arrangement between the United States and the foreign country, or in both.[44]

34.2[4][b] Basic Protection

National treatment is the nature of protection afforded by the foreign country. That means treatment on substantially the same basis as that on which the other country extends protection to works of its own nationals and domiciliaries and works first published in that nation. Some countries afford less than adequate protection to their own nationals, thus limiting protection for American works. In developing countries especially, rights of translation, generally out of or into the national language, are not recognized.[45] Also, the duration of protection, at least for specified classes of works, may be less than normal. On the other hand, many countries recognize copyrights for the life of the author plus fifty years without any formalities.

32.2[4][c] Formalities

Under national treatment, protection often accrues automatically upon creation or publication. Formalities are not required by most modern copyright laws. However, some countries do impose such formalities as local registration,

43. Such countries combine nationality-of-work and nationality-of-author principles. *See* notes 7, 10 *supra*.
44. *See* note 40 *supra*. For the converse, United States protection for foreign works, reciprocity is recognized by presidential proclamations. *See* chapter 6, note 17, *supra*.
45. The Berne Convention requires full-term protection for translation rights. Berne Convention art. 8. But see the Stockholm revision of 1967, arts. 22–38.

local deposit, local registration and deposit, notarial certificates, and special forms of notice of copyright.[46]

34.2[4][d] Bilaterally Related Countries

Countries that presumably protect American works are those identified by Presidential Proclamations as eligible for American protection on the basis of reciprocity under section 104.[47]

34.3 Summary

Since the United States became a Berne Union member on March 1, 1989, American works have become eligible for the maximum international copyright protection available under existing systems and circumstances.[48]

The scope and duration of protection varies from country to country, depending on the country's adherence to one or more multilateral or bilateral copyright arrangements with the United States and the other country's own domestic copyright laws. There are a few countries with which the United States has no copyright relations, notably China and Iran. There are a few countries that have not enacted any copyright laws.[49] Even some countries that appear to have

46. Not to mention use of national languages, customs duties, attorneys' fees.
47. *See* chapter 6, note 17, *supra*.
48. Including protection under the UNESCO "Phonogram" Convention of 1971, to which the United States adhered in 1974. *See* note 2 *supra*.
49. E.g., China (almost twenty drafts so far with enactment expected in the 1990s), Saudi Arabia (in drafting process with no deadline). Piracy of American works has been rampant in Brazil, China, Egypt, India, Indonesia, Malaysia, Nigeria, the Philippines, Saudi Arabia, South Korea, Taiwan, and Thailand. China, lacking a copyright law, was the most piratical country, depriving Americans of an estimated $400 million of royalties in 1988. As noted above, the country is working on a copyright law, with a view to adherence to the Berne

copyright systems do not afford much significant protection.

Works in the public domain in the United States may enjoy subsisting copyright protection in foreign countries, and vice versa.

Jurisdiction of American courts over actions for foreign copyright infringement raises many questions. There are complicated international law and procedural problems.[50]

Convention. Shou Kang, *The Berne Union and Developing Countries with Particular Reference to the Peoples' Republic of China*, 11 COLUM.–V.L.A. J.L. & ARTS 121 (1986). *Cf.* New York Chinese TV Programs, Inc. v. U.E. Enters., Inc., Copyright L. Rep. (CCH) ¶ 26,398 (S.D.N.Y. 1989) (Taiwanese films protected in United States under Taiwan Relations Act). The Copyright Office has designated as "unclear" the copyright relations of the United States with Angola, Antigua and Bermuda, Bahrain, Belau, Botswana, Brunei, Burma, Burundi, Cape Verde, Comoros, Djibouti, Dominica, Equatorial Guinea, Gambia, Grenada, Guinea-Bissau, Guyana, Indonesia, Jordan, Democratic People's Republic of Korea, Kuwait, Lesotho, Malaysia, Maldives, Mozambique, Nauru, Papua New Guinea, Saint Christopher and Nevis, Saint Lucia, Sao Tome and Principe, Seychelles, Solomon Islands, Somalia, Sudan, Switzerland, Syria, Tanzania, Tuvalu, Uganda, Vanuatu, Vietnam, Western Samoa, and Yeman (Aden). Designated as "None" were Afghanistan, Albania, Bhutan, Ethiopia, Iran, Iraq, Jamaica, Karibati, Mongolia, Nepal, Oman, Qatar, San Marino, Saudi Arabia, Sierra Leone, Tonga, United Arab Emirates, and Yemen (Sana). Copyright Office Circular 38a (July 1989). Indonesia since has become a presidentially proclaimed country. The "official" listing does not necessarily match the countries listed as problems on the United States Trade Representative's "Priority Watch Lists." *Will the Soviet Union and the People's Republic of China Follow the United States' Adherence to the Berne Convention?*, 13 B.C. INT'L & COMP. L. REV. 207 (1990).

50. Peter Starr Prod. Co. v. Twin Continental Films, Inc., 783 F.2d 1440 (9th Cir. 1986); London Film Prods. Ltd. v. Intercontinental Communications, Inc., 580 F. Supp. 47 (S.D.N.Y. 1984) (causes of action under copyright laws of foreign countries; personal jurisdiction over defendant; transitory cause of action; situs of copyright in domicile of copyright owner; no complexities of formalities in foreign countries involved; not transfer under forum non conveniens since no other available forum). For criticism of the holding of *London Film*, *see* Note, 70 CORNELL L. REV. 1165 (1985). There, of course, would have to

be some basis for federal court jurisdiction other than 28 U.S.C.A. § 1331 (since case not "arising under" 17 U.S.C.A.). Besides the defendant's amenability to process, service of process would be invoked under FED. R. CIV. P. 4; also venue under 28 U.S.C.A. §§ 1391, 1400; transfers under 28 U.S.C.A. § 1406(a).

Appendix A

Copyright Law of the United States of America (United States Code, Title 17 as of January 1, 1991)

Chapter 1—Subject Matter and Scope of Copyright

Sec. 101. Definitions

As used in this title, the following terms and their variant forms mean the following:

An "anonymous work" is a work on the copies or phonorecords of which no natural person is identified as author.

An "architectural work" is the design of a building as embodied in any tangible medium of expression, including a building, architectural plans, or drawings. The work includes the overall form as well as the arrangement and composition of spaces and elements in the design, but does not include individual standard features.

"Audiovisual works" are works that consist of a series of related images which are intrinsically intended to be shown by the use of machines or devices such as projectors, viewers, or electronic equipment, together with accompanying sounds, if any, regardless of the nature of the material objects, such as films or tapes, in which the works are embodied.

The "Berne Convention" is the Convention for the Protection of Literary and Artistic Works, signed at Berne, Switzerland, on September 9, 1986, and all acts, protocols, and revisions thereto.

A work is a "Berne Convention work" if—

(1) in the case of an unpublished work, one or more of the authors is a national of a nation adhering to the Berne Convention, or in the case of a published work, one or more of the authors is a national of a nation adhering to the Berne Convention on the date of first publication;

(2) the work was first published in a nation adhering to the Berne Convention, or was simultaneously first published in a nation adhering to the Berne Convention and in a foreign nation that does not adhere to the Berne Convention;

(3) in the case of an audiovisual work

(A) if one or more of the authors is a legal entity, that author has its headquarters in a nation adhering to the Berne Convention; or

(B) if one or more of the authors is an individual, that author is domiciled, or has his or her habitual residence in, a nation adhering to the Berne Convention;

(4) in the case of a pictorial, graphic, or sculptural work that is incorporated in a building or other structure, the building or structure is located in a nation adhering to the Berne Convention; or

(5) in the case of an architectural work embodied in a building, such building is erected in a country adhering to the Berne Convention.

For purposes of paragraph (1), an author who is domiciled in or had his or her habitual residence in, a nation adhering to the Berne Convention is considered to be a national of that nation. For purposes of paragraph (2), a work is considered to have been simultaneously published in two or more nations if its dates of publication are within 30 days of one another.

The "best edition" of a work is the edition, published in the United States at any time before the date of deposit, that the

Library of Congress determines to be most suitable for its purposes.

A person's "children" are that person's immediate offspring, whether legitimate or not, and any children legally adopted by that person.

A "collective work" is a work, such as a periodical issue, anthology, or encyclopedia, in which a number of contributions, constituting separate and independent works in themselves, are assembled into a collective whole.

A "compilation" is a work formed by the collection and assembling of preexisting materials or of data that are selected, coordinated, or arranged in such a way that the resulting work as a whole constitutes an original work of authorship. The term "compilation" includes collective works.

"Copies" are material objects, other than phonorecords, in which a work is fixed by any method now known or later developed, and from which the work can be perceived, reproduced, or otherwise communicated, either directly or with the aid of a machine or device. The term "copies" includes the material object, other than a phonorecord, in which the work is first fixed.

"Copyright owner," with respect to any one of the exclusive rights comprised in a copyright, refers to the owner of that particular right.

The "country of origin" of a Berne Convention work, for purposes of section 411, is the United States if—

(1) in the case of a published work, the work is first published

(A) in the United States;

(B) simultaneously in the United States and another nation or nations adhering to the Berne Convention, whose law grants a term of copyright protection that is the same as or longer than the term provided in the United States;

(C) simultaneously in the United States and a foreign nation that does not adhere to the Berne Convention; or

(D) in a foreign nation that does not adhere to the Berne Convention and all of the authors of the work are nationals, domiciliaries, or habitual residents of, or in the case of an audiovisual work legal entities with headquarters in, the United States;

(2) in the case of an unpublished work, all the authors of the work are nationals, domiciliaries, or habitual residents of the United States, or, in the case of an unpublished audiovisual work, all the authors are legal entities with headquarters in the United States; or

(3) in the case of a pictorial, graphic, or sculptural work incorporated in a building or structure, the building or structure is located in the United States.

For the purposes of section 411, the "country of origin" of any other Berne Convention work is not the United States.

A work is "created" when it is fixed in a copy or phonorecord for the first time; where a work is prepared over a period of time, the portion of it that has been fixed at any particular time constitutes the work as of that time, and where the work has been prepared in different versions, each version constitutes a separate work.

A "derivative work" is a work based upon one or more preexisting works, such as a translation, musical arrangement, dramatization, fictionalization, motion picture version, sound recording, art reproduction, abridgment, condensation, or any other form in which a work may be recast, transformed, or adapted. A work consisting of editorial revisions, annotations, elaborations, or other modifications which, as a whole, represent an original work of authorship, is a "derivative work.

A "device," "machine," or "process," is one now known or later developed.

To "display" a work means to show a copy of it, either directly or by means of a film, slide, television image, or any other device or process or, in the case of a motion picture or other audiovisual work, to show individual images nonsequentially.

A work is "fixed" in a tangible medium of expression when its embodiment in a copy or phonorecord, by or under the authority of the author, is sufficiently permanent or stable to permit it to be perceived, reproduced, or otherwise communicated for a period of more than transitory duration. A work consisting of sounds, images, or both, that are being transmitted, is "fixed" for purposes of this title if a fixation of the work is being made simultaneously with its transmission.

The terms "including" and "such as" are illustrative and not limitative.

A "joint work" is a work; prepared by two or more authors with the intention that their contributions be merged into inseparable or interdependent parts of a unitary whole.

"Literary works" are works, other than audiovisual works, expressed in words, numbers, or other verbal or numerical symbols or indicia, regardless of the nature of the material objects, such as books, periodicals, manuscripts, phonorecords, film, tapes, disks, or cards in which they are embodied.

"Motion pictures" are audiovisual works consisting of a series of related images which, when shown in succession, impart an impression of motion, together with accompanying sounds, if any.

To "perform" a work means to recite, render, play, dance, or act it, either directly or by means of any device or process or, in the case of a motion picture or other audiovisual work, to show its images in any sequence or to make the sounds accompanying it audible.

"Phonorecords" are material objects in which sounds, other than those accompanying a motion picture or other audiovisual work, are fixed by any method now known or later developed, and from which the sounds can be perceived, reproduced, or otherwise communicated, either directly or with the aid of a machine or device. The term "phonorecords" includes the material object in which the sounds are first fixed.

"Pictorial, graphic, and sculptural works" include two-dimensional and three-dimensional works of fine, graphic, and applied art, photographs, prints and art reproductions, maps, globes, charts, diagrams, models, and technical drawings including architectural plans. Such works shall include works of artistic craftsmanship insofar as their form but not their mechanical or utilitarian aspects are concerned; the design of a useful article, as defined in this section, shall be considered a pictorial, graphic, or sculptural work only if, and only to the extent that, such design incorporates pictorial, graphic, or sculptural features that can be identified separately from, and are capable of existing independently of, the utilitarian aspects of the article.

A "pseudonymous work" is a work on the copies or phonorecords of which the author is identified under a fictitious name.

"Publication" is the distribution of copies or phonorecords of a work to the public by sale or other transfer of ownership, or by rental, lease, or lending. The offering to distribute copies or phonorecords to a group of persons for purposes of further distribution, public performance, or public display, constitutes publication.

A public performance or display of a work does not of itself constitute publication.

To perform or display a work "publicly" means—

(1) to perform or display it at a place open to the public or at any place where a substantial number of persons outside of a normal circle of a family and its social acquaintances is gathered; or

(2) to transmit or otherwise communicate a performance or display of the work to a place specified by clause (1) or to the public, by means of any device or process, whether the members of the public capable of receiving the performance or display receive it in the same place or in separate places and at the same time or at different times.

"Sound recordings" are works that result from the fixation of a series of musical, spoken, or other sounds, but not including the sounds accompanying a motion picture or other audiovisual work, regardless of the nature of the material objects, such as disks, tapes, or other phonorecords, in which they are embodied.

"State" includes the District of Columbia and the Commonwealth of Puerto Rico, and any territories to which this title is made applicable by an Act of Congress.

A "transfer of copyright ownership" is an assignment, mortgage, exclusive license, or any other conveyance, alienation, or hypothecation of a copyright or of any of the exclusive rights comprised in a copyright, whether or not it is limited in time or place of effect, but not including a nonexclusive license.

A "transmission program" is a body of material that as an aggregate, has been produced for the sole purpose of transmission to the public in sequence and as a unit.

To "transmit" a performance or display is to communicate it by any device or process whereby images or sounds are received beyond the place from which they are sent.

The "United States" when used in a geographical sense, comprises the several States, the District of Columbia and the Commonwealth of Puerto Rico, and the organized territories under the jurisdiction of the United States Government.

A "useful article" is an article having an intrinsic utilitarian function that is not merely to portray the appearance of the article or to convey information. An article that is normally a part of a useful article is considered a "useful article."

The author's "widow" or "widower" is the author's surviving spouse under the law of the author's domicile at the time of his or her death, whether or not the spouse has later remarried.

A "work of visual art" is—

(1) a painting, drawing, print, or sculpture, existing in a single copy, in a limited edition of 200 copies or fewer that are signed and consecutively numbered by the author, or, in the case of a sculpture, in multiple cast, carved, or fabricated sculptures of 200 or fewer that are consecutively numbered by the author and bear the signature or other identifying mark of the author; or

(2) a still photographic image produced for exhibition purposes only, existing in a single copy that is signed by the author, or in a limited edition of 200 copies or fewer that are signed and consecutively numbered by the author.

A work of visual art does not include—

(A)(i) any poster, map globe, chart, technical drawing, diagram, model, applied art, motion picture or other audiovisual work, book, magazine, newspaper, periodical, data base, electronic information service, electronic publication, or similar publication;

(ii) any merchandising item or advertising, promotional, descriptive, covering, or packaging material or container;

(iii) any portion or part of any item described in clause (i) or (ii);

(B) any work made for hire; or

(C) any work not subject to copyright protection under this title.

A "work of the United States Government" is a work prepared by an officer or employee of the United States Government as part of that person's official duties.

A "work made for hire" is—

(1) a work prepared by an employee within the scope of his or her employment; or

(2) a work specially ordered or commissioned for use as a contribution to a collective work, as a part of a motion picture or other audiovisual work, as a translation, as a supplementary work, as a compilation, as an instructional text, as a test, as answer material for a test, or as an atlas, if the parties expressly agree in a written instrument signed by them that the work shall be considered a work made for hire. For the purpose of the foregoing sentence, a "supplementary work" is a work prepared for publication as a secondary adjunct to a work by another author for the purpose of introducing, concluding, illustrating, explaining, revising, commenting upon, or assisting in the use of the other work, such as forewords, afterwords, pictorial illustrations maps, charts, tables, editorial notes, musical arrangements, answer material for tests, bibliographies, appendixes, and indexes, and an "instructional text" is a literary pictorial, or graphic work prepared for publication with the purpose of use in systematic instructional activities.

A "computer program" is a set of statements or instructions to be used directly or indirectly in a computer in order to bring about a certain result.

Sec. 102. Subject Matter of Copyright: In General

(a) Copyright protection subsists, in accordance with this title, in original works of authorship fixed in any tangible medium of expression, now known or later developed, from which they can be perceived, reproduced, or otherwise communicated, either directly or with the aid of a machine or device. Works of authorship include the following categories:

(1) literary works;
(2) musical works, including any accompanying words;
(3) dramatic works, including any accompanying music;
(4) pantomimes and choreographic works;
(5) pictorial, graphic, and sculptural works;
(6) motion pictures and other audiovisual works;

(7) sound recordings; and
(8) architectural works.

(b) In no case does copyright protection for an original work of authorship extend to any idea, procedure, process, system, method of operation, concept, principle, or discovery, regardless of the form in which it is described, explained, illustrated, or embodied in such work.

Sec. 103. Subject Matter of Copyright: Compilations and Derivative Works

(a) The subject matter of copyright as specified by section 102 includes compilations and derivative works, but protection for a work employing preexisting material in which copyright subsists does not extend to any part of the work in which such material has been used unlawfully.

(b) The copyright in a compilation or derivative work extends only to the material contributed by the author of such work, as distinguished from the preexisting material employed in the work, and does not imply any exclusive right in the preexisting material. The copyright in such work is independent of, and does not affect or enlarge the scope, duration, ownership, or subsistence of, any copyright protection in the preexisting material.

Sec. 104. Subject Matter of Copyright: National Origin

(a) UNPUBLISHED WORKS.—The works specified by sections 102 and 103, while unpublished, are subject to protection under this title without regard to the nationality or domicile of the author.

(b) PUBLISHED WORKS.—The works specified by sections 102 and 103, when published, are subject to protection under this title if—

(1) on the date of first publication, one or more of the authors is a national or domiciliary of the United States, or is a national, domiciliary, or sovereign authority of a foreign nation that is a party to a copyright treaty to which the United States is also a party, or is a stateless person, wherever that person may be domiciled; or

(2) the work is first published in the United States or in a foreign nation that, on the date of first publications, is a party to the Universal Copyright Convention; or

(3) the work is first published by the United Nations or any of its specialized agencies, or by the Organization of American States; or

(4) the work is a Berne Convention work; or

(5) the work comes within the scope of a Presidential proclamation. Whenever the President finds that a particular foreign nation extends, to works by authors who are nationals or domiciliaries of the United States or to works that are first published in the United States, copyright protection on substantially the same basis as that on which the foreign nation extends protection to works of its own nationals and domiciliaries and works first published in that nation, the President may by proclamation extend protection under this title to works of which one or more of the authors is, on the date of first publication, a national, domiciliary, or sovereign authority of that nation, or which was first published in that nation. The President may revise, suspend, or revoke any such proclamation or impose any conditions or limitations on protection under a proclamation.

(c) EFFECT OF BERNE CONVENTION.—No right or interest in a work eligible for protection under this title may be claimed by virtue of, or in reliance upon, the provisions of the Berne Convention, or the adherence of the United States thereto. Any rights in a work eligible for protection under this title that derive from this title, other Federal or State statutes, or the common law, shall not be expanded or reduced by virtue of, or in reliance upon, the provisions of the Berne Convention, or the adherence of the United States thereto.

Sec. 105. Subject Matter of Copyright: United States Government Works

Copyright protection under this title is not available for any work of the United States Government, but the United States Government is not precluded from receiving and holding copyrights transferred to it by assignment, bequest, or otherwise.

Sec. 106. Exclusive Rights in Copyrighted Works

Subject to sections 107 through 120, the owner of copyright under this title has the exclusive rights to do and to authorize any of the following:

(1) To reproduce the copyrighted work in copies or phonorecords;

(2) to prepare derivative works based upon the copyrighted work;

(3) to distribute copies or phonorecords of the copyrighted work to the public by sale or other transfer of ownership, or by rental, lease, or lending;

(4) in the case of literary, musical, dramatic, and choreographic works, pantomimes, and motion pictures and other audiovisual works, to perform the copyrighted work publicly; and

(5) in the case of literary, musical, dramatic, and choreographic works, pantomimes, and pictorial, graphic, or sculptural works, including the individual images of a motion picture or other audiovisual work, to display the copyrighted work publicly.

[Note: section 106A becomes effective June 1, 1991.]

Sec. 106A. Rights of Certain Authors to Attribution and Integrity

(a) RIGHTS OF ATTRIBUTION AND INTEGRITY.—Subject to section 107 and independent of the exclusive rights provided in section 106, the author of a work of visual art—

(1) shall have the right—

(A) to claim authorship of that work, and

(B) to prevent the use of his or her name as the author of any work of visual art which he or she did not create;

(2) shall have the right to prevent the use of his or her name as the author of the work of visual art in the event of a distortion, mutilation, or other modification of the work which would be prejudicial to his or her honor or reputation; and

(3) subject to the limitations set forth in section 113(d), shall have the right

(A) to prevent any intentional distortion, mutilation, or

other modification of that work which would be prejudicial to his or her honor or reputation, and any intentional distortion, mutilation, or modification of that work is a violation of that right, and

(B) to prevent any destruction of a work of recognized stature, and any intentional or grossly negligent destruction of that work is a violation of that right.

(b) SCOPE AND EXERCISE OF RIGHTS.—Only the author of a work of visual art has the rights conferred by subsection (a) in that work, whether or not the author is the copyright owner. The authors of a joint work of visual art are coowners of the rights conferred by subsection (a) in that work.

(c) EXCEPTIONS.—(1) The modification of a work of visual art which is a result of the passage of time or the inherent nature of the materials is not distortion, mutilation, or other modification described in subsection (a)(3)(A).

(2) The modification of a work of visual art which is the result of conservation, or of the public presentation, including lighting and placement, of the work is not a destruction, distortion, mutilation, or other modification described in subsection (a)(3) unless the modification is caused by gross negligence.

(3) The rights described in paragraphs (1) and (2) of subsection (a) shall not apply to any reproduction, depiction, portrayal, or other use of a work in, upon, or in any connection with any item described in subparagraph (A) or (B) of the definition of "work of visual art" in section 101, and any such reproduction depiction, portrayal, or other use of a work is not a destruction, distortion mutilation, or other modification described in paragraph (3) of subsection (a).

(d) DURATION OF RIGHTS.—(1) With respect to works of visual art created on or after the effective date set forth in section 610(a) of the Visual Artists Rights Act of l990, the rights conferred by subsection (a) shall endure for a term consisting of the life of the author.

(2) With respect to works of visual art created before the effective date set forth in section 610(a) of the Visual Artists Rights Act of 1990, but title to which has not, as of such effective date, been transferred from the author, the rights conferred

by subsection (a) shall be coextensive with, and shall expire at the same time as, the rights conferred by section 106.

(3) In the case of a joint work prepared by two or more authors, the rights conferred by subsection (a) shall endure for a term consisting of the life of the last surviving author.

(4) All terms of the rights conferred by subsection (a) run to the end of the calendar year in which they would otherwise expire.

(e) TRANSFER AND WAIVER.—(1) The rights conferred by subsection (a) may not he transferred, but those rights may be waived if the author expressly agrees to such waiver in a written instrument signed by the author. Such instrument shall specifically identify the work, and uses of that work, to which the waiver applies, and the waiver shall apply only to the work and uses so identified. In the case of a joint work prepared by two or more authors, a waiver of rights under this paragraph made by one such author waives such rights for all such authors.

(2) Ownership of the rights conferred by subsection (a) with respect to a work of visual art is distinct from ownership of any copy of that work, or of a copyright or any exclusive right under a copyright in that work. Transfer of ownership of any copy of a work of visual art, or of a copyright or any exclusive right under copyright, shall not constitute a waiver of the rights conferred by subsection (a). Except as may otherwise be agreed by the author in a written instrument signed by the author, a waiver of the rights conferred by subsection (a) with respect to a work of visual art shall not constitute a transfer of ownership of any copy of that work, or of ownership of a copyright or of any exclusive right under a copyright in that work.

Sec. 107. Limitations on Exclusive Rights: Fair Use

Notwithstanding the provisions of sections 106 and 106A, the fair use of a copyrighted work, including such use by reproduction in copies or phonorecords or by any other means specified by that section, for purposes such as criticism, comment, news reporting, teaching (including multiple copies for classroom use), scholarship, or research, is not an infringement of copyright. In determining whether the use made of a work in any particular case is a fair use the factors to be considered shall include—

(1) the purpose and character of the use, including whether such use is of a commercial nature or is for nonprofit educational purposes;

(2) the nature of the copyrighted work;

(3) the amount and substantiality of the portion used in relation to the copyrighted work as a whole; and

(4) the effect of the use upon the potential market for or value of the copyrighted work.

Sec. 108. Limitations on Exclusive Rights: Reproduction by Libraries and Archives

(a) Notwithstanding the provisions of section 106, it is not an infringement of copyright for a library or archives, or any of its employees acting within the scope of their employment, to reproduce no more than one copy or phonorecord of a work, or to distribute such copy or phonorecord, under the conditions specified by this section, if—

(1) the reproduction or distribution is made without any purpose of direct or indirect commercial advantage;

(2) the collections of the library or archives are (i) open to the public, or (ii) available not only to researchers affiliated with the library or archives or with the institution of which it is a part, but also to other persons doing research in a specialized field; and

(3) the reproduction or distribution of the work includes a notice of copyright.

(b) The rights of reproduction and distribution under this section apply to a copy or phonorecord of an unpublished work duplicated in facsimile form solely for purposes of preservation and security or for deposit for research use in another library or archives of the type described by clause (2) of subsection (a), if the copy or phonorecord reproduced is currently in the collections of the library or archives.

(c) The right of reproduction under this section applies to a copy or phonorecord of a published work duplicated in facsimile form solely for the purpose of replacement of a copy or phonorecord that is damaged, deteriorating, lost, or stolen, if the library or archives has, after a reasonable effort, determined that an unused replacement cannot he obtained at a fair price.

(d) The rights of reproduction and distribution under this section apply to a copy, made from the collection of a library or archives where the user makes his or her request or from that of another library or archives, of no more than one article or other contribution to a copyrighted collection or periodical issue, or to a copy or phonorecord of a small part of any other copyrighted work, if

(1) the copy or phonorecord becomes the property of the user, and the library or archives has had no notice that the copy or phonorecord would be used for any purpose other than private study, scholarship, or research; and

(2) the library or archives displays prominently, at the place where orders are accepted, and includes on its order form, a warning of copyright in accordance with requirements that the Register of Copyrights shall prescribe by regulation.

(e) The rights of reproduction and distribution under this section apply to the entire work, or to a substantial part of it, made from the collection of a library or archives where the user makes his or her request or from that of another library or archives, if the library or archives has first determined, on the basis of a reasonable investigation, that a copy or phonorecord of the copyrighted work cannot be obtained at a fair price,

(1) the copy or phonorecord becomes the property of the user, and the library or archives has had no notice that the copy or phonorecord would be used for any purpose other than private study, scholarship, or research; and

(2) the library or archives displays prominently, at the place where orders are accepted, and includes on its order from, a warning of copyright in accordance with requirements that the Register of Copyrights shall prescribe by regulation.

(f) Nothing in this section—

(1) shall be construed to impose liability for copyright infringement upon a library or archives or its employees for the unsupervised use of reproducing equipment located on its premises: *Provided,* That such equipment displays a notice that

the making of a copy may be subject to the copyright law;

(2) excuses a person who uses such reproducing equipment or who requests a copy or phonorecord under subsection (d) from liability for copyright infringement for any such act, or for any later use of such copy or phonorecord, if it exceeds fair use as provided by section 107;

(3) shall be construed to limit the reproduction and distribution by lending of a limited number of copies and excerpts by a library or archives of an audiovisual news program, subject to clauses (1), (2), and (3) of subsection (a); or

(4) in any way affects the right of fair use as provided by section 107, or any contractual obligations assumed at any time by the library or archives when it obtained a copy or phonorecord of a work in its collections.

(g) The rights of reproduction and distribution under this section extend to the isolated and unrelated reproduction or distribution of a single copy or phonorecord of the same material on separate occasions, but do not extend to cases where the library or archives, or its employee—

(1) is aware or has substantial reason to believe that it is engaging in the related or concerted reproduction or distribution of multiple copies or phonorecords of the same material, whether made on one occasion or over a period of time, and whether intended for aggregate use by one or more individuals or for separate use by the individual members of a group; or

(2) engages in the systematic reproduction or distribution of single or multiple copies or phonorecords of material described in subsection (d): *Provided,* That nothing in this clause prevents a library or archives from participating in interlibrary arrangements that do not have, as their purpose or effect, that the library or archives receiving such copies or phonorecords for distribution does so in such aggregate quantities as to substitute for a subscription to or purchase of such work.

(h) The rights of reproduction and distribution under this section do not apply to a musical work, a pictorial, graphic or sculptural work, or a motion picture or other audiovisual work other than an audiovisual work dealing with news, except that no such limitation shall apply with respect to rights granted by subsections (b) and (c), or with respect to pictorial or graphic works published as illustrations, diagrams, or similar adjuncts to works of which copies are reproduced or distributed in accordance with subsections (d) and (e).

(i) Five years from the effective date of this Act, and at five-year intervals thereafter, the Register of Copyrights, after consulting with representatives of authors, book and periodical publishers, and other owners of copyrighted materials, and with representatives of library users and librarians, shall submit to the Congress a report setting forth the extent to which this section has achieved the intended statutory balancing of the rights of creators, and the needs of users. The report should also describe any problems that may have arisen, and present legislative or other recommendations, if warranted.

Sec. 109. Limitations on Exclusive Rights: Effect of Transfer of Particular Copy or Phonorecord

(a) Notwithstanding the provisions of section 106(3), the owner of a particular copy or phonorecord lawfully made under this title, or any person authorized by such owner, is entitled, without the authority of the copyright owner, to sell or otherwise dispose of the possession of that copy or phonorecord.

(b)(1)(A) Notwithstanding the provisions of subsection (a), unless authorized by the owners of copyright in the sound recording or the owner of copyright in a computer program (including any tape, disk, or other medium embodying such program), and in the case of a sound recording in the musical works embodied therein, neither the owner of a particular phonorecord nor any person in possession of a particular copy of a computer program (including any tape, disk, or other medium embodying such program), may, for the purposes of direct or indirect commercial advantage, dispose of, or authorize the disposal of, the possession of that phonorecord or computer program (including any tape, disk or other medium embodying such program) by rental, lease, or lending, or by any other act or practice in the nature of rental, lease, or lending. Nothing in the preceding sentence shall apply to the rental, lease, or lending of a phonorecord for nonprofit purposes by a nonprofit library or nonprofit educational institution. The transfer of possession of a lawfully made copy of a computer program by a nonprofit educational institution to another nonprofit educational institution or to faculty, staff, and students does not constitute rental, lease, or lending for direct or indirect commercial purposes under this subsection.

(B) This subsection does not apply to—

(i) a computer program which is embodied in a machine or product and which cannot be copied during the ordinary operation or use of the machine or product; or

(ii) a computer program embodied in or used in conjunction with a limited purpose computer that is designed for playing video games and may be designed for other purposes.

(C) Nothing in this subsection affects any provision of chapter 9 of this title [The Semiconductor Chip Protection Act of 1984].

(2)(A) Nothing in this subsection shall apply to the lending of a computer program for nonprofit purposes by a nonprofit library, if each copy of a computer program which is lent by such library has affixed to the packaging containing the program a warning of copyright in accordance with requirements that the Register of Copyrights shall prescribe by regulation.

(B) Not later than three years after the date of the enactment of the Computer Software Rental Amendments Act of 1990, and at such times thereafter as the Register of Copyrights considers appropriate, the Register of Copyrights, after consultation with representatives of copyright owners and librarians, shall submit to the Congress a report stating whether this paragraph has achieved its intended purpose of maintaining the integrity of the copyright system while providing nonprofit libraries the capability to fulfill their function. Such report shall advise the Congress as to any information or recommendations that the Register of Copyrights considers necessary to carry out the purposes of this subsection.

(3) Nothing in this subsection shall affect any provision of the antitrust laws. For purposes of the proceeding sentence, "antitrust laws" has the meaning given that term in the first section of the Clayton Act and includes section 5 of the Federal Trade Commission Act to the extent that section relates to unfair methods of competition

(4) Any person who distributes a phonorecord or a copy of a computer program (including any tape, disk, or other medium embodying such program) in violation of paragraph (1) is an infringer of copyright under section 501 of this title and is subject to the remedies set forth in sections 502, 503, 504, 505, and 509. Such violation shall not be a criminal offense under section 506 or cause such person to be subject to the criminal penalties set forth in section 2319 of title 18.

(c) Notwithstanding the provisions of section 106(5), the owner of a particular copy lawfully made under this title, or any person authorized by such owner, is entitled, without the authority of the copyright owner, to display that copy publicly, either directly or by the projection of no more than one image at a time, to viewers presently at the place where the copy is located.

(d) The privileges prescribed by subsections (a) and (c) do not, unless authorized by the copyright owner, extend to any person who has acquired possession of the copy or phonorecord from the copyright owner, by rental, lease, loan, or otherwise, without acquiring ownership of it.

[Note: subsection (e) becomes effective Dec. 1, 1991.]

(e) Notwithstanding the provisions of sections 106(4) and 106(5), in the case of an electronic audiovisual game intended for use in coin-operated equipment, the owner of a particular copy of such a game lawfully made under this title, is entitled, without the authority of the copyright owner of the game, to publicly perform or display that game in coin-operated equipment, except that this subsection shall not apply to any work of authorship embodied in the audiovisual game if the copyright owner of the electronic audiovisual game is not also the copyright owner of the work of authorship.

Sec. 110. Limitations on Exclusive Rights: Exemption of Certain Performances and Displays

Notwithstanding the provisions of section 106, the following are not infringements of copyright:

(1) performance or display of a work by instructors or pupils in the course of face-to-face teaching activities of a nonprofit educational institution, in a classroom or similar place devoted to instruction, unless, in the case of a motion picture or other audiovisual work, the performance, or the display of individual images, is given by means of a copy that was not lawfully made under this title, and that the person responsible for the performance knew or had reason to believe was not lawfully made;

(2) performance of a nondramatic literary or musical work or display of a work, by or in the course of a transmission, if—

(A) the performance or display is a regular part of the systematic instructional activities of a governmental body or a nonprofit educational institution; and

(B) the performance or display is directly related and of material assistance to the teaching content of the transmission; and

(C) the transmission is made primarily for—

(i) reception in classrooms or similar places normally devoted to instruction, or

(ii) reception by persons to whom the transmission is directed because their disabilities or other special circumstances prevent their attendance in classrooms or similar places normally devoted to instruction, or

(iii) reception by officers or employees of governmental bodies as a part of their official duties or employment;

(3) performance of a nondramatic literary or musical work or of a dramatico-musical work of a religious nature, or display of a work, in the course of services at a place of worship or other religious assembly;

(4) performance of a nondramatic literary or musical work otherwise than in a transmission to the public, without any purpose of direct or indirect commercial advantage and without

payment of any fee or other compensation for the performance to any of its performers, promoters, or organizers,

(A) there is no direct or indirect admission charge: or

(B) the proceeds, after deducting the reasonable costs of producing the performance, are used exclusively for educational, religious, or charitable purposes, and not for private financial gain, except where the copyright owner has served notice of objection to the performance under the following conditions;

(i) the notice shall be in writing and signed by the copyright owner or such owner's duly authorized agent: and

(ii) the notice shall be served on the person responsible for the performance at least seven days before the date of the performance, and shall state the reasons for the objection; and

(iii) the notice shall comply, in form, content, and manner of service, with requirements that the Register of Copyrights shall prescribe by regulation;

(5) communication of a transmission embodying a performance or display of a work by the public reception of the transmission on a single receiving apparatus of a kind commonly used in private homes, unless—

(A) a direct charge is made to see or hear the transmission; or

(B) the transmission thus received is further transmitted to the public;

(6) performance of a nondramatic musical work by a governmental body or a nonprofit agricultural or horticultural organization, in the course of an annual agricultural or horticultural fair or exhibition conducted by such body or organization; the exemption provided by this clause shall extend to any liability for copyright infringement that would otherwise be imposed on such body or organization, under doctrines of vicarious liability or related infringement, for a performance by a concessionnaire, business establishment, or other person at such fair or exhibition, but shall not excuse any such person from liability for the performance;

(7) performance of a nondramatic musical work by a vending

establishment open to the public at large without any direct or indirect admission charge, where the sole purpose of the performance is to promote the retail sale of copies or phonorecords of the work, and the performance is not transmitted beyond the place where the establishment is located and is within the immediate area where the sale is occurring;

(8) performance of a nondramatic literary work, by or in the course of a transmission specifically designed for and primarily directed to blind or other handicapped persons who are unable to read normal printed material as a result of their handicap, or deaf or other handicapped persons who are unable to hear the aural signals accompanying a transmission of visual signals, if the performance is made without any purpose of direct or indirect commercial advantages and its transmission is made through the facilities of: (i) a governmental body; or (ii) a noncommercial educational broadcast station (as defined in section 397 of title 47); or (iii) a radio subcarrier authorization (as defined in 47 CFR 73.293-73.295 and 73.593-73.595); or (iv) a cable system (as defined in section 111(f));

(9) performance on a single occasion of a dramatic literary work published at least ten years before the date of the performance, by or in the course of a transmission specifically designed for and primarily directed to blind or other handicapped persons who are unable to read normal printed material as a result of their handicap, if the performance is made without any purpose of direct or indirect commercial advantage and its transmission is made through the facilities of a radio subcarrier authorization referred to in clause (8)(iii), *Provided*, That the provisions of this clause shall not be applicable to more than one performance of the same work by the same performers or under the auspices of the same organization.

(10) notwithstanding paragraph 4 above, the following is not an infringement of copyright: performance of a nondramatic literary or musical work in the course of a social function which is organized and promoted by a nonprofit veterans' organization or a nonprofit fraternal organization to which the general public is not invited, but not including the invitees of the organizations, if the proceeds from the performance, after deducting the

reasonable costs of producing the performance, are used exclusively for charitable purposes and not for financial gain. For purposes of this section the social functions of any college or university fraternity or sorority shall not be included unless the social function is held solely to raise funds for a specific charitable purpose.

Sec. 111. Limitations on Exclusive Rights: Secondary Transmissions

(a) CERTAIN SECONDARY TRANSMISSIONS EXEMPTED.—The secondary transmission of a primary transmission embodying a performance or display of a work is not an infringement of copyright if—

(1) the secondary transmission is not made by a cable system, and consists entirely of the relaying, by the management of a hotel, apartment house, or similar establishment, of signals transmitted by a broadcast station licensed by the Federal Communications Commission, within the local service area of such station, to the private lodgings of guests or residents of such establishment, and no direct charge is made to see or hear the secondary transmission; or

(2) the secondary transmission is made solely for the purpose and under the conditions specified by clause (2) of section 110; or

(3) the secondary transmission is made by any carrier who has no direct or indirect control over the content or selection of the primary transmission or over the particular recipients of the secondary transmission, and whose activities with respect to the secondary transmission consist solely of providing wires, cables, or other communications channels for the use of others: *Provided,* That the provisions of this clause extend only to the activities of said carrier with respect to secondary transmissions and do not exempt from liability the activities of others with respect to their own primary or secondary transmissions; or

(4) the secondary transmission is not made by a cable system but is made by a governmental body, or other nonprofit organization, without any purpose of direct or indirect commercial advantage, and without charge to the recipients of the secondary transmission other than assessments necessary to defray the

actual and reasonable costs of maintaining and operating the secondary transmission service.

(b) SECONDARY TRANSMISSION OF PRIMARY TRANSMISSION TO CONTROLLED GROUP.—Notwithstanding the provisions of subsections (a) and (c), the secondary transmission to the public of a primary transmission embodying a performance or display of a work is actionable as an act of infringement under section 501, and is fully subject to the remedies provided by sections 502 through 506 and 509, if the primary transmission is not made for reception by the public at large but is controlled and limited to reception by particular members of the public: *Provided*, however, That such secondary transmission is not actionable as an act of infringement if—

(1) the primary transmission is made by a broadcast station licensed by the Federal Communications Commission; and

(2) the carriage of the signals comprising the secondary transmission is required under the rules, regulations, or authorizations of the Federal Communications Commission; and

(3) the signal of the primary transmitter is not altered or changed in any way by the secondary transmitter.

(c) SECONDARY TRANSMISSIONS BY CABLE SYSTEMS.—

(1) Subject to the provisions of clauses (2), (3), and (4) of this subsection, secondary transmissions to the public by a cable system of a primary transmission made by a broadcast station licensed by the Federal Communications Commission or by an appropriate governmental authority of Canada or Mexico and embodying a performance or display of a work shall be subject to compulsory licensing upon compliance with the requirements of subsection (d) where the carriage of the signals comprising the secondary transmission is permissible under the rules, regulations, or authorizations of the Federal Communications Commission.

(2) Notwithstanding the provisions of clause (1) of this subsection, the willful or repeated secondary transmission to the public by a cable system of a primary transmission made by a broadcast station licensed by the Federal Communications Commission or by an appropriate governmental authority of Canada or Mexico and embodying a performance or display of a work is actionable as an act of infringement under section 501, and is

fully subject to the remedies provided by sections 502 through 506 and 509, in the following cases:

(A) where the carriage of the signals comprising the secondary transmission is not permissible under the rules, regulations, or authorizations of the Federal Communications Commission; or

(B) where the cable system has not recorded the notice specified by subsection (d) and deposited the statement of account and royalty fee required by subsection (d).

(3) Notwithstanding the provisions of clause (1) of this subsection and subject to the provisions of subsection (e) of this section, the secondary transmission to the public by a cable system of a primary transmission made by a broadcast station licensed by the Federal Communications Commission or by an appropriate governmental authority of Canada or Mexico and embodying a performance or display of a work is actionable as an act of infringement under section 501, and is fully subject to the remedies provided by sections 502 through 506 and sections 509 and 510, if the content of the particular program in which the performance or display is embodied, or any commercial advertising or station announcements transmitted by the primary transmitter during, or immediately before or after, the transmission of such program, is in any way willfully altered by the cable system through changes, deletions, or additions, except for the alteration, deletion, or substitution of commercial advertisements performed by those engaged in television commercial advertising market research: *Provided*, That the research company has obtained the prior consent of the advertiser who has purchased the original commercial advertisement, the television station broadcasting that commercial advertisement, and the cable system performing the secondary transmissions: *And provided further*, That such commercial alteration, deletion, or substitution is not performed for the purpose of deriving income from the sale of that commercial time.

(4) Notwithstanding the provisions of clause (1) of this subsection, the secondary transmission to the public by a cable system of a primary transmission made by a broadcast station licensed by an appropriate governmental authority of Canada or Mexico and embodying a performance or display of a work is

actionable as an act of infringement under section 501, and is fully subject to the remedies provided by sections 502 through 506 and section 509, if (A) with respect to Canadian signals, the community of the cable system is located more than 150 miles from the United States-Canadian border and is also located south of the forty second parallel of latitude, or (B) with respect to Mexican signals, the secondary transmission is made by a cable system which received the primary transmission by means other than direct interception of a free space radio wave emitted by such broadcast television station, unless prior to April 15, 1976, such cable system was actually carrying, or was specifically authorized to carry, the signal of such foreign station on the system pursuant to the rules, regulations, or authorizations of the Federal Communications Commission.

(d) COMPULSORY LICENSE FOR SECONDARY TRANSMISSIONS BY CABLE SYSTEMS.—

(1) For any secondary transmission to be subject to compulsory licensing under subsection (c), the cable system shall, at least one month before the date of the commencement of operations of the cable system or within one hundred and eighty days after the enactment of this Act, whichever is later, and thereafter within thirty days after each occasion on which the ownership or control or the signal carriage complement of the cable system changes, record in the Copyright Office a notice including a statement of the identity and address of the person who owns or operates the secondary transmission service or has power to exercise primary control over it, together with the name and location of the primary transmitter or primary transmitters whose signals are regularly carried by the cable system, and thereafter, from time to time, such further information as the Register of Copyrights, after consultation with the Copyright Royalty Tribunal (if and when the Tribunal has been constituted), shall prescribe by regulation to carry out the purpose of this clause.

(2) A cable system whose secondary transmissions have been subject to compulsory licensing under subsection (c) shall, on a semiannual basis, deposit with the Register of Copyrights, in accordance with requirements that the Register shall, after consultation with the Copyright Royalty Tribunal (if and when the

Tribunal has been constituted), prescribe by regulation—

(A) a statement of account, covering the six months next preceding, specifying the number of channels on which the cable system made secondary transmissions to its subscribers, the names and locations of all primary transmitters whose transmissions were further transmitted by the cable system, the total number of subscribers, the gross amounts paid to the cable system for the basic service of providing secondary transmissions of primary broadcast transmitters, and such other data as the Register of Copyrights may, after consultation with the Copyright Royalty Tribunal (if and when the Tribunal has been constituted). from time to time prescribe by regulation. Such statement shall also include a special statement of account covering any nonnetwork television programming that was carried by the cable system in whole or in part beyond the local service area of the primary transmitter, under rules, regulations, or authorizations of the Federal Communications Commission permitting the substitution or addition of signals under certain circumstances, together with logs showing the times, dates, stations, and programs involved in such substituted or added carriage; and (B) except in the case of a cable system whose royalty is specified in subclause (C) or (D), a total royalty fee for the period covered by the statement, computed on the basis of specified percentages of the gross receipts from subscribers to the cable service during said period for the basic service of providing secondary transmissions of primary broadcast transmitters, as follows:

(i) 0.675 of 1 per centum of such gross receipts for the privilege of further transmitting any nonnetwork programing of a primary transmitter in whole or in part beyond the local service area of such primary transmitter, such amount to be applied against the fee, if any, payable pursuant to paragraphs (ii) through (iv);

(ii) 0. 675 of 1 per centum of such gross receipts for the first distant signal equivalent;

(iii) 0.425 of 1 per centum of such gross receipts for each of the second, third, and fourth distant signal equivalents;

(iv) 0.2 of 1 per centum of such gross receipts for the

fifth distant signal equivalent and each additional distant signal equivalent thereafter; and

In computing the amounts payable under paragraph (ii) through (iv), above, any fraction of a distant signal equivalent shall be computed at its fractional value and, in the case of any cable system located partly within and partly without the local service area of a primary transmitter gross receipts shall be limited to those gross receipts derived from subscribers located without the local service area of such primary transmitter; and

(C) if the actual gross receipts paid by subscribers to a cable system for the period covered by the statement for the basic service of providing secondary transmissions of primary broadcast transmitters total $80,000 or less, gross receipts of the cable system for the purpose of this subclause shall be computed by subtracting from such actual gross receipts the amount by which $80,000 exceeds such actual gross receipts, except that in no case shall a cable system's gross receipts be reduced to less than $3,000. The royalty fee payable under this subclause shall be 0.5 of 1 per centum, regardless of the number of distant signal equivalents, if any; and

(D) if the actual gross receipts paid by subscribers to a cable system for the period covered by the statement, for the basic service of providing secondary transmissions of primary broadcast transmitters, are more than $80,000 but less than $160,000, the royalty fee payable under this subclause shall be (i) 0.5 of 1 per centum of any gross receipts up to $80.000; and (ii) 1 per centum of any gross receipts in excess of $80,000 but less than $160,000, regardless of the number of distant signal equivalents, if any.

(3) The Register of Copyrights shall receive all fees deposited under this section and, after deducting the reasonable costs incurred by the Copyright Office under this section, shall deposit the balance in the Treasury of the United States, in such manner as the Secretary of the Treasury directs. All funds held by the Secretary of the Treasury shall be invested in interest-bearing United States securities for later distribution with interest by the Copyright Royalty Tribunal as provided by this title.

The Register shall submit to the Copyright Royalty Tribunal, on a semiannual basis, a compilation of all statements of account covering the relevant six-month period provided by clause (2) of this subsection.

(4) The royalty fees thus deposited shall, in accordance with the procedures provided by clause (5), be distributed to those among the following copyright owners who claim that their works were the subject of secondary transmissions by cable systems during the relevant semiannual period:

(A) any such owner whose work was included in a secondary transmission made by a cable system of a nonnetwork television program in whole or in part beyond the local service area of the primary transmitter; and

(B) any such owner whose work was included in a secondary transmission identified in a special statement of account deposited under clause (2)(A); and

(C) any such owner whose work was included in nonnetwork programing consisting exclusively of aural signals carried by a cable system in whole or in part beyond the local service area of the primary transmitter of such programs.

(5) The royalty fees thus deposited shall be distributed in accordance with the following procedures:

(A) During the month of July in each year, every person claiming to be entitled to compulsory license fees for secondary transmissions shall file a claim with the Copyright Royalty Tribunal, in accordance with requirements that the Tribunal shall prescribe by regulation. Notwithstanding any provisions of the antitrust laws, for purposes of this clause any claimants may agree among themselves as to the proportionate division of compulsory licensing fees among them, may lump their claims together and file them jointly or as a single claim, or may designate a common agent to receive payment on their behalf.

(B) After the first day of August of each year, the Copyright Royalty Tribunal shall determine whether there exists a controversy concerning the distribution of royalty fees. If the Tribunal determines that no such controversy exists, it shall, after deducting its reasonable administrative costs under this section, distribute such fees to the copyright owners entitled, or to their designated agents. If the Tribunal finds the existence of a controversy, it shall, pursuant to chapter 8 of this title, conduct a proceeding to determine the distribution of royalty fees.

(C) During the pendency of any proceeding under this subsection the Copyright Royalty Tribunal shall withhold from distribution an amount sufficient to satisfy all claims with respect to which a controversy exists, but shall have discretion to proceed to distribute any amounts that are not in controversy.

(e) NONSIMULTANEOUS SECONDARY TRANSMISSIONS BY CABLE SYSTEMS.—

(1) Notwithstanding those provisions of the second paragraph of subsection (f) relating to nonsimultaneous secondary transmissions by a cable system, any such transmissions are actionable as an act of infringement under section 501, and are fully subject to the remedies provided by sections 502 through 506 and sections 509 and 510, unless—

(A) the program on the videotape is transmitted no more than one time to the cable system's subscribers; and

(B) the copyrighted program, episode, or motion picture videotape, including the commercials contained within such program, episode, or picture, is transmitted without deletion or editing- and

(C) an owner or officer of the cable system (i) prevents the duplication of the videotape while in the possession of the system, (ii) prevents unauthorized duplication while in the possession of the facility making the videotape for the system if the system owns or controls the facility, or takes reasonable precautions to prevent such duplication if it does not own or control the facility, (iii) takes adequate precautions to prevent duplication while the tape is being transported, and (iv) subject to clause (2), erases or destroys, or causes the erasure or destruction of, the videotape; and

(D) within forty-five days after the end of each calendar quarter, an owner or officer of the cable system executes an affidavit attesting (i) to the steps and precautions taken to prevent duplication of the videotape, and (ii) subject to clause (2), to the erasure or destruction of all videotapes made or used during such quarter; and

(E) such owner or officer places or causes each such affidavit, and affidavits received pursuant to clause (2)(C), to be placed in a file, open to public inspection, at such system's main office in the community where the transmission is made or in the nearest community where such system maintains an office; and

(F) the nonsimultaneous transmission is one that the cable system would be authorized to transmit under the rules, regulations, and authorizations of the Federal Communications Commission in effect at the time of the nonsimultaneous transmission if the transmission had been made simultaneously, except that this subclause shall not apply to inadvertent or accidental transmissions.

(2) If a cable system transfers to any person a videotape of a program nonsimultaneously transmitted by it, such transfer is actionable as an act of infringement under section 501, and is fully subject to the remedies provided by sections 502 through 506 and 509, except that, pursuant to a written, nonprofit contract providing for the equitable sharing of the costs of such videotape and its transfer, a videotape nonsimultaneously transmitted by it, in accordance with clause (1), may be transferred by one cable system in Alaska to another system in Alaska, by one cable system in Hawaii permitted to make such nonsimultaneous transmissions to another such cable system in Hawaii, or by one cable system in Guam, the Northern Mariana Islands, or the Trust Territory of the Pacific Islands, to another cable system in any of those three territories, if—

(A) each such contract is available for public inspection in the offices of the cable systems involved, and a copy of such contract is filed within thirty days after such contract is entered into, with the Copyright Office (which Office shall make each such contract available for public inspection); and

(B) the cable system to which the videotape is transferred complies with clause (1)(A), (B), (C)(i), (iii), and (iv), and (D) through (F); and

(C) such system provides a copy of the affidavit required to be made in accordance with clause (1)(D) to each cable system making a previous nonsimultaneous transmission of the same videotape.

(3) This subsection shall not be construed to supersede the exclusivity protection provisions of any existing agreement, or any such agreement hereafter entered into, between a cable system and a television broadcast station in the area in which the cable system is located, or a network with which such station is affiliated.

(4) As used in this subsection, the term "videotape" and each of its variant forms, means the reproduction of the images and sounds of a program or programs broadcast by a television broadcast station licensed by the Federal Communications Commission, regardless of the nature of the material objects, such as tapes or films, in which the reproduction is embodied.

(f) DEFINITIONS.—As used in this section, the following terms and their variant forms mean the following:

A "primary transmission" is a transmission made to the public by the transmitting facility whose signals are being received and further transmitted by the secondary transmission service, regardless of where or when the performance or display was first transmitted.

A "secondary transmission" is the further transmitting of a primary transmission simultaneously with the primary transmission, or nonsimultaneously with the primary transmission if by a "cable system" not located in whole or in part within the boundary of the forty-eight contiguous States, Hawaii, or Puerto Rico: *Provided*, however, That a nonsimultaneous further transmission by a cable system located in Hawaii of a primary transmission shall be deemed to be a secondary transmission if the carriage of the television broadcast signal comprising such further transmission is permissible under the rules, regulations, or authorizations of the Federal Communications Commission.

A "cable system" is a facility located in any State, Territory, Trust Territory, or Possession, that in whole or in part receives signals transmitted or programs broadcast by one or more television broadcast stations licensed by the Federal Communications Commission, and makes secondary transmission of such signals or programs by wires, cables, or other communications channels to subscribing members of the public who pay for such service. For purposes of determining the royalty fee under subsection (d)(2), two or more cable systems in contiguous communities under common ownership or control or operating from one headend shall be considered as one system.

The "local service area of a primary transmitter" in the case of a television broadcast station, comprises the area in which such station is entitled to insist upon its signal being retransmitted by a cable system pursuant to the rules, regulations, and authorizations of the Federal Communications Commission in effect on April 15, 1976, or in the case of a television broadcast station licensed by an appropriate governmental authority of Canada or Mexico, the area in which it would be entitled to insist upon its signal being retransmitted if it were a television broadcast station subject to such rules, regulations, and authorizations. The "local service area of a primary transmitter" in the case of a radio broadcast station, comprises the primary service area of such station pursuant to the rules and regulations of the Federal Communications Commission. In the case of a low power television station, as defined by the rules and regulations of the Federal Communications Commission, the "local service area of a primary transmitter" comprises the area within 35 miles of the transmitter site, except that in the case of such a station located in a standard metropolitan statistical area which has one of the 50 largest populations of all standard metropolitan statistical areas (based on the 1980 decennial census of population taken by the Secretary of Commerce), the number of miles shall be 20 miles.

A "distant signal equivalent" is the value assigned to the secondary transmission of any nonnetwork television programing carried by a cable system in whole or in part beyond the local service area of the primary transmitter of such programming. It is computed by assigning a value of one to each independent station and a value of one-quarter to each network station and noncommercial educational station for the nonnetwork programming so carried pursuant to the rules, regulations, and authorizations of the Federal Communications Commission. The foregoing values for independent, network, and noncommercial educational stations are subject, however, to the following exceptions and limitations. Where the rules and regulations of the Federal Communications Commission require a cable system to omit the further transmission of a particular program and such rules and regulations also permit the substitution of another program embodying a performance or display of a work in place of the omitted transmission, or where such rules and regulations in effect on the date of enactment of this Act permit a cable system, at its election, to effect such deletion and substitution of a nonlive program or to carry additional programs not transmitted by primary transmitters within whose local service area the cable system is located, no value shall be assigned for the substituted or additional program; where the rules, regulations, or authorizations of the Federal Communications Commission in effect on the date of enactment of this Act permit a cable system, at its election, to omit the further transmission of a particular program and such rules, regulations, or authorizations also permit the substitution of another program embodying a performance or display of a work in place of the omitted transmission, the value assigned for the substituted or additional program shall be, in the case of a live program, the value of one full distant signal equivalent multiplied by a fraction that has as its numerator the number of days in the year in which such substitution occurs and as its denominator the number of days in the year. In the case of a station carried pursuant to the late-night or specialty programing rules of the Federal Communications Commission, or a station carried on a part-time basis where full-time carriage is not possible because the cable system lacks the activated channel capacity to retransmit on a full-time basis all signals which it is authorized to carry, the values for independent, network, and noncommercial educational stations set forth above, as the case may be, shall be multiplied by a fraction which is equal to the ratio of the broadcast hours of such station carried by the cable system to the total broadcast hours of the station.

A "network station" is a television broadcast station that is owned or operated by, or affiliated with, one or more of the television networks in the United States providing nationwide transmissions, and that transmits a substantial part of the programming supplied by such networks for a substantial part of that station's typical broadcast day. An "independent station" is a commercial television broadcast station other than a network station. A "noncommercial educational system" is a television station that is a noncommercial educational broadcast station as defined in section 397 of title 47.

Sec. 112. Limitations on Exclusive Rights: Ephemeral Recordings

(a) Notwithstanding the provisions of section 106, and except in the case of a motion picture or other audiovisual work, it is not an infringement of copyright for a transmitting organization entitled to transmit to the public a performance or display of a work, under a license or transfer of the copyright or under the limitations on exclusive rights in sound recordings specified by section 114(a), to make no more than one copy or phonorecord of a particular transmission program embodying the performance or display, if—

(1) the copy or phonorecord is retained and used solely by the transmitting organization that made it, and no further copies or phonorecords are reproduced from it; and

(2) the copy or phonorecord is used solely for the transmitting organization's own transmissions within its local service area, or for purposes of archival preservation or security; and

(3) unless preserved exclusively for archival purposes, the copy or phonorecord is destroyed within six months from the date the transmission program was first transmitted to the public.

(b) Notwithstanding the provisions of section 106, it is not an infringement of copyright for a governmental body or other nonprofit organization entitled to transmit a performance or display of a work, under section 110(2) or under the limitations on exclusive rights in sound recordings specified by section 114(a), to make no more than thirty copies or phonorecords of a particular transmission program embodying the performance or display, if—

(1) no further copies or phonorecords are reproduced from the copies or phonorecords made under this clause; and

(2) except for one copy or phonorecord that may be preserved exclusively for archival purposes, the copies or phonorecords are destroyed within seven years from the date the transmission program was first transmitted to the public.

(c) Notwithstanding the provisions of section 106, it is not an infringement of copyright for a governmental body or other nonprofit organization to make for distribution no more than one copy or phonorecord, for each transmitting organization specified in clause (2) of this subsection, of a particular transmission program embodying a performance of a nondramatic musical work of a religious nature, or of a sound recording of such a musical work, if—

(1) there is no direct or indirect charge for making or distributing any such copies or phonorecords; and

(2) none of such copies or phonorecords is used for any performance other than a single transmission to the public by a transmitting organization entitled to transmit to the public a performance of the work under a license or transfer of the copyright; and

(3) except for one copy or phonorecord that may be preserved exclusively for archival purposes, the copies or phonorecords are all destroyed within one year from the date the transmission program was first transmitted to the public.

(d) Notwithstanding the provisions of section 106, it is not an infringement of copyright for a governmental body or other nonprofit organization entitled to transmit a performance of a work under section 110(8) to make no more than ten copies or phonorecords embodying the performance, or to permit the use of any such copy or phonorecord by any governmental body or nonprofit organization entitled to transmit a performance of a work under section 110(8), if—

(1) any such copy or phonorecord is retained and used solely by the organization that made it, or by a governmental body or nonprofit organization entitled to transmit a performance of a work under section 110(8), and no further copies or phonorecords are reproduced from it; and

(2) any such copy or phonorecord is used solely for transmissions authorized under section 110(8), or for purposes of archival preservation or security; and

(3) the governmental body or nonprofit organization permitting any use of any such copy or phonorecord by any governmental body or nonprofit organization under this subsection does not make any charge for such use.

(e) The transmission program embodied in a copy or phonorecord made under this section is not subject to protection as a derivative work under this title except with the express consent of the owners of copyright in the preexisting works employed in the program.

Sec. 113. Scope of Exclusive Rights in Pictorial, Graphic, and Sculptural Works

(a) Subject to the provisions of subsections (b) and (c) of this section, the exclusive right to reproduce a copyrighted pictorial, graphic, or sculptural work in copies under section 106 includes the right to reproduce the work in or on any kind of article, whether useful or otherwise.

(b) This title does not afford, to the owner of copyright in a work that portrays a useful article as such, any greater or lesser rights with respect to the making, distribution, or display of the useful article so portrayed than those afforded to such works under the law, whether title 17 or the common law or statutes of a State, in effect on December 31, 1977, as held applicable and construed by a court in an action brought under this title.

(c) In the case of a work lawfully reproduced in useful articles that have been offered for sale or other distribution to the public, copyright does not include any right to prevent the making, distribution, or display of pictures or photographs of such articles in connection with advertisements or commentaries related to the distribution or display of such articles, or in connection with news reports.

[Note: subsection (d) becomes effective June 1, 1991.]

(d)(1) In a case in which—

(A) a work of visual art has been incorporated in or made part of a building in such a way that removing the work from the building will cause the destruction, distortion, mutilation, or other modification of the work as described in section 106A(a)(3), and

(B) the author consented to the installation of the work in the building either before the effective date set forth in section 610(a) of the Visual Artists Rights Act of 1990, or in a written instrument executed on or after such effective date that is signed by the owner of the building and the author and that specifies that installation of the work may subject the work to destruction, distortion, mutilation, or other modification, by reason of its removal, then the rights conferred by paragraphs (2) and (3) of section 106A(a) shall not apply.

(2) If the owner of a building wishes to remove a work of visual art which is a part of such building and which can be removed from the building without the destruction, distortion, mutilation, or other modification of the work as described in section 106A(a)(3), the author's rights under paragraphs (2) and (3) of section 106A(a) shall apply unless—

(A) the owner has made a diligent, good faith attempt without success to notify the author of the owner's intended action affecting the work of visual art, or

(B) the owner did provide such notice in writing and the person so notified failed, within 90 days after receiving such notice, either to remove the work or to pay for its removal.

For purposes of subparagraph (A), an owner shall be presumed to have made a diligent, good faith attempt to send notice if the owner sent such notice by registered mail to the author at the most recent address of the author that was recorded with the Register of Copyrights pursuant to paragraph (3). If the work is removed at the expense of the author, title to that copy of the work shall be deemed to be in the author.

(3) The Register of Copyrights shall establish a system of records whereby any author of a work of visual art that has been incorporated in or made part of a building, may record his or her identity and address with the Copyright Office. The Register shall also establish procedures under which any such author may update the information so recorded, and procedures under which owners of buildings may record with the Copyright Office evidence of their efforts to comply with this subsection.

Sec. 114. Scope of Exclusive Rights in Sound Recordings

(a) The exclusive rights of the owner of copyright in a sound recording are limited to the rights specified by clauses (1), (2), and (3) of section 106, and do not include any right of performance under section 106(4).

(b) The exclusive right of the owner of copyright in a sound recording under clause (1) of section 106 is limited to the right to duplicate the sound recording in the form of phonorecords, or of copies of motion pictures and other audiovisual works, that directly or indirectly recapture the actual sounds fixed in the recording. The exclusive right of the owner of copyright in a sound recording under clause (2) of section 106 is limited to the right to prepare a derivative work in which the actual sounds fixed in the sound recording are rearranged, remixed, or otherwise altered in sequence or quality. The exclusive rights of the owner of copyright in a sound recording under clauses (1) and (2) of section 106 do not extend to the making or duplication of another sound recording that consists entirely of an independent fixation of other sounds, even though such sounds imitate or simulate those in the copyrighted sound recording. The exclusive rights of the owner of copyright in a sound recording under clauses (1), (2), and (3) of section 106 do not apply to sound recordings included in educational television and radio programs (as defined in section 397 of title 472) distributed or transmitted by or through public broadcasting entitles (as defined by section 118(g)): *Provided,* That copies or phonorecords of said programs are not commercially distributed by or through public broadcasting entities to the general public.

(c) This section does not limit or impair the exclusive right to perform publicly, by means of a phonorecord, any of the works specified by section 106(4).

(d) On January 3, 1978, the Register of Copyrights, after consulting with representatives of owners of copyrighted materials, representatives of the broadcasting, recording, motion picture, entertainment industries, and arts organizations, representatives of organized labor and performers of copyrighted materials, shall submit to the Congress a report setting forth recommendations as to whether this section should be amended to provide for performers and copyright owners of copyrighted material any performance rights in such material. The report should describe the status of such rights in foreign countries, the views of major interested parties, and specific legislative or other recommendations, if any.

Sec. 115. Scope of Exclusive Rights in Nondramatic Musical Works: Compulsory License for Making and Distributing Phonorecords

In the case of nondramatic musical works, the exclusive rights provided by clauses (1) and (3) of section 106, to make and to distribute phonorecords of such works, are subject to compulsory licensing under the conditions specified by this section.

(a) AVAILABILITY AND SCOPE OF COMPULSORY LICENSE.—

(1) When phonorecords of a nondramatic musical work have been distributed to the public in the United States under the authority of the copyright owner, any other person may, by complying with the provisions of this section, obtain a compulsory license to make and distribute phonorecords of the work. A person may not obtain a compulsory license only if his or her primary purpose in making phonorecords is to distribute them to the public for private use. A person may obtain a compulsory license for use of the work in the making of phonorecords duplicating a sound recording fixed by another, unless: (i) such sound recording was fixed lawfully; and (ii) the making of the phonorecords was authorized by the owner of copyright in the sound recording or. if the sound recording was fixed before February 15, 1972, by any person who fixed the sound recording pursuant to an express license from the owner of the copyright in the musical work or pursuant to a valid compulsory license for use of such work in a sound recording.

(2) A compulsory license includes the privilege of making a musical arrangement of the work to the extent necessary to conform it to the style or manner of interpretation of the performance involved, but the arrangement shall not change the basic melody or fundamental character of the work, and shall not be subject to protection as a derivative work under this title, except with the express consent of the copyright owner.

(b) NOTICE OF INTENTION TO OBTAIN COMPULSORY LICENSE.—

(1) Any person who wishes to obtain a compulsory license under this section shall, before or within thirty days after making, and before distributing any phonorecords of the work, serve notice of intention to do so on the copyright owner. If the

registration or other public records of the Copyright Office do not identify the copyright owner and include an address at which notice can be served, it shall be sufficient to file the notice of intention in the Copyright Office. The notice shall comply, in form, content, and manner of service, with requirements that the Register of Copyrights shall prescribe by regulation.

(2) Failure to serve or file the notice required by clause (1) forecloses the possibility of a compulsory license and, in the absence of a negotiated license, renders the making and distribution of phonorecords actionable as acts of infringement under section 501 and fully subject to the remedies provided by sections 502 through 506 and 509.

(c) ROYALTY PAYABLE UNDER COMPULSORY LICENSE.—

(1) To be entitled to receive royalties under a compulsory license, the copyright owner must be identified in the registration or other public records of the Copyright Office. The owner is entitled to royalties for phonorecords made and distributed after being so identified, but is not entitled to recover for any phonorecords previously made and distributed.

(2) Except as provided by clause (1), the royalty under a compulsory license shall be payable for every phonorecord made and distributed in accordance with the license. For this purpose, a phonorecord is considered "distributed" if the person exercising the compulsory license has voluntarily and permanently parted with its possession. With respect to each work embodied in the phonorecord, the royalty shall be either two and three-fourths cents, or one-half of one cent per minute of playing time or fraction thereof, whichever amount is larger.

(3) A compulsory license under this section includes the right of the maker of a phonorecord of a nondramatic musical work under subsection (a)(1) to distribute or authorize distribution of such phonorecord by rental, lease, or lending (or by acts or practices in the nature of rental, leases, or lending). In addition to any royalty payable under clause (2) and chapter 8 of this title, a royalty shall be payable by the compulsory licensee for every act of distribution of a phonorecord by or in the nature of rental, lease, or lending, by or under the authority of the com-

pulsory licensee. With respect to each nondramatic musical work embodied in the phonorecord, the royalty shall be a proportion of the revenue received by the compulsory licensee from every such act of distribution of the phonorecord under this clause equal to the proportion of the revenue received by the compulsory licensee from distribution of the phonorecord under clause (2) that is payable by a compulsory licensee under that clause and under chapter 8. The Register of Copyrights shall issue regulations to carry out the purpose of this clause.

(4) Royalty payments shall be made on or before the twentieth day of each month and shall include all royalties for the month next preceding. Each monthly payment shall be made under oath and shall comply with requirements that the Register of Copyrights shall prescribe by regulation. The Register shall also prescribe regulations under which detailed cumulative annual statements of account, certified by a certified public accountant, shall be filed for every compulsory license under this section. The regulations covering both the monthly and the annual statements of account shall prescribe the form, content, and manner of certification with respect to the number of records made and the number of records distributed.

(5) If the copyright owner does not receive the monthly payment and the monthly and annual statements of account when due, the owner may give written notice to the licensee that, unless the default is remedied within thirty days from the date of the notice, the compulsory license will be automatically terminated. Such termination renders either the making or the distribution, or both, of all phonorecords for which the royalty has not been paid, actionable as acts of infringement under section 501 and fully subject to the remedies provided by sections 502 through 506 and 509.

Sec. 116. Scope of Exclusive Rights in Nondramatic Musical Works: Compulsory Licenses for Public Performances by Means of Coin-Operated Phonorecord Players

(a) LIMITATION ON EXCLUSIVE RIGHT.—In the case of a nondramatic musical work embodied in a phonorecord, the exclusive right under clause (4) of section 106 to perform the work publicly by means of a coin-operated phonorecord player is limited as follows:

(1) The proprietor of the establishment in which the public performance takes place is not liable for infringement with respect to such public performance unless

(A) such proprietor is the operator of the phonorecord player; or

(B) such proprietor refuses or fails, within one month after receipt by registered or certified mail of a request, at a time during which the certificate required by clause (1)(C) of subsection (b) is not affixed to the phonorecord player, by the copyright owner, to make full disclosure, by registered or certified mail, of the identity of the operator of the phonorecord player.

(2) The operator of the coin-operated phonorecord player may obtain a compulsory license to perform the work publicly on that phonorecord player by filing the application, affixing the certificate, and paying the royalties provided by subsection (b).

(b) RECORDATION OF COIN-OPERATED PHONORECORD PLAYER, AFFIXATION OF CERTIFICATE, AND ROYALTY PAYABLE UNDER COMPULSORY LICENSE.—

(1) Any operator who wishes to obtain a compulsory license for the public performance of works on a coin-operated phonorecord player shall fulfill the following requirements:

(A) Before or within one month after such performances are made available on a particular phonorecord player, and during the month of January in each succeeding year that such performances are made available on that particular phonorecord player, the operator shall file in the Copyright Office, in accordance with requirements that the Register of Copyrights, after consultation with the Copyright Royalty Tribunal (if and when the Tribunal has been constituted), shall prescribe by regulation, an application containing the name and address of the operator of the phonorecord player and the manufacturer and serial number or other explicit identification of the phonorecord player, and deposit with the Register of Copyrights a royalty fee for the current calendar year of $8 for that particular phonorecord player. If such performances are made available on a particular phonorecord player for the first time after July 1 of any year, the royalty fee to be deposited for the remainder of that year shall be $4.

(B) Within twenty days of receipt of an application and a royalty fee pursuant to subclause (A), the Register of Copyrights shall issue to the applicant a certificate for the phonorecord player.

(C) On or before March 1 of the year in which the certificate prescribed by subclause (B) of this clause is issued, or within ten days after the date of issue of the certificate, the operator shall affix to the particular phonorecord player, in a position where it can be readily examined by the public, the certificate, issued by the Register of Copyrights under subclause (B), of the latest application made by such operator under subclause (A) of this clause with respect to that phonorecord player.

(2) Failure to file the application, to affix the certificate, or to pay the royalty required by clause (1) of this subsection renders the public performance actionable as an act of infringement under section 501 and fully subject to the remedies provided by sections 502 through 506 and 509.

(c) DISTRIBUTION OF ROYALTIES.—

(1) The Register of Copyrights shall receive all fees deposited under this section and, after deducting the reasonable costs incurred by the Copyright Office under this section, shall deposit the balance in the Treasury of the United States, in such manner as the Secretary of the Treasury directs. All funds held by the Secretary of the Treasury shall be invested in interest-bearing United States securities for later distribution with interest by the Copyright Royalty Tribunal as provided by this title. The Register shall submit to the Copyright Royalty Tribunal, on an annual basis, a detailed statement of account covering all fees received for the relevant period provided by subsection (b).

(2) During the month of January in each year, every person claiming to be entitled to compulsory license fees under this section for performances during the preceding twelve-month period shall file a claim with the Copyright Royalty Tribunal, in accordance with requirements that the Tribunal shall prescribe by regulation. Such claim shall include an agreement to accept

as final, except as provided in section 810 of this title, the determination of the Copyright Royalty Tribunal in any controversy concerning the distribution of royalty fees deposited under subclause (A) of subsection (b)(1) of this section to which the claimant is a party. Notwithstanding any provisions of the antitrust laws, for purposes of this subsection any claimants may agree among themselves as to the proportionate division of compulsory licensing fees among them, may lump their claims together and file them jointly or as a single claim, or may designate a common agent to receive payment on their behalf.

(3) After the first day of October of each year, the Copyright Royalty Tribunal shall determine whether there exists a controversy concerning the distribution of royalty fees deposited under subclause (A) of subsection (b)(1). If the Tribunal determines that no such controversy exists, it shall, after deducting its reasonable administrative costs under this section, distribute such fees to the copyright owners entitled, or to their designated agents. If it finds that such a controversy exists, it shall, pursuant to chapter 8 of this title, conduct a proceeding to determine the distribution of royalty fees.

(4) The fees to be distributed shall be divided as follows:

(A) to every copyright owner not affiliated with a performing rights society, the pro rata share of the fees to be distributed to which such copyright owner proves entitlement.

(B) to the performing rights societies, the remainder of the fees to be distributed in such pro rata shares as they shall by agreement stipulate among themselves, or, if they fail to agree, the pro rata share to which such performing rights societies prove entitlement.

(C) during the pendency of any proceeding under this section, the Copyright Royalty Tribunal shall withhold from distribution an amount sufficient to satisfy all claims with respect to which a controversy exists, but shall have discretion to proceed to distribute any amounts that are not in controversy.

(5) The Copyright Royalty Tribunal shall promulgate regulations under which persons who can reasonably be expected to have claims may, during the year in which performances take place, without expense to or harassment of operators or proprie-

tors of establishments in which phonorecord players are located, have such access to such establishments and to the phonorecord players located therein and such opportunity to obtain information with respect thereto as may be reasonably necessary to determine, by sampling procedures or otherwise, the proportion of contribution of the musical works of each such person to the earnings of the phonorecord players for which fees shall have been deposited. Any person who alleges that he or she has been denied the access permitted under the regulations prescribed by the Copyright Royalty Tribunal may bring an action in the United States District Court for the District of Columbia for the cancellation of the compulsory license of the phonorecord player to which such access has been denied, and the court shall have the power to declare the compulsory license thereof invalid from the date of issue thereof.

(d) CRIMINAL PENALTIES.—Any person who knowingly makes a false representation of a material fact in an application filed under clause (1)(B) of subsection (b) or knowingly affixes such certificate to a phonorecord player other than the one it covers, shall be fined not more than $2,500.

(e) DEFINITIONS.—As used in this section and section 116A, the following terms and their variant forms mean the following:

(1) A "coin-operated phonorecord player" is a machine or device that—

(A) is employed solely for the performance of nondramatic musical works by means of phonorecords upon being activated by insertion of coins, currency, tokens, or other monetary units or their equivalent;

(B) is located in an establishment making no direct or indirect charge for admission:

(C) is accompanied by a list of titles of all the musical works available for performance on it, which list is affixed to the phonorecord player or posted in the establishment in a prominent position where it can be readily examined by the public; and

(D) affords a choice of works available for performance and permits the choice to be made by the patrons of the establishment in which it is located.

(2) An "operator" is any person who, alone or jointly with others:

(A) owns a coin-operated phonorecord player; or

(B) has the power to make a coin-operated phonorecord player available for placement in an establishment for purposes of public performance; or

(C) has the power to exercise primary control over the selection of the musical works made available for public performance on a coin-operated phonorecord player.

(3) A "performing rights society" is an association or corporation that licenses the public performance of nondramatic musical works on behalf of the copyright owners, such as the American Society of Composers, Authors and Publishers, Broadcast Music. Inc., and SESAC, Inc.

Sec. 116A. Negotiated Licenses for Public Performances by Means of Coin-Operated Phonorecord Players

(a) APPLICABILITY OF SECTION.—This section applies to any nondramatic musical work embodied in a phonorecord.

(b) LIMITATION ON EXCLUSIVE RIGHT IF LICENSES NOT NEGOTIATED.—

(1) Applicability.—In the case of a work to which tliis section applies, the exclusive right under clause (4) of section 106 to perform the work publicly by means of a coin-operated phonorecord player is limited by section 116 to the extent provided in this section.

(2) Determination by Copyright Royalty Tribunal.—The Copyright Royalty Tribunal, at the end of the 1-year period beginning on the effective date of the Berne Convention Implementation Act of 1988, and periodically thereafter to the extent necessary to carry out subsection (f), shall determine whether or not negotiated licenses authorized by subsection (c) are in effect so as to provide permission to use a quantity of musical works not substantially smaller than the quantity of such works performed on coin-operated phonorecord players during the 1-year period ending on the effective date of that Act. If the Copyright Royalty Tribunal determines that such negotiated licenses are not so in effect, the Tribunal shall, upon making the determination,

publish the determination in the Federal Register. Upon such publication, section 116 shall apply with respect to musical works that are not the subject of such negotiated licenses.

(c) NEGOTIATED LICENSES.—

(1) Authority for Negotiations.—Any owners of copyright in works to which this section applies and any operators of coin-operated phonorecord players may negotiate and agree upon the terms and rates of royalty payments for the performance of such works and the proportionate division of fees paid among copyright owners, and may designate common agents to negotiate, agree to, pay, or receive such royalty payments.

(2) Arbitration.—Parties to such a negotiation, within such time as may be specified by the Copyright Royalty Tribunal by regulation, may determine the result of the negotiation by arbitration. Such arbitration shall be governed by the provisions of title 9, to the extent such title is not inconsistent with this section. The parties shall give notice to the Copyright Royalty Tribunal of any determination reached by arbitration and any such determination shall, as between the parties to the arbitration, be dispositive of the issues to which it relates.

(d) LICENSE AGREEMENTS SUPERIOR TO COPYRIGHT ROYALTY TRIBUNAL DETERMINATIONS.—License agreements between one or more copyright owners and one or more operators of coin-operated phonorecord players, which are negotiated in accordance with subsection (c), shall be given effect in lieu of any otherwise applicable determination by the Copyright Royalty Tribunal.

(e) NEGOTIATION SCHEDULE.—Not later than 60 days after the effective date of the Berne Convention Implementation Act of 1988, if the Chairman of the Copyright Royalty Tribunal has not received notice, from copyright owners and operators of coin-operated phonorecord players referred to in subsection (c)(l), of the date and location of the first meeting between such copyright owners and such operators to commence negotiations authorized by subsection (c), the Chairman shall announce the date and location of such meeting. Such meeting may not be held more than 90 days after the effective date of such Act.

(f) COPYRIGHT ROYALTY TRIBUNAL TO SUSPEND VARIOUS ACTIVITIES.—The Copyright Royalty Tribunal shall not conduct any rate-making activity with respect to coin-operated phonorecord players unless, at any time more than one year after the effective date of the Berne Convention Implementation Act of 1988, the negotiated licenses adopted by the parties under this section do not provide permission to use a quality of musical works not substantially smaller than the quantity of such works performed on coin-operated phonorecord players during the one-year period ending on the effective date of such Act.

(g) TRANSITION PROVISIONS: RETENTION OF COPYRIGHT ROYALTY TRIBUNAL JURISDICTION.—Until such time as licensing provisions are determined by the parties under this section, the terms of the compulsory license under section 116, with respect to the public performance of nondramatic musical works by means of coin-operated phonorecord players, which is in effect on the day before the effective date of the Berne Convention Implementation Act of 1988, shall remain in force. If a negotiated license authorized by this section comes into force so as to supersede previous determinations by the Copyright Royalty Tribunal, as provided in subsection (d), but thereafter is terminated or expires and is not replaced by another licensing agreement, then section 116 shall be effective with respect to musical works that were the subject of such terminated or expired licenses.

Sec. 117. Limitations on Exclusive Rights: Computer Programs

Notwithstanding the provisions of section 106, it is not an infringement for the owner of a copy of a computer program to make or authorize the making of another copy or adaptation of that computer program provided:

(1) that such a new copy or adaptation is created as an essential step in the utilization of the computer program in conjunction with a machine and that it is used in no other manner, or

(2) that such new copy or adaptation is for archival purposes only and that all archival copies are destroyed in the event that continued possession of the computer program should cease to be rightful.

Any exact copies prepared in accordance with the provisions of this section may be leased, sold, or otherwise transferred, along with the copy from which such copies were prepared, only as part of the lease, sale, or other transfer of all rights in the program. Adaptations so prepared may be transferred only with the authorization of the copyright owner.

Sec. 118. Scope of Exclusive Rights: Use of Certain Works in Connection with Noncommercial Broadcasting

(a) The exclusive rights provided by section 106 shall, with respect to the works specified by subsection (b) and the activities specified by subsection (d), be subject to the conditions and limitations prescribed by this section.

(b) Not later than thirty days after the Copyright Royalty Tribunal has been constituted in accordance with section 802, the Chairman of the Tribunal shall cause notice to be published in the Federal Register of the initiation of proceedings for the purpose of determining reasonable terms and rates of royalty payments for the activities specified by subsection (d) with respect to published nondramatic musical works and published pictorial, graphic, and sculptural works during a period beginning as provided in clause (3) of this subsection and ending on December 31, 1982. Copyright owners and public broadcasting entities shall negotiate in good faith and cooperate fully with the Tribunal in an effort to reach reasonable and expeditious results. Notwithstanding any provision of the antitrust laws, any owners of copyright in works specified by this subsection and any public broadcasting entities, respectively, may negotiate and agree upon the terms and rates of royalty payments and the proportionate division of fees paid among various copyright owners, and may designate common agents to negotiate, agree to, pay, or receive payments.

(1) Any owner of copyright in a work specified in this subsection or any public broadcasting entity may, within one hundred and twenty days after publication of the notice specified in this subsection, submit to the Copyright Royalty Tribunal proposed licenses covering such activities with respect to such works. The Copyright Royalty Tribunal shall proceed on the basis of the proposals submitted to it as well as any other relevant information. The Copyright Royalty Tribunal shall permit any interested party to submit information relevant to such proceedings.

(2) License agreements voluntarily negotiated at any time be-

tween one or more copyright owners and one or more public broadcasting entities shall be given effect in lieu of any determination by the Tribunal: *Provided,* That copies of such agreements are filed in the Copyright Office within thirty days of execution in accordance with regulations that the Register of Copyrights shall prescribe.

(3) Within six months, but not earlier than one hundred and twenty days, from the date of publication of the notice specified in this subsection the Copyright Royalty Tribunal shall make a determination and publish in the Federal Register a schedule of rates and terms which, subject to clause (2) of this subsection, shall be binding on all owners of copyright in works specified by this subsection and public broadcasting entities, regardless of whether or not such copyright owners and public broadcasting entities have submitted proposals to the Tribunal. In establishing such rates and terms the Copyright Royalty Tribunal may consider the rates for comparable circumstances under voluntary license agreements negotiated as provided in clause (2) of this subsection. The Copyright Royalty Tribunal shall also establish requirements by which copyright owners may receive reasonable notice of the use of their works under this section, and under which records of such use shall be kept by public broadcasting entities.

(4) With respect to the period beginning on the effective date of this title and ending on the date of publication of such rates and terms, this title shall not afford to owners of copyright or public broadcasting entities any greater or lesser rights with respect to the activities specified in subsection (d) as applied to works specified in this subsection than those afforded under the law in effect on December 31, 1977, as held applicable and construed by a court in an action brought under this title.

(c) The initial procedure specified in subsection (b) shall be repeated and concluded between June 30 and December 31, 1982, and at five-year intervals thereafter, in accordance with regulations that the Copyright Royalty Tribunal shall prescribe.

(d) Subject to the transitional provisions of subsection (b)(4), and to the terms of any voluntary license agreements that have been negotiated as provided by subsection (b)(2), a public broadcasting entity may, upon compliance with the provisions of this section, including the rates and terms established by the Copyright Royalty Tribunal under subsection (b)(3), engage in the following activities with respect to published nondramatic musical works and published pictorial, graphic, and sculptural works:

(1) performance or display of a work by or in the course of a transmission made by a noncommercial educational broadcast station referred to in subsection (g); and

(2) production of a transmission program, reproduction of copies or phonorecords, where such production, reproduction, or distribution is made by a nonprofit institution or organization solely for the purpose of transmissions specified in clause (1); and

(3) the making of reproductions by a governmental body or a nonprofit institution of a transmission program simultaneously with its transmission as specified in clause (1), and the performance or display of the contents of such program under the conditions specified by clause (1) of section 110, but only if the reproductions are used for performances or displays for a period of no more than seven days from the date of the transmission specified in clause (1), and are destroyed before or at the end of such period. No person supplying, in accordance with clause (2), a reproduction of a transmission program to governmental bodies or nonprofit institutions under this clause shall have any liability as a result of failure of such body or institution to destroy such reproduction; *Provided,* That it shall have notified such body or institution of the requirement for such destruction pursuant to this clause; *And provided further,* That if such body or institution itself fails to destroy such reproduction it shall be deemed to have infringed.

(e) Except as expressly provided in this subsection, this section shall have no applicability to works other than those specified in subsection (b).

(1) Owners of copyright in nondramatic literary works and public broadcasting entities may, during the course of voluntary negotiations, agree among themselves, respectively, as to the terms and rates of royalty payments without liability under the antitrust laws. Any such terms and rates of royalty payments

shall be effective upon filing in the Copyright Office, in accordance with regulations that the Register of Copyrights shall prescribe.

(2) On January 3, 1980, the Register of Copyrights, after consulting with authors and other owners of copyright in nondramatic literary works and their representatives, and with public broadcasting entities and their representatives, shall submit to the Congress a report setting forth the extent to which voluntary licensing arrangements have been reached with respect to the use of nondramatic literary works by such broadcast stations. The report should also describe any problems that may have arisen, and present legislative or other recommendations, if warranted.

(f) Nothing in this section shall be construed to permit, beyond the limits of fair use as provided by section 107, the unauthorized dramatization of a nondramatic musical work, the production of a transmission program drawn to any substantial extent from a published compilation of pictorial, graphic, or sculptural works, or the unauthorized use of any portion of an audiovisual work.

(g) As used in this section, the term "public broadcasting entity" means a noncommercial educational broadcast station as defined in section 397 of title 47 and any nonprofit institution or organization engaged in the activities described in clause (2) of subsection (d).

Sec. 119. Limitations on Exclusive Rights: Secondary Transmissions of Superstations and Network Stations for Private Home Viewing

(a) SECONDARY TRANSMISSIONS BY SATELLITE CARRIERS.—

(1) Superstations.—Subject to the provisions of paragraphs (3), (4), and (6) of this subsection, secondary transmissions of a primary transmission made by a superstation and embodying a performance or display of a work shall be subject to statutory licensing under this section if the secondary transmission is made by a satellite carrier to the public for private home viewing, and the carrier makes a direct or indirect charge for such retransmission service to each household receiving the second-

ary transmission or to a distributor that has contracted with the carrier for direct or indirect delivery of the secondary transmission to the public for private home viewing.

(2) Network Stations.—

(A) In General.—Subject to the provisions of subparagraphs (B) and (C) of this paragraph and paragraphs (3), (4), (5), and (6) of this subsection, secondary transmissions of programming contained in a primary transmission made by a network station and embodying a performance or display of a work shall be subject to statutory licensing under this section if the secondary transmission is made by a satellite carrier to the public for private home viewing, and the carrier makes a direct or indirect charge for such retransmission service to each household receiving the secondary transmission.

(B) Secondary Transmission to Unserved Households.—The statutory license provided for in subparagraph (A) shall be limited to secondary transmissions to persons who reside in unserved households.

(C) Submission of Subscriber Lists to Networks.—A satellite carrier that makes secondary transmissions of a primary transmission made by a network station pursuant to subparagraph (A) shall, 90 days after the effective date of the Satellite Home Viewer Act of 1988, or 90 days after commencing such secondary transmissions, whichever is later, submit to the network that owns or is affiliated with the network station a list identifying (by street address, including county and zip code) all subscribers to which the satellite carrier currently makes secondary transmissions of that primary transmission. Thereafter, on the 15th of each month, the satellite carrier shall submit to the network a list identifying (by street address, including county and zip code) any persons who have been added or dropped as such subscribers since the last submission under this subparagraph. Such subscriber information submitted by a satellite carrier may be used only for purposes of monitoring compliance by the satellite carrier with this subsection. The submission requirements of this subparagraph shall apply to a satellite carrier only if the network to whom the submissions are to be made places on file with the Register of Copyrights, on or after the effective date of the Satellite Home Viewer Act of 1988, a document identifying the name and address of the person to whom such submissions are to be made. The Register shall maintain for public inspection a file of all such documents.

(3) Noncompliance With Reporting and Payment Requirements.—Notwithstanding the provisions of paragraphs (1) and (2), the willful or repeated secondary transmission to the public by a satellite carrier of a primary transmission made by a superstation or a network station and embodying a performance or display of a work is actionable as an act of infringement under section 501, and is fully subject to the remedies provided by sections 502 through 506 and 509, where the satellite carrier has not deposited the statement of account and royalty fee required by subsection (b), or has failed to make the submissions to networks required by paragraph (2)(C).

(4) Willful Alterations.—Notwithstanding the provisions of paragraphs (1) and (2), the secondary transmission to the public by a satellite carrier of a primary transmission made by a superstation or a network station and embodying a performance or display of a work is actionable as an act of infringement under section 501, and is fully subject to the remedies provided by sections 502 through 506 and sections 509 and 510, if the content of the particular program in which the performance or display is embodied, or any commercial advertising or station announcement transmitted by the primary transmitter during, or immediately before or after, the transmission of such program, is in any way willfully altered by the satellite carrier through changes, deletions, or additions, or is combined with programming from any other broadcast signal.

(5) Violation of Territorial Restrictions on Statutory License for Network Stations.—

(A) Individual Violations.—The willful or repeated secondary transmission by a satellite carrier of a primary transmission made by a network station and embodying a performance or display of a work to a subscriber who does not reside in an unserved household is actionable as an act of infringement under section 501 and is fully subject to the remedies provided by sections 502 through 506 and 509, except that—

(i) no damages shall be awarded for such act of infringement if the satellite carrier took corrective action by promptly withdrawing service from the ineligible subscriber, and

(ii) any statutory damages shall not exceed $5 for such subscriber for each month during which the violation occurred.

(B) Pattern of Violations.—If a satellite carrier engages in a willful or repeated pattern or practice of delivering a primary transmission made by a network station and embodying a performance or display of a work to subscribers who do not reside in unserved households, then in addition to the remedies set forth in subparagraph (A)—

(i) if the pattern or practice has been carried out on a substantially nationwide basis, the court shall order a permanent injunction barring the secondary transmission by the satellite carrier, for private home viewing, of the primary transmissions of any primary network station affiliated with the same network, and the court may order statutory damages of not to exceed $250,000 for each 6-month period during which the pattern or practice was carried out; and

(ii) if the pattern or practice has been carried out on a local or regional basis, the court shall order a permanent injunction barring the secondary transmission, for private home viewing in that locality or region, by the satellite carrier of the primary transmissions of any network station affiliated with the same network, and the court may order statutory damages of not to exceed $250,000 for each 6-month period during which the pattern or practice was carried out.

(C) Previous Subscribers Excluded.—Subparagraphs (A) and (B) do not apply to secondary transmissions by a satellite carrier to persons who subscribed to receive such secondary transmissions from the satellite carrier or a distributor before the date of the enactment of the Satellite Home Viewer Act of 1988.

(6) Discrimination by a Satellite Carrier.—Notwithstanding the provisions of paragraph (1), the willful or repeated secondary transmission to the public by a satellite carrier of a primary transmission made by a superstation or a network station and embodying a performance or display of a work is actionable as an act of infringement under section 501, and is fully subject to the remedies provided by sections 502 through 506 and 509, if the satellite carrier unlawfully discriminates against a distributor.

(7) Geographic Limitation on Secondary Transmissions.—The statutory license created by this section shall apply only to secondary transmissions to households located in the United States.

(b) STATUTORY LICENSE FOR SECONDARY TRANSMISSIONS FOR PRIVATE HOME VIEWING.—

(1) Deposits with the Register of Copyrights.—A satellite carrier whose secondary transmissions are subject a statutory licensing under subsection (a) shall, on a semiannual basis, deposit with the Register of Copyrights, in accordance with requirements that the Register shall, after consultation with the Copyright Royalty Tribunal, prescribe by regulation—

(A) a statement of account, covering the preceding 6-month period, specifying the names and locations of all superstations and network stations whose signals were transmitted, at any time during that period, to subscribers for private home viewing as described in subsections (a)(1) and (a)(2), the total number of subscribers that received such transmissions, and such other data as the Register of Copyrights may, after consultation with the Copyright Royalty Tribunal, from time a time prescribe by regulation; and

(B) a royalty fee for that 6-month period, computed by—

(i) multiplying the total number of subscribers receiving each secondary transmission of a superstation during each calendar month by 12 cents;

(ii) multiplying the number of subscribers receiving each secondary transmission of a network station during each calendar month by 3 cents; and

(iii) adding together the totals computed under clauses (i) and (ii).

(2) Investment of Fees.—The Register of Copyrights shall receive all fees deposited under this section and, after deducting the reasonable costs incurred by the Copyright Office under this section (other than the costs deducted under paragraph (4)), shall deposit the balance in the Treasury of the United States, in such manner as the Secretary of the Treasury directs. All funds held by the Secretary of the Treasury shall be invested in interest-bearing securities of the United States for later distribution with interest by the Copyright Royalty Tribunal as provided by this title.

(3) Persons to Whom Fees Are Distributed.—The royalty fees deposited under paragraph (2) shall, in accordance with the procedures provided by paragraph (4), be distributed a those copyright owners whose works were included in a secondary transmission for private home viewing made by a satellite carrier during the applicable 6–month accounting period and who file a claim with the Copyright Royalty Tribunal under paragraph (4).

(4) Procedures for Distribution.—The royalty fees deposited under paragraph (2) shall be distributed in accordance with the following procedures:

(A) Filing of Ciaims for Fees.—During the month of July in each year, each person claiming to be entitled a statutory license fees for secondary transmissions for private home viewing shall file a claim with the Copyright Royalty Tribunal, in accordance with requirements that the Tribunal shall prescribe by regulation. For purposes of this paragraph, any claimants may agree among themselves as to the proportionate division of statutory license fees among them, may lump their claims together and file them jointly or as a single claim, or may designate a common agent to receive payment on their behalf.

(B) Determination of Controversy; Distributions.—After the first day of August of each year, the Copyright Royalty Tribunal shall determine whether there exists a controversy concerning the distribution of royalty fees. If the Tribunal determines that no such controversy exists, the Tribunal shall, after deducting reasonable administrative costs under this paragraph, distribute such fees a the copyright owners entitled to receive them, or to their designated agents. If the Tribunal finds the existence of a controversy, the Tribunal shall, pursuant to chapter 8 of this title, conduct a proceeding to determine the distribution of royalty fees.

(C) Withholding of Fees During Controversy.—During the pendency of any proceeding under this subsection, the Copyright Royalty Tribunal shall withhold from distribution an amount sufficient to satisfy all claims with respect to which a controversy exists, but shall have discretion a proceed a distribute any amounts that are not in controversy.

(c) DETERMINATION OF ROYALTY FEES.—

(1) Applicability and Determination of Royalty Fees.—The rate of the royalty fee payable under subsection (b)(1)(B) shall be effective until December 31, 1992, unless a royalty fee is established under paragraph (2), (3), or (4) of this subsection. After that date, the fee shall be determined either in accordance with the voluntary negotiation procedure specified in paragraph (2) or in accordance with the compulsory arbitration procedure specified in paragraphs (3) and (4).

(2) Fee Set by Voluntary Negotiation.

(A) Notice of Initiation of Proceedings.—On or before July 1, 1991, the Copyright Royalty Tribunal shall cause notice to be published in the Federal Register of the initiation of voluntary negotiation proceedings for the purpose of determining the royalty fee to be paid by satellite carriers under subsection (b)(1)(B).

(B) Negotiations.—Satellite carriers, distributors, and copyright owners entitled a royalty fees under this section shall negotiate in good faith in an effort to reach a voluntary agreement or voluntary agreements for the payment of royalty fees. Any such satellite carriers, distributors, and copyright owners may at any time negotiate and agree to the royalty fee, and may designate common agents a negotiate, agree to, or pay such fees. If the parties fail to identify common agents, the Copyright Royalty Tribunal shall do so, after requesting recommendations from the parties a the negotiation proceeding. The parties to each negotiation proceeding shall bear the entire cost thereof.

(C) Agreements Binding on Parties; Filing of Agreements.—

Voluntary agreements negotiated at any time in accordance with this paragraph shall be binding upon all satellite carriers, distributors, and copyright owners that are parties thereto. Copies of such agreements shall be filed with the Copyright Office within 30 days after execution in accordance with regulations that the Register of Copyrights shall prescribe.

(D) Period Agreement Is in Effect.—The obligation to pay the royalty fees established under a voluntary agreement which has been filed with the Copyright Office in accordance with this paragraph shall become effective on the date specified in the agreement, and shall remain in effect until December 31, 1994.

(3) Fee Set by Compulsory Arbitration.—

(A) Notice of Initiation of Proceeding.—On or before December 31, 1991, the Copyright Royalty Tribunal shall cause notice to be published in the Federal Register of the initiation of arbitration proceeding for the purpose of determining a reasonable royalty fee to be paid under subsection (b)(1)(B) by satellite carriers who are not parties to a voluntary agreement filed with the Copyright Office in accordance with paragraph (2). Such notice shall include the names and qualifications of potential arbitrators chosen by the Tribunal from a list of available arbitrators obtained from the American Arbitration Association or such similar organization as the Tribunal shall select.

(B) Selection of Arbitration Panel.—Not later than 10 days after publication of the notice initiating an arbitration proceeding, and in accordance with procedures to be specified by the Copyright Royalty Tribunal, one arbitrator shall be selected from the published list by copyright owners who claim to be entitled to royalty fees under subsection (b)(4) and who are not party to a voluntary agreement filed with the Copyright Office in accordance with paragraph (2), and one arbitrator shall be selected from the published list by satellite carriers and distributors who are not parties to such a voluntary agreement. The two arbitrators so selected shall, within 10 days after their selection, choose a third arbitrator from the same list, who shall serve as chairperson of the arbitrators. If either group fail to agree upon the selection of an arbitrator, or if the arbitrators selected by such groups fail to agree upon the selection of a chairperson, the Copyright Royalty Tribunal shall promptly select the arbitrator or chairperson, respectively. The arbitrators selected under this subparagraph shall constitute an Arbitration Panel.

(C) Arbitration Proceeding.—The Arbitration Panel shall conduct an arbitration proceeding in accordance with such procedures as it may adopt. The Panel shall act on the basis of a fully documented written record. Any copyright owner who claims to be entitled to royalty fees under subsection (b)(4), any satellite carrier, and any distributor, who is not party to a voluntary agreement filed with the Copyright Office in accordance with paragraph (2), may submit relevant information and proposals to the Panel. The parties to the proceeding shall bear the entire cost thereof in such manner and proportion as the Panel shall direct.

(D) Factors for Determining Royalty Fees.—In determining royalty fees under this paragraph, the Arbitration Panel shall consider the approximate average cost to a cable system for the right to secondarily transmit to the public a primary transmission made by a broadcast station, the fee established under any voluntary agreement filed with the Copyright Office in accordance with paragraph (2), and the last fee proposed by the parties, before proceedings under this paragraph, for the secondary transmission of superstations or network stations for private home viewing. The fee shall also be calculated to achieve the following objectives:

(i) To maximize the availability of creative works to the public.

(ii) To afford the copyright owner a fair return for his or her creative work and the copyright user a fair income under existing economic conditions.

(iii) To reflect the relative roles of the copyright owner and the copyright user in the product made available to the public with respect to relative creative contribution, technological contribution, capital investment, cost, risk, and contribution to the opening of new markets for creative expression and media for their communication.

(iv) To minimize any disruptive impact on the structure of the industries involved and on generally prevailing industry practices.

(E) Report to Copyright Royalty Tribunal.—Not later than 60 days after publication of the notice initiating an arbitration proceeding, the Arbitration Panel shall report to the Copyright Royalty Tribunal its determination concerning the royalty fee. Such report shall be accompanied by the written record, and shall set forth the facts that the Panel found relevant to its determination and the reasons why its determination is consistent with the criteria set forth in subparagraph (D).

(F) Action by Copyright Royalty Tribunal.—Within 60 days after receiving the report of the Arbitration Panel under subparagraph (E), the Copyright Royalty Tribunal shall adopt or reject the determination of the Panel. The Tribunal shall adopt the determination of the Panel unless the Tribunal finds that the determination is clearly inconsistent with the criteria set forth in subparagraph (D). If the Tribunal rejects the determination of the Panel, the Tribunal shall, before the end of that 60–day period, and after full examination of the record created in the arbitration proceeding, issue an order, consistent with the criteria set forth in subparagraph (D), setting the royalty fee under this paragraph. The Tribunal shall cause to be published in the Federal Register the determination of the Panel, and the decision of the Tribunal with respect to the determination (including any order issued under the preceding sentence). The Tribunal shall also publicize such determination and decision in such other manner as the Tribunal considers appropriate. The Tribunal shall also make the report of the Arbitration Panel and the accompanying record available for public inspection and copying.

(G) Period During Which Decision of Panel or Order of Tribunal Effective.—The obligation to pay the royalty fee established under a determination of the Arbitration Panel which is confirmed by the Copyright Royalty Tribunal in accordance with this paragraph, or established by any order issued under subparagraph (F), shall become effective on the date when the decision of the Tribunal is published in the Federal Register under subparagraph (F), and shall remain in effect until modified in accordance with paragraph (4), or until December 31, 1994.

(H) Persons Subject to Royalty Fee.—The royalty fee adopted or ordered under subparagraph (F) shall be binding on all satellite carriers, distributors, and copyright owners, who are not party to a voluntary agreement filed with the Copyright Office under paragraph (2).

(4) Judicial Review.—Any decision of the Copyright Royalty Tribunal under paragraph (3) with respect to a determination of the Arbitration Panel may be appealed, by any aggrieved party who would be bound by the determination, to the United States Court of Appeals for the District of Columbia Circuit, within 30 days after the publication of the decision in the Federal Register. The pendency of an appeal under this paragraph shall not relieve satellite carriers of the obligation under subsection (b)(1) to deposit the statement of account and royalty fees specified in that subsection. The court shall have jurisdiction to modify or vacate a decision of the Tribunal only if it finds, on the basis of the record before the Tribunal and the statutory criteria set forth in paragraph (3)(D), that the Arbitration Panel or the Tribunal acted in an arbitrary manner. If the court modifies the decision of the Tribunal, the court shall have jurisdiction to enter its own determination with respect to royalty fees, to order the repayment of any excess fees deposited under subsection (b)(1)(B), and to order the payment of any underpaid fees, and the interest pertaining respectively thereto, in accordance with its final judgment. The court may further vacate the decision of the Tribunal and remand the case for arbitration proceeding in accordance with paragraph (3).

(d) Definitions.—As used in this section—

(1) Distributor.—The term "distributor" means an entity which contracts to distribute secondary transmissions from a satellite carrier and, either as a single channel or in a package with other programming, provides the secondary transmission either directly to individual subscribers for private home viewing or indirectly through other program distribution entities.

(2) Network Station.—The term "network station" has the meaning given that term in section 111(f) of this title, and in-

cludes any translator station or terrestrial satellite station that rebroadcasts all or substantially all of the programming broadcast by a network station.

(3) Primary Network Station.—The term "primary network station" means a network station that broadcasts or rebroadcasts the basic programming service of a particular national network.

(4) Primary Transmission.—The term "primary transmission" has the meaning given that term in section 111(f) of this title.

(5) Private Home Viewing.—The term "private home viewing" means the viewing, for private use in a household by means of satellite reception equipment which is operated by an individual in that household and which serves only such household, of a secondary transmission delivered by a satellite carrier of a primary transmission of a television station licensed by the Federal Communications Commission.

(6) Satellite Carrier.—The term "satellite carrier" means an entity that uses the facilities of a satellite or satellite service licensed by the Federal Communications Commission, to establish and operate a channel of communications for point-to-multipoint distribution of television station signals, and that owns or leases a capacity or service on a satellite in order to provide such point-to-multipoint distribution, except to the extent that such entity provides such distribution pursuant to tariff under the Communications Act of 1934, other than for private home viewing.

(7) Secondary Transmission.—The term "secondary transmission" has the meaning given that term in section 111(f) of this title.

(8) Subscriber.—The term "subscriber" means an individual who receives a secondary transmission service for private home viewing by means of a secondary transmission from a satellite carrier and pays a fee for the service, directly or indirectly, to the satellite carrier or to a distributor.

(9) Superstation.—The term "superstation" means a television broadcast station, other than a network station, licensed by the Federal Communications Commission that is secondarily transmitted by satellite carrier.

(10) Unserved Household.—The term "unserved household"

with respect to a particular television network, means a household that—

(A) cannot receive, through the use of a conventional outdoor rooftop receiving antenna, an over-the-air signal of grade B intensity (as defined by the Federal Communications Commission) of a primary network station affiliated with that network, and

(B) has not, within 90 days before the date on which that household subscribes, either initially or on renewal, to receive secondary transmissions by a satellite carrier of a network station affiliated with that network, subscribed to a cable system that provides the signal of a primary network station affiliated with that network.

(e) EXCLUSIVITY OF THIS SECTION WITH RESPECT TO SECONDARY TRANSMISSIONS OF BROADCAST STATIONS BY SATELLITE TO MEMBERS OF THE PUBLIC.—No provision of section 111 of this title or any other law (other than this section) shall be construed to contain any authorization, exemption, or license through which secondary transmissions by satellite carrier for private home viewing of programming contained in a primary transmission made by a superstation or a network station may be made without obtaining the consent of the copyright owner.

Sec. 120. Scope of Exclusive Rights in Architectural Works

(a) PICTORIAL REPRESENTATIONS PERMITTED.—The copyright in an architectural work that has been constructed does not include the right to prevent the making, distributing, or public display of pictures, paintings, photographs, or other pictorial representations of the work, if the building in which the work is embodied is located in or ordinarily visible from a public place.

(b) ALTERATIONS TO AND DESTRUCTION OF BUILDINGS.—Notwithstanding the provisions of section 106(2), the owners of a building embodying an architectural work may, without the consent of the author or copyright owner of the architectural work, make or authorize the making of alterations to such building, and destroy or authorize the destruction of such building.

Chapter 2—Copyright Ownership and Transfer

Sec. 201. Ownership of Copyright

(a) INITIAL OWNERSHIP.—Copyright in a work protected under this title vests initially in the author or authors of the work. The authors of a joint work are coowners of copyright in the work.

(b) WORKS MADE FOR HIRE.—In the case of a work made for hire, the employer or other person for whom the work was prepared is considered the author for purposes of this title, and, unless the parties have expressly agreed otherwise in a written instrument signed by them, owns all of the rights comprised in the copyright.

(c) CONTRIBUTIONS TO COLLECTIVE WORKS.—Copyright in each separate contribution to a collective work is distinct from copyright in the collective work as a whole, and vests initially in the author of the contribution. In the absence of an express transfer of the copyright or of any rights under it, the owner of copyright in the collective work is presumed to have acquired only the privilege of reproducing and distributing the contribution as part of that particular collective work, any revision of that collective work, and any later collective work in the same series.

(d) TRANSFER OF OWNERSHIP.—

(1) The ownership of a copyright may be transferred in whole or in part by any means of conveyance or by operation of law, and may be bequeathed by will or pass as personal property by the applicable laws of intestate succession.

(2) Any of the exclusive rights comprised in a copyright,

including any subdivision of any of the rights specified by section 106, may be transferred as provided by clause (1) and owned separately. The owner of any particular exclusive right is entitled, to the extent of that right, to all of the protection and remedies accorded to the copyright owner by this title.

(e) INVOLUNTARY TRANSFER.—When an individual author's ownership of a copyright, or of any of the exclusive rights under a copyright, has not previously then transferred voluntarily by that individual author, no action by any governmental body or other official or organization purporting to seize, expropriate, transfer, or exercise rights of ownership with respect to the copyright, or any of the exclusive rights under a copyright, shall be given effect under this title except as provided under title 11.

Sec. 202. Ownership of Copyright as Distinct from Ownership of Material Object

Ownership of a copyright, or of any of the exclusive rights under a copyright, is distinct from ownership of any material object in which the work is embodied. Transfer of ownership of any material object, including the copy or phonorecord in which the work is first fixed, does not of itself convey any rights in the copyrighted work embodied in the object; nor, in the absence of an agreement, does transfer of ownership of a copyright or of any exclusive rights under a copyright convey property rights in any material object.

Sec. 203. Termination of Transfers and Licenses Granted by the Author

(a) CONDITIONS FOR TERMINATION.—In the case of any work other than a work made for hire, the exclusive or nonexclusive grant of a transfer or license of copyright or of any right under a copyright, executed by the author on or after January 1, 1978, otherwise than by will, is subject to termination under the following conditions:

(1) In the case of a grant executed by one author, termination of the grant may be effected by that author or, if the author is dead, by the person or persons who, under clause (2) of this subsection, own and are entitled to exercise a total of more than

one-half of that author's termination interest. In the case of a grant executed by two or more authors of a joint work, termination of the grant may be effected by a majority of the authors who executed it; if any of such authors is dead, the termination interest of any such author may be exercised as a unit by the person or persons who, under clause (2) of this subsection, own and are entitled to exercise a total of more than one-half of that author's interest.

(2) Where an author is dead, his or her termination interest is owned, and may be exercised, by his widow or her widower and his or her children or grandchildren as follows:

(A) the widow or widower owns the author's entire termination interest unless there are any surviving children or grandchildren of the author, in which case the widow or widower owns one-half of the author's interest;

(B) the author's surviving children, and the surviving children of any dead child of the author, own the author's entire termination interest unless there is a widow or widower, in which case the ownership of one half of the author's interest is divided among them;

(C) the rights of the author's children and grandchildren are in all cases divided among them and exercised on a per stirpes basis according to the number of such author's children represented; the share of the children of a dead child in a termination interest can be exercised only by the action of a majority of them.

(3) Termination of the grant may be effected at any time during a period of five years beginning at the end of thirty-five years from the date of execution of the grant; or, if the grant covers the right of publication of the work, the period begins at the end of thirty-five years from the date of publication of the work under the grant or at the end of forty years from the date of execution of the grant, whichever term ends earlier.

(4) The termination shall be effected by serving an advance notice in writing, signed by the number and proportion of owners of termination interests required under clauses (1) and (2) of this subsection, or by their duly authorized agents, upon the grantee or the grantee's successor in title.

(A) The notice shall state the effective date of the termination, which shall fall within the five-year period specified by clause (3) of this subsection, and the notice shall be served not less than two or more than ten years before that date. A copy of the notice shall be recorded in the Copyright Office before the effective date of termination, as a condition to its taking effect.

(B) The notice shall comply, in form, content, and manner of service, with requirements that the Register of Copyrights shall prescribe by regulation.

(5) Termination of the grant may be effected notwithstanding any agreement to the contrary, including an agreement to make a will or to make any future grant.

(b) EFFECT OF TERMINATION.—Upon the effective date of termination, all rights under this title that were covered by the terminated grants revert to the author, authors, and other persons owning termination interests under clauses (1) and (2) of subsection (a), including those owners who did not join in signing the notice of termination under clause (4) of subsection (a), but with the following limitations:

(1) A derivative work prepared under authority of the grant before its termination may continue to be utilized under the terms of the grant after its termination, but this privilege does not extend to the preparation after the termination of other derivative works based upon the copyrighted work covered by the terminated grant.

(2) The future rights that will revert upon termination of the grant become vested on the date the notice of termination has been served as provided by clause (4) of subsection (a). The rights vest in the author, authors, and other persons named in, and in the proportionate shares provided by, clauses (1) and (2) of subsection (a).

(3) Subject to the provisions of clause (4) of this subsection, a further grant, or agreement to make a further grant, of any right covered by a terminated grant is valid only if it is signed by the same number and proportion of the owners, in whom the right has vested under clause (2) of this subsection, as are required to terminate the grant under clauses (1) and (2) of subsection (a). Such further grant or agreement is effective with respect to all of the persons in whom the right it covers has vested under

clause (2) of this subsection, including those who did not join in signing it. If any person dies after rights under a terminated grant have vested in him or her, that person's legal representatives, legatees, or heirs at law represent him or her for purposes of this clause.

(4) A further grant, or agreement to make a further grant, of any right covered by a terminated grant is valid only if it is made after the effective date of the termination. As an exception, however, an agreement for such a further grant may be made between the persons provided by clause (3) of this subsection and the original grantee or such grantee's successor in title, after the notice of termination has been served as provided by clause (4) of subsection (a).

(5) Termination of a grant under this section affects only those rights covered by the grants that arise under this title, and in no way affects rights arising under any other Federal, State, or foreign laws.

(6) Unless and until termination is effected under this section, the grant, if it does not provide otherwise, continues in effect for the term of copyright provided by this title.

Sec. 204. Execution of Transfers of Copyright Ownership

(a) A transfer of copyright ownership, other than by operation of law, is not valid unless an instrument of conveyance, or a note or memorandum of the transfer, is in writing and signed by the owner of the rights conveyed or such owner's duly authorized agent.

(b) A certificate of acknowledgement is not required for the validity of a transfer, but is prima face evidence of the execution of the transfer if—

(1) in the case of a transfer executed in the United States, the certificate is issued by a person authorized to administer oaths within the United States; or

(2) in the case of a transfer executed in a foreign country, the certificate is issued by a diplomatic or consular officer of the United States, or by a person authorized to administer oaths whose authority is proved by a certificate of such an officer.

Sec. 205. Recordation of Transfers and Other Documents

(a) CONDITIONS FOR RECORDATION.—Any transfer of copyright ownership or other document pertaining to a copyright may be recorded in the Copyright Office if the document filed for recordation bears the actual signature of the person who executed it, or if it is accompanied by a sworn or official certification that it is a true copy of the original, signed document.

(b) CERTIFICATE OF RECORDATION.—The Register of Copyrights shall, upon receipt of a document as provided by subsection (a) and of the fee provided by section 708, record the document and return it with a certificate of recordation.

(c) RECORDATION AS CONSTRUCTIVE NOTICE.—Recordation of a document in the Copyright Office gives all persons constructive notice of the facts stated in the recorded document, but only if—

(1) the document, or material attached to it, specifically identifies the work to which it pertains so that, after the document is indexed by the Register of Copyrights, it would be revealed by a reasonable search under the title or registration number of the work; and

(2) registration has been made for the work.

(d) RECORDATION AS PREREQUISITE TO INFRINGEMENT SUIT.—No person claiming by virtue of a transfer to be the owner of copyright or of any exclusive right under a copyright is entitled to institute an infringement action under this title until the instrument of transfer under which such person claims has been recorded in the Copyright Office, but suit may be instituted after such recordation on a cause of action that arose before recordation.

(e) PRIORITY BETWEEN CONFLICTING TRANSFERS.—As between two conflicting transfers, the one executed first prevails if it is recorded, in the manner required to give constructive notice under subsection (c), within one month after its execution in the United States or within two months after its execution outside the United States, or at any time before recordation in such manner of the later transfer. Otherwise the later transfer prevails if recorded first in such manner, and if taken in good faith, for valuable consideration or on the basis of a binding promise to pay royalties, and without notice of the earlier transfer.

(f) PRIORITY BETWEEN CONFLICTING TRANSFER OF OWNERSHIP AND NONEXCLUSIVE LICENSE.—A nonexclusive license, whether recorded or not, prevails over a conflicting transfer of copyright ownership if the license is evidenced by a written instrument signed by the owner of the rights licensed or such owner's duly authorized agent, and if—

(1) the license was taken before execution of the transfer; or

(2) the license was taken in good faith before recordation of the transfer and without notice of it.

Chapter 3—Duration of Copyright

Sec.

Sec. 301. Preemption with Respect to Other Laws

(a) On and after January 1, 1978, all legal or equitable rights that are equivalent to any of the exclusive rights within the general scope of copyright as specified by section 106 in works of authorship that are fixed in a tangible medium of expression and come within the subject matter of copyright as specified by sections 102 and 103, whether created before or after that date and whether published or unpublished, are governed exclusively by this title. Thereafter, no person is entitled to any such right or equivalent right in any such work under the common law or statutes of any State.

(b) Nothing in this title annuls or limits any rights or remedies under the common law or statutes of any State with respect to—

(1) subject matter that does not come within the subject matter of copyright as specified by sections 102 and 103, including

works of authorship not fixed in any tangible medium of expression; or

(2) any cause of action arising from undertakings commenced before January 1, 1978;

(3) activities violating legal or equitable rights that are not equivalent to any of the exclusive rights within the general scope of copyright as specified by section 106; or

(4) State and local landmarks, historic preservation, zoning, or building codes, relating to architectural works protected under section 102(a)(8).

(c) With respect to sound recordings fixed before February 15, 1972, any rights or remedies under the common law or statutes of any State shall not be annulled or limited by this title until February 15, 2047. The preemptive provisions of subsection (a) shall apply to any such rights and remedies pertaining to any cause of action arising from undertakings commenced on and after February 15, 2047. Notwithstanding the provisions of section 303, no sound recording fixed before February 15, 1972, shall be subject to copyright under this title before, on, or after February 15, 2047.

(d) Nothing in this title annuls or limits any rights or remedies under any other Federal statute.

(e) The scope of Federal preemption under this section is not affected by the adherence of the United States to the Berne Convention or the satisfaction of obligations of the United States thereunder.

[Note: subsection (f) becomes effective on June 1, 1991.]

(f)(1) On or after the effective date set forth in section 610(a) of the Visual Artists Rights Act of 1990, all legal or equitable rights that are equivalent to any of the rights conferred by section 106A with respect to works of visual art to which the rights conferred by section 106A apply are governed exclusively by section 106A and section 113(d) and the provisions of this title relating to such sections Thereafter, no person is entitled to any such right or equivalent right in any work of visual art under the common law or statutes of any State.

(2) Nothing in paragraph (1) annuls or limits any rights or remedies under the common law or statutes of any State with respect to—

(A) any cause of action from undertakings commenced before the effective date set forth in section 610(a) of the Visual Artists Rights Act of 1990;

(B) activities violating legal or equitable rights that are not equivalent to any of the rights conferred by section 106A with respect to works of visual art; or

(C) activities violating legal or equitable rights which extend beyond the life of the author.

Sec. 302. Duration of Copyright: Works Created on or After January 1, 1978

(a) IN GENERAL.—Copyright in a work created on or after January 1, 1978, subsists from its creation and, except as provided by the following subsections, endures for a term consisting of the life of the author and fifty years after the author's death.

(b) JOINT WORKS.—In the case of a joint work prepared by two or more authors who did not work for hire, the copyright endures for a term consisting of the life of the last surviving author and fifty years after such last surviving author's death.

(c) ANONYMOUS WORKS, PSEUDONYMOUS WORKS, AND WORKS MADE FOR HIRE.—In the case of an anonymous work, a pseudonymous work, or a work made for hire, the copyright endures for a term of seventy-five years from the year of its first publication, or a term of one hundred years from the year of its creation, whichever expires first. If, before the end of such term, the identity of one or more of the authors of an anonymous or pseudonymous work is revealed in the records of a registration made for that work under subsections (a) or (d) of section 408, or in the records provided by this subsection, the copyright in the work endures for the term specified by subsection (a) or (b), based on the life of the author or authors whose identity has been revealed. Any person having an interest in the copyright in an anonymous or pseudonymous work may at any time record, in records to be maintained by the Copyright Office for that purpose, a statement identifying one or more authors of the work; the statement shall also identify the person filing it, the nature of that person's interest, the source of the information recorded, and the particular work affected, and shall comply in form and content with requirements that the Register of Copyrights shall prescribe by regulation.

(d) RECORDS RELATING TO DEATH OF AUTHORS.—Any person having an interest in a copyright may at any time record in the Copyright Office a statement of the date of death of the author of the copyrighted work, or a statement that the author is still living on a particular date. The statement shall identify the person filing it, the nature of that person's interest, and the source of the information recorded, and shall comply in form and content with requirements that the Register of Copyrights shall prescribe by regulation. The Register shall maintain current records of information relaxing to the death of authors of copyrighted works, based on such recorded statements and, to the extent the Register considers practicable, on data contained in any of the records of the Copyright Office or in other reference sources.

(e) PRESUMPTION AS TO AUTHOR'S DEATH.—After a period of seventy-five years from the year of first publication of a work, or a period of one hundred years from the year of its creation, whichever expires first, any person who obtains from the Copyright Office a certified report that the records provided by subsection (d) disclose nothing to indicate that the author of the work is living, or died less than fifty years before, is entitled to the benefit of a presumption that the author has been dead for at least fifty years. Reliance in good faith upon this presumption shall be a complete defense to any action for infringement under this title.

Sec. 303. Duration of Copyright: Works Created but Not Published or Copyrighted Before January 1, 1978

Copyright in a work created before January 1, 1978, but not theretofore in the public domain or copyrighted, subsists from January 1, 1978, and endures for the term provided by section 302. In no case, however, shall the term of copyright in such a work expire before December 31, 2002; and, if the work is published on or before December 31, 2002, the term of copyright shall not expire before December 31, 2027

Sec. 304. Duration of Copyright: Subsisting Copyrights

(a) COPYRIGHTS IN THEIR FIRST TERM ON JANUARY 1, 1978.—Any copyright, the first term of which is subsisting on January 1, 1978, shall endure for twenty-eight years from the date it was originally secured: *Provided,* That in the case of any posthumous work or of any periodical, cyclopedic, or other composite work upon which the copyright was originally secured by the proprietor thereof, or of any work copyrighted by a corporate body (otherwise than as assignee or licensee of the individual author) or by an employer for whom such work is made for hire, the proprietor of such copyright shall be entitled to a renewal and extension of the copyright in such work for the further term of forty-seven years when application for just renewal and extension shall have been made to the Copyright Office and duly registered therein within one year prior to the expiration of the original term of copyright: *And provided further,* That in the case of any other copyrighted work, including a contribution by an individual author to a periodical or to a cyclopedic or other composite work, the author of such work, if still living, or the widow, widower, or children of the author, if the author be not living, or if such author, widow, widower, or children be not living, then the author's executors, or in the absence of a will, his or her next of kin shall be entitled to a renewal and extension of the copyright in such work for a further term of forty-seven years when application for such renewal and extension shall have been made to the Copyright Office and duly registered therein within one year prior to the expiration of the original term of copyright: *And provided further,* That in default of the registration of such application for renewal and extension, the copyright in any work shall terminate at the expiration of twenty-eight years from the date copyright was originally secured.

(b) COPYRIGHTS IN THEIR RENEWAL TERM OR REGISTERED FOR RENEWAL BEFORE JANUARY 1, 1978.—The duration of any copyright, the renewal term of which is subsisting at any time between December 31, 1976, and December 31, 1977, inclusive, or for which renewal registration is made between December 31, 1976, and December 31, 1977, inclusive, is extended to endure for a term of seventy-five years from the date copyright was originally secured.

(c) TERMINATION OF TRANSFERS AND LICENSES COVERING EXTENDED RENEWAL TERM.—In the case of any copyright subsisting in either its first or renewal term on January 1, 1978, other than a copyright in a work made for hire, the exclusive or nonexclusive grant of a transfer or license of the renewal copyright or any right under it, executed before January 1, 1978, by any of the persons designated by the second proviso of subsection (a) of this section, otherwise than by will, is subject to termination under the following conditions:

(1) In the case of a grant executed by a person or persons other than the author, termination of the grant may be effected by the surviving person or persons who executed it. In the case of a grant executed by one or more of the authors of the work, termination of the grant may be effected, to the extent of a particular author's share in the ownership of the renewal copyright, by the author who executed it or, if such author is dead, by the person or persons who, under clause (2) of this subsection, own and are entitled to exercise a total of more than one-half of that author's termination interest.

(2) Where an author is dead, his or her termination interest is owned, and may be exercised, by his widow or her widower and his or her children or grandchildren as follows:

(A) the widow or widower owns the author's entire termination interest unless there are any surviving children or grandchildren of the author, in which case the widow or widower owns one-half of the author's interest;

(B) the author's surviving children, and the surviving children of any dead child of the author, own the author's entire termination interest unless there is a widow or widower, in which case the ownership of one-half of the author's interest is divided among them;

(C) the rights of the author's children and grandchildren are in all cases divided among them and exercised on a per stirpes basis according to the number of such author's children represented; the share of the children of a dead child in a termination interest can be exercised only by the action of a majority of them.

(3) Termination of the grant may be effected at any time during a period of five years beginning at the end of fifty-six years from the date copyright was originally secured, or beginning on January 1, 1978, whichever is later.

(4) The termination shall be effected by serving an advance notice in writing upon the grantee or the grantee's successor in

title. In the case of a grant executed by a person or persons other than the author, the notice shall be signed by all of those entitled to terminate the grant under clause (1) of this subsection, or by their duly authorized agents. In the case of a grant executed by one or more of the authors of the work, the notice as to any one author's share shall be signed by that author or his or her duly authorized agent or, if that author is dead, by the number and proportion of the owners of his or her termination interest required under clauses (1) and (2) of this subsection, or by their duly authorized agents.

(A) The notice shall state the effective date of the termination, which shall fall within the five-year period specified by clause (3) of this subsection, and the notice shall be served not less than two or more than ten years before that date. A copy of the notice shall be recorded in the Copyright Office before the effective date of termination, as a condition to its taking effect.

(B) The notice shall comply, in form, content, and manner of service with requirements that the Register of Copyrights shall prescribe by regulation.

(5) Termination of the grant may be effected notwithstanding any agreement to the contrary, including an agreement to make a will or to make any future grant.

(6) In the case of a grant executed by a person or persons other than the author, all rights under this title that were covered by the terminated grant revert, upon the effective date of termination, to all of those entitled to terminate the grant under clause (1) of this subsection. In the case of a grant executed by one or more of the authors of the work, all of a particular author's rights under this title that were covered by the terminated grant revert, upon the effective date of termination, to that author or, if that author is dead, to the persons owning his or her termination interest under clause (2) of this subsection, including those owners who did not join in signing the notice of termination under clause (4) of this subsection. In all cases the reversion of rights is subject to the following limitations:

(A) A derivative work prepared under authority of the grant before its termination may continue to be utilized under the terms of the grant after its termination, but this privilege does not extend to the preparation after the termination of other derivative works based upon the copyrighted work covered by the terminated grant.

(B) The future rights that will revert upon termination of the grant become vested on the date the notice of termination has been served as provided by clause (4) of this subsection.

(C) Where the author's rights revert to two or more persons under clause (2) of this subsection, they shall vest in those persons in the proportionate shares provided by that clause. In such a case, and subject to the provisions of subclause (D) of this clause, a further grant, or agreement to make a further grant, of a particular author's share with respect to any right covered by a terminated grant is valid only if it is signed by the same number and proportion of the owners, in whom the right has vested under this clause, as are required to terminate the grant under clause (2) of this subsection. Such further grant or agreement is effective with respect to all of the persons in whom the right it covers has vested under this subclause, including those who did not join in signing it. If any person dies after rights under a terminated grant have vested in him or her, that person's legal representatives, legatees, or heirs at law represent him or her for purposes of this subclause.

(D) A further grant, or agreement to make a further grant, of any right covered by a terminated grant is valid only if it is made after the effective date of the termination. As an exception, however, an agreement for such a further grant may be made between the author or any of the persons provided by the first sentence of clause (6) of this subsection, or between the persons provided by subclause (C) of this clause, and the original grantee or such grantee's successor in title, after the notice of termination has been served as provided by clause (4) of this subsection.

(E) Termination of a grant under this subsection affects only those rights covered by the grant that arise under this title, and in no way affects rights arising under any other Federal, State, or foreign laws.

(F) Unless and until termination is effected under this subsection, the grant, if it does not provide otherwise, continues in effect for the remainder of the extended renewal term.

Sec. 305. Duration of Copyright: Terminal Date

All terms of copyright provided by sections 302 through 304 run to the end of the calendar year in which they would otherwise expire.

Chapter 4—Copyright Notice, Deposit, and Registration

Sec. 401. Notice of Copyright: Visually Perceptible Copies

(a) GENERAL REQUIREMENT.—Whenever a work protected under this title is published in the United States or elsewhere by authority of the copyright owner, a notice of copyright as provided by this section shall be placed on all publicly distributed copies from which the work can be visually perceived, either directly or with the aid of a machine or device.

(b) FORM OF NOTICE.—The notice appearing on the copies shall consist of the following three elements:

(1) the symbol © (the letter C in a circle), or the word "Copyright," or the abbreviation "Copr."; and

(2) the year of first publication of the work; in the case of compilations or derivative works incorporating previously published material, the year date of first publication of the compilation or derivative work is sufficient. The year date may be omitted where a pictorial, graphic, or sculptural work with accompanying text matter, if any, is reproduced in or on greeting cards, postcards, stationery, jewelry, dolls, toys, or any useful articles; and

(3) the name of the owner of copyright in the work, or an abbreviation by which the name can be recognized, or a generally known alternative designation of the owner.

(c) POSITION OF NOTICE.—The notice shall be affixed to the copies in such manner and location as to give reasonable notice of the claim of copyright. The Register of Copyrights shall prescribe by regulation, as examples, specific methods of effectuation and positions of the notice on various types of works that will satisfy this requirement, but these specifications shall not be considered exhaustive.

Sec. 402. Notice of Copyright: Phonorecords of Sound Recordings

(a) GENERAL REQUIREMENT.—Whenever a sound recording protected under this title is published in the United States or elsewhere by authority of the copyright owner, a notice of copyright as provided by this section shall be placed on all publicly distributed phonorecords of the sound recording.

(b) FORM OF NOTICE.—The notice appearing on the phonorecords shall consist of the following three elements:

(1) the symbol ℗ (the letter P in a circle); and

(2) the year of first publication of the sound recording; and

(3) the name of the owner of copyright in the sound recording, or an abbreviation by which the name can be recognized, or a generally known alternative designation of the owner; if the producer of the sound recording is named on the phonorecord labels or containers, and if no other name appears in conjunction with the notice, the producer's name shall be considered a part of the notice.

(c) POSITION OF NOTICE.—The notice shall be placed on the surface of the phonorecord, or on the phonorecord label or container, in such manner and location as to give reasonable notice of the claim of copyright.

Sec. 403. Notice of Copyright: Publications Incorporating United States Government Works

Whenever a work is published in copies or phonorecords consisting preponderantly of one or more works of the United States Government, the notice of copyright provided by sections 401 or 402 shall also include a statement identifying, either affirmatively or negatively, those portions of the copies or phonorecords embodying any work or works protected under this title.

Sec. 404. Notice of Copyright: Contributions to Collective Works

(a) A separate contribution to a collective work may bear its own notice of copyright as provided by sections 401 through 403. However, a single notice applicable to the collective work as a whole is sufficient to satisfy the requirements of sections 401 through 403 with respect to the separate contributions it contains (not including advertisements inserted on behalf of persons other than the owner of copyright in the collective work), regardless of the ownership of copyright in the contributions and whether or not they have been previously published.

(b) Where the person named in a single notice applicable to a collective work as a whole is not the owner of copyright in a separate contribution that does not bear its own notice, the case is governed by the provisions of section 406(a).

Sec. 405. Notice of Copyright: Omission of Notice on Certain Copies and Phonorecords

(a) EFFECT OF OMISSION ON COPYRIGHT.—The omission of the copyright notice prescribed by sections 401 through 403 from copies or phonorecords publicly distributed by authority of the copyright owner does not invalidate the copyright in a work if—

(1) the notice has been omitted from no more than a relatively small number of copies or phonorecords distributed to the public; or

(2) registration for the work has been made before or is made within five years after the publication without notice, and a reasonable effort is made to add notice to all copies or phonorecords that are distributed to the public in the United States after the omission has been discovered; or

(3) the notice has been omitted in violation of an express requirement in writing that, as a condition of the copyright owner's authorization of the public distribution of copies or phonorecords, they bear the prescribed notice.

(b) EFFECT OF OMISSION ON INNOCENT INFRINGERS.—Any person who innocently infringes a copyright, in reliance upon an authorized copy or phonorecord from which the copyright notice has been omitted, incurs no liability for actual or statutory damages under section 504 for any infringing acts committed before receiving actual notice that registration for the work has been made under section 408, if such person proves that he or she was misled by the omission of notice. In a suit for infringement in such a case the court may allow or disallow recovery of any of the infringer's profits attributable to the infringement, and may enjoin the continuation of the infringing undertaking or may require, as a condition [of] permitting the, continuation of the infringing undertaking, that the infringer pay the copyright owner a reasonable license fee in an amount and on terms fixed by the court.

(c) REMOVAL OF NOTICE.—Protection under this title is not affected by the removal, destruction, or obliteration of the notice, without the authorization of the copyright owner from any publicly distributed copies or phonorecords.

Sec. 406. Notice of Copyright: Error in Name or Date on Certain Copies and Phonorecords

(a) ERROR IN NAME.—Where the person named in the copyright notice on copies or phonorecords publicly distributed by authority of the copyright owner is not the owner of copyright, the validity and ownership of the copyright are not affected. In such a case, however, any person who innocently begins an undertaking that infringes the copyright has a complete defense to any action for such infringement if such person proves that he or she was misled by the notice and began the undertaking in good faith under a purported transfer or license from the person named therein, unless before the undertaking was begun—

(1) registration for the work had been made in the name of the owner of copyright; or

(2) a document executed by the person named in the notice and showing the ownership of the copyright had been recorded.

The person named in the notice is liable to account to the copyright owner for all receipts from transfers or licenses purportedly made under the copyright by the person named in the notice.

(b) ERROR IN DATE.—When the year date in the notice on copies or phonorecords distributed by authority of the copyright owner is earlier than the year in which publication first occurred, any period computed from the year of first publication under section 302 is to be computed from the year in the notice. Where the year date is more than one year later than the year in which publication first occurred, the work is considered to have been published without any notice and is governed by the provisions of section 405.

(c) OMISSION OF NAME OR DATE.—Where copies or phonorecords publicly distributed by authority of the copyright owner contain no name or no date that could reasonably be considered a part of the notice, the work is considered to have been published without any notice and is governed by the provisions of section 405.

Sec. 407. Deposit of Copies or Phonorecords for Library of Congress

(a) Except as provided by subsection (c), and subject to the provisions of subsection (e), the owner of copyright or of the exclusive right of publication in a work published with notice of copyright in the United States shall deposit, within three months after the date of such publication—

(1) two complete copies of the best edition; or

(2) if the work is a sound recording, two complete phonorecords of the best edition, together with any printed or other visually perceptible material published with such phonorecords.

Neither the deposit requirements of this subsection nor the acquisition provisions of subsection (e) are conditions of copyright protection.

(b) The required copies or phonorecords shall be deposited in the Copyright Office for the use or disposition of the Library of Congress. The Register of Copyrights shall, when requested by the depositor and upon payment of the fee prescribed by section 708, issue a receipt for the deposit.

(c) The Register of Copyrights may by regulation exempt any categories of material from the deposit requirements of this section, or require deposit of only one copy or phonorecord with respect to any categories. Such regulations shall provide either for complete exemption from the deposit requirements of this section or for alternative forms of deposit aimed at providing a satisfactory archival record of a work without imposing practical or financial hardships on the deposition where the individual author is the owner of copyright in a pictorial, graphic, or sculptural work and (i) less than five copies of the work have been published, or (ii) the work has been published in a limited edition consisting of numbered copies, the monetary value of which would make the mandatory deposit of two copies of the best edition of the work burdensome, unfair, or unreasonable.

(d) At any time after publication of a work as provided by subsection (a), the Register of Copyrights may make written demand for the required deposit on any of the persons obligated to make the deposit under subsection (a). Unless deposit is made within three months after the demand is received, the person or persons on whom the demand was made are liable—

(1) to a fine of not more than $250 for each work; and

(2) to pay into a specially designated fund in the Library of

Congress the total retail price of the copies or phonorecords demanded, or, if no retail price has been fixed, the reasonable cost of the Library of Congress of acquiring them; and

(3) to pay a fine of $2,500, in addition to any fine or liability imposed under clauses (1) and (2), if such person willfully or repeatedly fails or refuses to comply with such a demand.

(e) With respect to transmission programs that have been fixed and transmitted to the public in the United States but have not been published, the Register of Copyrights shall, after consulting with the Librarian of Congress and other interested organizations and officials, establish regulations governing the acquisition through deposit or otherwise of copies or phonorecords of such programs for the collections of the Library of Congress.

(1) The Librarian of Congress shall be permitted, under the standards and conditions set forth in such regulations, to make a fixation of a transmission program directly from a transmission to the public, and to reproduce one copy or phonorecord from such fixation for archival purposes.

(2) Such regulations shall also provide standards and procedures by which the Register of Copyrights may make written demand, upon the owner of the right of transmission in the United States, for the deposit of a copy or phonorecord of a specific transmission program. Such deposit may, at the option of the owner of the right of transmission in the United States, be accomplished by gift, by loan for purposes of reproduction, or by sale at a price not to exceed the cost of reproducing and supplying the copy or phonorecord. The regulations established under this clause shall provide reasonable periods of not less than three months for compliance with a demand, and shall allow for extensions of such periods and adjustments in the scope of the demand or the methods for fulfilling it, as reasonably warranted by the circumstances. Willful failure or refusal to comply with the conditions prescribed by such regulations shall subject the owner of the right of transmission in the United States to liability for an amount, not to exceed the cost of reproducing and supplying the copy or phonorecord in question, to be paid into a specially designated fund in the Library of Congress.

(3) Nothing in this subsection shall be construed to require the making or retention, for purposes of deposit, of any copy or phonorecord of an unpublished transmission program, the transmission of which occurs before the receipt of a specific written demand as provided by clause (2).

(4) No activity undertaken in compliance with regulations prescribed under clauses (1) or (2) of this subsection shall result in liability if intended solely to assist in the acquisition of copies or phonorecords under this subsection.

Sec. 408. Copyright Registration in General

(a) REGISTRATION PERMISSIVE.—At any time during the subsistence of copyright in any published or unpublished work, the owner of copyright or of any exclusive right in the work may obtain registration of the copyright claim by delivering to the Copyright Office the deposit specified by this section, together with the application and fee specified by sections 409 and 708. Subject to the provisions of section 405(a), such registration is not a condition of copyright protection.

(b) DEPOSIT FOR COPYRIGHT REGISTRATION.—Except as provided by subsection (c), the material deposited for registration shall include—

(1) in the case of an unpublished work, one complete copy or phonorecord;

(2) in the case of the published work, two complete copies or phonorecords of the best edition;

(3) in the case of a work first published outside the United States, one complete copy or phonorecord as so published;

(4) in the case of a contribution to a collective work, one complete copy or phonorecord of the best edition of the collective work.

Copies or phonorecords deposited for the Library of Congress under section (407 may be used to satisfy the deposit provisions of this section, if they are accompanied by the prescribed application and fee, and by any additional identifying material that the Register may, by regulation, require. The Register shall also prescribe regulations establishing requirements under which copies or phonorecords acquired for the Library of Congress under subsection (e) of section 407, otherwise than by deposit, may be used to satisfy the deposit provisions of this section.

(c) ADMINISTRATIVE CLASSIFICATION AND OPTIONAL DEPOSIT.—(1) The Register of Copyrights is authorized to specify by regulation the administrative classes into which works are to be placed for purposes of deposit and registration, and the nature of the copies or phonorecords to be deposited in the various classes specified. The regulations may require or permit, for particular classes, the deposit of identifying material instead of copies or phonorecords, the deposit of only one copy or phonorecord where two would normally be required, or a single registration for a group of related works. This administrative classification of works has no significance with respect to the subject matter of copyright or the exclusive rights provided by this title.

(2) Without prejudice to the central authority provided under clause (1), the Register of Copyrights shall establish regulations specifically permitting a single registration for a group of works by the same individual author, all first published as contributions to periodicals, including newspapers, within a twelve-month period, on the basis of a single deposit, application, and registration fee, under all of the following conditions—

(A) if each of the works as first published bore a separate copyright notice, and the name of the owner of copyright in the work, or an abbreviation by which the name can be recognized, or a generally known alternative designation of the owner was the same in each notice; and

(B) if the deposit consists of one copy of the entire issue of the periodical, or of the entire section in the case of a newspaper, in which each contribution was first published; and

(C) if the application identifies each work separately, including the periodical containing it and its date of first publication.

(3) As an alternative to separate renewal registrations under subsection (a) of section 304, a single renewal registration may be made for a group of works by the same individual author, all first published as contributions to periodicals, including newspapers, upon the filing of a single application and fee, under all of the following conditions:

(A) the renewal claimant or claimants, and the basis of

claim or claims under section 304(a), is the same for each of the works: and

(B) the works were all copyrighted upon their first publication, either through separate copyright notice and registration or by virtue of a general copyright notice in the periodical issue as a whole; and

(C) the renewal application and fee are received not more than twenty-eight or less than twenty-seven years after the thirty-first day of December of the calendar year in which all of the works were first published; and

(D) the renewal application identifies each work separately, including the periodical containing it and its date of first publication.

(d) CORRECTIONS AND AMPLIFICATIONS.—The Register may also establish, by regulation, formal procedures for the filing of an application for supplementary registration, to correct an error in a copyright registration or to amplify the information given in a registration. Such application shall be accompanied by the fee provided by section 708, and shall clearly identify the registration to be corrected or amplified. The information contained in a supplementary registration augments but does not supersede that contained in the earlier registration.

(e) PUBLISHED EDITION OF PREVIOUSLY REGISTERED WORK.—Registration for the first published edition of a work previously registered in unpublished form may be made even though the work as published is substantially the same as the unpublished version.

Sec. 409. Application for Copyright Registration

The application for copyright registration shall be made on a form prescribed by the Register of Copyrights and shall include—

(1) the name and address of the copyright claimant;

(2) in the case of a work other than an anonymous or pseudonymous work, the name and nationality or domicile of the author or authors, and, if one or more of the authors is dead, the dates of their deaths;

(3) if the work is anonymous or pseudonymous, the nationality or domicile of the author or authors;

(4) in the case of a work made for hire, a statement to this effect;

(5) if the copyright claimant is not the author, a brief statement of how the claimant obtained ownership of the copyright;

(6) the title of the work, together with any previous or alternative titles under which the work can be identified;

(7) the year in which creation of the work was completed;

(8) if the work has been published, the date and nation of its first publication;

(9) in the case of a compilation or derivative work, an identification of any preexisting work or works that it is based on or incorporates, and a brief, general statement of the additional material covered by the copyright claim being registered;

(10) in the case of a published work containing material of which copies are required by section 601 to be manufactured in the United States, the names of the persons or organizations who performed the processes specified by subsection (c) of section 601 with respect to that material, and the places where those processes were performed; and

(11) any other information regarded by the Register of Copyrights as bearing upon the preparation or identification of the work or the existence, ownership, or duration of the copyright.

Sec. 410. Registration of Claim and Issuance of Certificate

(a) When, after examination, the Register of Copyrights determines that, in accordance with the provisions of this title, the material deposited constitutes copyrightable subject matter and that the other legal and formal requirements of this title have been met, the Register shall register the claim and issue to the applicant a certificate of registration under the seal of the copyright Office. The certificate shall contain the information given in the application, together with the number and effective date of the registration.

(b) In any case in which the Register of Copyrights determines that, in accordance with the provisions of this title, the material deposited does not constitute copyrightable subject matter or that the claim is invalid for any other reason, the Register shall refuse registration and shall notify the applicant in writing of the reasons for such refusal.

(c) In any judicial proceedings the certificate of a registration made before or within five years after first publication of the work shall constitute prima facie evidence of the validity of the copyright and of the facts stated in the certificate. The evidentiary weight to be accorded the certificate of a registration made thereafter shall be within the discretion of the court.

(d) The effective date of a copyright registration is the day on which an application, deposit, and fee, which are later determined by the Register of Copyrights, or by a court of competent jurisdiction to be acceptable for registration, have all been received in the Copyright Office.

Sec. 411. Registration and Infringement Actions

(a) Except for actions for infringement of copyright in Berne Convention works whose country of origin is not the United States, and an action brought for a violation of the rights of the author under section 106A(a) and subject to the provisions of subsection (b), no action for infringement of the copyright in any work shall be instituted until registration of the copyright claim has been made in accordance with this title. In any case, however, where the deposit, application, and fee required for registration have been delivered to the Copyright Office in proper form and registration has been refused, the applicant is entitled to institute an action for infringement if notice thereof, with a copy of the complaint, is served on the Register of Copyrights. The Register may, at his or her option, become a party to the action with respect to the issue of registrability of the copyright claim by entering an appearance within sixty days after such service, but the Register's failure to become a party shall not deprive the court of jurisdiction to determine that issue.

(b) In the case of a work consisting of sounds, images, or both, the first fixation of which is made simultaneously with its transmission, the copyright owner may, either before or after such fixation takes place, institute an action for infringement under section 501, fully subject to the remedies provided by sections 502 through 506 and sections 509 and 510, if, in accordance with requirements that the Register of Copyrights shall prescribe by regulation, the copyright owner—

(1) serves notice upon the infringer, not less than ten or more than thirty days before such fixation, identifying the work and the specific time and source of its first transmission, and declaring an intention to secure copyright in the work; and

(2) makes registration for the work, if required by subsection (a), within three months after its first transmission.

Sec. 412. Registration as Prerequisite to Certain Remedies for Infringement

In any action under this title, other than an action brought for a violation of the right of the author under section 106A(a) or an action instituted under section 411(b), no award of statutory damages or of attorney's fees, as provided by sections 504 and 505, shall be made for—

(1) any infringement of copyright in an unpublished work commenced before the effective date of its registration; or

(2) any infringement of copyright commenced after first publication of the work and before the effective date of its registration, unless such registration is made within three months after the first publication of the work.

Chapter 5—Copyright Infringement and Remedies

Sec.

Sec. 501. Infringement of Copyright

(a) Anyone who violates any of the exclusive rights of the copyright owner as provided by sections 106 through 118 or of the author as provided in section 106A(a) or who imports copies or phonorecords into the United States in violation of section 602, is an infringer of the copyright or right of the author, as the case may be. For purposes of this chapter (other than section 506), any reference to copyright shall be deemed to include the rights conferred by section 106A(a). As used in this subsection the term "anyone" includes any State, any instrumentality of a State, and any officer or employee of a State or instrumentality of a State acting in his or her official capacity. Any State, and any such instrumentality, officer, or employee, shall be subject to the provisions of this title in the same manner and to the same extent as any nongovernmental entity.

(b) The legal or beneficial owner of an exclusive right under a copyright is entitled, subject to the requirements of section 411, to institute an action for any infringement of that particular right committed while he or she is the owner of it. The court may require such owner to serve written notice of the action with a copy of the complaint upon any person shown, by the records of the Copyright Office or otherwise, to have or claim an interest in the copyright, and shall require that such notice be served upon any person whose interest is likely to be affected by a decision in the case. The court may require the joinder, and shall permit the intervention, of any person having or claiming an interest in the copyright.

(c) For any secondary transmission by a cable system that embodies a performance or a display of a work which is actionable as an act of infringement under subsection (c) of section 111, a television broadcast station holding a copyright or other license to transmit or perform the same version of that work shall, for purposes of subsection (b) of this section, be treated as a legal or beneficial owner if such secondary transmission occurs within the local service area of that television station.

(d) For any secondary transmission by a cable system that is actionable as an act of infringement pursuant to section 111(c)(3), the following shall also have standing to sue: (i) the primary transmitter whose transmission has been altered by the cable system; and (ii) any broadcast station within whose local service area the secondary transmission occurs.

(e) With respect to any secondary transmission that is made by a satellite carrier of a primary transmission embodying the performance or display of a work and is actionable as an act of infringement under section 119(a)(5), a network station holding a copyright or other license to transmit or perform the same version of that work shall for purposes of subsection (b) of this section, be treated as a legal or beneficial owner if such secondary transmission occurs within the local service area of that station.

Sec. 502. Remedies for Infringement: Injunctions

(a) Any court having jurisdiction of a civil action arising under this title may, subject to the provisions of section 1498 of title 28, grant temporary and final injunctions on such terms as it may deem reasonable to prevent or restrain infringement of a copyright.

(b) Any such injunction may be served anywhere in the United States on the person enjoined; it shall be operative throughout the United States and shall be enforceable, by proceedings in contempt or otherwise, by any United States court having jurisdiction of that person. The clerk of the court granting the injunction shall, when requested by any other court in which enforcement of the injunction is sought, transmit promptly to the other court a certified copy of all the papers in the case on file in such clerk's office.

Sec. 503. Remedies for Infringement: Impounding and Disposition of Infringing Articles

(a) At any time while an action under this title is pending, the court may order the impounding, on such terms as it may deem reasonable, of all copies or phonorecords claimed to have been made or used in violation of the copyright owner's exclusive rights, and of all plates, molds, matrices, masters, tapes, film negatives, or other articles by means of which such copies or phonorecords may be reproduced.

(b) As part of a final judgment or decree, the court may order the destruction or other reasonable disposition of all copies or phonorecords found to have been made or used in violation of the copyright owner's exclusive rights, and of all plates, molds, matrices, masters, tapes, film negatives, or other articles by means of which such copies or phonorecords may be reproduced.

Sec. 504. Remedies for Infringement: Damages and Profits

(a) IN GENERAL.—Except as otherwise provided by this title, an infringer of copyright is liable for either—

(1) the copyright owner's actual damages and any additional profits of the infringer, as provided by subsection (b); or

(2) statutory damages, as provided by subsection (c).

(b) ACTUAL DAMAGES AND PROFITS.—The copyright owner is entitled to recover the actual damages suffered by him or her as a result of the infringement, and any profit of the infringer that are attributable to the infringement and are not taken into account in computing the actual damages. In establishing the infringer's profits, the copyright owner is required to present proof only of the infringer's gross revenue, and the infringer is required to prove his or her deductible expenses and the elements of profit attributable to factors other than the copyrighted work.

(c) STATUTORY DAMAGES.—

(1) Except as provided by clause (2) of this subsection, the copyright owner may elect, at any time before final judgment is rendered, to recover, instead of actual damages and profits, an award of statutory damages for all infringements involved in the action, with respect to any one work, for which any one infringer is liable individually, or for which any two or more infringers are liable jointly and severally, in a sum of not less than $500 or more than $20,000 as the court considers just. For the purposes of this subsection, all the parts of a compilation or derivative work constitute one work.

(2) In a case where the copyright owner sustains the burden of proving, and the court finds, that infringement was committed willfully, the court in its discretion may increase the award of statutory damages to a sum of not more than $100,000. In a case where the infringer sustains the burden of proving, and the court finds, that such infringer was not aware and had no reason to believe that his or her acts constituted an infringement of copyright, the court in its discretion may reduce the award of statutory damages to a sum of not less than $200. The court shall remit statutory damages in any case where an infringer believed and had reasonable grounds for believing that his or her use of the copyrighted work was a fair use under section 107, if the infringer was: (i) an employee or agent of a nonprofit educational institution, library, or archives acting within the scope of his or her employment who, or such institution, library, or archives itself, which infringed by reproducing the work in copies or phonorecords; or (ii) a public broadcasting entity which or a person who, as a regular part of the nonprofit activities of a public broadcasting entity (as defined in subsection (g) of section 118) infringed by performing a published nondramatic literary work or by reproducing a transmission program embodying a performance of such a work.

Sec. 505. Remedies for Infringement: Costs and Attorney's Fees

In any civil action under this title, the court in its discretion may allow the recovery of full costs by or against any party other than the United States or an officer thereof. Except as otherwise provided by this title, the court may also award a reasonable attorney's fee to the prevailing party as part of the costs.

Sec. 506. Criminal Offenses

(a) CRIMINAL INFRINGEMENT.—Any person who infringes a copyright willfully and for purposes of commercial advantage or private financial gain shall be punished as provided in section 2319 of title 18.

(b) FORFEITURE AND DESTRUCTION.—When any person is convicted of any violation of subsection (a), the court in its judgment of conviction shall, in addition to the penalty therein prescribed, order the forfeiture and destruction or other disposition of all infringing copies or phonorecords and all implements, devices, or equipment used in the manufacture of such infringing copies or phonorecords.

(c) FRAUDULENT COPYRIGHT NOTICE.—Any person who, with fraudulent intent, places on any article a notice of copyright or words of the same purport that such person knows to be false, or who, with fraudulent intent, publicly distributes or imports for public distribution any article bearing such notice or words that such person knows to be false, shall be fined not more than $2,500.

(d) FRAUDULENT REMOVAL OF COPYRIGHT NOTICE.—Any person who, with fraudulent intent, removes or alters any notice of copyright appearing on a copy of a copyrighted work shall be fined not more than $2,500.

(e) FALSE REPRESENTATION.—Any person who knowingly makes a false representation of a material fact in the application for copyright registration provided for by section 409, or in any written statement filed in connection with the application, shall be fined not more than $2,500.

(f) RIGHTS OF ATTRIBUTION AND INTEGRITY.—Nothing in this section applies to infringement of the rights conferred by section 106A(a).

Sec. 507. Limitations on Actions

(a) CRIMINAL PROCEEDINGS.—No criminal proceeding shall be maintained under the provisions of this title unless it is commenced within three years after the cause of action arose.

(b) CIVIL ACTIONS.—No civil action shall be maintained under the provisions of this title unless it is commenced within three years after the claim accrued.

Sec. 508. Notification of Filing and Determination of Actions

(a) Within one month after the filing of any action under this title, the clerks of the courts of the United States shall send written notification to the Register of Copyrights setting forth, as far as is shown by the papers filed in the court, the names and addresses of the parties and the title, author, and registration number of each work involved in the action. If any other copyrighted work is later included in the action by amendment, answer, or other pleading, the clerk shall also send a notification concerning it to the Register within one month after the pleading is filed.

(b) Within one month after any final order or judgment is issued in the case, the clerk of the court shall notify the Register of it, sending with the notification a copy of the order or judgment together with the written opinion, if any, of the court.

(c) Upon receiving the notifications specified in this section, the Register shall make them a part of the public records of the Copyright Office.

Sec. 509. Seizure and Forfeiture

(a) All copies or phonorecords manufactured, reproduced, distributed, sold, or otherwise used, intended for use, or possessed with intent to use in violation of section 509(a), and all plates, molds, matrices, masters, tapes, film negatives, or other articles by means of which such copies or phonorecords may be reproduced, and all electronic, mechanical, or other devices for manufacturing, reproducing, or assembling such copies or phonorecords may be seized and forfeited to the United States.

(b) The applicable procedures relating to (i) the seizure, summary and judicial forfeiture, and condemnation of vessels, vehicles, merchandise, and baggage for violations of the customs laws contained in title 19, (ii) the disposition of such vessels vehicles, merchandise, and baggage or the proceeds from the sale thereof, (iii) the remission or mitigation of such forfeiture, (iv) the compromise of claims, and (v) the award of compensation to informers in respect of such forfeitures, shall apply to seizures and forfeitures incurred, or alleged to have been incurred, under the provisions of this section, insofar as applicable and not inconsistent with the provisions of this section; except that such duties as are imposed upon any officer or employee of the Treasury Department or any other person with respect to the seizure and forfeiture of vessels, vehicles, merchandise, and baggage under the provisions of the customs laws contained in title 19 shall be performed with respect to seizure and forfeiture of all articles described in subsection (a) by such officers, agents, or other persons as may be authorized or designated for that purpose by the Attorney General.

Sec. 510. Remedies for Alteration of Programming by Cable Systems

(a) In any action filed pursuant to section 111(c)(3), the following remedies shall be available:

(1) Where an action is brought by a party identified in subsections (b) or (c) of section 501, the remedies provided by sections 502 through 505, and the remedy provided by subsection (b) of this section; and

(2) When an action is brought by a party identified in subsection (d) of section 501, the remedies provided by sections 502 and 505, together with any actual damages suffered by such party as a result of the infringement, and the remedy provided by subsection (b) of this section.

(b) In any action filed pursuant to section 111(c)(3), the court may decree that, for a period not to exceed thirty days, the cable system shall be deprived of the benefit of a compulsory license for one or more distant signals carried by such cable system.

Sec. 511. Liability of States, Instrumentalities of States, and State Officials for Infringement of Copyright

(a) IN GENERAL.—Any State, any instrumentality of a State, and any officer or employees of a State or instrumentality of a State acting in his or her official capacity, shall not be immune, under the Eleventh Amendment of the Constitution of the United States or under any other doctrine of sovereign immunity, from suit in Federal court by any person, including any governmental or nongovernmental entity, for a violation of any of the exclusive rights of a copyright owner provided by sections 106 through 119, for importing copies of phonorecords in violation of 602, or for any other violation under this title.

(b) REMEDIES.—In a suit described in subsection (a) for a violation described in that subsection, remedies (including remedies both at law and in equity) are available for the violation to the same extent as such remedies are available for such a violation in a suit against any public or private entity other than a State, instrumentality of a State, or officer or employee of a State acting in his or her official capacity. Such remedies include impounding and disposition of infringing articles under section 503, actual damages and profits and statutory damages under section 504, costs and attorney's fees under section 505, and the remedies provided in section 510.

Chapter 6—Manufacturing Requirements and Importation

Sec.

Sec. 601. Manufacture, Importation, and Public Distribution of Certain Copies

(a) Prior to July 1, 1986, and except as provided by subsection (b), the importation into or public distribution in the United States of copies of a work consisting preponderantly of nondramatic [*sic*] literary material that is in the English language and is protected under this title is prohibited unless the portions consisting of such material have been manufactured in the United States or Canada.

(b) The provisions of subsection (a) do not apply—

(1) where, on the date when importation is sought or public distribution in the United States is made, the author of any substantial part of such material is neither a national nor a domiciliary of the United States or, if such author is a national of the United States, he or she has been domiciled outside the United States for a continuous period of at least one year immediately preceding that date; in the case of a work made for hire, the exemption provided by this clause does not apply unless a substantial part of the work was prepared for an employer or other person who is not a national or domiciliary of the United States or a domestic corporation or enterprise;

(2) where the United States Customs Service is presented with an import statement issued under the seal of the Copyright Office, in which case a total of no more than two thousand copies of any one such work shall be allowed entry; the import statement shall be issued upon request to the copyright owner or to a person designated by such owner at the time of registration for the work under section 408 or at any time thereafter;

(3) where importation is sought under the authority or for the use, other than in schools, of the Government of the United States or of any State or political subdivision of a State;

(4) where importation, for use and not for sale, is sought—

(A) by any person with respect to no more than one copy of any work at any one time;

(B) by any person arriving from outside the United States, with respect to copies forming part of such person's personal baggage; or

(C) by an organization operated for scholarly, educational, or religious purposes and not for private gain, with respect to copies intended to form a part of its library;

(5) where the copies are reproduced in raised characters for the use of the blind; or

(6) where, in addition to copies imported under clauses (3) and (4) of this subsection, no more than two thousand copies of any one such work, which have not been manufactured in the United States or Canada, are publicly distributed in the United States; or

(7) where, on the date when importation is sought or public distribution in the United States is made—

(A) the author of any substantial part of such material is an individual and receives compensation for the transfer or license of the right to distribute the work in the United States; and

(B) the first publication of the work has previously taken place outside the United States under a transfer or license granted by such author to a transferee or licensee who was not a national or domiciliary of the United States or a domestic corporation or enterprise; and

(C) there has been no publication of an authorized edition

of the work of which the copies were manufactured in the United States; and

(D) the copies were reproduced under a transfer or license granted by such author or by the transferee or licensee of the right of first publication as mentioned in subclause (B), and the transferee or the licensee of the right of reproduction was not a national or domiciliary of the United States or a domestic corporation or enterprise.

(c) The requirement of this section that copies be manufactured in the United States or Canada is satisfied if—

(1) in the case where the copies are printed directly from type that has been set, or directly from plates made from such type, the setting of the type and the making of the plates have been performed in the United States or Canada; and

(2) in the case where the making of plates by a lithographic or photoengraving process is a final or intermediate step preceding the printing of the copies, the making of the plates has been performed in the United States or Canada.

(3) in any case, the printing or other final process of producing multiple copies and any binding of the copies have been performed in the United States or Canada.

(d) Importation or public distribution of copies in violation of this section does not invalidate protection for a work under this title. However, in any civil action or criminal proceeding for infringement of the exclusive rights to produce and distribute copies of the work, the infringer has a complete defense with respect to all of the nondramatic literary material comprised in the work and any other parts of the work in which the exclusive rights to reproduce and distribute copies are owned by the same person who owns such exclusive rights in the nondramatic literary material, if the infringer proves—

(1) that copies of the work have been imported into or publicly distributed in the United States in violation of this section by or with the authority of the owner of such exclusive rights; and

(2) that the infringing copies were manufactured in the United States or Canada in accordance with the provisions of subsection (c); and

(3) that the infringement was commenced before the effective date of registration for an authorized edition of the work, the copies of which have been manufactured in the United States or Canada in accordance with the provisions of subsection (c).

(e) In any action for infringement of the exclusive rights to reproduce and distribute copies of a work containing material required by this section to be manufactured in the United States or Canada, the copyright owner shall set forth in the complaint the names of the persons or organizations who performed the processes specified by subsection (c) with respect to that material, and the places where those processes were performed.

Sec. 602. Infringing Importation of Copies or Phonorecords

(a) Importation into the United States, without the authority of the owner of copyright under this title, of copies or phonorecords of a work that have been acquired outside the United States is an infringement of the exclusive right to distribute copies of phonorecords under section 106, actionable under section 501. This subsection does not apply to—

(1) importation of copies or phonorecords under the authority or for the use of the Government of the United States or of any State or political subdivision of a State, but not including copies or phonorecords for purposes other than archival use;

(2) importation, for the private use of the importer and not for distribution, by any person with respect to no more than one copy or phonorecord of any one work at any one time, or by any person arriving from outside the United States with respect to copies or phonorecords forming part of such person's personal baggage; or

(3) importation by or for an organization operated for scholarly, educational, or religious purposes and not for private gain, with respect to no more than one copy of an audiovisual work solely for its archival purposes, and no more than five copies or phonorecords of any other work for its library lending or archival purposes, unless the importation of such copies or phonorecords is part of an activity consisting of systematic reproduction or distribution, engaged in by such organization in violation of the provisions of section 108(g)(2).

(b) In a case where the making of the copies or phonorecords would have constituted an infringement of copyright if this title had been applicable, their importation is prohibited. In a case where the copies or phonorecords were lawfully made, the United States Customs service has no authority to prevent their importation unless the provisions of section 601 are applicable. In either case, the Secretary of the Treasury is authorized to prescribe, by regulation, a procedure under which any person claiming an interest in the copyright in a particular work may, upon payment of a specified fee, be entitled to notification by the Customs Service of the importation of articles that appear to be copies or phonorecords of the work.

Sec. 603. Importation Prohibitions: Enforcement and Disposition of Excluded Articles

(a) The Secretary of the Treasury and the United States Postal Service shall separately or jointly make regulations for the enforcement of the provisions of this title prohibiting importation.

(b) These regulations may require, as a condition for the exclusion of articles under section 602—

(1) that the person seeking exclusion obtain a court order enjoining importation of the articles; or

(2) that the person seeking exclusion furnish proof, of a specified nature and in accordance with prescribed procedures, that the copyright in which such person claims an interest is valid and that the importation would violate the prohibition in section 602; the person seeking exclusion may also be required to post a surety bond for any injury that may result if the detention or exclusion of the articles proves to be unjustified.

(c) Articles imported in violation of the importation prohibitions of this title are subject to seizure and forfeiture in the same manner as property imported in violation of the customs revenue laws. Forfeited articles shall be destroyed as directed by the Secretary of the Treasury or the court, as the case may be; however, the articles may be returned to the country of export whenever it is shown to the satisfaction of the Secretary of the Treasury that the importer had no reasonable grounds for believing that his or her acts constituted a violation of law.

Chapter 7—Copyright Office

Sec.

Sec. 701. The Copyright Office: General Responsibilities and Organization

(a) All administrative functions and duties under this title, except as otherwise specified, are the responsibility of the Register of Copyrights as director of the Copyright Office of the Library of Congress. The Register of Copyrights, together with the subordinate officers and employees of the Copyright Office, shall be appointed by the Librarian of Congress, and shall act under the Librarian's general direction and supervision.

(b) The Register of Copyrights shall adopt a seal to be used on and after January 1, 1978, to authenticate all certified documents issued by the Copyright Office.

(c) The Register of Copyrights shall make an annual report to the Librarian of Congress of the work and accomplishments of the Copyright Office during the previous fiscal year. The annual report of the Register of Copyrights shall be published separately and as a part of the annual report of the Librarian of Congress.

(d) Except as provided by section 706(b) and the regulations issued thereunder, all actions taken by the Register of Copyrights under this title are subject to the provisions of the Administrative Procedure Act of June 11, 1946, as amended (c. 324, 60 Stat. 237, title 5, United States Code, Chapter 5, Subchapter II and Chapter 7).

Sec. 702. Copyright Office Regulations

The Register of Copyrights is authorized to establish regulations not inconsistent with law for the administration of the functions and duties made the responsibility of the Register under this title. All regulations established by the Register under this title are subject to the approval of the Librarian of Congress.

Sec. 703. Effective Date of Actions in Copyright Office

In any case in which time limits are prescribed under this title for the performance of an action in the Copyright Office, and in which the last day of the prescribed period falls on a Saturday, Sunday, holiday, or other nonbusiness day within the District of Columbia or the Federal Government, the action may be taken on the next succeeding business day, and is effective as of the date when the period expired.

Sec. 704. Retention and Disposition of Articles Deposited in Copyright Office

(a) Upon their deposit in the Copyright Office under section 407 and 408, all copies, phonorecords, and identifying material, including those deposited in connection with claims that have been refused registration, are the property of the United States Government.

(b) In the case of published works, all copies, phonorecords, and identifying material deposited are available to the Library of Congress for its collections, or for exchange or transfer to any other library. In the case of unpublished works, the Library is entitled, under regulations that the Register of Copyrights shall prescribe, to select any deposits for its collections or for transfer to the National Archives of the United States or to a Federal records center, as defined in section 2901 of title 44.

(c) The Register of Copyrights is authorized, for specific or general categories of works, to make a facsimile reproduction of all or any part of the material deposited under section 408, and to make such reproduction a part of the Copyright Office records of the registration, before transferring such material to the Library of Congress as provided by subsection (b), or before destroying or otherwise disposing of such material as provided by subsection (d).

(d) Deposits not selected by the Library under subsection (b), or identifying portions or reproductions of them, shall be retained under the control of the Copyright Office, including retention in Government storage facilities, for the longest period considered practicable and desirable by the Register of Copyrights and the Librarian of Congress. After that period it is within the joint discretion of the Register and the Librarian to order their destruction or other disposition; but, in the case of unpublished works, no deposit shall be knowingly or intentionally destroyed or otherwise disposed of during its term of copyright unless a facsimile reproduction of the entire deposit has been made a part of the Copyright Office records as provided by subsection (c).

(e) The depositor of copies, phonorecords, or identifying material under section 408, or the copyright owner of record, may request retention, under the control of the Copyright Office, of one or more of such articles for the full term of copyright in the work. The Register of Copyrights shall prescribe, by regulation, the conditions under which such requests are to be made and granted, and shall fix the fee to be charged under section 708(a)(11) if the request is granted.

Sec. 705. Copyright Office Records: Preparation, Maintenance, Public Inspection, and Searching

(a) The Register of Copyrights shall provide and keep in the Copyright Office records of all deposits, registrations, recordations, and other actions taken under this title, and shall prepare indexes of all such records.

(b) Such records and indexes, as well as the articles deposited in connection with completed copyright registrations and retained under the control of the Copyright Office, shall be open to public inspection.

(c) Upon request and payment of the fee specified by section 708, the Copyright Office shall make a search of its public records, indexes, and deposits, and shall furnish a report of the information they disclose with respect to any particular deposits, registrations, or recorded documents.

Sec. 706. Copies of Copyright Office Records

(a) Copies may be made of any public records or indexes of the Copyright Office; additional certificates of copyright registration and copies of any public records or indexes may be furnished upon request and payment of the fees specified by section 708.

(b) Copies or reproductions of deposited articles retained under the control of the Copyright Office shall be authorized or furnished only under the conditions specified by the Copyright Office regulations.

Sec. 707. Copyright Office Forms and Publications

(a) Catalog of Copyright Entries — The Register of Copyrights shall compile and publish at periodic intervals catalogs of all copyright registrations. These catalogs shall be divided into parts in accordance with the various classes of works, and the Register has discretion to determine, on the basis of practicability and usefulness, the form and frequency of publication of each particular part.

(b) Other Publications — The Register shall furnish, free of charge upon request, application forms for copyright registration and general informational material in connection with the functions of the Copyright Office. The Register also has the authority to publish compilations of information, bibliographies, and other material he or she considers to be of value to the public.

(c) Distribution of Publications. — All publications of the Copyright Office shall be furnished to depository libraries as specified under section 1905 of title 44, and, aside from those furnished free of charge, shall be offered for sale to the public at prices based on the cost of reproduction and distribution.

Sec. 708. Copyright Office Fees

(a) The following fees shall be paid to the Register of Copyrights:

(1) on filing each application for registration of a copyright claim or a supplementary registration under section 408, including the issuance of a certificate of registration if registration is made, $10;

(2) on filing each application for registration of a claim to renewal of a subsisting copyright in its first term under section 304(a), including the issuance of a certificate of registration if registration is made, $6;

(3) for the issuance of a receipt for a deposit under section 407, $2;

(4) for the recordation, as provided by section 205, of a transfer of copyright ownership or other document of six pages or less, covering no more than one title, $10; for each page over six and each title over one, 50 cents additional;

(5) for the filing, under section 115(b), of a notice of intention to make phonorecords, $6;

(6) for the recordation, under section 302(c), of a statement revealing the identity of an author of an anonymous or pseudonymous work, or for the recordation, under section 302(d), of a statement relating to the death of an author, $10 for a document of six pages or less, covering no more than one title; for each page over six and for each title over one, $1 additional;

(7) for the issuance, under section 601, of an import statement, $3;

(8) for the issuance, under section 706, of an additional certificate of registration, $4;

(9) for the issuance of any other certification, $4; the Register of Copyrights has discretion, on the basis of their cost, to fix the fees for preparing copies of Copyright Office records, whether they are to be certified or not;

(10) for the making and reporting of a search as provided by section 705, and for any related services, $10 for each hour or fraction of an hour consumed;

(11) for any other special services requiring a substantial

amount of time or expense, such fees as the Register of Copyrights may fix on the basis of the cost of providing the service.

(b) The fees prescribed by or under this section are applicable to the United States Government and any of its agencies, employees, or officers, but the Register of Copyrights has discretion to waive the requirement of this subsection in occasional or isolated cases involving relatively small amounts.

(c) All fees received under this section shall be deposited by the Register of Copyrights in the Treasury of the United States and shall be credited to the appropriation for necessary expenses of the Copyright Office. The Register may, in accordance with regulations that he or she shall prescribe, refund any sum paid by mistake or in excess of the fee required by this section.

Sec. 709. Delay in Delivery Caused by Disruption of Postal or Other Services

In any case in which the Register of Copyrights determines, on the basis of such evidence as the Register may by regulation require, that a deposit, application, fee, or any other material to be delivered to the Copyright Office by a particular date, would have been received in the Copyright Office in due time except for a general disruption or suspension of postal or other transportation or communications services, the actual receipt of such material in the Copyright Office within one month after the date on which the Register determines that the disruption or suspension of such services has terminated, shall be considered timely.

Sec. 710. Reproduction for Use of the Blind and Physically Handicapped: Voluntary Licensing Forms and Procedures

The Register of Copyrights shall, after consultation with the Chief of the Division for the Blind and Physically Handicapped and other appropriate officials of the Library of Congress, establish by regulation standardized forms and procedures by which, at the time applications covering certain specified categories of nondramatic literary works are submitted for registration under section 408 of this title, the copyright owner may voluntarily grant to the Library of Congress a license to reproduce the copyrighted work by means of Braille or similar tactile symbols, or by fixation of a reading of the work in a phonorecord, or both, and to distribute the resulting copies or phonorecords solely for the use of the blind and physically handicapped and under limited conditions to be specified in the standardized forms.

Chapter 8—Copyright Royalty Tribunal

Sec.

Sec. 801. Copyright Royalty Tribunal: Establishment and Purpose

(a) There is hereby an independent Copyright Royalty Tribunal in the legislative branch.

(b) Subject to the provisions of this chapter, the purposes of the Tribunal shall be—

(1) to make determinations concerning the adjustment of reasonable copyright royalty rates as provided in sections 115 and 116, and to make determinations as to reasonable terms and rates of royalty payments as provided in section 118. The rates applicable under sections 115 and 116 shall be calculated to achieve the following objectives.

(A) To maximize the availability of creative works to the public;

(B) To afford the copyright owner a fair return for his creative work and the copyright user a fair income under existing economic conditions;

(C) To reflect the relative roles of the copyright owner and the copyright user in the product made available to the public with respect to relative creative contribution, technological contribution, capital investment, cost, risk, and contribution to the opening of new markets for creative expression and media for their communication;

(D) To minimize any disruptive impact on the structure of the industries involved and on generally prevailing industry practices.

(2) to make determinations concerning the adjustment of the copyright royalty rates in section 111 solely in accordance with the following provisions:

(A) The rates established by section 111(d)(2)(B) may be adjusted to reflect (i) national monetary inflation or deflation or (ii) changes in the average rates charged cable subscribers for the basic service of providing secondary transmissions to maintain the real constant dollar level of the royalty fee per subscriber which existed as of the date of enactment of this Act: *Provided,* That if the average rates charged cable system subscribers for the basic service of providing secondary transmissions are changed so that the average rates exceed national monetary inflation, no change in the rates established by section 111(d)(2)(B) shall be permitted: *And provided further,* That no increase in the royalty fee shall be permitted based on any reduction in the average number of distant signal equivalents per subscriber. The Commission may consider all factors relating to the maintenance of such level of payments including, as an extenuating factor, whether the cable industry has been restrained by subscriber rate regulating authorities from increasing the rates for the basic service of providing secondary transmissions.

(B) In the event that the rules and regulations of the Federal Communications Commission are amended at any time after April 15, 1976, to permit the carriage by cable systems of additional television broadcast signals beyond the local service area of the primary transmitters of such signals, the royalty rates established by section 111(d)(2)(B) may be adjusted to insure that the rates for the additional distant signal equivalents resulting from such carriage are reasonable in the light of the changes effected by the amendment to such rules and regulations. In determining the reasonableness of rates proposed following an amendment of Federal Communications Commission rules and regulations, the Copyright Royalty Tribunal shall consider, among other factors, the economic impact on copyright owners and users: *Provided*, That no adjustment in royalty rates shall be made under this subclause with respect to any distant signal equivalent or fraction thereof represented by (i) carriage of any signal permitted under the rules and regulations of the Federal Communications Commission in effect on April 15, 1976, or the carriage of a signal of the same type (that is, independent, network, or noncommercial educational) substituted for such permitted signal, or (ii) a television broadcast signal first carried after April 15, 1976, pursuant to an individual waiver of the rules and regulations of the Federal Communications Commission, as such rules and regulations were in effect on April 15, 1976.

(C) In the event of any change in the rules and regulations of the Federal Communications Commission with respect to syndicated and sports program exclusivity after April 15, 1976, the rates established by section 111(d)(2)(B) may be adjusted to assure that such rates are reasonable in light of the changes to such rules and regulations, but any such adjustment shall apply only to the affected television broadcast signals carried on those systems affected by the change.

(D) The gross receipts limitations established by section 111(d)(2)(C) and (D) shall be adjusted to reflect national monetary inflation or deflation or changes in the average rates charged cable system subscribers for the basic service of providing secondary transmissions to maintain the real constant dollar value of the exemption provided by such section; and the royalty rate specified therein shall not be subject to adjustment; and

(3) to distribute royalty fees deposited with the Register of Copyrights under sections 111 and 116, and to determine, in cases where controversy exists, the distribution of such fees.

(c) As soon as possible after the date of enactment of this Act, and no later than six months following such date, the President shall publish a notice announcing the initial appointments provided in section 802, and shall designate an order of seniority among the initially-appointed commissioners for purposes of section 802(b).

Sec. 802. Membership of the Tribunal

(a) The Tribunal shall be composed of five commissioners appointed by the President with the advice and consent of the Senate for a term of seven years each; of the first five members appointed, three shall be designated to serve for seven years from the date of the notice specified in section 801(c), and two shall be designated to serve for five years from such date, respectively. Commissioners shall be compensated at the highest rate now or hereafter prescribe [sic] for grade 18 of the General Schedule pay rates (5 U.S.C. 5332).

(b) Upon convening the commissioners shall elect a chairman from among the commissioners appointed for a full seven-year term. Such chairman shall serve for a term of one year. Thereafter, the most senior commissioner who has not previously served as chairman shall serve as chairman for a period of one year, except that, if all commissioners have served a full term as chairman, the most senior commissioner who has served the least number of terms as chairman shall be designated as chairman.

(c) Any vacancy in the Tribunal shall not affect its powers and shall be filled, for the unexpired term of the appointment, in the same manner as the original appointment was made.

Sec. 803. Procedures of the Tribunal

(a) The Tribunal shall adopt regulations, not inconsistent with law, governing its procedure and methods of operation. Except as otherwise provided in this chapter, the Tribunal shall be subject to the provisions of the Administrative Procedure Act of June 11, 1946, as amended (c. 324, 60 Stat. 237, title 5, United States Code, chapter 5, subchapter II and chapter 7).

(b) Every final determination of the Tribunal shall be published in the Federal Register. It shall state in detail the criteria that the Tribunal determined to be applicable to the particular proceeding, the various facts that it found relevant to its determination in that proceeding, and the specific reasons for its determination.

Sec. 804. Institution and Conclusion of Proceedings

(a) With respect to proceedings under section 801(b)(1) concerning the adjustment of royalty rates as provided in sections 115 and 116, and with respect to proceedings under section 801(b)(2)(A) and (D)—

(1) on January 1, 1980, the Chairman of the Tribunal shall cause to be published in the Federal Register notice of commencement of proceedings under this chapter; and

(2) during the calendar years specified in the following schedule, any owner or user of a copyrighted work whose royalty rates are specified by this title, or by a rate established by the Tribunal, may file a petition with the Tribunal declaring that the petitioner requests an adjustment of the rate. The Tribunal shall make a determination as to whether the applicant has a significant interest in the royalty rate in which an adjustment is requested. If the Tribunal determines that the petitioner has a significant interest, the Chairman shall cause notice of this determination, with the reasons therefor, to be published in the Federal Register, together with notice of commencement of proceedings under this chapter.

(A) In proceedings under section 801(b)(2)(A) and (D), such petition may be filed during 1985 and in each subsequent fifth calendar year.

(B) In proceedings under section 801(b)(1) concerning the adjustment of royalty rates as provided in section 115, such petition may be filed in 1987 and in each subsequent tenth calendar year.

(C) In proceedings under section 801(b)(1) concerning the adjustment of royalty rates under section 116, such petition may be filed in 1990 and in each subsequent tenth calendar year.

(b) With respect to proceedings under subclause (B) or (C) of section 801(b)(2), following an event described in either of those subsections, any owner or user of a copyrighted work whose royalty rates are specified by section 111, or by a rate established by the Tribunal, may, within twelve months, file a petition with the Tribunal declaring that the petitioner requests an adjustment of the rate. In this event the Tribunal shall proceed as in subsection (a)(2), above. Any change in royalty rates made by the Tribunal pursuant to this subsection may be reconsidered in 1980, 1985, and each fifth calendar year thereafter, in accordance with the provisions in section 801(b)(2)(B) or (C), as the case may be.

(c) With respect to proceedings under section 801(b)(1), concerning the determination of reasonable terms and rates of royalty payments as provided in section 118, the Tribunal shall proceed when and as provided by that section.

(d) With respect to proceedings under section 801(b)(3), concerning the distribution of royalty fees in certain circumstances under sections 111 or 116, the Chairman of the Tribunal shall, upon determination by the Tribunal that a controversy exists concerning such distribution, cause to be published in the Federal Register notice of commencement of proceedings under this chapter.

(e) All proceedings under this chapter shall be initiated without delay following publication of the notice specified in this section, and the Tribunal shall render its final decision in any such proceeding within one year from the date of such publication.

Sec. 805. Staff of the Tribunal

(a) The Tribunal is authorized to appoint and fix the compensation of such employees as may be necessary to carry out the provisions of this chapter, and to prescribe their functions and duties.

(b) The Tribunal may procure temporary and intermittent services to the same extent as is authorized by section 3109 of title 5.

Sec. 806. Administrative Support of the Tribunal

(a) The Library of Congress shall provide the Tribunal with necessary administrative services, including those related to budgeting, accounting, financial reporting, travel, personnel, and procurement. The Tribunal shall pay the Library for such services, either in advance or by reimbursement from the funds of the Tribunal, at amounts to be agreed upon between the Librarian and the Tribunal.

(b) The Library of Congress is authorized to disburse funds for the Tribunal, under regulations prescribed jointly by the Librarian of Congress and the Tribunal and approved by the Comptroller General. Such regulations shall establish requirements and procedures under which every voucher certified for payment by the Library of Congress under this chapter shall be supported with a certification by a duly authorized officer or employee of the Tribunal, and shall prescribe the responsibilities and accountability of said officers and employees of the Tribunal with respect to such certifications.

Sec. 807. Deduction of Costs of Proceedings

Before any funds are distributed pursuant to a final decision in a proceeding involving distribution of royalty fees, the Tribunal shall assess the reasonable costs of such proceeding.

Sec. 808. Reports

In addition to its publication of the reports of all final determinations as provided in section 803(b), the Tribunal shall make an annual report to the President and the Congress concerning the Tribunal's work during the preceding fiscal year, including a detailed fiscal statement of account.

Sec. 809. Effective Date of Final Determinations

Any final determination by the Tribunal under this chapter shall become effective thirty days following its publication in the Federal Register as provided in section 803(b), unless prior to that time an appeal has been filed pursuant to section 810, to vacate, modify, or correct such determination, and notice of such appeal has been served on all parties who appeared before the Tribunal in the proceeding in question. Where the proceeding involves the distribution of royalty fees under sections 111 or 116, the Tribunal shall, upon the expiration of such thirty-day period, distribute any royalty fees not subject to an appeal filed pursuant to section 810.

Sec. 810. Judicial Review

Any final decision of the Tribunal in a proceeding under section 801(b) may be appealed to the United States Court of Appeals, within thirty days after its publication in the Federal Register by an aggrieved party. The judicial review of the decision shall be had, in accordance with chapter 7 of title 5, on the basis of the record before the Tribunal. No court shall have jurisdiction to review a final decision of the Tribunal except as provided in this section.

Appendix B

Transitional and Supplementary Provisions (Pub. L. 94-553, 90 Stat. 2598 (1976))

SEC. 102. This Act becomes effective on January 1, 1978, except as otherwise expressly provided by this Act, including provisions of the first section of this Act. The provisions of sections 118, 304(b), and chapter 8 of title 17, as amended by the first section of this Act, take effect upon enactment of this Act.

SEC. 103. This Act does not provide copyright protection for any work that goes into the public domain before January 1, 1978. The exclusive rights, as provided by section 106 of title 17 as amended by the first section of this Act, to reproduce a work in phonorecords and to distribute phonorecords of the work, do not extend to any nondramatic musical work copyrighted before July 1, 1909.

SEC. 104. All proclamations issued by the President under section 1(e) or 9(b) of title 17 as it existed on December 31, 1977, or under previous copyright statutes of the United States, shall continue in force until terminated. suspended, or revised by the President.

SEC. 105. (a)(1) Section 505 of title 44 is amended to read as follows:

"§ 505. Sale of duplicate plates

"The Public Printer shall sell, under regulations of the Joint Committee on Printing to persons who may apply, additional or duplicate stereotype or electrotype plates from which a Government publication is printed, at a price not to exceed the cost of composition, the metal, and making to the Government, plus 10 per centum, and the full amount of the price shall be paid when the order is filed."

(2) The item relating to section 505 in the sectional analysis at the beginning of chapter 5 of title 44, is amended to read as follows:
"505. Sale of duplicate plates."

(b) Section 2113 of title 44 is amended to read as follows:

"§ 2113. Limitation on liability

"When letters and other intellectual productions (exclusive of patented material, published works under copyright protection, and unpublished works for which copyright registration has been made) come into the custody or possession of the Administrator of General Services, the United States or its agents are not liable for infringement of copyright or analogous rights arising out of use of the materials for display, inspection, research, reproduction, or other purposes."

(c) In section 1498(b) of title 28, the phrase "section 101(b) of title 17" is amended to read "section 504(c) of title 17".

(d) Section 543(a)(4) of the Internal Revenue Code of 1954, as amended, is amended by striking out "(other than by reason of section 2 or 6 thereof)".

(e) Section 3202(a) of title 39 is amended by striking out clause (5). Section 3206 of title 39 is amended by deleting the words "subsections (b) and (c)" inserting "subsection (b)" in subsection (a), and by deleting subsectio Section 3206(d) is renumbered (c).

(f) Subsection (a) of section 290(e) of title 15 is amended by deleting the phrase "section 8" and inserting in lieu thereof the phrase "section 105".

(g) Section 131 of title 2 is amended by deleting the phrase "deposit to secure copyright," and inserting in lieu thereof the phrase "acquisition of material under the copyright law,".

SEC. 106. In any case where, before January 1, 1978, a person has lawfully made parts of instruments serving to reproduce mechanically a copyrighted work under the compulsory license provisions of section 1(e) of title 17 as it existed on December 31, 1977, such person may continue to make and distribute such parts embodying the same mechanical reproduction without obtaining a new compulsory license under the terms of section 115 of title 17 as amended by the first section of this Act. However, such parts made on or after January 1, 1978, constitute phonorecords and are otherwise subject to the provisions of said section 115.

SEC. 107. In the case of any work in which an ad interim copyright is subsisting or is capable of being secured on December 31, 1977, under section 22 of title 17 as it existed on that date, copyright protection is hereby extended to endure for the term or terms provided by section 304 of title 17 as amended by the first section of this Act.

SEC. 108. The notice provisions of sections 401 through 403 of title 17 as amended by the first section of this Act apply to all copies or phonorecords publicly distributed on or after January 1, 1978. However, in the case of a work published before January 1, 1978, compliance with the notice provisions of title 17 either as it existed on December 31, 1977, or as amended by the first section of this Act, is adequate with respect to copies publicly distributed after December 31, 1977.

SEC. 109. The registration of claims to copyright for which the required deposit, application, and fee were received in the Copyright Office before January 1, 1978, and the recordation of assignments of copyright or other instruments received in the Copyright Office before January 1, 1978, shall be made in accordance with title 17 as it existed on December 31, 1977.

SEC. 110. The demand and penalty provisions of section 14 of title 17 as it existed on December 31, 1977, apply to any work in which copyright has been secured by publication with notice of copyright on or before that date, but any deposit and registration made after that date in response to a demand under that section shall be made in accordance with the provisions of title 17 as amended by the first section of this Act.

SEC. 111. Section 2318 of title 18 of the United States Code is amended to read; as follows:

§ 2318. Transportation, sale or receipt of phonograph records bearing forged or counterfeit labels

"(a) Whoever knowingly and with fraudulent intent transports, causes to be transported receives, sells, or offers for sale in interstate or foreign commerce any phonograph record, disk, wire, tape, film, or other article on which sounds are recorded, to which or upon which is stamped, pasted, or affixed any forged or counterfeited label, knowing the label to have been falsely made, forged, or counterfeited shall be fined not more than $10,000 or imprisoned for not more than one year, or both, for the first such offense and shall be fined not more than $25,000 or imprisoned for not more than two years, or both, for any subsequent offense.

(b) When any person is convicted of any violation of subsection (a), the court in its judgment of conviction shall, in addition to the penalty therein prescribed, order the forfeiture and destruction or other disposition of all counterfeit labels and all articles to which counterfeit labels have been affixed or which were intended to have had such labels affixed."

(c) Except to the extent they are inconsistent with the provisions of this title all provisions of section 509, title 17, United States Code, are applicable to violations of subsection (a).“

SEC. 112. All causes of action that arose under title 17 before January 1, 1978 shall be governed by title 17 as it existed when the cause of action arose.

[American Television and Radio Archives Act, 2 U.S.C. § 170]

SEC. 113. (a) The Librarian of Congress (hereinafter referred to as the "Librarian") shall establish and maintain in the Library of Congress a library to be known as the American Television and Radio Archives (hereinafter referred to as the "Archives“). The purpose of the Archives shall be to preserve a perrnanent record of the television and radio programs which are the heritage of the people of the United States and to provide access to such programs to historians and scholars without encouraging or causing copyright infringement.

(1) The Librarian, after consultation with interested organizations and individuals, shall determine and place in the Archives such copies and phonorecords of television and radio programs transmitted to the public in the United States and in other countries which are of present or potential public or cultural interest, historical significance, cognitive value, or otherwise worthy of preservation, including copies and phonorecords of published and unpublished transmission programs—

(A) acquired in accordance with sections 407 and 408 of

title 17 as amended by the first section of this Act; and

(B) transferred from the existing collections of the Library of Congress; and

(C) given to or exchanged with the Archives by other libraries, archives, organizations, and individuals; and

(D) purchased from the owner thereof.

(2) The Librarian shall maintain and publish appropriate catalogs and indexes of the collections of the Archives, and shall make such collections available for study and research under the conditions prescribed under this section.

(b) Notwithstanding the provisions of section 106 of title 17 as amended by the first section of this Act, the Librarian is authorized with respect to a transmission program which consists of a regularly scheduled newscast or on-the-spot coverage of news events and, under standards and conditions that the Librarian shall prescribe by regulation—

(1) to reproduce a fixation of such a program, in the same or another tangible form, for the purposes of preservation or security or for distribution under the conditions of clause (3) of this subsection; and

(2) to compile, without abridgment or any other editing, portions of such fixations according to subject matter, and to reproduce such compilations for the purpose of clause (1) of this subsection; and

(3) to distribute a reproduction made under clause (1) or (2) of this subsection—

(A) by loan to a person engaged in research; and

(B) for deposit in a library or archives which meets the requirements of section 108(a) of title 17 as amended by the first section of this act, in either case for use only in research and not for further reproduction or performance.

(c) The Librarian or any employee of the Library who is acting under the authority of this section shall not be liable in any action for copyright infringement committed by any other person unless the Librarian or such employee knowingly participated in the act of infringement committed by such person. Nothing in this section shall be construed to excuse or limit liability under title 17 as amended by the first section of this Act for any act not authorized by that title or this section, or for any act performed by a person not authorized to act under that title or this section.

Appendix C

Non-amendatory Provisions of Berne Convention Implementation Act of 1988 (Pub. L. 100-568, 102 Stat. 2853 (1988))

Sec. 1. Short Title and References to Title 17, United States Code.

(a) SHORT TITLE.—This Act may be cited as the "Berne Convention Implementation Act of 1988." (b) REFERENCES TO TITLE 17, UNITED STATES CODE.—Whenever in this Act an amendment or repeal is expressed in terms of an amendment to or a repeal of a section or other provision, the reference shall be considered to be made to a section or other provision of title 17, United States Code.

Sec. 2. Declarations

The Congress makes the following declarations:

(1) The Convention for the Protection of Literary and Artistic Works, signed at Berne, Switzerland, on September 9, 1886, and all acts, protocols, and revisions thereto (hereafter in this Act referred to as the "Berne Convention") are not self-executing under the Constitution and laws of the United States.

(2) The obligations of the United States under the Berne Convention may be performed only pursuant to appropriate domestic law.

(3) The amendments made by this Act, together with the law as it exists on the date of the enactment of this Act, satisfy the obligations of the United States in adhering to the Berne Con-

vention and no further rights or interests shall be recognized or created for that purpose.

Sec. 3. Construction of the Berne Convention

(a) RELATIONSHIP WITH DOMESTIC LAW.—The provisions of the Berne Convention—

(1) shall be given effect under title 17, as amended by this Act, and any other relevant provision of Federal or State law, including the common law; and

(2) shall not be enforceable in any action brought pursuant to the provisions of the Berne Convention itself.

(b) CERTAIN RIGHTS NOT AFFECTED.—The provisions of the Berne Convention, the adherence of the United States thereto, and satisfaction of United States obligations thereunder, do not expand or reduce any right of an author of a work, whether claimed under Federal, State, or the common law—

(1) to claim authorship of the work; or

(2) to object to any distortion, mutilation, or other modification of, or other derogatory action in relation to, the work, that would prejudice the author's honor or reputation.

Sec. 12 Works in the Public Domain

Title 17, United States Code, as amended by this Act, does not provide copyright protection for any work that is in the public domain in the United States.

Sec 13. Effective Date; Effect on Pending Cases

(a) EFFECTIVE DATE.—This Act and the amendments made by this Act take effect on the date on which the Berne Convention (as defined in section 101 of title 17, United States Code) enters into force with respect to the United States.

(b) EFFECT ON PENDING CASES.—Any cause of action arising under title 17, United States Code, before the effective date of this Act shall be governed by the provisions of such title as in effect when the cause of action rose.

Appendix D

Non-amendatory Provisions of Judicial Improvements Act of 1990 (Pub. L. 101-650, 104 Stat. 5089, 5128 (1990))

TITLE VI– VISUAL ARTISTS RIGHTS

Sec. 601. Short Title

This title may be cited as the "Visual Artists Rights Act of 1990."

Sec. 608. Studies by Copyright Office

(a) STUDY ON WAIVER OF RIGHTS PROVISION.—

(1) Study.—The Register of Copyrights shall conduct a study on the extent to which rights conferred by subsection (a) of section 106A of title 17, United States Code, have been waived under subsection (e)(1) of such section.

(2) Report to Congress.—Not later than 2 years after the date of the enactment of this Act, the Register of Copyrights shall submit to the Congress a report on the progress of the study conducted under paragraph (1). Not later than 5 years after such date of enactment, the Register of Copyrights shall submit to the Congress a final report on the results of the study conducted under paragraph (1), and any recommendations that the Register may have as a result of the study.

(b) STUDY ON RESALE ROYALTIES.—

(1) Nature of Study.—The Register of Copyrights, in consulta-

tion with the Chair of the National Endowment for the Arts, shall conduct a study on the feasibility of implementing

(A) a requirement that, after the first sale of a work of art, a royalty on any resale of the work, consisting of a percentage of the price, be paid to the author of the work; and

(B) other possible requirements that would achieve the objective of allowing an author of a work of art to share monetarily in the enhanced value of that work.

(2) Groups to Be Consulted.—The study under paragraph (1) shall be conducted in consultation with other appropriate departments and agencies of the United States, foreign governments, and groups involved in the creation, exhibition, dissemination, and preservation of works of art, including artists, art dealers, collectors of fine art, and curators of art museums.

(3) Report to Congress.—Not later than 18 months after the date of the enactment of this Act, the Register of Copyrights shall submit to the Congress a report containing the results of the study conducted under this subsection.

Sec. 609. First Amendment Application

This title does not authorize any governmental entity to take any action or enforce restrictions prohibited by the First Amendment to the Constitution of the United States.

Sec. 610. Effective Date

(a) In General.—Subject to subsection (b) and except as provided in subsection (c), this title and the amendments made by this title take effect 6 months after the date of the enactment of this Act.

(b) Applicability.—The rights created by section 106A of title 17, United States Code, shall apply to—

(1) works created before the effective date set forth in subsection (a) but title to which has not, as of such effective date, been transferred from the author, and

(2) works created on or after such effective date, but shall not apply to any destruction, distortion, mutilation, or other modifi-

cation (as described in section 106A(a)(3) of such title) of any work which occurred before such effective date.

(c) SECTION 608.—Section 608 takes effect on the date of the enactment of this Act.

TITLE VII—ARCHITECTURAL WORKS

Sec. 701. Short Title

This title may be cited as the "Architectural Works Copyright Protection Act."

Sec. 706. Effective Date

The amendments made by this title apply to—

(1) any architectural work created on or after the date of the enactment of this Act; and

(2) any architectural work that, on the date of the enactment of this Act, is unconstructed and embodied in unpublished plans or drawings, except that protection for such architectural work under title 17, United States Code, by virtue of the amendments made by this title, shall terminate on December 31, 2002, unless the work is constructed by that date.

TITLE VIII—COMPUTER SOFTWARE

Sec. 801. Short Title

This title may be cited as the "Computer Software Rental Amendments Act of 1990."

Sec. 804. Effective Date

(a) IN GENERAL.—Subject to subsection (b), this title and the amendments made in section 802 shall take effect on the date of enactment of this Act. The amendments made by section 803 shall take effect one year after such date of enactment.

(b) PROSPECTIVE APPLICATION.—Section 109(b) of title 17, United States Code, as amended by section 802 of this Act, shall not affect the right of a person in possession of a particular copy of a computer program, who acquired such copy before the date of the enactment of this Act to dispose of the possession of that copy on or after such dale of enactment in any manner permitted by section 109 of title 17, United States Code, as in effect on the day before such date of enactment.

(c) TERMINATION.—The amendment made by section 802 shall not apply to rentals, leasings, or lendings (or acts or practices in the nature of rentals, leasings, or lendings) occurring on or after October 1, 1997. The amendments made by section 803 shall not apply to public performances or displays that occur on or after October 1, 1995.

Sec. 805. Recordation of Shareware [sic]

(a) IN GENERAL.—The Register of Copyrights is authorized, upon receipt of any document designated as pertaining to computer shareware and the fee prescribed by section 708 of title 17, United States Code, to record the document and return it with a certificate of recordation.

(b) MAINTENANCE OF RECORDS; PUBLICATION OF INFORMATION.—The Register of Copyrights is authorized to maintain current, separate records relating to the recordation of documents under subsection (a), and to compile and publish at periodic intervals information relating to such recordations. Such publications shall be offered for sale to the public at prices based on the cost of reproduction and distribution.

(c) DEPOSIT OF COPIES IN LIBRARY OF CONGRESS.—In the case of public domain computer software, at the election of the person recording a document under subsection (a), two complete copies of the best edition (as defined in section 101 of title 17, United States Code) of the computer software as embodied in machine-readable form may be deposited for the benefit of the Machine-readable Collections Reading Room of the Library of Congress.

(d) REGULATIONS.—The Register of Copyrights is authorized to establish regulations not inconsistent with law for the administration of the functions of the Register under this section. All regulations established by the Register are subject to the approval of the Librarian of Congress.

Appendix E

Semiconductor Chip Protection Act of 1984 (Pub. L. 98-620, 98 Stat. 3347 (1984) adding to 17 U.S.C., chapter 9, entitled "Protection of Semiconductor Chip Products")

Semiconductor Chip Protection Act of 1984

Sec.

Sec. 901. Definitions

(a) As used in this chapter—

(1) a "semiconductor chip product" is the final or intermediate form of any product—

(A) having two or more layers of metallic, insulating, or semiconductor material, deposited or otherwise placed on, or etched away or otherwise removed from, a piece of semiconductor material in accordance with a predetermined pattern; and

(B) intended to perform electronic circuitry functions;

(2) a "mask work" is s series of related images, however fixed or encoded—

(A) having or representing the predetermined, three-dimensional pattern of metallic, insulating, or semiconductor material present or removed from the layers of a semiconductor chip product; and

(B) in which series the relation of the images to one another is that each image has the pattern of the surface of one form of the semiconductor chip product;

(3) a mask work is "fixed" in a semiconductor chip product when its embodiment in the product is sufficiently permanent or stable to permit the mask work to be perceived or reproduced from the product for a period of more than transitory duration;

(4) to "distribute" means to sell, or to lease, bail, or otherwise transfer, or to offer to sell, lease, bail, or otherwise transfer;

(5) to "commercially exploit" a mask work is to distribute to the public for commercial purposes a semiconductor chip product embodying the mask work; except that such term includes an offer to sell or transfer a semiconductor chip product only when the offer is in writing and occurs after the mask work is fixed in the semiconductor chip product;

(6) the "owner" of a mask work is the person who created the mask work, the legal representative of that person if that person is deceased or under a legal incapacity, or a party to whom all the rights under this chapter of such person or representative are transferred in accordance with section 903(b); except that, in the case of a work made within the scope of a person's

employment, the owner is the employer for whom the person created the mask work or a party to whom all the rights under this chapter of the employer are transferred in accordance with section 903(b);

(7) an "innocent purchaser" is a person who purchases a semiconductor chip product in good faith and without having notice of protection with respect to the semiconductor chip product;

(8) having "notice of protection" means having actual knowledge that, or reasonable grounds to believe that, a mask work is protected under this chapter; and

(9) an "infringing semiconductor chip product" is a semiconductor chip product which is made, imported, or distributed in violation of the exclusive rights of the owner of a mask work under this chapter.

(b) For purposes of this chapter, the distribution or importation of a product incorporating a semiconductor chip product as a part thereof is a distribution or importation of that semiconductor chip product.

Sec. 902. Subject Matter of Protection

(a)(1) Subject to the provisions of subsection (b), a mask work fixed in a semiconductor chip product, by or under the authority of the owner of the mask work, is eligible for protection under this chapter if—

(A) on the date on which the mask work is registered under section 908, or is first commercially exploited anywhere in the world, whichever occurs first, the owner of the mask work is (i) a national or domiciliary of the United States, (ii) a national, domiciliary, or sovereign authority of a foreign nation that is a party to a treaty affording protection to mask works to which the United States is also a party, or (iii) a stateless person, wherever that person may be domiciled;

(B) the mask work is first commercially exploited in the United States; or

(C) the mask work comes within the scope of a Presidential proclamation issued under paragraph (2).

(2) Whenever the President finds that a foreign nation ex-

tends, to mask works of owners who are nationals or domiciliaries of the United States protection (A) on substantially the same basis as that on which the foreign nation extends protection to mask works of its own nationals and domiciliaries and mask works first commercially exploited in that nation, or (B) on substantially the same basis as provided in this chapter, the President may by proclamation extend protection under this chapter to mask works (i) of owners who are, on the date on which the mask works are registered under section 908, or the date on which the mask works are first commercially exploited anywhere in the world, whichever occurs first, nationals, domiciliaries, or sovereign authorities of that nation, or (ii) which are first commercially exploited in that nation. The President may revise, suspend, or revoke any such proclamation or impose any conditions or limitations on protection extended under any such proclamation.

(b) Protection under this chapter shall not be available for a mask work that—

(1) is not original; or

(2) consists of designs that are staple, commonplace, or familiar in the semiconductor industry, or variations of such designs, combined in a way that, considered as a whole, is not original.

(c) In no case does protection under this chapter for a mask work extend to any idea, procedure, process, system, method of operation, concept, principle, or discovery, regardless of the form in which it is described, explained, illustrated, or embodied in such work.

Sec. 903. Ownership, Transfer, Licensing, and Recordation

(a) The exclusive rights in a mask work subject to protection under this chapter belong to the owner of the mask work.

(b) The owner of the exclusive rights in a mask work may transfer all of those rights, or license all or less than all of those rights, by any written instrument signed by such owner or a duly authorized agent of the owner. Such rights may be transferred or licensed by operation of law, may be bequeathed by will, and may pass as personal property by the applicable laws of intestate succession.

(c)(1) Any document pertaining to a mask work may be recorded in the Copyright Office if the document filed for recordation bears the actual signature of the person who executed it, or if it is accompanied by a sworn or official certification that it is a true copy of the original, signed document. The Register of Copyrights shall, upon receipt of the document and the fee specified pursuant to section 908(d), record the document and return it with a certificate of recordation. The recordation of any transfer or license under this paragraph gives all persons constructive notice of the facts stated in the recorded document concerning the transfer or license.

(2) In any case in which conflicting transfers of the exclusive rights in a mask work are made, the transfer first executed shall be void as against a subsequent transfer which is made for a valuable consideration and without notice of the first transfer, unless the first transfer is recorded in accordance with paragraph (1) within three months after the date on which it is executed, but in no case later than the day before the date of such subsequent transfer.

(d) Mask works prepared by an officer or employee of the United States Government as part of that person's official duties are not protected under this chapter, but the United States Government is not precluded from receiving and holding exclusive rights in mask works transferred to the Government umder subsection (b).

Sec. 904. Duration of Protection

(a) The protection provided for a mask work under this chapter shall commence on the date on which the mask work is registered under section 908, or the date on which the mask work is first commercially exploited anywhere in the world, whichever occurs first.

(b) Subject to subsection (c) and the provisions of this chapter, the protection provided under this chapter to a mask work shall end ten years after the date on which such protection commences under subsection (a).

(c) All terms of protection provided in this section shall run to the end of the calendar year in which they would otherwise expire.

Sec. 905. Exclusive Rights in Mask Works

The owner of a mask work provided protection under this chapter has the exclusive rights to do and to authorize any of the following:

(1) to reproduce the mask work by optical, electronic, or any other means;

(2) to import or distribute a semiconductor chip product in which the mask work is embodied; and

(3) to induce or knowingly to cause another person to do any of the acts described in paragraphs (1) and (2).

Sec. 906. Limitation on Exclusive Rights: Reverse Engineering; First Sale

(a) Notwithstanding the provisions of section 905, it is not an infringement of the exclusive rights of the owner of a mask work for—

(1) a person to reproduce the mask work solely for the purpose of teaching, analyzing, or evaluating the concepts or techniques embodied in the mask work or the circuitry, logic flow, or organization of components used in the mask work; or

(2) a person who performs the analysis or evaluation described in paragraph (1) to incorporate the results of such conduct in an original mask work which is made to be distributed.

(b) Notwithstanding the provisions of section 905(2), the owner of a particular semiconductor chip product made by the owner of the mask work, or by any person authorized by the owner of the mask work, may import, distribute, or otherwise dispose of or use, but not reproduce, that particular semiconductor chip product without the authority of the owner of the mask work.

Sec. 907. Limitation on Exclusive Rights: Innocent Infringement

(a) Notwithstanding any other provision of this chapter, an innocent purchaser of an infringing semiconductor chip product—

(1) shall incur no liability under this chapter with respect to

the importation or distribution of units of the infringing semiconductor chip product that occurs before the innocent purchaser has notice of protection with respect to the mask work embodied in the semiconductor chip product; and

(2) shall be liable only for a reasonable royalty on each unit of the infringing semiconductor chip product that the innocent purchaser imports or distributes after having notice of protection with respect to the mask work embodied in the semiconductor chip product.

(b) The amount of the royalty referred to in subsection (a)(2) shall be determined by the court in a civil action for infringement unless the parties resolve the issue by voluntary negotiation, mediation, or binding arbitration.

(c) The immunity of an innocent purchaser from liability referred to in subsection (a)(1) and the limitation of remedies with respect to an innocent purchaser referred to in subsection (a)(2) shall extend to any person who directly or indirectly purchases an infringing semiconductor chip product from an innocent purchaser.

(d) The provisions of subsections (a), (b), and (c) apply only with respect to those units of an infringing semiconductor chip product that an innocent purchaser purchased before having notice of protection with respect to the mask work embodied in the semiconductor chip product.

Sec. 908. Registration of Claims of Protection

(a) The owner of a mask work may apply to the Register of Copyrights for registration of a claim of protection in a mask work. Protection of a mask work under this chapter shall terminate if application for registration of a claim of protection in the mask work is not made as provided in this chapter within two years after the date on which the mask work is first commercially exploited anywhere in the world.

(b) The Register of Copyrights shall be responsible for all administrative functions and duties under this chapter. Except for section 708, the provisions of chapter 7 of this title relating to the general responsibilities, organization, regulatory authority, actions, records, and publications of the Copyright Office shall apply to this chapter, except that the Register of Copyrights may make such changes as may be necessary in applying those provisions to this chapter.

(c) The application for registration of a mask work shall be made on a form prescribed by the Register of Copyrights. Such form may require any information regarded by the Register as bearing upon the preparation or identification of the mask work, the existence or duration of protection of the mask work under this chapter, or ownership of the mask work. The application shall be accompanied by the fee set pursuant to subsection (d) and the identifying material specified pursuant to such subsection.

(d) The Register of Copyrights shall by regulation set reasonable fees for the filing of applications to register claims of protection in mask works under this chapter, and for other services relating to the administration of this chapter or the rights under this chapter, taking into consideration the cost of providing those services, the benefits of a public record, and statutory fee schedules under this title. The Register shall also specify the identifying material to be deposited in connection with the claim for registration.

(e) If the Register of Copyrights, after examining an application for registration, determines, in accordance with the provisions of this chapter, that the application relates to a mask work which is entitled to protection under this chapter, then the Register shall register the claim of protection and issue to the applicant a certificate of registration of the claim of protection under the seal of the Copyright Office. The effective date of registration of a claim of protection shall be the date on which an application, deposit or identifying material, and fee, which are determined by the Register of Copyrights or by a court of competent jurisdiction to be acceptable for registration of the claim, have all been received in the Copyright Office.

(f) In any action for infringement under this chapter, the certificate of registration of a mask work shall constitute prima facie evidence (1) of the facts stated in the certificate, and (2) that the applicant issued the certificate has met the requirements of this chapter, and the regulations issued under this chapter, with respect to the registration of claims.

(g) Any applicant for registration under this section who is dissatisfied with the refusal of the Register of Copyrights to issue a certificate of registration under this section may seek judicial review of that refusal by bringing an action for such review in an appropriate United States district court not later than sixty days after the refusal. The provisions of chapter 7 of title 5 shall apply to such judicial review. The failure of the Register of Copyrights to issue a certificate of registration within four months after an application for registration is filed shall be deemed to be a refusal to issue a certificate of registration for purposes of this subsection and section 910(b)(2), except that, upon a showing of good cause, the district court may shorten such four-month period.

Sec. 909. Mask Work Notice

(a) The owner of a mask work provided protection under this chapter may affix notice to the mask work, and to masks and semiconductor chip products embodying the mask work, in such manner and location as to give reasonable notice of such protection. The Register of Copyrights shall prescribe by regulation, as examples, specific methods of affixation and positions of notice for purposes of this section, but these specifications shall not be considered exhaustive. The affixation of such notice is not a condition of protection under this chapter, but shall constitute prima facie evidence of notice of protection .

(b) The notice referred to in subsection (a) shall consist of

(1) the words "mask work", the symbol *M*, or the symbol˜ (the letter M in a circle); and

(2) the name of the owner or owners of the mask work or an abbreviation by which the name is recognized or is generally known.

Sec. 910. Enforcement of Exclusive Rights

(a) Except as otherwise provided in this chapter, any person who violates any of the exclusive rights of the owner of a mask work under this chapter, by conduct in or affecting commerce, shall be liable as an infringer of such rights. As used in this subsection, the term "any person" includes any State, any instrumentality of a State, and any officer or employee of a State or instrumentality of a State acting in his or her official capacity. Any State, and any such instrumentality, officer, or employee, shall be subject to the provisions of this chapter in the same manner and to the same extent as any nongovernmental entity.

(b)(1) The owner of a mask work protected under this chapter, or the exclusive licensee of all rights under this chapter with respect to the mask work, shall, after a certificate of registration of a claim of protection in that mask work has been issued under section 908, be entitled to institute a civil action for any infringement with respect to the mask work which is committed after the commencement of protection of the mask work under section 904(a).

(2) In any case in which an application for registration of a claim of protection in a mask work and the required deposit of identifying material and fee have been received in the Copyright Office in proper form and registration of the mask work has been refused, the applicant is entitled to institute a civil action for infringement under this chapter with respect to the mask work if notice of the action, together with a copy of the complaint, is served on the Register of Copyrights, in accordance with the Federal Rules of Civil Procedure. The Register may, at his or her option, become a party to the action with respect to the issue of whether the claim of protection is eligible for registration by entering an appearance within sixty days after such service, but the failure of the Register to become a party to the action shall not deprive the court of jurisdiction to determine that issue.

(c)(1) The Secretary of the Treasury and the United States Postal Service shall separately or jointly issue regulations for the enforcement of the rights set forth in section 905 with respect to importation. These regulations may require, as a condition for the exclusion of articles from the United States, that the person seeking exclusion take any one or more of the following actions:

(A) Obtain a court order enjoining, or an order of the International Trade Commission under section 337 of the Tariff Act of 1930 excluding, importation of the articles.

(B) Furnish proof that the mask work involved is protected

under this chapter and that the importation of the articles would infringe the rights in the mask work under this chapter.

(C) Post a surety bond for any injury that may result if the detention or exclusion of the articles proves to be unjustified.

(2) Articles imported in violation of the rights set forth in section 905 are subject to seizure and forfeiture in the same manner as property imported in violation of the customs laws. Any such forfeited articles shall be destroyed as directed by the Secretary of the Treasury or the court, as the case may be, except that the articles may be returned to the country of export whenever it is shown to the satisfaction of the Secretary of the Treasury that the importer had no reasonable grounds for believing that his or her acts constituted a violation of the law.

Sec. 911. Civil Actions

(a) Any court having jurisdiction of a civil action arising under this chapter may grant temporary restraining orders, preliminary injunctions, and permanent injunctions on such terms as the court may deem reasonable to prevent or restrain infringement of the exclusive rights in a mask work under this chapter.

(b) Upon finding an infringer liable, to a person entitled under section 910(b)(1) to institute a civil action, for an infringement of any exclusive right under this chapter, the court shall award such person actual damages suffered by the person as a result of the infringement. The court shall also award such person the infringer's profits that are attributable to the infringement and are not taken into account in computing the award of actual damages. In establishing the infringer's profits, such person is required to present proof only of the infringer's gross revenue, and the infringer is required to prove his or her deductible expenses and the elements of profit attributable to factors other than the mask work.

(c) At any time before final judgment is rendered, a person entitled to institute a civil action for infringement may elect, instead of actual damages and profits as provided by subsection (b), an award of statutory damages for all infringements involved in the action, with respect to any one mask work for which any one infringer is liable individually, or for which any two or more infringers are liable jointly and severally, in an amount not more than $250,000 as the court considers just.

(d) An action for infringement under this chapter shall be barred unless the action is commenced with three years after the claim accrues.

(e)(1) At any time while an action for infringement of the exclusive rights in a mask work under this chapter is pending, the court may order the impounding, on such terms as it may deem reasonable, of all semiconductor chip products, and any drawings, tapes, masks, or other products by means of which such products may be reproduced, that are claimed to have been made, imported, or used in violation of those exclusive rights. Insofar as practicable, applications for orders under this paragraph shall be heard and determined in the same manner as an application for a temporary restraining order or preliminary injunction.

(2) As part of a final judgment or decree, the court may order the destruction or other disposition of any infringing semiconductor chip products, and any masks, tapes, or other articles by means of which such products may be reproduced.

(f) In any civil action arising under this chapter, the court in its discretion may allow the recovery of full costs, including reasonable attorney's fees, to the prevailing party.

(g)(1) Any State, any instrumentality of a State, and any officer or employee of a State or instrumentality of a State acting in his or her official capacity, shall not be immune, under the Eleventh Amendment of the Constitution of the United States or under any other doctrine of sovereign immunity, from suit in Federal court by any person, including any governmental or nongovernmental entity, for a violation of any of the exclusive rights of the owner of a mask work under this chapter, or for any other violation under this chapter.

(2) In a suit described in paragraph (1) for a violation described in that paragraph, remedies (including remedies both at law and in equity) are available for the violation to the same extent as such remedies are available for such a violation in a suit against any public or private entity other than a State, instrumentality of a State, or officer or employee of a State

acting in his or her official capacity. Such remedies include actual damages and profits under subsection (b), statutory damages under subsection (c), impounding and disposition of infringing articles under subsection (e), and costs and attorney's fees under subsection (f).

Sec. 912. Relation to Other Laws

(a) Nothing in this chapter shall affect any right or remedy held by any person under chapters 1 through 8 of this title, or under title 35.

(b) Except as provided in section 908(b) of this title, references to "this title" or "title 17" in chapters 1 through 8 of this title shall be deemed not to apply to this chapter.

(c) The provisions of this chapter shall preempt the laws of any State to the extent those laws provide any rights or remedies with respect to a mask work which are equivalent to those rights or remedies provided by this chapter, except that such preemption shall be effective only with respect to actions filed on or after January 1, 1986.

(d) Notwithstanding subsection (c), nothing in this chapter shall detract from any rights of a mask work owner, whether under Federal law (exclusive of this chapter) or under the common law or the statutes of a State, heretofore or hereafter declared or enacted, with respect to any mask work first commercially exploited before July 1, 1983.

Sec. 913. Transitional Provisions

(a) No application for registration under section 908 may be filed, and no civil action under section 910 or other enforcement proceeding under this chapter may be instituted until sixty days after the date of the enactment of this chapter.

(b) No monetary relief under section 911 may be granted with respect to any conduct that occurred before the date of the enactment of this chapter, except as provided in subsection (d).

(c) Subject to subsection (a), the provisions of this chapter apply to all mask works that are first commercially exploited or are registered under this chapter, or both, on or after the date of the enactment of this chapter.

(c)(1) Subject to subsection (a), protection is available under this chapter to any mask work that was first commercially exploited on or after July 1, 1983, and before the date of the enactment of this chapter, if a claim of protection in the mask work is registered in the Copyright Office before July 1, 1985, under section 908.

(2) In the case of any mask work described in paragraph (1) that is provided protection under this chapter, infringing semiconductor chip product units manufactured before the date of the enactment of this chapter may, without liability under sections 910 and 911, be imported into or distributed in the United States, or both, until two years after the date of registration of the mask work under section 908, but only if the importer or distributor, as the case may be, first pays or offers to pay the reasonable royalty referred to in section 907(a)(2) to the mask work owner, on all such units imported or distributed, or both, after the date of the enactment of this chapter.

(3) In the event that a person imports or distributes infringing semiconductor chip product units described in paragraph (2) of this subsection without first paying or offering to pay the reasonable royalty specified in such paragraph, or if the person refuses or fails to make such payment, the mask work owner shall be entitled to the relief provided in sections 910 and 911.

Sec. 914. International Transitional Provisions

(a) Notwithstanding the conditions set forth in subparagraphs (A) and (C) of section 902(a)(1) with respect to the availability of protection under this chapter to nationals, domiciliaries, and sovereign authorities of a foreign nation, the Secretary of Commerce may, upon the petition of any person, or upon the Secretary's own motion, issue an order extending protection under this chapter to such foreign nationals, domiciliaries, and sovereign authorities if the Secretary finds—

(1) that the foreign nation is making good faith efforts and reasonable progress toward—

(A) entering into a treaty described in section 902(a)(1)(A); or

(B) enacting legislation that would be in compliance with subparagraphs (A) and (B) of section 902(a)(2); and

(2) that the nationals, domicilaries, and sovereign authorities of the foreign nation, and persons controlled by them, are not engaged in the misappropriation, or unauthorized distribution or commercial exploitation, of mask works; and

(3) that issuing the order would promote the purposes of this chapter and international comity with respect to the protection of mask works.

(b) While an order under subsection (a) is in effect with respect to a foreign nation, no application for registration of a claim for protection in a mask work under this chapter may be denied solely because the owner of the mask work is a national, domiciliary, or sovereign authority of that foreign nation, or solely because the mask work was first commercially exploited in that foreign nation.

(c) Any order issued by the Secretary of Commerce under subsection (a) shall be effective for such period as the Secretary designates in the order, except that no such order may be effective after the date on which the authority of the Secretary of Commerce terminates under subsection (e). The effective date of any such order shall also be designated in the order. In the case of an order issued upon the petition of a person, such effective date may be no earlier than the date on which the Secretary receives such petition.

(d)(1) Any order issued under this section shall terminate if—

(A) the Secretary of Commerce finds that any of the conditions set forth in paragraphs (1), (2), and (3) of subsection (a) no longer exist; or

(B) mask works of nationals, domiciliaries, and sovereign authorities of that foreign nation or mask works first commercially exploited in that foreign nation become eligible for protection under subparagraph (A) or (C) of section 902(a)(1).

(2) Upon the termination or expiration of an order issued under this section, registrations of claims of protection in mask works made pursuant to that order shall remain valid for the period specified in section 904

(e) The authority of the Secretary of Commerce under this section shall commence on the date of the enactment of this chapter, and shall terminate on July 1, 1991.

(f)(1) The Secretary of Commerce shall promptly notify the Register of Copyrights and the Committees on the Judiciary of the

Senate and the House of Representatives of the issuance or termination of any order under this section, together with a statement of the reasons for such action. The Secretary shall also publish such notification and statement of reasons in the Federal Register.

(2) Two years after the date of the enactment of this chapter, the Secretary of Commerce, in consultation with the Register of Copyrights, shall transmit to the Committees on the Judiciary of the Senate and the House of Representatives a report on the actions taken under this section and on the current status of international recognition of mask work protection. The report shall include such recommendations for modifications of the protection accorded under this chapter to mask works owned by nationals, domiciliaries, or sovereign authorities of foreign nations as the Secretary, in consultation with the Register of Copyrights, considers would promote the purposes of this chapter and international comity with respect to mask work protection. Not later than July 1, I990, the Secretary of Commerce, in consultation with the Register of Copyrights, shall transmit to the Committees on the Judiciary of the Senate and the House of Represenlatives a report updating the matters contained in the report transmitted under the preceding sentence.

Appendix F

TABLE OF CONTENTS COPYRIGHT OFFICE APPLICATION FORMS, CIRCULARS, REGULATIONS, AND ANNOUNCEMENTS (as of January 7, 1991)

APPLICATION FORMS

FORM CA:	For supplementary registration to correct or amplify information given in the copyright record of an earlier registration
FORM SE:	For registration of each individual issue of a serial
FORM SE/GROUP: and SHORT FORM SE	Specialized SE forms for use when certain requirements are met
FORM GR/CP:	An adjunct application to be used for registration of a group of contributions to periodicals
FORM PA:	For published and unpublished works of the performing arts (musical and dramatic works, pantomimes and dramatic works, motion pictures, and other audiovisual works)

FORM RE:	For claims to renewal of copyright in works copyright under the law in effect through December 31, 1977 (1909 Copyright Act)
FORM SR:	For published and unpublished sound recordings
FORM TX:	For published and unpublished nondramatic literary works
FORM VA:	For published and unpublished works of the visual arts (pictorial, graphic, and sculptural works)

CIRCULARS

SL9	General Announcement
TSL -92	Copyright Law
1	Copyright Basics
1b	Limitations on the Information Furnished by the Copyright Office
1e	The Certification Space of the Application Form
2	Publications on Copyright
2b	Selected Bibliographies on Copyright
3	Copyright Notice
SL - 4	Copyright Fees Increase
5	How to Open and Maintain a Deposit Account in the Copyright Office
6	Obtaining Copies of Copyright Office Records and Deposits
7b	"Best Edition" of Published Copyrighted Works for the Collections of the Library of Congress
7c	The Effects of Not Replying Within 120 Days to Copyright Office Correspondence

7d	Mandatory Deposit of Copies or Phonorecords for the Library of Congress
8	Supplementary Copyright Registration
9	Works-Made-for-Hire Under the 1976 Copyright Act
12	Recordation of Transfers & Other Documents
13	Trademarks
14	Copyright Registration for Derivative Works
15	Renewal of Copyright
15a	Duration of Copyright
15t	Extension of Copyright Terms
21	Reproduction of Copyrighted Works by Educators and Librarians
22	How to Investigate the Copyright Status of a Work
23	The Copyright Card Catalog and the Online Files of the Copyright Office
30	Special Postage Rates for Deposit Copies Mailed to the Copyright Office
31	Ideas, Methods, or Systems
32	Blank Forms and Other Works Not Protected by Copyright
33	Computing and Measuring Devices
34	Copyright Protection Not Available for Names, Titles, or Short Phrases
38a	International Copyright Relations of the United States
40	Copyright Registration for Works of the Visual Arts
40a	Deposit Requirements for Registration of Claims to Copyright in Visual Arts Material
41	Copyright Claims in Architectural Works

44	Cartoons and Comic Strips
45	Copyright Registration for Motion Pictures Including Video Recordings
50	Copyright Registration for Musical Compositions
51	Repeal of Notice of Use Requirements
55	Copyright Registration for Multimedia Works
56	Copyright for Sound Recordings
56a	Copyright Registration of Musical Compositions and Sound Recordings
61	Copyright Registration for Computer Programs
62	Copyright Registration for Serials on Form SE
63	Reproductions of Copyrighted Works for Blind and Physically Handicapped Individuals
64	Copyright Registration for Secure Tests
65	Copyright Registration for Automated Databases
93	Highlights of U.S. Adherence to the Berne Convention
93a	The United States Joins The Berne Union
96 Sec. 201.1	Communications with the Copyright Office;
201.2	Information Given by the Copyright Office
96 Sec. 201.4	Recordation of Transfers and Certain Other Documents
96 Sec. 201.5	Corrections and Amplifications of Copyright Registrations; Applications for Supplementary Registration
96 Sec. 201.6	Payment and Refund of Copyright Office Fees
96 Sec. 201.7	Cancellation of Completed Registrations
96 Sec. 201.9	Recordation of Agreements Between Copyright Owners and Public Broadcasting Entities
96 Sec. 201.10	Notices of Termination of Transfers and Licenses Covering Extended Renewal Term

96 Sec. 201.12	Recordation of Certain Contracts by Cable Systems Located Outside of the Forty-Eight Contiguous States
96 Sec. 201.13	Notices of Objection to Certain Noncommercial Performances of Nondramatic Literary or Musical Works
96 Sec. 201.14	Warnings of Copyright for Use by Certain Libraries and Archives
96 Sec. 201.15	Voluntary License to Permit Reproduction of Nondramatic Literary Works Solely for Use of the Blind and Physically Handicapped
96 Sec.201.17	Statements of Account Covering Compulsory Licenses for Secondary Transmission by Cable Systems
96 Sec. 201.18	Notice of Intention to Obtain a Compulsory License for Making and Distributing Phonorecords of Nondramatic Musical Works
96 Sec. 201.19	Royalties and Statements of Account under Compulsory License for Making and Distributing Phonorecords of Nondramatic Musical Works
96 Sec. 201.20	Methods of Affixation and Positions of the Copyright Notice on Various Types of Works
96 Sec. 201.22	Advance Notices of Potential Infringement of Works Consisting of Sounds, Images, or Both
96 Sec. 201.23	Transfer of Unpublished Copyright Deposits to the Library of Congress
96 Sec. 202.1	Material Not Subject to Copyright
96 Sec. 202.2	Copyright Notice
96 Sec. 202.3	Registration of Copyright
96 Sec. 202.10	Pictorial, Graphic, and Sculptural Works
96 Sec. 202.17	Renewals
96 Sec. 202.19	Deposit of Published Copies or Phonorecords for the Library of Congress

96 Sec. 202.20	Deposit of Copies and Phonorecords for Copyright Registration
96 Sec. 202.21	Deposit of Identifying Material Instead of Copies
96 Sec. 202.22	Acquisition and Deposit of Unpublished Television Transmission Programs
96 Sec. 202.23	Full-Term Retention of Copyright Deposits
96 Part 203	Freedom of Information Act: Policies and Procedures
96 Part 204	Privacy Act: Policies and Procedures
96 Part 211	Mask Work Protection
100	Federal Statutory Protection for Mask Works

ANNOUNCEMENTS

ML - 319	Policy Decision Announcing an Increase in the Fee for Special Handling of Applications for Copyright Registration
ML - 341	Policy Decision Fixing Fees for the Special Handling of Import Statements and Documents
ML - 345	Policy Decision Regarding Mandatory Deposit of Books and Other Printed Works Published with Notice of Copyright in the United States After First Publication Abroad
ML - 354	Notice of Policy Decisions Regarding Searches of Certain In-Process Materials
ML - 380	Notice of Policy Decisions, Compulsory License for Cable Systems: Reporting of Gross Receipts
ML - 387	Notice of Policy Decision, Registration Decision; Registration and Deposit of Computer Screen Displays
ML - 392	Notice of Change in Procedure, Mandatory Deposit; New Procedure for Requesting Prompt Exercise of

	Right to Demand Under the Motion Picture Agreement
ML - 393	Notice of Policy Decision on Copyrightability of Digitized Typefaces
ML - 402	Final Regulations: Statements of Account and Filing Requirements For Satellite Carrier Statutory License
ML - 406	Final Regulations: Registration of Claims to Copyright; Mandatory Deposits of Machine-Readable Copies
ML - 413	Technical Amendment To Final Regulations: Statements of Account and Filing Requirements for Satellite Carrier Statutory License
ML - 414	Final Regulation: Adjustment of the Syndicated Exclusivity Surcharge
ML - 415	Final Regulation: Registration of Claims to Copyright; Effective Date of Registration
ML - 416	Final Regulation: Registration of Claims to Copyright: Group Registration of Serials

Tables of Authorities

(References are to pages and footnotes.)

Table of Cases

A

B

C

D

E

F

G

H

I

J

K

L

M

N

O

P

Q

R

S

T

U

V

W

Berne Act

Code of Federal Regulations

19 CFR

28 CFR

37 CFR

47 CFR

1909 Act

Trademark Act of 1946 (Lanham Act)

United States Code

Title 1

Title 5

Title 9

Title 15

Title 17 (Trademark Act)

1976 Act

Transitional & Supplementary Provisions

Title 18

Title 19

Title 28

Title 35

Title 44

Title 47

Title 48

Index

(References are to pages.)

A

Index

B

F

G

H

I

J

L

N

Index

O

P

S

T

V

Y